PROVERBS

PROVERBS

A SHORTER COMMENTARY

Bruce K. Waltke and Ivan D. V. De Silva

WILLIAM B. EERDMANS PUBLISHING COMPANY

GRAND RAPIDS, MICHIGAN

Wm. B. Eerdmans Publishing Co.
4035 Park East Court SE, Grand Rapids, Michigan 49546
www.eerdmans.com

27 26 25 24 23 22 21   1 2 3 4 5 6 7

ISBN 978-0-8028-7503-7

Library of Congress Cataloging-in-Publication Data

Names: Waltke, Bruce K., author. | De Silva, Ivan D. V., 1961– author. |
   Waltke, Bruce K. Book of Proverbs.
Title: Proverbs : a shorter commentary / Bruce K. Waltke and Ivan D. V. De Silva.
Description: Grand Rapids, Michigan : William B. Eerdmans Publishing Com-
   pany, [2021] | Includes bibliographical references and index. | Summary:
   "An abridged and more accessible version of Bruce Waltke's magisterial
   two-volume commentary on the book of Proverbs from the New Interna-
   tional Commentary on the Old Testament series"—Provided by publisher.
Identifiers: LCCN 2020038629 | ISBN 9780802875037 (paperback)
Subjects: LCSH: Bible. Proverbs—Commentaries.
Classification: LCC BS1465.53 .W353 2021 | DDC 223/.7077—dc23
LC record available at https://lccn.loc.gov/2020038629

Contents

TEXT AND COMMENTARY

Contents

Contents

Preface

This commentary seeks to make Prof. Bruce Waltke's two-volume commentary titled *The Book of Proverbs* (Eerdmans, 2004) more accessible to students, pastors, and Bible readers in general.

The original commentary was a major scholarly work that sought to break new ground in its affirmation that the authors and redactors of Proverbs organized their material into discernible clusters or groupings. While peer reviews largely lauded the commentary, it proved challenging for the general reader. Its length, complex analysis, and use of the Hebrew text to demonstrate its main affirmation meant that some people found it too intricate and detailed for their purposes. Thus, the need for a simplified, abridged version accessible to a wider audience became apparent. The challenge of abridging the commentary centered on how to maintain the erudition, exegetical precision, and poetic insights of the original commentary while condensing it and simplifying its technical elements. Prof. Waltke invited his friend and former student, Ivan De Silva (ThM), to assist in the work. Ivan teaches in the Religious Studies departments at Trinity Western University and Pacific Life Bible College in British Columbia and serves as a detective in the Vancouver Police Department.

In 2016, Eerdmans approved the project, and we undertook the work in earnest. As the project progressed, we realized that mere condensation was not sufficient, as the commentary was by then more than ten years old, and new secondary literature on Proverbs had emerged. In addition, Waltke felt that the new work would benefit from revision of some of his earlier interpretations of the proverbs based on his further reflections. Accordingly, we decided that the abridged commentary would take into account both of these elements. Especially significant was the publication in 2009 of Michael Fox's second volume on Proverbs, covering chapters 10–31, which was not available in 2004. However, in order to maintain the concise nature of the commentary we limited our selection from new research to topics such as the nature of the "foreign woman," the *Sitz im Leben* (setting in life) for the dissemination of Proverbs in ancient Israel, the existence of doublets, and some newer exegetical insights on a few words and verses (e.g., 1:5; 8:30). Overall, however, the new research does not significantly alter the substance of the original commentary.

This work is intended for the Bible lover who is looking for a commentary on Proverbs that handles the introductory issues concisely and the contents faithfully. The current work, like the original, is divided into two parts: an introduction and an exegesis of the text. The introduction deals with issues of authorship, date, structure, and the character of Hebrew poetry, albeit more concisely than in the original. The introduction also includes theological reflection on topics such as God, humans, speech, and wealth, and includes word studies of many wisdom terms that appear frequently in the Proverbs (e.g., "wisdom," "the wicked," "righteousness," "the fear of *I AM*," etc.). Providing the word studies in the introduction eliminates the need to keep defining them each time they appear in the commentary. Instead, when a word appears in the commentary that we have described in the introduction, we will direct the reader to it by citing its page number in the introduction.

Most importantly, this is a Christian commentary. A whole section of the introduction compares the proverbs of Solomon and the sayings of the wise with the person and teaching of the Lord Jesus Christ.

The commentary proper divides the book of Proverbs into poems (chs. 1–9; 30–31), collections, sections, and units on the basis of thematic and poetic considerations. A translation is provided for each unit, followed by exegetical comments on each verse and an assessment of whether the meaning of the verse is enhanced by its place in the unit. As appropriate, we offer theological reflections and anecdotes.

Readers familiar with the original work will notice some differences in this abridged version. First, in response to Eerdmans's request that its authors conform their style to the *Chicago Manual of Style*, Waltke's translation of the original Hebrew is here rendered more gender neutral, often by using plural pronouns to translate the original masculine singular pronouns. Likewise, in the commentary itself we have tried to achieve gender neutrality as much as possible by rendering the masculine singular pronoun by various other, more inclusive terms. However, many poems, such as those in the Prologue (1:8–9:18), and some aphorisms are addressed to the son, and so the masculine gender has been retained in those cases.

Second, the divine name, represented by the Hebrew consonants *yhwh* (the Tetragrammaton) and commonly rendered by the titular LORD, has been rendered here by its divinely revealed *meaning* of *I AM* (see Exod. 3:13–15). Unfortunately, the scribes did not preserve the pronunciation of the divine name, and names such as Jehovah and Yahweh are speculative. What we do know is that God's name is a sentence and in his own mouth (that is, in its first-person form) means "*I AM*."[1] Therefore, we chose to translate, instead of transliterating, God's name according to how it appears in his own mouth.

Third, one of the prime contributions of the original commentary was to demonstrate that the proverbs have been arranged into meaningful clusters that require them to be interpreted both individually and in their larger context. In the case of many of the groupings, the demonstration of this requires detailed analysis of the Hebrew text. That is not possible in a concise commentary. Therefore, this aspect of the original is only reflected in the current volume to the extent that groupings can be easily discerned in the translation.

Fourth, in order to aid preachers and teachers, we have included a subject index that seeks to reference all the proverbs related to a topic. While no such index can be exhaustive in its coverage of subjects, we hope that the topics covered will aid in the study and preaching of the book. In addition, we added a few memorable citations and insightful illustrations.

Finally, a word must be said about the relationship between this abridged commentary and its two-volume predecessor. The nature of an abridged commentary is such that it cannot provide the detailed analysis and argumentation required to justify all of its conclusions. Thus, the concise commentary provides the meaning and interpretation of the Proverbs without a lot of the detailed research that demonstrates many of its conclusions. Readers requiring the exegetical background to the interpretation offered here should consult the major two-volume work, which functions as a massive footnote to this abridged commentary.

As is the case in any meaningful undertaking, behind the originators stand numerous supporters without whose help no work can reach completion. In our case, Bruce dedicated his first work to Elaine, his wife, but she can no longer participate in his work. Bruce takes this opportunity to thank the Northwest University Library for assisting him in accessing books and periodical literature. Carol, Ivan's wife, has been a constant source of encouragement and support that has empowered him to keep moving to the work's completion, and so he gives much of the credit for his work to Carol. In addition, Ivan was assisted by his friend Ruben Sorge, who undertook to carefully read the work and offer constructive criticism. His suggestions have made the work better. We would also like to thank Andrew Knapp, acquisitions editor at Eerdmans,

---

1. For a fuller defense of this decision to render the divine name as *I AM*, see Bruce K. Waltke with Charles Yu, *An Old Testament Theology: An Exegetical, Thematic and Canonical Approach* (Grand Rapids: Zondervan, 2007), 11–12.

for his patient shepherding of this work through a long and drawn-out process. Without his patience when deadlines could not be met this work would not have seen the light of day. Our copyeditor, Sam Kelly, expertly edited the original manuscript to ensure we achieved our goal of making the work accessible to a broader readership. Ivan's former student, Roland Messier, a skilled software engineer, helped with the creation of the indexes. In this work he was aided by the scripture indexing tool developed by gracelife.org. Any remaining deficiencies, however, remain the responsibility of its two authors. In the end, it is our majestic and loving Triune God who deserves all praise and honor. Without his providential preservation of Proverbs as canonical Scripture, there would be no book of Proverbs to comment on. And without his providential preservation of its commentators, there would be no commentary.

Bruce Waltke and Ivan De Silva

Abbreviations

ABD	*Anchor Bible Dictionary*. Edited by David Noel Freedman. 6 vols. New York: Doubleday, 1992
AEL	*Ancient Egyptian Literature*. Miriam Lichtheim. 3 vols. Berkeley: University of California Press, 1971–1980
ANEP	*The Ancient Near East in Pictures Relating to the Old Testament*. 2nd ed. Edited by James B. Pritchard. Princeton: Princeton University Press, 1994
ANET	*Ancient Near Eastern Texts Relating to the Old Testament*. Edited by James B. Pritchard. 3rd ed. Princeton: Princeton University Press, 1969
BAGD	Bauer, Walter, William F. Arndt, F. Wilbur Gingrich, and Frederick W. Danker. *Greek-English Lexicon of the New Testament and Other Early Christian Literature*. 2nd ed. Chicago: University of Chicago Press, 1979
BBRSup	Bulletin for Biblical Research, Supplements
BDB	Brown, Francis, S. R. Driver, and Charles A. Briggs. *A Hebrew and English Lexicon of the Old Testament*
Bib	*Biblica*
BiBh	*Bible Bhashyam*
BibOr	Biblica et Orientalia
BKAT	Biblischer Kommentar: Altes Testament
BR	*Biblical Research*
BSac	*Bibliotheca Sacra*
BT	*The Bible Translator*
CAT	Commentaire de l'Ancien Testament
CBQ	*Catholic Biblical Quarterly*
ConBOT	Coniectanea Biblica, Old Testament Series
DOTWPW	*Dictionary of the Old Testament: Wisdom, Poetry and Writings*. Edited by Scott C. Jones, Tremper Longman III, and Peter Enns. Downers Grove, IL: InterVarsity Press, 2008

EBC	*Expositor's Bible Commentary*. Edited by Frank E. Gaebelein. 12 vols. Grand Rapids: Zondervan, 1979–1988
EvQ	*Evangelical Quarterly*
GKC	*Gesenius' Hebrew Grammar*. Ed. E. Kautzsch. Tr. A. E. Cowley. 2nd ed. Oxford: Clarendon, 1910
GUOST	*Glasgow University Oriental Society Transactions*
HALOT	*The Hebrew and Aramaic Lexicon of the Old Testament*. Ludwig Koehler, Walter Baumgartner, and Johann J. Stamm. Translated and edited under the supervision of Mervyn E. J. Richardson. 4 vols. Leiden: Brill, 1994–1999
HAT	Handbuch zum Alten Testament
HeyJ	*Heythrop Journal*
HTR	*Harvard Theological Review*
HUCA	*Hebrew Union College Annual*
IBHS	*An Introduction to Biblical Hebrew Syntax*. Bruce K. Waltke and Michael O'Connor. Winona Lake, IN: Eisenbrauns, 1990
ICC	International Critical Commentary
ISBE	*International Standard Bible Encyclopedia*. Edited by Geoffrey W. Bromiley. 4 vols. Grand Rapids: Eerdmans, 1979–1988
JAOS	*Journal of the American Oriental Society*
JBL	*Journal of Biblical Literature*
JETS	*Journal of the Evangelical Theological Society*
JM	P. Joüon and T. Muraoka, *A Grammar of Biblical Hebrew*. Editrice Pontificio Istituto Biblico. Rom, 1911
JNSL	*Journal of Northwest Semitic Languages*
JSOTSup	Journal of the Society of Old Testament Supplement Series
JSS	*Journal of Semitic Studies*
LUÅ	Lunds universitets årsskrift
LXX	Septuagint
MT	Masoretic Text
NAC	New American Commentary
NBD	*New Bible Dictionary*. Edited by D. R. W. Wood, Howard Marshall, J. D. Douglas, and N. Hillyer. 3rd ed. Downers Grove, IL: InterVarsity Press, 1996
NCBC	New Century Bible Commentary
NIB	*The New Interpreter's Bible*. Edited by Leander E. Keck. 12 vols. Nashville: Abingdon, 1994–2004
NICOT	New International Commentary on the Old Testament
NIDOTTE	*New International Dictionary of Old Testament Theology and Ex-*

	egesis. Edited by Willem A. VanGemeren. 5 vols. Grand Rapids: Zondervan, 1997
OTL	Old Testament Library
OTS	Old Testament Studies
OtSt	*Oudtestamentische Studiën*
RB	*Revue biblique*
SBL	Society of Biblical Literature
SJT	*Scottish Journal of Theology*
Syr.	Syriac
Targ.	Targum
TDOT	*Theological Dictionary of the Old Testament*. Edited by G. Johannes Botterweck and Helmer Ringgren. Translated by John T. Willis et al. 8 vols. Grand Rapids: Eerdmans, 1974–2006
TLOT	*Theological Lexicon of the Old Testament*. Edited by Ernst Jenni, with assistance from Claus Westermann. Translated by Mark E. Biddle. 3 vols. Peabody, MA: Hendrickson, 1997
TLZ	*Theologische Literaturzeitung*
TOTC	Tyndale Old Testament Commentaries
TWOT	*Theological Wordbook of the Old Testament*. Edited by R. Laird Harris, Gleason L. Archer Jr., and Bruce K. Waltke. 2 vols. Chicago: Moody Press, 1980
TynBul	*Tyndale Bulletin*
VT	*Vetus Testamentum*
VTSup	Supplement to Vetus Testamentum
Vulg.	Vulgate
WBC	Word Biblical Commentary
WIANE	*Wisdom in Israel and in the Ancient Near East*. Edited by M. Noth and D. Winton Thomas. Leiden: Brill, 1969
WMANT	Wissenschaftliche Monographien zum Alten und Neuen Testament
WTJ	*Westminster Theological Journal*
WWis	*Way of Wisdom: Essays in Honor of Bruce K. Waltke*. Edited by J. I. Packer and Sven K. Soderlund. Grand Rapids: Zondervan, 2000
ZAH	*Zeitschrift für Althebräistik*
ZAW	*Zeitschrift für die alttestamentliche Wissenschaft*
ZBK	Zürcher Bibelkommentare
ZTK	*Zeitschrift für Theologie und Kirche*

Bibliography

Aitken, Kenneth T. *Proverbs*. Philadelphia: Westminster John Knox, 1986.

Albright, William Foxwell. "Some Canaanite-Phoenician Sources of Hebrew Wisdom." Pages 1–15 in *WIANE*.

Andrews, M. E. "Variety of Expression in Proverbs XXIII 29–35." *VT* 28 (1978): 102–3.

Atkinson, David. *The Message of Proverbs*. Downers Grove, IL: InterVarsity, 1997.

Barr, James. "Prov. XI.31, 1 Pet IV.18." *JSS* 20 (1975): 149–64.

Barrett, J. Edward. "Can Scholars Take the Virgin Birth Seriously?" *BR* 4 (1988): 10–15.

Bartholomew, Craig G., and Ryan O'Dowd. *Old Testament Wisdom Literature: A Theological Introduction*. Downers Grove, IL: IVP Academic, 2011.

Bauckham, Richard. *Jesus and the God of Israel: God Crucified and Other Studies on the New Testament's Christology of Divine Identity*. Grand Rapids: Eerdmans, 2008.

Berlin, Adele. "Introduction to Hebrew Poetry." Pages 167–81 in *The New Interpreter's Bible: Old Testament Survey*. Edited by Leander E. Keck. Nashville: Abingdon, 2005.

———. *Poetics and Interpretation of Biblical Narrative*. JSOTSup 9. Sheffield: Almond, 1983.

Blocher, Henri. "The Fear of the LORD as the 'Principle' of Wisdom." *TynBul* 28 (1977): 3–28.

Bodenheimer, F. S. "Fauna and Flora of the Bible." Page 1 in *Helps for Translators*. Vol. 11. London: United Bible Societies, 1972, 1980.

Boström, G. *Proverbiastudien: Die Weisheit und das fremde Weib in Spr. 1–9*. LUÅ. Lund: Gleerup, 1935.

Boström, Lennart. *The God of the Sages: The Portrayal of God in the Book of Proverbs*. ConBOT 29. Stockholm: Almqvist Wiksell, 1990.

Bratcher, Robert G. "Biblical Words Describing Man: Breath, Life, Spirit." *BT* 34 (1983): 201–13.

Brenner, Athaliah, and Fokkelien van Dijk-Hemmes. *On Gendering Texts: Female and Male Voices in the Hebrew Bible*. Leiden: Brill, 1993.

Brettler, M. Z. God Is King: Understanding an Israelite Metaphor. JSOTSup 76. Sheffield: JSOT Press, 1989.

Bridges, Charles. *An Exposition of Proverbs*. Evansville: Sovereign Grace Book Club, 1959; preface 1846.

Brongers, H. A. "Die Partikel *lmʿn* in der biblisch-hebraischen Sprache." *OtSt* 18 (1973): 84–96.

Brown, Raymond E. *The Gospel According to John: A New Translation with Commentary*. AB 29. Garden City, NY: Doubleday, 1966.

Brown, William P. *Character in Crisis: A Fresh Approach to the Wisdom Literature*. Grand Rapids: Eerdmans, 1996.

Brueggemann, Walter. "A Neglected Sapiential Word Pair." *ZAW* 89 (1977): 234–58.

Budge, E. A. W. *Second Series of Facsimiles of Egyptian Hieratic Papyri in the British Museum*. London: British Museum, 1923.

Camp, Claudia V. "Woman Wisdom as Root Metaphor: A Theological Consideration." Pages 45–76 in *The Listening Heart: Essays in Wisdom and the Psalms in Honor of Roland E. Murphy, O. Carm*. Edited by K. G. Hoglund et al. JSOTSup 58. Sheffield: JSOT Press, 1987.

Cansdale, G. S. *Animals of Biblical Lands*. Exeter: Paternoster, 1970.

Carr, David M. *Formation of the Hebrew Bible*. New York: Oxford University Press, 2011.

——. *Writing on the Tablet of the Heart: Origins of Scripture and Literature*. New York: Oxford University Press, 2005.

Childs, Brevard S. *Introduction to the Old Testament as Scripture*. Philadelphia: Fortress, 1979.

Clayton, Allen Lee. "The Orthodox Recovery of a Heretical Proof-Text: Athanasius of Alexandria's Interpretation of Proverbs 8:22–30 in Conflict with the Arians." PhD diss., Southern Methodist University, 1988.

Clifford, Richard J. *Proverbs*. OTL. Louisville: Westminster John Knox, 1999.

Cody, A. "Notes on Proverbs 22,21 and 22,23b." *Bib* 61 (1980): 418–26.

Cohen, Abraham. *Proverbs*. London: Soncino, 1967.

Conybeare, F. C., J. Redel Harris, and Agnes Smith Lewis, eds. "The Story of Ahikar." Pages 715–84 in *The Apocrypha and Pseudepigrapha of the Old Testament*. Edited by R. H. Charles. Oxford: Clarendon, 1976.

Cosser, William. "The Meaning of 'Life' (*Ḥayyîm*) in Proverbs, Job, and Ecclesiastes." *GUOST* 15 (1955): 48–53.

Crown, A. D. "Messengers and Scribes: The *Sopher* and *Mazkir* in the Old Testament." *VT* 24 (1974): 366–70.

Dahood, Mitchell. *Proverbs and Northwest Semitic Philology*. Rome: Biblical Institute, 1963.

Delitzsch, Franz. *Biblical Commentary on the Proverbs of Solomon*. Translated by M. G. Easton. Edinburgh: T & T Clark, 1874; repr., Grand Rapids: Eerdmans, 1983.

Donald, Trevor. "The Semantic Field of 'Folly' in Proverbs, Job, Psalms, and Ecclesiastes." *VT* 13 (1963): 285–92.

Dorsey, David A. *The Roads and Highways of Ancient Israel*. Baltimore: John's Hopkins University Press, 1991.

Emerton, John A. "Note on Proverbs 12:26." *ZAW* 101 (1989): 190–98.

Farmer, K. *Who Knows What Is Good? A Commentary on the Books of Proverbs and Ecclesiastes* (Grand Rapids: Eerdmans, 1991).

Fee, Gordon D. "Wisdom Christology in Paul: A Dissenting View." Pages 251–79 in *WWis*.

Finkelstein, J. "The Middle Assyrian Shulmanu-Texts," *JAOS* 72 (1952): 77–80.

Follis, E. *Directions in Biblical Hebrew Poetry*. JSOTSup 40. Sheffield: Sheffield Academic, 1987.

Fox, Michael V. "Pedagogy of Proverbs 2." *JBL* 113 (1994): 233–43.

———. *Proverbs 1–9: A New Translation with Introduction and Commentary*. AB 18A. New York: Doubleday, 2000.

———. *Proverbs 10–31: A New Translation with Introduction and Commentary*. AB 18B. New Haven, CT: Yale University Press, 2009.

———. "The Social Location of the Book of Proverbs." Pages 227–39 in *Texts, Temples, and Traditions: A Tribute to Menahem Haran*. Edited by Michael V. Fox, Victor Avigdor Hurowitz, Avi M. Hurvitz, Michael L. Klein, Baruch J. Schwartz, and Nili Shupak. Winona Lake, IN: Eisenbrauns, 1996.

———. "Words for Wisdom." *ZAH* 6 (1993): 158–59.

Freedman, H., trans. "*Kiddushin*." In *The Babylonian Talmud*. Edited by I. Epstein. Vol. 4. London: Soncino, 1948.

Gadamer, Hans-Georg. *Truth and Method*. Edited and translated by J. Weinsheimer and D. Marshall. 2nd ed. New York: Continuum, 1989.

Garrett, Duane A. *Proverbs, Ecclesiastes, Song of Songs*. NAC 14. Nashville: Broadman, 1993.

———. "Votive Prostitution Again: A Comparison of Proverbs 7:13–14 and 21:28–29." *JBL* 190 (1990): 681–82.

Gasper, J. *Social Ideas in the Wisdom Literature of the Old Testament*. Washington, DC: The Catholic University of America, 1947.

Gemser, Bernard. *Sprüche Salomos*. HAT 16. Tübingen: J. C. B. Mohr, 1963; preface, 1937.

Gevirtz, Stanley. *Patterns in Early Hebrew Poetry*. Chicago: University of Chicago Press, 1964.

Giese, Ronald L., Jr. "'Iron Sharpens Iron' as a Negative Image: Challenging the Common Interpretation of Proverbs 27:17." *JBL* 135 (2016): 61–76.

Gladson, J. A. "Retributive Paradoxes in Proverbs 10–29." PhD diss., Vanderbilt University, 1978.

Goldingay, John. "The Arrangement of Sayings in Proverbs 1–15." *JSOT* 61 (1994): 75–83.

——. "The 'Salvation History' Perspective and the 'Wisdom' Perspective within the Context of Biblical Theology." *EvQ* 51 (1979): 194–207.

Greenstone, Julius H. *Proverbs with Commentary*. Philadelphia: The Jewish Publication Society of America, 1950.

Grollenberg, R. P. L. "A propos de Prov. VIII,6 et XVII,27." *RB* 59 (1962): 40–43.

Habel, Norman C. "Wisdom, Wealth and Poverty: Paradigms in the Book of Proverbs." *BiBh* 14 (1988): 26–49.

Heaton, E. W. *The Hebrew Kingdoms*. Oxford: Oxford University Press, 1986.

Heim, Knut Martin. "A Closer Look at the Pig in Proverbs xi 22." *VT* 58 (2008): 13–27.

——. Poetic Imagination in Proverbs: *Variant Repetitions and the Nature of Poetry*. BBRSup 4. Winona Lake, IN: Eisenbrauns, 2013.

——. "Structure and Context in Proverbs 10:1–22:16." PhD diss., University of Liverpool, 1996.

Herbert, A. S. "The 'Parable' (MĀŠĀL) in the Old Testament." *SJT* 7 (1954): 180–96.

Hillers, D. *Covenant: The History of a Biblical Idea*. Baltimore: Johns Hopkins University Press, 1969.

Hubbard, D. A. *Proverbs*. Dallas: Word, 1989.

Irwin, William H. "The Metaphor in Prov. 11,30." *Bib* 65 (1984): 97–100.

Janzen, J. Gerald. "The Root *pr'* in Judges v 2 and Deuteronomy xxxii 42." *VT* 39 (1989): 393–406.

Janzen, Walsemar. "'AŠRÊ in the Old Testament." *HTR* 58 (1965): 215–26.

Jobes, Karen H. "Sophia Christology: The Way of Wisdom?" Pages 226–50 in *WWis*.

Kayatz, Christa B. *Studien zu Proverbien 1–9: Eine form- und motivgeschichtliche Untersuchung unter Einbeziehung ägyptischen Vergleichsmaterials*. WMANT 11. Neukirchen-Vluyn: Neukirchener, 1966.

Keel, Othmar. *The Symbolism of the Biblical World*. New York: Seabury, 1978.

Kidner, Derek. *The Proverbs*. TOTC. Downers Grove, IL: InterVarsity, 1964.

Kitchen, K. A. "Proverbs 2: Ancient Near Eastern Background." Pages 552–53 in *DOTWPW*.

———. "Proverbs and Wisdom Books of the Ancient Near East: The Factual History of a Literary Form." *TynBul* 28 (1977): 69–114.

Koch, Klaus. "Is There a Doctrine of Retribution in the Old Testament?" Pages 57–87 in Issues in Religion and Theology 4: Theodicy in the Old Testament. Edited by J. L. Crenshaw. Philadelphia: Fortress; London: SPCK, 1983. Orig. "Gibt es ein Vergeltungsdogma im Alten Testament?" *ZTK* 52 (1955): 1–42.

Kruger, Paul A. "Promiscuity or Marriage Fidelity? A Note on Prov 5:15–18." *JNSL* 13 (1987): 61–68.

Liew, Sow-Phen. "Social and Literary Context of Proverbs 28–29." PhD diss., Westminster Theological Seminary, 1991.

Longman, Tremper, III. *Proverbs*. Grand Rapids: Baker Academic, 2006.

———. "Woman Wisdom and Woman Folly." Pages 912–16 in *DOTWPW*.

Lucas, Ernest C. *Exploring the Old Testament: A Guide to the Psalms and Wisdom Literature*. Downers Grove, IL: InterVarsity, 2003.

———. *Proverbs*. The Two Horizons Old Testament Commentary. Grand Rapids: Eerdmans, 2015.

Lyons, Maurice. "Rashi's Commentary on the Book Proverbs." Paper submitted in partial fulfillment of the requirements for the degree of rabbi, 1936.

Malbim, Meir Leibush. *The Book of Proverbs*. Edited by Charles Wengrov and Avival Gottlieb Zornberg. Jerusalem: Feldheim, 1973.

Malchow, Bruce V. "A Manual for Future Monarchs." *CBQ* 47 (1985): 238–45.

Martens, Elmer A. "The Way of Wisdom." Pages 75–90 in *WWis*.

McCreesh, T. T. "Wisdom as Wife: Proverbs 31:10–31." *RB* 92 (1985): 25–46.

McKane, William. *Prophets and Wise Men*. London: SCM, 1965.

———. *Proverbs: A New Approach*. OTL. Philadelphia: Westminster, 1970.

Meinhold, Arndt. *Die Sprüche*. 2 vols. ZBK. Zurich: Theologischer, 1991.

Morenz, S. "Feurige Kohlen auf dem Kaput." *TLZ* 78 (1953): 187–92.

Moss, A. "Wisdom as Parental Teaching in Proverbs 1–9." *HeyJ* 38 (1997): 426–39.

Murphy, Ronald E. *Proverbs*. WBC 22. Nashville: Thomas Nelson, 1998.

———. "Wisdom and Eros in Proverbs 1–9." *CBQ* 50 (1998): 600–603.

Nel, Philip. *The Structure and Ethos of the Wisdom Admonitions in Proverbs*. Berlin: de Gruyter, 1982.

Newsom, Carol A. "Woman and the Discourse of Patriarchal Wisdom: A Study of Proverbs 1–9." Pages 142–60 in *Gender and Difference in Ancient Israel*. Edited Peggy L. Day. Minneapolis: Fortress, 1989.

Overland, Paul B. "Literary Structure in Proverbs 1–9." PhD diss., Brandeis University, 1988.

Pan, Chou-Wee. "A Study of the Vocabulary of Education in Proverbs." PhD diss., University of Newcastle upon Tyne, 1987.

Pauls, Jerry V. "Proverbs 30:1–6: 'The Words of Agur' as Epistemological Statement." ThM thesis, Regent College, 1998.

Peels, Hendrik G. L. "Passion or Justice? The Interpretation of *beyôm nāqām* in Proverbs VI 34." *VT* 44 (1994): 270–72.

Perdue, Leo G. *Wisdom and Cult: A Critical Analysis of the Views of Cult in the Wisdom Literature of Israel and the Ancient Near East.* Missoula, MT: Scholars Press, 1977.

Plaut, Gunther W. *Book of Proverbs: A Commentary.* New York: Union of American Hebrew Congregations, 1941.

Plöger, Otto. *Sprüche Salomos (Proverbia).* BKAT 17.2–4. Neukirchen-Vluyn: Neukirchener, 1984.

Rad, Gerhard von. *Wisdom in Israel.* London: SCM, 1972.

Ross, Allen P. *Proverbs.* EBC. Grand Rapids: Zondervan, 1991.

Roth, Wolfgang M. W. "NBL." *VT* 10 (1960): 394–409.

Saggs, H. W. F. *The Greatness That Was Babylon.* New York: New American Library, 1962.

Sawyer, J. F. A. "The Role of Jewish Studies in Biblical Semantics." Pages 201–8 in *Scripta Signa Vocis: Studies about Scripts, Scriptures, Scribes and Languages in the Near East Presented to J. H. Hospers by His Pupils, Colleagues, and Friends.* Edited by H. Vanstiphout and Johannes Hendrik Hospers. Groningen: E. Forsten, 1986.

Shupak, Nili. "The Instruction of Amenemope and Proverbs 22:17–24:22 from the Perspective of Contemporary Research." Pages 117–33 in *Seeking Out the Wisdom of the Ancients: Essays Offered to Honor Michael V. Fox on the Occasion of His 65th Birthday.* Edited by Ronald L. Troxel, Kelvin G. Friebel, and Dennis R. Magary. Winona Lake, IN: Eisenbrauns, 2005.

Snijders, L. A. "The Meaning of *Zār* in the Old Testament." *OtSt* 10 (1954): 1–54.

Surls, Austin. *Making Sense of the Divine Name in Exodus: From Etymology to Literary Onomastics.* BBRSup 17. Winona Lake, IN: Eisenbrauns, 2017.

Thomson, James G. "Sleep: An Aspect of Jewish Anthropology." *VT* (1955): 421–33.

Toy, C. H. *The Book of Proverbs.* ICC. Edinburgh: T&T Clark, 1899.

Van Leeuwen, Raymond C. "The Book of Proverbs." Pages 239–48 in *The New Interpreter's Bible: Old Testament Survey.* Edited by Leander E. Keck. Nashville: Abingdon, 2005.

———. "The Book of Proverbs." Pages 17–264 in *NIB* 5. Nashville: Abingdon, 1997.

———. "Context and Meaning in Proverbs 25–27." PhD diss., University of St. Michael's College, 1984.

———. "Wisdom Literature." Pages 847–50 in *Dictionary for Theological Interpretation of the Bible*. Edited by Kevin J. Vanhoozer, Craig G. Bartholomew, Daniel J. Treier, and N. T. Wright. Grand Rapids: Baker Academic, 2005.

Vuilleumier, Rene. "*Michèe*." CAT 11b. Neuchatel: Delachaux & Niestle, 1971.

Wakeman, Mary K. *God's Battle with the Monster: A Study in Biblical Imagery*. Leiden: E. J. Brill, 1973.

Waltke, Bruce K. "Abomination." Page 13 in *ISBE*, vol. 1.

———. *The Book of Proverbs: Chapters 1–15*. NICOT. Grand Rapids: Eerdmans, 2004.

———. *The Book of Proverbs: Chapters 15–31*. NICOT. Grand Rapids: Eerdmans, 2005.

———. "The Book of Proverbs and Old Testament Theology." *BSac* 136 (1979): 302–17.

———. "The Fear of the Lord." Pages 17–33 in *Alive to God: Essays in Honour of James D. Houston*. Edited by J. I. Packer and Loren Wilkinson. Downers Grove, IL: InterVarsity, 1992.

———. *Finding the Will of God: A Pagan Notion?* 2nd ed. Grand Rapids: Eerdmans, 2016.

———. "Righteousness in Proverbs." *WTJ* 70 (2008): 225–37.

Waltke, Bruce K., and James M. Houston. *The Psalms as Christian Praise*. Grand Rapids: Eerdmans, 2019.

Waltke, Bruce K., with Cathi Fredricks. *Genesis: A Commentary*. Grand Rapids: Zondervan, 2001.

Waltke, Bruce K., with Charles Yu. *An Old Testament Theology*. Grand Rapids: Zondervan, 2007.

Washington, Harold C. "Wealth and Poverty in the Instruction of Amenemope and the Hebrew Proverbs: A Comparative Case Study in the Social Location and Function of Ancient Near Eastern Wisdom Literature." PhD diss., Princeton Theological Seminary, 1992.

Whybray, R. N. *Proverbs*. NCBC. London: Marshall Pickering; Grand Rapids: Eerdmans ,1999.

———. *Wealth and Poverty in the Book of Proverbs*. JSOTSup 99. Sheffield: Sheffield Academic, 1990.

———. *Wisdom in Proverbs: The Concept of Wisdom in Proverbs 1–9*. London: SCM, 1965.

Wiles, John Keating. "The 'Enemy' in Israelite Wisdom Literature." PhD diss., Southern Baptist Theological Seminary, 1982.

Wilson, Lindsay. *Proverbs*. TOTC. Downers Grove, IL: InterVarsity, 2017.

Wolters, Al. "The Meaning of *Kîšôr*." HUCA 65 (1994): 91–104.

———— "Proverbs XXI 10–31 as Heroic Hymn." *VT* 38 (1988): 446–57.

Yee, Gale A. "'I Have Perfumed My Bed with Myrrh': The Foreign Woman (ʾ*Iššâ Zārâ*) in Proverbs 1–9." *JSOT* 43 (1989): 53–68.

Yoder, Christine Roy. "The Woman of Substance (אשת־חיל): A Socioeconomic Reading of Proverbs 31: 10–31." *JBL* (2003): 427–47.

Introduction

I. Title

The English name "Book of Proverbs" is a translation of *Liber Proverbiorum*, its title in the Latin Vulgate, translated by Jerome (ca. A.D. 400). Its title in the Hebrew Bible is *mišlê* ("Proverbs"),[1] the first word of the book. Proverbs belongs to the third division of the Hebrew canon: the Writings. English Bibles, however, follow the order of the LXX and place it among the Poetical Books, in between Psalms and Ecclesiastes.

II. Texts and Versions

Most English translations of the Proverbs are based on the Masoretic Text (MT). According to the common-sense rules for establishing an original text, it is superior to the other versions even though the earliest extant manuscripts of the MT date to ca. A.D. 1000, more than 500 years after the earliest extant Greek texts. Both the MT and the LXX follow the same arrangement of content up to Prov. 24:22. After that, they significantly differ, as the following diagram shows:

MT	LXX
1:1–24:22	1:1–24:22
24:23–34 (Further sayings of the wise)	30:1–14 (Sayings of Agur)
25:1–29:27 (Sayings gathered by Hezekiah's men)	24:23–34 (Further sayings of the wise)
30:1–33 (All the sayings of Agur)	30:15–33 (Agur's numerical sayings)

1. We refer to the book of Proverbs as "Proverbs" (capitalized) and individual proverbs as "proverbs."

31:1–31 (On being a noble king and finding a valiant wife)

31:1–9 (On being a noble king)

25:1–29:27 (Sayings gathered by Hezekiah's men)

31:10–31 (On finding a valiant wife)

H. C. Washington argues convincingly that the structure of the LXX aims to give the whole book of Proverbs the illusion of being authored by Solomon.[2] It does so by suppressing the authorship of Agur (30:1) and Lemuel (31:1), rendering "the words of Agur" as "fear my words, son" and "the sayings of Lemuel, a king" as "my words have been spoken by God"; and by interlacing their sayings among "the sayings of the wise," which it attributes to Solomon.

There are also scores of additions, omissions, transpositions, and other differences between the LXX and the MT. Some are accidental, others deliberate. James Barr, a Scottish liberal Old Testament scholar, convincingly argues that the LXX translator sometimes so creatively renders proverbs that they become "an original composition rather than a rendering."[3] Nevertheless, the LXX occasionally preserves the original readings. Moreover, since centuries separate Solomon (ca. 950 B.C.) from the earliest extant Hebrew manuscripts and ancient versions, the extant text should be emended according to accredited principles of textual criticism to establish the original text.[4]

III. STRUCTURE

Proverbs contains six headings naming the genre and authorship of distinct collections within the book (1:1; 10:1; 24:23; 25:1; 30:1, 31:1). No heading occurs in 22:17, but the distinctive form of these "thirty sayings of the wise" in 22:17–24:22, including its own preamble, fully justifies recognizing it as a distinct collection. Thus, the book of Proverbs consists of seven collections.

Collection I (1:1–9:18)

This collection consists of three subsections: Title and Preamble (1:1–7), Prologue (1:8–8:36), and Epilogue (9:1–18). The Title (1:1) identifies the author

2. H. C. Washington, "Wealth and Poverty in the Instruction of Amenemope and the Hebrew Proverbs: A Comparative Case Study in the Social Location and Function of Ancient Near Eastern Wisdom Literature" (PhD diss., Princeton Theological Seminary, 1992), 194–97.

3. J. Barr, "Prov. XI.31, 1 Pet IV.18," *JSS* 20 (1975): 158–59.

4. Proverbs is poorly attested in a few fragments of the Dead Sea Scrolls.

(Solomon) and the genre (proverbs); the Preamble identifies its purpose (1:2–6), its addressees (youths, both uncommitted and wise), and the theological foundation of the book ("the fear of *I AM*," 1:7). The Prologue consists of ten lectures by a fictional father and mother to their son and two sermons by Woman Wisdom to uncommitted youths. The Epilogue features metaphorical invitations by Woman Wisdom and Woman Folly to uncommitted youths to enter their houses of life and death respectively and feast on their life-giving or death-dealing food.

Collection I differs markedly from the other collections. Whereas the other collections consist mainly of aphorisms (or epigrams: terse and witty statements of truth), its lectures and sermons are extended encomiums to wisdom to motivate the son to embrace the proverbs and sayings[5] in the following collections. Moreover, as Brevard Childs observes, chapters 1–9 function as "the 'hermeneutical guide' for understanding the rest of the book."[6]

Collection II (10:1–22:16)

The heading "The proverbs of Solomon" in 10:1a and the marked change from lengthy, unified lectures to aphorisms sharply separate Collection II from Collection I. Its one verse epigrams consist mainly of bicolons (the two halves, or versets, of a verse).[7] Scholars debate whether these aphorisms are a haphazard collection or are meaningfully grouped into larger clusters.[8] At the least, they are often associated with one another by sound and sense and occur in pairs. We seek to interpret the proverbs individually first and, where appropriate, within a larger meaningful cluster.

This collection is commonly divided into sections A (10:1–15:33) and B (16:1–22:17). However, 15:30–33 is better analyzed as a prologue to section B. The proverbs of section A are mostly antithetic while those of section

---

5. We commonly use "proverbs" for Solomon's aphorisms and "sayings" for the aphorisms of other sages.

6. B. S. Childs, *Introduction to the Old Testament as Scripture* (Philadelphia: Fortress, 1979), 553, citing W. Zimmerli.

7. They are sometimes referred to as "sentence proverbs." See E. C. Lucas, *Proverbs*, The Two Horizons Old Testament Commentary (Grand Rapids: Eerdmans, 2015), 3.

8. To summarize the history of scholarship on this topic, which according to Michael V. Fox goes back to the twelfth century, is beyond the scope of this commentary. Fox (*Proverbs 10–31: A New Translation with Introduction and Commentary*, AB 18B [New Haven: Yale University Press, 2009]) recognizes proverb clusters according to associative thinking but not as meaningful larger groupings. But Fox's dismissal depends on several assumptions that I (Bruce) critique in my review of Fox, *Proverbs 10–31* in *Review of Biblical Literature* (February, 2010).

B are mostly synthetic and show a much greater concern for the king and future functionaries at the royal court.

Collection III (22:17–24:22)

Collection III is commonly referred to as the "Thirty Sayings of the Wise." Its own preamble (22:17–21) debatably refers to thirty sayings (22:20). Its preamble and especially its first ten sayings have striking similarities with the thirty sayings of the Egyptian *Instruction of Amenemope* (ca. 1186–1069 B.C.) as selected examples in the following table show:

Instruction of Amenemope	Proverbs
"Look to these thirty chapters; they inform, they educate." (30.7)	"Have I not written for you thirty sayings of advice and knowledge . . . ?" (22:20)
"Guard yourself from robbing the poor, from being violent to the weak." (4.4–5)	"Do not rob poor people because they are poor and do not crush the afflicted in the gate." (22:22)
"As for the scribe who is experienced in his office, he will find himself worthy to be a courtier." (22.16–17)	"Do you see people who are skillful in their commission? They will present themselves before kings." (22:29)
"They [riches] made themselves wings like geese and flew away to the sky." (10.4–5)	"Will you let your eyes glance at riches? [If you do], they are not. Surely, without question, they will make a set of wings for themselves; like an eagle, they will fly toward the heavens." (23:5)

Solomon *adopted* from pagan cultures the wise sayings informed by God's common grace and *adapted* them to Israel's faith in *I AM*.

The style of Collection III differs from that of Collection II. Gone are the short, pithy epigrams of Collection II. In their place are more flowing shorter sayings, often in pairs consisting of admonition and motivating reason.

Collection IV (24:23–34)

The heading of this short collection identifies its genre and authors: "These also are sayings of the wise." For the collection's alternating structure, see p. 1.

The similarity between its last two verses (24:33–34) and 6:10–11 shows how the same material can be used in different contexts.

Collection V (25:1–29:27)

The heading ("These also are proverbs of Solomon, which the men of Hezekiah the king of Judah copied and collected" [ca. 700 B.C.]) resembles the short aphorisms of Collection II. The heading shows that the proverbs of Solomon were still open to additions more than two centuries after Solomon. This collection consists of two clusters: Va (chs. 25–27) and Vb (chs. 28–29). Va virtually lacks proverbs mentioning *I AM* and commonly uses similes and metaphors, while Vb focuses on *I AM*, rearing, and rulership. Raymond Van Leeuwen argues convincingly that Va consists of meaningful groupings: 25:2–27; 26:1–12; 26:13–16; and 26:17–28.[9] Bruce Malchow argues that Vb has a unique structure to develop its main theme: to wit, the education of young rulers.[10] A long poem (27:23–27) functions as a janus (see p. 14) linking the two clusters.

Collection VI (30:1–33)

An editorial prose heading ("The sayings of Agur son of Jakeh. An oracle.") marks off Collection VI. Many scholars deny the unity of this collection, but we will argue its sayings are united structurally and thematically (see pp. 411–12).

Collection VII (31:1–31)

"The sayings of Lemuel, a king—an oracle that his mother taught him" contains two distinct poems: the first a poem on the noble king (vv. 2–9) and the second an acrostic on the noble wife (vv. 10–31). Many scholars attribute only the first poem to King Lemuel, but we will argue with K. Kitchen that the heading pertains to both poems (see p. 426).

IV. Authorship

The headings in Proverbs name four authors: Solomon (Collections I and II), "men of Hezekiah" who collected and edited some of Solomon's proverbs (Col-

---

9. R. C. Van Leeuwen, "Context and Meaning in Proverbs 25–27" (PhD diss., University of St. Michael's College, 1984), 57–85.

10. Bruce V. Malchow, "A Manual for Future Monarchs," *CBQ* 47 (1985): 238–45.

lection V), Agur (Collection VI), and King Lemuel (Collection VII). Collection III and IV, identified as "sayings of the wise," were probably adopted, adapted and appended by Solomon. If so, Solomon authored Collections I–IV (chs. 1–24), and other editors collected his proverbs in Collection V (chs. 25–29). In other words, Solomon's fingerprint can be found in all but the last two collections.

A. Solomon

Most scholars agree with the attribution of Collections V, VI, and VII to Hezekiah, Agur, and Lemuel respectively, but they inconsistently deny the Solomonic authorship of Collections I and II. Some grant that a small nucleus of Solomon's proverbs are preserved in these collections. We contend, however, that the book's claim of Solomon's authorship should be taken at face value, although it's possible some proverbs were reshaped by later editors, even as compositions by English poets have been.[11]

The Old Testament claims Solomon was very wise and authored many proverbs (1 Kgs. 3:5-12 [= 2 Chr. 1:7-12]; 4:29-34; 5:7, 12; 10:1-12 [= 2 Chr. 9:1-9]; 11:41), and the New Testament accepts the historicity of these narratives (Matt. 6:29 [= Lk. 12:27]; 12:42 [= Lk. 11:31]; Acts 7:47). Similarities in the structure and content of Proverbs to comparable instructional literature from Egypt, Mesopotamia, and the Levant dating from the third millennium B.C. to Greco-Roman times substantiate the plain sense of the headings in Proverbs.

According to Egyptologist Kenneth Kitchen, the wisdom literature of Egypt exhibits two structures, which he labels type A and type B. Type A has a formal authorial title followed immediately by the main body. Type B has a formal authorial title followed by a prologue and then the main body, which may also contain short subtitles. The two types occur simultaneously and in roughly equal proportion from the third millennium B.C. to the Greco-Roman period, except that type A is unattested in the early second century B.C.[12]

The collections of Proverbs fall into either of these types. Collections IV–VII are like type A, while Collections I–II, consisting of author (1:1) + prologue (1:8–9:18) + main body (10:1–22:16) with terse subtitle (10:1), and III,

---

11. T. S. Eliot dedicated *The Waste Land* to Ezra Pound as "ll miglior fabbro" ("the better craftsman"). Pound's revisions were so significant that some critics believe he deserves co-author credit. Mabel Loomis Todd infamously edited Emily Dickinson's poems to make them suitable for nineteenth-century publication. (Thanks to Prof. Jeremiah Webster of Northwest University in Kirkland, Washington, for pointing me to these two cases.)

12. K. Kitchen, "Proverbs 2: Ancient Near Eastern Background," in *DOTWPW*, 552–53.

consisting of prologue (22:17–21) and main body (22:22–24:22) are essentially like type B. This comparative empirical evidence supports, but doesn't prove, the biblical claim.

Other correlations between Solomon and Egypt support the claims of Solomonic authorship. In 1922, E. A. Wallis Budge published what came to be known as *The Instruction of Amenemope*, which is from about the time of Solomon.[13] Its teachings, as noted above, resemble those of Collection III, further substantiating Solomon's connection to Prov. 22:17–24:22 as author or compiler. In 1966, Christa Kayatz noted many similarities in form and motifs between Proverbs 1–9 and Egyptian instructional wisdom, leading her toward a preexilic dating of Collection I.[14]

The similarities between the Solomonic proverbs and Egyptian wisdom are unsurprising given that Solomon married an Egyptian princess (1 Kgs. 3:1) and modeled his administration on that of Egypt. Scribes in Israel's courts must have been fluent in several languages, including Egyptian. Moreover, one can easily imagine the brilliant Solomon learning Egyptian from schoolboy texts, which consisted of instruction literature, in his preparation to head Israel's administration.

Solomonic authorship is also supported by linguistic evidence. Proverbs teems with Canaanitisms[15] and makes use of Ugaritic (ca. 1400 B.C.). This is consistent with the Solomonic era.[16]

The attributions in Proverbs to "Solomon son of David, king of Israel" (1:1; cf. 10:1), to "King Hezekiah" (25:1), and to "King Lemuel" (31:1), all royal figures, match the attributions of much ANE wisdom literature to royalty: in Egypt, for example, Khety I (ca. 2100 B.C.), Merikare (ca. 2000 B.C.), and Amenemhat I (ca. 1900 B.C.). The limited evidence from Mesopotamia also associates its wisdom with the legendary Sumerian king Shuruppak. The Aramaic collection of proverbial sayings is attributed to Ahiqar, a senior advisor to the Assyrian kings Sennacherib and Esarhaddon. In sum, the evidence from the ancient

13. E. A. W. Budge, *Second Series of Facsimiles of Egyptian Hieratic Papyri in the British Museum* (London: British Museum, 1923), plates 1–14.

14. C. B. Kayatz, *Studien zu Proverbien 1–9: Eine form- und motivgeschichtliche Untersuchung unter Einbeziehung ägyptischen Vergleichsmaterials*, WMANT 11 (Neukirchen-Vluyn: Neukirchener, 1966).

15. W. F. Albright, "Some Canaanite-Phoenician Sources of Hebrew Wisdom," in *WIANE*, 9.

16. M. J. Dahood, *Proverbs and Northwest Semitic Philology* (Rome: Biblical Institute, 1963); W. A. van der Weiden, *Le Livre des Proverbs: Notes philolgiques*, BibOr 23 (Rome: Biblical Institute, 1970).

Near East indicates that wisdom literature is typically associated with a court setting, and a court setting is opaquely present throughout Proverbs. Of all Israelite royal figures, Solomon best fits this setting.

David M. Carr cautiously suggests that parts of Proverbs "have the best claim to being datable . . . to the time of David and Solomon."[17] In a subsequent monograph, he argues that explicit and implicit historical references in Proverbs, such as attribution of major collections to Solomon, should be taken prima facie: "Perhaps we should start with the assumption that substantial portions of Proverbs date to the early preexilic period."[18]

In short, there is indisputable evidence that supports the Bible's claim that Solomon authored the bulk of Proverbs and no evidence that refutes it.[19]

To a scroll containing Collections I and II, Solomon probably appended the Thirty Sayings of the Wise (Collection III). Its author speaks of himself in the first person: "I cause you to know," (22:19) and "have I not written for you thirty sayings" (22:20). Solomon is the only named antecedent of "I." To this collection, he appended Collection IV, introducing it with: "these also are sayings of the wise" (24:23), which assumes the existence of Collection III. If Collections III and IV are anonymous, they are unique.

B. Men of Hezekiah

To the scroll of proverbs by Solomon (Collections I and II) and of sayings of the wise that Solomon appended to it (Collections III and IV), the men of Hezekiah king of Judah compiled "more proverbs of Solomon" (Collection V). When Collection V was added to the Proverbs is unknown. Although Solomon composed the proverbs of Collection V, their compilation is an act of authorship.

17. D. M. Carr, *An Introduction to the Old Testament: Sacred Texts and Imperial Contexts of the Hebrew Bible* (Malden, MA: Wiley-Blackwell, 2010), 76.

18. D. M. Carr, *Formation of the Hebrew Bible* (New York: Oxford University Press, 2011), 408.

19. Solomonic authorship is contested primarily on the existence of pseudepigraphal writings in the ancient Near East and the Bible (especially Ecclesiastes) and on linguistic data. For a refutation arguing that Ecclesiastes is not a pseudepigraph, see B. K. Waltke, *Proverbs: Chapters 1–15*, NICOT (Grand Rapids: Eerdmans, 2004), 34–36; and Waltke, *An Old Testament Theology* (Grand Rapids: Zondervan, 2007), 948.

C. Agur and Lemuel

Agur son of Jakeh, unknown and undated, is not a king. He was likely a court official, since he supports dynastic succession and strong kingship (30:22, 31) and his son Ithiel seems to be a budding court official (30:32–33). Lemuel, also unknown, is referred to as a king (31:1), which is in keeping with the royal context of wisdom literature.

D. The Final Editor

An anonymous final editor must have appended at the end of an expanding scroll the Sayings of Agur and Sayings of King Lemuel. The final editor also probably added the preamble (1:1–7) since it refers to the substance of the book as proverbs (of Solomon) and sayings of the wise (1:6). He may have allowed the original heading, "proverbs of Solomon" (1:1), to stand as the title to the whole book. This follows the practice of other biblical books. The editor who compiled the book of Job names Job as the author (cf. 31:40b) even though the book contains speeches from Job's friends. Similarly, the editor of Psalms names David as the author (72:20) of a collection that includes psalms by the sons of Korah and by Asaph.

This final editor—the real author of Proverbs but not of its collections— probably lived during the Persian period (ca. 540 B.C. – 322 B.C.) or in the Hellenistic era and expanded and updated the book to its present form. This inspired editor mediated the proverbs and sayings, originally addressed to historical persons such as Ithiel, to the universal covenant community of all ages. More specifically, according to the book's preamble, it is addressed to Israel's youths (1:4) and the wise (1:5, 8) to enable them to attain wisdom and to safeguard them against pagan worldviews in any age. The Holy Spirit, through the church, then sanctioned the work as canonical.

V. Ancient Near Eastern Wisdom Literature

Sound interpretation requires that words be interpreted in light of their historical context. The comparative ANE wisdom literature sheds light on Proverbs's authorship, literary forms, arrangement, textual transmission, philology, and figures of speech and also profiles its theology. For example, in Egypt, the number 30 was considered holy and symbolizes a complete and perfect teaching. Probably, Solomon meant the same in Prov. 22:20. In Prov. 24:12, *I AM* is represented as the one "who weighs the heart" (NIV). This imagery can be traced to the Egyptian god Thoth, who is represented as standing at the judgment of the dead beside the scales with the human heart.[20]

VI. Poetry

A. Characteristics of Biblical Poetry

Apart from the prose headings (1:1; 10:1a; 24:23a; 25:1; 30:1; 31:1), Proverbs is written in poetry. Three elements characterize biblical poetry: terseness, imagery, and parallelism.

1. Terseness

A poet states things in as few words as possible.[21] Terseness is achieved within the poetic line by commonly omitting the definite article, conjunctions, and relative pronouns and occasionally gapping whole words or phrases. Terseness between the lines is achieved by the omission of conjunctions and logical particles such as "and" or "therefore."

For Proverbs, terseness is the hallmark of its lines. The sage teaches truth through aphorisms that are also epigrams. Consequently, a single proverb may not express the whole truth about a subject; other proverbs are needed to complete

20. According to N. Shupak ("The Instruction of Amenemope and Proverbs 22:17–24:22 from the Perspective of Contemporary Research," in *Seeking Out the Wisdom of the Ancients: Essays Offered to Honor Michael V. Fox on the Occasion of His 65th Birthday*, ed. Ronald L. Troxel, Kelvin G. Friebel, and Dennis R. Magary [Winona Lake, IN: Eisenbrauns, 2005], 216), the borrowing of Egyptian imagery "was done in a careful and considered manner: the Hebrew author or editor made changes and adapted the instructions of the Egyptian sage to the world of monotheistic belief."

21. Adele Berlin ("Introduction to Hebrew Poetry," in *The New Interpreter's Bible: Old Testament Survey*, ed. Leander E. Keck [Nashville: Abingdon, 2005], 169) offers a good example of terseness by comparing the prose version of Judges 4:19 with its poetic equivalent in 5:19:

> Then he said to her; "Please give me a little water to drink; for I am thirsty."
> So she opened a skin of milk, gave him a drink, and covered him. (Judg. 4:19)
>   "Water," he asked; milk she gave;
>   in a princely bowl she brought him curds. (Judg. 5:25)

The prose version carries the reader step by step along the narrative sequence of Jael's providing for Sisera's need, but the terse poetic version highlights her largess to put him at ease for the kill. Prose is like a film; poetry is like a slide show, in which each verse closes with a click.

the picture.[22] For example, "Dedicate youth according to what their way dictates; even when they become old, they will not depart from it" (22:6) expresses the truth (or promise) that parenting has lifelong effects on a youth, but it does not exhaust the biblical truth about child-raising. Rather, it is one of many components that must be fitted together with other components in order to comprehend the comprehensive, confused pattern of real life. A failure to recognize *terseness* and how it asserts truth baldly has led to many errors in interpreting Proverbs.

2. Imagery or Figures

Proverbs is filled with figures of speech (e.g., simile, metaphor, metonymy, etc.), and even sustained figures—especially in the Prologue. In addition to being evocative, imagery contributes to terseness by enabling the author to communicate much with little. Familiarity with figures of speech is an essential part of the propaedeutic for interpreting any poem.

3. Parallelism

Whereas English poetry is marked by a sustained meter and rhyme, Hebrew poetry is marked by parallelism. Parallelism occurs when a line of poetry is divided into half lines—what we call versets—with each corresponding to the other in some way.[23] The two versets together constitute a bicolon. Prov. 15:4 is a typical bicolon:

> Verset A: The soothing tongue is a tree of life,
> Verset B: but perversity in it fractures the spirit.

In this example, the bicolon consists of two versets, which we designate verset A (or 15:4a) and verset B (or 15:4b).

Semantically, verset B both corresponds in thought with verset A and in some way advances or escalates it, often specifying or intensifying it. The versets commonly move from general to specific, from abstract to concrete, or from less intense to more intense.[24] Traditionally, the parallelism in the versets has been classified into three main types:

22. This may be why the sages call on their disciples to memorize all of the proverbs (22:18).

23. L. Wilson (*Proverbs*, TOTC [Downers Grove, IL: InterVarsity, 2017], 7) refers to parallelism as "a kind of 'thought rhyme.'"

24. James Kugel (*The Idea of Biblical Poetry: Parallelism and Its History* [Baltimore:

- Synonymous—Verset B repeats the same thought as verset A in different words:

    Verset A: Let a stranger and not your own mouth praise you,
    Verset B: an outsider, and let not your own lips praise you. (27:2)

- Antithetical—The thought of verset B is opposed to that of verset A. Usually the contrast is marked by "but":

    Verset A: A poor person is made with a slack hand,
    Verset B: but the hand of diligent people brings wealth. (10:4)

- Synthetic—Verset B expands the thought of verset A:

    Verset A: Commit to *I AM* your works
    Verset B: and your thoughts will be established. (16:3)

Two subtypes are also worth noting:

- Better-Than Proverbs—A subtype of antithetical parallelism, this type provides two negative situations in its versets and calls the reader to choose the better of the two, which is usually stated in verset A:

    Verset A: Better a little with the fear of *I AM*
    Verset B: than great treasure and turmoil with it. (15:16)

- Comparative Proverbs—In this subtype of synthetic parallelism, the reader is called to compare two situations to note what is similar in them:

    Verset A: [Like] a gold ring in a snout of a pig
    Verset B: [is] a beautiful woman who turns aside from discretion. (11:22)

The above classifications of parallelism are not hard and fast, and no complete taxonomy of parallelism is possible since the variations are too many.

Sometimes two bicola stand in parallel, forming a quatrain. Consider Prov. 23:4-5 (NIV):

The Johns Hopkins University Press, 1981]) contends that in parallelism, the second line expands upon the first in a multitude of ways. He articulates the way in which the second line develops the first with the phrase: "A is so, and *what's more*, B is so" (his emphasis).

Do not wear yourself out to get rich;
    do not trust your own cleverness.
Cast but a glance at riches, and they are gone,
    for they will surely sprout wings and fly off to the sky like an
        eagle.

Semantically, not formally, v. 5 gives the reason for heeding the admonition in v. 4, albeit each verse is a saying in its own right.

B. Poetics

Through the study of poetics, connections between the verses are discerned. Biblical sages used a variety of literary techniques to give their compositions coherence and unity and to protect the vulnerable epigrams against misinterpretation. According to Adele Berlin, poetics is "an inductive science that seeks to abstract the general principles of literature from many different manifestations of those principles as they occur in actual literary texts." Its essential aim is not "to elicit meaning of any given text" but "to find the building blocks of literature and the rules by which they are assembled." Thus, "poetics is to literature as linguistics is to language."[25] If linguistics is the science of language (a study of the meaning of words and the rules that govern their interrelationship), then poetics is the science of literature (a study of how basic components of writing interrelate to create meaning). In other words, poetics is a grammar of literature. Just as we need grammar to make sense of a language, we need poetics to make sense of a literary text. To know what a text means, we must first know how it means.

In a poem, the verses are usually connected. For example, in Prov. 2, the conditional clauses introduced by "if" in vv. 1–4 are followed by the consequential clauses introduced by "then" in vv. 5 and 9. Two closely connected verses (or bicola) are called a *quatrain*, a smaller collection of verses a *strophe*, and a larger division a *stanza*. The twelve lectures and sermons of the Prologue are all poems.

In contrast to the poems, the proverbs of Solomon and the sayings of the wise are mostly collections of individual proverbs and sayings, expressing a complete thought by themselves and only secondarily to be interpreted in connection with other proverbs or sayings. The connections between the units are less obvious,

---

25. A. Berlin, *Poetics and Interpretation of Biblical Narrative*, JSOTSup 9 (Sheffield: Almond Press, 1983), 15.

creating the impression that they are atomistic and without coherence. However, the study of poetics provides a lens to see unstated connections between them. This means the interpreter must interpret each proverb and saying not only on its own but also in light of the group to which it is connected.

Verses are linked by words, syntax, sense, and repetitive phonology. Other literary devices are also used to create connections. A sampling of such devises includes:

- Inclusio—Marking off a literary unit by matching the end with the beginning. The preamble to the book (1:2–7) begins and ends with the words "wisdom and instruction" (2a; 7b).
- Key word (German *Leitwort*)—A word that highlights the unit's topic. In Prov. 30:18–20, the key word "way" is used to contrast the four ways admired by Agur (30:18–19) with the despicable way of the adulteress.
- Catchword—A word that stitches the sayings together. Prov. 16:1–9 is connected by the catchword "*I AM*" which occurs in every verse except 8, the second from the end. Prov. 16:10–15 is held together by the catchword "king," which occurs in every verse except 11, the second from the beginning. Thus, the two units (16:1–9, 10–15) complement each other by respectively trumpeting the themes of God's sovereign rule and the king's mediatorial rule.
- Janus—A transition that looks back to the preceding text and ahead to the proceeding text. Thus, 31:19 is a janus because it functions as a seam transitioning from the valiant wife's sources of income (vv. 13–18) to her contributions to her household and to the wider community (vv. 20–27).

In addition to the techniques listed above, structures of patterning are used to bind proverbs or sayings together around a specific topic or theme that is only discernible when the pattern is recognized. Patterns help to establish the boundaries of a unit. Scholars have recognized a variety of such patterns in Proverbs:

- An alternating pattern (A-B::A'-B') can be described as one wave following another.[26] This pattern requires the reader to compare the parallel elements to discern progression. For example, in 4:5–9, the admonition to get wisdom (A, A') progresses in the motivation from protection (B) to honor (B'):

26. Waltke, *Old Testament Theology*, 119.

A			Admonition: Get wisdom	v. 5
	B		Motivation: She will protect her lover	v. 6
A'			Admonition: Get wisdom	v. 7
	B'		Motivation: She will honor her lover	vv. 8–9

• A concentric pattern (A-B-C::C'-B'-A') can be described as the tide coming in and then going back out. This pattern provides a sense of completeness and enables the reader to focus on comparison and contrast. The Prologue (1:8–9:18) may be arranged in a concentric pattern:

A				Rival invitations of parents and gang to son	1:8–19
	B			Wisdom's rebuke of uncommitted	1:20–33
		C		Janus: Father's command to heed teaching as safeguard against evil men and unchaste wife	2:1–22
			D	Father's command to heed teaching	3:1–4:27
			D'	Father's warnings against unchaste wife	5:1–6:35
		C'		Janus: Father's warnings against Wisdom's rival	7:1–27
	B'			Wisdom's invitation to uncommitted	8:1–36
A'				Rival invitations of Wisdom and Folly to uncommitted	9:1–18

• A chiastic pattern (A-B-C-X-C'-B'-A') has a pivot (X) as the focus of the message. It can be described as the ripples from a rock thrown in a pond.[27] The five sayings of Prov. 26:6–10 are arranged in a chiastic pattern, as shown by Duane Garrett,[28] to emphasize the point that honoring a fool is unfitting.

A			Committing important business to a fool	v. 6
	B		A proverb in a fool's mouth	v. 7
		X	Honoring a fool	v. 8
	B'		A proverb in a fool's mouth	v. 9
A'			Committing important business to a fool	v. 10

27. Waltke, *Old Testament Theology*, 120.
28. D. Garrett, *Proverbs, Ecclesiastes, Song of Solomon*, NAC 14 (Nashville: Broadman, 1983), 212.

VII. The Wisdom Genre

A. What Is Wisdom Literature?

Understanding the literary genre of a text is essential to properly interpret it. Each genre contains distinctive characteristics that require unique interpretative approaches.[29] The exact nature and setting of the wisdom literature of the Old Testament is debated. It is often said to be characterized by features such as being humanistic in orientation, international in scope, non-historical in emphasis, eudaemonistic in practice, concerned with a search for order, and instructional in tone. However, what radically distinguishes biblical wisdom literature from other biblical genres is its unique inspiration.[30] Unlike the visions and dreams given to the prophet, the face-to-face encounter given to Moses, and the poetic imagination given to David, sages gained revelation through keen observations of nature and humanity and their cogitations upon them, which are informed by the fear of *I AM*.[31]

This psychology of inspiration is showcased in 24:30–34. After passing the field of a sluggard, which once was a productive and profitable vineyard but under the sluggard's management has devolved into a weed patch, the sage says: "I saw; I paid attention; I observed; I accepted a lesson" (v. 32), whereupon the sage either coins or cites a proverb (vv. 33–34):

> A little sleep, a little slumber,
>> a little folding of the arms to lie down,
> and poverty will come on you like a vagrant,
>> and scarcity like an armed man.

The sages' wisdom, however, is not based on natural theology. They view creation and all human activity through the lens of faith in Israel's covenant-

---

29. For example, in Proverbs, the word *petî*, from a root meaning "open," means open to other worldviews (i.e., "uncommitted" to truth) and so is related to the fool. In the Psalms, however, *petî* has the sense of open to God (i.e. "pious").

30. The author of Hebrews recognized that "in the past God spoke to our ancestors through the prophets at many times and *in various ways*" (1:1, our emphasis).

31. Similarly, Qoheleth ("teacher" or "gatherer") begins his treatise in Ecclesiastes by observing the cycles of creation that appear to him a "chasing after wind"/"vexation of spirit." He tells of his quest for wisdom by reflecting on his experiences under the sun. Job also bases his reflections on his experience of misery, for which he found no relief until *I AM* opened his eyes to observe that chaos and death in creation are not absolute but are divinely bounded by order and life (Job 38–41).

keeping God. Without this point of view, observing nature could teach the "law of the survival of the fittest" and not the way of righteousness, leading them to commend the use of power and dominance. When Solomon uses the ant as a paragon of industry and prudence (6:6-11), he ignores the ant's destructive capabilities. In fact, both Agur (30:1-6) and Job (Job 8:31-41) claim that creation teaches the impossibility of attaining true wisdom apart from special revelation.

B. Genres in Proverbs

1. Proverbs

Proverbs classifies its genre as *mišlê* (a plural form of *māšāl*, meaning "proverb"). Both in English language and culture and in the book of Proverbs, a proverb is a short, pithy saying. In English, it has popular currency, whereas in Proverbs, it has currency only with those who fear *I AM*. For example, the first proverb ("Treasures gained by wickedness are of no eternal value," 10:2) is not popular among the masses, since many seek precisely such treasure. Similarly, Wisdom restricts the acceptance of her wisdom "to those who understand" (8:9). Were it popular among the masses, she would not need to stand at the gate of the city pleading her cause (1:20-21; 8:1-3).

The verbal root of the noun *māšāl* may mean "to be like," in which case the noun would mean "a comparison or analogy [constructed] for the purpose of conveying a model, exemplar, or paradigm."[32] Thus, the purpose of a proverb is to compel the readers or hearers to compare their lives to the truth of the proverb.[33] Because the proverbs and sayings ask the reader to "see" the connection between the proverb and themselves, they are also called "parables" or "riddles" (1:6).The result depends sometimes on the reader's particular life situation. For example, in Psalm 49, the proverb (*māšāl* in v. 4) that a person without understanding "is like" the beasts that perish (vv. 12, 20) will comfort the low and sober the high, warn the rich and console the poor.

Although proverbs assert truths, using them without discerning one's situation can have dire consequences. The proverb "A thornbush in the hand of a drunkard, and a proverb in the mouth of fools" (26:9) is illustrated by Job's

---

32. G. M. Landers, "Johan: A māšāl?," in *Israelite Wisdom*, ed. J. G. Gammie et al. (Missoula, MT: Scholars, 1978), 140, following W. McKane, *Proverbs: A New Approach*, OTL (Philadelphia: Westminster, 1970), 23-33.

33. A. S. Herbert, "The 'Parable' (MĀŠĀL) in the Old Testament," *SJT* 7 (1954): 180-96.

friends' misuse of proverbs (see Job 18:5). R. Van Leeuwen notes, "Users of proverbs must choose from the diverse sayings and admonitions the one that best 'hits the nail on the head.' . . . Proverb use is always situational."[34] A proverb is always true, but it may not be true for a given situation.

2. Short Sayings and Long Admonitions

Proverbs contains two primary literary forms: longer units in admonitory style (Collections I, III–IV) and short aphorisms or epigrams in the third person (Collections II and V), albeit exceptions occur (6:12–19; 31:10–31). The longer, admonitory type is similar to the Egyptian instructions, while the shorter sentence proverbs are similar to those from Mesopotamia. As noted, the epigrammatic proverbs must be qualified by other proverbs (cf. Prov. 14:20–21). Also, the epigrammatic proverbs require more wit to interpret them. Consequently, the Prologue's longer, clearer, admonitory poems prepare the reader to interpret the more elusive shorter sayings.

This distinction, however, can be misleading. Admonitions may seem more instructive and authoritative than the shorter sayings, but the preamble to Proverbs makes clear that all proverbs and sayings are to make youth prudent and the wise wiser (1:4–5). The Prologue refers to both forms as commands and teaching (1:8). Moreover, both forms are authoritative because they are both inspired by God (2:6) and handed down by faithful parents through the generations (4:3–4). They are not based on human traditions nor on common sense.

C. Setting

Two issues concern us here: In what context were proverbs composed, and in what context were they circulated?

1. Setting of Composition

The attributions of proverbs and sayings to Solomon (1:1; 10:1), the men of Hezekiah (25:1), and King Lemuel (31:1) suggest they were composed in a court setting. Agur (30:1) was probably a court official (see exposition). As argued above (see p. 4), the Thirty Sayings of the Wise (22:17) were

34. R. C. Van Leeuwen, "The Book of Proverbs," in *The New Interpreter's Bible: Old Testament Survey*, ed. Leander E. Keck (Nashville: Abingdon, 2005), 241.

probably adopted and adapted by Solomon, and he himself probably appended the "further sayings of the wise" (24:23–34). And as noted above (see p. 7) the collections of Egyptian instructional literature were composed in court settings.

Scholars who reject the book's attribution to Solomon disagree as to where the book's sayings were composed. Among the proposed settings, two are worth noting: the folk setting and the school setting.

Those who propound a folk setting argue that many of the book's sayings originate from observations on life by ordinary people functioning in the agricultural sector of society. One reason they prefer this setting is that many of the sayings do not speak directly of the king and are more appropriate to a rural, agricultural context. As for those sayings that do speak directly of the king (and they are a significant number), Whybray explains them as the observations on monarchy by ordinary people.[35] Fox notes, however, that this conclusion overlooks clues for an urban setting, such as "references to goldsmiths and messengers which have no place in the small village."[36] Moreover, the content of a proverb does not establish its setting. "Strike while the iron is hot" may not have originated in a blacksmith's shop any more than "look before you leap" originated at a swimming hole.

Those who propound a school setting argue on the basis that such schools existed in Egypt. However, as Lucas notes, following others, "The fact is there is no unambiguous reference to a wisdom school in Israel until Jesus Ben Sirach's 'house of instruction' in the early second century B.C. (Sir. 51:23)."[37] Of course, much depends on one's definition of "school." If by school one understands a standalone building staffed by professional "teachers," then the evidence of such schools in ancient Israel is still forthcoming.[38]

Although it is hazardous to establish setting by content, many sayings and proverbs unmistakably point to a royal setting. For example, "When you sit

35. R. N. Whybray, *Wealth and Poverty in the Book of Proverbs*, JSOTSup 99 (Sheffield: Sheffield Academic, 1990), 47.

36. M. V. Fox, "The Social Location of the Book of Proverbs," in *Texts, Temples, and Traditions: A Tribute to Menahem Haran*, ed. M. V. Fox et al. (Winona Lake, IN: Eisenbrauns, 1996), 233. Fox also notes that in Proverbs, when an agricultural setting is the context, the saying usually addresses wealthy landowners and not peasants.

37. E. C. Lucas, *Exploring the Old Testament: A Guide to the Psalms and Wisdom Literature* (Downers Grove, IL: InterVarsity, 2003), 82. Similarly, Fox, "Social Location," 231: "Apart from the supposed Egyptian analogy, there is nothing in Proverbs to point to a school origin."

38. D. M. Carr, *Writing on the Tablet of the Heart: Origins of Scripture and Literature* (New York: Oxford University Press, 2005), 12.

down to eat with a ruler, mark well what is before you" (23:1) does not pertain to Mr. Everyman. So, given the lack of consensus for another setting and on the basis of the named authors, the analogy of other collections of instructional literature for budding officials, and the content of many sayings, we contend that the sayings of Proverbs originated in a court setting.

2. Setting of Dissemination

Where were the proverbs disseminated? The references to the father and the mother and their son(s) (e.g., 1:8; 6:20; 10:1) point to the home as the setting for the dissemination of the book's wisdom. As noted above, ancient Israel had no schools.[39] Moreover, in Egyptian and Mesopotamian wisdom literature, the speaker is almost always a father speaking to his son. Furthermore, the fact that the mother is also mentioned as teaching the son wisdom puts the home setting beyond reasonable doubt (4:3; 6:20; 23:25; 31:1, 26–28; cf. 10:1; 15:20). Carr comments, "It is highly unlikely that female teachers would have taken on the epithet 'mother' who were not the actual 'mother' of a student, and Proverbs 31:1 even mentions a mother responsible for a given written teaching attributed to King Lemuel."[40] The home setting is further corroborated in 4:1–9, where the godly family—including grandfather, father, mother, and son—is fictitiously represented as transmitting the family's spiritual inheritance. Fox finds a strong analogy to the ancient wisdom instructions in the medieval Jewish ethical testament.[41] Thus, it appears Solomon intended to pass his wisdom to Israel's youths by putting his proverbs in the mouths of godly parents (1:8–9), even as Moses disseminated the law in the home (cf. Deut. 6:7–9). Wisdom's call in the public places to the masses (1:20–33; 8:1–31) are fictional and in fact intended for the son, as the conclusion of her address in 8:32–36 shows. Finally, the fact that the book does not name a specific recipient—unlike other ANE wisdom texts—indicates the final editor wished to democratize the book so it would be continually taught in all godly homes.

---

39. According to H. Freedman ("Kiddushin," in *The Babylonian Talmud*, ed. I. Epstein, vol. 4 [London: Soncino, 1948], 140 n. 8), the introduction of schools in Judaism is variously ascribed to the reforms of R. Simeon b. Shetah and the high priest Joshua b. Gamala.

40. Carr, *Writing*, 129–30.

41. Fox, "Social Location," 232: "Ethical testaments are instructions written by men in their maturity for the religious-ethical guidance of their sons and, sometimes, daughters. These texts are, in fact, descendants of ancient Wisdom Literature, since they use Proverbs as a model. . . . The father addresses his son (or sons) and through him speaks to a larger audience."

VIII. Theology

A. Introduction

To better understand Proverbs, we step back briefly and consider some of the book's theological presuppositions and teachings utilizing three of the categories of systematic theology: theology proper (God), anthropology, and soteriology. Under the category of theology proper, we also consider the sub-categories of revelation, inspiration, and tradition.

But first, two other theological matters should be dealt with: What is the relationship of Proverbs to the rest of the Old Testament? And how do we explain Proverbs's relationship to the wisdom literature of the surrounding cultures?

1. The Relationship of Proverbs to the Old Testament

Two facts have led to the problem of how to relate Proverbs to the rest of the Old Testament: the book's lack of reference to the history of Israel and its many similarities with the wisdom literature of the surrounding cultures, especially Egypt. These two facts lead scholars to connect Proverbs more to the international wisdom scene than to the rest of the Old Testament. So how holy is Proverbs? Is it Scripture, or merely an expression of human wisdom like other ancient instructional literature?

In fact, Proverbs has many significant connections with other Old Testament literature.[42] First, its identification of Solomon as "son of David, king of Israel" (1:1) both locates Proverbs within the flow of Israel's narrative history and implies its audience is God's mediatorial "kingdom of priests" (see Exod. 19:6).

Second, Proverbs joins the rest of the Old Testament in calling its audience to "fear *I AM*" (*yir'at yhwh*; Prov. 1:7; cf. Deut. 6:5; Josh. 24:14; Isa. 29:13). The use of God's personal name, YHWH ("He is," translated "*I AM*"), in Prov. 1:7 signals his unique covenant relationship with his son, Israel. And the call to fear him pertains to submitting to his revealed will—whether it is revealed in the laws of Moses or in the proverbs of Solomon.

Third, the theology of Proverbs refines the theology of Moses and of the prophets. The bottom line for all three—Moses, the prophets, and the sages—is to create a nation that in its theology fears God, in its praxis reflects God's

---

42. See B. K. Waltke, "The Book of Proverbs and Old Testament Theology," *BSac* 136 (1979): 302-17.

character by doing righteousness and justice, and in its purpose extends true Israel to the ends of the earth. The law does it through its commandments and stipulations, the prophets, through their oracles, and Solomon through his proverbs.[43] Derek Kidner notes about Proverbs, "There are details of character small enough to escape the mesh of the law and the broadsides of the prophets, and yet decisive in personal dealings. Proverbs moves in this realm, asking what a person is like to live with, or to employ; how he manages his affairs, his time and himself."[44]

The refinement of the Law of Moses by the proverbs of Solomon may be compared to learning to drive a car.[45] The comprehensive rule "drive carefully" is refined by road signs: "STOP," "YIELD," "Speed Limit 35 mph," and so on. This is further refined by passing a written test and a road test, requiring such knowledge as how far to park from a corner, how to change lanes, and how to merge onto a four-lane highway. Similarly, the comprehensive commandments "love God" and "love your neighbor" (see Deut. 6:5; Lev. 19:18) are refined in the Law of Moses by the Ten Commandments: "You shall have no other gods before me" (Exod. 20:3); "you shall not murder" (Exod. 20:13). And these commandments are further refined in Proverbs: "If those who hate you are hungry, give them food to eat " (25:21); and "Her husband [rises] and praises her: 'Many daughters do valiantly, but you surpass them all'" (31:28–29). Thus, if the son obeys Proverbs, he will, *ipso facto*, fulfill the Law.

Fourth, Solomon ascribes the same attributes and actions to God as do Moses and the prophets. To all three, God is the Creator (Deut. 10:14; Prov. 1:7; 3:19–20; Isa. 40:28), the just Avenger (Deut. 32:35, 40–41; Prov. 5:21–22; Nah. 1:2), the Sovereign of history (Deut. 4:19; 29:1; Prov. 16:1–9; 19:21; Isa. 45:1), the disciplinary Father (Deut. 8:5; Prov. 3:11–12; Isa. 1:4–6), and the merciful Responder who answers prayer (Deut. 4:29–31; Prov. 15:8, 29; Isa. 56:7).[46]

Fifth, Agur's relationship to the rest of the Old Testament is indicated in Prov. 30:5–6, where Agur cites two Scriptures from the Old Testament. After confessing his despair of finding wisdom and a knowledge he can trust, he

43. Childs (*Introduction*, 558) states, "It is striking that the patterns of human behavior which the Proverbs inculcate overlap to a large extent with that set of ethical standards prescribed in the Pentateuch for the covenant people. . . . Both the Proverbs and the Law call for a commitment to God and his divine order."

44. D. Kidner, *The Proverbs*, TOTC (Downers Grove, IL: InterVarsity, 1964), 13. Cf. John Goldingay, "The 'Salvation History' Perspective and the 'Wisdom' Perspective within the Context of Biblical Theology," *EvQ* 51 (1979): 194ff.

45. See B. K. Waltke, "Righteousness in Proverbs," *WTJ* 70 (2008): 225–37.

46. See Waltke, "Proverbs and Old Testament Theology," 305.

arrives at an answer in discovering that God has spoken in the Bible, citing Ps. 18:30 in v. 5 and the canonical formula of Deut. 4:2 in v. 6a. Thus, we can extrapolate that his search for knowledge is satisfied in Scripture found in the canon as it was then known to him.[47] In sum, Solomon, Moses, and the prophets speak out of the same worldview, but they express it in different forms: proverbs, laws, and oracles.

2. The Relationship of Proverbs to the Wisdom Literature of the Surrounding Cultures

But how do we explain and understand the undoubtable similarities in expression and in theology between the inspired book of Proverbs and the non-inspired wisdom of Israel's neighbors? None doubts that the instruction literature from Egypt's Old Kingdom (ca. 2686–2181 B.C.) and Middle Kingdom (ca. 1975–1640 B.C.), and from the Ebla and Sumerian collections, predates and so is not dependent on Solomon's proverbs. The Thirty Sayings of the Wise and The *Instructions of Amenemope* originate at about the same time and may both depend on a common earlier source.

The first explanation is cultural. The Old Testament is embedded in the culture of the ancient Near East. Hebrew is a Canaanite language, and its forms of literature (e.g., law codes, hymns, and prophecies) are also found in pagan cultures. Thus, its uniqueness is found not in transcending its culture but in its subjection of that culture to the transcendent, living God. It borrows *and adapts* ideas, language, sayings, laws, and mythological allusions from its neighbors, but purges them of their pagan theology to serve the purposes of *I AM*. This is the case also with Proverbs. Some of its wisdom is borrowed, but all of the borrowed material is brought under the affirmation that it is *I AM* who is the Creator and Revealer of wisdom. In Prov. 22:17, Solomon states that he has borrowed and adapted the sayings of other wise men but immediately adds, "In order that your trust may be in *I AM*."[48]

The second explanation is theological and rests in the distinction between the concepts of the "fear of *I AM* [*yhwh*]" and the "fear of God ['*ĕlōhîm*]." The Bible distinguishes between them. The former is seen as unique to Israel and pertains to special revelation, whereas the latter is seen as the general revelation of God to all humans, which is accessible through conscience and

---

47. Waltke, *Old Testament Theology*, 903.
48. Childs (*Introduction*, 548) concurs: "Of course the uniquely Hebrew stamp which Israel gave its borrowed material has not been denied."

the created order.[49] According to R. N. Whybray, "fear of God" refers "to a standard of moral conduct known and accepted by men in general" and "motivates people to right behavior even when there are no legal codes."[50] And Yale psychology professor Paul Bloom finds that "at birth, babies are endowed with compassion, with empathy, with the beginnings of a sense of fairness."[51] Thus, foreign sages such as Amenemope, who possess the "fear of God," can produce wisdom that agrees in some moral matters with the wisdom of Proverbs. The difference is that in *Amenemope*, God is opaque, a generic being, while in Proverbs he is specifically named as YHWH, the God of Israel.

B. God

1. Names of God

Proverbs refers to God in 100 of its 915 verses—over 10 percent—and, more specifically, eighty-seven times by his covenant-with-Israel name YHWH (*I AM*). In contrast, the name "God" (*ĕlōhîm*) occurs only five times and signifies God's eternal might and power over all mortals (cf. Num. 23:19).

2. God as Creator

The concept of creation is mentioned ten times in Proverbs. The citations in Collection I, the Prologue, refer to God's creation of the world (Prov. 3:19–20; 8:22–31), while those in Solomon's proverbs (Collections II and V) refer to his creation of human beings (Prov. 14:31; 16:11; 17:5; 20:12; 22:2; 29:13). These references are consistent with the creation theology of the rest of the Bible (e.g., that Israel's God is the solitary and sovereign Creator), albeit some poems of the Bible may use the terminology, but not the theology, of pagan myths (cf. 3:20; 8:29; 30:4).

In 3:19–20, the Hebrew verb used for splitting the primeval waters retains the imagery of battle myths. Unlike the psalmists, who point to *I AM*'s creation and his sustenance of the earth to glorify him (see Ps. 104) or to argue for the steadfastness of the Creator's laws (see Ps. 93),[52] Solomon points to

---

49. R. N. Whybray, *Wisdom in Proverbs: The Concept of Wisdom in Proverbs 1–9* (London: SCM, 1965), 96.

50. See Whybray, *Wisdom in Proverbs*, 96.

51. Gareth Cook, "The Moral Life of Babies," *Scientific American*, November 12, 2013.

52. B. K. Waltke and J. M. Houston, *The Psalms as Christian Praise* (Grand Rapids: Eerdmans, 2019), 131–42.

God's wisdom, which enables the world to endure in such a finely balanced manner. The application, then, is that the same wisdom which established a creation that endures is also what is needed, and what is available, to establish a life that will endure. The Creator made humans with eyes and ears in order to grasp wisdom (20:12).

3. God as Sovereign, Transcendent, and Immanent

I AM is sovereign. Nothing is hidden from his eyes (5:21; 15:3; 22:12), and nothing operates outside of his will. Even the king's heart, inscrutable to other humans (25:3), is but a stream of water in *I AM's* hands that he directs as he sees fit (21:1), meriting him the title King of kings.[53] *I AM* even rules over chance. Humans may throw a die and call it chance, but it is *I AM* who determines which way it ends up (16:33). His sovereignty over history means that everything, even the wicked, will be directed to an end appropriate to itself (16:4). He made the scales that the king uses to administer fair weights and measures, and under his king's administration, no cheat escapes judgment (16:4, 14). The Sovereign created all humans, rich and poor, investing both with dignity and requiring the wealthy to take care of the poor (22:2; 29:13). Whoever mocks the poor reviles *I AM* since he created the poor in his image (17:5). The human thinks and plans, but the answer of his tongue is from *I AM*, who also establishes his steps (16:1, 9). Thus, the only sensible response for humankind is to commit their ways to *I AM* (16:3), who searches them out (15:11; 20:27) and blesses or punishes humans for their works and words (3:13, 18; 8:34; 12:14; 19:3; 20:25; 21:16; 24:12; 28:14, 17; 29:23).

I AM's sovereignty entails his transcendence. This is seen in his role as Creator; he is not bound by the spatial or temporal limits of his creation. His existence before time contributes to his comprehensive and therefore infallible knowledge—a fact that filled Agur with humility and hope and lays the foundation for an orthodox epistemology (see 30:1–4). It hardly needs saying that in the theology of Proverbs, there are no other gods to compete with *I AM*.

Paradoxically, *I AM*, transcendent in heaven, is immanent on earth. His immanence means he knows the sufferings of the oppressed. He is near to them, feels their misery, and will punish their oppressors just as certainly as he will reward those who have compassion on them (19:17). The saying "ignorance of the law is no excuse" comes home to roost in Proverbs, where the immanent *I AM* holds the ignorant accountable for not delivering the helpless

---

53. Kidner, *Proverbs*, 141.

and oppressed (24:11–12). Only an immanent God, fully involved in the life of the world, would care enough to hold people accountable for their deeds. All who choose wisdom will find *I AM* at their side (3:26) and be, as his friends, taken into his confidence (3:32).

4. God as Judge

In Proverbs, God's transcendence provides the theological rationale for his role as judge. "Only a transcendent God," states Bostrom, "can be trusted with the 'impossible' task of dispensing justice to each individual and situation!"[54] But precisely how does God dispense justice? To some scholars, Proverbs presents a world order that is so impersonal and deistic that the dispensing of justice becomes merely a matter of an inexorable "deed and destiny": you reap what you sow. In such a scheme, *I AM*'s connection to justice is at best no more than that of a first cause. Does Proverbs teach that the fate of the wicked is simply a matter of some inescapable destiny or karma that automatically follows their deeds? A superficial reading could lead to such a view—"He who sows iniquity will reap calamity" (cf. 1:19; 10:2, 4; 11:5–6; etc.)—but a deeper reading shows that *I AM* is no Olympian removed from the active dispensation of justice.

First, recall the epigrammatic nature of the proverbs, which bars an individual saying from expressing the complete truth of a matter. Proverbs need to be read together.[55] Proverbs that seem to present an impersonal world order (10:2) are followed by proverbs that speak of *I AM*'s involvement in peoples' lives, as in 10:3.[56]

Second, as noted above, one cannot enter Proverbs without its key: "the fear of *I AM*" (1:7). This programmatic phrase, discussed below, emphasizes that a reverent, awestruck trust in *I AM*, who upholds his proverbs promising life or threatening death, is the lens through which to read Proverbs, and it rules out the notion that justice is meted out by the impersonal forces of fate or karma.

---

54. Lennart Boström, *The God of the Sages: The Portrayal of God in the Book of Proverbs*, ConBOT 29 (Stockholm: Almqvist Wiksell, 1990), 145.

55. Van Leeuwen ("Proverbs," in *NIB: Old Testament Survey*, 244) comments, "One saying calls for another to qualify it, or for a biblical story to flesh it out. . . . Brief as proverbs are, no one saying contains the whole truth. Reality is too rich and complex for that." McKane (*Proverbs*) built his commentary on separating humanistic sayings from theological sayings. His new approach floundered because rhetorical criticism demonstrates the two types are intentionally unified.

56. Cf. J. Goldingay, "The Arrangement of Sayings in Proverbs 1–15," *JSOT* 61 (1994): 75–83.

Third, some proverbs of Solomon explicitly assert *I AM*'s involvement in judgment (10:3; 12:2; 15:3; 16:7; 19:17; 25:21–22; 28:25; 29:25, 26), and the twenty-fifth saying of the wise (24:12) asks rhetorically, "Will he not repay people according to their conduct?"

Proverbs makes clear, however, that retribution does not operate like clockwork. Sayings that seem to indicate that righteousness is immediately rewarded and wickedness immediately punished (e.g., 11:5–6) need to be read along with other proverbs that assert that retribution, like many of God's actions, is inscrutable and only grasped by faith. Proverbs knows all too well we live in a topsy-turvy world where the wicked seem to operate with impunity while the righteous suffer for doing good. But Proverbs assures the reader that this present state of affairs will not be the final state. We will return to this issue below under the heading "Does Proverbs Promise Too Much" (pp. 42–45).

C. Revelation, Inspiration, Woman Wisdom, and Tradition

God revealed his word through a variety of means. Sometimes he appeared in a theophany, as with Moses at the burning bush; other times in dreams and visions, as with the prophets. With the sages, he used their keen observations and their faith-informed reflections. Let us flesh out this notion, which entails the sages' epistemology. We begin by defining wisdom and then examine the nature of its revelation and inspiration. We will also try to identify who Woman Wisdom is and the role of tradition in the formation and transmission of wisdom.

1. What Is "Wisdom"?

"Wisdom" (*ḥokmâ*) is a difficult concept to define since, as Van Leeuwen and others note, it is a totalizing concept that seeks to bring all of life's activities into harmony with God's created order.[57] At its core is the belief that God has made the world in, with, and by wisdom (3:19–20; Ps. 104:24). The wise, therefore, seek to orientate all their being and actions to conform to this wisdom. The word's use in the Bible suggests the meaning "masterful understanding," "expertise," "skill." People are called wise who possessed technical and artistic skills (Exod.

---

57. R. C. Van Leeuwen, "Wisdom Literature," in *Dictionary for Theological Interpretation of the Bible*, ed. K. J. Vanhoozer et al. (Grand Rapids: Baker Academic, 2005), 847. Cf. C. G. Bartholomew and R. O'Dowd, *Old Testament Wisdom Literature: A Theological Introduction* (Downers Grove, IL: IVP Academic, 2011), 23–31.

28:3; 31:6), who displayed diplomacy in government (1 Kgs. 5:7), who gave wise judgments (1 Kgs. 3:28), and who possessed encyclopedic knowledge (2 Sam. 14:20; 1 Kgs. 4:29–34). The possession of wisdom enables humans to cope with life[58] and to achieve what would otherwise be impossible—to wit, eternal life.

In Proverbs, "wisdom" mainly denotes the skill to navigate through the maze of life so that one conducts one's life to the greatest benefit of oneself and the community; it is the way of eternal life. Through wisdom, one is able to read circumstances and interpret situations so as to act correctly, speak properly, and respond appropriately to each situation so that beneficial consequences ensue to self and community. This reveals a further understanding of "wisdom": namely, insight into the deed-destiny nexus (2:20–21; 22:8). In 30:24–28, it is depicted as the skill to survive even when the odds are stacked against you—as in the examples of the ant, rock badger, locust, and lizard. These creatures are vulnerable; they have almost no personal defense systems. Yet by their *wisdom*, they survive, and the lizard even lives in a palace.

Biblical wisdom also has companions. The book's preamble (1:1–7) includes among them "knowledge" (*da'at*), "instruction" (*mûsār*), "understanding" (*bînâ*), "prudence" (*haśkēl*), "subtlety" (*'ormâ*), "discretion" (*məzimmâ*). We unpack each of these words and its context in the commentary.

Some of these words by themselves are morally neutral; they can describe even Satan (see Gen. 3:1) and the wicked. Therefore, these wisdom terms are safeguarded by their correlative (that is, words that have the same referent but are not synonyms) ethical and moral companions: righteousness (*ṣedeq*), justice (*mišpāṭ*), and fairness (*mêšārîm*) (1:3). In other words, in Proverbs, if a person is righteous, that person is also wise. Notice the matching of "righteous" with "wise" in 10:1–2. These *ethical* correlative terms lift the wisdom terms from the morally neutral realm of skill into the realm of God's character and actions.

2. Revelation

Proverbs claims that its wisdom comes from God: "For *I AM* gives wisdom; from his mouth come knowledge and understanding" (2:6). But this wisdom, says the sage, comes through a human's mouth (1:1), indicating that the revelation from God is communicated through the inspired sage. In short, the sage's mouth is God's mouth.

While it can be inferred that God in common grace has revealed wisdom to humans in and through the created order (Prov. 6:6; 30:24–28), special rev-

---

58. E. W. Heaton, *The Hebrew Kingdoms* (Oxford: Oxford University Press, 1986), 165.

elation of wisdom is needed to be truly wise. On one hand, the created order is marred by evil, alienated from God, and not in humankind's interest; on the other, human beings are totally infected by this evil and thus deluded in their understanding of creation. Additionally, the finite mind cannot achieve comprehensive knowledge, and without comprehensive knowledge, humans cannot attain certainty or see clearly. For example, people used to think using asbestos was good and that forest fires were bad. With more knowledge, they learned that the former is bad and the latter may be good. For the epistemology of Proverbs, see the exposition at 8:22–31; 30:1–6.

3. Inspiration

But how did the sages of Proverbs receive this revelation? Many scholars claim that it was through their research into the created order and rational reflection upon it. The problem with this notion is twofold: it is not taught in Proverbs, and it reduces the authority of Proverbs to merely human advice.

However, Solomon, in the guise of the wise father, urges his son to accept his proverbs because "*I AM* gives wisdom; from his mouth comes understanding" (2:6; cf. vv. 1–6). Here, "wisdom" and its companion, "understanding," refer to Proverbs. In short, what the sages in Proverbs say, *I AM* says (see "Author," p. 6). From the time of its composition, God's people have recognized in Proverbs the voice of God and have accepted it as part of their canon of Scripture.

4. Illumination and Woman Wisdom

"Woman Wisdom" plays a prominent role in the Prologue. Who is she? She makes her debut immediately after the parents' first lecture to their son (1:8–19) in a passionate call, complete with withering warnings, to the uncommitted to commit to her (1:20–33). She appears again in ch. 8, where she extols her virtues and promises profound premiums for those who embosom her. Elsewhere in the Prologue, she appears in other guises: a divine guide (ch. 6), a beloved sister (= bride, ch. 7). Finally and climactically, we meet her in the epilogue to Collection I (9:1–18), where she offers a compelling invitation to the youth to come and dine with her (9:1–6). However, here she is not alone, as Woman Folly also makes an appearance in 9:13–18 with a rival invitation.

Scholars have posited various identities for Woman Wisdom:[59] a prophetess

---

59. For a summary of the various scholarly proposals, see Lucas, *Proverbs*, 251–73.

because she sounds like the prophet (e.g., compare "how long" in 1:22 with 1 Kgs. 18:21; Jer. 4:14; Hos. 8:5); a sage because her jargon is the same as in the book's preamble (1:1–7); and a hypostasis of God (of the same substance but independent from God) because of her promise to provide life. Moreover, her claim to laugh at the calamity of the wicked (1:26) reflects on action elsewhere attributed only to God (Pss. 2:4; 59:8).[60] Still others see her as the ideal woman and wise wife.[61]

In truth, she is a unique woman who speaks with the passion of a prophet, reasons like a sage, exercises the authority of God, and honors those who cherish her. In this, she is a heavenly go-between who mediates God's wisdom to humans. This is the role of Proverbs according to its preamble: to wit, that its reader/hearers may know wisdom and instruction with understanding (1:1–2). Thus, the preamble identifies "wisdom" with Proverbs, and we have no reason to think its personification as Woman Wisdom differs from this equation. Moreover, there are similarities between Proverbs and Woman Wisdom: both address the uncommitted (1:4, 22, 32; 8:5) and teach the fear of *I AM* (1:7, 29). Woman Wisdom's admonitions, motivations, promises, and speech style are virtually indistinguishable from those of the parents' lectures. Heeding her sermon and the parents' lectures is a matter of life and death (e.g. 2:20–22; 8:32–36). Compare the grandfather's words in 4:5–6, where he equates his teaching ("Do not forget and do not turn aside from the words of my mouth!" v. 5b) with personified Wisdom ("Do not leave [Wisdom], and she will keep you; love her, and she will guard you," v. 6).

These striking parallels between the lectures of the father (Solomon's alter ego) and the sermons of Woman Wisdom are best explained by recognizing Woman Wisdom as a *personification of Proverbs*. Thus, when the son is enjoined to marry Wisdom (7:4), it is a metaphorical way of saying he should become intimately acquainted with Proverbs, which would then provide him with both guidance (6:22) and nutrition (9:1–6) on the way of eternal life.

5. Tradition

Some scholars, who deny an inspired Solomon composed the bulk of Proverbs (see "Author," p. 6), maintain that the composers of Proverbs derived their

60. T. Longman III ("Woman Wisdom and Woman Folly," in *DOTWPW*, 913) bases this identification on the location of Woman Wisdom's house at the highest point in the city—a location only occupied by the palace in the ancient Near East.

61. See Fox, *Proverbs 1–9: A New Translation with Introduction and Commentary*, AB 18A (New York: Doubleday, 2000); Wilson, *Proverbs*, 11, 319.

sayings from human tradition. Apart from the fifth lecture (4:1–9), however, there is no evidence within the book of an appeal to a "wisdom tradition" as the original source of the book's proverbs and sayings. In this fifth lecture, a fictive father expects the son to receive and pass on his teaching even as he received it from his father, the son's grandfather. The point of this lecture is that Solomon expected his teaching to be passed on by tradition, not that his wisdom derives from tradition.

Nevertheless, Collections III (22:17–24:22) and IV (24:23–34) consist of sayings that the inspired Solomon adopted and adapted from other sages, and Collection V (25:1–29:27) contains Solomon's sayings that Hezekiah's officials copied. In Collection VII (ch. 31), King Lemuel passes on the sayings that his mother taught him. But tradition is not the original source of these collections; rather *I AM* inspired them, and he stands behind their threats and promises, according to the Prologue (3:1–5).

D. Anthropology

Here, we will analyze humankind in general and then differentiate between the wise and fools and male and female.

1. Human Beings in General

a. Words for "Humankind" in Proverbs

The word '*ādām* ("humankind"), occurring forty-four times in Proverbs, differentiates the mortal on earth from God in heaven, who is sovereign over all human potentialities and limitations. The word '*îš*, occurring ninety times in Proverbs, designates an individual vis-à-vis society. It is used variously to designate a male ("man"/"husband") in contrast to an '*iššâ* ("woman"/"wife"; see 7:19), though in 2 Sam. 6:19, '*îš* refers to "each one" of men and women. It too may distinguish the human from the divine, making the human conscious of the vast distinction (see 5:21; 14:12; 21:2; 30:2–4).

Geber refers to the male in his strength, and '*ănôš* refers to the male in his weakness.

Throughout the Old Testament, human beings are conceptualized as a psychosomatic unity, but the fundamental components of their beings in Proverbs, besides their bodies, are *nepeš* (traditionally "soul"), *lēb* ("heart"), and *rûaḥ* ("spirit").

b. *Nepeš* (Traditionally, "Soul")

Nepeš, occurring fifty-six times in Proverbs, has the same meaning as in the rest of the Old Testament. In English versions, it is traditionally glossed "soul," which can mislead the reader to conceptualize the "soul" in the New Testament sense of *psychē*, the "seat and center of life that transcends the earthly."[62] But in the Old Testament, *nepeš* refers to the passionate drives and appetites of all breathing creatures, including their drive for food and sex (6:30; 10:3; 12:10; 16:26; 19:15; 25:25; 27:7; cf. Deut. 23:24; Ps. 78:18; Isa. 5:14; Jer. 2:24). A glutton is a *ba'al nepeš* ("owner of appetite/hunger," 23:2). A greedy person with an unrestrained appetite is a *rəḥab-nepeš* ("wide of throat/appetite," 28:25). *Nepeš* often predicates words denoting yearning (13:19; 21:10). The craving for God distinguishes a human *nepeš* from an animal *nepeš*. Since it refers to the basic nature of humans as having and being "passionate yearning," it is best rendered according to context by "hunger," "self" (see 1:18, 19), "life" (22:5), and "soul" when it clearly refers to the appetite (see 13:19; 16:24).

c. Heart

"Heart" (*lēb/lēbāb*), occurring forty-six times in Proverbs and 858 times in the Old Testament, is the most important anthropological term in the Old Testament (see 4:20–27, esp. v. 23) but has no equivalent in English. The ancients attributed *bodily functions* to the heart, not the brain. Nabal's body became like stone (paralyzed) because his *heart* died (1 Sam. 25:37–38). The heart controls facial expressions (Prov. 15:13), the tongue (15:28; 12:23), and all other members (4:23–27; 6:18).

Psychological functions are also ascribed to the heart. It is the seat of a person's disposition (23:7; cf. Rom 1:21). The complex interplay of intellect, sensibility, will and disposition occurs in the heart; it prompts all we do (4:23). Thus, planning and decision-making are actions of the heart (6:14, 18; 16:9). *I AM* knows (17:3; 24:12) and experiences all of its emotions (cf. 12:25; 14:10, 30; 15:15). Lack of insight or judgment is called "lacking heart" (10:13).

The heart also has *spiritual functions*; it accepts and trusts in the religious sphere (3:5). It feels all modes of desire and is responsible for ethical activity. The teacher warns the son not to let *his heart* covet the adulteress's beauty (6:25) and not to let it envy sinners (23:17). The heart's psychological and spiritual functions are closely connected to its *spiritual state*. It can be wise (14:33)

---

62. BAGD, 893, s.v. *psychē*.

and pure (20:9) or perverse (17:20; 26:23–25). The bent of one's heart can determine one's actions (Exod. 14:5; 35:21; Num. 32:9; 1 Kgs. 12:27; 18:37). Therefore, Solomon seeks to bend the spiritual condition of the heart by repeated appeals to accept his wisdom (2:10; 3:1; 22:17; 23:12; 24:32). But the heart can spurn correction (5:12) and become so hardened that it cannot move in a new spiritual direction (28:14; cf. Isa. 6:10; Matt. 13:15). The centrality of the heart to a person's emotional-intellectual-religious-moral activity demands its utmost safeguarding (4:23).

Paradoxically, while the eye and the ear are gates to the heart and shape it (see 2:2; 4:21–23), the heart decides what they will see and hear (4:25–26). Egyptian wisdom resolved the paradox by perceiving God as the ultimate cause of the good: "The one whom God loves can hear; but the one whom God hates cannot hear."[63] Prov. 20:12 traces the teachable ear and the morally insightful eye to God. The king's heart is in *I AM*'s hand (21:1). But Proverbs negates fatalism by placing the emphasis on the audience's responsibility to choose the teaching.

d. Spirit

In Proverbs, *rûaḥ* ("wind" or "spirit," occurring twenty-one times) is used literally of the wind, which sets other things in motion (25:23; 27:16). But, apart from Agur's reference to God's control of the wind (30:4a), Proverbs, unlike other biblical books, does not associate *rûaḥ* with *I AM*.

Rûaḥ also denotes "breathing," and the manner of breathing indicates one's mindset: if "short," nervousness (14:29); if "long," patience (17:27). This dynamic vitality becomes attenuated into the psychic designation of "mood" or "spirit." In contexts where the person's physical vitality is paramount, *rûaḥ* is best rendered by "breath" (e.g., Judg. 15:19 [= "strength," NIV]; 1 Sam. 30:12 [= "revived," NIV]); where psychical vitality is paramount, it is best rendered by "spirit" (e.g., Gen. 45:27).

Rûaḥ can also function as a synecdoche for a person's entire disposition (Eccl. 7:8, 9; Ezek. 11:19; 18:31; 36:26) or the whole inner life (Job 7:11; Ps. 78:8), including opinions or desires (Ezek. 13:3), mind (Ps. 77:6), will (Prov. 16:32), and motives (Prov. 16:2; cf. 2 Chr. 36:22).[64] The plural of *rûaḥ* in 16:2, paralleling "ways," denotes that complex patterns of behavior depend on complex motives.

---

63. Kayatz, *Proverbien 1–9*, 45.

64. See R. G. Bratcher, "Biblical Words Describing Man: Breath, Life, Spirit," *BT* 34 (1983): 204.

2. The Wise and Fools

a. Introduction: Correlative Terms

Proverbs divides humans into the "wise and righteous" and the "fools and wicked." We are indebted to Knut Heim for his cogent recognition that these word pairs are correlative terms—that is to say, they differ in their semantic domains ("skill" versus "ethics") but refer to the same person and so are inseparable.[65] For example, "Vice President of the US" and "President of the US Senate" are correlative terms since they do not belong to the same semantic domain but refer to the same person.[66] So a wise person is righteous, and a fool is wicked. Synonyms belong to the same semantic domain and often, but not always, refer to the same person or thing (cf. 1:3–6; 8:12). So, a righteous person is also "good" and "upright" while the wicked are also "bad" and "crooked." These synonyms often occur as parallels. Apart from these two classes, there is no other category in Proverbs. A person uncommitted to wisdom is not in a category in between the wise and the fool but is categorized as a fool and suffers the fate of fools (1:22–33), even though they do not despise wisdom, unlike the fool. The following are the more frequent synonyms of these correlative terms.

b. The Wise and Righteous

i. Intellectual Terms for the Wise and Righteous

The *wise* person (*ḥākam*) possesses and exhibits the traits of wisdom in its religious-social-ethical sense. Instead of being wise in their own opinion (26:5, 11, 12, 16), they are teachable, seek knowledge (18:15), and store it up (10:4). They listen to instruction (13:1; 22:17) and counsel (12:5), accept commands (10:8), love reproof (9:8), walk with the wise (13:20), and ever increase their wisdom (1:5; 4:18; 15:31–32).[67] The wise grow to become exceedingly wise (cf. 30:24) and become teachers (4:1–4). Having gained knowledge, they spread it

---

65. K. M. Heim, "Structure and Context in Proverbs 10:1–22:16" (PhD diss., University of Liverpool, 1996), 54–86.

66. See Waltke, "Righteousness," 233.

67. Lucas (*Proverbs*, 219) notes that "teachableness" is the most frequently mentioned attribute of the wise in Proverbs: "About 40 percent of the sayings which explicitly mention the wise refer to this in one way or another."

(15:7) and become a fountain of life to the community (13:14). Their mastery of the moral order enables them to control their emotions (29:11) and to rule fools (11:29). They bring joy to their parents (15:20; 23:24) and healing to others (12:18) and are themselves protected (13:14).

The wise are also *prudent* (*maśkîl*), having "wise behavior" and "good sense" (1:3; cf. 10:5, 19; 14:35; 15:24; 17:2; 19:14; 21:16). The prudent person pays attention to a threatening situation, gets insight into its solution, acts on it decisively, and thereby gains success and life while preventing failure and death. David's success against the Philistines is a textbook example of prudence (see 1 Sam. 18:5, 14, 15).[68]

According to Fox, *'ormâ* (*shrewdness* or "cunning") "is the talent for devising and using adroit and wily tactics in the attaining of one's goals, whatever these may be. . . . Lady Wisdom herself legitimizes *'ormâ* when she boasts of proximity to it (8:12)."[69] The shrewd scheme to achieve their desires (14:8, 15), ignore insults (12:16), look where they are going (14:15), and spot danger and avoid it (22:3; 27:12). Being cunning entails acting with "knowledge" (13:16) while refraining from vaunting it (12:23).

Discretion (or "caginess," *mzimmâ*) is defined by Fox as "private, unrevealed thinking and the faculty for it"[70]—usually in the sense of making plans.[71] If the plans are hostile and full of intrigue (24:8), they are condemned by God (12:2) and the community (14:17). But if discretion is in accord with the sages' wisdom (1:4; 2:11; 3:21; 5:2), it is inseparable from it (8:12).

The *insightful* person (*nābôn*, 1:5) "has a penetrating and foreseeing mind (15:21; 20:5; 28:11) . . . [and] speaks and acts sensibly (11:12; 17:28)."[72] They are so because they have the perspective of wisdom and therefore the mental and intellectual ability to distinguish between right and wrong, good and bad. The insightful can perceive things from the divine viewpoint and do not rely on

---

68. So W. McKane, *Prophets and Wise Men* (London: SCM, 1965), 67.

69. M. V. Fox, "Words for Wisdom," *ZAH* 6 (1993): 158–59.

70. Fox, "Words for Wisdom," 160–61, who says further, "This power will protect you from the temptations of the wicked man and woman (2:11; 5:2f), because when they try to seduce you to their ways, you will be able to look inward, maintain independence of thought, and stand up to their inveiglements."

71. In the Prologue (1:4; 2:11; 3:21; 5:2: 8:12) and Collection VII (31:16), *mzimmâ* has a positive connotation. In the rest of the collections, it has a negative connotation (10:23; 21:27; 24:8, 9; 30:32).

72. Chou-Wee Pan, "A Study of the Vocabulary of Education in Proverbs" (PhD diss., University of Newcastle upon Tyne, 1987), 106.

their own relative perspective. They seek and obtain knowledge (14:6; 15:14; 18:15), readily accept rebuke (19:25), enshrine the book's wisdom in the heart (14:33), wear it as the badge of their character (16:21), and keep silent (17:28) unless they can speak wisely (10:13).

The insightful acquire *guidance* (*taḥbulôt*, 1:5). The word may be a nautical term, referring to the steering ropes of a ship. The LXX renders the word by the Greek *kybernēsis* ("steering" or "navigation").

Understanding (*təbûnâ*) occurs nineteen times, thirteen of which are in parallel with "wisdom" (2:2, 6; 3:13, 19; 5:1; 8:1; 24:3; cf. 21:30) or one of its synonyms. According to Fox, who renders it with "competence" or "know-how," the distinction between *təbûnâ* and *bînâ* is that the former "designates the pragmatic, applied aspect of thought, operating in the field of action; it aims at efficacy and accomplishment. [The latter] is the conceptual, interpretive activity of thought, operating in the field of meaning; it aims at perception and comprehension."[73]

People with *təbûnâ* have insight into the moral order and a social conscience that guides their actions. They have self-control (17:27), are patient (14:29), hold their tongues (11:29), can discern the hearts of others (20:5), and keep a straight path (15:21). Fools couldn't care less for *təbûnâ* (18:2), and without it, rulers become tyrants (28:16).

ii. Ethical Terms for the Wise and Righteous

According to Lucas, explicit references to "the righteous" and "the wise" are approximately equal in Proverbs.[74] *Righteousness* is "doing what is right in a social relationship, as defined by God's standard of what is right behavior . . . , [namely] depriving self to benefit others. Put simply, the righteous disadvantage themselves to advantage the community; the wicked disadvantage the community to advantage themselves."[75]

---

73. Fox, "Words for Wisdom," 154. In the parlance of modern neuroscience, *təbûnâ* could be correlated with the task-oriented, problem-solving, pragmatic network of the brain—what neuroscientists call the task-positive network. *Bînâ* roughly correlates with the creative, emotionally self-aware, ethical decision-making network labelled the default mode network. Ancients may have been aware of these two aspects of human thinking that modern brain physiology is now discovering and labelling. See R. Boyatzis, K. Rochford and A. I. Jack, "Review Article: Antagonistic Neural Networks Underlying Differentiated Leadership Roles," *Frontiers in Human Neuroscience*, March 4, 2014.

74. Lucas, *Proverbs*, 222.

75. Waltke, "Righteousness," 236.

Furthermore, righteousness must be "put on" (Job 29:14), a metaphor signifying it is the very essence of a person, not merely an outward performance. It is a matter of the heart (10:20) gained through the sages' words (2:1–11) and so promotes a relationship with God (15:9). The wicked forsake God, while the righteous cling to him. Righteousness also profits self because *I AM* guarantees that it will result in true profit and security (2:11; 10:2, 3). Finally, being righteous is a matter of life and death (11:19; 15:9; 21:12).

If righteousness establishes right order, *justice* (*mišpāṭ*) restores the violated order by delivering the victim and punishing the offender to produce shalom. But justice is more than legal action; it is a moral quality, coming from the heart. To live rightly is to do justice and righteousness (cf. Gen. 18:19; Ps. 106:3; Prov. 1:3; 2:3; 8:20; 16:8; 21:3; Isa. 5:7; 58:2). To judge rightly is to judge in accordance with justice and righteousness (cf. Lev. 19:15; Deut. 1:16, 17; Ps. 9:4, 7–8), as is to govern rightly (cf. 2 Sam. 8:15; 1 Kgs. 10:9; Ps. 72:1–12; Eccl. 3:16; Isa. 9:7)—just as God governs all his realm in accordance with justice and righteousness (cf. Job 8:3; Pss. 33:5; 36:6; 89:14).

Uprightness (*mêšārîm*, often translated "equity" in the sense of being fair or impartial) derives from the root *yāšār*, which has the geometrical notion of being straight, whether vertically or horizontally. The geometric use assumes a fixed order to which something can be compared. Proverbs uses the term primarily in an ethical figurative sense that assumes a fixed moral order by which actions can be judged as straight, upright, and level (Prov. 8:6).[76] Conduct that does not stray from or go outside of this fixed moral order can be called "upright." Paraphrasing a public lecture by Raymond C. Van Leeuwen, true freedom is found within form, liberty within law, lovemaking within marriage.

Blameless(ness) (*tām* [adj.]; *tōm* [n.]) denotes completeness and integrity in the sense of a process that has already been accomplished in a person (see 1:12, where it is translated "whole" in the NIV). The basic meaning of the root (*tmm*) is "to be complete, finished, perfect."[77] When used with "walk," it denotes consistent behavior—doing things with the whole of one's heart as opposed to acting with a double heart. In Proverbs, *tōm* is a comprehensive term for total commitment to *I AM*. The word occurs always with "walk" or "way" (2:7; 10:9, 29; 13:6; 19:1; 28:6).

Good (*ṭôb*) denotes anything or anyone as desirable on account of being

---

76. There is one nonethical, metaphorical use in 23:31, where it refers to wine that goes down "smoothly."

77. Cf. K. Koch, *TLOT*, 3:1427, s.v. *tmm*; B. K. Waltke with C. J. Fredricks, *Genesis: A Commentary* (Grand Rapids: Zondervan, 2001), 362.

aesthetically pleasing and ethically beneficial. The "good" unselfishly act in the best interest of God and neighbor.

Trustworthy (*ʾəmûnâ*; also "honest" or "conscientious") designates a person's character and conduct, not just their words. Trustworthiness is not an abstract quality but springs from inner stability—the inner attitude that produces honest and conscientious conduct.[78]

Finally, *kindness* (*ḥesed*) essentially means "help to the needy" and has no precise English equivalent. It refers to a situation where someone needs help and another provides it without compulsion, out of their better spiritual and inward instincts. Since the helper is under no obligation to help, *faithfulness* or "reliability" (*ʾemet*) is added to *ḥesed* twenty-one times in the Old Testament. The resulting combination (*ḥesed weʾemet*) means to exercise "unfailing kindness."

iii. Fear of I AM

Fear of I AM (*yirʾat yhwh*) is the key that opens the door to understanding Proverbs.[79] The expression is a collocation, a combination of words that has a unique meaning. For example, one will not understand "butterfly" by analyzing "butter" and "fly" independently. So also "fear of *I AM*" cannot be understood by analyzing "fear" and "*I AM*" separately. The expression is a compound. "Fear of *I AM*" involves both rational and non-rational aspects simultaneously.

Rationally, the collocation entails an objective revelation that can be taught (Ps. 34:11ff.) and memorized (Prov. 2:1–5). In Ps. 19:7–9, it is used as an equivalent of "law," "statutes," "commands," and "ordinances" of *I AM*. As noted above under "Names of God" (see p. 26), "fear of *I AM*" differs somewhat from "fear of God."

Psychologically, the "fear of *I AM*" entails responding to the revelation in fear, love, and humility. According to Prov. 2:1–5, "the fear of *I AM*" is found through heartfelt prayer and diligent seeking for the sages' words. In 15:33, "humility" and "the fear of *I AM*" are parallel terms, and "humility" in 22:4 is further defined as "the fear of *I AM* sort" (our translation).

Whoever fears *I AM* trusts him, for they are confident that he upholds the

---

78. Cf. A. Jepsen, *TDOT*, 1:317, s.v. *ʾāman*.

79. Bartholomew and O'Dowd (*Old Testament Wisdom*, 80–81) questionably use "fear of *I AM*" (1:7; 9:10; 10:27; 31:30) as a literary marker to divide the book into three major collections (1–9; 10–29; 30–31).

teachings that promise life to the obedient and threaten death to the disobedient. So paradoxically, because of their faith in *I AM*, whoever fears *I AM* also loves him (cf. Deut. 5:29 with 6:2; Deut. 6:5 with Josh. 24:14; cf. Prov. 10:12, 20; 13:5).[80] C. Bridges writes, "[The fear of YHWH is] that affectionate reverence, by which the child of God bends himself humbly and carefully to his Father's law."[81]

iv. The Wise and Words

The behavior of the wise/righteous is often assumed and not defined in Proverbs. But two areas stand out in contrasting the wise/righteous and the fools/wicked: namely, how they handle words and wealth.

The Bible's ideal of wise speech is similar to the humanistic ideal of *eloquentia*, or talking well, which Gadamer identifies as having two meanings: "not merely rhetorical ideal [but] also . . . saying the right things—that is the truth."[82]

The importance of *eloquentia* cannot be overemphasized. All social relationships depend on communication. "Speech and communication go hand in hand. Community depends on communication"[83] (see Prov. 11:30; 15:4). Here we consider the value of wise speech, its characteristics, and its sources.

Concerning value, first, the tongue has the power of life and death (18:21; cf. 10:19; 17:27–28) because it has the power to shape beliefs and convictions that affect eternal destinies. Parents utilize the good power of the tongue (that is, speech) to influence their children to accept wisdom and life. However, fools starve to death because they refuse to eat the good fruit of sound teaching (10:21). Good speech is both a "tree of life" (11:30) and a "fountain of life"

80. See B. K. Waltke, "The Fear of the Lord," in *Alive to God: Essays in Honour of James D. Houston*, edited by J. I. Packer and L. Wilkinson (Downers Grove, IL: InterVarsity Press, 1992).

81. C. Bridges, *An Exposition of Proverbs* (Evansville: Sovereign Grace Book Club, 1959), 3–4.

82. H.-G. Gadamer, *Truth and Method*, trans. J. Weinsheimer and D. Marshall, 2nd rev. ed. (New York: Continuum, 1989), 17.

83. D. A. Hubbard, *Proverbs* (Dallas: Word, 1989), 214. The British anthropologist and evolutionary psychologist Robin Dunbar, in his book *Grooming, Gossip, and the Evolution of Language* (Cambridge, MA: Harvard University Press, 1996), argues that human language evolved from gossip to maintain the harmony and balance of social networks—which otherwise would devolve into violence. While Dunbar's evolutionary presuppositions are debatable, his main point that language *primarily* serves to bond and cohere humans is one that Proverbs affirms.

(13:14) available now. Second, the tongue has the power to heal and to destroy (6:12–15, 16–19; 10:14; 11:9; 12:18; 16:24). The child's proverb "Sticks and stones may break my bones, but words will never hurt me" is not true, for, as Kidner says, "What is done *to* you is of little account beside what is done *in* you."[84] Third, the tongue has the power to reward or damage its owner (10:10; 12:14; 18:6–7). A fool's tongue is long enough to cut his throat.

Concerning its characteristics, one of Bruce's students formulated the acronym Gentle B-R-E-A-T-H to make some of the features of wise speech memorable. Such speech is *gentle*, not harsh or quarrelsome (15:1); *boasts* not (27:1–2); is *restrained*, not blabby (10:19; 17:14, 27, 28); *eavesdrops* not (that is, is not given to gossip or rumor; 11:12–13); is *apt* (uses the right word at the right time in the right way; 15:2); is *thoughtful*, not rash (15:28; 18:13); and is *honest*, not false (8:7; 12:17, 19, 22).

Concerning sources, wise speech comes from the heart (16:23) and is realized by walking with the wise (13:20), by maintaining sound doctrine (22:17–19), and by prayer (15:29; cf. Jas. 1:5).

v. The Wise and Wealth

In their lectures, the parents aim to protect their son from the dangers of easy sex (2:16–19) and easy money (1:10–19). Here, the topic of wealth is analyzed in terms of its danger, limitation, value and management.

As to money's dangers, it tends to supplant trust in God. That happens to the *rich person* (*ʿāšîr*) in Proverbs. The meanings of "rich person" in English and in Proverbs differ significantly. In the former, "rich person" has only a material sense; the rich have superfluous money. In Proverbs, however, "the rich" also has the spiritual connotation of trusting money, not *I AM*, for one's security and significance (10:15; 18:10–11; cf. Ps. 49:6). Instructively, the NIV changed Prov. 28:11 from "the rich *may be* wise in their own eyes" (1984) to "the rich *are* wise in their own eyes" (2011). Instead of depending on *I AM*, the rich think of themselves as self-made. So they are fools, living in the realm of death. Agur recognized this danger of wealth and prayed to be kept from too much of it (30:7–9). As one seminary ad says, under an image of a stack of bills, "It's put more Christians at stake than Nero."

Proverbs also recognizes the limitations of money (3:13–18). It can build a house but not a home; put food on the table but not fellowship around the table; give a woman diamonds and furs but not the love she really wants. Wisdom, however, gives both material well-being and spiritual life.

---

84. Kidner, *Proverbs*, 46.

Yet Proverbs is realistic about the value of money. It saves one from the *spiritual* losses associated with poverty. Too little money leads people to steal and so defile their consciences and alienate themselves from God (30:9). The poor lack social power (18:23; 22:7). Moreover, Proverbs candidly recognizes that poverty hampers friendship: people dodge the destitute (14:20), albeit Proverbs promotes kindness to them (14:21). Some wealth, therefore, is necessary to enjoy life more fully (12:9) and to be righteous in the sense of serving and supporting the community (11:23–28; cf. Eph. 4:28).

Enduring wealth is obtained through honoring God with one's firstfruits (3:9–10), generosity rather than stinginess (11:23–28; 28:22), hard and timely work (10:4–5), contentment rather than indulgence (21:17), patience rather than haste (13:11; 21:5), and securing one's income before building a home (24:27). In other words, the key is character, not method. Proverbs is a "how to be" book, not a "how to get" book.

vi. *The Wise and Their Rewards: Life*

The sage's nexus between deed-destiny (see "What Is 'Wisdom'?" pp. 27–28) entails the doctrines of retribution for the wicked (see "God as Judge," p. 26) and of reward for the righteous (10:2; 11:5–6, 23, 27)—to wit, "life" (*ḥayyîm*).

The noun *ḥayyîm* occurs thirty-three times in Proverbs and the verb *ḥāyâ* four times.[85] Sometimes it refers to physical life (31:12), but most often *ḥayyîm* is unqualified and refers to "life" that is added to physical (that is, clinical) life—apparently an abundant life of health, prosperity, and social esteem (3:21–22; 4:13; 8:35; 16:15; 21:21; 22:4). Other than 16:15, these passages point to "life" as wisdom's reward—a reward never said to be tarnished by death (4:22; 6:23; 10:17; 11:19; 12:28; 13:14; 15:31; 19:23; 22:4). This is true also for all four uses of the verb (4:4; 7:2; 9:6; 15:27). Moreover, the "tree of life" (3:18; 11:30; 13:12; 15:4; cf. Gen. 2:9; 3:24) figuratively represents perpetual healing, ensuring eternal life, as is probably also true of the "wellspring of life" (16:22).

In the proverb "The wages of the righteous is life, but the earnings of the wicked are sin and death" (10:16), "life" is in antithetic parallelism to "death," implying that the former is life apart from death. In biblical theology, life is essentially a relationship with the living and eternal God, and the disruption of that relationship means death (Gen. 2:17). Wisdom's concern is in maintaining this relationship (Prov. 2:5–8) and thus with experiencing life in God's favor. In sum, "life" mostly refers to abundant life in fellowship with God—a living,

---

85. W. Cosser, "The Meaning of 'Life' (*Ḥayyîm*) in Proverbs, Job, and Ecclesiastes," *GUOST* 15 (1955): 48–53.

eternal relationship in contrast to the eternal "death" of the wicked. As Jesus said, "He is not the God of the dead but of the living" (Matt. 22:32).

Prov. 12:28 affirms that the righteous are rewarded with immortality ('al-māwet). Prov. 14:32 says, "Even in death the righteous seek refuge in God," and 23:17 asserts that their future hope will not be disappointed. In contrast, the wicked have no future hope (11:7a; 12:28; 24:19-20). What Proverbs teaches, then, is immortality, not resurrection, unlike Job 19:25-27; Pss. 49:15 (cf. v. 8); 73:23-24; Isa. 14:13-15; and Dan. 12:2 (cf. Gen. 5:24; 2 Kgs. 2:1). However, Prov. 15:24, if taken at face value, implies an ascent from the grave. The movement from below (that is, the grave— *šə'ôl*) "upward" fits the biblical teaching that the godly terminate their journey in the presence of God himself (Pss. 16:9-11; 73:23-26; John 14:1-4; 2 Tim. 4:18; Heb. 12:2). Thus, "life" in Proverbs has to be more than being spared an untimely death, for otherwise "the path of life" terminates in death. But death is not God and does not have the last word in this book any more than in any other biblical book.

Furthermore, the hope of life after death in Proverbs comports with the well-known Egyptian belief in an afterlife. The hymns and prayers of the Egyptians witness to their hope for a blessed future beyond death. Since Proverbs shows a heavy dependence on Egyptian instructions, it would be surprising if "life" meant less with the living God than the Egyptian hope of life with a "no-god" (Deut. 32:21). Finally, humanity's intuitive notion of justice and the assurance of it in Proverbs (16:15) demand the doctrine (see "Ethical Terms for the Wise and Righteous," pp. 36-38).

Nevertheless, it is true that Proverbs and the Egyptian instructions focus on health, prosperity, and social honor *in this life* in contrast to the Christian focus on the resurrection. Perhaps this is due to the opaqueness of the hope before the resurrection of Jesus Christ (Titus 1:2-3).

vii. Does Proverbs Promise Too Much?

The heavenly promises of life, health, prosperity, and honor given in Proverbs to the wise/righteous, appear unrealistic in light of earth's harsh realities. Human experience sometimes contradicts them—as Job (9:22-23) and Qoheleth (the "Preacher"/"Gatherer," Eccl. 9:2-3) complained. Often, the righteous suffer and the wicked prosper (cf. Heb. 11:35-38). The following reflections on whether Proverbs promises too much explore, first, three unsatisfactory and untenable solutions to this apparent contradiction and, second, four better solutions.

First, the three untenable solutions:

VIII. Theology

1. The problem is human depravity. This was the solution of Eliphaz: "Consider now: Who, being innocent, has ever perished? Where were the upright ever destroyed? As I have observed, those who plow evil and those who sow trouble reap it" (Job 4:7-8). There is a large element of truth to Eliphaz's proposition that sin has its consequences in this life (see "God as Judge," p. 26). However, it is not the whole answer, and it is debunked, first by the narrator of Job (1:8) and later by *I AM* himself (42:7): Job was a righteous man and suffered uncommonly.

2. The sages are dullards who cannot see or think straight[86] and are looking at the world through rose-tinted glasses. This solution contradicts the principle of the inspiration of the sage, which entails cogent reflection upon keen observation (see "Inspiration," p. 29). Moreover, this solution undermines the authority of Proverbs and the canon, as well as Christ and his apostles' claim that all Scripture is inspired of God, who neither lies (1 Sam. 15:29) nor authors confusion (1 Cor. 14:33; 2 Tim. 3:16).

3. A popular evangelical solution is that these are not promises but probabilities. Though this solution contains an element of truth, it also raises theological, practical, and psychological problems. Stated this way, humans are expected to keep their obligations perfectly (3:1, 3, 5, 7, 9), but God may keep his obligations imperfectly (3:2, 4, 6, 8, 10). The truth is, "though we are faithless, he will remain faithful" (2 Tim. 2:13). Moreover, a risk-taker would like to know the odds, and a person of sound mind could scarcely trust a God who will "probably" keep his promises.

From among the better solutions that have been suggested, we present four:

1. The promises are mostly validated by experience. The sober person, not the drunkard (cf. 23:29-35); the cool-tempered person, not the hothead (15:18; 19:19; 22:24; 29:22); and the diligent person, not the sluggard, usually experience health and prosperity. Moreover, even apart from a future that outlasts death (see the fourth solution, below), history shows that people may not pay the price for vice immediately, but over time the harm is realized.

---

86. K. T. Aitken (*Proverbs* [Philadelphia: Westminster John Knox Press, 1986], 43) suggested that the sages were too optimistic: "There is a strong suspicion here that Israel's sages have confused their belief about what ought to be the case with what actually is the case." G. Von Rad (*Wisdom in Israel* [London: SCM, 1972], 233) goes further. Pitting Qoheleth against the sages, he accuses the latter of becoming "entangled in a single false doctrine."

2. The epigrammatic nature of the proverbs means that a proverb represents the truth but not the whole truth. Proverbs that promise health and wealth must be balanced by other proverbs that qualify these promises. For example, note that the first proverb pair (10:2–3) is a unity. Proverbs 10:2a asserts that the wicked do have treasures gained by wickedness (plundering the innocent) for a season, but 10:2b says that it will not deliver them from death. To this, 10:3 adds that (afterward) the cravings of the wicked will be frustrated, while the righteous, who may now be afflicted, will later be fed. Moreover, several better-than proverbs assume that at present the wicked have material possessions while the righteous do not: "Better a little with righteousness than a large income with injustice" (16:8; see 16:19; 17:1; 19:1, 19; 22:1; 25:24; 28:6; cf. Ps. 37:16; Eccl. 4:6).

3. As a primer on morality for youth, Proverbs focuses on a future when the righteous rise (see "The Wise and Their Rewards: Life," pp. 41–42), not the present when they fall: "For if the righteous fall seven times, then they rise; but the wicked stumble in calamity" (24:16). "Seven" signifies completeness, like the count of ten for the downed boxer. Here, the complete fall of the righteous is assumed, but so is their future rise, phoenix-like, from the ashes. Job and Qoheleth, instead of noting the fall of the righteous in a concessive clause, feature their fall in the main clause, as it were. This by-faith religious instruction of Proverbs (to wit, the fear of *I AM*) reinforces youth's intuitive grasp of right and wrong.

4. Finally, as argued under the heading "The Wise and Their Rewards: Life" (pp. 41–42), the righteous person rises in a blessed future that surpasses death. The book's concept of justice demands such a hope. Instructively, in his first lecture warning the son against criminal gangs, the father imagines a situation very much like that of the first situation of humanity outside the garden. Just as the righteous Abel was dispatched to an early grave by the wicked Cain, who then lived a normal span of life, in the father's first lecture, an innocent victim is depicted as prematurely dispatched by wicked gangsters. This initial situation debunks the popular view that, in Proverbs, "life" refers to long life while "death" refers to dying prematurely. For justice to be done, as Proverbs assures it will be (e.g., 3:31–35; 16:4–5), Abel and the innocent victim must be vindicated and delivered from death in a future that lies beyond their graves. If physical death is the last word for innocent victims, then the first story outside the Garden and the first lecture, along with other biblical stories about the martyrs, undermine the Bible's claim that God upholds

justice. Farmer rightly comments, "One either has to give up the idea of justice or one has to push its execution into some realm beyond the evidence of human experience."[87] Prov. 23:18 puts it more explicitly: "Surely there is a latter end [for the wise]; your hope will not be cut off." So "do not fret because of those who forge evil; do not envy the wicked; for the evil person has no blessed future; the lamp of the wicked will be snuffed out" (24:19–20). Obviously, that future is not accessible to verification, as Gladson complained,[88] but without such faith, one cannot be justified (Rom. 4:5–25), cannot be saved (Rom. 10:6–13), cannot please God (Heb. 11:6). If these promises were infallibly validated by experience, then the father's command for the son to trust in *I AM* (3:5) is pointless.

If God were to reward virtue instantly, humankind would confound pleasure with piety and would use piety to satisfy its prurient interests. Instead, God develops the character of his saints by calling them to suffer for the sake of righteousness while living in the hope of eternal life (see Rom. 8:18; 2 Cor. 4:17). In sum, Proverbs characterizes the wise as living by faith entirely ("with all your heart," 3:5a), exclusively ("lean not on your own understanding," 3:5b), and exhaustively ("in all your ways" 3:6a).

c. The Wicked and Fools

i. Ethical Terms for Wicked and Fools

Those called *wicked* (*rəšāʿîm*), according to K. H. Richards, are the guilty and are always seen as such vis-à-vis the community.[89] *Rešāʿ* ("wickedness") is the most important antonym of *ṣedeq* ("righteousness"). Van Leeuwen writes, "Rš̆ expresses negative behavior—evil thoughts, words, and deeds—antisocial behavior that simultaneously betrays a person's inner disharmony and unrest (Isa. 57:20)."[90] If the righteous advantage the community, even at the expense of disadvantaging themselves, then the wicked advantage themselves by disadvantaging the community. In Proverbs, "the wicked" is used of impious

---

87. K. Farmer, *Who Knows What Is Good? A Commentary on the Books of Proverbs and Ecclesiastes* (Grand Rapids: Eerdmans, 1991), 206.

88. J. A. Gladson, "Retributive Paradoxes in Proverbs 10–29" (PhD diss., Vanderbilt University, 1978).

89. K. H. Richards, "A Form and Traditio-Historical Study of *Rš̆*" (PhD diss., Claremont, 1970).

90. R. C. Van Leeuwen, *TLOT*, 3:1262, s.v. *rš̆*.

people who are greedy (10:3; 21:10), violent (10:6), threaten innocent life (12:6; 24:15), practice deceit (12:5) and cruelty (12:10), and speak perversely (10:32; 11:11; 15:28; 19:28). *I AM* detests them and their ways (15:9, 29).

Perversity (*tahpūkôt*) is an abstract noun designating the action of its verbal root *hāpak*: "to overturn, overthrow," as when bread is turned over when baked (Hos. 7:8) and bowls are turned upside down (2 Kgs. 21:13). In Proverbs, it is used as a general term of reproach for speech (8:13; 10:31; cf. 17:20) coming from a perverse heart (cf. 6:14; 16:30) that seeks to overthrow the established order. Such a tongue will be "cut out" (10:31)—a radical punishment but proportional to the threat to public safety. The perverse act against the community and for their own selves.[91] The word combines the moral perverseness of what people say and do (Prov. 8:8; 19:1; 28:6) with the calamitous result of their lifestyle, which trips them up and makes them stumble headlong (4:12; 22:5).

The verbal root of *treacherous* (*bôgədîm*, 11:3, 6; 13:2, 15; 21:18; 22:12; 23:28; 25:19) expresses unfaithfulness to an established relationship. Specifically, it refers to those "who abandon" their heritage of having a relationship with God and with their teachers (2:13, 17; cf. Ps. 25:3). Prov. 2:21–22 divides the covenant community into two groups: those wholly committed to *I AM* and the treacherous who refuse to honor the covenant given them by faithful parents.

Those called *evildoers* are literally "those who do iniquity (*ʾāwen*)." They use the negative power of violence and deception against all humanity; they even hound the blameless (3:34; 6:12 ["villain," NIV]; 10:29; 21:15b).

For *sinners*, see on 1:10.

ii. Intellectual Terms for the Wicked and Fools

The above ethical terms for the unwise refer to fools' moral culpability, not their lack of intelligence.[92] The intellectual terms, however, are not correlatives, but distinguish several classes of fools according to their teachableness: the uncommitted, the fool, and the mocker. As for the "sluggard" and the "sense-

---

91. W. Brueggemann ("A Neglected Sapiential Word Pair," *ZAW* 89 [1977]: 244) notes that the perverse act is apart from and against the community in favor of self (see 10:9).

92. Fools may have a high IQ, but they don't know how to live. D. Goleman (*Emotional Intelligence* [New York: Bantam Books, 1995]) speaks of "emotional intelligence" (EQ). EQ refers to social skills and so is similar to "wisdom" in Proverbs. Goleman discovered that "the men with the highest test scores in college were not particularly successful compared to their lower-scoring peers in terms of salary, productivity, or status in their field. Nor did they have great life satisfaction, nor the most happiness with friendship, family, and romantic relationships" (35).

less" (see the next section, pp. 49–50), the former is worse than the fool (cf. 28:12, 16) but not as incorrigible or vile as the latter.

The personal term *uncommitted* (*pətî/pətā'yīm* [pl.]) occurs fourteen times in Proverbs, and the related abstract nouns *petî* and *pətayyût* ("simplicity") once each. Basically, the word means "to be open" and so in Proverbs describes a person who is not committed to the sages' teachings. Such a character is in danger of being easily misled. I (Bruce) earlier suggested the translation "gullible," but upon further reflection, the notion of being uncommitted is more fundamental to the meaning of *pətî/pətā'yim*. The uncommitted are the mildest sort of fools, and their state is not hopeless; they can still repent and be taught (1:4, 22–23; 8:5; 21:11) and so join the wise (cf. 1:22; 9:4). Both Wisdom and Folly vie for their allegiance (ch. 9), but until they make the decision to accept wisdom, they are wayward (see 1:32). Descriptive terms used with *petî* describe their character as youthful (1:4; 7:7) and senseless (7:7; 9:4, 16); neither shrewd (14:15, 18) nor "insightful" (19:25); not "wise" (21:11); weak-willed (22:3; 27:12); and easily seduced (7:7, 21–22).[93]

The uncommitted are a danger to themselves and their associates. Until they repent, they are on a slippery slope and are grouped with fools and mockers (1:22, 32; 8:5). What they need most is "shrewdness" (1:4). They naively trust every word (14:15), bumble into misfortune (22:3; 27:13), and inherit folly (14:18). Their "open-to-everything" attitude kills them (1:32). "Simplicity" (*pətayyût*) characterizes Woman Folly, whose way leads to death (9:13). Only by abandoning their peers, embarking on the way of insight, and learning cunning can they live (8:5; 9:4, 6, 16). Put colloquially, Woman Wisdom's message to them is, "Turn or burn" (1:25–32).

Two Hebrew terms are commonly translated *fool* (*ĕwîl* and *kəsîl*). Unlike the uncommitted, the fool is fixed in the infallibility of their own opinion, even when it contravenes the established moral order revealed through the sage. Ptahhotep noted, "A fool sees knowledge in ignorance, usefulness in harmfulness. . . . He lives on that by which one dies, his food is distortion of speech."[94] Both Hebrew words are derogatory, describing people who act irrationally due to their morally deficient characters. They are deaf to wisdom but cocksure of their distorted moral vision from which they love to twist the beneficial values of the community.

A clear distinction between *ĕwîl* and *kəsîl* cannot be drawn, because both

93. T. Donald, "The Semantic Field of 'Folly' in Proverbs, Job, Psalms, and Ecclesiastes," *VT* 13 (1963): 287.

94. *AEL*, 1:74–75.

share the same moral deficiencies and fate. Respectively in the citations, note that ’ĕwîl and kəsîl are characterized by "folly" (’iwwelet, 16:22 and 14:24; 17:12; 26:4, 5, 11), despise discipline and correction (15:5 and 15:20), lack wisdom (10:14, 21 and 14:33), speak poorly (10:8, 10; 17:28; 27:3 and 10:18; 12:23; 15:2; 19:1), lack self-control and are hot-tempered (12:16; 20:3 and 19:11), and are morally insolent, intractable, and incorrigible (12:15; 24:7 and 15:14; 17:10; 18:2; 26:5, 11; 28:26). Hopelessly bound to their folly (27:22 and 14:24; 17:10, 16; 23:9; 26:11), they cannot manage their homes and finances (11:29 and 21:20), have no honor (20:23; 29:9 and 3:35), and are punished for their folly (10:14; 14:3 and 19:29; 26:3).

The ’ĕwîl uniquely has no interest in rectifying wrongs (14:9). Such a person's provocations are worse than carrying sand and stones (27:3), and their vexations upset others (12:16; 17:25; 26:4). (The same is probably true of the kəsîl.) The ’ĕwîl is self-sufficient, rejects counsel (12:15), and disdains wisdom (1:7).

The nominal equivalent of the "fool" is *folly, foolishness* (’iwwelet), which, according to Fox, signifies "moral corruption from the standpoint of its impact on judgment and reason."[95] While the disciplining rod may remove folly from a youth (22:15), not even pounding fools in a pestle removes their folly (27:22). The deed-destiny nexus ensures that the fool's folly is transformed into a chastening discipline (16:22). The fool's mouth is a cherry bomb (10:14); their ignorance kills them (10:21).

Fools (pl. kəsîlîm) are cocksure of their own point of view (18:2; 26:12; 28:26; 30:32), have no heart for education, disregard moral truth, and recklessly vent their folly (12:23; 15:2; 26:9). As they spout their own opinions, they get others (14:7) and themselves into trouble (18:6, 7). They are hotheaded (29:11) and reckless (14:16), and delight in evil conduct (10:23). They waste money (17:16) and are prone to stupid amusements (19:10). Their ways are clear to all (13:16). It is "better to meet a bear robbed of her cubs than a fool bent on folly" (17:12, NIV). Instead of valuing knowledge and pursuing it, fools are repulsed by it and seek to rid themselves of it, doubling down on folly "as a dog returns to its vomit" (26:11).

Mockers (lēṣîm) occurs fourteen times in Proverbs and refers to the most hardened apostates. The noun "mocking" (lāṣôn) occurs in 1:22; 29:8. The mocker, the direct opposite of the wise (Prov. 9:12; 13:1; 20:1; 21:4) and of the discerning (14:6; 19:25), hates the wise should they try to correct them (9:7-8; 15:12). Their spiritual problem is rooted in their overweening pride (21:24),

95. Fox, *Proverbs 1–9*, 40.

and their arrogance keeps them from wisdom (14:6). It is futile to punish or discipline a mocker, but watching a mocker being disciplined may enlighten the uncommitted (19:25; 21:11). A mocker has a big mouth and unleashes strife upon the community (22:10; 29:8), destroying it in the process (21:24; 22:10; 29:8). Their negative influence is clear to most (24:9). According to McKane, "No man earns more universal detestation or deserves it more than he who wears a perpetual sneer, who is himself incapable of deep loyalty and reverence and who supposes that it is his mission in life to promote the corrosion of the values by which individuals and society lives."[96] To save the community, a mocker must be forcefully driven out (22:10). In the end, God himself scoffs at the mocker (3:34), thus ensuring they will disappear (Isa. 29:20).

iii. The Sluggard and the Senseless

The term *sluggard* (*ʿāṣēl*)[97] occurs thirteen times in the Old Testament, all in the book of Proverbs (6:6, 9; 10:26; 13:4; 15:19; 19:24; 20:4; 21:25; 22:13; 24:30; 26:13, 14, 16). Another term for the sluggard is *rəmiyyâ* (10:4; 12:24, 27; 19:15). Other circumlocutions for the sluggard are "slack in his work" (18:9) and "a man of want" (21:17). The antonym of the sluggard is the "diligent" (*ḥārûṣ*), which also only occurs in Proverbs and always as the antithetic parallel to sluggard. Only in 21:5 is a clear contrast to the sluggard missing, but the sluggard's shadow is still discernible. The sluggard is the subject of two main units: 6:6-11 and 24:30-34.

Sluggards irritate all who do business with them because they are unreliable and procrastinate (10:26; cf. 26:15). They bring shame to their parents (10:5) because they destroy the family inheritance (19:13-15; 24:31). Sluggards view hard workers as fools; otherwise they would stand self-condemned. The sluggard irrationally excuses not going to work: "I can't go to work today; I might get hit by a truck!" (see 22:13).

Laziness in Proverbs is more than a character flaw. It is a moral issue, for it takes away freedom (12:24), causes frustration because of the sense of getting nowhere (24:34), and eventually results in death (see 6:6-11; 10:4; 18:9; 20:13; 21:25-26; 24:30-34; cf. 28:24). Sluggards stand in contrast to the "upright" in 15:19 and the "righteous" in 21:25-26 because they give nothing to society. Sluggards are never equated with the "poor," who are so because of circum-

---

96. McKane, *Proverbs*, 399.

97. Here, we lean heavily on a paper by Bruce's student, D. Phillip Roberts, "The Sluggard in Proverbs" (unpublished term paper, OT 813, Westminster Theological Seminary, 1994).

stances beyond their control, such as tyranny (13:23; cf. 28:3); sluggards are poor because they are morally degenerate. They are not worthy to be called "poor," which is why the book does not instruct the disciple to feed them (13:4; 16:26; 19:17). The sluggard is left begging in harvest and has "plenty of poverty," a telling oxymoron (20:4; 28:19).

The *senseless* (*ḥăsar-lēb*, "lacking heart/sense") occurs only in wisdom literature (thirteen times in Proverbs; cf. Eccl. 10:3 and Sirach). Here the word "heart" (*lēb*) carries its psychological meaning (see "Heart," p. 32). In Collection I, this moral flaw is ascribed to the uncommitted (7:7; 9:4, 16) and the unchaste wife (6:32). The former is weak in temptation, lacking the foresight to see the fatal consequences of adultery (6:32; 7:7). In Collection II, the senseless despise their neighbors (11:12), chase fantasies (12:11), find joy in folly (15:21), put themselves up as security (17:18), and are the antithesis of the righteous (10:20, 21) and wise (10:13). In Collection IV, senselessness is ascribed to the sluggard (24:30). In short, fools have this moral flaw.

iv. Retribution for the Wicked

The wicked are already dead, for they have no relationship with the living God. The texts predicting the death of the wicked do not refer to a premature death but represent this present state of death, terminating with a tragic, final end. While the pursuit of wisdom and practice of righteousness save the wise from the realm and destiny of death, nothing can deliver the wicked (1:4, 19; 10:2; 13:14; 14:27; 15:24). Their physical death is a land of no return, without a second chance (1:20-33; 2:19, 22; cf. Ps. 49:8, 15; Isa. 26:19). If death is the final destiny of the wicked, we should assume that life is the final destiny of the righteous (cf. Matt. 25:46).

v. The Grave (Traditionally, "Sheol")

Sheol (*šə'ôl*), which occurs nine times in Proverbs, describes the destiny of all humanity (23:14; 27:20; 30:16), both the fools/wicked (5:5; 7:27; 9:18) and, temporarily, the wise/righteous (1:12; cf. Ps. 49:9, 15, a wisdom psalm). In most English translations, *šə'ôl* is transliterated as "Sheol," but the NIV (1984) justly renders it by "Grave." The prepositions attached to Sheol indicate that it is the physical grave below the earth. The varied and rich figures that the biblical poets use to depict it transform it from the physical realm of the dead to the metaphorical, transcendent realm—a place distinct from both the earth where the living are and the heavenly realm where God is.[98] The Grave, like the Jordan River and Mount Zion, symbolizes eternal realities that transcend its physical space, and so it is rendered with the upper case, "Grave."[99]

3. Male and Female

Finally, humankind is divided into male and female, distinguishing them sexually as man and woman, socially as husband and wife, and parentally as father and mother.[100] The complex character of the unfaithful wife will be discussed separately, since the father lectures against her more than any other person.

a. Man and Woman

Proverbs is a book oriented to the male. In the lectures of the Prologue, the father is always mentioned, the mother rarely so (however, see below). The addressee is always his son, never his daughter; and in the father's warning, he warns his son against an unfaithful wife (chs. 5, 7), never his daughter against an adulterous husband. Woman Wisdom addresses the males in the gate, not the women in the market (8:4). The unfaithful wife and Woman Folly go after the uncommitted male, but no equivalent male seduces the uncommitted girl. In Collection II, Solomon continues to address the son (10:1; 19:27), not the daughter. He warns against the unfaithful (22:14) and quarrelsome woman (19:13; 21:9, 19; 25:24; 27:15) while commending marriage to a good woman (12:4; 18:22; 19:14). He never mentions a good or bad husband. Collections III, VI, and

---

98. E.g., Sheol has a "mouth" (Ps. 141:7), which it "enlarges" (Isa. 5:14). It is "never satisfied" (Prov. 27:20; 30:16) and lets no one out of its "grip" (Ps. 89:48; Song 8:6), although some are redeemed from it (Ps. 49:15; Prov. 23:14; Hos. 13:14). It is like a prison with "cords" (2 Sam. 22:6) and a land that has "gates" (Isa. 38:10) with "bars" (Job 17:16). In Sheol, corruption is "the father" and the worm "the mother and sister" (Job 17:13ff.). It is a "land" from which none return to this life (Job 7:9). It equalizes all: rich and poor (Job 3:18–19), righteous and wicked (3:17), regardless of their moral choices, lie together. It is a land of silence (Ps. 94:17), darkness (13:13), weakness, and oblivion (Ps. 88:11–19). Sheol's destructive nature is highlighted by the addition of "Abaddon" (Prov. 15:11; 27:20).

99. The NIV (2011) translates *šə'ōl* with "realm of the dead." It is problematic to speculate about an intermediate state from the figurative descriptions of Sheol.

100. Here, we reflect the normative biblical assumption that biological sex and gender identity do not vary independently (cf. Gen. 1:27). While some contest this assumption today, this commentary is not the place to debate it.

VII are addressed to the son (23:15; 30:1; 31:1), and the book closes with a portrait of an ideal wife, with no mention of an ideal husband for a woman.[101]

Yet the woman was not excluded from being taught the book's wisdom. The reference to "your mother" (1:8; 4:3; 6:20; 10:1) points to the home, with mother and father, as the place in which wisdom was taught. The fact that some lectures of the Prologue mention the mother (1:8; 4:3; 6:20) implies that in the other lectures, too, she is engaged with the father in teaching their son. The poet gaps her presence in the other lectures due to the epigrammatic nature of proverbs.[102] In the book's concluding poem, the noble wife is praised for having faithful instruction on her tongue (31:26). These references to the mother/noble wife as a teacher in the home imply that when she was a daughter, she too was taught the proverbs by both her parents, since to be a teacher of wisdom, she herself had to be taught.

One reason only the son is addressed is the expectation that it is the male offspring who will assume leadership in defining the family's identity and values (4:3-4; cf. Num. 30). E. Follis argues another reason: speaking in general terms, males are the more adventuresome of the sexes by nature, tending to press beyond existing boundaries and stray from the inherited tradition. By contrast, daughters tend to nurture the home and community.[103] In sum, the proverbs are also addressed to the daughter and need to be applied appropriately in a way that looks at men through a woman's eyes.

b. Husband and Wife

A wise man is prayerful (15:8, 29; 16:3) and depends on God for a prudent wife (18:22). He searches for one who is noble and competent (31:10-31) and rejects

---

101. Of course, the whole book is addressed to the son with the implication that wisdom will make him an ideal husband, but that point is not made explicitly.

102. So A. Moss, "Wisdom as Parental Teaching in Proverbs 1-9," *HeyJ* 38 (1997): 426-39. The mention of the mother at the book's seams—at the beginning of the Prologue (1:8) and of the proverbs (10:1)—validates this interpretation.

103. E. Follis, *Directions in Biblical Hebrew Poetry*, JSOTSup 40 (Sheffield: Sheffield Academic, 1987), 178. The gender differences noted by Follis appear to be supported by numerous social-scientific studies, which show that these differences are not primarily due to socialization but are biologically based. See Y. Weisberg, C. DeYoung, and J. Hirsh, "Gender Differences in Personality across the Ten Aspects of the Big Five," *Frontiers in Psychology*, August 1, 2011; D. Schmitt et al., "Personality and gender differences in global perspective," *International Journal of Psychology* 52 (2016): 45-56; M. Del Giudice, T. Booth, and P. Irwing, "The Distance Between Mars and Venus: Measuring Global Sex Differences in Personality," *PLOS One*, January 4, 2012.

one who is unloved by the godly community (30:23). Because he is wise and teachable, he listens to his wife's good and earnest correction and counsel (9:8, 9; 13:14, 20) as he would to a friend (27:6, 9)—as David listened to Abigail (1 Sam. 25:32–35). If his wife is foolish, we assume he would reject her counsel as Job refuted his wife's (Job 2:9–10), as David rebuffed Michal's (2 Sam. 6:21–22), and as Adam and Abraham should have done to their wives (Gen. 3:6, 12; 16:2). The wise husband becomes intoxicated with his wife's love, and the father prays that the son will find a wife who fully satisfies his God-given sexual appetite (5:18–19). A good wife does not shame him (12:4) or tear down her house (14:1), and he praises her by publicly standing up in her presence and proclaiming her virtue (31:28–31).

A wise wife fears *I AM*, is wise and righteous in general (see 31:31b) and so accepts her husband's godly teaching and correction. He can trust her as he does *I AM* (31:11). Unlike the unfaithful wife, she keeps her marriage covenant (2:17; 15:4) and desires to be a crown on her husband's head (12:4). She works to supplement the family income so that her husband is free to serve the public good (31:13–25, esp. v. 23). She teaches and manages her whole household (31:28) and finds her fulfillment in enriching others.

In sum, husband and wife dwell together in a spirit of humility (15:33) and faith in God (16:3). They express their love in each other's embrace and in open correction of each other (27:5; cf. Lev. 19:17–18). And they confess and renounce their inevitable sins while extending mercy to each other (28:13).

c. Father and Mother

Wise parents build their house (14:1; 24:27), value their children (4:3), and raise them in *I AM*. They recognize the depravity of human nature (14:12; 19:27; 20:9; 22:15; 29:18) but believe wise parenting is effective (22:6) and so give their children moral instruction (1:2–6; 30:1; 31:1). They use verbal instruction to form the child's character (chs. 1–10) and the rod to prevent repeated folly (13:24). They regard their values as God-given (2:6) and therefore as absolute and not relative to the whims of secular society. They are united in their instruction (1:8; 31:26), were exemplary in their own submission when they were children (4:3–4), and are diligent in their pedagogy—as seen in the repetitive pattern of the ten lectures. Far from overly safeguarding the child from real-world evil, they take the risk and allow the child to feel its tempting power by re-creating the words of wicked men and the unfaithful wife while simultaneously developing repulsion to them (1:10–19; 7:1–27).

d. The Unchaste ("Strange") Wife

Who is the woman from whose wiles the father seeks to protect his son through repeated warnings in chapters 5–7?[104] He introduces her in 2:16–19 and then expands her profile in three lectures (5:1–23; 6:20–35; 7:1–27; cf. 22:14; 23:33).[105] He introduces her as an "unchaste wife" (*'iššâ zāra'*), a "foreigner" (*nokrîâ*), "who abandons the companion of her youth," and "forgets her covenant with God" (2:16–17). The last two reveal her as an unfaithful, apostate wife. When all the lectures about her are analyzed, they present a portrait of an unchaste wife, an outsider to the covenant community, who betrayed her faithful covenant husband (2:16; 5:20; 6:24; 7:5) and remarried outside the covenant community.[106] Her remarriage can be inferred from the fact that she now has a foreign husband (6:29; 7:19). She is a prostitute *at heart* (6:26)[107] who lustfully stalks the streets and attempts to seduce young men (7:10–21). Let us analyze the four descriptors used to introduce her.

104. Fox (*Proverbs 1–9*, 134–41) lists six ways of understanding this figure and concludes that she is "strange" (*zārâ*) because she is another man's wife and therefore "strange" to all men but her husband.

105. According to R. E. Murphy and O. Carm ("Wisdom and Eros in Proverbs 1–9," *CBQ* 50 [1998]: 600), this woman is the subject of some sixty-five verses, more than "any other figure, even . . . Lady Wisdom."

106. G. Yee ("'I Have Perfumed My Bed with Myrrh': The Foreign Woman [*'Iššâ Zārâ*] in Proverbs 1–9," *JSOT* 43 [1989]: 54) argues that the adulteress in the Prologue is one woman described variously.

107. Here a "prostitute" signifies one who engages in sex with no intention of an enduring relationship, not one who engages in sex for payment. The Akkadian Counsel of Wisdom warns youths not to marry a (temple) prostitute, and the Proverbs of Ahikar warns them not to lust after her (see H. W. F. Saggs, *The Greatness That Was Babylon* [New York: New American Library; Times Mirror, 1962], 332; F. C. Conybeare, J. R. Harris, A. S. Smith, "The Story of Ahikar," in *The Apocrypha and Pseudepigrapha of the Old Testament*, ed. R. H. Charles, vol. 2 [Oxford: Clarendon, 1976], 728–29). Prostitution was accepted and regulated in the ancient Near East (see J. Gasper, *Social Ideas in the Wisdom Literature of the Old Testament* [Washington, DC: The Catholic University of America, 1947], 11 n. 49). The Mosaic law, however, strictly prohibited Israelite women from roles as prostitutes (Lev. 19:29), prohibited and condemned cultic prostitution (Deut. 23:18), and presented monogamy as the ideal (Gen. 2:18–25). No law, however, explicitly prohibited harlotry with a foreigner, as do these texts in Proverbs. The New Testament threatens God's judgment for all sorts of sexual immorality outside of marriage (1 Cor. 6:9–20) and prescribes marriage as an anodyne against sexual uncleanness (1 Cor. 7:2).

VIII. Theology

i. The "Unchaste Woman" ('iššâ zārâ, 2:16a)

According to Snijders, "the participle zār ('strange' [fem. zārâ]) must be translated 'one who distances or removes himself.'"[108] This definition fits well the sketch in 2:17 ("[She] abandons the companion of her youth"), matching the depiction in the parallel sketch of the perverse men as apostates from the right way (2:15–18). Furthermore, the zārâ is hostile to the covenant community and endangers it because her behavior is outside the laws of the community.[109]

ii. The "Outsider" (nokriyyâ, 2:16b)

Is this unchaste woman also a foreigner in the literal sense?[110] In covenantal contexts, nokrî signifies a "foreigner" not incorporated within Israel (Exod. 2:22; Deut. 14:21; Judg. 19:12; 1 Kgs. 8:41; Isa. 2:6). Based on this, some contend she is a cult prostitute.[111] However, the father does not label her as such, and she never tempts the son religiously but only with sensual pleasure. The father warns of the danger posed by her husband, not by apostasy from I AM. The father's warning does not pertain to her ethnicity but to the negative social and economic consequences of adultery. In sum, in Proverbs, she is probably not a pagan foreigner but an unfaithful wife who stands outside the community of the wise.

iii. The Unfaithful Wife (2:17a)

The woman is also described as willfully violating her commitment to her godly husband. "Companion of her youth" ('allûp nəʿûrêhā) is a metonymy for her husband as a teacher. 'Allûp denotes "a [personal] friend, confidante,

---

108. L. A. Snijders, *TDOT*, 4:53, s.v. *zûr/zār*.

109. R. Martin-Achard (*TLOT*, 1:391–92, s.v. *zār*) writes, "The other is the outsider whose behavior endangers the existence of the group because he/she stands outside the laws of the community.... Thus *zār* 'other' can acquire a rather negative meaning ('dangerous, hostile')."

110. Snijders ("The Meaning of *Zār* in the Old Testament," *OtSt* [1954]: 1–54) says no, while J. K. Wiles ("The 'Enemy' in Israelite Wisdom Literature" [PhD diss., Southern Baptist Theological Seminary, 1982], 50) says yes: "She is an unfaithful foreigner married to an Israelite."

111. G. Boström, *Proverbiastudien: Die Weisheit und das fremde Weib in Spr. 1–9*, LUÅ (Lund: Gleerup, 1935).

[bosom] companion, comrade" and is used six other times (cf. 16:28; 17:9; Ps. 55:14; Jer. 3:4; 13:21; Mic. 7:5).[112] Its verbal root means "to instruct" and may refer to the intimate fellowship that develops from people sharing and getting to know each other. In such a relationship, friends become vulnerable to each other because their trust can be misused. Indeed, in all seven occurrences of *'allûp*, it refers to the betrayed confidence of a close friend. As Hosea guided Gomer (Hos. 3:2–3), so this woman's husband faithfully instructed her in the right way, but she spurned his loyalty with betrayal.

iv. The Apostate Wife (2:17b)

In the phrase "forgets her covenant with God," the word "forgets" (*šākēḥâ*) means that she dismembers herself from her allegiance to her marriage covenant; it is synonymous with "abandon." "Covenant" (*bərît*) means "imposition" or "obligation" and here refers to her marriage obligations. The addition of "with her God" suggest that the Creator is the witness to, guarantor, and possibly author of her marriage vows.[113] Thus, this depiction presents her as a woman who in her youth had accepted *I AM* and his wisdom as taught her by her husband but refuses to honor her commitment. Turning her back on her husband, she has also turned her back on *I AM* and his covenant community. The unfaithful wife of the Prologue is an adulteress among people and an apostate against God.

v. Conclusion

The unchaste wife is not simply an "adulteress" (that is, "someone else's wife").[114] The various descriptions of her in the Prologue present her as a lustful apostate from the godly community and an unrestrained wife who has betrayed the faithful husband of her youth (2:16–17; 5:20; 6:24; 7:5), as Gomer did Hosea (Hos. 1:2–11). Throughout the Prologue, she is *at heart* a prostitute (6:26), lustfully stalking the streets to seduce young men (7:10–21). This description fits the biblical world. She is a *femme fatale* who will bring disaster to the son if he becomes involved with her—namely, ruin from the community

---

112. Kühlewein, *TLOT*, 3:1243–44, s.v. *rēaʿ*.

113. M. Weinfeld, *TDOT*, 2:255, 256, 261, s.v. *bərît*. Ezek. 16:8 uses *bərît* in reference to marriage.

114. Pace Fox, *Proverbs 1–9*, 139–40.

(5:17), insatiable vengeance from her current husband (6:32–35), and ultimately death from God (5:21–23; 7:23–27).

The unchaste wife is also a paradigm for spiritual infidelity to *I AM*. This interpretation is fortified in the unchaste wife's personification as Woman Folly at the end of the Prologue. Sexual and spiritual faithfulness interpenetrate each other. A sexual adulterer shows himself incapable of having a single eye toward God. Solomon's sexual unfaithfulness stole away his heart from loving God because his sex life was married to his spiritual life. The prophets frequently used marriage as a metaphor for Israel's relationship to *I AM*. However, these warnings against the literal adulteress must not be minimized, as seen by the father's detailed description of her allurements and the economic, not religious, nature of his warnings.

E. Christology

Proverbs is directly relevant to the Christian, albeit it is surpassed in the life and teachings of Jesus Christ. Moreover, Woman Wisdom is a type of Lord Jesus Christ and, along with the rest of Scripture, speaks of his death and resurrection, as Jesus said (Luke 24:44).

1. The Enduring Relevance of Proverbs to Christians

Four arguments establish the enduring importance of Proverbs.

1. By nature, proverbs express eternal, unchanging truth applicable to many situations, but the way they express that truth is historically, politically, and culturally conditioned.
2. The Holy Spirit caused its inclusion in the canon of Scripture and thus affirmed its relevance. Jews and Christians have universally recognized Proverbs as part of the Bible. And the New Testament includes Proverbs in the statement, "All Scripture is God-breathed and is useful for teaching, rebuking, correcting and training in righteousness, so that the servant of God may be thoroughly equipped for every good work" (2 Tim. 3:16–17).
3. The apostles apply the book to the church. Peter uses Prov. 26:11 and Jude uses Prov. 25:14 with reference to false teachers (2 Pet. 2:22; Jude 12). The apostles generally use proverbs to teach the church godly living (cf. Prov. 3:7 with 2 Cor. 8:12; Prov. 3:34 with Jas. 4:5 and 1 Pet. 5:5; Prov.

4:26 with Heb. 12:13; Prov. 10:16 with Rom. 6:23; Prov. 24:21 with 1 Pet. 2:17; Prov. 25:21–22 with Rom. 12:20; Prov. 26:11 with 2 Pet. 2:2; Prov. 30:8 with Matt. 6:11).

4. The author of Hebrews interprets the father's lecture to his son in Prov. 3:11–12 as addressing the church (Heb. 12:5–6).

2. The Superiority of Jesus Christ to Solomon's Wisdom

Jesus Christ claimed superiority to Solomon and his wisdom (Matt. 12:42). This superiority is evident in a number of ways:

- The Queen of Sheba praised Solomon's wisdom, but she will rise at the judgment to condemn those who do not listen to Christ's superior wisdom (cf. 1 Kings 10:7 with Matt. 12:42).
- Solomon taught that *I AM* would repay the wrongdoer, but Christ says he himself will repay them (cf. Prov. 24:12 with Matt 25:41–46; Rev. 2:23; 22:12; see also Rom. 2:6–8; 2 Thess. 1:8; 2 Tim. 4:14; 1 Pet. 1:17; Rev. 20:12–13).
- Solomon depended on God to discipline those he loves, but Christ himself disciplines those he loves (cf. Prov. 3:11–12 with Rev. 3:19).
- Solomon emphasized health and wealth now while minimizing present sufferings; Christ emphasized present suffering for righteousness while maximizing future glory (cf. Prov. 3:1–10, 34 with Matt. 5:3–12; 25:1–13).
- Solomon speaks opaquely of eternal life, but Christ, by his resurrection, brought eternity into present history (cf. Prov. 8:35 with Matt. 25:46; 2 Tim. 1:10; see also John 11:25–26; Rom. 6:1–4; Col. 3:1–3).
- Solomon promotes pleasing parents, but Christ, while upholding the honor of parents, gives higher priority to loving and serving the triune God (cf. Prov. 10:1; 19:13; 23:22–25; 27:11; 29:3 with Matt. 5:45; 7:21; 10:32, 33, 35, 37; 15:4; 23:9; 25:34; Mark 3:31–35; Luke 9:60).
- Solomon's wisdom is brought into being by God, but Christ is God.
- Solomon offers a banquet of food and drink, but Christ himself is the Christian's food and drink (cf. Prov. 9:1–3 with John 6:53; see also Matt. 26:26–28 parr.; 1 Cor. 11:23–27).
- No human ascended into heaven to gain comprehensive knowledge, but Christ both descended from heaven and ascended into it (cf. Prov. 30:4 with John 6:33; Eph. 4:9–10).

- Solomon himself failed to obey his wisdom, but Christ perfectly exemplified his teachings (cf. Prov. 3:2; 25:26 with 1 Kgs. 11:19–10; Luke 2:52; Heb. 4:15).
- Solomon taught his disciples to feed their enemies, but Christ died for his enemies (cf. Prov. 25:21 with Rom. 5:8; see also Eph. 2:1–10; 1 Tim. 1:12–17).

Nevertheless, we do not discard Solomon's wisdom on the grounds that Christ's wisdom is superior any more than we would throw away a ten-dollar bill because we had a hundred-dollar bill. Jesus himself undoubtedly devoted much time to studying and memorizing Proverbs; the disciple is not above the master.

3. Woman Wisdom as a Type of Jesus Christ

a. Historical Background

From about the time of Justin Martyr (A.D. 125), most Christians[115] identified Woman Wisdom (*Sophia*, the Greek equivalent of the Hebrew *ḥokmâ*) in Prov. 8 with Jesus Christ. This fateful interpretation embroiled the church in controversy about the nature of the relationship between God and Christ.[116]

The Nicene fathers equated Wisdom and Christ on the basis of their preexistence and their assumed roles as agents in the creation (cf. Prov. 3:19–20; 8:22–31 with John 1:3; 1 Cor. 8:6; Col. 1:15–16; Heb. 1:3). However, as we will show in the commentary, exegesis of Proverbs 8:22–31 does not support identifying Wisdom with Christ. As we argued above (see pp. 29–30), Solomon identifies Woman Wisdom with his teachings, not with a hypostasis of God.

Furthermore, the apostles do not build their high Christology by identifying Jesus with Wisdom. Jewish wisdom literature provides no sure foundation, if any, for the high Christology of the New Testament as found in John 1:3, Phil. 2:6, and Col. 1:15–16.[117] By contrast, the Wisdom of Solomon represents

115. Irenaeus equated Wisdom with the Holy Spirit. See *Against Heresies* 4.20.

116. A. L. Clayton, "The Orthodox Recovery of a Heretical Proof-Text: Athanasius of Alexandria's Interpretation of Proverbs 8:22–30 in Conflict with the Arians" (PhD diss., Southern Methodist University, 1988), 32–51.

117. There is no direct evidence in Hellenistic Jewish wisdom literature that links Wisdom in Prov. 8 to Wisdom as an agent in creation. If there were, it might have led the apostles to link Jesus the Creator with Wisdom.

Wisdom as a mediator between God and creation, and the Jerusalem Targum renders Gen. 1:1 in conjunction with Prov. 8:22: "*I AM* created the heavens and the earth by wisdom." Such writings, while not contributing directly to the high Christology of the New Testament, may have provided the apostles with a paradigm for expressing the doctrine of the Trinity, with Jesus Christ represented as the agent through whom all things were created; but the apostles do not cite or build their high Christology on Prov. 8:22–31.[118]

A lot has been made of John's use of Wisdom in his Gospel, but nowhere does he equate Jesus Christ with the figure of Wisdom in Prov. 8. In fact, he never uses the word *sophia* in his Gospel (or epistles), which, as Karen Jobes notes, would be "beyond comprehension" if John were trying to present Jesus in the categories of Wisdom.[119] According to Jobes, the *logos* in John's prologue differs so markedly from Woman Wisdom that "the prologue is, in fact, a polemic against viewing Jesus Christ through the lens of Jewish Wisdom as refracted by Greek philosophy."[120]

Neither does Paul build his high Christology on Prov. 8 or on any other Jewish wisdom literature.[121] Gordon Fee examines the crucial wisdom texts in

---

118. R. Bauckham (*Jesus and the God of Israel: God Crucified and Other Studies on the New Testament's Christology of Divine Identity* [Grand Rapids: Eerdmans, 2008]) argues an original thesis that in Second Temple Judaism, Wisdom was seen as an intermediary who was intrinsic to God's divine identity, thus revealing distinctions within God's identity which then enabled the apostles to construct their high Christology of Jesus as sharing in the divine identity of God.

119. K. Jobes, "Sophia Christology: The Way of Wisdom?," in *WWis*, 239. However, Bartholomew and O'Dowd (*Old Testament Wisdom Literature*, 245) write, "John's prologue (Jn. 1:1–18; cf. Heb. 1:1–3) presents the strongest blend of Greek and Hebrew wisdom in the New Testament. . . . Not only is Genesis 1 evident in John's prologue, so too is the passage in Proverbs 8:22–31, where we read Woman Wisdom was created by God in the beginning and became an agent in his original creation of the world." But a careful exegesis of Prov. 8:22–31, as we shall see, does not say Wisdom was "created"—she was given birth—nor that she was an agent in the creation.

120. Jobes, "Sophia Christology," 242. Jobes notes the following main differences between Wisdom and *logos*: (1) Wisdom was brought into being by God, but the *logos* was God; (2) Wisdom witnessed the creation, but the *logos* was the Creator; (3) Wisdom-Sophia in Wisdom of Solomon 7:26 is a reflection of eternal light, but the *logos* is the light. To these, we add that Wisdom laughs at the time of judgment (1:26), but the *logos* is the judge (John 5:23–24, 27).

121. Bartholomew and O'Dowd (*Old Testament Wisdom Literature*, 247) provide a contrary voice: "While the Gospels only make implicit use of wisdom to understand Jesus, the Pauline epistles make explicit use of wisdom theology." Unfortunately, Bartholomew and

the Pauline corpus (1 Cor. 8:6; Col. 1:15–17) along with the crucial wisdom texts in the Jewish tradition where Wisdom is personified and said to be present with God when he created (Prov. 8:22–31; Sir. 24:3–22; Wis. 6:1–10:21). Fee's conclusion is that "Wisdom is of virtually no—or very little—help in understanding Paul's view of the preexistent Christ."[122]

b. Woman Wisdom a Type of Jesus Christ

Nevertheless, the striking similarities between Solomon's literary personification of his wisdom and John's representation of Jesus Christ argue that Woman Wisdom is a type—that is to say, a divinely intended exemplar—of Jesus Christ:

- Both existed with God before all things.
- Both played some role in creation.
- Both descended from heaven to dwell with humanity and were rejected by the masses.
- Both teach heavenly wisdom.
- Both call those who listen "children."
- Both lead those who listen to life and immortality and threaten death to those who do not.
- Both offer blessings in the symbols of food and drink.[123]

Typology, however, is not identity. Rather, the antitype will be similar and yet superior to the type.

c. Conclusion

"In Christ," says Paul, "are hidden all the treasures of wisdom and knowledge" (Col. 2:3–4). Therefore, while Christians prize Solomon's wisdom, they do

---

O'Dowd fail to interact with G. Fee's previously published essay, "Wisdom Christology in Paul," in *WWis*, 251–79, where Fee argues against Paul's reliance on Jewish wisdom traditions for his Christology.

122. Fee, "Wisdom Christology in Paul," 265. Fee draws the conclusion that "what is most lacking in all of this material [wisdom literature] is a verbal or conceptual linkage between Wisdom and creation of the kind explicitly found in Paul with reference to Christ."

123. See R. E. Brown, *The Gospel According to John: A New Translation with Commentary*, AB 29 (Garden City, NY: Doubleday, 1966), cxxii–cxxvii.

not substitute it for the person and work of Jesus Christ. Instead, they come to Proverbs recognizing that they now live in the heavenly Jerusalem with a greater-than-Solomon—with Jesus the mediator of a superior covenant—and with the sprinkled blood that speaks a better word than the blood of Abel (Matt. 12:42; Heb. 12:22–24). In love and faith, Christians hold fast what is good from the past and grasp the presence of Christ's kingdom now, and with a certain hope they anticipate the consummation of all things.

TEXT AND COMMENTARY

N

Preamble and Prologue
(1:1–9:18)

For the structure of this collection, see "Structure," pp. 2–3.

TITLE AND PREAMBLE: 1:1–7

¹The proverbs of Solomon son of David, king of Israel:
²to know wisdom and instruction
   in understanding words of insight;
³to accept instruction in prudent behavior:
   what is right and just and fair;
⁴to give to the uncommitted shrewdness,
   to the young knowledge and discretion.
⁵Let the wise hear and add to their learning,
   and let the insightful acquire guidance
⁶in understanding a proverb, namely a parable—
   the sayings of the wise, namely their riddles.
⁷The fear of *I AM* is the beginning of knowledge,
   but fools despise wisdom and instruction.

Title (1:1)

The Proverbs of Solomon son of David is a cover title for the whole book, for Solomon is the principal, but not the sole nor the final, author of the book's seven collections (see "Solomon," p. 6). *King of* all *Israel* (966 to 926 B.C.) locates Proverbs within the flow of Israel's salvation history. When Solomon took the throne of Israel, he copied the Book of the Law of Moses, which would have shaped his worldview and values (see Deut. 17:18–20), and his dying father, King David, reinforced those values, charging Solomon to obey the Book of the Law (1 Kings 2:1–4).

Preamble (1:2–7)

The chiastic structure (see "Poetics," p. 15) of the preamble, noted by William Brown,[1] binds together as correlative terms (see p. 34) the abstract terms for wisdom and the terms for its practical application in ethics, with the focus on the latter: "what is right and just and fair."

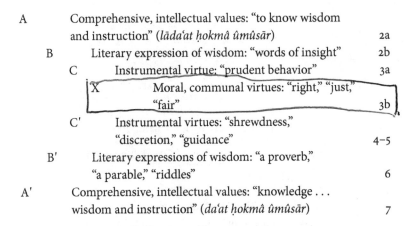

A	Comprehensive, intellectual values: "to know wisdom and instruction" (*lāda'at ḥokmâ ûmûsār*)	2a
	B	Literary expression of wisdom: "words of insight"	2b
		C	Instrumental virtue: "prudent behavior"	3a
			X	Moral, communal virtues: "right," "just," "fair"	3b
		C'	Instrumental virtues: "shrewdness," "discretion," "guidance"	4–5
	B'	Literary expressions of wisdom: "a proverb," "a parable," "riddles"	6
A'	Comprehensive, intellectual values: "knowledge . . . wisdom and instruction" (*da'at ḥokmâ ûmûsār*)	7

A/A' form an inclusio around the preamble with the verbal sequence of "to know"/"knowledge,"[2] "wisdom," and "instruction." B/B' are bound together by "understanding words of insight" (v. 2b), sharpened to "understanding a proverb," "a parable," and "riddles" in v. 6. Instrumental terms for wisdom—"prudence" (v. 3a) sharpened to "shrewdness," "discretion," and "guidance" (vv. 4–5)—bind C/C'. X is the pivot, focusing on the book's practical aim of producing a righteous, just, and fair community.[3]

Aim and Addressees (1:2–6)

Verses 2–6 state the book's aim and in that connection identify its addressees as Israel's youth. Verse 2 is a summary statement of the book's purpose, pre-

---

1. W. Brown, *Character in Crisis: A Fresh Approach to the Wisdom Literature* (Grand Rapids: Eerdmans, 1996), 25.

2. Hebrew *da'at* is a homonym for both an infinitive, "to know" (v. 2), and the noun "knowledge" (v. 7).

3. See Waltke, "Righteousness," 225–37.

senting the two sides of acquiring wisdom: its substance ("wisdom," v. 2a) and its *expression* ("words of insight," v. 2b). Wisdom's substance is unpacked in vv. 3–5 by synonyms and by poetics, and its expression is unpacked in v. 6, which repeats the catchword "in understanding" and identifies "words" in v. 2b as "a proverb" and "sayings." Verses 2a and 3–5 pertain to moral acumen; vv. 2b and 6 pertain to mental acumen.

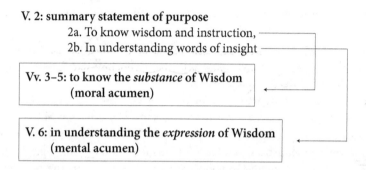

V. 2: summary statement of purpose
        2a. To know wisdom and instruction,
        2b. In understanding words of insight

Vv. 3–5: to know the *substance* of Wisdom
    (moral acumen)

V. 6: in understanding the *expression* of Wisdom
    (mental acumen)

As for the poetics of vv. 3–5, the catchword "instruction" links vv. 2 and 3. Verses 3–4 are linked by the two aspects of learning: "to accept" by the student (v. 3) and "to give" by the teacher (v. 4). Verses 4–5 are linked by the book's two addressees, the "uncommitted" (v. 4) and the "wise" (v. 5). Finally, the inclusio of "wisdom" and "wise" in vv. 2a and 5a and of "insight" and "insightful" in vv. 2b and 5b moves the unit from the substance of wisdom to the person who incarnates it.

Summary of Purpose: The Substance and Expression of Wisdom (1:2)

To know means to have personal, experiential knowledge of the thing known, namely *wisdom* (see "What Is 'Wisdom,'" pp. 27–28). *Instruction* (*mûsār*; see "What Is 'Wisdom,'" p. 28; "The Wise and Fools," p. 28; cf. 15:33; 19:25) can be imparted either verbally to prevent acts of folly or with the correcting rod to prevent the repetition of folly. To convey the latter notion, *mûsār* is translated "discipline" (cf. 13:24; 22:15; 23:13, 14; 29:15). *Understanding* (see p. 36) requires mental skill wherein something is contemplated with the senses as described in 2:1–4. *Words* (*'imrê*) signifies the complete statements—the full thoughts rather than individual words—and these give *insight* or *understanding* (see "The Wise and Fools," pp. 35–36).

The Substance of Wisdom and the Addressees (1:3–5)

The book's addressees are "the young" (v. 4b). Those "uncommitted" to its teachings (v. 4) become "the wise" by embracing its instruction (v. 5). (For these and other terms in this section, see "The Wise and Fools," p. 34.) Those who remain uncommitted into adulthood are lumped among the fools (see 1:20–33). Unlike the sage-kings or high officials of Solomon's world who composed their wisdom texts for their sons or other budding court officials— whom they name as the recipients of their wisdom—the preamble does not name a specific recipient (e.g., Rehoboam) and so "democratizes" the sages' collected sayings and places them in the mouths of all Israel, and today the church, to shape its character.

3 To begin to know wisdom, one has *to accept* (lit., "to take"; see 2:1) the book's *instruction* (see v. 2), which produces *prudent behavior*. Since wisdom and some of its synonyms are morally neutral, v. 3b qualifies them by *what is right* (or "righteousness") *and just* (or "justice") *and fair* (or "upright").

4 Proverbs aims *to give to the uncommitted shrewdness*. The parallel, *the young* (*na'ar*) includes all youth. *Na'ar* can refer to baby Moses (Exod. 2:6), the child Samuel (1 Sam. 1:22, 24; cf. 4:21), a seventeen-year-old Joseph (Gen. 37:2; cf. 1 Sam 30:17), and presumably a young adult (e.g., Zadok, 1 Chr. 12:28; Absalom, 2 Sam 18:5; and Solomon, 1 Kgs. 3:7). Men were registered in the military and held accountable at twenty years of age (Num. 1:3; 14:29), and the son addressed in the Prologue has likely reached puberty. *Knowledge* is a metonymy for the book's inspired proverbs and sayings. Wisdom without knowledge is impossible. As knowledge of the laws of aerodynamics is essential to build an airplane, so building a wise life demands knowledge of the revealed divine moral order—the deed-destiny nexus—taught in Proverbs. The substance of wisdom also includes *discretion*.

5 *Let the wise hear* and so obey implies that Proverbs was meant to be heard as well as read. *And add to their learning* implies a lifelong process (see 4:18). *The insightful acquire*—that is, exert effort and pay a cost "to purchase" (cf. 2:4; 4:5)—*guidance*.

The Expression of Wisdom (1:6)

The "words" of v. 2b are now specified as proverbs, parables, and riddles (see "Genres in Proverbs," pp. 17–18). The single poem in Hab. 2:6 is described using these words, suggesting that they are not distinct genres of wisdom but synonyms. *Proverb* refers exclusively to Solomon's aphorisms. *Parable* elaborates that the proverb requires the addressees to compare their situation to the aphorism. *The sayings of the wise* refers to the moral aphorisms of other sages. Their sayings are called *riddles*, for they too demand interpretation.

The Foundation of Wisdom: The Fear of *I AM* (1:7)

The fear of I AM (see "Fear of *I AM*," pp. 38–39) is the quintessential expression of the spiritual grammar for understanding Proverbs. The catchword *instruction* also links vv. 7b and v. 8a; thus v. 7 also functions as a janus between the preamble and the Prologue. *Beginning of knowledge* refers to the epistemological foundation of Proverbs.[4] What the alphabet is to reading, what notes are to music, what numerals are to mathematics, the fear of *I AM* is to gaining the book's *wisdom and instruction. Fools* (see "The Wise and Fools," p. 34) lack this prerequisite. They *despise* (regard as worthless and vile) God's revelation.

THE PROLOGUE (1:8–9:18)

Adolescence, according to Erik Erikson, is the quest for a sense of identity.[5] The son stands on the threshold of adulthood, where he must choose between the way of his parents or the way of sinners. The choice is a matter of life and death. Exacerbating youths' vulnerability is their budding sexuality, their innate greed, and their need for peer approval.

Lecture 1: Reject the Gang's Invitation (1:8–19)

> [8]Listen, my son, to your father's instruction, [MUSAR] [TORAH]
>   and do not let go of your mother's teaching.
> [9]For they are an attractive garland for your head
>   and a necklace for your neck.
> [10]My son, if sinful men tempt you,
>   do not yield.
> [11]If they say, "Come with us;
>   let's set an ambush for blood;
>   let's lie in wait for the innocent with no reason at all;

---

4. The word for "beginning" here is *rēšit*. The variant in 9:10a, *təhillat*, has only a temporal sense; *rēšit* probably includes that notion.

5. E. Erikson, *Childhood and Society* (London: Triad; Granada, 1977), 222ff.; cited by D. Atkinson, *The Message of Proverbs* (Downers Grove, IL: InterVarsity, 1997), 70.

¹²let's swallow them alive, like Sheol—
  even whole, like those who go down to the pit;
¹³all kinds of precious things we will find;
  we will fill our houses with plunder;
¹⁴cast lots with us;
  all of us will divide up one purse—"
¹⁵my son, do not go on the way with them;
  withhold your foot from their byway;
¹⁶for their feet rush into evil,
  and they hasten to shed blood.
¹⁷Surely a net is spread out in vain
  in the sight of any flying creature,
¹⁸but they set an ambush for their own blood;
  they lie in wait for their own lives.
¹⁹Such are the paths of everyone who is greedy for gain:
  it takes away the life of the one who gets it.

The parents' lectures typically include an introduction, a main lesson, and a conclusion. The introduction consists of an *address* ("my son") followed by an *admonition* ("listen" or "pay attention") and a *motivation*.

Introduction (1:8–9)

This introduction contains the typical motifs: an address and an admonition to listen (v. 8) with motivation (v. 9). But it uniquely objectifies the father as "your father," giving the impression that Solomon himself is speaking to every youth in Israel as "my son," admonishing them to listen to their wise parents. If so, this introduction introduces the whole Prologue, not just the first lecture.

8 The catchword *listen* (*šamaʿ*) links the introduction with the preamble (see 1:5) and resonates with the famous *šamaʿ* of Deut. 6:4: "*Hear*, O Israel." The tender address, *my son*, refers to the child not merely as a biological offspring but as a spiritual heir (see on 4:3). The inclusion of *your mother* shows that women as well as men were taught (see "Man and Woman," p. 52) and that both parents were involved in teaching the children (cf. Deut. 21:18–21). The parents stand under God as they teach the sages' inspired wisdom, and the child stands under the parents. In the new Israel, Jesus Christ subordinates himself to the Father (1 Cor. 11:3), the elders of the church to Christ and his inspired apostles, the church body to the elders (Heb. 13:17), the wife to her husband (1 Cor. 11:3; Eph. 5:22–24; Col. 3:18; 1 Tim. 2:11–12), and the children to their parents (Eph. 6:1; Col. 3:20; cf. 1 Tim. 5:4). *Instruction* (see on 1:2). *Do not let go . . . teaching* (*tôrâ*) means to not neglect, leave unattended or uncared for, the parent's teaching.

9 The antecedent of *they* is the content of the parents' instruction, to wit, the proverbs and sayings of Proverbs. *An attractive garland*—more precisely a wreath—*for your head*, if interpreted against an Egyptian background, as seems probable, symbolizes power, life, victory, and vindication over enemies, as well as prestige and high social status.[6] *A necklace for your neck* should also probably be interpreted within this historical context: Egyptian high judges and viziers wore symbols of Ma'at, the goddess of right order, as a symbolic expression that they lived an exemplary life serving her.[7]

Lesson (1:10–18)

In short, the first lecture warns the son against easy money. Simmering in the background is the tension between the parents' authority and the peer pressure of the gang. The father fortifies the son to resist the gang's enticements by first exposing the gang's belying words and then debunking them. The gang's repeated use of "we" and "us" aims to seduce the son to join them. They offer immediate wealth outside the law rather than gradually accumulating it through development of character in hard, often frustrating work under the law. Also, they promise a counterfeit, egalitarian community in which all share the loot equally. They do not fear *I AM*. Verse 10 summarizes the lesson: "if tempted" (v. 10a), "do not give in" (v, 10b). These are unpacked in two equal sections: the gang's temptation (vv. 11–14) and the admonition, with reasons not to give in (vv. 15–18).

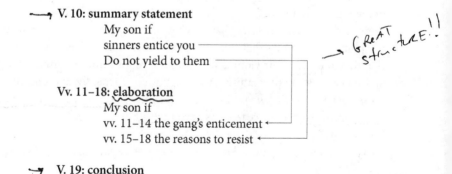

V. 10: summary statement
My son if
sinners entice you
Do not yield to them

→ GREAT structure!!

Vv. 11–18: elaboration
My son if
vv. 11–14 the gang's enticement
vv. 15–18 the reasons to resist

V. 19: conclusion

---

6. See K. Kayatz, *Proverbien 1–9*, 111–17.
7. Kayatz, *Proverbien 1–9*, 107–11.

Summary Statement (1:10)

The father's tender epithet, *my son*, links the introduction and the lesson. Although *if* presents the lesson as a hypothetical situation, the scenario all too often proves real. *Sinful men* denotes those who miss the mark of God's standard of doing what is right and just and fair and so wrong their community. Sinners seek company and so *tempt* the son to join them. As Aristotle noted, humans are political animals. As such, they want others to value what they value, confirm their worldview by a consensus, and increase their joy in sharing a common endeavor.

The Sinners' Temptation Elaborated (1:11–14)

The enticement is elaborated in two couplets: the invitation to join them (vv. 11–12) and the reasons to yield (vv. 13–14).

11–12 The father brilliantly re-creates the sinners' invitation to join them in a way that both exposes the gang's attraction and makes them repulsive. *Come* implies that there is another "way" than the way of wisdom. *With us* indicates their gang mentality. *Let's set an ambush* may connote their brutishness, since the term is used mostly of animals lurking for their prey (cf. Ps. 10:9; Lam. 3:10–11). *Blood* refers to a violent death and is a synecdoche for the murdered victim. *Let's lie in wait for* shows their crime is premeditated murder. They incriminate themselves by acknowledging their victim as *innocent*, or guiltless. *With no reason at all* shows that their motive is naked greed (see vv. 14–15, 19).

Let's swallow them . . . like Sheol suggests that they are in league with the grave (see "The Grave," p. 50).[8] *Alive* implies that they coldly plot to blitz their victim so that the target has no chance to escape or resist. The switch to the plural *them* shows that this is not their first victim. *Even whole* specifies that they plunder their victims without reserve. In sum, the sinners dispatch an innocent victim prematurely, thoroughly, unexpectedly, and unjustly. *Like those who go down to the pit* in v. 12b intensifies 12a. Like Abel, the innocent victim must await a justice that lies beyond death (see "Does Proverbs Promise Too Much?," p. 44).

13–14 Having dispatched the owner, the greedy gang are now free to plun-

---

8. O. Plöger, *Sprüche Salomos (Proverbia)*, BKAT 17.2–4 (Neukirchen-Vluyn: Neukirchener, 1984), 16.

der the victim's house, taking *all kinds of precious things* (cf. Matt. 12:29). *We will fill our houses* implies they have houses and so are part of society, not outsiders. *Plunder*, normally used to describe spoil taken from a conquered enemy, connotes how these sinners regard their neighbor. *Cast lots with us* refers to casting a small stone to divide plunder by chance and so fairly (cf. Ps. 22:18; Matt. 27:35), as explained by *all of us will divide up one purse.*

The Father Nerves the Son to Fidelity (1:15–18)

At the lesson's midpoint, the father shifts his focus from the sinners' entice-ments to his reasoned rebuttal. It also consists of two couplets (vv. 15–16, 17–18), linked respectively by *for* and *but.*

15–16 *Do not go . . . with them* stoutly counters the sinners' call to "come with us" in 11a. *On the way* is the first of many uses of the prologue's multifac-eted metaphor. The figurative "way" evokes the notions of (1) character and orientation of life, (2) the social context with which one identifies, (3) conduct (that is, specific choices and behavior), and (4) the inevitable consequences of that conduct. Put simply, "way" is a metaphor for the deed-destiny nexus upheld by God (see "What Is 'Wisdom,'" pp. 27–28). The vivid metaphor *with-hold your foot from their byway* means to not even entertain the temptation. Temptation entertained stimulates a person's evil desires and drags them away into sin and death (James 1:14–15).

Their feet rush into evil implies that these gangsters, like addicts, are driven to wrongdoing (see 4:10–17, esp. v. 16). "Evil" (*ra'*) denotes what in God's and his people's eye is ugly. In v. 16, *ra'* is a double entendre that refers both to the moral evil of the deed and the physical evil (calamity) it generates. In God's economy, the two are inseparable. *And they hasten to shed blood* is ambigu-ous since it does not specify whose blood—the gangsters' or the victim's. The otherwise identical Isaiah 59:7 removes the ambiguity by adding "innocent" to "blood," specifying it is the blood of the victims. The medieval Jewish com-mentator Rashi thinks the omission shows that here it refers to the criminal's blood, as is made plain in v. 18. More probably, in light of the lesson's two halves, the ambiguity is intentional.

17–18 The couplet of vv. 17–18 contrasts the folly of the sinners (v. 18) with the insight of birds (v. 17). Even a bird understands the deed-destiny nexus. Every bird that sees a trap has enough sense to avoid it, but these gangsters set a trap for themselves and walk lockstep into it! *Surely* emphasizes the birds' logical instincts. *A net is spread out* probably refers to throwing a net over grazing birds.[9] *In vain* shows that it is fruitless to spread the net *in the sight of any flying creature*. Whereas God has given birds the discernment to avoid lethal nets, in the case of humans, the father must teach the son to see or discern the sinners' lethal "trap of words" in order to avoid it.

The father then takes up the gangsters' proposition in v. 11b ("let us set an ambush for blood") and, in a marvelous bait and switch, changes it so that in place of the innocent victims, the gangsters are the ones caught in their own ambush: *they set an ambush for their own blood; they lie in wait for their own lives.*

Conclusion: The Lesson's Moral (1:19)

The lesson is universalized by *everyone. Such* functions to draw an intuitive analogy between the particular scenario and a universal truth. The "way" is expanded to the plural *paths* to include all lethal behavior prompted by greed. *Who is greedy for gain* is literally "who makes a rip off" (see 15:27; 28:16). *It* (the "rip off") *takes away the life of the one who gets it.* The moral is clear: unjust gain clings to the criminal and eventually destroys him (see Matt. 26:52).

Wisdom's First Speech: Rebuke of the Uncommitted (1:20-33)

> [20]Wisdom cries aloud in the street;
> in the public squares she raises her voice;
> [21]on the highest walls she calls out;
> at the entrance of the gates to the city she makes her speech:
> [22]"How long, you uncommitted, will you love being
> uncommitted—
> and mockers delight themselves with mocking,
> and fools hate knowledge?
> [23]Turn back, [you who are uncommitted], to my rebuke.
> Then I will pour forth my thoughts to you;
> I will make you know my words.
> [24][But] since I cry out, and you refuse [to repent],
> and when I stretch out my hand none pays attention,
> [25]and you flout all my counsel

9. Egyptian art depicts hunters with nets approaching birds from behind to throw the nets over them. See the art on the burial chapel of Nefermaat I at Meidum.

and do not consent to my rebuke,

²⁶I in turn will laugh when your disaster happens;
   I will scoff when your calamity comes—
²⁷when your calamity comes like a storm,
   and your disaster arrives like a whirlwind,
   when distress and anguish come upon you."
²⁸Then they will call on me, but I will not answer;they will look
     diligently for me but will not find me,
²⁹because they hated knowledge,
   and they did not choose the fear of *I AM.*
³⁰They did not consent to my advice;
   they spurned my every rebuke;
³¹so they will eat from the fruit of their way,
   and from their schemes they will be filled.
³²Surely the turning away of the uncommitted will kill them,
   and the complacency of fools will destroy them;
³³but the who listens and obeys will dwell in security
   even at ease, without fear of harm.

Personified Wisdom's sermon (see "Illumination and Woman Wisdom," pp. 29-30) to uncommitted fools (vv. 20-27) is meant to be heard by all youths (1:28-33; cf. 1:4-5). Her message in a nutshell is "repent *now*, because at the time of judgment there will be no second chance."

After setting the scene in vv. 20-21, Solomon (see "Solomon," pp. 6-8) develops this philippic of sermon (vv. 22-27) and reflection (vv. 28-33) in a concentric structure. With this doubling, he intensifies and expands the message.   *Bitter Attack*

I		Wisdom's Sermon		vv. 22-27
	A		Wisdom calls uncommitted fools to repent	vv. 22-23
		B	The uncommitted reject her rebuke	vv. 24-25
			C Wisdom rejects the uncommitted at the time of judgment	vv. 26-27
II		Wisdom's Reflections		vv. 28-33
			C' Wisdom rejects the uncommitted at the time of judgment	vv. 28-29
		B'	The uncommitted reject her rebuke	vv. 30-31
	A'		The death of uncommitted fools vs. the security of the wise	vv. 32-33

The Setting (1:20–21)

Wisdom does not wait for an audience to come to her; she goes to them in the most public places: *in the street* (that is, "out of doors"; cf. 5:16; 7:12; 22:13; 24:27); *in the public squares* where people assemble; *on the highest walls* so that all will hear; *at . . . the gates to the city* where officials meet. She *cries aloud* with passion and urgency; *she raises her voice* with fervency and strong emotions. "Lady Wisdom," says Aitken, "is no gentle persuader. She shouts, pleads, scolds, reasons, threatens, warns, and even laughs. . . . Pulpit bashing and hell-fire preaching if ever there were! All quite unladylike; and nowadays also quite unfashionable, even frowned upon."[10]

LoL!

The Sermon (1:22–27)

Introductory Accusation (1:22–23)

22 Wisdom starts with a strident appeal to the uncommitted to stop rejecting her. Her exasperated question, "*How long?*", along with the ensuing condemnation (vv. 24–27), indicates the uncommitted have been rejecting her for a long time, including when they were instructed in their nurturing homes. Now that the *uncommitted* (see "Intellectual Terms for the Wicked and Fools," p. 47) have passed the age of accountability without identifying with wisdom, she calls them to repent so that they can begin to learn the sages' inspired knowledge.

She lumps these uncommitted with fools and mockers in 22b. They are uncommitted fools and will face the punishment of fools. One must make a decision to be wise or remain a fool. Apathy reinforces, not constrains, the unbelieving consensus. Their identification with fools will lead to their progressive hardening in folly, culminating in hating and mocking Wisdom. *Mockers* (see "Intellectual Terms for the Wicked and Fools," pp. 48–49) *delight themselves with mocking* (see p. 48). "Delight" more literally means "covet." Here it indicates a strong craving for mocking. Smug *fools* (see p. 48) *hate God's knowledge.*

23 *Turn back*, or "repent," implies there is still hope (see ch. 9). Her sermon is a *rebuke* (that is, a correction, reprimand) and a call to account to these free-spirited Peter Pans. As Christ did, Woman Wisdom humbles herself to

10. Aitken, *Proverbs*, 22.

step into the messed-up world of the fools and offers the uncommitted her saving words of wisdom. If they humble themselves and repent, she promises to *pour forth*, or drench them with, her internal *thoughts* and external *words*— her sayings in the following sections of the book. Wisdom's spiritual words can be heard only by those sharing her spirit (cf. Prov. 8:9; John 8:37, 42, 47; 18:37; 1 Cor. 1:11–16). *I will make you know* means that she will communicate spiritually, in such a way that they will internalize the book's proverbs and sayings (see 1:6).

Condemnation (1:24–27)

Wisdom's condemnation consists of an accusation (vv. 24–25) and a judicial sentence (26–27). Tragically, her shift from an invitation to condemnation implies the uncommitted had no taste for her invitation.

24 *Since* introduces four conditions of her accusation (vv. 24a, 24b, 25a, 25b) that lead to the dreadful judicial consequences (vv. 26–27). *I cry out*, a repetition of v. 21a, reflects the truth that God only punishes after he has properly warned (cf. Ezek. 33:7–8; Jonah 3:4). That the uncommitted *refuse [to repent]* indicates their willful obstinacy. *When I stretch out my hand* connotes hostility toward the ones against whom the hand is stretched (cf. Exod. 7:5; 9:22; 15:12; Isa. 5:25; Josh. 8:18, 19) and matches the rest of her sermon and reflection. Fox observes, "Wisdom does not threaten to harm the fools herself, but she does warn them of disaster in a caustic and menacing manner."[11] And still *none pays attention*.

25 To *flout* means "to let go, let alone, disregard" and so rebel against structure and constraints.[12] *All my counsel* refers to Wisdom's plan that the uncommitted save themselves by listening to her *rebuke*. But they do not *consent*—translated "yield" in 1:10.

26 *I in turn* shifts the condemnation from accusation to punishment. Her schadenfreude, *I will laugh when your disaster happens*, is right and just because she celebrates the triumph of right over wrong (cf. Pss. 2:4; 37:13; 59:8). *I will scoff* expresses her disdain of fools, a correlative term for the wicked (see "Correlative Terms," p. 34) who harm the innocent (see 1:10–19). The rebellion is so ridiculous and the victory so victorious that there is a

11. Fox, *Proverbs 1–9*, 100.
12. Cf. J. G. Janzen, "The Root *prʿ* in Judges v 2 and Deuteronomy xxxii 42," *VT* 39 (1989): 393-406.

comic aspect to it all. "Disaster" refers to a sudden, calamitous event that brings great loss, damage, and destruction (cf. 6:15; 17:5; 24:22; 27:10). *When your calamity comes* aims to knock sense into uncommitted fools. The Hebrew *paḥad* ("calamity") signifies "dread" (Deut. 28:66; Isa. 33:14). "Your" indicates that it is "the calamity coming upon you" and probably "the calamity you deserve." In wisdom literature "come" frequently expresses the nexus between deed and destiny (see 6:10–11). Its threefold repetition in vv. 26–27 implies certainty.

27 In a final flourish, Wisdom uses vivid storm imagery to waken her insouciant addressees to their impending judgment. The violent similes *like a storm* (*šôʾâ*) and *like a whirlwind* (*sûpâ*) expand and intensify the coming judgment. The "storm" is one that wreaks havoc, and its parallel "whirlwind" means "come to an end," "cease." Together they signify a catastrophic storm that, like a tornado, destroys everything in its path. Then, mimicking the actions of a chaotic storm herself, Wisdom breaks the structure of her symmetric parallelism with a third jarring verset, in which she adds to the assonant *šôʾâ* and *sûpâ* two more words: *ṣārâ* (*distress*) and *ṣûqâ* (*anguish*).[13] In sum, when the judgment finally comes, the smug attitude of the uncommitted will suddenly change to extreme terror. But then it will be too late—the point Wisdom makes in her reflection.

Wisdom's Reflection on Her Sermon (1:28–33)

In this literary fiction, Wisdom, by shifting from speaking directly to "you" to speaking about "them," "breaks the fourth wall"—the invisible wall that separates the actor from her audience (in this case, Israel's youth; see 1:4). Offstage, she reflects upon her sermon delivered onstage. The connection between sermon and reflection is established subtly by a quid pro quo:

24	I cry out	You refuse to repent
28	They will call on me	I will not answer

Her reflection is structured in a concentric pattern of consequence (judgment) in the outer frame (vv. 28, 31) and cause (accusation) in the inner core (vv. 29, 30). When disaster strikes:

---

13. "Anguish" occurs exclusively in combination with "distress," reinforcing the already strong notion of fear.

A	The uncommitted will seek but not find Wisdom	v. 28
	B Since the uncommitted hated knowledge and the fear of *I AM*	v. 29
	B' Since the uncommitted did not accept Wisdom's advice	v. 30
A'	The uncommitted will suffer the consequence of rejecting Wisdom	v. 31

The reflection adds the uncommitted's hatred of wisdom to the accusation and adds finality (vv. 28–29) and certainty (vv. 30–31) to the judgment. The conclusion expands the judgment of eternal death to all fools (v. 32a; cf. 1:22) in contrast to the eternal security of the wise (v. 33).

The Finality and Certainty of Judgment (1:28–31)

28 Judgment is final. *Then* (that is, at the time of judgment, vv. 26–27) explicitly links the reflection with the sermon. *They will call on me* means they will use their voice to seek Wisdom's attention and implies that, when they are stricken with judgment, they will finally realize that Wisdom possessed the life and security they spurned. *But,* she quickly adds, *I will not answer.* "Prayer, once omnipotent, will then be powerless," says Bridges.[14] Reinforcing this harsh and hard reality, she adds, *They will look diligently for me,* implying their desperation. *But will not find me* makes frighteningly clear that her saving voice is not at human disposal and can be forfeited. Similarly, Jesus taught that at his Parousia it will be too late (Matt. 25:1–13). No one is "left behind" for a second chance.[15]

29 Wisdom explains why. The crux of the uncommitted fools' problem is that *they hated knowledge* (see p. 47), *and they did not choose the fear of* I AM (see "Fear of *I AM*," p. 38) when they had the opportunity to repent.

The harsh reality of this reflection is that there will be no second chance at the time of the judgment. Why that is can be discerned from the following theological reflections:

---

14. Bridges, *Proverbs*, 11.

15. In the logic of Jesus's discourse on his return (Matt. 24:36ff.), it is those "taken away" who are destroyed in judgment (v. 39) while those "left behind" are the saved, even as Noah was "left behind" after the waters receded.   ↳ *Really?!*

- It would make God an accomplice to their folly.
- It would mean that only after death would decisions really matter; everything before is merely a trial run.
- If choices made now had no eternal consequences, they lose their awesome dignity and worth.
- It would validate the fools' belief that their careless treatment of this life is justified.
- If pursuing a foolish life did not result in irreversible negative consequences, the wise would be the fools.

People deny the doctrine of final judgment because they do not want to believe that this life has awesome dignity—a dignity that invests their current decisions with consequence that is eternal.

30–31 Final judgment is certain. The repetition of v. 25 in v. 30—albeit v. 30 uses "spurn" instead of "flout"—underscores that the judgment is also just. To *spurn* something is "to fail to appreciate," "to undervalue," and so to despise it.[16]

So links the cause (v. 30) and consequence (v. 31). The poet represents the consequence by an evocative metaphor: *they will eat from the fruit . . . they will be filled.* This points to the inexorable nexus between foolish deeds and fatal destiny. The metaphor implies the damned will experience their punishment with their whole being (cf. v. 27). *Of their way* (see p. 73) is defined by the parallel *and from their schemes*, that is, their many plans to have abundant life without God and without his wisdom.

Conclusion (1:32–33)

Wisdom's draws her reflections to conclusion with a plain, bald summary of the baneful end of all fools (v. 32; cf. v. 22) and of the beneficent destiny of the wise (v. 33).

32 *Surely* certifies Wisdom's sweeping conclusion. Instead of the uncommitted turning toward Wisdom's correction and finding life (v. 23), their *turning away . . . will kill them* (cf. Exod. 32:27; Num. 25:5; Deut. 13:9). The *complacency of fools* implies their sense of false security, which prevents them from repenting. *Will destroy them* (lit. "annihilate them") implies the finality of their death.

16. H. Wildberger, *TLOT*, 2:695, s.v. *n'ṣ*.

33 The shift from the plural with reference to the death of fools to the singular *one who listens and obeys* (*šōmēaʿ*, see p. 70) resembles Israel's history, in which only a remnant remains at the end (cf. Matt. 7:14). The remnant, however, will live interminably because they will physically *dwell* (or *remain*) *in security* and psychologically be *at ease, without fear of harm* (v. 33b).

Lecture 2: A Safeguard against the Wicked (2:1–22)

¹My son, if you accept my words,
    and my commands you store up with you—
²by making your ear attentive to wisdom
    you will apply your heart to understanding—
³indeed, if you call out to insight,
    raise your voice to understanding,
⁴if you seek it as for silver,
    and search for it as for hidden treasures,
⁵then you will understand the fear of *I AM*,
    and find the knowledge of God;
⁶for *I AM* gives wisdom;
    from his mouth come knowledge and understanding.
⁷He holds success in store for the upright—
    he is a shield to those who walk in blamelessness
⁸by guarding the paths of justice—
    and he watches over the way of his loyal ones.
⁹Then you will understand what is right and just
    and fair, every good track;
¹⁰for wisdom will enter your heart,
    and knowledge will be pleasant to your appetite.
¹¹Shrewdness will watch over you;
    understanding will guard you,
¹²to deliver you from the way of the evil man,
    from the man who speaks perversions;
¹³those who abandon straight paths
    to walk in ways of darkness;
¹⁴those who are joyful in doing evil
    [and] rejoice in evil perversions;
¹⁵whose paths are crooked

and who are devious in their tracks;
¹⁶to deliver you from the unchaste wife,
from the foreigner who causes her words to be smooth;
¹⁷who abandons the companion of her youth
and forgets her covenant with God.
¹⁸Surely her byway[a] leads down into death
and her tracks to the realm of the dead.
¹⁹All who enter into her will not return,
and they will not reach the paths of life.
²⁰And so you will walk in the way of good people,
and the paths of the righteous you will keep.
²¹Surely the upright will dwell in the land,
and the blameless will be left in it;
²²but the wicked will be cut off from the earth,
and the treacherous will be torn from it.

a. Emending *byth* ("her house") by *ntybth* "her byway"; see Waltke, *Proverbs 1–15*, 215–16 n. 24.

The father's important second lecture tells the son both how to know God (v. 5b)—what Agur on his own could not achieve (30:4)—and how to achieve the book's key to understanding: the fear of *I AM* (v. 5a; cf. 1:7). Furthermore, it empowers the son to achieve the book's objective: to understand what is right and just and fair (v. 9; cf. 1:3).

In Hebrew, the lecture is a single, complex sentence of twenty-two verses, the number of letters in the Hebrew alphabet. This is an intentional rhetorical feature, albeit it is not an acrostic poem. The lecture is marvelously symmetrical, reflecting the orderly moral world. Logically and semantically, it has two equal stanzas[17] of eleven verses. Verses 1–11 concern the development of a godly character; vv. 12–22 concern the defenses ensuing from a godly character: namely, defenses against the evil man (vv. 12–15) and the evil woman (vv. 16–19). Furthermore, each stanza is symmetrically divided into two strophes of four verses and a climactic third strophe of three verses, as in the following table.

17. For the definitions of "stanza" and "strophe," see "Poetics," p. 13.

	Stanza 1 (vv. 1–11) The Development of a Godly Character	Stanza 2 (vv. 12–22) The Defenses Ensuing from Godly Character
Strophe 1	*The Conditions (vv. 1–4)* "if . . ." "if . . ." "if . . ."	*Defense against the Evil Man* *(vv. 12–15)* "to deliver you . . ."
Strophe 2	*Consequence 1: Theological* *Education (vv. 5–8)* "then you will understand . . ."	*Defense against the Evil Woman* *(vv. 16–19)* "to deliver you . . ."
Strophe 3	*Consequence 2: Ethical Education* *(vv. 9–11)* "Then you will understand . . ."	*Conclusion: Eternal Life* *(vv. 20–22)* "And so you will . . ."

The first strophe of stanza 1 (vv. 1–4) describes the conditions the son is asked to internalize ("My son, if . . ."); the second and third strophes (vv. 5–8, 9–11) describe the resulting benefits and their outcomes. Two profound benefits and two outcomes are promised: a theological education that results in protection from God (vv. 5–8) and an ethical education that results in protection through the son's own godly character (vv. 9–11). These benefits follow an alternating pattern:

A		Summary of benefit: A theological education ("then you will understand")		v. 5
	B	Substantiation: "For *I AM* gives wisdom"		v. 6
		C	Outcome: Protection from God ("guarding . . . watches")	v. 8
A'		Summary of benefit: An ethical education ("then you will understand")		v. 9
	B'	Substantiation: "For wisdom will enter your heart"		v. 10
		C'	Outcome: Protection from own character ("watch . . . guard")	v. 11

As for A/A', a personal knowledge of God is foundational to an intuitive discerning of right and wrong. As for B/B', wisdom proceeds from *I AM* through Solomon's inspired words and then enters the son's willing heart. As for C/C', a chiasm tightly links the protection from *I AM* with the son's formed character.

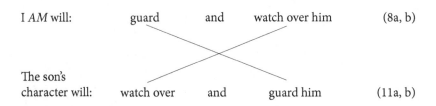

I AM will:	guard	and	watch over him	(8a, b)
The son's character will:	watch over	and	guard him	(11a, b)

These consequences segue into the son's deliverance from the evil man and the unchaste wife. The two deliverances are also developed in an alternating pattern:

A		"To deliver you from the way of the evil man"		v. 12
	B	"Those who abandon straight paths"		v. 13
		C	Description of the "crooked paths"	vv. 14–15
A'		"To deliver you from the unchaste wife"		v. 16
	B'	"Who abandons the companion of her youth"		v. 17
		C'	Description of her deadly "paths"	v. 18–19

The final stanza (vv. 20–22) brings the lecture to its climax: the son walks on the righteous way (v. 20) and so lives (v. 21) in contrast to the wicked who die (v. 22). The youth must choose between the way of life and the paths to death.

Conditions (2:1–4)

The lecture again asserts the logic of wisdom literature: the nexus of deed (vv. 1–4) and destiny (5–22). The destiny itself, as seen in the lesson's structure, is an unfolding of consequences, each of which becomes the cause of the next.

1–2 The first condition requires the son to become like Solomon's Temple, which housed God's word in its innermost sanctum. *If you accept* lays the foundation for all subsequent conditions and consequences. It entails heartfelt faith in and commitment to the father's teaching. This faith is provoked by the father's thoughtful words and effected by God (cf. 16:1; 1 Cor. 2:14). *My words* are qualified as "wisdom" in v. 2, and that wisdom comes from God (v. 6). So "my words" are in fact God's words. The father bases his authority on *I AM* himself (see v. 6), not, as is often alleged, on his patriarchal position or tradition or an impersonal moral order. Ultimately, the son's faith is in God's word as known through the father's words. In form, the father's words may be sayings, but in function they are *commands* from a superior to a subordinate[18] and so must be obeyed to avoid being a traitor. To *store up* or to "treasure," is a metaphor signifying memorizing the book with affection. Solomon's "sound bites" are to be *with you*—ready at hand wherever he goes (cf. 6:22; Deut. 6:6-9).

Accepting the commands entails *making your ear attentive* (that is, paying attention) *to wisdom*, the substance of Solomon's words (see 1:2). *You will apply* (or "incline") means to yield or turn to someone or something (cf. Judg. 9:3; 2 Sam. 19:14; 1 Kgs. 11:3; Ps. 119:36) and hence to the resulting actions.[19] *Your heart* (see "Heart," p. 32). *Understanding* (see "Intellectual Terms for the Wise and Righteous," p. 36) is a metonymy of effect for the proverbs and sayings.

3-4 *Indeed* marks an escalation from passive reception (vv. 1-2) to aggressive initiatives (vv. 3-4). *If you call out* (see 1:21) for personified *insight* is the appropriate response to Wisdom, who called out vainly to the fools in 1:20-33. *Raise your voice* intensifies "call out." *Understanding* (see above on v. 2).

If you seek it means to search diligently to fulfill the wish and to realize the plan to attain understanding. The similes, *as for silver* (that is, refined silver) escalated in verset B to *as for hidden treasures*, assume that precious metals are valuable and imply that great effort and sacrifice must be expended to get them (cf. 4:7; see Matt. 13:45-46). In short: no pain, no gain.

Consequences: Protection (2:5-11)

Theological Education Leading to Divine Protection (2:5-8)

5 A logical *then* binds the spiritual conditions to the first spiritual consequence: *you will understand* (see 1:2, 6) *the fear of I AM*, the key to the book's treasures (see 1:7), and *you will find*, as a result of diligent search, *the personal knowledge* (see 1:2, 7) *of God* (see "God as Sovereign, Transcendent, and Immanent," p. 25), who is otherwise personally inaccessible to mortals. Probably both the knowledge that he possesses and the experience of knowing him are intended.

---

18. F. Stolz, *TLOT*, 2:1062, s.v. *ṣwh*.
19. Cf. Fox, *Proverbs 1–9*, 109.

6 This relational knowledge results because *I AM gives* the insuperable virtues of *wisdom* and *knowledge and understanding*, to gain which is the purpose of the book according to 1:2. God alone has access to wisdom (Job 28:12–28) since he gave birth to it from his own being (Prov. 8:22–24). In view here is not the wisdom that God gives in common grace to all, such as the animal's instinctual wisdom (cf. 30:24–28) or the farmer's practical knowledge of raising crops (Isa. 28:26, 29) or the human's conscience that causes even children to cry out that something is unfair (Job 22:22; 32). Rather, in this context, the wisdom is what he revealed to Solomon and the sages whose proverbs and sayings comprise this book. Thus, the father's words carry the authority of God, for they are *from his (I AM's) mouth*—an anthropomorphism that suggests the father's mouth is a surrogate for God's mouth. This makes clear that Proverbs is an inspired, God-breathed book, as is all Scripture (2 Tim. 3:16).

7 An outcome of this religious education is, among other things, God's protection from the deadly apostasy of wicked men and the deadly immorality of the adulteress (vv. 12–19). The metaphor *he holds success* or "sound judgment" (see "The Wise and Their Rewards," p. 41) *in store for the upright* reciprocates the son's storing up of wisdom. *I AM* himself is the *shield* gripped in the hands of *those who walk in blamelessness* (see "Ethical Terms for the Wise and Righteous," p. 37). Fox helpfully comments, "God's protection is not a reward extraneous to the knowledge, but rather a consequence intrinsic to it."[20]

8 As a shield, *I AM* is *guarding the paths of justice* (see 1:3) to protect from harm those who walk on them so that they arrive at their appointed destiny of eternal life. The ethical terms "upright" and "justice" segue nicely from religious education (vv. 6–8) to ethical practice (9–11). The "upright" and "blameless" of v. 7 are now identified as *his loyal ones*—that is, those in covenant with God who practice loyal love for him and acts of costly kindness for others (see 17:17). His guarding entails that he *watches over* (that is, observes and carefully protects) them. The combination of the singular *way* (the highway, 8b) and plural "paths" (branches off the main road, 8a), depicts life as a basic commitment with many derivative choices. However, in essence there are only two ways: wisdom and righteousness or folly and wickedness (see 4:26).

Ethical Education Leading to Character Protection (2:9–11)

9 A logical *then* links ethical education to both the fundamental conditions of vv. 1–4 and the theological education of vv. 5–8. *You will understand* or "dis-

---

20. M. V. Fox, "Pedagogy of Proverbs 2," *JBL* 113 (1994): 239.

cern" (see 1:5) *what is right and just and fair*, a repetition of 1:3b, the purpose of Proverbs. These are expanded to *every good track*, a metaphor for "course of life" (see 16:17). "Good" signifies beauty or benefit and, therefore, something desirable. Its Latin equivalents are *util* (benefit) and *frui* (beauty): the sun is *util*, the sunset *frui*.

10 *For* introduces the explanation. I AM's *wisdom*, through the father's words, *will enter your heart*, thus explaining the personal relationship between God and the wise. This spiritual *knowledge will be pleasant to your appetite* (see "*nepeš*," p. 32) because the religious affections have been transformed. The prophets referred to this as a "new heart" that enables covenant keeping (Jer. 24:7; 31:31–34; 32:37–41; Ezek. 36:26), and Jesus called it being born again (John 3:7; cf. 2 Cor. 3:3). To the regenerate, the word of God is sweeter than honey (Ps. 19:10), and his commands are not burdensome or impossible. Sinners, by contrast, delight in perversity (2:14; 9:17), and to them, God's law is a galling bondage (Ps. 2:1–3).

11 The outcome of the son's morally formed character is that *shrewdness* (see "Intellectual Terms for the Wise and Righteous," p. 35) *will watch over* him to empower him to withstand temptation, not necessarily to escape it. *Understanding*, which is now in the heart (1:2), *will guard him.* As the wisdom of God became audible in the teacher's words, so God's protection becomes effective through the son's formed character.

The Purpose of Protection (2:12–22)

The protection is now revealed as deliverance from the temptations of wicked men and women for easy money and easy sex respectively. Thus delivered, the son continues his walk on the way of good and righteous people that leads to the abundant life (vv. 20–22).

Defense from Wicked Men (2:12–15)

12 Collapsing the parallels, the purpose of the divine protection is *to deliver you from* going on *the way of the evil man . . . who speaks perversions*, such as the tempting invitation to grab the wealth of the innocent without fear of punishment (1:10–14). The lecture implies that on his own, the son is unable to escape temptation. If even innocent Adam and Eve in the idyllic Garden of Eden could not resist Satan's temptation, how much more will the depraved son in a depraved society be unable? ➔ learned this is Genesis class

13 The perverse tempter is typified as *those who abandon straight* (= "up-

right"; see "Ethical Terms for the Wise and Righteous," p. 37) *paths* (see v. 8). "Abandon" is often used of apostasy from *I AM* (Deut. 28:20; 29:24; 31:16; Jer. 1:16; 9:12). Implicitly, the apostates were raised in covenant homes but are like Ishmael and Esau, who had no appetite for Abraham's faith and morality (see Gen. 18:19).[21] Having rejected the sages' moral light, the apostates *walk in ways of darkness* (see v. 15).

14 Their description as being *joyful in doing evil* points to their overripe inward impiety and immorality, which they express outwardly when they *rejoice in evil perversions*. Fox notes, "The wicked not only do evil for the sake of its supposed rewards, they positively enjoy it."[22] Aitken writes, "Like Milton's Satan, their watchword is, 'Evil, be thou my Good.'"[23]

15 Their *paths are crooked*, in contrast to "smooth" or "straight paths" (v. 13a). Brueggemann defines a "crooked" act as a perverse one, apart from and against the community in favor of self (see 10:9).[24] These *devious* (that is, errant) crooks are perverse in word and deed (8:8; 19:1; 28:6). Whoever walks in darkness along their crooked paths and *tracks* (see on v. 9) stumbles into death (4:12; 22:5). *I AM* detests the devious (3:32).

Defense from the Unchaste Wife (2:16–19)

The second promised defense is from the unchaste wife, who is now introduced for the first time. The degree of her danger can be inferred from the fact that she is the subject of the parents' last three lectures (chs. 5–7).

16 The unfolding conditions of vv. 1–9 also aim *to deliver* the son from the temptations of illicit sex, *from the unchaste wife*, a *foreigner* to Israel's covenant values (see " The Unchaste Wife," p. 54). Her lure is *her words* that are *smooth* as olive oil (cf. the English "to butter-up"). The parents arm the son by quoting her smooth and deceitful words in their last lecture (7:13–21). She promises to give herself to her paramour, but in reality she hates him (26:28) and intends to use him for her own ends. She inflicts death intentionally on the innocent and unwittingly on herself within God's just and moral order.

17 *Who abandons* deftly exposes her fatal flaw of infidelity (see v. 13). A society that does not value keeping verbal agreements will quickly unravel (cf.

---

21. Many youths in today's Western culture no longer have a Christian heritage. This is partially the fault of the church. Nevertheless, the youth are not exculpated, since even the light of conscience teaches them the difference between right and wrong (Rom. 2:14–15).

22. Fox, *Proverbs 1–9*, 117.

23. Aitken, *Proverbs*, 32.

24. W. Brueggemann, "A Neglected Sapiential Word Pair," *ZAW* 89 (1977): 244.

Mic. 7:1–7). *The companion of her youth* is a metonymy for her husband, who was her leader and teacher (see "Husband and Wife," p. 52). *Forgets* signifies both a mental and moral lapse. Morally, it means she dismembers herself—the opposite of "re-membering"—from her former allegiance. *Her covenant* refers to the "imposition" or "obligation" she most likely undertook when she married. The addition of *with God* suggests that the Creator was the guarantor, witness, and possibly author of her marriage vow (see "The Apostate Wife," p. 56).

18 The witless youth who joins this woman, thinking she will take him to sexual heaven, will find *her byway leads down into death.* This is so because *I AM* ensures the voluptuary's death (5:21–23; cf. Judg. 16:1–22). Emphatically, her *tracks* slope steeply to *the realm of the dead (rəpā'îm).*[25]

19 *All*—without exception—*who enter into her (bāʾĕhā;* cf. Gen. 16:2; Prov. 16:19) is a powerful image for carnal knowledge. They *will not return* from the realm of the dead, making the woman herself the portal to the land of no return. Emphatically, *they will not* escape and *reach* again *the paths of life.*

Since the root meaning of a "proverb" is a comparison or analogy (see "Proverbs," pp. 17–18), the specific, literal truth stated in this lecture may, by analogy, be used to judge one's life more broadly. Sexual unfaithfulness on the historical plane may be seen as a paradigm for spiritual unfaithfulness to *I AM.* Solomon's sexual infidelity contributed to his spiritual infidelity because the sexual and the spiritual interpenetrate one another existentially. The prophets frequently used marriage as a metaphor for Israel's relationship to *I AM.* This woman's breaking her marriage contract is comparable to covenant children today breaking their contract with Christ. The end result will be death. However, the primary level of meaning is the historical, as indicated by the father's detailed description of her allurements and his economic—not religious—arguments in the following lectures.

Conclusion: Life on Earth versus Death (2:20–22)

As Wisdom did in her sermon (see 1:32–33), and as they also did in their first lecture (see 1:19), the parents cap off their second lecture with an embracive

---

25. The common rendering of *rəpā'îm* as "shades" or "spirits of the dead" can lead to a flawed doctrine of the afterlife in the Old Testament. In the Historical Books, *rəpā'îm* refers to an ethnic group or groups that settled in specific areas of Canaan. In its eight occurrences in Hebrew poetry (Job 26:5; Ps. 88:10; Prov. 2:18; 9:18; 21:16; Isa. 14:9; 26:14, 19), it is used figuratively and as stock-in-trade parallel of death/the dead. It occurs in the pagan Ugaritic texts for divine beings in the underworld and for dead kings.

promise that the wise live with an open-ended future and the wicked die in a terminal death.

20 *And so* ("the consequences of all that has been said"[26]) *you will walk in the way* (see 1:15) *of good people* (see 2:9). And safeguarded against evil people, *you will keep* ("observe carefully," see 2:8) *the paths of the righteous.* Christ is the exemplar (Phil. 2:5ff.).

21 *Surely* emphatically confirms the subsequent promise. *The upright* (linked with v. 7) *will dwell in the land* (cf. 10:30; Ps. 37:9, 11, 22, 28, 29, 34). "Land" here is a metonymy for the life it sustains.[27] The land stands in striking contrast to the grave filled with corpses (vv. 18–19). *And the blameless* (see "Ethical Terms for the Wise and Righteous," p. 37) *will be left* (lit. "left over"). Greenstone observes, "The picture presented here is that of a land which has been purified of all the wicked people, leaving only the pure and the righteous dwellers therein."[28] The final word spoken over the righteous will be "Life!"

22 In contrast to the dazzling destiny of the righteous, *the wicked* (see "Ethical Terms for the Wicked and Fools," p. 45) *will be cut off* (that is, annihilated) *from the earth,* their life source (10:30; 14:32; 15:25; Matt. 3:10). This is *I AM*'s judicial sentence against them. "Cut off" (*kārat*) here signifies annihilation[29] and excommunication.[30] According to R. Vuilleumier, it can mean to excommunicate by extermination.[31] If so, it connotes that the wicked will be cut off because they pollute the land and threaten the relationship of the righteous with their God. The passive is a divine passive: God is the Agent (cf. 5:21). The wicked are also labelled *the treacherous* (meaning "unfaithful to an existing and established relationship"), an apt term for the apostates (vv. 13, 17). Emphatically, they *will be torn from it* and so not continue their life in the good earth (cf. Deut. 28:63; Matt. 5:5; Rev. 21:7–8).

---

26. So H. A. Brongers, "*Die Partikel lm'n in der biblisch-hebraischen Sprache,*" *OtSt* 18 (1973): 89.

27. Compare Ps. 37:9, 11, 29, 34 with Matt. 5:5. "Land" in the law and the prophets often refers to the physical land of Canaan covenanted to Israel, but Proverbs rarely refers to Israel's historic covenants.

28. J. H. Greenstone, *Proverbs with Commentary* (Philadelphia: The Jewish Publication Society of America, 1950), 24.

29. *Kārat* can have this meaning in the Niphal stem with personal subjects.

30. So J. L. Mayes, *Micah*, OTL (Philadelphia: Westminster, 1976), 125–26.

31. R. Vuilleumier, "Michée," in *Michée, Nahoum, Habacuc, Sophonie,* by R. Vuilleumier and C.-A. Keller, CAT 11b (Neuchâtel: Delachaux & Niestle, 1971), 66.

Lecture 3: I AM's *Promises and the Son's Obligations (3:1–12)*

¹My son, do not forget my teaching,
  and let your heart guard my commandments;
²for length of days and years of life
  and peace and prosperity they will add to you.
³Let kindness and faithfulness not leave you;
  bind them upon your neck,³²
⁴and find favor³³ and good repute
  in the eyes of God and humankind.
⁵Trust in *I AM* with all your heart,
  and do not rely on your own understanding;
⁶in all your ways experience his presence,
  and he will make your paths straight and smooth.
⁷Do not be wise in your own eyes;
  fear *I AM* and shun evil;
⁸let there be healing to your navel
  and refreshment to your bones.
⁹Honor *I AM* from your wealth,
  from the firstfruits of all your produce;
¹⁰and your granaries will be filled with plenty,
  and your vats will overflow with new wine.
¹¹The discipline of *I AM*, my son, do not reject,
  and do not loathe his correction;
¹²because whom *I AM* loves, he corrects,
  even as a father the son in whom he delights.

Lecture 3 consists of six quatrains (see "Poetics," p. 13). Each double verse presents a command in the odd verse and *I AM*'s motivating promises in the even verse. The structure includes an *introduction* (keep the father's teaching,

---

32. The MT, Vulg., Targ., and Syr. add, "Write them on the tablet of your heart," but this is omitted in Old Greek. It is probably an early gloss from 7:3, not a haplography in the original due to homoioteleuton (*grgrwtyk . . . lbk*). K. Heim (*Poetic Imagination in Proverbs: Variant Repetitions and the Nature of Poetry*, BBRSup 4 [Winona Lake, IN: Eisenbrauns, 2013], 111) alleges that since all the repetitions in Proverbs may be considered glosses, "it seems arbitrary to exclude one of the partial lines here." However, we do not consider other repetitions glosses; this one is missing in Old Greek, and a tricola in this pericope is exceptional.

33. The grammatical imperative indicates purpose or result.

vv. 1–4), a *body* (trust *I AM*, vv. 5–10), and a *conclusion* (do not reject *I AM*'s discipline, vv. 11–12). This structure is illustrated in the table below.

Commands (Odd Verses)		Motivating Promises (Even Verses)	
Introduction			
v. 1	Keep my command	v. 2	Life and peace
v. 3	Don't let go of unfailing love	v. 4	Favor with God and men
Body			
vv. 5–6a	Trust in *I AM*	v. 6b	Straight paths
v. 7	Fear *I AM*	v. 8	Healing
v. 9	Honor *I AM*	v. 10	Prosperity
Conclusion			
v. 11	Don't reject discipline	v. 12	Proof of "Father's" love

The father's commands progress from preserving teaching (3:1) to retaining ethical behavior (v. 3) to active piety (v. 5), humility (v. 7), worship (v. 9), and submissiveness (v. 11). Only *I AM* can vouchsafe the promises, but he mediates them through the son's obedience to the father's teaching. Linking the father's teaching with trust in *I AM* and his promises anchors the father's commands in *I AM*'s authority. The lecture begins with the human teaching father and ends with the heavenly disciplining Father (see 2:6).[34] The conclusion implies that the Father, out of love, disciplines a flawed son to ensure he inherits the father's promises. However, these promises need to be nuanced by counter-proverbs that speak of privation before realization (see "Does Proverbs Promise Too Much?," pp. 42–45).

Introduction: Commands to Preserve the Parent's Teaching (3:1–4)

1–2 *My teaching* and *my commandments* repeat 1:8. *Do not forget* (see 2:17) but *let your heart* (see "Heart," p. 32) *guard* implies the son has memorized the commands, and they have safeguarded him. *For* introduces the promise of *length of days and years of life*, which is long, abundant life (see "The Wise

---

34. C. A. Newsom, "Woman and the Discourse of Patriarchal Wisdom: A Study of Proverbs 1–9," in *Gender and Difference in Ancient Israel*, ed. P. L. Day (Minneapolis: Fortress, 1989), 149–51.

and Their Rewards," pp. 41–42) and is elsewhere attributed both to wisdom (3:16) and to the fear of *I AM* (10:27). This command and promise reprises the fourth of the Ten Commandments (Deut. 5:16; cf. Exod. 20:12; Eph. 6:2). *Peace* (*šālôm*) *and prosperity* qualifies "life" as free from turmoil and lack. Long life without peace is not good. *Will add to you* signifies an increase in quantity ("days and years") and in quality ("peace and prosperity").

3–4 The teaching is now characterized practically as *kindness and faithfulness* (see p. 38),[35] which is fleshed out in 3:27–30 as helping the helpless. According to D. A. Hubbard, these virtues "influence every choice and movement" (cf. Hos. 4:1–3).[36] The sage personifies the two virtues and urgently commands *let* them *not leave you* (that is, do not forget them, as in v. 1; see 2:17 for the same parallelism). *Bind them upon your neck* implicitly likens the teachings to a necklace that symbolizes protection, guidance, eternal life, and social exaltation (see. 1:9). *And find* introduces the reciprocal promise (see 2:5), which pertains to humanity's two fundamental relationships: with *God* and with *humankind* (see p. 31; cf. Luke 2:52; Rom. 12:17). *Favor* (a positive disposition toward something or someone) cannot be compelled; it is extended voluntarily and unilaterally to preserve a valued relationship. *Repute* (esteem) refers to "the way others see a person,"[37] and is in this case *good. In the eyes of* signifies "in the opinion of" but may be literal—that is to say, "the look in someone's eyes," such as when one person smiles at another.[38]

Body: Trust, Fear, and Honor *I AM* (3:5–10)

5 To *trust in* I AM means to rely on him out of a sense of security, often in the presence of danger. The command is a platitude, however, without *I AM*'s specific teachings through the inspired parents in Proverbs (see 2:6). Proverbs is good only to the extent that God backs it up, so the son's trust is ultimately in God, not in Proverbs per se. In fact, Proverbs is written to teach a life of faith in Israel's covenant-keeping God (22:19). The wise trust *I AM* to uphold the moral order sovereignly (in his own time and way) and contingently (in response to human actions), despite contrary appearances such as the wicked

---

35. Fox goes against the majority of commentators when he argues that "kindness and faithfulness" refers to God's kindness toward the pupil. See Waltke's arguments against this interpretation in *The Book of Proverbs: Chapters 1–15*, NICOT (Grand Rapids: Eerdmans, 2004), 241.

36. Hubbard, *Proverbs*, 70

37. Fox, *Proverbs 1–9*, 147.

38. J. Fabry, *TDOT*, 5:24, s.v. *ḥānan*.

prospering and the godly suffering. *With all your heart* means with all one's being and actions, for all actions flow from the heart (see 4:23). To *rely on your own understanding* stands in strong opposition to trusting in *I AM*. A complete commitment to trust *I AM* entails an exclusive commitment. To *not* rely means to not lean on it as on a broken crutch. Only fools rely on their thimble of knowledge or on their incomplete and fallible understanding (26:5, 12, 16; 28:26a; esp. 30:1–6; Job 38:4–5).

6 To entire and exclusive commitment, the father now adds exhaustive commitment—*in all your ways* (see 1:15; 2:8) *Experience his presence (dā'ēhû,* from the root *yd':* lit. "know him") is commonly translated "acknowledge him" (e.g., NIV, NASB, NKJV, NRSV), implying "confess him." But this gloss does not fully represent the meaning of *dā'ēhû,*[39] which refers more to personal knowledge—intimate experience with a person's being (see 1:2). Botterweck says, "To know Yahweh refers to a practical, religio-ethical relationship."[40] John F. Evans agrees: "*Yd'* has far more to do with one's experience of God than with comprehension of doctrinal points about God."[41] *And* so, in your experience of his presence, *he will make your paths straight and smooth.* "Straight" figuratively denotes behavior that is right, honest, upright, and does not go astray or out of bonds (2:13; 9:15), and "smooth" denotes "the success of an undertaking or action (cf. 3:23; 4:12; Isa. 40:3)."[42] "Your paths" is a standard parallel to "your ways." The immensity of this promise is only seen when viewing one's life from a bird's-eye view, not from a worm's-eye view. Only then will it be seen how "God writes straight with crooked lines."[43]

7 The negative and positive admonitions in this verse chiastically define the positive and negative admonitions in vv. 5–6. *Do not be wise in your own eyes* (that is, don't rely on your own cleverness rather than on God's Word; cf. Isa. 5:21) prohibits being a pretentious individualist who does it "my way"[44]—a state worse than being a fool (26:12; cf. Rom. 12:16). The expression

---

39. F. Delitzsch, *Biblical Commentary on the Proverbs of Solomon*, trans. M. G. Easton (Edinburgh: T & T Clark, 1874; repr., Grand Rapids: Eerdmans, 1983), 81.

40. Botterweck, *TDOT*, 5:469, s.v. *yāda';* cf. Terence Fretheim, *NIDOTTE*, 2:413, s.v. *yd'.*

41. John F. Evans, *You Shall Know That I AM Yahweh: An Inner-Biblical Interpretation of Ezekiel's Recognition Formula* BBRSup 25 (University Park, PA: Eisenbrauns, 2019), 228.

42. L. Alonso-Schökel, *TDOT*, 6:466, s.v. *yāšar.*

43. A Portuguese proverb.

44. The folly from which the father wishes to safeguard his son by this admonition is well illustrated in the song "My Way," made famous by Frank Sinatra in 1969. That song, which even today ranks among the most popular songs in the United Kingdom and is the one most played at funerals, extols the rugged individual who "planned each charted course, each careful step along the byway, and more, much more than this . . . did it my

also has an ethical dimension in that God instructs people to seek the good of others. But humans displace this dictum with their own wisdom to gratify themselves (Jas. 3:14–16). In antithetical parallelism, the father gives the positive admonition, *fear I AM* (see "Fear of *I AM*," p. 38) which complements "trust in *I AM*" in v. 5a. The final negative command, *shun evil*, is inseparable from the positive command to fear God. They are the two sides of a coin. To "shun" is to turn aside from one's set-upon direction (1 Sam. 6:12) and connotes the notion of "to avoid."

8 The reciprocal promise for fearing *I AM* and avoiding evil (v. 7) is the experience of spiritual, psychological, and physical *healing* (the restoration to a former state of well-being). Sin sickens humans and puts them on the road to death. However, when they put their trust in *I AM* and shun their endemic evil, they experience total healing, as expressed by the merism of *to your navel* and *to your bones*. The former (elsewhere only in Ezek. 16:4; Song 7:2) is a synecdoche for the whole body, while the latter metaphorically refers to the psyche (cf. Ps. 51:8). In sum, a right relationship with God leads to a state of complete physical and psychological well-being, not simply to the absence of illness.

9 The next admonition calls the son to show his inner piety (vv. 5, 7) in outward worship. *Honor* whose root means "to be heavy," here refers to esteeming a person as having value by the concrete act of presenting tribute to him *from your wealth*, specifically *from the firstfruits—the best* (cf. Num. 18:12–13; Ezek. 48:14)*—of all your produce*, whether of crops or of the womb. However, sacrifice without zeal is unacceptable. Unless the son drenches his offering with the oil of love, trust, and devotion, *I AM* cares nothing for it, as Cain learned (Gen. 4:3–5).

10 As the human partners offer their best, the divine partner promises to reciprocate in kind. *And . . . will be filled with* states the logical consequence of obeying the admonition of v. 9. *Granaries* stored the produce of the field, including both grain and legumes. *Plenty* indicates abundance and may be a metonymy for grain. The assumption is that God will reward the true worshippers by sustaining their lives (Deut. 28:8; 2 Chr. 31:5–10; Mal. 3:10; Phil. 4:10–19). Along with "plenty," *new wine* functions as a merism for a complete supply of food and drink. "New wine" refers to "wine made from the first

---

way." The final stanza reaches a crescendo with the questions, "What is a man? What has he got?" answered, "If not himself, then he has naught. To say the things he truly feels and not the words of one who kneels." To Sinatra's credit, his daughter later acknowledged that her father "always thought that song was self-serving and self-indulgent. . . . He didn't like it. That song stuck, and he couldn't get it off his shoe" ("Sinatra 'Loathed' My Way," BBC News, October 30, 2000)

drippings of the juice before the winepress was trodden. As such it would be particularly potent."[45] *Your vats* refer to the troughs hewn from the rock where the juice of the grapes was collected after treading. The plural indicates the need for several such hollows because the abundant yield from the *untrampled* grapes *will overflow* their confines.

Conclusion: Do Not Reject *I AM*'s Discipline (3:11–12)

11 The lecture that started with the father teaching his son during the latter's formative years concludes with attention to *I AM*'s loving discipline during the rest of the son's life. The conclusion presupposes that the son has strayed and that *I AM* has meted out punishment instead of blessings. *Discipline* (or "instruction," see 1:2) may be verbal or corporal (22:15; 23:13). The punishment *of I AM* aims to restore the afflicted person to proper conduct. The admonition *do not reject* is clarified in an ancient Egyptian wisdom text, Papyrus Insinger 8:24: "No instruction can succeed if there is dislike."[46] The parallel, *and do not loathe*, intensifies the admonition. *His correction* may be verbal or some sort of affliction (cf. 5:12) or both (2 Sam. 7:14; Ps. 141:5; Prov. 19:25). If the son violates the father's admonitions, he can expect *I AM* to back it up with a "spanking" to prevent the provocation from becoming permanent.

12 A logical *because* assures the son that though the discipline may be harsh, it is, oxymoronically, *I AM*'s "severe mercy."[47] It is reserved for *those whom I AM loves*. Plaut comments: "Verse 12 is 'deservedly famous . . . one of the deepest sayings of the Bible' (Montefiore)."[48] C. S. Lewis illustrates this truth by noting the care an artist takes over a beloved work of art. If the work of art were alive, as "the artist rubbed and scraped off and recommenced for the tenth time," it would cry out in pain. When we complain about our sufferings, Lewis concludes, we are in fact asking for less love.[49] Verset 12b represents *I AM* as a loving *father* (see 1:22; cf. 13:25; Deut. 8:5; Heb. 12:3–12) who wants *the son* to experience the blessings of the even verses. However, for that, the son must obey the commands of the odd verses. God's discipline, therefore, is to ensure the son fulfills his obligations. The addition *in whom he delights* could also be rendered "whom he favorably accepts."

---

45. F. S. Fitzsimmonds, "Wine and Strong Drink," in *NBD*, 1254.

46. *AEL*, 3:192: "Dislike" means "resentment, blame" (214 n. 28).

47. See S. Vanauken, *A Severe Mercy* (San Francisco: Harper and Row, 1977).

48. Cited by G. W. Plaut, *Book of Proverbs: A Commentary* (New York: Union of American Hebrew Congregations, 1941), 58.

49. C. S. Lewis, *The Problem of Pain* (London: Geoffrey Bles and Centenary, 1940), 30–33.

Lecture 4: The Value of Wisdom (3:13–35)

¹³Blessed is the human being who finds wisdom,
> the human being who obtains understanding;

¹⁴for the profit she gives[50] is better than the profit of silver,
> and her revenue than gold.

¹⁵She is more precious than corals;[51]
> all desirable things cannot compare with her.

¹⁶Long life is in her right hand;
> in her left, wealth and honor.

¹⁷Her ways are pleasant ways,
> and all her byways are peace and prosperity.

¹⁸She is a tree of life to those who take hold of her;
> and those who hold her fast are each declared blessed.

¹⁹*I AM* by wisdom founded the earth,
> established the heavens by understanding;

²⁰by his knowledge the depths were split open
> and the clouds drip dew.

²¹My son, let them [wisdom and understanding] not depart from
> your eyes;
> guard sound judgment and discretion;

²²and let them become[52] life for you
> [and] an attractive ornament[53] for your neck.

²³Then you will walk securely in your way,
> and your foot will not stumble.

²⁴When you lie down, you will not dread;
> and when you fall asleep, your sleep will be pleasing.

²⁵Do not be afraid of sudden calamity
> or the ruin of the wicked when it comes;

---

50. Lit. "her profit." The parallel, "her revenue," supports interpreting "her profit" and "profit of silver" to mean "the profit wisdom/silver give," not "the profit of gaining her/silver."

51. The meaning of Heb. *mippĕnîyîm* (K) and *mippĕnînîm* (Q) is uncertain. In Lam. 4:7 *pnynym* are said to be red, suggesting rubies or coral, both of which were highly prized by ancients. Rubies, however, appear to be unknown until first mentioned by Theophrastus in the third century B.C. Since coral is no longer precious, many translations substitute "rubies" as a dynamic equivalent.

52. The volitional form connotes purpose or result (= "so that"; see 3:4).

53. Lit. "grace" or "favor" in its aesthetic sense (cf. 3:4) and a metonymy of adjunct for the ornament.

²⁶for *I AM* will be at your side
  and he will guard your foot from capture.
²⁷Do not withhold [doing] good from those to whom it is due
  when you have the power to do [good].
²⁸Do not say to your neighbor, "Go and come back, and tomorrow
    I will give,"
  and all the while you have it with you.
²⁹Do not plan evil against your neighbors
  while they are dwelling trustfully with you.
³⁰Do not bring an accusation against a person without reason
  if they have not done you evil.
³¹Do not envy a violent person,
  and do not choose any of his ways;
³²for the devious are an abomination to *I AM*,
  but his counsel is with the upright.
³³*I AM*'s curse is on the house of the wicked,
  but he blesses the abode of the righteous.
³⁴If it is a matter of mockers, he mocks;
  and if it is a matter of the humble and oppressed, he shows
    favor.
³⁵The wise will inherit honor,
  but fools are those who acquire only disgrace.

Seemingly, four originally independent pericopes have been brought together to create lecture 4 (3:13–18, 19–20, 21–26, 27–35). The first three function as strophes of a first stanza on the value of wisdom (vv. 13–26), and the fourth functions as the second stanza on being a good neighbor (vv. 27–35). This history of composition may explain why the address "my son" is not encountered until the third strophe (v. 21). We lean heavily on Paul Overland for the analysis of the lecture's rhetoric.[54]

The Value of Wisdom (3:13–26)

Unlike lecture 3, which placed the admonitions in the odd verses and the promises in the even verses, this stanza moves logically, progressing from substantiation in vv. 13–20 to admonition in v. 21, with further substantiation in vv. 22–26. Paul Overland divides the poem into three parts:

54. P. B. Overland, "Literary Structure in Proverbs 1–9" (PhD diss., Brandeis University, 1988), 285–328. Overland disengages 3:1–26 from 3:27–35.

I	The Value of Wisdom to Humanity	vv. 13–18
II	The Value of Wisdom to *I AM* as Creator	vv. 19–20
III	The Value of Wisdom to the Son	vv. 21–26

Overland's structure shows how the exordium escalates to a climax: wisdom's great value to humanity and even to the Creator can be the son's if he guards it.

The Value of Wisdom to Humanity (3:13–18)

In addition to the escalation from "find" (v. 13) to "hold fast" (v. 18), and the inclusio of "blessed," its first and last words, this pericope is also unified by its concentric pattern:

A	The person who finds wisdom pronounced blessed	v. 13
	B Wisdom's superiority to precious metals	vv. 14–15
	B' Wisdom's benefits in detail	vv. 16–18a
A'	All who hold fast to wisdom pronounced blessed	v. 18b

13 *Blessed* ('*ašrê*) is a laudatory exclamation reserved for people who experience life optimally.[55] This declaration has in view a person's near or distant beneficent destiny due to their present relationship with God.[56] Eliphaz calls "blessed" those *I AM* disciplines (Job 5:17; cf. Prov. 3:11–12), and Jesus Christ, using the Greek equivalent *makarios*, refers to the persecuted and mourners as blessed because, though suffering in the present, joy is their destiny. *Finds* (see 2:5) *wisdom* (see "What Is 'Wisdom,'" pp. 27–29) and *obtains understanding* (see "Intellectual Terms for the Wise and Righteous," p. 36) entail a decision to accept the inspired teaching by faith (see 2:1–4).

14–15 *Surely*, or "for," unpacks the blessedness that personified wisdom bestows. The *profit she gives* to one who buys her (cf. 4:7) *is better than the profit of silver*. Money can put food on the table, but not the fellowship around it; can buy a house, but not a home; can give a woman jewelry, but not the love she really wants. Wisdom bestows both material and spiritual benefits. The comparison presumes that material wealth helps one to experience a full life (cf. 16:16). Habel says, "If wealth is a bonum, wisdom is the *summum bonum*" (cf. 8:10–11).[57] *Her revenue* is a metonymy for the benefits specified in vv. 16–18. *She*

---

55. An appropriate gloss is: "How rewarding is the life of . . ."

56. W. Janzen, "'*AŠRÊ* in the Old Testament," *HTR* 58 (1965): 223.

57. N. C. Habel, "Wisdom, Wealth and Poverty: Paradigms in the Book of Proverbs," *BiBh* 14 (1988): 30.

is more precious presumes her high quality and scarcity.[58] *All desirable things*, such as Satan illegitimately offered Jesus Christ (Luke 4:5–6), sums up all her legitimate material benefits. A Talmudic proverb says, "Lackest thou wisdom, what has thou acquired? Hast thou acquired wisdom, what lackest thou?"[59]

16–17 Specifically, wisdom is personified as holding *long life . . . in her right hand* and *in her left, wealth and honor* (see 3:9). According to C. Kayatz, this imagery is derived from the figure of Ma'at, the Egyptian goddess of wisdom and justice. Ma'at is pictured holding the ankh, the symbol of life, in her left hand and the scepter, the symbol of order and dominion, in her right.[60] Placing life in Woman Wisdom's right hand gives it greater value than wealth (see Gen. 48:14; Eccl. 10:2; Matt. 25:33). But longevity without *peace* and *prosperity* (*šālôm*; see 3:2) is not ideal. Wealth is the reward of wisdom, not the goal of life (cf. 1 Kings 3:9). *Her ways* (see 1:15) *are pleasant ways*—that is, kind and beneficial.[61] *All her byways* refers to the many individual proverbs that guide one's behavior along the way of wisdom (see 2:8).

18 *Tree of life* is a common ANE image that represents the inseparable notions of healing (Prov. 13:12; 15:4; Rev. 2:7; cf. Ezek. 47:12) and eternal life (Gen. 2:9; 3:22; Prov. 11:30; 13:12; 15:4).[62] Adam and Eve, humanity's representatives, lost access to the tree of life by their hubris. Humans can regain it by humbling themselves and receiving by faith the words of eternal life, which are inseparable from the Word, the Lord Jesus Christ. Having found wisdom (v. 13), the wise *take hold of her* and *hold her fast*. The incomplete metaphor equates "her" (Wisdom) with the tree of life. Human beings can regain the lost "tree of life" through humbly accepting God's Word. Although faith in Proverbs is inseparable from faith in Jesus Christ, Christ is better (see "The Superiority of Jesus Christ to Solomon's Wisdom," p. 58). *Are each declared blessed* (see 3:13).

The Value of Wisdom to *I AM* (3:19–20)

As *I AM* used wisdom to make (3:19) and sustain the earth (8:22–31), so also the son can establish and preserve his life through it.

---

58. S. Wagner, *TDOT*, 6:280, s.v. *yqr*.

59. Cited in A. Cohen, *Proverbs* (London: Soncino, 1967), 17.

60. Kayatz, *Proverbien 1–9*, 105; O. Keel, *The Symbolism of the Biblical World* (New York: Seabury, 1978), 96.

61. *HALOT*, 2:706, s.v. *nō'am*.

62. This interpretation is supported by the religious literature of the ancient Near East (see Prov. 1:9 above, p. 71), other wisdom literature of the Old Testament (e.g. Ps. 49; Job 19:25–27), and the book of Proverbs itself (12:28; 14:32).

19 Initial *I AM* (*yhwh*) is juxtaposed with initial *ʾādām* ("humankind") in v. 13. The rest of the verse is arranged concentrically:

> *I AM*
>> by wisdom
>>> founded the earth,
>>> established the heavens
>> by understanding.

By wisdom and its stock-in-trade parallel, *understanding*, *I AM* created a functioning cosmos in which all its myriad, complex parts fit together and work to sustain life. "By wisdom" he established the physical constants that control the nature of interactions between matter and the way energy behaves so that complex life can flourish.[63] If by wisdom *I AM* created a wondrous creation, imagine what his revealed wisdom will do in the lives of those who obtain it.[64] The merism, *founded the earth* and *established the heavens*, sums up the entire cosmos as firmly fixed on a permanent and stable foundation.[65]

20 *I AM* also sustains his creation with life-giving springs from below the earth and dew from above it. *By his knowledge* (see 1:2, 7). *The depths* denotes the primeval depths that *were split open* at the time of creation (Ps. 104:8–13). The verb has a hostile sense because the poet utilizes the imagery, not the theology, of ANE cosmogonic battle myths, wherein a heroic deity splits open the "abyss," a restraining deity, to release the essential life forces, including life-giving water.[66] *And the clouds drip dew* (Ps. 77:17; Job 36:28),[67] the moisture from wind off the Mediterranean Sea after sunset.

The Value of Wisdom to the Son (3:21–26)

The meanings of *nāṣar* (v. 21) and *šāmar* (v. 26)—that is, to observe carefully and to protect (both translated "guard" in our translation)—create an inclusio around the final strophe (see 2:8, 11). If the son "guards" *I AM*'s wisdom (v. 21),

---

63. Cf. Waltke and Yu, *Old Testament Theology*, 175; Francis Collins, "Religion and Science: Conflict or Harmony," Pew Research Center, May 4, 2009, http://www.pewforum.org/2009/05/04/religion-and-science-conflict-or-harmony/.

64. Hubbard, *Proverbs*, 75.

65. R. Mosis, *TDOT*, 6:114, s.v. *ysd*; E. Gerstenberger, *TLOT*, 2:604, s.v. *kûn*.

66. See Mary K. Wakeman, *God's Battle with the Monster: A Study in Biblical Imagery* (Leiden: E. J. Brill, 1973).

67. *HALOT*, 4:1465, s.v. *šaḥaq*.

I AM will "guard" him from being "captured" (v. 26). The strophe consists of three quatrains: the admonition to heed the teaching (vv. 21–22), the argument that it leads to security (vv. 23–24), and consequently the admonition not to fear because *I AM* gives security (vv. 25–26).

21–22 Uniquely, *my son* (see 1:8) occurs in the third strophe instead of at the beginning of the lecture (see above, p. 98). In addition to the noted progression to *and let . . . not depart,* the antecedent of *them* is "wisdom and understanding," as it is at the beginning of the other strophes (vv. 13, 19). *From your eyes* may signify the sayings were written to be read (cf. 22:20) as well as recited to be heard (22:17). In any case, constant and diligent attention to the teachings is required. *Guard* (see 2:8; 3:1) *sound judgment* (see 2:7) *and discretion* (see "Intellectual Terms for the Wise and Righteous," p. 35) *so that they may become life* (see pp. 41–42) *for you.* Corresponding to the inward "life" is the outward *attractive ornament for your neck* (cf. 1:9; 3:3).[68]

23–24 Logical *then* (see 2:5, 9) binds the consequence of security (vv. 23–24) to the conditions of guarding (vv. 21–22). The merism of walking (23a) and lying down (24a) unites the quatrain and signifies round-the-clock security. The metaphor *you will walk securely* (see 1:33) *in your way* (see 1:15) is followed by the concretion *and your foot will not stumble* (cf. Ps. 91:12).[69] *When* (or "if") hypothetically refers to the most vulnerable time: when *you lie down.* Nevertheless, *you will not dread.* On the contrary, *when you fall asleep, your sleep will be pleasing*—free of real dangers and of nightmares (Job 7:13–15) and terrors (Ps. 91:5). Refreshing sleep is refused to addicts (Prov. 4:16) and the rich (Eccl. 5:12). Sweet sleep is the fruit of faith in God (Pss. 3:5; 4:8) and of wisdom (Prov. 6:22; 19:23).

25–26 *Do not be afraid* is likely a real command (cf. Deut. 20:3; Isa. 10:24), the complement of the positive command to "trust *I AM*" (3:5). *Sudden calamity* refers to the *ruin of the wicked when it comes* unexpectedly (see 1:27; 1 Thess. 5:3). The son need not fear because I AM *will be at your side* (Lev. 3:4, 10, 15; Ps. 38:7; Job 15:27), as he was with Noah and Lot and their families (2 Pet. 2:5-9). Jesus assures his people that on judgment day he will separate the sheep from the goats (Matt. 25:31–46), the wheat from the tares (13:24–30), and the good fish from the bad (13:47–50). *And,* as a result of God's presence, *he will guard your foot from capture,* clarifies it is *I AM* who is the unseen source of sure-footedness.

---

68. The assertion by Heim (*Poetic Imagination,* 114) that the metaphor of binding the teachings "around the neck" (along with its minor variations in 1:9; 3:3; 3:22; 6:21) foregrounds different characteristics of the teachings is not convincing.

69. *HALOT,* 2:669, s.v. *nāgāph.*

Lesson: Obligations to Neighbors (3:27–35)

The meaning of "wisdom and understanding" in stanza 1 is now concretized in stanza 2 as being a good neighbor to a needy or trusting neighbor and so winning *I AM*'s blessing, not his curse (vv. 32–35; cf. 3:3, 4). The notion of a needy neighbor who deserves help (3:27–28), however, stands in tension with the promises of the first stanza. The tension represents the two faces of truth: *I AM* protects his covenant partner from the doom of the wicked, but in the interim the good may suffer, as implied in v. 34. The stanza can be analyzed as having two equal-length strophes united by a middle line, a janus.

A	Commands: Obligations to good neighbors	vv. 27–30
B	Janus: Do not envy a violent neighbor	v. 31
C	Argument: *I AM* punishes the wicked but blesses the righteous	vv. 32–35

The logical connection between the ethical commands and the theological argument shows that social behavior and theology are inextricably intertwined.

Commands: Obligations to Good Neighbors (3:27–30)

Syntactically, each verse of the strophe begins with a negative command: "do not" in verset A followed by a qualification in verset B. Semantically, the strophe consists of two quatrains, teaching not to withhold "good" (i.e., help) from good neighbors (vv. 27–28) and not to harm a trusting and innocent neighbor (vv. 29–30). The quatrains juxtapose the sin of omission (vv. 27–28) with sins of commission (vv. 29–30).

27 *Do not withhold good* implies neighbors in need. "Good" (see 2:9) stands for whatever tangible help the situation requires. *From those to whom it is due*, or "from those who deserve it" (NIV). Fox observes that the neighbor has a moral claim to this " good," as in the case of a person whose donkey has wandered off (Exod. 23:4): "If you can help this man, you are obliged to do so *even if he is your enemy*."[70] However, Exod. 23:5 qualifies "your enemy" as someone "who hates you"; you may be hated for overstaying your visit (cf. Prov. 25:17, 21). Morally evil people, however, such as the sluggard (cf. 19:24; 2 Thess. 3:10, 12), the leech (Prov. 30:15), and the pampered servant (29:21) are

---

70. Fox, *Proverbs 1–9*, 164–65, his Italics.

neither good nor possess a legal claim of benefit. *When you have the power to do [good]*: God does not ask people to give what they do not have (2 Cor. 8:12; Gal. 6:10) and forbids them from risking themselves as security for a stranger (see 6:1–5). John Milton, in his sonnet "On His Blindness," asked: "Doth God exact day-labour, light denied?"

28 *Do not say* . . . *"Go and come back, and tomorrow I will give,"* which is a delaying or denying tactic, not a promise (cf. Luke 18:2–3), as indicated by the qualifying clause *and all the while you have it with you.* Aitken comments, "Help which is long on the road is no help at all."[71] Publilius Syrus (50 B.C.) said, "He gives twice who gives quickly."[72] *Your neighbor* is a broad term embracing a close friend (see 17:17) and extending to anyone who has a relationship with you (see 6:1). Jesus answers the question "who is my neighbor" by the question "who behaves as a neighbor" (Luke 10:29–36). In other words, if you have the heart of being a neighbor, there are no boundaries to whom you help. In sum, the proverb commands giving practical and prompt help to a deserving neighbor.

29-30 *Plan* means, concretely, "to plow" and, figuratively, "to prepare." Rashi plausibly connects the two concepts by noting "plowing" is preparation for sowing.[73] *Evil* (or harm; see 1:16) *against your neighbors* (see v. 28) *while they are dwelling . . . with you* is tautological but serves to underscore *trustingly* (see 3:5). They feel secure because they have done no harm and so do not expect treachery.[74] Trust, says McKane, is "an indispensable condition of community."[75] *Do not bring an accusation against a person* illustrates a planned evil by a gratuitous accusation, as in a legal case, initiated by an oral complaint. *Without reason* (see 1:11) is clarified by *if they have not done you evil.* To bring a legal charge willfully against an innocent neighbor must be chalked up to malice or avarice (see 1:19).

Middle Line (Janus): Do Not Envy a Violent Man (3:31)

The initial *do not* with regard to ethical behavior in both versets of v. 31 links the middle line to vv. 27–30; the subject "a violent person," abetted by explanatory "for" in v. 32, links it to vv. 32–35. *Envy* denotes zeal for a rival's property.

---

71. Aitken, *Proverbs*, 51.

72. Cited in Cohen, *Proverbs*, 19.

73. Cited by H. Ringgren, *TDOT*; 5:222, s.v. *ḥāraṣ*.

74. The Bible gives many examples of despicable treachery. See 17:13; cf. Gen. 34:13–29; 1 Sam. 18:17–18; 2 Sam. 3:27; 11:14–15; 20:9–10; Ps. 55:12–14; Jer. 41:12; Mic. 2:9; John 13:2.

75. McKane, *Proverbs*, 300.

Envy is the root of a miscellany of sins. It incited Cain to kill Abel (Gen. 4). A *violent person* describes a person who cold-bloodedly and brutally infringes the rights of others, often out of greed and hate. According to Haag, in 3:31, it "can only be concerned with wealth that is wrung from others" (cf. 10:6; 16:29).[76] *Choose* means to make a well-thought-out decision.[77] Success and surfeit may crown the violent for now, but the son must beware the cruel end to which *I AM* will consign them (see "Retribution for the Wicked," p. 50). To mimic *any of his ways* is to be his comrade and so to place oneself under divine damnation (3:32–35).

Argument: *I AM* Punishes the Wicked but Rewards the Righteous (3:32–35)

"For" introduces the theological reasons for the ethical admonitions. Gemser notes that the violent person of v. 31 is looked at from different viewpoints in vv. 32–35: as "devious" (v. 32), "wicked" (v. 33), "the mocker" (v. 34), and "the fool" (v. 35), all of whom disrespect God and ethical values to enrich themselves.[78] Except for the last verse, *I AM* is present in every verse as the one who justly rewards or punishes people. The A versets of vv. 32–34 feature the wicked and their punishment; the B versets feature the righteous and their rewards. Verse 35 reverses the pattern to signal the poem's end.

32 From one perspective, the violent are *devious* (see 2:7, 15; 3:21), polar opposites to *the upright* (2:7). That they are an *abomination* to *I AM* means their antisocial behavior offends his sensibilities[79] and turns his stomach.[80] It is a metonymy of cause for their punishment; otherwise, as Koch notes, *I AM* "is relegated to the position of a spectator."[81] Whereas "abomination" entails social distance, *his counsel* entails social intimacy (cf. Gen. 18:17).[82] Guided by the Wonderful Counselor, the upright are guaranteed protection, success, and eternal life.

---

76. H. Haag, *TDOT*, 4:479–83, s.v. *ḥāmās*.

77. H. Seebass, *TDOT*, 2:75, s.v. *bāḥar*.

78. B. Gemser, *Sprüche Salomos*, HAT 16 (Tübingen: J. C. B. Mohr, 1963), 24. Gemser also notes that v. 31 is connected in this way to vv. 32–35.

79. B. Waltke, "Abomination," in *IBSE*, 1:13.

80. Aitken, *Proverbs*, 52.

81. K. Koch, "Is There a Doctrine of Retribution in the Old Testament?" in *Issues in Religion and Theology 4: Theodicy in the Old Testament*, ed. J. L. Crenshaw (Philadelphia: Fortress; London: SPCK, 1983), 62.

82. *HALOT*, 2:745, s.v. *sôd*.

33 From another perspective, the violent are viewed as *wicked* (see "Ethical Terms for the Wicked and Fools," pp. 45–46), in contrast to the *righteous* (see "Ethical Terms for the Wise and Righteous," pp. 36–37), and "abomination" and "counsel" become "*I AM*'s curse" and "he blesses." *Curse* signifies *I AM*'s pronouncing the curse formula, "cursed be," against them—a speech act[83] that consigns the wicked to misfortune.[84] *I AM*, not chance or magic, is the agent of the misfortune. *On the house of the wicked* refers to everything he treasures and possesses—life, health, family, and security. As he plundered others so, *quid pro quo*, *I AM* does to him. The proverb assumes the corporate solidarity of the family (cf. Num. 16:32; Josh. 7:24–25; Esth. 8:1). *The abode of the righteous* connotes sustenance and security. *He blesses* means he fills their abode with the potency for life (vitality, fertility, prosperity) that enables them to overcome their enemies (see Gen. 22:17).

34 The repetition of *if it is a matter of* contrasts the treatment of the wicked and the righteous. The violent are now viewed as *mockers* (see "Intellectual Terms for the Wicked and Fools," pp. 48–49), and the blessed include "the humble and oppressed" (cf. 3:13). In another *lex talionis*, *he* (I AM) *mocks*. What the mockers gave to others, God will give to them. Until then, however, they get away with their treachery. *The humble and oppressed*, a hendiadys for "the oppressed poor," in this context are righteous (cf. 22:22–23). To them, I AM *shows favor* (see 3:4). James (4:6) and Peter (1 Pet 5:5) quote this verse to encourage Christians to submit to God and to one another respectively. Mary, the mother of Jesus, incarnates this truth (Luke 1:46–55).

35 In the climactic verse, the violent are viewed as *fools* (see "Intellectual Terms for the Wicked and Fools," p. 46–49) in contrast to *the wise* (see "Intellectual Terms for the Wise and Righteous," pp. 34–35). *Will inherit* refers to being permanently awarded a share in a possession. Here the share awarded the wise is lasting *honor*, a metonymy for the property that gives them social esteem and signals their success. Fools, by contrast, *acquire* (earn, not inherit) public *disgrace* (being held in ignominy and dishonor for a failed venture).

Lecture 5: Get the Family Heritage (4:1–9)

> [1]Listen, sons, to a father's instruction,
>> and pay attention to knowledge that gives insight.

---

83. For example, the speech act, "I pronounce you man and wife," legally effects a marriage.

84. Cf. J. Scharbert, *TDOT*, 1:411, s.v. 'rr.

²Because I give to you a good education,
do not leave my teaching.
³When I was a son to my father,
tender and cherished by my mother,
⁴then he taught me, and he said to me,
"Let your heart take hold of my words;
keep my commands and live.
⁵Get wisdom! Get insight!
Do not forget and do not turn aside
from the words of my mouth!
⁶Do not leave her, and she will keep you;
love her, and she will guard you.
⁷The beginning of wisdom is [this:] get wisdom!
In exchange for all your acquisitions, get insight.
⁸Cherish her, and she will exalt you;
she will honor you if you embrace her.
⁹She will bestow a garland to grace your head;
a splendid crown she will give you."

The fifth lecture, as is typical, includes an introduction (vv. 1–2) and the lesson (vv. 3–9). But uniquely, the lesson is the grandfather's to the father. In autobiographical style, the father introduces that lecture, naming himself as its addressee (vv. 3–4a), and then quotes his father (vv. 4b–9). The grandfather's lecture also has the typical introduction (v. 4b) and lesson (vv. 5–9), which is brought to a climactic conclusion with the promise that wisdom will give the son the victor's crown (see 1:9). The inclusio formed by "I give" (v. 2a) and "she will give" (v. 9b) helps unify the lecture's two parts. By quoting his father and setting himself up as an example, the father implies the antiquity of the teaching and his own sympathetic experience within the tradition, giving it authority and credibility. Chesterton wrote, "Tradition means giving votes to the most obscure of all classes, our ancestors. It is the democracy of the dead. Tradition refuses to submit to the small and arrogant oligarchy of those who merely happen to be walking about. . . . We will have the dead at our councils."[85] Tradition, however, can become "a cycle of deprivation" or, as here, "a

---

85. G. K. Chesterton, *Orthodoxy* (New York: John Lane, 1909), 85; quoted by B. G. Harrison, "Arguing with the Pope," *Harper's Magazine*, April 1994, 56; cited by R. C. Van Leeuwen, "The Book of Proverbs," in *NIB* 5, 62.

cycle of affirmation."[86] "Breaking the bad cycles and continuing the good ones are what wise parenting entails."[87]

Introduction: Addressees and Admonitions (4:1–2)

Every word of the introduction echoes the preamble (1:2–7) and the preceding introductions.

1 Uniquely, the father uses the indefinite *sons*, not "*my* sons," and the indefinite *a father's instruction*, not "*your* father's," to typify the lecture. Thus, the plural "sons" probably addresses the entire lineage of sons, not just contemporaries, suiting well a lecture about the generational transfer of wisdom. *Listen* (see 1:8) . . . *and pay attention* (see 1:23). *To knowledge that gives insight* is a synthetic parallel to "instruction" (cf. 1:2).

2 *Because I give to you* emphasizes that the *education* is passed down in an intimate father-son encounter. *Good* (see 2:9) implies that it serves the family's interest (see 2:20); hence the escalation *do not leave my teaching* (see 2:13; 3:3).

The Lesson: The Grandfather's Lecture (4:3–9)

Narrative Introduction to the Grandfather's Lecture (4:3–4)

3 *When* or "for" introduces the lesson's implied motivation. *I was a son to my father* connotes their spiritual, not just biological, relationship. J. E. Barrett writes, "In Hebrew thought sonship was understood not as a matter of biology but as a matter of obedience."[88] A rebellious child was disowned (Deut. 21:18–21; 32:19–20; Hos. 1:9; Mark 3:35; Luke 15:18–19).[89] Teaching began soon after the child was weaned.[90] To his *mother* (see 1:8) he was *tender* (that is, pliable). *Cherished* highlights his incomparable and beloved status. This beautiful peek into a pious Israelite home segues into the grandfather's lecture.

---

86. Atkinson, *Proverbs*, 68.

87. Hubbard, *Proverbs*, 81.

88. J. E. Barrett, "Can Scholars Take the Virgin Birth Seriously?" *BR* 4 (1988): 15. The LXX paraphrases 4:3 with "obedient son."

89. Ptahhotep counsels: "If he [a man's seed] goes astray and transgresses thy plans and does not carry out thy instruction . . . thou shouldst cast him off; he is not thy son at all. He was not really born to thee" (*ANET*, 413).

90. Probably at three years. The Egyptian *Instruction of Any* 7.19 speaks of "the mother's breast in your mouth for three years."

4 *Then he taught me* refers to the catechetical teaching. *And he said* underscores the oral tradition learned by rote. His admonitions move logically from receiving the teaching (*let your heart take hold of my words*) to retaining it (*keep my commands*). *And live*, or "and so live," functions as motivation (see 3:4).

The Grandfather's Lecture: Get Wisdom (4:5-9)

The lecture follows an alternating pattern of two cycles:

Cycle 1	A	Admonition: Get wisdom	v. 5
	B	Motivation: She will protect her lover	v. 6
Cycle 2	A'	Admonition: Get wisdom	v. 7
	B'	Motivation: She will honor her lover	vv. 8-9

5 The key word *get*, or "buy," (*qānē*) is repeated four times, twice in both v. 5a and v. 7. "Get" means to purchase goods deliberately through financial transactions and often includes the price (Gen. 33:19; 47:20; Lev. 25:14; Neh. 5:8). According to Meinhold, *wisdom* (see "What Is 'Wisdom'?," pp. 27–28), a synonym with *insight*, is here imagined as a bride for whom a dowry must be paid, namely, "all your acquisitions" (v. 7)—everything he owns.[91] The figure becomes mixed by shifting from *do not forget* (see 3:1) to *do not turn aside*, an incomplete, implied comparison to a path (see 17:23). Wisdom is equated with *the words of my mouth*.

6 The motivation is mixed with admonitions. In the admonitions, Wisdom is presented as a bride to be cherished, in the motivations as a patroness who rewards her lover. The negative admonition *do not leave her* and the positive parallel *love her* escalate the command in v. 5 to "get wisdom." Judging from Deut. 6:5 as well as other ANE treaties,[92] "love," as Hillers notes, is legal language that shapes the emotional term and so can be commanded. "To love is to set one's sincere affections on the covenant Lord and to give this affection its expression in loyal service."[93] The motivating, reciprocal promise is *she will keep you*, her lover, and emphatically, *she will guard you* (see 2:8, 11), presumably from any loss.

91. A. Meinhold, *Die Sprüche*, 2 vols., ZBK (Zurich: Theologischer, 1991), 91–92.

92. The El Amarna suzerainty treaties typically call upon the vassal to love the suzerain: "May my brother preserve love toward me ten times more than did his father" (29.166).

93. D. Hillers, *Covenant: The History of a Biblical Idea* (Baltimore: Johns Hopkins, 1969), 154.

7 *The beginning of wisdom* can mean its starting point (see 1:7), its first principle, or its chief thing (cf. NIV: "wisdom is supreme"). All three fit the context, suggesting "beginning" is polysemous. Commenting on the blunt *get wisdom*, Kidner says: "What it takes is not brains or opportunity, but a decision. Do you want it? Come and get it."[94] The admonition repeats the first cycle (v. 5a) but adds the purchase price: *in exchange for all your acquisitions*—a high cost, but none is too high for this treasure (see 2:4; cf. 3:13–18; 31:10). The dowry that this "type of Christ" demands is nothing less than one's heart (see "Woman Wisdom as a Type of Jesus Christ," p. 61).

8 *Cherish her*, escalates "love her" (v. 6). "Cherish" is an intelligent and compromising guess for a unique verb that means either "esteem her" or "caress/ cuddle her," an inchoate personification of wisdom as a woman or bride.[95] *And she will exalt you* mixes the figure of a bride with a patroness, who bestows upon her lover a high position—a connotation clarified by its parallel *she will honor you* (see 3:9), or better, "make you honored." So esteemed, her lover will become an influential leader (cf. 14:34). But this is only *if you embrace her*. In 5:2, "embrace her" has an erotic sense (cf. Eccl. 3:5; Song 2:6; 8:3), suggesting that Wisdom is here personified as a wife.

9 The lover's exalted position is symbolized in *she will bestow a garland to grace your head*. A victor's "garland" (see 1:9) nicely matches "exaltation" and "honor." Its depiction as *a splendid crown* enhances the garland's beauty and authority (cf. Isa. 9:15). *Give you* means to give as a gift.[96]

✦ Lecture 6: Stay Off the Wrong Way (4:10–19)

[10]Listen, my son, and accept my words,
> that the years of life may be many for you.
[11]I instruct you in the way of wisdom;
> I lead you along straight tracks.
[12]When you walk, your step will not be hampered,
> and if you run, you will not stumble.
[13]Hold on to instruction; do not stop;
> guard it, for it is your life.
[14]Do not enter the path of the wicked,
> and do not take strides in the way of evil men.

---

94. Kidner, *Proverbs*, 67.
95. Cf. Fox, *Proverbs 1–9*, 175.
96. *HALOT*, 2:545, s.v. *mgn*; M. A. Grisanti, *NIDOTTE*, 2:846, s.v. *māgēn*.

> ¹⁵Flout it; do not travel on it;
>> turn aside from going upon it and pass on.
> ¹⁶For they are robbed of sleep until they forge evil,
>> and their sleep is torn away unless they make [somebody]
>> stumble.
> ¹⁷For they eat the bread of wickedness,
>> and the wine of violent acts they drink.
> ¹⁸Now the path of the righteous is like the morning sun,
>> shining ever brighter until the day is firm.
> ¹⁹The way of the wicked is like darkness;
>> they do not know what trips them up.

Apart from a conclusion, lecture 6 is divided into two equal halves. The first pertains to accepting the way of wisdom (vv. 10–13); the second warns against going on the path the wicked (vv. 14–17). The conclusion contrasts the increasing light in the path of wisdom with the deepening darkness in the way of the wicked (vv. 18–19).

In lecture 1, the father grimly described the sinners as stone-cold killers (1:10–19); in this lecture, he grimly describes them as addicts, as "evilholics." Evil is their sedative by night and their bloody stimulant by day. These gruesome portrayals aim to so horrify the son that he recoils from evil.

Introduction and Body (4:10–17)

Admonitions to Walk in the Way of Wisdom (4:10–13)

Verses 10 and 13 form an inclusio around the first half, escalating from admonitions to accept the father's instruction (v. 10a) to persevering in it (v. 13a) with the motivating promise of life (vv. 10b, 13b). Within this frame, the father describes his teaching as a straight path (v. 11) on which the son can securely walk (v. 12).

10 Lecture 6, as is typical, begins *listen, my son* but atypically adds *and accept* (see 2:1). *Words* make abstract wisdom (v. 11) available to the senses. *That the years of your life may be many for you* does not entail a limitation by death (see "The Wise and Their Rewards: Life," pp. 41–42). The rest of the lecture showcases the enjoyable quality of this unrestricted quantity.

11 *I instruct you* implies a deliberate catechism that demands compliance, not "coaching" the child to discover their own way. *In the way* introduces the metaphor that unifies the lecture (see 1:15). *Of wisdom* sharply contrasts with the path of the wicked (v. 14). The metaphor connotes an ongoing, practical lifestyle, not theoretical contemplation. *I lead you along straight tracks* (see 2:8) states wisdom's first benefit: namely, it is free of treacherous turns and so ends in life, not death. Tracks are created by people repeatedly walking the same path—that is to say, wisdom is a tried and true way.

12 *When you walk* shifts the focus from the road to the son's activity on it. *Your step* refers to each decision. *Will not be hampered* (not cramped, restricted, or impeded), making progress easy and its end certain. To *run* is more dangerous than walking; nevertheless, *you will not stumble* and so not reach the goal: abundant life.

13 The lecture began with two commands to encourage total commitment to wisdom; it ends with three commands to encourage perseverance in it. *Do not stop* colors its parallel *hold on to instruction* (see 1:2) to mean keep holding on, not to initially take hold of (cf. 3:18). The two commands are akin to accepting the rigorous regimen of athletes, who by disciplining themselves in their diet, exercise, and training, are free to run at top form without "stumbling."[97] Ezekiel gives the reason: if the righteous let go of their righteousness they will die (18:26–27). *Guard* (see v. 21) *it* (fem.) refers to "wisdom" (11a), not "instruction" (masc.). *For it is your life* (see 3:22; 4:22; 8:35) completes the frame and reinforces the motivation in v. 10b.

Admonitions to Avoid the Way of the Wicked (4:14–17)

The second half of lecture 6 also has two halves: admonitions to avoid the way of the wicked (vv. 14–15) and validations that evil is addictive (vv. 16–17).

14 The metaphor *the path*, no different from "way," unites the two halves. *Of the wicked* (see "Ethical Terms for the Wicked and Fools," pp. 45–46) signifies their path as the wrong one, which must be avoided. To highlight its danger, the father piles on six intensifying imperatives, doubling their number from two (v. 14) to four (v. 15). This is to counter the enthralling power of the wicked. They must be vigorously resisted, without yielding them even an inch. First, *do not enter* denotes both not entering and not continuing in the realm of the wicked. Second, *and do not take strides* escalates the first. *In the way of evil men* paints the path of the wicked as moral evil (see 1:16; 3:7).

15 Third, to *flout it* (see 1:25) is to rebel against it—namely that which masquerades as what is true and right.[98] Fourth, to *not travel on* means to

---

97. Van Leeuwen, "Proverbs," in *NIB* 5, 59.
98. J. Janzen, "The Root *prʿ*," *VT* 39 (1989): 406.

not pass through (cf. Exod. 12:12) or traverse (cf. Job 33:18) a designated area. Fifth, to *turn aside from* means to deliberately redirect one's course from *going upon it*—namely, the path of the wicked. Sixth, *and pass on* brings the son's attention back to the right way. In sum, the son is told, "Don't step off the path of wisdom. Keep going!"

16 *For* introduces the other reason why evil should be avoided: it is so addictive that at night its victims cannot sleep unless they design devilry (v. 16), and by day they are nourished by executing it (v. 17). *They are robbed of sleep until they forge evil* signifies that they can sleep only after they have planned how to injure others to advantage themselves (see 3:7). The parallel, *and their sleep is torn away*, magnifies the fact that they are sociopaths.[99] *Unless they make [somebody] stumble* clarifies their wicked plans.

17 By day they nourish themselves by carrying out what they planned. *For they eat the bread of wickedness* is a deliberately ambiguous expression meaning, literally, "bread obtained through wickedness" or, more likely, figuratively, that "wickedness constitutes their regular diet (cf. Job 15:16)."[100] Nefariousness has become their necessary nutrient. The parallel, *and the wine . . . they drink* forms a merism with "the bread" they eat, signifying a complete meal. They crave brutality, as when criminals build magnificent casinos by exploiting addicts, or the rich build mansions by underpaying their employees, or gangsters drive luxurious cars by selling drugs. *Of violent acts* clarifies that the wickedness that stimulates them may involve murder and mayhem (cf. 1:10–15; Mic. 3:2–3). The plural "acts" may be to draw a comparison between the crushing of many grapes to put one glass of wine on the table and the exploitation of many victims to acquire wealth. In the Greek myth of Medusa, the heart of anyone who stared at its hideous face turned to stone; so too the son runs the risk of lithifying his heart by becoming involved with the wicked.

Conclusion (4:18–19)

The conclusion of the lecture, like its body, first describes the righteous and then the wicked. The initial word "path/way" and the concluding verb "trips" clearly link the way of wisdom (vv. 10–13) with light (v. 18) and the way of the wicked (v. 14–17) with darkness (v. 19).

18 *Now the path of the righteous,* in marked contrast to the "path of the

---

99. We are using the word here phenomenologically, not in its technical psychoanalytic sense.

100. Greenstone, *Proverbs,* 42.

wicked" (v. 14), *is like the morning sun* whose light increases. There are no clouds, not even shadows, on this path (cf. 2 Sam. 23:4; Isa. 62:1). Light symbolizes true piety and morality along with safety, salvation, and well-being (Ps. 43:3; Job 22:28; 29:2–3; Isa. 9:2; 42:16). *I AM* himself is light (Ps. 27:1). Thus, the road of the wise is doubly safe: obstacle free and brilliantly bright. *Shining ever brighter* implies that there is growth in righteousness and its benefits. *Until the day is firm* implies that the righteous eventually comes to perfect illumination and full salvation. As Saadia comments, "The righteous are like the light of morning that keeps on increasing, and not like the afternoon light which is constantly diminishing."[101]

19 By contrast, *the way of the wicked is like darkness*—the same word used for the dreadful darkness of Egypt (Exod. 10:22) and for the darkness of the blind who at noon grope and cannot find their way (Deut. 28:29). Devoid of moral light in their conscience within or of revelation without, *they do not know what trips them up.* They do not see the nexus between deed and destiny, sin and death—the divine moral order (cf. 5:21–23; Deut. 28:28–29; Job 5:23–24; 12:24–25; Jer. 13:16; 23:12). "What trips them up" refers to the cause of their demise. Their blindness is momentary bliss but eternal death. Sadly, today, many see no connection between sexual immorality and sexually transmitted diseases, between extravagant greed and national debt, between atheism and amorality—and it is killing them.

Lecture 7: Do Not Swerve from the Right Way (4:20–27)

> [20]My son, pay attention to my words;
> > turn your ear to my sayings.
> [21]Do not allow them to depart from before your eyes;
> > keep them within your heart;
> [22]for they are life to those who find them
> > and a remedy for one's whole body.
> [23]Above every watch, guard your heart,
> > for everything you do flows from it.
> [24]Keep a crooked mouth away from you,
> > and devious lips put far away from you.
> [25]Let your eyes look straight ahead,
> > and let your pupils look straight in front of you.
> [26]Watch the track for your foot,

---

101. Cited by Greenstone, *Proverbs*, 43.

and let all your ways be steadfast.
  [27]Do not turn to the right or to the left;
  keep your foot from evil.

Lecture 6 warned the son against entering the wicked path; lecture 7 admonishes him to walk straight ahead in the father's teaching, without swerving to the right or the left. "Turn" forms an inclusio: "turn . . . to" (v. 20b) and "do not turn . . ." (v. 27a). This lecture could also be labelled "the anatomy of discipleship."[102] As Carol Newsom notes, the disciple's self is rewritten as a series of body parts: the ear (v. 20b), the eyes (v. 21a), the heart (vv. 21b, 23a), the body (v. 22b), the mouth and lips (v. 24), the eyes and pupils (v. 25), and the foot (v. 26a, 27b). She adds, "Intertwined with this inventory of the body are terms from a code of physical orientation (incline, extend, twist away, turn aside, twistedness, crookedness, makes distant, straight, in front, straight before, swerve to right or left)."[103]

Verses 20–22 contain the typical introductory motifs of a lecture (address, admonitions, and motivations), but since all its verses, apart from v. 22, are admonitions, and since vv. 20–22 constitute almost half of the lecture, they are better considered as also part of the lesson. The lecture begins with the passive body parts—the hearing ear (v. 20) and the seeing eyes (v. 21)—that receive the teaching which enlivens the body (v. 22). Verse 23 features the heart in both versets and is a janus: the heart is both the receptacle of what the passive body parts receive and the agent that controls the active body parts: the speaking mouth (v. 24), directing eyes (v. 25), and walking foot (vv. 26–27).

The inclusio formed by "to turn to" the father's words (20b) and "do not turn to the right or left" (27a) summarizes the message. What one is and what one does are inseparable.

Passive Anatomy (4:20–22)

20 *My son* (see 1:8), *pay attention* (see 2:2) *to my words* (the act of speaking; see 1:6), reinforced by *turn your ear to my sayings* (their content), introduces the lecture in a typical manner, albeit with somewhat unique vocabulary.

21 *Do not allow them to depart* personifies the sayings as having fleeing feet and advances the admonition to retain the words (see 1:8; 3:13, 18, 21; 4:4, 6, 10, 13). *From before your eyes* presumes the sayings were written for literate youth.

---

102. Hubbard, *Proverbs*, 87. Newsom, "Woman and the Discourse," 152.
103. Newsom, "Woman and the Discourse," 152.

Keep (*šāmar*; see 2:8, 11) *them within your heart* (see "Heart," p. 32) makes the heart like the ark of the covenant that housed the tablets on which the Ten Commandments were written.

22 An explanatory *for* introduces the only motivation in the lecture, but what a motivation it is: *they are life* (see "The Wise and Their Rewards: Life," pp. 41–42) *for those who find them* (see 3:13). A *remedy* restores to full life. One's *whole body* includes both the physical and the psychological. The verse interprets what the figurative tree of life signifies (see 3:18).

Janus: The Heart (4:23)

23 *Above every watch* (that is, more than everything else that needs guarding) *guard your heart.* Keeping the commands within the heart protects it from evil. *For* introduces the reason. *Everything you do flows from it* assumes the heart controls all the members of the body (see "Heart," p. 32).

Active Anatomy (4:24–27)

The lecture's second part is framed by the inclusio of negative commands—to keep away, in connection with the mouth (v. 24a) and foot (v. 27b)—around a core of positive commands.

24 Although the heart controls the body, the body's members must themselves be watched.[104] The list of body parts is not exhaustive but exemplary of practical living.[105] Nevertheless, v. 24 is the only verse that specifies a specific ethical behavior. As in Egyptian instruction literature, the mouth comes first because it is the direct pipeline to and from the heart. While this metonymy for speech allows one to test what is in the heart (cf. Luke 6:45; Rom. 10:10),[106] the sage probably also has in view the mouth's influence upon the heart. As Kidner rightly notes, "cynical chatter, fashionable grumbles, flippancy, half-truths . . . harden into well-established habits of thought."[107] *Keep . . . away from you* is a better translation than "remove from you," since the address "my son" places the son among the wise.[108] *Crooked mouth* denotes speech that distorts or deforms

---

104. Gemser, *Sprüche*, 27.
105. Plöger, *Sprüche*, 49.
106. Plöger, *Sprüche*, 49.
107. Kidner, *Proverbs*, 68.
108. Further corroborating this translation is that in the inclusio, the same construction must mean "keep away," not remove.

the truth (see "The Wise and Words," pp. 39–40). Being *devious* means diverging or departing from what is right and true. *Lips* is a stock-in-trade parallel to mouth. *Put far away from you* escalates keeping evil speech away (24a) to making it remote. Proverbs is full of straight talk about talking straight.

25 *Let your eyes look straight ahead* resumes the metaphor of a straight road, to which the eyes must give undivided attention and from which the foot must not stray. Since the eyes have an insatiable appetite for stimuli (27:20), the disciple must concentrate their gaze on the ways of wisdom. Unlike the discerning, who keep wisdom in view, fools look everywhere else (17:24). *Pupils* is a stock-in-trade parallel to eyes. The synonymous parallel *look straight in front of you* emphasizes the admonition (cf. Matt. 6:22). As long as people fix themselves on heavenly truth, Satan has no advantage over them. Eve sinned after she focused on the forbidden fruit.

26 Verses 26 and 27 are framed by the repetition of "your foot" in 26a and 27b. Verse 26 positively admonishes commitment to the right way; v. 27 warns against deviating from it to evil. To *watch the track* is to conform every step to the conduct laid out by the father; one false step could prove fatal. *Your foot* entails each step on the road of life. *And let . . . be steadfast* calls for a firm commitment to the father's wisdom. *All your ways* refers to the many facets of the son's behavior.

27 *Do not turn* assumes the son is walking on the straight path. *To the right or the left*, a merism for moral deviation of any sort (Deut. 5:29; 17:11, 20; 28:14; Josh. 1:7; 23:6; 2 Kgs. 22:2), refutes the abuse of Aristotle's middle path between two harmful extremes: there is no third way. *Keep* [away] *your foot from evil* could be translated "turn your foot away from evil" (ESV), but that might imply the son's foot is on an evil path, contrary to the implication of the address "my son" (v. 20).

Lecture 8: Folly of Adultery, Wisdom of Marriage (5:1–23)

> ¹My son, pay attention to my wisdom;
>> turn your ear to my words of understanding,
> ²that you may keep discretion
>> and that your lips may guard knowledge.
> ³For the lips of the unchaste wife drip honey,
>> and her palate is smoother than oil,
> ⁴but in the end she is bitter like wormwood,
>> sharp like a double-edged sword.

⁵Her feet are going down to death;
    her steps lay hold of the grave.
⁶The path of life she does not watch;
    her tracks meander aimlessly; she does not know it.
⁷So now, sons, listen to me,
    and do not turn aside from the words of my mouth.
⁸Keep your way far from her,
    and do not draw near to the door of her house,
⁹lest you give your splendor to others
    and your dignity to the cruel;
¹⁰lest strangers be filled with your strength,
    and your strenuous labors be in an outsider's house.
¹¹And you will groan at the end of your life,
    when your body and your flesh are spent,
¹²and you will say, "How I hated instruction;
    [how] my heart spurned rebuke.
¹³And I did not listen to the voice of my teachers;
    I did not turn my ear to those who taught me.
¹⁴I was soon in serious trouble
    in the midst of the congregation and the assembly."
¹⁵Drink water from your own cistern
    and flowing streams from the midst of your own well.
¹⁶Should your springs overflow without?
    Your channels of water in the open squares?
¹⁷Let them be for yourself alone,
    and have no strangers with you.
¹⁸May your wellspring be blessed,
    and get pleasure from the wife of your youth.
¹⁹[May she be] a lovemaking doe, a graceful mountain goat;
    may her breasts drench you at all times;
    and with her caresses may you always become intoxicated.
²⁰Now why be intoxicated, my son, with an unchaste wife?
    [Why] embrace the bosom of an unfaithful woman?
²¹For a man's ways are before the eyes of *I AM*;
    he is watching all his tracks.
²²His iniquities will catch him,
    and with the cords of his sin he will be held fast.
²³He will die in his lack of instruction,
    and in the abundance of his folly he will be led astray.

Lecture 8 is the father's "robust man-to-man warning"[109] to the son against adultery. It consists of three parts: the typical introduction (vv. 1–6), the lesson describing the folly of adultery (vv. 7–14) and the wisdom of sex within marriage (vv. 15–20), and the conclusion consisting of a sober prediction about the fatal consequences of sinning against God and spurning instruction (vv. 21–23). Van Leeuwen comments, "The opposition of adultery to married love concretely shows that sin and folly cross created boundaries, while the play of eros within marriage illustrates freedom within form."[110] → *Love!!*

A subtheme punctuating the whole is that of accepting the father's teaching (vv. 1, 7), which rejecting leads to regret (vv. 12–13) and death (vv. 21–23). This subtheme is crucial because the father is countering the mellifluent speech of the adulteress.

Introduction (5:1–6)

Address, Admonition, and Aim (5:1–2)

1 The introduction *my son, pay attention . . . turn your ear* repeats 4:20 but replaces the external expressions of wisdom, "sayings" and "words," with *my wisdom* and *my words of understanding*, the substance and end result of the father's words. Although a youth, the son is old enough to experience sexual temptation; he is either married or on the verge of marrying (see 1:4).

2 The admonition's aim is *that you may keep discretion* (see "Intellectual Terms for the Wise and Righteous," p. 35). Its parallel, *lips* (that is, speech) *may guard knowledge* (see p. 28), means they *speak* forthrightly in accord with the sages' religious and ethical teachings (cf. 22:18). Fox explains the idea based on Mal. 2:7: "The lips of the priest keep knowledge, and [people] seek instruction from his mouth" (cf. Prov. 22:18). "The priest 'keeps' knowledge by *speaking*. . . ."[111] By speaking up, the son's lips resist the honeyed "lips of the unchaste wife" (v. 3).

Motivation (5:3–6)

3 *For* introduces the argument for heeding the admonition. Implicitly, without wisdom and speaking up for what is right, the son will be no match for the

---

109. McKane, *Proverbs*, 312.
110. Van Leeuwen, "Proverbs," in *NIB* 5, 66.
111. Fox, *Proverbs 1–9*, 191.

enchantress. He must speak the truth, as Joseph did with Potiphar's wife (Gen. 39:8–9), to counter the evil, buttery speech from *the lips of the unchaste wife* (see "The Unchaste Wife," p. 54). Newsom notes the inseparable connection between speech and sexuality: "Sexuality is by its nature dialogical, as the term 'intercourse' well suggests. Culturally, it is closely associated with speech: courting speech, seductive speech, love songs, whispered sweet nothings." She further notes, "The point at which the horizontal speech of the woman's sexuality comes into conflict with the vertical speech of the father's authority is precisely the point of generational transition when the boy becomes a man."[112] *Drip honey* refers to honey that falls drop by drop directly from the honeycomb—the purest and sweetest. McKane comments, "She speaks in accents which ooze seductive charm."[113] *Her palate* (i.e., her speech) *is smoother than oil,*[114] a metaphor for fraudulent flattery (2:16; 29:5). Her oleaginous speech "draws her victim irresistibly towards mystery, excitement and delight."[115]

4 *But* jarringly contrasts her promising start with her dreadful end. *In the end she is* points to the final judgment of illicit sex with the adulteress. The gustatory metaphor *bitter* describes the pains enumerated in vv. 7–14 and the final death predicted in v. 23. The simile *like wormwood* intensifies the metaphor.[116] The military metaphor *sharp* implies a sword that kills efficiently (cf. 7:23f.). The intensifying simile *like a double-edged sword* literally denotes "a sword of mouths," which, according to Isaiah 1:20, "devours" people. Her smooth lips and palate will become a devouring mouth on judgment day.

5 The focus now shifts down to *her* deadly *feet*, a metonymy for her path (2:18).[117] *Are going down to death* denotes the final destruction of the adulteress and all her lovers. *Her steps* depict her deliberate stride toward the grave. *Lay hold of* escalates "going down" to her final stygian destiny, namely, *the grave* (see p. 50), the terminus of her lewd life.

6 *The path of life* ("The Wise and Their Rewards: Life," p. 41). *she does not watch.* Having abandoned God and her marital vows, she ambles in amorality. *Her tracks,* a metaphorical metonymy for all her behaviors, *meander aimlessly* (cf. 2 Sam. 15:20; Ps. 109:10; Lam. 4:15), connoting her homeless, hapless state.

112. Newsom, "Woman and the Discourse," 153.

113. McKane, *Proverbs*, 314.

114. Unless stated otherwise, all references to oil in the Bible are to olive oil.

115. McKane, *Proverbs*, 314.

116. By itself, wormwood is not poisonous, but it is often linked with "gall," which refers to a bitter and poisonous plant.

117. "Feet" may be a euphemism for the genitalia of both males (Exod. 4:25; Judg. 3:24; Isa. 7:20; cf. Gen. 49:19) and females (Deut. 28:56; Ezek. 16:25). See *HALOT*, 3:1185, s.v. *regel*.

Without home or hope, the strumpet staggers about in her sin (Jer. 14:10; Amos 4:8). *She does not know it*—namely, her total moral failure wherein she can no longer tell right from wrong and so strays into death.

Lesson (5:7–20)

The Folly of Adultery (5:7–14)

The father now specifies the deadly effects of the adulteress. After another urgent call to listen (v. 7) and a command to avoid her (v. 8), he replaces the figurative language of the introduction with facts: economic ruin by strangers without (vv. 9–10) and social ruin by the community within. Verse 11 is a janus between the sinner's economic and social losses. Both will leave him physically and psychologically wrecked as he confesses his regret of refusing instruction (vv. 12–14). In that confession, however, is hope.

7 So now shifts the argumentative tack while continuing with the same subject.[118] The plural *sons* (see 4:1) for lineal descent is appropriate in an argument for retaining the family's wealth and reputation garnered over generations. But the argument shifts to the singular in the rest of the lecture, suggesting that each successive son is addressed. One weak link in the line and generations of prosperity could evanesce. The admonition *listen to me* calls for initial obedience to the teaching and perseverance in it. *And do not turn aside* strikingly contrasts with the straying tracks of the adulteress. *From the words of my mouth* may be added to contrast the father's words with those of the adulteress.

8 The command *keep your* (singular) *way far from her* states the whole lesson in a nutshell (cf. Matt. 5:28–29; 2 Tim. 2:22). People often find their biological drives and social responsibilities in conflict—all the more reason to channel their innate drives within the right form, just as a train engine functions best on tracks. *And to not draw near to the door*, the entry point of *her house*, the place of danger. In short, avoid her entirely.

9 Verses 9 and 10, linked by the repetition of *lest*, introduce the negative results of disobeying the command of v. 8. This repetition suggests that the four groups—"others" and "the cruel" (v. 9), "strangers" and "outsiders" (v. 10)—refer to the same group and the same individuals.[119] The verses proclaim the

---

118. *IBHS* §§39.3.4–5.

119. All four substantive adjectives are masculine, ruling out the possibility that they are references to the adulteress.

son's economic ruin (v. 9) while castigating foreigners (v. 10). Verse 9 refers to the loss of splendor; v. 10 to the loss of strength by which it is acquired. *You give* accuses the adulterer for his own impoverishment. *To others* plausibly refers to the family of the adulteress's husband (cf. 6:24, 29, 34). *Your splendor* designates regal, lofty, or stately dignity and is a metonymy for "the product of the best years of his life."[120] *Your dignity* is a metonymy for the strength that produces wealth; *to the cruel* is a metonymy for the brutal husband who willfully and unrelentingly punishes the voluptuary. Through one generational failure, years of accumulated wealth pass into the hands of an outsider.

10 *Lest strangers be filled* introduces another disadvantage of disobeying the dictum of v. 8. *Your strength* is another metonymy of cause for the product of the son's vital powers. *And your strenuous labors* adds to the figure the pain associated with the hard work. The same word is used in Genesis 3:16 to describe the woman's labor pains in childbearing. His painful acquisitions will be *in an outsider's house*. Evidently, the custom of that day allowed the outraged husband the remedy of subjugating the adulterer to slavery. Today—albeit fornication may not result in slavery—it may lead to alimony, child support, broken homes, hurt, jealousy, loneliness, venereal disease, and sometimes to murder.[121]

11 *And you will groan*, that is, cry in extreme destitution due to belated regret and remorse (cf. Heb. 12:17). *At the end of your life* is when the damages of adultery will be revealed "in terms of destitution and hunger."[122] The "end" refers to the outcome, the future in light of which the whole must be evaluated. "One can never judge life in accordance with the appearance of the moment, but one must keep 'the end' in view."[123] *When your body and your flesh are spent* connotes that the physical body, once vibrant and energetic, is wasted away, exhausted, and about to fail.

12 *And you will say* expresses the profligate's groanings and his fourfold self-condemnation (vv. 12–13). Had the father not warned him, the father

---

120. Gemser, *Sprüche*, 34.

121. Still today in some states there are "alienation of affection" and "criminal conversation"—an old term for illicit sexual intercourse—statutes that allow a jilted party to sue the illicit lover of his or her spouse. In a recent North Carolina case the husband was awarded $8,800,000 against the man who carried on an affair with his wife: https://www.washington-post.com/news/morning-mix/wp/2018/07/31/8-8-million-alienation-of-affection-award-another-reason-not-to-have-an-affair-in-north-carolina/.

122. R. N. Whybray, *Proverbs*, NCBC (London: Marshall Pickering; Grand Rapids: Eerdmans, 1994), 88.

123. Von Rad, *Wisdom in Israel*, 202.

would be guilty (Ezek. 33:1–9). *How* is an exclamation of lamentation. *I hated* reveals an unregenerate heart that rejects the holy. *Instruction* and its parallel *rebuke* (see 3:11) summarize the teachings of his teachers (see v. 13). *My heart* (see "Heart," p. 32) *spurned* further emphasizes his depravity. The confession, however, suggests that the chastisement of losing all led to his salvation (cf. 28:13). It takes humility, repentance, and accepting rebuke to confess like this.

13 *And* connects the fool's rejection of the teaching with his rejection of the teachers. *I did not listen to the voice*—that is, "I did not obey." *My teachers* refers to his parents and to the sages at the gate. *I did not turn my ear to those who taught me* magnifies his *mea culpa*.

14 The profligate's private disgrace now becomes a public disgrace. *I was* looks back to the time he slaved in the stranger's house. *Soon* refers to the speed by which his sin found him out. The metonymy *in serious trouble* may refer to his public humiliation, his excommunication, his flogging (cf. 6:33), or the expropriation of his remaining possessions (cf. Pss. Sol. 16:13–14). Meinhold thinks that the opaqueness of the danger makes it worse.[124] *In the midst of the congregation* denotes a legal gathering at a public trial (also 26:26; cf. Sir. 7:7), as clarified by the parallel *and the assembly*, which denotes a legal body appointed to examine judicial matters and which most likely imposed the "trouble" upon him.

The Wisdom of Marriage (5:15–20)

The father now shifts from the folly of adulterous sex to the joy of marital sex. Using an allegory (vv. 15–17), he teaches marital faithfulness as a prophylactic to the elementary sex urge (vv. 18–19; cf. 1 Cor. 7:9). The joy of lovemaking with one's own wife is a concrete protection from the temptation of sex with the adulteress.

15 The figure, *drink water*, creates ambiguity, but the father risks it to stimulate the son's thinking. The key to its interpretation is given in its parallel in v. 18b: "get pleasure from the wife of your youth." Here, similar to Song 5:1, "drinking water" stands for slaking one's sexual thirst. Satisfying sexual desires is likened to eating food in 30:20 and drinking water in 9:17. *From your own cistern* likens his wife to the prized and private cistern for gathering rainwater in arid Canaan, dug from the rocky ground. Verset b intensifies the imagery from water gathered from rain to *flowing streams* that flow *from the midst*

124. Meinhold, *Sprüche*, 103.

of your own well. Such water, from underground streams that replenish the well, was of better quality. "The image suggests cool, limpid refreshment for hot desires, which are slaked by 'drinking,' that is, lovemaking."[125] While the text assumes the wife belongs to the husband, it is also true that the husband belongs to the wife (cf. 1 Cor. 7:4–5).

16 The ambiguous *should . . . overflow* is best taken as a rhetorical question expecting the answer "No!" (so NIV, NRSV), not as a command, "and let your springs overflow . . ." (so KJV). Many interpreters think *your springs* is an allusion to "generative power" (i.e., male sperm[126]) or to numerous offspring. Thus, the plural subject of v. 17 ("them") is seen as referring to children (i.e. let the children belong to the son alone and not to other families [v. 17]). This interpretation explains the shift from the singular (v. 15) to plural (vv. 16–17) but its flaw is to shift the topic back and forth between sexual refreshment (vv. 15, 18) and offspring (vv. 16–17).

Others think the "springs/channels of water" signify the wife and that the verse is a warning that if the husband abandons his wife for pleasure with an adulteress, other men will sleep with her, since, presumably, she will seek sexual gratification with them. This view keeps the water imagery consistent to the wife and satisfies v. 17b, "have no strangers with you," but it does not explain the shift from singular images for the wife in vv. 15 and 18 to plural images for her in vv. 16–17. Moreover, this view assumes the virtuous wife will become a harlot if neglected.

P. A. Kruger helpfully suggests that the whole allegory depends on the idea of private (in contrast to common) property: a private cistern as opposed to "springs" and *channels of water in the open squares.*[127]

Most likely, then, "springs" refers to *any* female source of sexual satisfaction. The plural precludes the implication that the virtuous wife becomes a harlot. "Open squares" are precisely where harlots plied their trade, while "your channels of water" is another image for the son's sexual satisfaction, which he must not seek *without,* that is, outside his marriage.

17 *Let them* continues the admonition to connubial pleasure, which of necessity must be exclusive: *for yourself alone*—a notion emphasized by the addition *and have no strangers with you.*[128]

---

125. Fox, *Proverbs 1–9,* 199.

126. So Lucas, *Proverbs,* 70.

127. P. A. Kruger, "Promiscuity or Marriage Fidelity?" *JNSL* 13 (1987): 60.

128. In light of the current push to mainstream polygamy and polyamory as superior sexual unions to heterosexual, monogamous marriage, the wisdom of v. 17 is especially

18 The wise father understands his son needs a passionate wife. Therefore, he prays for a wife who will sexually satisfy him quantitatively (at all times) and qualitatively (in the best manner). *May . . . be* is implicitly directed to heaven as a prayer for continual blessing (cf. 1 Kgs. 10:9; Ruth 2:19). *Your wellspring* (see v. 15b). The meaning of *blessed* (see 3:13) is spelled out in v. 19, from which it is evident that it uniquely refers to erotic gratification in this case. *And* (i.e., as a result of the wife's blessed state) the son will *get pleasure* (ebullient, exuberant, and enduring ecstasy) from *the wife*, who mediates sensual pleasure. The father focuses on the son's pleasure to teach the point that sensual man can find a delectation from his wife that no other woman can provide—a point strongly supporting heterosexual monogamous marriage. *Of your youth* may also be "your youthful wife," but the similar expression in 2:17 and Mal. 2:14 validates the given translation. The phrase envisions a lifelong marriage that begins at an early age (see 2:17), and it represents (or, better, anticipates) the son as married.

19 The blessing of v. 18 is now elaborated. *Lovemaking* refers to sensual love in Hos. 8:9, and its congener in Prov. 7:18 refers to physical lovemaking. *Doe* is probably the Iranian fallow deer, which in the adult female reaches a height of 2 ½ ft. and weighs between 64 and 121 pounds. *A graceful mountain goat*, only mentioned here in the Bible, is, according to Meinhold, the ibex or Capricorn. The imagery reflects that culture's use of animals as evocative metaphors of erotica (cf. Song 2:9; 4:5). I (Bruce) appreciated the imagery when I encountered a flock of mountain goats on Tel Hesi and observed their bright, black eyes, their graceful limbs, and their silky hair. *Her breasts*, more precisely the nipples, represents the wife's erogenous members and is associated with sex in its only other uses (Ezek. 23:3, 8, 21).[129] *Drench you* continues the imagery of drinking. The implied liquid, according to the parallel (v. 19c), is the wife's caresses. *At all times*—that is, whenever the son is thirsty. The father prays their lovemaking will be satisfying in quality and continuous in quantity. In the New Testament, the apostle Paul enjoins Christian couples not to deprive one another of connubial sex and to maintain a robust and regular sex life (1 Cor. 7:1–5). *And with her caresses* interprets a word that simply means "love." *May you . . . become intoxicated* (lit. "go astray") likens the drenching from the wife's breasts to intoxicating wine. Fox comments, "The term connotes no disapproval here, but perhaps it bears a slightly 'naughty' overtone by suggestions

---

apt. See for example https://thefederalist.com/2019/11/15/no-human-beings-arent-happier
-when-we-ditch-monogamy-for-polyamory/

129. *HALOT*, 1:214, s.v. *dād*.

of 'straying' deliciously dazed on the ecstasies of lovemaking."[130] The father insists that the marriage bed is not a place for inhibitions. *Always* repeats the father's prayer that the blessed wife's lovemaking always be there to drench and intoxicate her thirsty husband. The Song of Solomon describes the woman's delight in sex, especially through verbal foreplay.

20 *Now* connects the allegory with the lecture. In view of the delights of marital sex, adultery is absurd. *Why* signals a rhetorical question expressing incredulity at the possibility. *Be intoxicated, my son* (see v. 19c). *With* identifies the intoxicant as "the caresses" (omitted through ellipsis) of *the unchaste wife.* "Why" (gapped in verset B) *embrace* (a physical expression of love) *the bosom* (the area below the breasts where loved ones are nuzzled). "Giving into the bosom" is a euphemism for sex in Gen. 16:5. *Of an unfaithful woman*—that is, a woman holding a different worldview.

Conclusion (5:21-23)

In conclusion, the father grounds his lecture in *I AM*'s omniscience (v. 21) and his just moral order (v. 23).

21 *For* introduces the summarizing argument: the omniscient *I AM* upholds moral order wherein the sinner reaps what he sows (Gal. 6:7). *A man's ways* broadens the lecture to everyone; and *all his tracks* broadens it to all behavior. *Are before* (directly in front of) *the eyes of* I AM is a metonymy for God's presence and judgment that upholds the moral order of vv. 22–23. *He is watching*—constantly scrutinizing.

22 *His* narrows the focus to the wicked who commits the *iniquities*, a holistic term that encompasses both the misdeeds and their punishment. Within *I AM*'s moral order, the iniquities themselves entrap the sinner and kill him (cf. 1:18). No thunderbolt from heaven is necessary; rather, sin (personified) *will catch him*—trap him like an animal. *And with the cords of his sin* (see 1:10) depicts sin as holding the cords that capture the sinning sinner. *He will be held fast* for the slaughter. Capture by one's sin is both inevitable and inescapable.

23 *He* (the wicked) *will die* an eternal death, not just a premature physical death. Other than 30:7, where "to die" refers to clinical death, "death" refers to rejection or lack of life-giving instruction (see 10:21; 15:10; 19:16; 23:13). *In his lack of instruction* (see 1:2) refers to the wicked's refusal to imbibe wisdom's

130. Fox, *Proverbs 1–9*, 203.

discipline. *And in the abundance of his folly* (see "Intellectual Terms for the Wicked and Fools," p. 48) *he will be led astray* to death, as shown by the parallel "will die."

❘Appendix: Three Inferior Types of People (6:1–19)

¹My son, if you have become surety for your neighbor,
   [if] you have struck your palm for a stranger,
²you have been ensnared by the word of your lips;
   you have been captured by the words of your mouth.
³So do this, my son, and deliver yourself,
   for you have come into the hand of your neighbor:
   go, weary yourself, and badger your neighbors.
⁴Do not give sleep to your eyes
   nor slumber to your pupils.
⁵Deliver yourself as a gazelle from someone's hand,
   and as a bird from the hand of the fowler.
⁶Go to the ant, you sluggard;
   observe its ways and become wise.
⁷It has no overseer,
   officer, or ruler.
⁸It provides for its grain in summer;
   it gathers in its food in the harvest.
⁹How long, you sluggard, will you keep lying down?
   When will you rise from your sleep?
¹⁰A little sleep, a little slumber,
   a little folding of the arms to lie down,
¹¹and your poverty will come on you like a vagrant,
   your scarcity like an armed man.
¹²A rebel, a malevolent person
   is one who goes with a crooked mouth,
¹³maliciously winks his eyes, shuffles his feet,
   and points with his fingers.
¹⁴Perversions are in his heart; he plans evil at all times.
   He unleashes conflicts.
¹⁵Therefore, suddenly his calamity will come;
   in an instant he will be broken, and without a remedy.
¹⁶There are six [abominations] *I AM* hates;

yea, [they are] seven abominations to him:
¹⁷haughty eyes, a lying tongue,
   and hands that shed innocent blood;
¹⁸a heart that plans malevolent schemes,
   feet that hasten to run to evil,
¹⁹a lying witness—a perjurer—
   and one who unleashes conflicts among relatives.

An appendix to lecture 8 indicts three more inferior types or persons, escalating from the surety (vv. 1–5), to the sluggard (vv. 6–11), and to the malevolent rebel (vv. 12–19). The first two harm themselves; the third harms society. Like the adulterer, the surety risks impoverishment while enriching the "stranger"; the sluggard will be ruined by poverty; and the malicious rebel will be broken by *I AM*. Only the surety is addressed as "my son" (see 4:3). The surety risks his future well-being, and the sluggard does not provide for it; both are warned against untimely sleep. As for the rebel, *I AM* abhors him and will destroy him. The surety and sluggard are not wicked, but their delinquency, if unchecked, could land them in full blown wickedness.

Warning against Becoming Surety (6:1–5)

This lesson consists of an introduction that includes an address and presents the foolish situation of becoming surety to a stranger (vv. 1–2), a main lesson admonishing escape forthwith (vv. 3–4), and a summarizing admonition to extricate oneself immediately from the trap (v. 5).

The Mosaic Law prescribes liberality to the needy (Deut. 15:7–11; cf. Prov. 3:27–28), proscribes taking interest from the poor (Exod. 22:25; Lev. 25:35–36), and allows creditors to take a pledge to secure their loan (Exod. 22:26–27; Deut. 24:10–13, 17; cf. 2 Kgs. 4:1; Neh. 5:3) but does not mention becoming security. Proverbs, however, condemns the practice (6:1; 11:15; 17:18; 20:16; 22:26). Sirach commends the practice as an act of kindness (Sir. 29:14) but warns it has ruined many (Sir. 29:18). The practice is well known in Babylonian and Greco-Roman law. Paul accepted Onesimus's past liabilities but, as Kidner notes, not his future ones (Phm. 18–19).[131]

---

131. Kidner, *Proverbs*, 72.

Introduction: The Foolish Situation (6:1–2)

1 The tender address *my son* shows that becoming security, though imprudent, does not lump the offender with the wicked and fools.[132] *If* (cf. 1:10). To *become surety* is to pledge oneself as a guarantee to pay another's debts should the debtor default. *Your neighbor* (see 3:28) is more narrowly defined by *a stranger* (*zār*)—someone outside the surety's family and community (see 2:16; 5:10; cf. 20:16). *You have struck your palm*—a gesture for sealing the deal (cf. 2 Kgs. 10:15). The surety's motives are not given.

2 A trapping metaphor depicts the danger and the dire consequences of becoming surety: *you have been ensnared.* Snares take victims by surprise and destroy them before they can save themselves. *By the words of your lips* refers to the surety's verbal pledge to the debtor that is sealed by striking hands, probably like today's handshake. The synonymous parallel *captured by the words of your mouth* emphasizes that the surety destroys himself only by his own words.

Lesson: Urgent Admonitions to Resolve the Situation (6:3–4)

3 *So do this my son*: as your careless words entrapped you, so *deliver yourself* by urgent and energetic words. *For you have come into the hand* explains that the surety has lost his freedom and is now in the power of the secured neighbor. Becoming surety is double folly: the surety makes promises for a future he does not control and hands himself to a potential fool. The three commands in verset C aim to rouse the careless son to energetic action. *Go* (act immediately), *weary yourself* (exhaust yourself in giving your neighbor no rest), *and badger* (lit. "rush upon him boisterously"; cf. Isa. 3:5). Like the unjust judge who could not resist the chivying widow (Luke 18:1–5) and the man who could not withstand his pestering friend (Luke 11:8), the secured debtor will be unable to resist the incessant badgering of the surety. The plural *your neighbors* (see 6:1) implies others, such as witnesses, are associated with the secured debtor (see 17:18).

4 *Do not give sleep to your eyes* underscores acting immediately. *Nor slumber to your pupils* probably refers to the period before deep sleep and thus intensifies the urgency to act immediately, while still awake.

---

132. Meinhold (*Sprüche*, 111) interprets the surety as a speculator looking for profit apart from work.

Conclusion: Summary of the Lecture (6:5)

The conclusion recapitulates the admonition *deliver yourself* and the imagery of being trapped in the "hand" of another. The simile *as a gazelle* signifies quick flight, and *from someone's hand* probably refers to hunting gazelles by driving them into natural stone corrals, where they become trapped and from which they are taken by hand to be slaughtered.[133] The additional simile, *as a bird from the hand of the fowler*, intensifies the need for urgent action. Gazelles and birds, once aware they are trapped, fully focus on escaping.

Warning to the Sluggard (6:6–11)

The theme of self-inflicted economic risk and the need for urgent action continues in the lesson on the sluggard, but the agent of affliction is the created order. The sluggard challenges this order, which yields its largess to honest workers but withholds it from those who defy it. Meinhold overstates the case when he says that the surety and the sluggard are similar because both want something but not through honest work.[134] The similarity is rather that both can reverse their plight through diligence.

The lesson's two equal parts (vv. 6-8, 9-11) begin with the vocative "you sluggard" (vv. 6, 9). The first admonishes the sluggard to go and consider the wisdom and energy of the ant, and the second condemns him for his folly and indolence. Nevertheless, Solomon does not render the sluggard hopeless but offers constructive criticism to make him wise before it is too late. All youth are warned against laziness through this fictive admonition (see 1:4; cf. 10:4-5; 13:4; 15:19).

Admonition to Learn Wisdom from the Ant (6:6–8)

6 Again, three commands energize the addressee to industry. *Go* (cf. v. 3) startles the deviant out of his lethargy (cf. Eph. 5:14). *The ant* is probably the harvester ant,[135] which stores grain within its nest and so is a model of prudent industry. *Sluggard* (see "The Sluggard and the Senseless," pp. 49–50). *Observe* connotes looking with moral discernment (cf. 20:12). The ant's *ways* teach

---

133. E. Firmage, "Zoology (Animal Profiles)," in *ABD*, 6:141.

134. Meinhold, *Sprüche*, 111.

135. F. S. Bodenheimer, "Fauna and Flora of the Bible," in *Helps for Translators*, vol. 11 (London: United Bible Societies, 1972), 1.

self-discipline, foresight, and (prudent) industry (cf. 30:25). The sluggard is thus to *become wise* (see "The Wise and Righteous," pp. 34–35). The next two verses detail the ant's wisdom.

7 The ant *has no overseer, officer, or ruler* because it has no need for anyone to force it to work or to deal with disputes about timing, distribution, and division of labor. Instead of needing external control, God has endowed the ant with innate wisdom to work diligently at the right time. Hopefully, through this lesson, the sluggard will internalize this wisdom.

8 The activity leaders perform over a workforce is now detailed and applied to the ant. *It provides for* (i.e., prepares) *its grain* (nourishment) *in summer*, or the *harvest* of April-May—the only available time before winter scarcity (cf. Exod. 16:5; Prov. 30:25). *It gathers in* describes how it prepares *its food*. God provides the food (Pss. 104:14–15; 136:25; 146:7; 147:9), but the ant must diligently harvest it in the right way at the right time and store it for the bad times. Simply put, the ant knows "to make hay while the sun shines."[136]

Condemnation of the Sluggard (6:9–11)

This rebuke of the sluggard presumes his indolence.

9 The accusatory *how long* (see 1:22) presumes the harvest has been ongoing for some time and aims to awaken the sluggard and save him in what little time remains. The repeated vocative *you sluggard* holds him accountable by demanding an answer. *Lying down* in sleep is a sign of carelessness and indolence (cf. Ps. 68:13). *When will you rise?* "Rise" is a metonymy for going to work immediately (see 6:4).

10 The sage now perceptively penetrates the sluggard's psyche, analyzing his behavior and its outcome. *A little* means a small amount. *Sleep* is plural (elsewhere only in 24:33) and refers to a few untimely instances of sleep (see 20:13; 26:14). Sleep is to the sluggard what narcotics are to an addict: the means of escaping the world (26:14). In contrast to the laborer, who has sweet sleep (4:16; Eccl. 5:12), the sluggard craves ever more of his soporific sleep to escape the hard work of living (19:15). *A little slumber* (cf. 6:4; Job 33:15) underscores that the sluggard loses by small surrenders. *A little folding of the arms* (see Eccl. 4:5) signifies his refusal to work in order *to lie down* in sleep. The sluggard's hands betray him (cf. 10:4; 19:24; 21:25). The threefold repetition of "a little" shows, according to Kidner, that "he does not commit himself to a refusal, but

---

136. The Egyptian *Instruction of Ankhsheshonq* 9:17 says, "Whoever does not collect wood in the summer, has no warmth in the winter."

deceives himself by the smallness of his surrenders. So, by inches and minutes, his opportunity slips away."[137]

11 *Poverty* denotes destitution, not merely reduced circumstances (cf. 25:21). It is not luxuries the sluggard lacks; it is food—the basic necessities of life (19:15; 20:13). The sluggard, however, is never described as "poor" or "oppressed," which are terms reserved in Proverbs for those impoverished through no fault of their own and who are a special concern to *I AM* (19:17) and deserve charity. The sluggard may become a beggar, but the sluggard is not a case for charity. *And . . . will come* communicates that destitution is inexorable. Proverbs, unlike Ecclesiastes, is silent about poverty due to natural disasters because it concerns itself solely with improving the morals of youth. However, unlike Job's friends, it does not commit the logical fallacy of attributing all poverty to folly. *Like a vagrant* personifies poverty as a parasitic vagabond panhandling for whatever he can get. *Scarcity* is the lack of life-sustaining essentials. *An armed man* is someone who forcefully takes things and against whom resistance is futile. The simile may paint the vagabond with a sinister color. Ironically, the robber's easiest victim is the sleeping sluggard, who lacks both the vigilance and the diligence to sustain life.

Warning against the Malevolent Rebel (6:12–19)

The lesson on the third and most inferior type of person consists of two strophes of equal length. They were probably originally independent sayings about the malevolent rebel (vv. 12–15) and what *I AM* hates (vv. 16–19). Although the second strophe does not name the agitator, its list of unhealthy body members so closely matches the first strophe's list of abhorrent actions by body parts that the malevolent rebel is the subject of both (cf. lying mouth/tongue, vv. 12b, 17; eyes and hands/fingers, vv. 13, 17; feet, vv. 13, 18; evil-devising heart, vv. 14, 18). The subject of both strophes "unleashes conflict" (14, 19). And so the first strophe predicts the rebel's sudden death (v. 15), and *I AM's* hate (v. 16), by metonymy, is the cause of his death.

Seven Marks of the Malevolent Rebel (6:12–15)

The rebel's seven malevolent body parts, each in its own way, unjustly aims to overthrow the divinely established social order (vv. 12b–14). But in the end, he will be permanently destroyed.

---

137. Kidner, *Proverbs*, 42.

12 A *rebel* (*'ādām bəliyya'al*) denotes one who is implacably evil and who agitates against the good. The term is applied to rebels against God and people (Deut. 13:13; 1 Sam. 2:12; Nah. 1:11, 15), against God's anointed king (1 Sam. 10:27; 2 Sam. 20:1; 2 Chr. 13:7), against justice (1 Kgs. 21:10; Prov. 19:28), against community solidarity (Deut. 15:9; 1 Sam. 30:22; Ps. 101:3), against social propriety (Judg. 19:22; 1 Sam. 1:16), and even against life itself (2 Sam. 22:5; Ps. 41:8). In later Jewish literature and the New Testament, *bəliyya'al* became explicitly a term for the devil, the chief of demons (see 2 Cor. 6:15).[138] *Malevolent person* describes someone who uses power negatively against others.[139] *Who goes with a crooked mouth* metaphorically describes their fraudulent speech that distorts the truth on which a healthy society stands.

13 The agitator gestures sinisterly behind the victim's back (vv. 12b–13) to cohorts who understand his nonverbal speech and conspire with him. *Maliciously winks his eyes* denotes insidious, antisocial behavior. The English "winks" normally connotes playfulness, hence "malicious" is added to clarify its nefarious nature. *Shuffles his feet* may be intended to form a merism with "eyes" to denote all nefarious gestures. *He points his fingers* indicates he is giving instruction to cohorts. Plaut comments: "By his devious and invidious motions he attempts to derogate others and thereby to lower their status in the eyes of associates. In turn, a troublemaker feels superior, and this ego satisfaction is his ultimate desire and goal."[140]

14 By observing the agitator's use of his body parts, the sage penetrates into his heart: *perversions* (see 2:12) *are in his heart* (see "Heart," p. 32). *He plans evil at all times* likens the agitator to those in Noah's time: every imagination of his heart is only evil continually (see Gen. 6:5). *He unleashes conflicts* describes the bitter discord the wicked agitator brings on society.

15 *Therefore* links the agitator's destiny with his deeds. As he abruptly overthrew God's order, *suddenly his calamity will come*. "Suddenly" and its parallel *in an instant* highlight the unexpected nature of the judgment. *He will be broken* metaphorically compares his deserved destruction to his being broken apart violently and rendered as wreckage. The divine passive is made explicit in the next strophe. *And* adds permanence to the suddenness of his ruin: it will be *without remedy*. Nothing can cure or curb the coming calamity (cf. 1:26–28). His ensured end is eternal death.

---

138. Fox, *Proverbs 1–9*, 220.
139. K. H. Bernhardt, *TDOT*, 1:143, s.v. *āven*.
140. Plaut, *Proverbs*, 88.

Catalog of Seven Abominations to *I AM* (6:16–19)

This numerical catalog of what *I AM* abhors (v. 16) is a list of five misused body parts (vv. 17–18) and of two antisocial actions (v. 19). Each abomination ruins its victims and boomerangs to ruin the troublemaker.[141] McKane notes their common elements: "They are all disruptive in their tendency . . . characterized by self-assertiveness or malice or violence, and . . . they break the bond of confidence and loyalty between man and man."[142] At the center of the list is the troublemaker's evil heart, framed by matching pairs hands/feet and the lying tongue/lying witness. "Haughty eyes" and "unleashes conflicts" begin and end the catalog.

16 Collapsing the parallels, *there are six . . . yea, [they are] seven*, the actual number *abominations. I AM hates* means they are separated from his life-giving presence and so consigned to perdition (cf. Pss. 1:6; 104:29).

17 *Haughty eyes*, used of the Assyrian invader in Isa. 10:12–14 and of the proud king in Dan. 11:12, describes one who denies *I AM*'s authority (Job 21:22; 38:15; Ps. 101:5; Isa. 2:11–17; 10:33) and disregards human rights. Gemser thinks this tops the list of abominations because no other vice stands more opposed to wisdom and fear of God,[143] but Meinhold thinks the reason is that the list moves from the top of the body to the bottom.[144] Both may be right. *Lying* signifies "aggressive deceit intended to harm the other . . . even when only the result of words"[145] (cf. Ps. 109:2). *Tongue*—that is, speech. *Hands that shed innocent blood* refers to intentional murder (see 1:11–14). "Contempt for others and for the sanctity of their reputation is but a step away from contempt for the sanctity of life itself."[146]

18 The *heart* (see "Heart," p. 32) *that plans malevolent* (see 6:12) *schemes* is the literary and psychological center of the list. That his *feet . . . hasten to run to evil* is a metaphorical way of describing his zeal to carry out the heart's schemes as soon as possible (cf. 1:16; Ps. 147:15b; Isa. 59:7).

19 *A lying witness* is someone who knowingly lies. Its appositive, *a perjurer*, signifies a deceptive witness and clarifies that the liar is seeking to endanger

---

141. Plöger (*Sprüche*, 65) notes that this list is a summary since some of the vices are individually mentioned in the rest of the Proverbs as abomination sayings: perversity of heart (11:20), false lips (12:19), evil attacks (15:26), and arrogance (16:5).

142. McKane, *Proverbs*, 326.

143. Gemser, *Sprüche*, 31.

144. Meinhold, *Sprüche*, 115.

145. M. A. Klopfenstein, *TLOT*, 3:1400, s.v. *šeqer*.

146. Plaut, *Proverbs*, 89.

the life or property of someone else (cf. Exod. 20:16; Deut. 29:15–21). The *one who unleashes conflicts* (see v. 14) brings the docket of diabolical distinctions to a climactic conclusion. The narrowing of the conflict to *among relatives* describes the worst kind of villainy (cf. 3:27–32) since it destroys the social harmony between closely connected people. Amenemope (ch. 13) warns against deceit because social harmony is its first casualty.[147]

Lecture 9: The High Price of an Unchaste Wife (6:20–35)

[20]Guard my son, your father's commandment,
  and do not let go of your mother's teaching.
[21]Bind them regularly upon your heart;
  fasten them upon your throat.
[22]When you walk, she will lead you;
  when you lie down, she will guard you.
  Then you will awake, [and] she will speak to you.
[23]For the commandment is a lamp, and the teaching is a light,
  and corrections of instruction are the way of life,
[24]to guard you from your neighbor's wife
  and from the smoothness of the unfaithful wife's tongue.
[25]Do not covet her beauty in your heart,
  and do not let her capture you with the pupils of her eyes;
[26]for the price of a prostitute can be reduced to a loaf of bread,
  but the wife of a man hunts for precious life.
[27]Can a man carry fire in his bosom
  and his clothes not be burned?
[28]Or can a man walk about on glowing coals
  and his feet not be branded?
[29]So is the one who enters into his neighbor's wife;
  all who touch her will not escape punishment.
[30]People do not show contempt for a thief if he steals
  to satisfy his appetite when he is hungry;
[31]but if he is caught, he must repay sevenfold;
  all the wealth of his household he will give.
[32]The adulterer is one who lacks sense;
  as for one who ruins his own life, he does it.

147. Cf. Fox, *Proverbs 1–9*, 224.

³³He will find strokes and shame,
>   and his reproach will not be wiped away.
³⁴For jealousy [arouses] the wrath of a man,
>   and he will not show compassion when he exacts revenge.
³⁵He will not accept any compensation,
>   and he will not yield though you enlarge the bribe.

Lecture 9 consists of a typical introduction (vv. 20–24) and a lesson against adultery (vv. 25–35). Matching lecture 8 (5:1–23), it completes the frame around a threefold collection describing inferior types of people (6:1–19). The lesson proper is given in the third person (vv. 25–34), but the last verse forges an inclusio by returning to the second person address of the introduction.

Introduction (6:20–24)

As is typical, the introduction includes an address to the son, an admonition to preserve the parental teaching (vv. 20–21), and a motivation: their teaching guides and protects the faithful son (vv. 22–24)—here, specifically, from the "unfaithful wife" (v. 24; see 2:16–19). "Guard" the teaching (v. 20) and the teaching will "guard" you (v. 24) frames the introduction.[148] The call to heed the father's teaching matches Moses's call to Israel to heed the Law. Both the father's teaching and the Law are to be bound on the person (cf. v. 21; Deut. 6:6–9; 11:8, 18–20), to give constant guidance (v. 21; Deut. 6:7; 11:19), and to be a lamp and a light (see Ps. 119:105).

20 *Guard* (naṣōr; see 3:1), *my son* (see 1:8), *your father's commandment, and do not let go of your mother's teaching* repeats 1:8.

21 *Bind them regularly* (or "constantly") *upon your heart* (see "Heart," p. 32) is a metaphorical reference to memorizing the teaching so that it permanently permeates the heart, from which spring all actions (see 4:23). *Fasten them upon your throat* (see 1:9).

22 *Walk* means "to walk with, commune."[149] The antecedent of the singular *she* implies the parental "command" and "teaching" (v. 20), a hendiadys for their authoritative teaching, and subtly pits their teaching against the rival, the adulteress (see 1:8–9:18). *Will lead you* personifies their authoritative teaching as a shepherdess (cf. Pss. 23:1; 77:20), who will lead the son through dangers

---

148. Two synonymous Hebrew words for "guard" are used to create a frame around the introduction.

149. *IBHS* §§26.1.2b, d.

to a good destiny (Exod. 15:13; 32:34; Deut. 32:12; Pss. 5:8; 23:3; 78:14, 53). *When you lie down, she will guard* (see 2:8, 11; 3:21, 26; 4:6) communicates her protection even when the son is most vulnerable. *Then you will awake* implies protection during the dangerous night (see 3:24) and connotes attentiveness to the teaching as the first task of the day. The metaphor *speak* refers to the internalized wisdom and means loud, enthusiastic speech that is as good as being audible. In sum, the internalized, authoritative parental teaching functions as a superego that leads, protects, and counsels (cf. Deut. 11:18–20).

23 *For* explains, by a new metaphor, the reason: *the commandment is a lamp* and *the teaching is a light*. Exposing dark wrongdoings and showing the right way (cf. Job 18:5–6; 29:3; Prov. 13:9), they become the *corrections* (see 1:23) *of instruction*, a collocation for correcting what is wrong and establishing what is right (see 3:11 and 5:12). The plural implies that the authoritative teaching rights all wrongs, not just adultery. And so, resuming the metaphor of a "way" implied in "when you walk" (v. 22), they *are the way* (see 1:15) *of life* ("The Wise and Their Rewards: Life," p. 41). In sum, the authoritative parental teaching illuminates the way of abundant life on which the son will be protected from hidden danger.

24 Exposing the dark, nefarious ways of the adulteress and providing the way of life, the authoritative parental teaching functions *to guard you from your neighbor's wife*, more specifically from *the smoothness of the unfaithful wife's* (see "The Unfaithful Wife," pp. 55–56; 2:16; 5:20; 7:5) *tongue*, a metonymy for her talk, which is dramatically illustrated in the next lecture (7:13–21). To the tempted, her speech is smooth and seductive; to the parents it is slippery and sly. All four passages on the adulteress describe her speech as "smooth" (2:16; 5:3; 6:24; 7:5). Her weaponized tongue aims to rip apart the godly home at the seam where the generations are sewn together.

Lesson (6:25–35)

The admonition to the son not to desire the adulteress (v. 25) is supported by the argument: it will cost the son his life (vv. 26, 32–35). Within that frame, the argument is developed that the cost of adultery is severe, certain, and ceaseless (vv. 26–31). The lesson ends with the explanation that the cuckold will settle for nothing other than the total destruction of the adulterer (vv. 32–35).

Admonition (6:25)

25 The admonition is pointedly brief. *Do not covet* (or "crave"; see 1:22)—a desire induced by *her* physical *beauty*. Only when attended by the fear of

I AM does beauty represent the biblical feminine ideal (5:18–20; 11:22; 31:30; Cf. 1 Sam. 25:3). The command assumes people can govern their hearts (Prov. 4:23) by binding the parental teaching to it (6:21). Paul knew from experience that one needs the empowering Holy Spirit, not just volition, to resist temptation (Rom. 8:13; 2 Cor. 3:7–18). *And do not let her capture you* shifts the perspective from the man's role to the woman's role. *The pupils of her eyes* are the means by which she arouses lust. Verses 24 and 25 reverse the actual sequence: coveting begins with eye contact leading to desire, followed by sweet talk. The son must guard himself against both her verbal and nonverbal modes of seduction. Sin begins in lust and in the imagination and must be nipped in the bud (Jas. 1:14–16).

Argument (6:26–35)

The *severity* of the penalty for adultery is illustrated by contrasting the price of a prostitute, a meal, with the price of the adulteress, one's life (v. 26); its *certainty* by comparing adultery to getting burned when playing with fire (vv. 27–29); and its *ceaselessness* by contrasting adultery with thievery: a thief can make restitution, the adulterer cannot (vv. 30–31).

The Severe Price of Adultery: One's Life (6:26)

26 Logical *for* introduces the first argument. *The price of a prostitute,* who offers sex for hire, *can be reduced to a loaf of bread* (i.e., a meal), *but the wife of a man* (the adulteress) *hunts for precious life.* As Plöger notes, whereas a prostitute is satisfied with a relatively small payment, a "loaf of bread," the adulteress hunts for the most precious thing of all: life.[150] The metaphor "hunts" signifies the use of her voice and eyes to stalk her prey (the son, v. 25; cf. 7:6–20). As for the morality of this argument, by this contrast the father no more endorses prostitution than his contrasting adultery with thievery endorses stealing. The New Testament warns that those who engage in prostitution will meet God's wrath and be excluded from his kingdom (1 Cor. 6:13–20; Gal. 5:19–21; Eph. 5:5; 1 Thess. 4:1–8). Nevertheless, adultery is worse because it involves breaking the marriage vow, wronging a spouse, destroying a home, and paying the ultimate price: one's precious life.[151]

---

150. Plöger, *Sprüche,* 69.

151. This was illustrated by the hack of a prominent website dedicated to providing adulterous liaisons. Ashley Madison, which justifies its immorality with the diabolical

The Certainty of the Punishment (6:27–29)

27–29 The argument now shifts to the certainty of the penalty, with two illustrations from fire (vv. 27, 28). The question *can*—an invitation to think—*a man carry fire in his bosom and his clothes not be burned* demands the experiential answer "of course not." "Fire" should be carried in a firepan (Exod. 27:3; Lev. 10:1) or clay shard (25:22; Isa. 30:14). "Burned" represents the permanent, painful, and life-threatening damage of foolish behavior (cf. 2:19; 5:9–14). *Or can a man walk about on glowing coals and his feet not be branded?* "Feet" may evoke an association with the sexual organ (see 5:5), in which case, touching this "hot" woman will burn more than the "feet." *So* draws out the moral from the two illustrations. *The one who enters into*—a powerful metonymy for sex (see 2:19). *His neighbor's wife* clarifies that adultery, not prostitution, is in view. *All who touch her* (that is, have sex with her; see Gen. 20:6; 1 Cor. 7:1) *will not escape punishment* (the literal reality behind "not be burned/branded"). Verses 30–35 clarify the form of permanent punishment.

The Penalty Is Unceasing (6:30–31)

30–31 The ceaselessness of the adulterer's pain is argued by contrasting the temporary social stigma of the thief who transgresses to satisfy alimentary hunger with that of the adulterer who transgresses to satisfy sexual hunger. *People do not show contempt for a thief if he steals.* Even godly Agur assumes that if he becomes too poor, he will steal (30:9). While stealing is a crime under any circumstance (Exod. 20:15; Deut. 5:19; Prov. 30:8–9; Eph. 4:28), society is willing to cut the thief some slack due to exigent circumstances, such as *to satisfy his appetite when he is hungry* (i.e., famished, as in a famine; see Gen. 41:55; Isa. 8:21; 9:20). *But,* even though he is not despised, *if he is caught,* the thief *must repay,* a technical term for making restitution. The Law prescribes penalties for stealing ranging from double to fivefold depending on the circumstances (Exod. 22:7, 9; 22:1; cf. Luke 19:8), but never *sevenfold,* which

---

copyrighted epigram, "Life is short. Have an affair," and boasts a client list in excess of 57 million, guaranteed its clients 100 percent confidence. However, in 2015 it was hacked, and many of its clients were outed, including some prominent evangelical leaders. Some clients committed suicide as a result. See Abby Phillip, "Why the wife of a pastor exposed in Ashley Madison hack spoke out after his suicide," *The Washington Post*, September 9 2015, https://www.washingtonpost.com/news/acts-of-faith/wp/2015/09/09/why-the-wife -of-a-pastor-exposed-in-ashley-madison-leak-spoke-out-after-his-suicide/?noredirect=on &utm_term=.5fac4fa4795f.

symbolically represents full compensation (cf. Gen. 4:15; Lev. 26:28; cf. Matt. 18:21–22). The parallel *all the wealth of his household he will give* indicates that he loses everything, and thus his freedom, and so becomes a slave (see Exod. 22:3b; Mic. 2:2).

Explanation of the Penalty: The Cuckold Will Exact Revenge (6:32–35)

32 The argument climaxes with an explanation of why the penalty for adultery is so severe, inevitable, and endless. *The adulterer is one who lacks sense* (that is, lacks good judgment). He is *one who ruins* (totally devastates) *his own life* (see v. 26). *He* (the adulterer) *does it* (the self-destruction). The unfaithful wife tempts him, but the resulting ruin is his responsibility.

33 His ruin is elaborated. *He will find* physical and social ruin (see 5:9–10). *Strokes* refers to a violent and painful assault; it may be inflicted by others (Deut. 17:8; 21:5; 2 Sam. 7:14), by God (Exod. 11:2), or by disease (Lev. 13–14). *Shame* (see 3:35) and "strokes" are felt as a hendiadys: strokes that shame. Perhaps a pagan court and a public flogging are in view. If the son's adultery had been with an Israelite woman, not a pagan, the punishment in the Israelite court would be death (see 5:14; cf. Lev. 20:10; Deut. 22:22; Ezek. 23:45–47). Prostitution and marriage to foreign women, though forbidden, were not capital offenses (cf. Gen. 38:15; Lev. 19:29; 21:7, 9; Deut. 23:17–18; Ezra 9:1; Neh. 13:23–27).[152] *And his reproach* (the unending disgrace a healthy society piles on one who threatens to destroy its fabric) *will not be wiped out*. The punishment is designed to nullify the adulterer's significance, worth, and influence.

34 A logical *for* introduces the reason: The adulterer is unable to compensate the cuckold's implacable *jealousy*—his zeal for that which rightly belongs to him (Num. 5:14–15, 18, 25, 29–30; Prov. 27:4). His strong passion inflames his *wrath* against the rake who wronged him (Prov. 15:18; Isa. 34:2; Jer. 6:11). By its nature, "wrath" is cruel, merciless, and exacerbated when fanned by jealousy (27:4). The infuriated husband is designated a strong *man* (*geber*). *And he will not show compassion when he exacts revenge*, meaning his wrath is implacable, and he will not be bought off or hold back any pain he can inflict on the rake. According to Peels, 'vengeance' refers to "the legitimate righteous execution of punishment by a competent authority." Accordingly, the vengeful husband

---

152. The account of Jesus and the woman caught in adultery in John 8:3–11 is not found in the earliest manuscripts. In any case, Jesus spared her because the hypocrites who would stone her were as guilty as she.

will not strike a blow, but makes the case public after which the community is to execute the sentence.[153]

35 The cuckold will use the courts to exact his pound of flesh and *will not accept* (will not be favorably disposed to) *any compensation* to reduce the pain he can inflict on the cad. "Compensation" denotes a gift that assuages a plaintiff; here it refers to a ransom for one's life. *And he will not yield* (not consent to reduce the pain) *though you* (the father now addresses the son directly as if the son were the adulterer) *enlarge the bribe.* Bribery was forbidden in the Mosaic law (Exod. 23:8; Deut. 10:17; 16:19; 27:25; Prov. 17:8, 23; 21:14) but not in other ANE cultures. According to J. Finkelstein, "[Bribery] was not only a common practise, but was recognized as a legal transaction."[154] That view fits well this context pertaining to foreigners.

Lecture 10: The Adulteress's Seductive Tactics (7:1–27)

> [1]My son, keep my sayings,
>> and my commands store up with you;
> [2]keep my commands and live.
>> and [protect] my teaching as the pupil[155] of your eye;
> [3]bind them upon your fingers.
>> Write them on the tablet of your heart;
> [4]say to wisdom, "You are my sister,"
>> and call out to insight, "You are my relative,"
> [5]to keep you from the unfaithful wife,
>> from the unchaste wife who causes her words to be smooth.
> [6]For standing at the window of my house,
>> through the opening I looked down.
> [7]And I saw among the uncommitted,
>> I gave heed among the sons to a youth who lacked sense.
> [8]He was passing through the street beside her corner;
>> he was taking strides on the way to her house,
> [9]at dusk, in the evening of the day,
>> with the approach of night and darkness.
> [10]And look! A woman comes out to face him

---

153. H. G. L. Peels, "Passion or Justice? The Interpretation of *beyôm nāqām* in Proverbs VI 34," *VT* 44 (1994): 270–72.

154. J. Finkelstein, "The Middle Assyrian *Shulmanu*-Texts," *JAOS* 72 (1952): 77–80.

155. Lit. "apple," a figure for pupil. "Protect" is added to signify the meaning of the figure.

in the garb of a harlot and with a cunning heart.
[11]She is unruly and defiant;
    her feet do not settle down in her house;
[12]now in the street, now in the squares,
    and beside every corner she lies in wait.
[13]And she grabbed him and kissed him;
    she hardened her face and said to him:
[14]"I owed a fellowship sacrifice;
    today I fulfilled my vows.
[15]Therefore, I came out to face you,
    to seek your face diligently, and I found you!
[16]I have provided my couch with coverlets,
    embroidered stuff, the linen of Egypt.
[17]I have perfumed my bed
    with myrrh, lign-aloes, and cinnamon.
[18]Come, let us drink our fill with making love until morning;
    let us enjoy each other with love;
[19]for my husband is not at home;
    he went on a distant journey.
[20]He took in his hand a purse filled with silver;
    he will come home at full moon."
[21]She turned him aside with her immense persuasiveness;
    with the blandishments of her lips she routed him.
[22]He went after her suddenly,
    as an ox enters a slaughterhouse,
    and as a stag stepping into a noose[156]
[23]until an arrow splits open his liver;
    as a bird hastens into a trap.
    And he does not know [he acts] against his own life.
[24]So now, sons, listen to me;
    pay attention to the words of my mouth.
[25]Do not let your heart turn aside into her ways;
    do not go astray into her paths.
[26]For she has toppled many slain [victims],
    even the powerful, all those killed by her.
[27]Her house presents the ways to the grave,
    descending to the chambers of death.

---

156. The text of v. 22c is uncertain, but its meaning is clear.

This fourth (cf. 2:16–19; 5:1–23; 6:20–35) and climactic lecture warning the son against the adulteress exposes her seductive tactics. In a gripping eyewitness narrative, the father graphically delineates the danger of the adulteress by narrating how she seduced a susceptible dimwit. Though given as an eyewitness account, it is artistic fiction. Yet the account is true to life. Against her tempting images of dining on savory meats, smelling rare spices, and making love on a lush lounge, he launches counter images of an ox going to the slaughter, a stag stepping into a noose, and a bird flying into a trap. With the climactic last word, he exposes her for what she is: a lush in league with death.

The lesson's structure suggests the father's urgency to protect his son. The introduction (vv. 1–4) calls the son to attention, first plainly (vv. 1–2), then figuratively (vv. 3–4). The lesson (vv. 6–23) presents the argument in the form of an autobiographical, eyewitness account in which the father characterizes the adulteress's dress, cunning, essential nature, and aggressive actions. Most of all, he attends to her words, which compete with his to woo the son away from wisdom. The conclusion (vv. 24–27) admonishes him to stay clear of her. The janus (v. 5) states the father's aim of protecting his son against the smooth talk of the adulteress, who may also function as a symbolic representation of a seductive worldview alien to true Israel, God's son.[157]

Introduction: Address and Admonition to Hear (7:1–5)

1 The address and admonition, *my son, keep my sayings,* emphasized by the synonymous parallelism of 1b, *and my commands store up with you,* stand in sharp opposition to the adulteress's words (7:5, 13; cf. v. 21).

2 The unique repetition of *keep* (vv. 1a, 2a) and *my commands* (vv. 1b, 2a) emphasizes the importance of the parental teaching. *And live*—memorizing and obeying the teaching will lead to abundant life, a stark contrast with the threat of eternal death from listening to the adulteress (v. 27; cf. 2:16–17). *My teaching* (the commands) is so precious that the son is ordered to protect it *as the pupil of your eye,* the most precious part of the human anatomy (cf. 3:14–26; 8:11; 31:10). The pupil is essential for illumination and guidance. Without it—darkness (cf. Deut. 32:10). The imagery emphasizes what requires the most protection.

3 *Bind them upon your fingers* is a metaphor for memorizing, and constantly recalling, the commands. *Write them on the tablet of your heart* escalates the

---

157. Since it is a narrative, the reader must utilize the poetics appropriate to interpreting narrative theology (see "Poetics," pp. 13–15).

outward metaphor for memorizing and retaining the teaching to the inward governing center of the being. The figure connotes the indelible impression of the instruction on one's character so that one keeps it from within (2:2; 4:23; cf. Jer. 31:31–34). Christian theologians substitute the concept of regeneration for this metaphor (cf. John 3:1–16).

4 The impersonal metaphor of writing the teaching now changes to the personal metaphor of marrying it and thus avoiding the temptation to lust. *Say* indicates a performative speech act that entails marrying *wisdom* (see "What Is 'Wisdom'?" pp. 27–28). *You are my sister* is probably love language signifying the groom's commitment to his bride (Song 4:9, 10, 12; 5:1, 2; Sir. 15:2; cf. Tob. 7:16).[158] *Call out to insight* intensifies "say" while adding the notion of intellectual discernment and interpretation to wisdom. *You are my relative*, the parallel to "you are my sister," underscores the son's commitment to the parental teaching as to a family member. Such a committed and endearing relationship with wisdom will provide a powerful prophylactic to the attractive allurements of the adulteress.

5 The janus verse concludes the introduction by making plain the purpose of embracing the teaching: *to keep you from the unfaithful wife*. Meanwhile, *from the unchaste wife who causes her words to be smooth* transitions to the lesson featuring her smooth speech.

Lesson: The Adulteress's Seductive Tactics (7:6–23)

The lesson has three parts: (1) the encounter as witnessed by the father (vv. 6–13); (2) the woman's smooth talk (vv. 14–20); and (3) the father's concluding statement of how well it worked (vv. 21–23).

Encounter (7:6–13)

The father describes the setting of the encounter (vv. 6–9) and the character of the woman (vv. 10–13).

6 *For* is explanatory. *At the window* symbolically represents the father's separation from the adulteress's world and his looking down upon it from a different worldview (cf. 2 Sam. 6:16). *Of my house* contrasts the domiciled father with the streetwalker. *Opening* is a synonym for "window." *I looked down* presumes a two-story house and transitions to the rest of the lecture, which is vividly narrated in the first person.

---

158. In Eighteenth Dynasty Egyptian material (ca. 1500–1300 B.C.), "sister" is a term of endearment for one's beloved.

7 The father draws the lesson from the street scene occurring below him. *The uncommitted* (see "Intellectual Terms for the Wicked and Fools," p. 47) are those youth who refuse to commit to wisdom prior to entering the city and so make easy pickings for the wicked (cf. 1:20). *I gave heed* means the father used all his faculties to understand (cf. 24:23). *Sons*, a parallel to "the uncommitted," brings to mind the loving filial relationship that the uncommitted youth should have had with his parents (cf. 1:8; 4:3) and thus the failure to pass wisdom between the generations. The *youth* is about to betray that relationship and squander the family's heritage. Furthermore, *he lacked sense* (see p. 50).

8 *He was passing through the street beside her corner*, where she resided, not where she met him (v. 12). Here we see his fundamental flaw: without wisdom the youth is clueless as to the danger of wandering through darkening streets in her "hood." *He was taking strides* suggests a pompous gait. *On the way to her house* does not mean he deliberately headed to her house, since she has to come out to meet him and persuade him to accompany her. Rather, his folly is leading him into moral jeopardy.

9 And so he ends up in the wrong place at the wrong time. Every phrase or word in the scenic depiction of v. 9 pertains to darkness. *At dusk* refers to the onset of evening darkness. Since "dusk" can mean either morning or evening twilight, *in the evening of the day* disambiguates it. *With the approach of night and darkness* clarifies it even further. The darkness simultaneously symbolizes the moral darkness of the foreign adulteress and the dark destiny now "approaching" her victim.

10 With an exclamation *and look!*, the father brings his audience into the scene to see with their own eyes the sudden appearance of *a woman* (see 2:16). Placing her center-stage, he characterizes her by her bold approach in a provocative dress, her deep-seated motives, and her brazen, confrontational kiss (v. 13). She knows her victim and so boldly *comes out to face him in the garb of a harlot*, which simultaneously draws his attention and stimulates his lust. Through observing her dress, the father insightfully understands her *cunning heart*. To him, her outrageous outfit outs her inner intentions, but to the morally stupid, it is a camouflage.[159] She is only interested in satisfying her own lusts. When her husband is at home, she feigns fidelity to him, but when he is away, she flatters her paramour as her one true love. She uses both and loves none. She knows that, if caught, her hard-fisted husband will take all that her victim owns while society will strip him of all his dignity (5:7–14; 6:33–35). But

---

159. Plöger, *Sprüche*, 78.

she does not fear or care. If caught, she knows how to frame him, as Potiphar's wife framed Joseph.

11 In a parenthetical aside, the sage, by his powers of keen observation and cogent reflection, exposes two more characteristics of the adulteress's psyche. *She is unruly* denotes ceaseless, tumultuous movement—opposite behavior to that of the peaceful woman (cf. 1 Pet. 3:1–6). *And defiant* indicates her rebellion against propriety. Her insurrection is confirmed by observing that *her feet do not settle down in her house*, even as night approaches. She is not the religious woman she pretends to be.

12 Verset A further develops her unruly disposition. She is constantly on the prowl, *now in the street, now in the squares*. Had the gullible youth observed and reflected on this behavior, he would not have been deceived when she told him she sought him out. Verset B documents her rebellion against ordered society: *she lies in wait* (or "ambush"; see 1:11, 18; 12:6) *beside every corner*. She is a predator, and as predators lurk where game is thick, she lurks at street corners where people congregate. The uncommitted youth naively strays into territory unknown to him but home turf to her.

13 After the aside, this verse picks up the narrative of v. 10. *And*, upon meeting him (v. 10a), *she grabbed him and kissed him*, presumably on the lips. Though holding and kissing are normally acts of tenderness (Song 3:4; 8:1), here it is a rapacious act meant to overpower her prey. *She hardened her face*—that is, became brazen and shameless in behavior (cf. Deut. 28:50; Eccl. 8:1, 2a; Ezek. 3:7–9; Jer. 3:3). Garrett argues that the phrase also means she told a bold-faced lie.[160] *And she said to him* transitions to her speech in vv. 14–20. Her tactics are predatory.[161]

Seduction: The Adulteress's Smooth Speech (7:14–20)

Her seduction has two phases. First (vv. 14–17), she convinces him that her intentions are sincere by telling him she needs a sexual partner for religious reasons (v. 14), that he is the ideal partner (v. 15), and that she has the ideal place for uninhibited lovemaking (vv. 16–17). Second (vv. 18–20), she seals the deal by propositioning him with the assurance that they have nothing to fear.

14 Disguising her true intentions, she masks her lust with piety. *I owed a*

---

160. D. Garrett, "Votive Prostitution Again: A Comparison of Proverbs 7:13–14 and 21:28–29," *JBL* 109 (1990): 681–82.

161. A. Brenner and F. van Dijk-Hemmes, *On Gendering Texts: Female and Male Voices in the Hebrew Bible* (Leiden: Brill, 1993), 59.

fellowship sacrifice is a reference to the peace offering practiced by both Israelites and Canaanites that was meant to unite deity, priests, worshipper, and guests through the sharing of the sacrifice (Lev. 7:11-21; 1 Sam. 9:11-13; Jer. 7:21). After the deity consumed the burning fat and intestines and the priests took their share of the meat, the rest was eaten as a communal meal at home by the worshipper and invited guests. Ironically, this woman cares nothing for true community. A specific type of fellowship sacrifice was the votive sacrifice, in which a person vowed to offer a sacrifice if the deity granted a request. She claims, *Today I fulfilled my vows*, implying she has food at home that needs to be consumed. According to Mosaic law, and presumably Canaanite practice, the sacrificial meal had to be eaten on the day of the sacrifice or on the following day. The connection here between sex and religion has led some scholars to posit that she is inviting the youth to participate in foreign fertility religion.[162] If she is a Canaanite, then the communal meal would also have involved sexual intercourse (Exod. 32:1-6; Num. 25:1ff.)—hence her need for a sexual partner. But is she really religious or merely pretending? She lies about how she happened to meet the young man (vv. 11-13, 15), and probably also about her husband, since the youth is caught (vv. 19-23). So why should she be believed about her piety?

15 *Therefore* assumes her connection to fertility religion. *I came out to face* confirms the father's observation (v. 10). She now flatters him by saying she came out *to seek . . . your face diligently*, an idiom meaning "to request" and connoting it was his looks that made him stand out from the crowd, when in fact it was his dimwitted naivety that made him the ideal dupe. Thus, she says climactically, *I found you*—"you alone, you hunk of a man"—idolizing him in an effort to mask her concupiscence.

16 Following the flattery, she fans his lust with a vision of her luxurious lounge. *I have provided my couch with coverlets* means she has provided a bed with covers; the phrase points to its sensual comfort. She highlights its aesthetic appeal: *embroidered stuff, the linen of Egypt*, referring to the red-colored linen exported by Egypt.

17 Next, she stimulates his olfactory senses. She names three perfumes, which are all found in Song 4:14 as aromatic images of sex. *I perfumed my bed*, if bed is a synonym for "couch" (v. 16), now portrays it as a place for making love (Gen. 49:4; Isa. 57:7-8). The perfumes are *myrrh*, a fragrant gum-resin obtained from tapping Arabian or African balsam trees; *lign-aloes*, a precious

---

162. Leo G. Perdue, *Wisdom and Cult: A Critical Analysis of the Views of Cult in the Wisdom Literature of Israel and the Ancient Near East* (Missoula, MT: Scholars, 1977), 150.

spice from the Southeast Asian and north Indian eaglewood tree; and *cinnamon*, obtained from the bark of the cinnamon tree, native to Sri Lanka and the Indian coast. These perfumes would have been obtained at great cost from merchants traveling great distances. The merchant's wife alleges she is willing to spend all this to satisfy her lust.

In vv. 18–20, she makes her proposition.

18 *Come* suggests they do it immediately. To *drink our fill of lovemaking* means "to be saturated" with erotic love. The word *dōdîm*, here rendered "lovemaking," always refers to a sexual relationship, and in the Song of Solomon it is strongly erotic (Song 5:1). *Until morning* suggests they pass the night slowly, trying every form of lovemaking. *Let us enjoy each other with love* focuses on the reciprocal pleasure of erotic love awaiting them. She promises him unrestrained sex while withholding the fundamental commitment of self that is the basis of true love. She wants his body, not him.

19 Her final argument aims to remove any fear of her husband catching them *in flagrante delicto* (6:34-35). *For* introduces why they have nothing to fear. Her reason, similar to that which Satan gave to Eve ("You will not die," Gen 3:4) denies the deed-destiny nexus, the absence of which undermines the whole basis of biblical ethics. "In Proverbs 7 . . . the woman does not seek to convince her prey that adultery is right, but only that they can get away with it because her husband is not at home."[163] She calls *my husband* "the man," but the idiom is normal in Hebrew and does not indicate disparagement. Similarly, *at home* is a dynamic equivalent translation for the Hebrew "his house," another idiom that does not suggest they are emotionally alienated. She clearly states that she is only after sex and is not interested in divorcing her husband and marrying the dimwit. She tells him her husband will be back in two weeks, indicating she intends to stay married, albeit unfaithfully. This renders the gullible youth without moral excuse for his adultery. He should have known not to trust her when her very argument reveals she is deceptive and unfaithful. Her proof that *he went on a distant journey* is probably a lie, judging from the quick and dire consequences (v. 22-23; cf. 5:9-10).

20 To reinforce the fact that they have nothing to fear, she adds that not only is her husband physically distant (v. 19), he is also temporally distant. *He took in his hand a purse* indicates he is on a business trip. *Filled with silver* means he has a lot of business and so will be long away. But *he will come home*

---

163. C. V. Camp, "Woman Wisdom as Root Metaphor: A Theological Consideration," in *The Listening Heart: Essays in Wisdom and the Psalms in Honor of Roland E. Murphy, O. Carm.*, ed. K. G. Hoglund et al., JSOTSup 58 (Sheffield: Sheffield Academic, 1987), 51.

and will find things status quo. All she wants is to indulge her lusts for one night, not to change her life—certainly not for a dimwit like this young man. *At full moon* implies he is gone for a fortnight. Her argument is plausible in that travelers preferred traveling during the full moon, as it was less dangerous. She does not care about other witnesses who may report them to the husband. Should her husband break in on them, we may assume she will accuse the youth of rape (cf. Gen. 39:6b-20).

The Uncommitted Youth's Submission (7:21-23)

The father concludes his narrative with the deadly effectiveness of her speech.

21 Her speech works. *She turned him aside* actually and metaphorically; by turning his lust toward her, she also turned his steps to her boudoir. *With her immense persuasiveness* denotes she took control of him with her extensive smooth talk. *With the blandishments of her lips* further qualifies her effective speech. *She routed him* signifies that her seduction drove the sucker from the way of life into her house, the gateway to death.

22 *He went after her suddenly* implies that the dimwit acted impulsively, without reflection, allowing his glands to do the thinking for him. The sage then interprets the encounter by three animal comparisons that illustrate how the dimwit ignorantly rushes to death. The first simile, *as an ox enters a slaughterhouse,* compares the victim to the powerful king of domesticated animals, which is nevertheless dispatched to an instant death when its neck is slit beneath the jugular. The image implies that the dimwit, by following his animal instincts, sacrifices all his endowed opportunities, his strength, and even his life. The second simile, *and as a stag,* intensifies the fatal reality and adds to the bull's strength the deer's grace, while *stepping into a noose* adds the idea of entrapment.

23 *Until an arrow splits open his liver* is best connected to the trapped stag in v. 22c. The meaning is clear: the victim meets a fatal end (see vv. 26-27). The aim of the text is not to identify the shooter, only the deadly effect of the shot. The Hebrew word "liver" is derived from the Semitic root "to be heavy," implying it is full of blood. Thus, to split open the core of the animal's blood supply means instant death. The third simile, *as a bird hastens into a trap,* highlights the speed with which the dimwit meets his end. The implied notion of the ignorance of the doomed animals is now made explicit as the sage wraps up the lesson: *and he does not know he [acts] against his own life.* Dumb animals, blinded by the trap, see no connection between traps and death, and morally stupid people, blinded by Satan, see no connection between sin and death (cf. 1:17-18; Hos. 7:11).

Conclusion (7:24-27)

The father draws the lecture to a conclusion with a renewed double admonition to stay clear of the adulteress (vv. 24–25), fortified by a renewed double motivation (vv. 26–27).

24 The conclusion emphatically repeats the call to listen to the father's teaching. *So now, sons* extends the teaching to the lineage of sons. *Listen to me* repeats verbatim the exhortation of 5:7, the first full lecture against the adulteress. In the emphatic parallel, *the words of my mouth* are needed to counter the adulteress's mouth.

25 *Your heart* (see "Heart," p. 32). *Her ways* is an incomplete metaphor for her dark deceptions, unrestrained lust, betrayal of her husband, tyranny against society, and calloused indifference to the youth's fate. The synonymous parallel, *do not go astray into her paths*, emphasizes the prohibition and implies a warning to stick to the straight path of wisdom.

26 *For* introduces the two reasons for the two admonitions in vv. 24–25. First, *she has toppled* summarizes her deceptive and effective tactics (vv. 6–23) by which she has vanquished *many* men. *Slain*, a technical term for those "pierced" in battle and a figure of speech for corpses, implies that she leads men uncommitted to wisdom to a violent, unnatural death. *Powerful* refers to power through numbers. Despite their numerical superiority, these men, like a herd of bulls, are led to the slaughter by this one aggressive adulteress. *All* of them, without exception, are *killed by her*. Her record is perfect; she has vanquished them all.

27 The scene, which now shifts to *her house*, provides the second reason to keep clear of the adulteress. She portrays her pad as a pleasure palace (vv. 16–18), but in fact, it *presents the ways to the grave*. The plural "ways" connotes that her house contains many wrong ways (the many aspects of her foolish behavior), all of which lead to the grave. *Descending to the chambers of death* unpacks the notion of leading to the grave. The plural "chambers" envisions the grave divided into several chambers; the lowest, where her victims lie, is the worst (see 9:18). There may be a correlation between the grave and her body, for elsewhere in Proverbs "chamber" (*ḥeder*) refers to "innermost parts of the body" (18:8 [= 26:22]; 20:27, 30). According to Price, "In the Mishnaic and Talmudic literature *ḥeder* took on the additional connotation of the inner part of the female genitals."[164] Thus, as Newsom observes, "The father's concluding words . . . expose the monstrous, mythic dimension of the strange woman. She

---

164. J. D. Price, *NIDOTTE*, 2:28–30, s.v. *ḥdr*.

is not just a woman. . . . She is a predator who has slain multitudes. Indeed her vagina is the gate of Sheol. Her womb, death itself."[165] Finally, although God is not mentioned in the chapter, other clear expressions of the sage's worldview show that Solomon assumes that God is the ultimate Agent who condemns the gullible to death (e.g., 5:21–23).

Wisdom's Second Speech: Her Self-Praise to the Uncommitted (8:1–36)

¹Does not Wisdom call out
and Understanding raise her voice?
²On the highest points beside the way,
at the crossroads she takes her stand.
³Beside the gates, at the entries of the city,
at the entrances of the openings she cries aloud:
⁴"To you, people, I call out;
indeed, I cry aloud [to you] humanity.
⁵You uncommitted, understand shrewdness,
and you fools, set[166] your hearts on it.
⁶Listen, because I speak what is right,
and the opening of my lips speaks what is upright.
⁷Surely my palate utters truth,
and wickedness is an abomination to my lips.
⁸All the words of my mouth are spoken in righteousness,
and there is not one among them that is deceitful or perverse.
⁹All of them are straight to those who understand—
yes, upright to those who have found knowledge.
¹⁰Choose my instruction instead of silver
and knowledge rather than choice gold.[167]
¹²I, Wisdom, dwell with shrewdness;
and knowledge and discretion I find.
¹³The fear of *I AM* is hating evil—
pride and arrogance and an evil way
and a perverse mouth I hate.

165. Newsom, "Woman and the Discourse," 155–56.
166. Reading *hākînû* from LXX *enthesthe*, not *hābînû* of MT.
167. All MSS and versions add v. 11: "Because wisdom is better than corals, and all the things one desires do not compare with her." It is better omitted as a gloss from 3:15 because (1) after the mention of "silver" and "gold" in v. 10, matching 3:14, it essentially repeats 3:15; (2) apart from v. 11, the poem consists of seven stanzas of five verses each; and (3) only in v. 11, matching 3:13–21, is Wisdom's encomium in the third and not the first person.

¹⁴Counsel and resourcefulness belong to me;
 I am insight; heroic strength is mine.
¹⁵Through me kings reign
 and potentates decree what is right.
¹⁶Through me rulers govern,
 and nobles—all the judges on the earth.
¹⁷As for me, those who love me I love,
 and those who seek me diligently will find me.
¹⁸Riches and honor are with me,
 enduring wealth and prosperity.
¹⁹My fruit is better than gold, even pure gold,
 and my yield than choice silver.
²⁰I walk about in the path of righteousness,
 in the midst of the byways of justice,
²¹so that I bequeath property to those who love me,
 and I fill their treasuries.
²²*I AM* brought me forth as the first of his way,
 the earliest of his deeds from of old.
²³In the remotest time I was formed,
 at the beginning, from the earliest times of the earth.
²⁴When there were no depths, I was brought forth,
 when there were no fountains abounding with water.
²⁵Before the mountains had been planted,
 before the heights, I was brought forth.
²⁶Before he made the earth and the open fields
 and the world's first clods of dirt—
²⁷when he fixed the heavens, I was there;
 when he inscribed a circle on the face of the deep;
²⁸when he made the clouds firm above
 and he fixed fast the fountains of the deep;
²⁹when he set for the sea its limits—
 and the waters cannot go beyond his command—
 when he marked out the foundations of the earth.
³⁰And I was beside him constantly;
 I was delighting [before him] day after day,
 celebrating before him at all times,
³¹celebrating his inhabited earth,
 and my delight was humanity.
³²So now, sons, listen to me—

and blessed are those who keep my ways.
[33]Listen to instruction and become wise,
   and do not flout it.
[34]Blessed is the person who listens to me,
   keeping vigil at my doors day by day,
   observing the doorposts of my doorways;
[35]for the one who finds me finds life
   and so obtains favor from *I AM*.
[36]But the one who misses me is the one who does violence against
      himself;
   all who hate me love death."

This great encomium of Woman Wisdom stands in contrast to the previous poem on the adulteress (ch. 7). The adulteress moves stealthily at dusk and speaks deceitfully; Wisdom moves publicly and speaks truthfully. The adulteress leads her victims to slavery and death; Wisdom leads her disciples to kingship, wealth, and life. The adulteress lives, moves, and has her being in the earthly, mundane sphere; Wisdom soars in heaven, above space and time. The uncommitted youth needs to make a critical decision to love Wisdom before he enters the danger-laden city. Wisdom trumpets her words, virtues, and rewards since she has a hard sell against the adulteress's sweet talk and sexual excitement. The adulteress pitches her pleasure, which ends in death. Wisdom demands discipline, which ends in life.

In Van Leeuwen's analysis, the encomium consists of seven sections of five verses each.[168] All but the last are subdivisions of the poem's three stanzas: the introduction, lesson, and conclusion:

I	Introduction		vv. 1–10
	A	The Setting and Addressees of Wisdom's Speech	vv. 1–5
	B	Wisdom's Exhortation to Listen with Motivations	vv. 6–11
II	Lesson		vv. 12–31
	A	Wisdom's Communicable Attributes in Historical Time	vv. 12–21
		1 Wisdom's Role in Civil Order	vv. 12–16
		2 Wisdom's Gifts of Material Glory for Her Lovers	vv. 17–21

---

168. Van Leeuwen, "Proverbs," in *NIB* 5, 88.

Personified Wisdom addressing fools and uncommitted youths at the city gate is the penultimate poem in the Prologue, balancing the parallel personification in the second poem from the beginning (1:20–33). Though similar in settings, addressees, and vocabulary, they also differ. In the former, she denounces the dimwits for dismissing her; in the latter, she wants to win them to listen to her.

Introduction (8:1–11)

Solomon introduces Wisdom's two speeches by identifying her as the speaker (1:20; 8:1), her location at the city gate (1:20–21; 8:3), and her zealous locution (1:20–21; 8:1, 3). Following this introduction, Wisdom herself uses the father's typical introduction of naming her addressees and an admonition to listen (vv. 4–5) followed by motivation (vv. 6–10).

The Setting and Addressees of Wisdom's Speech (8:1–5)

1 The rhetorical question, *Does not Wisdom call out?*, emphatically asserts that Wisdom widely broadcasts her proclamation, not waiting for an audience to come to her. *Understanding raises her voice* (see 1:20).

2 Six adverbial phrases (vv. 2, 3) describe the public, prominent location of her speech. *On the highest points* to maximize visibility and audibility (see 1:21). *Beside the way*, where the masses walk. *At the crossroads*—the point at which they must choose wisdom or folly (cf. Ps. 1:1–2)—*she takes her stand* to persuade them to pursue her paths.

3 *Beside the gates* where people congregate to trade, settle disputes, and conduct politics. *At the entries of the city* before they enter the dangerous city. *At the entrances of the openings*—the portals accessing the gate where "decisions are made and people 'enter into' new situations and even embark on new journeys."[169] *She cries aloud* (see 1:20a).

---

169. Van Leeuwen, "Proverbs," in *NIB* 5, 89.

4 *People* glosses a term for individuals in social relationships. *I call out* (see v. 1a); its intensive parallel is *I cry aloud*. *Humanity* signifies common people.

5 *You uncommitted* (see "Intellectual Terms for the Wicked and Fools," p. 47). *Understand* (see "Intellectual Terms for the Wise and Righteous," p. 36). *shrewdness* (see "Intellectual Terms for the Wise and Righteous," p. 35). The parallel lumps the uncommitted together with *fools* (see pp. 47–48). *Set your hearts on it.* Unlike in her first address, she does not assume the uncommitted have rejected her; there is still hope for them.

Wisdom's Exhortation to Listen with Motivation (8:6–11)

The stanza's framing commands "listen" (v. 6) and "choose" (v. 10) move Wisdom's admonition from listening to her words to accepting her lesson. The motivations are twofold: "because" her words are flawless (vv. 6–9) and her instruction is priceless (v. 10).

6 *Listen* (see 1:8). *Because* introduces the first set of motivations (vv. 6–9), which contain eight qualifications commending her ethical speech. An oral appeal, *I speak . . . the opening of my lips*, is harder to avoid than a written message, which can be thrown unopened into a fire (Jer. 36). *What is right* is the first qualification, *what is upright* (see 1:4) the second.

7 *Surely* (or "because") *my palate* (speech) *utters truth* (what is reliable) is the third qualification. In Ps. 51:6, "truth" occurs as a parallel to wisdom. *Wickedness*, an antonym of "truth," refers to wicked speech such as the speech of the gangsters (1:11–15) and the adulteress (7:14–21). It is condemned because it is anti-God and anti-humankind and denies the ordained connection between unethical behavior and death. Such spurious speech, which is the fourth—and in this case negative—qualification, *is an abomination* (see 3:32; 6:16) *to my lips*, as it is also to *I AM*, who begot Wisdom from his own being (cf. 6:16–17; 8:22).

8 The fifth qualification, *all the words of my mouth are spoken in righteousness* (see pp. 36–37), qualifies the realm within which Wisdom speaks or the norm according to which she speaks. The sixth qualification, *there is not one among them that is deceitful or perverse*, is another negative. "Deceitful" and "perverse/crooked" (see 2:15) occur together often (Deut. 32:5; Ps. 18:26). In ethical contexts "deceitful" means tricky, and to be "perverse" is to distort norms. Wisdom needs no such "terminological inexactitudes" because she has no self-serving agenda.

9 *All of them* (without exception) *are straight* is the seventh qualification. "Straight" is a synonym for "right" (see v. 6), which started the series. The proliferation of these qualities emphasizes that the style and substance of Wisdom's speech upholds the ethical ideal of doing what is best for society. But she restricts the recognition of this truth only *to those who understand*, which is those who have "insightful, reasonable, intelligent discerning."[170] What is known is relative to the knower, and knowing operates within spiritual commitments (see 2:5; John 8:31–32). Those unwilling to embrace wisdom distort even her plain and truthful speech. *Upright*, the final qualification, means that her speech comports to *I AM*'s religious-ethical order. *Those who have found knowledge* refers to those who have committed themselves to Wisdom and so attained the knowledge communicated through this book (see 1:2, 7, 28; 2:5, 9; 3:3; 4:22; 8:35).

10 The focus now shifts from Wisdom's flawless speech to her priceless rewards. *Choose*, the telic counterpart to "listen" in v. 6, has the nuance of accepting what is true (cf. 1:5; 2:1; 24:32) or false (6:25; 7:21; 22:24–25). *My instruction* refers to the proverbs and sayings of the remaining sections (chs. 10–31; see on 1:2, 3). *Instead of silver . . . rather than choice gold* (see 3:14) does not condemn material wealth; it is an important part of Wisdom's reward to her lovers (vv. 17–21a). When material wealth is the reward of wisdom, it edifies (see vv. 17–21; cf. Matt. 6:33); but when it is made life's pursuit, it corrupts (1 Tim. 6:9–10). Wisdom will brook no rival (cf. 3:4). If riches are loved, Wisdom withdraws, leaving the person at best a rich fool, frolicking to eternal death (see "The Wise and Their Rewards: Life," pp. 41–42). "Acquire" (gapped) *knowledge* (see "What Is 'Wisdom'?" pp. 27–28). which is inseparable from instruction (see 12:13; cf. 23:12).

11 This verse is a late gloss (see p. 151 n. 167).

Lesson (8:12–31)

The lesson develops in two equal halves of ten verses each. The first pertains to historic time (vv. 12–21); the second to primordial time (vv. 22–31). The first features Wisdom's communicable attributes of counsel and understanding that empower kings to rule and that bestow wealth and honor upon her lovers. The second pertains first to her divine birthing before the rest of creation, giving her dignity, competence, and authority; and then to her delight in how *I AM* ordered the cosmos. The governing skills she gives to rulers in historic time (vv. 12–21) stem from her rank and authority from being begotten in primordial time and for this reason omniscient about the cosmos and humanity (vv. 22–31).

170. *HALOT*, 1:118.

Wisdom's Communicable Attributes in Historical Time (8:12–21)

The first part of Wisdom's lesson (vv. 12–21) can be divided into two equal stanzas of five verses each, respectively dealing with her communicable attributes whereby kings govern (vv. 12–16) and the material rewards she bestows on those who love her (vv. 17–21). They are demarcated by the repetition of "I" at the beginning of each stanza (vv. 12, 17) and by the frame "those who love me" around the second (vv. 17–21).

Wisdom's Role in Civil Order (8:12–16)

12 *I, Wisdom* (see "What Is 'Wisdom'?" pp. 27–28). In addition to identifying a person, biblical names may remember or anticipate events, or as with Wisdom, describe a person's essential characteristic.[171] The figure *dwell with* signifies that *shrewdness* (see "Intellectual Terms for the Wise and Righteous," p. 35) is inseparably connected with wisdom. *Knowledge* (see "Intellectual Terms for the Wise and Righteous," pp. 34–35) accompanies both since it is essential to both (see 1:4; 8:9). Hebrew *məzimmâ* denotes the ability to devise plans—a virtue in the Prologue (chs. 1–9), and so glossed *discretion*, and a vice in the other sections (12:2; 14:17; 24:8), and so glossed "crafty" or "schemer." "Knowledge and discretion" is a hendiadys for "mental agility, versatility and adroitness."[172] The figure *I find* signifies that these virtues are also inseparable from wisdom and are communicated through inherited wisdom (cf. 1:4; 2:10–11; 5:1–2).

13 *The fear of* I AM (see "Fear of *I AM*," pp. 38–39) *is hating evil.* The rest of the verse adumbrates the evil but as an object of what *I* (Wisdom) *hate*, moving logically from *pride* and *arrogance*, which abhor God's authority in pursuit of self-interests (cf. 16:19; 29:23), to *walking on an evil way* (see 1:15) and to *a perverse mouth* (speech) that covers it up.

14 *Counsel* (see 1:25) *and resourcefulness* (see 2:7) here may refer to political and military advice given to a king (2 Sam. 7:7; 1 Kgs. 1:12; Prov. 20:18). *Belong to me* means she owns them and so can give them to her lovers. Her declaration *I am insight* (see "Intellectual Terms for the Wise and Righteous," pp. 35–36) signifies she is totally such a person. Her attributes are communicable, since those who accept her share in her being. *Heroic strength (gəbûrâ)* means both "valor,"

---

171. Austin Surls, *Making Sense of the Divine Name in Exodus: From Etymology to Literary Onomastics*, BBRSup 17 (Winona Lake, IN: Eisenbrauns, 2017), 38.
172. McKane, *Proverbs*, 347.

which makes a person brave and able to confront redoubtable enemies, and the strength to implement a strategy in spite of opposition. Rulers need these divine qualities (Job 12:13). According to Isaiah, the spirit of *I AM* mediates them to Messiah (11:2); but here Wisdom mediates them to her lovers through inspired proverbs. Only Jesus Christ, the Son of God, achieved them perfectly, becoming the "wisdom of God" for his church (1 Cor. 1:23–30; see pp. 58–59).

15 The focus now shifts from Wisdom's skills (vv. 12–14) to her political usefulness (vv. 15–16). The repetition of *through me* at the beginning of vv. 15 and 16 links them on the topic of statecraft. These verses assume personal leadership by wise leaders, not by impersonal law codes. All rulers are the visible tools of hidden Wisdom's work.[173] Keep in mind Wisdom addresses the person in the street, not just elites; that is to say, the success rulers achieve in good government she offers, mutatis mutandis, to all her lovers. Wisdom's skills for statecraft are expanded to all rulers by five synonyms, beginning with the most important: *kings* [who] *reign*. Marc Brettler documents that the king was invested with supreme authority by virtue of his ability to lead, especially in war and in the administration of justice. And his ability to lead depends on his noble qualities: strength, justice, majesty, and longevity.[174] *Potentates*, a common parallel to "kings,"[175] *decree*, meaning "to fix, to determine"[176] (the same word used of *I AM*'s decrees at creation, v. 29). *What is right* (see 1:4) is a metonymy for just laws and actions.

16 *Rulers* refers to officials in a king's house. *Nobles*, when used in poetry, denotes noblemen—powerful officials in the royal court (see 17:7). The word can mean either noble by disposition (that is, generous) or noble by birth (see Isa. 32:8). *All the judges on the earth* refers to all sorts of governors, administrators of justice, and rulers.

Wisdom's Gifts of Material Glory for Her Lovers (8:17–21)

The frame, "those who love me" (vv. 17a, 21a), states the essential condition for receiving Wisdom's material rewards.

17 An initial *as for me* (simply "I" in Hebrew; see v. 12) demarcates the stanza. *Those who love me* are those with the heart's affection for receiving

---

173. So Plöger, *Sprüche*, 90.

174. M. Z. Brettler, *God Is King: Understanding an Israelite Metaphor*, JSOTSup 76 (Sheffield: JSOT Press, 1989), 31, 109–16.

175. S. Gevirtz, *Patterns in Early Hebrew Poetry* (Chicago: University of Chicago, 1964), 3 n. 11.

176. H. Ringgren, *TDOT*, 5:141, s.v. *ḥāqaq*.

Wisdom's virtues. If they have not loved her previously, repentance is necessary. This personification signifies that when the sages' teachings are lovingly memorized, they will become assimilated into one's character (2:1–5). *I love* signifies complete reciprocity between seeker and sought. While Wisdom offers herself to all humanity, her offer is only efficacious for those whose hearts have been regenerated to love her, a regeneration she effects through speech. "Those who love me" are by definition *those who seek me diligently.*[177] Likewise, "I love" is matched by the effective consequence: they *will find me.*

18 *Riches and honor* denotes material well-being that gives dignity and social status. *Are with me*: enduring wealth is inseparable from possessing wisdom. They are hers to bestow and cannot be coerced, but she does not withhold them from her lovers. Although during a time of testing and of character development they may seem separable (see 3:12), ultimately they are not. *Enduring wealth* refers to future wealth that will become venerable. The Hebrew word glossed *prosperity* is commonly rendered "righteousness"; it entails the inevitable and inviolable success that comes from ethical behavior. Paradoxically, when one pursues wealth, it corrupts, but when one pursues wisdom, it comes with edifying wealth (cf. 1 Kgs. 3:12–13). Those who achieve wealth and power by striving after wisdom will be humane and civilized.

19 The incomplete metaphors *my fruit* and *my yield* refer to Wisdom's external, material benefits to those who inwardly and spiritually seek her. *Is better than gold, even pure gold* (see v. 10). *Choice silver* is refined silver, which is free of impurities.

20 Wisdom says of herself, *I walk about in the path of righteousness,* wherein ethical behavior is combined with benefits (see on v. 18). *In the midst of the byways* refers to every situation in which she sought out *justice.*

21 Wisdom walks in righteousness and justice so as to *bequeath property.* But only to *those who love me,* since they alone have a rightful claim to her rewards. Such will not be denied, since Wisdom is just and righteous. *I fill their treasuries* confirms that real property is in view and that Wisdom's inheritance is superabundant.

Wisdom's Birth and Celebration in Primordial Time (8:22–31)

This highly imaginative and figurative poem is marked by the change from "I" (vv. 12–21) to "*I AM*" (vv. 22–31) and by other changes noted above. The poem

177. C. H. Toy, *The Book of Proverbs,* ICC (Edinburgh: T&T Clark, 1899), 169.

begins with "*I AM*" and ends with "humanity," the climax of God's creative works and Wisdom's audience.

Structurally, the poem falls into two equal stanzas of five verses each: Wisdom's origin before creation (vv. 22–26) and her presence and celebration during it (vv. 27–31). Wisdom's relationship with God's creative works unifies the two halves.

Functionally, this poem transcendentalizes Solomon's teaching (see "Illumination and Woman Wisdom," pp. 29–30) in three ways. First, it exalts Solomon's wisdom by tracing its antiquity to the time before creation (vv. 22–26). This is confirmed by the Egyptian background; in those texts, a god's nobility is based on their preexisting creation. Second, only Wisdom has the knowledge to competently counsel, because only she has observed creation from the start and so knows the whole story. Since she knows comprehensively, she can speak dogmatically (cf. 30:1–6). Third, the verbal link "to decree" in vv. 15 and 29 illuminates the poem's function. Wisdom, who relished in God's creative decrees that wisely structured the enduring cosmos (vv. 27–31), in turn enables rulers to issue decrees that wisely structure an enduring society (vv. 12–16).

Wisdom's Genesis before the Creation of the Cosmos (8:22–26)

The first stanza (vv. 22–26) establishes that Wisdom's preeminence in rank and dignity over the rest of creation is both qualitative (begotten, not created) and temporal (she preexists any creature). The stanza consists of two strophes. The first strophe (vv. 22–23) asserts that Wisdom's divine birth occurred in the primordial past. The second strophe (vv. 24–26) demonstrates Wisdom's existence prior to the creation with five markers of origin—"when there were no" (twice in v. 24) and prepositions meaning "before" (thrice in vv. 25–26)—and so emphasize wisdom's priority in time and rank over the rest of the creation. ANE cosmogonies commonly begin with the negative state (cf. Gen. 1:2; 2:5). Similarly, after describing what did not exist, Wisdom depicts the panorama of God's creative acts in a movement from below the earth to above it.[178] Fox notes that this unified representation impresses on the audience that "the creation is a coherent panorama rather than an assemblage of phenomena."[179]

22 The meaning of Hebrew *qānānî* (here translated *brought me forth*), from the root *qānâ*, has been hotly debated since the time of the Arian heresy (see

178. Meinhold, *Sprüche*, 145.
179. Fox, *Proverbs 1–9*, 282.

"Woman Wisdom as a Type of Jesus Christ," pp. 59–62).[180] While *qānâ* often means "to acquire or possess" (cf. Prov. 4:5, 7), here it has its rarer meaning of "to beget, bring forth"—in a procreative, not a creative, sense. In Gen. 4:1, Deut. 32:6, and Ps. 139:13, *qānâ* occurs in birth contexts, suggesting the meaning "to procreate." This meaning of *qānâ* is certified by the parallels "I was formed" (v. 23) and "I was brought forth" (vv. 24–25). But any thought involving *I AM* with a sexual partner in begetting Wisdom is unthinkable in this book. The metaphor signifies that wisdom comes organically from God's essential being, not from outside of himself, unlike the rest of the creation. Moreover, since this wisdom predates creation and is independent of it, it is only available to humanity by revelation and so must be accepted by faith. *As the first* probably means first in time ("as the beginning" or "in the beginning"). *His way* is a metaphor probably with the specific sense of "activity" or "works," as indicated by the parallel "his deeds" in verset B. *The earliest* designates the remotest (that is, the primordial) past (see v. 23; cf. Deut. 33:15; Pss. 44:2; 68:34; 74:2, where it modifies *qānâ*; 78:2; 119:152).[181] *Of his deeds* distinguishes wisdom from *I AM*. *From of old* is relative to the context (cf. 2 Sam. 15:34; Isa. 44:8; 45:21), and here refers to when God gave birth to Wisdom (i.e., Solomon's wisdom).

23 *In* (lit. "from"). *The remotest time* designates the indeterminate distant past; the figure accommodates the human incapacity to comprehend infinity in time. The translation of the Heb. verb *nissaktî* with *I was formed* takes it as derived from the verb *sākak* ("to be woven, shaped").[182] Another option is to render it "I was installed," assuming it is derived from a homonym meaning "to install, set up" (cf. Ps. 2:6).[183] But the former is preferable because the notion that Wisdom was installed into an office is absent in this stanza. *Sākak* is also used figuratively in Ps. 139:13 and Job 10:11 for God "weaving" together the embryo in the mother's womb, and that notion comports well with the birth imagery of vv. 22 and 24, an image that connotes Wisdom's close relationship to *I AM*. *At the beginning* is defined as *from the earliest times of the earth* (that is, from primeval time), when humankind began to move and have its being.

24 *When there were no* appears twice—the first two negative markers of the second strophe. *Depths* (or "floods") may refer to the primeval abyss or to the present oceans. In Gen. 1:1–3, the primeval depths were part of the chaotic earth prior to God's word transforming it into cosmos. Wisdom, however,

---

180. For the full discussion of the meanings of *qānâ* and for the arguments supporting the interpretation adopted here, See Waltke, *Proverbs 1–15*, 408–9.

181. Jenni, *TLOT*, 3:1103, s.v. *qedem.*

182. So *HALOT*, NAB, NIV, REB, HCSB.

183. So BDB, KJV, JPS, ESV, NLT, NET.

preexisted these primeval depths, whose origin is indeterminate in time and inexplicable in reasoning. *I was brought forth* is a divine passive (see on vv. 22, 26). *Fountains* denotes the places where the subterranean water erupts upon the earth to nourish it. *Abounding with water* probably emphasizes their fecundity.

25 The third negative marker, *before the mountains had been planted*, refers in non-scientific language to the sinking of the earth's foundations in the ocean depths (cf. Jonah 2:6; Ps. 93). But the mountains also rise above the waters (Ps. 104:6–8) and thus form a merism with the "depths." As the depths represent primeval time, the mountains connote the oldest aspects of the earth (cf. Ps. 90:1–2). *Before the heights*—a stock-in-trade poetical parallel to "mountains"—*I was brought forth* (see v. 24a), is the fourth and intensifying negative marker.

26 *Before* is the fifth negative marker of Wisdom's priority. The antecedent of *he* is "*I AM*" in v. 22. This verse, for the first time in the stanza, identifies him as the Agent of creation. *Made* is a common word associated with God's creative work (e.g., Gen. 1:31). *The earth* is the land—both arable and non-arable. *The open fields* (cf. 1:20) are outside the city (Job 5:10), where flocks grace (Ps. 144:13). *The first* (or "the beginning") *of the world's clods of dirt* are those from which humankind was made, which it cultivates and to which it will return.

Wisdom's Delight in the Created Order (8:27–31)

The second stanza, of two strophes, shifts the focus to Wisdom's presence (vv. 27–29) and celebration (vv. 30–31)—probably in dance—when *I AM* created everything, especially humankind. The strophes are linked by the frame "I was there" (v. 27a) and "I was beside him" (v. 30a).

The first strophe hymns *I AM*'s establishment of the cosmic elements that sustain human life. All the metaphors for creation in vv. 27–29 signify that each element is so firmly fixed that none can overreach or transgress another. Otherwise the cosmos would crumble into chaos. Human existence requires such a firmly fixed universe. This divinely fixed order serves as a model of *I AM*'s fixed moral boundaries that prevent human society from atomizing into anarchy.

In the second strophe, Wisdom celebrates each of God's creative acts—especially his making of humanity. If Job spoke ignorantly because he was not present at the creation (Job 38:1–2), Wisdom speaks authoritatively because she was there and has the comprehensive knowledge he lacked. Without comprehensive knowledge, a person lacks absolute knowledge. A concentric pattern (delight, celebrate, celebrate, delight) unifies the strophe.

27 First, *he fixed* (a metaphor for "made permanent") *the heavens* (in contrast to the earth). *I was there*, gapped in 27b, implies Wisdom's omniscience about the creation. *He inscribed* (as with a compass) *a circle* (that is, the horizon; cf. Job. 22:14; 26:10; Isa. 40:22). *The face of the deep* is the ring of water encompassing the earth beyond the coastlines. "A circle on the face of the deep" is a metaphor for the boundary between the two cosmic spheres of sea and sky.

28 Next, he provided the waters of rain and of the fountains to sustain life on the earth. *He made the clouds firm above* means he made the rain clouds stay suspended, not motionless, above the earth. *The fountains of the deep* are the water supply from the subterranean depths.

29 The focus now shifts to the habitable land. *He set* (he ordained or decreed[184]) *for the sea its limits* to restrain it from overflowing onto the earth. The sea embodies the primordial chaos. *And the waters cannot go beyond his command* confirms that the Creator decreed the earth's boundaries, which the hostile sea cannot transgress (see Job 38:8–11). The chaotic energy of the sea, while retaining an element of freedom, operates within strict limits. In Gen. 1:9–10, God called the sea restrained by the land "good"—it functions within his purpose. *Marked* is the same word as that glossed "inscribed" in v. 27b. *The foundations of the earth* signifies the lowest parts of the mountains, rooted in the sea's depths.

30 *I was beside him*, along with the parallel "I was there" (v. 27a), underscores Wisdom's preexistence to the creation and her closeness to the Creator. The Hebrew word *ʾāmôn*, here translated *constantly*, is much debated. The word occurs only here in the Old Testament, and four feasible interpretations have been offered:[185]

1. "Craftsman" (so NASB, NLT, HCSB, NIV footnote) lacks good lexical support and jars with the broader context by suddenly making Wisdom the artisan of creation even though the claim of Prov. 8:22–29 is that *I AM* is the Creator of all things.

2. An alternate interpretation of the translation "craftsman" is that the word

---

184. *BDB*, 963, s.v. *śûm*.

185. For the full discussion of the four feasible interpretations of *ʾāmôn* and the arguments for the interpretation adopted here, consult Waltke, *Proverbs 1–15*, 417–20.

is in apposition to "him" and so refers to God ("I was beside him, the Craftsman"). While this fits the context, it still lacks lexical support.

3. "Nursling" or "child," achieved by emending *'āmôn* to *'amûn* (so RSV and NRSV footnotes, REB), has the difficulty not only of lacking textual support but also that *'amûn* is a masculine participle and poetry demands that Wisdom (*ḥokmâ*, a feminine Hebrew noun) be personified as a female.

4. "To be firm, faithful" ("faithfully/constantly," NIV) has solid lexical support in the root *'mn* ("to be firm"; cf. "amen") and best suits both the broader context of vv. 22–31 and the immediate context of v. 30. Note its parallels: "day after day" (v. 30b); "at all times" (v. 30c).

I was delighting is literally "I was delights," an idiom meaning "I was wholly delighting." To delight in God's work is healthy. To not do so is unhealthy.[186] *Day after day* assumes the creation took place over several days, as in Gen. 1. *Celebrating* means expressing exuberant joy in actions such as dancing and music (1 Sam. 18:6). To delight and dance *before him* as in worship is found elsewhere only in 2 Sam. 6:5, 21 (cf. Job 38:7). Wisdom (Solomon's teachings) celebrates God's inviolably ordered cosmos. *At all times* means unceasingly. Implicitly, as Wisdom rejoiced ceaselessly at God's cosmos, so her lovers rejoice constantly at God's well-ordered cosmos and social structures.

31 More specifically, she was *celebrating his . . . earth*, or better, "his earth-disk." *Humanity* at the beginning (v. 4b) and end (v. 31b) frames Wisdom's encomium and segues into the conclusion. The weak earthling is the object of Wisdom's *delight* and is offered her absolute knowledge to live abundantly. The mortal has not yet rejected her and realized his mortality (cf. 1:20–33). Her final appeal in vv. 32–36 will divide this humanity into those who love her and live and those who deny her and die.

Conclusion: Wisdom's Final Invitation and Warning (8:32–36)

Following the logical particle *so now* (v. 32), the conclusion Wisdom draws to her self-encomium mirrors the characteristic motifs of the father's lectures: addressees ("the sons"), admonitions to "listen" (vv. 32–34), and motivation introduced by *for* (vv. 35–36). Wisdom, however, changes her persona, setting, and addressees in the conclusion. From a mediatrix at the city gate calling to the

186. Waltke and Houston, *Psalms as Christian Praise*, 6–7.

masses (vv. 1–21) and from a primordial figure beside the Creator (vv. 22–31), she changes to a patroness who invites the sons to find her by watching at her door. Her initial words, "so now, sons, listen to me," and her final word, "death," exactly match the father's conclusion in the preceding speech (cf. 7:24a, 27b). In the former, the father asks his son to marry Wisdom (7:4); now Wisdom asks him to find her as she dwells in her house (8:34). This precise intertextuality between these paired poems (chs. 7 and 8) further confirms that Wisdom personifies Solomon's teachings, which he puts into the mouth of the parents.

32 Wisdom's original addressees, the masses, are in part a foil to her other addressees, the *sons* who overhear or read her encomium (see on 1:4–5, 8; cf. 1:20–27, 28–33). *Listen* frames her speech (vv. 6, 32). The repeated "Listen *to me*" in the conclusions of chs. 7 and 8 (also see 5:7) strongly suggests that to listen to the sage and to Wisdom amount to the same thing. *And blessed are those who keep my ways* is Wisdom's beatitude to motivate obedience (see on 3:13).

33 *Listen*, emphatically repeated, *to instruction* (*mûsār*, 1:2; see "What Is 'Wisdom'?" p. 28) interprets her metaphor "my ways" in v. 32. Since she has not yet given any instructions, it refers to the following collections of Proverbs. *And become wise* (see "What Is 'Wisdom'?" p. 28; cf. 23:1). *Do not flout it* (see on 1:25).

34 *Blessed is the person* and *who listens to me* parallel the beatitude of v. 32b and the command of v. 32a, thus linking vv. 32 and 34. *Keeping vigil* denotes intently looking out for something. *Doors* are the mechanisms that permit or prevent passage into Wisdom's house, and the word probably foreshadows Wisdom's invitation to her banquet in 9:1–6. Probably, the sons are represented as suitors, like those of Penelope in Homer's *Odyssey* (see v. 35; 18:22; cf. 4:6; 7:4; 8:17, 21; Song 8:8–10). *Day by day* (see v. 30a) connotes constancy. The blessed person is *observing* lest they miss the opportunity to enter. *The doorposts of my doorways*—a metonymy for the doors—intensifies the imagery of their eager anticipation to enjoy her banquet (see 8:17; cf. Matt. 25:1–13).

35–36 To eagerly watch at Wisdom's door is a matter of life and death. *The one who finds me* (by loving Wisdom and diligently seeking her) *finds life* (that is, eternal life; cf. 3:18, where wisdom is declared a tree of life; see "The Wise and Their Rewards: Life," p. 41). *And so obtains favor from* I AM through the inspired sages' wisdom. *But the one who misses me*, due to lack of diligence, *is the one who does violence against himself*. *All* (in contrast to singular "one") *who hate me* includes the uncommitted and apathetic. Already dead spiritually, they *love death*, the climactic word of the address (see 7:27).

Epilogue: Rival Banquets of Wisdom and Folly (9:1–18)

[1]Wisdom has built her house;
    she has erected its seven pillars.
[2]She has slaughtered her animals; she has mixed her wine;
    and she has prepared her table.
[3]She has sent out her servant girls; she cries out
    on the tops of the heights of the city:
[4]"Whoever is uncommitted, let him turn aside here."
    To the one who has no sense, she says,
[5]"Come, dine on my food,
    and drink the wine I have mixed.
[6]Leave your ways, you uncommitted ones, and live,
    and proceed on the way of insight."
[7]Whoever chastises a mocker gets shame,
    and whoever corrects a wicked person gets hurt.
[8]Do not correct a mocker lest he hate you;
    correct a wise person so that he will love you.
[9]Give [instruction] to the wise so that he may become wiser still;
    inform the righteous and he will increase in learning.
[10]The fear of *I AM* is the beginning of wisdom,
    and knowledge of the Holy One is insight.
[11]Surely through wisdom your days will be many,
    and years of life will be added to you.
[12]If you are wise, you are wise for yourself;
    but [if] you mock, you alone will incur guilt.
[13]The woman Folly is turbulent;
    she is totally uncommitted and does not know anything.
[14]And she sits at the opening of her house,
    on a throne on the heights of the city,
[15]calling out to those who pass along the way,
    to those who make their paths straight,
[16]"Whoever is uncommitted, let him turn aside here."
    As for the one who has no sense, she says,
[17]"Stolen water is sweet;
    and hidden food is pleasant."
[18]But he does not know that the dead are there;
    those she invited are in the depths of the grave.

The contest between the adulteress and Wisdom for the hearts of the uncommitted reaches its climax in the epilogue. It is in the form of an allegory that represents the rivals giving banquets: Wisdom as a noble patroness and Folly as a pretentious hostess. They represent two views of reality: "fear of *I AM*," which entails faith that he upholds the teachings of Proverbs, and flouting revealed wisdom for a life of sensuality. Wisdom invites the uncommitted to leave behind their old identification and become wise at her sumptuous feast; Folly lures them to turn aside to enjoy her profligate, self-indulgent meal. The repentant will live; the apostates will die. The wise sons are not mentioned, for they hate Folly and are already seated at Wisdom's table.

The rival invitations (vv. 1–6 and 13–18) are almost identically framed.

	Wisdom	Folly
1. Preparation for the Meal	1–3	13–15
Designation	1aα	13aα
Activity/attributes	1aβ–3	13aβ–15
Calling out	3a	15
Location	3b	14b
2. Invitation	4–5	16–17
Invitation to uncommitted	4a	16a
Invitation to brainless	4b	16b
Offer of symbolic foods	5	17
3. Conclusion: Life or Death	6	18

The intervening section (vv. 7–12), equal in length to the invitations, explains why mockers are not invited: they are beyond repentance.

The allegory of Wisdom having built her house and prepared her banquet may represent, respectively, the Prologue (chs. 1–9) and the collections that follow. The house (the Prologue) is now finished, and the banquet (the proverbs of Solomon) is about to start. Wisdom's messengers (the sages) have been sent to invite the uncommitted youth to feast on her fare. The sage has done his part; now the uncommitted must decide.

Wisdom's Banquet (9:1-6)

Preparation for the Meal (9:1-3)

Wisdom (that is, Solomon's teachings on how to skillfully navigate life and so live), now donning the persona of an aristocratic hostess from whom *noblesse oblige* is expected (see pp. 29–30) prepares to throw a lavish banquet. She has built her expansive house (v. 1), prepared her lavish feast (v. 2), and issued an open invitation (v. 3) to turn aside and dine at her banquet (vv. 4–6).

1 *Has built* denotes bringing something into existence through craftsmanship. *She has erected* contrasts Wisdom's industry with Folly's indolence. Folly merely "sits" at the door of her house (v. 14). *Pillars* refers to the pillars supporting the roof over an open room facing a courtyard. Normally a house has four pillars; *seven* symbolizes divine perfection (cf. 6:16; 24:16; 26:16, 25). The house has room for all who turn aside (that is, repent; cf. John 14:2).

2 *She has slaughtered her animals* is a synecdoche for the preparation of a festal banquet (cf. Gen. 43:16; Exod. 22:1; Deut. 28:31; Matt. 22:4; Luke 15:23). For the allegory to work, Wisdom does the work of men: building a house and slaughtering animals (cf. Gen. 18:7; Judg. 6:19; 1 Sam. 25:11). *She has mixed her wine* refers to adding honey, herbs, or spices to contribute to its sweetness. The meat and the wine, a complete meal, represent enjoying the higher spiritual realities of Solomon's teachings that gladden and strengthen, in contrast to Folly's water and food (9:17). Illicit sex and easy money are water compared to the wine and meat of Wisdom. *Her table* is a metonymy for the nutriments on it.

3 Wisdom's *servant girls* are a metaphor for the teachers of Proverbs (cf. Matt. 22:1–14; Luke 14:15–24). She *has sent* them *out* to invite the uncommitted. According to McKane, these female servants "have an educational mission; they invite the young men not to bed, but to school."[187] *Cries out* in the context of a feast means "to invite." *On the tops of the heights* is a metonymy for the walls *of the city* (see 1:20–21).

Wisdom's Invitation: 9:4–6

Wisdom's invitation comes with great promises: if the uncommitted turn aside (that is, repent or change direction, v. 4) and dine on her dishes (the proverbs, v. 5), they will live forever (v. 6a) as they steadily stride on the path of insight (v. 6b).

4 *Whoever* extends the invitation to all the *uncommitted*, implying they have not yet rejected her (cf. 1:22; 8:5). The invitation forces a decision upon them. *Let him turn aside here* (to Wisdom's house) is an invitation to repent now of being uncommitted. The uncommitted is equated with *the one who has no sense* (see p. 50). With amazing grace, *she* who belongs to the heavenlies speaks (*says*) to those numbered among the fools.

5 *Come*—her appeal is urgent. *Dine on my food, and drink the wine I have*

187. McKane, *Proverbs*, 360.

mixed signifies that her sumptuous banquet is free of charge (cf. Isa. 55:1–3; Sir. 15:3; 24:19; Luke 14:15–24; John 6:35) but costs entrusting your whole life to the fear of *I AM*. Food and drink give physical life; Solomon's teachings give spiritual life (cf. Deut. 8:3).

6 *Leave your ways* escalates "turn aside" (v. 4). *You uncommitted ones* (see "Intellectual Terms for the Wicked and Fools," p. 47). *Live* (see "The Wise and Their Rewards: Life," pp. 41–42) finds its deepest exposition in John 6. The stakes are high: it is a life and death matter (see 3:18; 4:13, 22; 5:6; 6:23; 8:32–35). *Proceed on the way* entails that the repentant are on the path of life and must persevere on it. McKane comments, "No man stands still. He must journey on and, if he loses his way, he may lose his life."[188] *Insight* (see pp. 35–36).

really?

The Sage's Supplement to the Invitations (9:7–12)

This reflection on the contrasting responses of mockers and the wise to corrective instruction intrudes between the invitations of Wisdom and Folly. Neither mockers nor the wise have been invited to Wisdom's house. The intrusive supplement explains why and enriches the allegorical drama. The interlude has three parts:

I	Consequences to the Sage for Correcting the Proud and the Wise	vv. 7–9
II	Janus: The Beginning and Gain of Wisdom	v. 10
III	The Consequences to Oneself of Being Wise or a Mocker	vv. 11–12

Consequences to the Sage for Correcting the Proud and the Wise (9:7–9)

Verses 7–9 contrast the opposing responses of the mocker and the wise and the corresponding negative and positive effects that their responses have on the sage, to wit, rejection and shame versus acceptance and love.

7 *Whoever chastises* connotes a superior correcting an inferior's folly (see 22:15). The uncommitted may humble themselves, but *a mocker* is so self-involved and contemptuous of others as to be unable to humble him or herself, even to God, who gives breath (see "Intellectual Terms for the Wicked and Fools," pp. 48–49). Instead, the mocker's disciplinarian only *gets shame* for im-

---

188. McKane, *Proverbs*, 365.

prudently wasting time and energy on a futile cause (cf. 14:6; 15:12; 21:24; Matt. 7:6)—or, judging from v. 8, from the mocker's verbal attacks and attempts to publicly shame the wise (see 22:10). *Whoever corrects* (see on 3:12) denotes one who applies *I AM*'s teachings to rectify a wrong. The mocker, who loves self, not God and people, is *a wicked person* (see "Intellectual Terms for the Wicked and Fools," p. 48) on a perverse path; whoever corrects such a person *gets hurt*.

8 The advice to *not correct a mocker lest he hate you* means one should avoid the negative emotions of a rejected relationship. The command to correct one's neighbor frankly in Lev. 19:17 must be nuanced by this proverb. The wise aim to reorient people to the path of life and thereby form spiritual relationships with them (cf. Amos 3:2). If a rebuke defeats this aim, then it is better not to express it (cf. 17:14). *Correct a wise person* (see "What Is 'Wisdom'?" p. 28) implies he is imperfect but able to learn (1:5; 12:1; 13:1; 15:31; 19:25; 21:11; Matt. 13:12; Acts 18:26). The aim of correction is to establish a warm relationship so that *he will love you*—be your committed friend.

9 *Give [correction[189]] to the wise* links v. 9a with v. 8b. *So that he may become wiser still* assumes the wise are not static but, as imperfect persons, grow and develop (see 4:18; cf. Matt. 25:29). *The righteous* is the correlative ethical term for the sapiential term "the wise" (see "Introduction: Correlative Terms," p. 34). *So that he might increase learning* (see on 1:5; see Matt. 13:12; 25:29).

Janus: The Beginning and Gain of Wisdom (9:10)

The sage now traces the wisdom of the wise back to *the beginning of wisdom* (that is, the foundation of their masterful understanding and skill in abundant living) and uncovers its source, its fundamental principle: *the fear of I AM* (see 1:7). The wise, who accepts Wisdom's invitation to dine at her table, begin and continue by submitting to the highest authority: *I AM*. The parallel, *knowledge of the Holy One*, unpacks the cognitive and affective aspects of the "fear of *I AM*." The title "Holy One" underscores both *I AM*'s separation from the mundane and profane and, unlike pagan gods, his ethical otherness from mortals.

Consequences to Oneself of Being Wise or a Mocker (9:11–12)

11 The argument now shifts to the profit gained by the teachable wise—to wit, abundant life: *Surely through wisdom your days will be many* (cf. 3:2). In

---

189. "To the wise" links v. 9a to v. 8b and suggests that the nominal form of *ykḥ* (*tôkaḥat*, "correction"; see 1:25) is the gapped object of "to give."

Proverbs, those many days end in life. *Years of life will be added to you* mixes phrases from 3:2 and 4:10.

12 *If you are wise, then you are wise for yourself*—that is to say, the person who chooses Solomon's teaching is the beneficiary of that wisdom. But, *if you mock, you alone will incur guilt* has the sense of "will bear the responsibility of a capital punishment." "Alone" underscores the doctrine of individual accountability: that each one bears the consequences of his own sin (cf. 15:32; Ezek. 18:20; Gal. 6:4–5). The conclusion (v. 12), like the introduction (vv. 7–9), emphasizes personal responsibility.

Folly's Banquet (9:13–18)

The Pretentious Hostess (9:13–15)

As a background to understanding Folly's invitation (vv. 16–17), Solomon first describes her character as a turbulent moral ignoramus (v. 13), then her pompous posturing and prominent position (v. 14), and finally her addressees—to wit, the uncommitted who happen to be going on the right path (v. 15).

13 *The woman Folly* elevates the adulteress from the heretofore historical register to the symbolic register in the persona of Folly. The addition of "woman" connects personified Folly to the adulteress with whom she shares many traits. Both are *turbulent* (or "unruly"; see 7:11), lustful lovers panting after the uncommitted youth's body (7:13; 9:17), and so both proposition him (7:7, 18; 9:15–16). Both are married (7:19; 9:17) and, above all, deadly (2:18–19; 5:23; 7:27; 9:18). Paradoxically, Folly is committed to being *totally uncommitted* and so has no desire or will to leave her ignorance and do what is right (cf. 1:32). That she *does not know anything*, a corollary to her being uncommitted, refers in this context to moral knowledge and the connection between wisdom and life—and inversely, sin and death. Consequently, left to her own lust and will, she is willfully blind to lust's deadly end.

14 In 7:6–15, the adulteress was portrayed as approaching her prey on the city streets at dusk. Here she is portrayed as sitting prominently at the front of her house on the highest point of the city. The two portrayals present different aspects of the foolish woman. Folly, having built no house, prepared no meat nor wine, and sent no messengers, slovenly *sits at the opening of her house.* Her lifestyle is so titillating and morally undemanding that all she needs is her crude invitation to attract the uncommitted. *A throne* is a seat of honor normally occupied by kings and the highest of noblemen.[190] The pretentious

190. An exception to this may be 2 Kgs. 4:10.

imposter presents herself as an empress, and the ignorant masses bow to her authority. Like her rival, Wisdom, Folly too sits *on the heights of the city* to compete for the attention of the masses.

15 Folly, seeking to divert those going about their own business, is *calling out to those who pass along the way.* But she has no political and spiritual power over them until they pay her attention, even as the serpent had no power over Eve until he diverted her attention to the forbidden tree (Gen. 3:1–3). The appositional phrase *those who make their paths straight* signifies the youths who follow Wisdom's teachings without personally committing to them. Folly tests their mettle. Tragically, since they are uncommitted, they are no match for her, who, committed to no absolutes, follows her own lust (see 7:10–22). The art of seduction consists in skillfully dissuading someone from a former way.

Folly's Invitation (9:16–17)

16 Folly's invitation repeats Wisdom's almost verbatim (see on v. 4). The addressees are again challenged to evaluate themselves by deciding whether or not to turn aside from their way. People demonstrate their identity by their responses to temptation (see 1 Cor. 15:2; Col. 1:22–23; 2 Tim. 2:12; Heb. 3:14). Those who outwardly turn aside from the righteous congregation were inwardly never part of it (1 John 2:19). But those who persevere in the right path when tested prove themselves wise (Matt. 13:1–9).

17 Folly states her invitation in the form of a proverb. The proverb presents a half-truth: illicit sex, like wine (see 23:29–35), is pleasurable. What is left unsaid is that in the end it is repulsive. *Water,* an incomplete metaphor for sexual pleasure, is qualified by *stolen* to underscore that the pleasure is being taken from the spouse to whom it rightfully belongs. Because it *is sweet,* it tempts the victim with the pleasure of sin (Heb. 11:25), but like Satan (cf. Gen. 3:4), Folly denies sin's connection to death. *Food* is another incomplete metaphor for sexual gratification (see on 30:20). *Hidden* complements "stolen," for as the thief steals under concealment, so the adulterer hides his "theft" (see 7:19–20). Adultery *is pleasant* to sinful taste buds.

Conclusion: Death (9:18)

With *but,* Solomon steps in and corrects Folly's half-truth. The scene of sensual delight morphs into a scene of corpses in the depths of the grave. *He does not know that* exposes the fool's fatal flaw: his disregard of the deed-destiny nexus, wherein *I AM* upholds the moral order, rewarding the righteous with life and the wicked with death. *The dead* depicts the youth, specifically *those she* (Folly) *invited* to turn aside and enter her house, as corpses (see 2:18). And her brothel is compared to *the depths of the grave*. This ghoulish depiction of her guests as corpses in the depths of the grave is a prolepsis (that is, a statement made as though it were already fulfilled: "He was a dead man when he walked into the room"). Ross comments, "Many 'eat' on earth what they 'digest' in hell."[191] With this grim warning, Solomon closes the curtain on the Prologue, hoping to goad the uncommitted to choose the life he offers in his subsequent proverbs (Collections II–IV).

---

191. A. P. Ross, *Proverbs*, EBC (Grand Rapids: Zondervan, 1991), 951.

Antithetic and Synthetic Proverbs
(10:1–22:16)

For the structure of this collection, see "Structure," pp. 3–4.

SECTION A: MOSTLY ANTITHETIC PROVERBS (10:1–15:28)

Superscription (10:1a)

¹ᵃThe proverbs of Solomon:ᵃ

a. Were this superscription more than three words long in Hebrew, it would have been designated a separate verse in the Masoretic tradition.

This short superscription essentially repeats 1:1a (see the exposition there). Collection II consists of 375 proverbs, probably to correspond with the numerical value of the Hebrew consonants of Solomon's name.[1]

The Wise and the Fool in Relation to Wealth and Speech (10:1b–16)

¹ᵇA wise son makes a father glad,
  but a foolish son brings grief to his mother.
²Treasures gained by wickedness are of no eternal value,
  but righteousness delivers from death.
³*I AM* does not let the appetite of the righteous go unsatisfied,
  but what the wicked crave he thrusts aside.
⁴A poor person is made with a slack hand,
  but the hand of diligent people brings wealth.
⁵He who gathers [food] in summer is a prudent son,

1. *š* (= 300), *l* (= 30), *m* (= 40), *h* (= 5).

but he who sleeps in harvest is a shameful son.
⁶Blessings come to the head of the righteous,
    but violence overwhelms the mouth of the wicked.
⁷A righteous person is invoked in blessings,
    but the names of wicked people decay.
⁸The wise in heart accepts commands,
    but the babbling fool comes to ruin.
⁹Whoever walks in blamelessness walks securely,
    but whoever twists their ways will be known.
¹⁰Whoever maliciously winks the eye causes trouble,
    but the babbling fool comes to ruin.
¹¹The mouth of a righteous person is a wellspring of life,
    but the mouth of wicked people conceals violence.
¹²Hatred awakens conflicts,
    but love conceals all transgressions.
¹³On the lips of an insightful person, wisdom is found,
    but a rod is for the back of one who lacks sense.
¹⁴Wise people store up knowledge,
    but the mouth of a fool is imminent terror.
¹⁵The wealth of the rich is their fortified city;
    the terror of the poor is their poverty.
¹⁶The wage of the righteous is surely life;
    the earnings of the wicked are surely sin and death.

Following an introductory educational proverb (v. 1b), this unit consists of three subunits. The first and third subunits (vv. 2–5, 15–16), both on the topic of wealth and poverty, form a frame around the second subunit on communication (vv. 6–14). All three contrast the righteous and the wicked and are concerned with "life" (vv. 11, 16). The stakes are high; one's conduct in money (vv. 2–5; 15–16) and speech (vv. 6–14) are matters of life and death (v. 2).

The Introductory Educational Proverb (10:1b)

The introductory proverb again mentions both parents (see 1:8) and the contrasting psychological effects a *wise son* and a *foolish son* have upon them. The stereotyped phrase "father and mother" is broken apart so that *father* and "wise" occur in verset A and *mother* and "foolish" in verset B (cf. 1:8; 6:20; 15:20; 19:26; 23:22; 30:11, 17). *Makes . . . glad* and *brings grief* each pertain to both parents. Other proverbs ascribe grief to the father (17:21, 25) and joy to the mother (23:25). The Law of Moses commands sons to honor parents (Exod. 20:12; Deut. 5:16), but Proverbs motivates them by tender family affections (cf. 15:20; 17:21, 25; 19:26; 23:15–16, 24–25; 27:11; 28:7; 29:3). Proper rearing is essential because it affects society spatially (from the home to the community) and temporally (from generation to generation).

↳ Parenting
Impact!

Wisdom and Wealth (10:2–5)

The first subunit's theme pertains to acquiring wealth, the consequences of wisdom, and avoiding poverty, the consequence of folly. Verses 2–5 consist of two antithetical couplets (vv. 2–3 and 4–5) with antithetical parallels that alternate in a stitching pattern between vice (−) and virtue (+). The first couplet (vv. 2–3) links ethics with theology to show that those who strive to be righteous rather than rich will be rewarded by I AM with life-sustaining resources, though for a time they may suffer. In contrast, self-serving fools discover that in the end, their tarnished wealth will not save them from eternal death. The second couplet (v. 4–5) makes the practical point that the wise accumulate wealth through diligent and timely work.

Ethical and Theological Foundations of Wealth (10:2–3)

2 What saves a person from eternal death is righteousness, not illegal wealth. *Treasures gained by wickedness* (see "Ethical Terms for Wicked and Fools," pp. 45–46) *are of no eternal value* because, although such ill-gotten gain affords some protection from the vicissitudes of life (see 11:4), it will not protect anyone on the day of God's wrath. In contrast, *righteousness* (see "Ethical Terms for the Wise and Righteous," pp. 36–37) *delivers from death.* The proverb is not promising long life for the righteous or a short life for the wicked. Neither is it saying that one cannot accumulate great wealth through wickedness or experience want in righteousness. The point is what will save a person from eternal death. The proverb negates the wicked's hope that wealth will protect against death. What protects against eternal death is righteousness. See Jesus's parable against the rich fool in Luke 12:13–21.

3 The eschatological basis of v. 2 is given its theological rationale in v. 3. The contrasting destinies of those who acquire wealth wickedly and those who serve the community are not due to fate, karma, or chance but to I AM, who *does not let the appetite* (see "*Nepeš* [Traditionally, 'Soul']," p. 31) *of the righteous go unsatisfied.* In the end, he feeds the hungry righteous and starves the greedy wicked. The "appetite of the righteous" is for life, and they will be satisfied with an eternity of it, even if, like Job, they may suffer for a while. Albeit, unlike Job, they suffer at the hands of the wicked. In contrast to the righteous, *what the wicked crave*, that is, their riches, *he thrusts aside*. In the end, *I AM* will repossess all their gains and send them empty to eternal death.

The Practical Foundation of Wealth (10:4–5)

4 *A poor person is made with a slack hand* is an oxymoron, since a slack hand making anything is a contradiction. "Hand," when combined with "slack" (that is, sluggish, careless, characterized by lax behavior; cf. Jer. 48:10; Prov. 12:24, 27; 19:15), is a synecdoche for the sluggard (cf. 15:19). The only thing the sluggard makes is a poor person. *But the hand of diligent people brings wealth*, because the diligent are thoughtful, not hasty (see 21:5), and through their constancy, attentiveness, and persistence, they produce great quantities of wealth and valuable possessions.

5 Verse 4 contrasts what the sluggard and the diligent produce; this proverb contrasts how they produce it. It all has to do with their sense of timing: *He who gathers [food] in summer is a prudent son* because he not only works hard but also works at the right time, namely, in summer—the optimal time for gathering food. The cliché *carpe diem* characterizes the prudent son. He is one who is cognizant of time and takes advantage of it. Such a son—a parent's dream—earns the high honor bestowed by wisdom: "prudent." By contrast, *he who sleeps in harvest* and thus misses it *is a shameful son* because he brings public shame upon his parents and himself.

Effects of Speech on Self and Others (10:6–14)

At first glance, this subunit appears to be an *omnium gatherum* of unrelated proverbs. However, a closer look shows carefully worked-out patterns that reveal its topic and theme. The unit consists of two equal halves of four antithetical proverbs each ("but" in the B versets of vv. 6–9 and 11–14) around a central pivot proverb of synthetic parallelism ("and" in v. 10b).

Six references to body parts unite the subunit: head, mouth, heart, lips, eyes, and back. "Mouth" is mentioned four times (vv. 6b, 11a, 11b, 14b) and "lips" three times (vv. 8b, 10b, 13a). Six of the ten verses explicitly refer to communication, and the key word "mouth/lips," often a metonymy for speech, reveals the unit's topic.

The structure reveals the theme: how one's speech affects self and others. The first half (vv. 6–9) focuses on the results of good and bad speech on oneself, the second half (vv. 11–14) on their results on others. The pivot proverb,

v. 10, chiastically reverses the pattern so that v. 10a points to the effect of bad communication on others and v. 10b to its effect on oneself. The unit trumpets the message, often overlooked, that one's evil speech intended to harm others will inevitably boomerang to devastating effect upon oneself.

On Self (10:6–9)

6 This antithetic proverb shows the effects of good and bad speech on the speaker: speak well, get blessed; speak badly, get blasted. *Blessings* refer to the ability to reproduce life, obtain wealth, and overcome obstacles. According to Hebrew idiom, blessings *come to the head of the righteous* (cf. Gen. 49:26), probably a reference to the words of blessing people pray over the wise speaker. But only God can grant blessing—in his way and in his time.[2] In sum, God mediates his blessings through the prayers of others. The "righteous" bring prosperity to the community, and in return the community's blessings reward them. *But violence overwhelms the mouth of the wicked* (see "Ethical Terms for Wicked and Fools," pp. 45–46). The same God who rewards the wise speaker through the prayers of others also ensures the foolish speech of the wicked will boomerang to ensnare them. He will not allow them to indefinitely speak evil with impunity.

7 How will you be remembered after death? With love or with loathing? This proverb shows that the blessings of the righteous and the failures of the wicked go beyond clinical death. *The righteous person* (lit. "the memory of the righteous person") *is invoked* (or "mentioned") *in blessings*. The righteous will be rewarded even after their deaths because the community will remember and mention their names when blessing others, thereby ensuring they live on in the memory of the community. In contrast, *the names* (that is, memory; cf. Exod. 3:15; Pss. 97:12; 102:12; Hos. 12:5) *of wicked people decay*. Their memory goes the way of their corpses: they rot and stink. Mother Teresa's name is recalled with honor, Adolf Hitler's name with horror.

8–9 These verses form a couplet linked syntactically and conceptually. The A versets represent the way of the wise while the B versets represent the demise of the depraved. Verse 8a shows a fundamental characteristic of the wise—to wit, their teachability; v. 9a shows their consequent security. Verses 8b and 9b continue the topic of bad speech.

Those aspiring to be *the wise in heart,* as opposed to "the wise in their own eyes," know they need teaching and so *accept* the *commands* of the inspired sages. This leads to growth in wisdom and the power to speak wisely. *The bab-*

---

2. LXX makes this overly clear by paraphrasing, "Blessing from *I AM.*"

bling fool, however, is a know-it-all who stubbornly refuses to learn. Instead of wisdom, fools broadcast their own opinions. However, their rejection of wisdom has dire consequences: not only does their foot-in-mouth disease harm others, but they themselves come *to ruin*. As someone has aptly said, some people's tongues are long enough to cut their own throats.

Verse 8 highlights the teachability of the wise; v. 9 highlights their security. *Whoever walks in blamelessness* is a figure of speech for a person who, out of total commitment to *I AM*, consistently behaves with integrity in the community. That person *walks securely*—lives without fear of harm. This proverb offers immense comfort. To go through life without having to look over your shoulder to see which of your misdeeds is about to catch up with you is an inestimable amenity. By contrast, *whoever twists their ways* refers to the person who acts against the community in favor of the self. The plural "ways" denotes the varied schemes perpetrated to self-advantage. *Will be known* is likely a metonymy for "come to ruin." The point is clear: there is no security for the wicked.

Janus (10:10)

10 This central, synthetic proverb functions as the janus (transitional pivot) in the unit (vv. 6–14). Its versets chiastically reverse the unit's pattern: the A verset pertains to the effects of bad speech on others (vv. 11–14) while the B verset pertains to the effects of bad speech on self (vv. 6–9). The proverb shows the effect to others and to oneself of two types of bad communication: malicious, secretive gestures and vain babblings. *Whoever maliciously winks the eye* refers to those whose insidious, antisocial behavior *causes trouble* (see 15:13; Job 9:28; Pss. 16:4; 147:3) to the community. But the community is not the only sufferer; the *babbling fool* also *comes to ruin*. As in v. 8b, once again the boomeranging of socially destructive communication is emphasized. God, the Guardian of the social order according to the book of Proverbs, will ensure such people reap what they sow.

On Others (10:11–14)

11 *The mouth of the righteous* is a metonymy for wise speech that blesses and builds the community. Such speech is compared to a *wellspring* (or "fountain") *of life.*[3] A fountain is a source of fresh, refreshing water, which, especially in

---

3. The mouth of the righteous, the teaching of the wise (13:14) and the fear of *I AM* (14:27) are all said to be "a fountain of life."

the arid biblical world, is a welcome source of life for the community. The open and virtuous speech of the righteous, like an oasis in the desert, draws the community to gather around and receive moral, intellectual, physical, and temporal sustenance. Not so the *mouth of the wicked*. Their speech hypocritically *conceals violence*; it edifies self at the expense of tearing the fabric of society. Those who gather around it find themselves withering and dying.

12 This proverb examines how we treat those who have wronged us. Two possibilities are revealed: one leads to violence and further conflict, the other to reconciliation and harmony. When wronged, we can respond in hate or in love. Verset A shows where the former option leads, verset B where the latter leads. *Hatred* is personified as someone who, having been wronged, is now seeking revenge. Such hatred looks for company and soon *awakens* dormant *conflicts* in the community. The graphic picture trails off here, but we can imagine a lynch mob forming when such a sleeping giant is awakened and prodded on by hatred. By contrast, *love*, also personified, cherishes the wrongdoer as a friend to be won. Love *conceals* (draws a veil over) *all* kinds of *transgressions*. Instead of exposing the wrongdoers on the front page of the tabloids, love, at great cost to self, absorbs the wrong in order to reconcile and save the offender from death. The resulting rewards both to self and to the community are priceless! The apostle Paul's question to a cheated brother, "Why not rather be wronged?" (1 Cor. 6:7), echoes the intent of this proverb admirably.

In today's culture of mass communication, we possess the power to expose anyone's sin or weakness to millions of people. Sometimes such public shaming may achieve just ends, but most often it unleashes a monster that can destroy a person unmercifully and without due process. And unlike God's forgiveness, which includes his promise to forget the penitent's sins, the internet never forgets. Once something is posted, it is there forever. In such a culture, God's people will have to carefully consider the wisdom of this proverb before participating in any such use of mass media.

13–14 These verses are linked by "wisdom" (v. 13a) and "wise" (v. 14a) and by two metonymies of speech, "lips" (v. 13a) and "mouth" (v. 14b). Together, they show that fools must be corrected both by caning and by rebuke. They cannot save themselves since they return to their folly as dogs to vomit (26:11).

On the lips of an insightful person reveals another source of wise speech: the character of one who considers and understands a situation and its outcome. Through submission to divinely revealed wisdom, such a person has attained a heavenly perspective from which to evaluate the fallen world. Thus, an insightful person is able to penetrate situations to discern right and wrong, good and evil. In the mouth of such a character *wisdom is found*, to which, it is implied, the humble and teachable will pay attention. Fools, however, are never persuaded by mere words—not even the words of the insightful. As a police detective I (Ivan) have often sat in court and listened to judges lecture wrongdoers in the hope that their mere words will persuade the fool to do right. Each time the words of this proverb have echoed in my mind. The fool is not persuaded by mere words, as is demonstrated when I arrest the recidivist again. Sometimes physical discipline is required: *A rod is for the back of one who lacks sense* (see 10:13; 14:3; 18:6–7; 19:29; esp. 26:3; cf. Ps. 32:9). The "rod" is a metonymy for physical punishment intended to correct the senseless. While many in today's society disapprove of physical punishment, the wise understand that its careful use may turn away a youth who otherwise will not listen, from death to life.

Verse 14 admonishes the *wise* to *store up* (that is, to memorize) the *knowledge* of this book (see 2:1). Such memorization is needed for the situation revealed in verset B: *The mouth of a fool is imminent terror.* A fool's mouth is a threat to a community. When it finally erupts, the wise person's knowledge will be called upon to mitigate the damage. The NIV translation of v. 14b gives the impression that the fool's folly will be the source of the fool's own ruin; hence the fool's mouth "invites ruin." However, this is not the proverb's point. The Hebrew *qĕrōbâ* is better translated as "imminent," indicating the ever-present danger to the community from the fool's mouth.

Wealth and Security (10:15–16)

The topic of the last subunit shifts back to riches (see vv. 2–5). The catchword "terror" links vv. 13–14 with vv. 15–16 to show that both bad speech and poverty can be a terror, just as "blessing" is due to both work (vv. 4–5) and words (vv. 6–9).

15 This proverb asserts both the positive and negative features of *wealth*:[4] in the hands of the righteous, it fosters life; in the hands of the *rich person* (*ʿāšîr*) death. Proverbs treats all occurrences of *ʿāšîr* with hostility. Their wealth deceives them into thinking it provides real security (18:11); seduces them into becoming wise in their own eyes (28:11) and leads them to lord it over the poor (22:7; cf. 2 Sam. 12:1ff.) and to reply harshly (18:23). Moreover, 28:6 probably refers to all rich persons with the observation that their "ways are perverse" (cf. Isa. 53:9). Here, their fatal flaw is to think their wealth provides them an

---

4. Half of the occurrences of "wealth" in the book of Proverbs praise its value (12:27; 13:7; 19:14; 29:3; cf. 19:4) and the other half warn against trusting in it (11:4; 13:11; 18:11; 23:4; cf. 28:8, 22; 29:4).

unbreachable *fortified city*. Their wealth may provide them with temporary security because, in contrast to the poor, they can hire lawyers to protect their possessions and doctors to prolong their lives. But their eternal security is only imaginary, as the verbatim parallel in 18:11 makes plain (cf. Job 27:19). Obviously, poverty is not the answer. That state induces *terror* (constant suspense, fear and worry due to imminent ruin). Thus, *the poor* are in a state of panic because their *poverty* threatens to deprive them of the necessities of life.

16 Enduring wealth must be achieved through righteousness, not wickedness. The *wage* (reward for hard work; see 2 Chr. 15:7; Jer. 31:16) *of the righteous is surely* nothing less than eternal *life*. Only *I AM* can pay this wage. In contrast, *the earnings of the wicked*, gained though antisocial, self-serving labor, *are surely sin and death*. In this state, sin begets more sin, resulting in ultimate death (cf. Rom. 6:23).

The Deeds and Destinies of the Righteous and the Wicked Contrasted (10:17–11:31)

> [10:17]Whoever keeps instruction is a path to life,
> but whoever abandons correction leads astray.
> [18]Whoever conceals hatred with lying lips
> and whoever publishes an injurious report is a fool.
> [19]By multiplying words transgression does not cease,
> but the prudent restrain their lips.
> [20]The tongue of the righteous is choice silver;
> the heart of the wicked is of little worth.
> [21]The lips of the righteous person shepherd many,
> but fools die through lack of sense.
> [22]As for the blessing of *I AM*, it brings wealth,
> and he does not add painful toil with it.
> [23]To commit villainy is like [the pleasure of] laughter to a fool,
> but wisdom [is like the pleasure of laughter] to an understand-
> ing person.
> [24]As for the terror of the wicked, it will come to them,
> but that which the righteous desire will be given.
> [25]As soon as the storm passes by, the wicked person is no more,
> but the righteous is an everlasting foundation.
> [26]As vinegar to the teeth and as smoke to the eyes,
> so are sluggards to those who send them.
> [27]The fear of *I AM* adds days,
> but the years of the wicked are short.

²⁸The expectation of the righteous ends in joy,
  but the hope of the wicked perishes.
²⁹The way of *I AM* is a mountain fortress for the blameless
  but terror for those who do iniquity.
³⁰The righteous is never toppled,
  and the wicked will not dwell in the earth.
³¹The mouth of the righteous person yields wisdom,
  but the tongue of perverse people will be cut out.
³²The lips of the righteous person know what is pleasing,
  but the mouth of the wicked [knows] what is perverse.
¹¹·¹Deceptive balances are an abomination to *I AM*,
  but a full weight finds his favor.
²Pride comes, and then comes disgrace,
  but with modest people is wisdom.
³The integrity of the upright leads them,
  but the perversity of the treacherous devastates them.
⁴Wealth does not profit in the day of wrath,
  but righteousness delivers from death.
⁵The righteousness of the blameless makes their way straight,
  but by their own wickedness the wicked fall.
⁶The righteousness of the upright delivers them,
  but through [their] craving, the treacherous are captured.
⁷When a human being dies, hope perishes,
  and the expectation from strength perishes.
⁸A righteous person is delivered from adversity,
  and it falls on the wicked person instead.
⁹With their mouths, deceivers destroy their neighbors,
  but through knowledge the righteous deliver themselves.
¹⁰In the prosperity of the righteous a city exults,
  and when the wicked perish, there is a shout of praise.
¹¹By the blessing of the upright a city is exalted,
  but by the mouth of the wicked it is destroyed.
¹²Those who have no sense despise their neighbors,
  but the understanding hold their tongues.
¹³Whoever goes about as a slanderer is one who reveals a secret,
  but the faithful in spirit conceals a word.
¹⁴Where there is no guidance, a people falls,
  but safety [lies] in a multitude of counselors.
¹⁵One suffers harm grievously when one becomes surety for a
    stranger,

but one who hates clapping [hands] is one who is secure.

[16] A gracious woman lays hold of honor,
  but violent men lay hold of wealth.

[17] Those who are kind benefit themselves,
  but the cruel harm their own flesh.

[18] A wicked person is one who works for a deceptive wage,
  but one who sows righteousness [works] for true pay.

[19] Yes, indeed! The righteous attain life,
  but whoever pursues evil attains death.

[20] People with perverse hearts are an abomination to *I AM*,
  but those who are blameless in their way find his favor.

[21] Be sure of this: an evil person will not go unpunished,
  but such as are righteous will escape.

[22] [Like] a gold ring in a snout of a pig [is]
  a beautiful woman who turns aside from discretion.

[23] The desire of the righteous is only good,
  but the hope of the wicked is wrath.

[24] There is one who scatters and who is increased still more,
  and one who withholds from what is right comes only to lack.

[25] A life-bestowing blessing will be fattened,
  and as for those who drench [others], they in turn will be
    soaked.

[26] As for those who withhold grain, people curse them,
  but blessing [is] on the head of one who sells it.

[27] Whoever diligently seeks good will find favor,
  but whoever searches for evil—it will come to them.

[28] As for those who rely on their wealth, they will fall.
  but like foliage the righteous sprout.

[29] Those who ruin their household inherit the wind,
  and a fool is slave to the wise in heart.

[30] The fruit of a righteous person is a tree of life,
  and the one who "takes lives" is wise.

[31] If the righteous person is repaid in the earth,
  how much more the wicked and the sinner.

Poetic analysis of this unit points to seven more or less clearly marked sub-units, some with their own subunits, not counting the introductory proverb in 10:17 or the janus in 11:9.

Educational Proverb (10:17)

A single educational proverb again introduces a new unit pertaining broadly to the contrasting deeds and destinies of the righteous and the wicked (see 10:1b).

Verse 17 asserts that a person's choice to keep or reject the sage's teaching affects the eternal destiny of others. *Whoever keeps instruction* by memorizing, observing and practicing it, *is a path to life* (see "The Wise and Their Rewards: Life," pp. 41–42). The faithful son who "keeps instruction" becomes a means of salvation for others. The metaphor "path to life" matches the metaphor "fountain of life" in v. 11. By contrast, *whoever abandons correction leads astray* others or himself from the path of life into sin and death. The imprecise antithesis of "path to life" and "lead astray" implies the latter is the path to death.

The Speech and Expectations of the Righteous and the Wicked Contrasted (10:18–32)

This unit is framed by proverbs pertaining to organs of speech: their effects on others (vv. 18–22) and their endurance (vv. 31–32). Its core addresses expectations with regard to pain and pleasure (vv. 23–26) and security (vv. 27–30).

The Effects of Good and Bad Speech on Others (10:18–21)

This section may consist of two couplets. The first (vv. 18–19) focuses on the deadly effect evil speech has on others, the second (vv. 20–21) on the life-giving effect good speech has on others. A multitude of words by the imprudent are worthless and harmful, but the few choice words of the prudent give life to all who accept them.

18–19 Fools use their lips to spread slander; the prudent restrain their speech. Fools spread injurious slander, concealing their hatred behind lies. The enjambment of v. 18 combines the liar (*whoever conceals hatred with lying lips*) with the slanderer (*whoever publishes an injurious report*), implying that fools' hatred motivates their disingenuous speech consisting of innuendoes, half-truths, distortions, and exaggerations.

Verse 19 teaches that you cannot curtail sin merely *by multiplying words* (that is, with effusive speech). In fact, loquaciousness can increase *transgression* (see 10:11) because it may be rash and depend on rhetoric, not on *I AM* (see 12:6; 15:23; 25:11; cf. 12:25; 18:4; 24:26; Job 15:3; Eccl. 10:12ff.; Isa. 32:4, 6). The litotes (an understatement using the negative) *does not cease* signifies that the more one babbles, the more one may offend. By contrast, *the prudent restrain their lips.* They control their speech because they know the lethality of rash words (see "The Wise and Words," pp. 39–40) and so depend on *I AM* for a good and effective word in the situation (cf. 16:1).

20–21 Nevertheless, though it is restrained, the speech of the righteous is needed to counter the bad speech of fools. The juxtaposition of *the tongue,* the organ of speech, and *the heart,* the organ of planning, implies that the heart informs the tongue. Both organs pertain to both *the righteous* and *the wicked.* Words reveal hearts. The metaphor *choice silver* signifies the words of the righteous are of extreme value because they are devoid of evil intentions and, as v. 21 explains, "shepherd many." By contrast, the heart of the wicked *is of little worth,* a litotes signifying their speech is utterly worthless. That the speech of a creature made in God's image is condemned as trifling is frightening. The heart and speech of the wicked are capable of great inventions but are worthless because of sin and violence (v. 11b).

The metaphor, *the lips of the righteous person "shepherd" many,* expands the preceding metaphor of "choice silver." Out of pure and loving hearts that produce the words of their mouth, the righteous lead, revive, guide, and defend people. Nevertheless, *fools die through lack of sense.* Though surrounded by the life-giving words of the righteous, the senseless fool refuses to feed on them and so starves to death. Fools can neither receive life nor give it. The proverb encourages youth to store up the parents' ethical wisdom so that they, and as many as want their words, may live and not die.

The Expectations of the Righteous and the Wicked (10:22–32)

The two subunits of this section pertain to the expectations of the righteous and the wicked. The first (vv. 22–26) focuses on their pain and pleasure and the second (vv. 27–32) on their security. An *I AM* saying begins each subunit (vv. 22, 27), showing that *I AM* upholds the moral order which rewards the righteous and punishes the wicked. In vv. 22–25, the reward of the righteous is stated in the emphatic B verset; in vv. 27–32, the punishment of the wicked is emphasized in the B verset.

Pain and Pleasure (10:22–26)

22 *The blessing of* I AM . . . *brings wealth* means that *I AM,* the ultimate Agent of prosperity, does not require the diligent wise and righteous to slave for prosperity; he blesses them with it. This does not mean he blesses apart from diligent work. Fox writes, "The way God grants prosperity is by blessing the work of one's hands (e.g., Deut. 2:7 [8:10–18]; 15:10; 28:2; Job 1:10)."[5] Lasting wealth comes from righteousness that uses wealth to serve others (cf. 10:1–4; 11:22–27; 21:17; 23:4; 28:20), and *I AM* is its ultimate source (cf. 1 Sam. 2:7). *He does not add painful toil with it.* "Painful toil" here denotes strenuous work that stems from self-ambition (10:3). Such striving is under God's judgment, not his blessing (cf. 20:21; 28:22; Ps. 127:1; 1 Tim. 6:9–10; Jas. 3:1–16).

23 *To commit villainy* here denotes committing any crass offense against people and community. *To a fool* such offenses are *like [the pleasure of] laughter.* What is an abomination to the righteous is amusement to the fool. In contrast, *wisdom,* which entails serving God and community, gives delightful pleasure *to an understanding person.* The proverb admonishes youth to guard their inner spiritual state since it determines what activities they find pleasurable (4:16; 15:21a; 21:10a).

24 This verse nuances v. 23 by affirming that although the fool presently takes pleasure in villainy, thoughts of a dreadful destiny bedevil him. *The terror of the wicked* probably refers to inward terror and differs radically from the fear of *I AM. It will come to them.* The terror anticipated by the wicked will strike them, and when it does, it will fit the crime. In contrast, *that which the righteous desire will be given.* "Desire" denotes deep-rooted aspirations, which in the case of the righteous is a yearning for God's righteous rule (10:3; cf. Matt. 5:6). "Will be given" connotes that it is God's gracious reward (see 2:6; 10:22; cf. Ps. 37:4). However, until *I AM* effects these differing destinies, the world may be morally upside-down.

25 The terrible terror of the wicked and pleasant pleasure of the righteous are now escalated to their ultimate end. That it happens *as soon as* the storm *passes by* denotes that the elimination of the wicked immediately follows the final judgment. The incomplete metaphor of *the storm* evokes the sudden, all-encompassing destruction of the wicked's final judgment, after which *the wicked person is no more* (cf. 1:27; Ps. 1:4). Verset B lacks a counterpart for "as soon as the storm passes by," suggesting this phrase modifies both clauses. The storm breaks on the *righteous* too, but it cannot dislodge them because they are *an everlasting foundation* (cf. Matt. 7:24–27). So firm and secure are the righteous that no misfortune can shake them. On such people one can build a kingdom. The picture anticipates the age to come, when the wicked are purged from the earth and only the righteous remain (see 2:21–22).

26 This proverb compares irritations to the physical body with irritations

---

5. Fox, *Proverbs 10–31*, 523.

in social relationships. What vinegar to teeth, smoke to eyes, and a sluggard to a sender have in common is irritation and hurt. *Vinegar* refers to wine turned acidic from fermentation (cf. 25:20). Psalm 69:21 refers to drinking vinegar as a form of punishment. *To the teeth,* such a drink would have been highly irritating and painful, especially if we assume that adults in the ancient Near East lacked proper dental care, resulting in bad teeth. *As smoke to the eyes* makes a similar comparison. In the same way, *sluggards* (see 6:6; "The Sluggard," pp. 49–50) disappoint, exasperate, and irritate *those who send them.* According to A.D. Crown, royal messengers in the ancient Near East could be highly regarded. They were often privy to the innermost thoughts of the king and were entrusted with the most difficult tasks.[6] It took a diligent messenger to carry forth messages accurately and promptly. If he turned out to be a sluggard, the effect could be calamitous. Fox writes, "Hence, it is foolish to employ one and dangerous to be one!"[7]

The Security of the Righteous and Transience of the Wicked (10:27–30)

Whybray notes four features that unite these verses: (1) they are all antithetical parallels with the negative stated in the B verset; (2) each one uses ethical terms, not intellectual terms; (3) the words "righteous" and "wicked" predominate; and (4) they are oriented toward Yahwistic piety. "The fear of *I AM*" at the beginning sets the tone for the whole subunit.[8]

27–28 These verses are linked by the topic of destiny and the catchword "wicked" in their B versets. The contrast between the parallels *fear of* I AM (see "The Fear of *I AM*," pp. 38–39) and *the wicked* (see "Ethical Terms for Wicked and Fools," pp. 45–46) is imprecise, suggesting the wicked have no fear of *I AM.* The *days* in the predicate of v. 27a are specified as eternal in v. 30, and *years . . . are short,* the predicate of 27b, is equivalent to "is no more" in v. 25.

Fulfilled versus unfulfilled hope is the topic of v. 28. *The expectation* refers to hope (cf. Ps. 39:7, where "expectation" is parallel with "to hope"). *Of the righteous* qualifies the hope as what honors God and serves the community. Such hope ends in *joy,* a metonymy for all the future blessings when the righteous triumph over the wicked (cf. 3:34). In contrast, *the hope of the wicked perishes.* The imprecise parallelism of "perish" with "joy" suggests that the wicked hope

---

6. A.D. Crown, "Messengers and Scribes: The *Sopher* and *Mazkir* in the Old Testament," *VT* 24 (1974): 366–70.

7. Fox, *Proverbs 10–31,* 526.

8. Whybray, *Proverbs,* 172.

for joy. But there will be a reversal of fortunes, as indicated by the antithesis in the B verset. The hope of the righteous that their lives will climax in joyful celebration will be fulfilled (23:18; 24:14) while the hope of the wicked for the same joyful end will be shattered. The use of "expectation" to describe the hope of the righteous may imply that in the present, the righteous suffer (see "Does Proverbs Promise Too Much," pp. 42–45). The Lord Jesus, "for the joy set before him, endured the cross" (Heb. 12:2). The wicked hope their present pleasures will last forever, but their hope will evanesce in a dying gasp (Job 11:20) because their delight is inconsistent with the character of the Holy One (Prov. 11:7, 23).

29–30 The antithetical parallels of these verses contrast the stability of the blameless/righteous with the transience of the wicked. *The way of* I AM guarantees the security of the righteous and the destruction of the wicked. The metaphor refers to God's character and government, which upholds his moral order, and his determination to bless the righteous and curse evildoers (Ps. 27:11; 67:2; 119:27; 143:8; Matt. 22:16; Acts 9:2; 18:25–26; 24:14). This government *is a mountain fortress*, a metaphor implying security for *the blameless* even in a storm (see v. 25). By contrast, the same government is *terror for those who do iniquity.*

Verse 30 pushes the salvation of the righteous and the destruction of the wicked into eternity. The powerful moral government of *I AM* (v. 29) guarantees that *the righteous is never* ("not for eternity"; see v. 25; Pss. 15:5; 30:6; 112:6) *toppled.* The implied agent of the passive verb "be toppled" is *I AM*'s final judgment (see. v. 25; cf. Rom. 8:37–39), which is also why *the wicked will not dwell in the earth* (see 2:21–22).

The Permanence of Righteous and Impermanence of Wicked Mouths (10:31–32)

The subject continues to be the righteous and the wicked, and the topic returns to organs of speech (vv. 17–21), but now in connection with their destiny (cf. vv. 22–30). Verses 31–32 are tightly linked. Both have "righteous" in their A versets and "perverse" in their B versets, and each verset begins with an organ of speech.

31 *The mouth of the righteous person* is precisely contrasted with *the tongue of perverse people*, but the predicates naming their destinies are imprecisely contrasted. The imprecision suggests that *will be cut out* does not apply to the righteous and *yield wisdom* does not apply to the perverse. "Wisdom" here is a metonymy for speech that brings the speaker into harmony with *I AM* and his moral government. By contrast, the speech of the perverse seeks to overthrow *I AM*'s moral government (see 6:24). *I AM*, the implied Agent, will cut their tongues out. He will uphold his moral government by purging it of subversive speech.

32 People's characters are defined by the nature of their speech. As Seneca observed, "Speech is the index of the mind."[9] *The lips of the righteous person* stand opposed to *the mouth of the wicked*. But again, their predicates are imprecise, suggesting that *know what is pleasing* signifies that the righteous do not engage in *what is perverse*. Here "pleasing" is a metonymy for speech that *I AM* favors. Such a speaker is blessed by him. By contrast, the wicked speak to confuse others and to overthrow God's rule. Their ruin is certain because *I AM* denies them his favor.

Security through Honesty and Righteousness (11:1–8)

This subunit trumpets the theme of security through honesty (vv. 1–2) and righteousness (vv. 3–8).

Security through Honesty (11:1–2)

Verse 1 pertains to honesty in the marketplace and v. 2 to honesty with oneself. The explicit mention of *I AM*'s moral repugnance in v. 1 highlights his agency in determining the destiny of the righteous and the wicked in the rest of vv. 1–8. Otherwise, he is mostly hidden in the shadows of this subunit.

1 Something that is *deceptive* has an evil design to hoodwink and so harm a victim. Here it refers to the opposite of a full measure (see 20:23; Hos. 12:7; Amos 8:5). *Balances* could be falsified by inaccurate pans, a bent crossbow, or mishandling. They are *an abomination to* I AM, which is to say they excite his moral outrage and punishment (see 3:32; 20:10, 23; cf. Lev. 19:35–36; Deut. 25:13–16; Ezek. 45:10–11; Hos. 12:7; Amos 8:5; Mic. 6:10–11). By contrast *a full weight finds his favor*. Deceitful traders would carry a heavy stone for buying and a light one for selling (Deut. 25:13; Prov. 16:11). Such people outwardly defraud their neighbors and inwardly mock God. *I AM* abhors them and must respond, otherwise he remains a spectator. The fear of God embedded in conscience teaches honesty in measuring.[10]

2 *Pride* denotes a psychological state: an unrealistic and exaggerated opin-

---

9. Cited by Cohen, *Proverbs*, 64.

10. The Egyptian *Instruction of Amenemope* (17:15–20) also calls for accurate measurements.

ion of oneself. *Comes* personifies pride, implying that the wicked favor it and invite it in as their guest. But *then comes disgrace* (social failure). When the wicked invite pride, disgrace, like an inseparable twin, comes with it as an uninvited guest.[11] The text does not say how the wicked will be disgraced. Ultimately, *I AM* effects disgrace, as is stated explicitly in 3:34 (cf. Gen. 11:5–8; Num. 12:2, 10; 2 Chr. 26:16–21; Esth. 5:11; 7:10; Dan. 5; Luke 18:14; Acts 12:22–23). By contrast, *with modest people is wisdom* because they know their limits, accept them, and confidently comport themselves to them. The imprecise contrast between "comes disgrace" and "is wisdom" suggests that wisdom ends in honor, folly in disgrace (cf. 16:18).

Security through Righteousness (11:3–8)

Verses 3–8 advance the theme of security through righteousness and the certainty that death is God's final no to the wicked. Two proverbial pairs (vv. 3–4, 5–6) emphasize by repetition that integrity and righteousness save the upright. By contrast, the treachery of the treacherous betrays them with ultimate ruin. Two caveats draw the section to a close. First, no mortal can save another (v. 7); second, when *I AM* saves the righteous from their position of present distress, he replaces them with the wicked (v. 8).

3 The proverb states the contrasting internal principles of the righteous and the wicked. *The integrity* (wholeness or totality that manifests itself in concrete deeds; see 2:7) *of the upright* (see p. 37) *leads them* through difficulties to final glory. They display a lifestyle of complete loyalty to *I AM* and to others. That lifestyle shepherds them in the way of salvation. By contrast, the perfidy of the perverse powerfully boomerangs to shatter them. The Hebrew root of *perversity* denotes twisting, distorting, and so overthrowing truth through speech (Exod. 23:8; Prov. 15:4) or other behaviors that cause ruin (Job 12:19; Prov. 13:6; 19:3; 21:12). Perversity is the inalienable possession of *the treacherous*, and it *devastates them*.

4 This verse contrasts two causes, tainted *wealth* and *righteousness*, and their respective effects, *does not profit* versus *delivers from death* (final ruin). This proverb is equivalent to 10:2, which substitutes "treasures of wickedness" for "wealth." Here, such wealth is connected with *the day of* God's *wrath*, an escalation from 10:2a, which affirms only that it does not profit. The wicked,

---

11. So Meinhold, *Sprüche*, 186. In some Greek mythology, the person who succumbs to hubris (pride) is visited by Nemesis, the goddess who exacts revenge upon those who harbor hubris.

who unrighteously pile up wealth to fortify themselves, displease *I AM* and will not be saved when he unleashes his pent-up anger.

5 The common theme that righteousness saves and apostasy damns unites vv. 5 and 6. *Righteousness* is an inalienable possession *of the blameless* and *makes their way straight* (that is, free of pitfalls; see on 3:6). But *by their own wickedness*—the inalienable possession of *the wicked*—they *fall* (go violently to death and destruction). The contrast between "makes their way straight" and "fall" implies there are no stumbling blocks to trip up the righteous as they proceed on their way.

6 This verse nuances how the blameless avoid stumbling blocks. When they are confronted with deadly traps, their righteousness extricates them. *Righteousness* is also the inalienable possession of *the upright*, and it *delivers them*. As integrity is decisive for the upright's way of life (cf. v. 3), righteousness is decisive in their deliverance (v. 6a). What they are delivered from is unstated, but the metaphor of the antithetical parallel, *are captured*, suggests that deadly traps are in view (see 10:2; 11:4). By contrast, *through [their] craving* (probably a metonymy for what they stole) *the treacherous* (see 11:3b) *are captured*. Wickedness is motivated by addictive greed and unwillingness to be restrained by God's laws. The wicked's cavernous craving catches them.[12]

7 In the midst of antithetical proverbs on the fateful consequences of righteousness and wickedness, this synonymous proverb asserts the futility of trusting in mortals. Hope in them dies with them (cf. 10:28; Ps. 49:5–12). *Human being* here must refer to a wicked person. The wicked's hope perishes when they perish since, unlike the righteous, they do not trust in God but in humans (Prov. 3:5; 18:10; cf. Ps. 49:5–12).[13] *Dies* refers to clinical death and *hope* to the expectation of good that the wicked place on a mortal's continuing life. *Perishes* parallels "dies." The *expectation*, in synonymous parallel with "hope," is for something good. It is *from strength* because it is expected through the resources of a mortal's physical strength (see Job 40:16; Isa. 40:29; Hos. 12:4). This expectation also *perishes* upon the mortal's death (see 10:28).

8 When *I AM* delivers the righteous from their adversity, he plops the

---

12. So Meinhold, *Sprüche*, 188.

13. Ancient translators mistakenly thought that the original text of v. 7a meant that the hope of any person, including the righteous, perishes at death. To remove this unorthodox meaning (cf. 10:28; 12:28; 14:32: 23:17–18), they added "wicked" to "human being." Most manuscripts of the MT read "a wicked person"; so KJV, NASB, NRSV, RSV, ESV. Because internal evidence favors the omission of "wicked," the translation adopted here is based on two Heb. MSS that do so.

wicked into their place. Verset A implies that the wicked person nearly succeeds in harming the *righteous person*. But the latter *is delivered from adversity* by *I AM*. *And* signifies that at the time *I AM* delivers the righteous person, *it falls on the wicked person instead*. For example, according to the Law, the perjurer who intends death for the innocent is the one who is to be sentenced to death (Deut. 19:16–18); Haman is hanged on the very gallows he intends for Mordecai (Esth. 7:10); and Daniel's enemies are thrown into the lions' den to die the death they decreed for Daniel (Dan. 6:24). This tidy justice must be viewed in light of eternity. In the present, it is possible for the righteous to suffer under the wicked (cf. 10:2–3; Acts 2:22–23).

Security from Destructive Speech through Knowledge (11:9–15)

Janus (11:9)

Verse 9 is a janus between vv. 1–8 and 10–15. On the one hand, it is concentrically connected to 11:1–8 by the words "righteous" and "deliver" (vv. 8a, 9b).

A	*A righteous person* is *delivered* from adversity,	v. 8a
B	and it falls on the wicked person instead.	v. 8b
B'	With their mouths, deceivers destroy their neighbors,	v. 9a
A'	but through knowledge *the righteous deliver* themselves.	v. 9b

The concentric pattern implies that the delivery of the righteous envisioned in v. 8a is through the knowledge in v. 9b. Similarly, the adversity into which the wicked come (v. 8b) is brought about by their self-destroying speech (v. 9a; see vv. 10–11).

On the other hand, v. 9 is connected to vv. 10–15 by the theme of "words in community."

The antithetical parallelism of verse 9 juxtaposes the subjects, *the deceiver* and *the righteous*; their respective actions, *destroy their neighbors* and *deliver themselves*; and their respective means, *with the mouth* and *through knowledge*. The imprecise antithetic parallelism implies that the neighbor is not righteous and, thus unfortified by righteousness, is led astray by the deceiver's professed friendship. But the knowledgeable righteous (10:14) see through the deceiver's masks (28:11) and through the knowledge of wise speech, by which they know when, how, and what to speak, they save themselves from the trap (see 12:6, 13; 14:3).

Words in Community (11:10–15)

This subunit reaffirms the power of speech to revive or ravage the community. Verse 15 pertains to becoming surety, but recall that this happens by words and must be resolved by speech (see 6:1–5).[14] The subunit consists of three quatrains.

10–11 This couplet strengthens the appeal to be righteous, not wicked, by contrasting the social assessment of their fates. The righteous prosper with the community's full approval (cf. 10:8; 28:12, 28; 29:2, 16), but the wicked perish in opprobrium.

Prosperity denotes all the concrete good things people desire (cf. Jer. 31:12). God gives these to the *righteous* (Job 2:10). And when he does, *a city exults*—it celebrates the triumph of morality. The exultation in v. 10a is paired with *a shout of praise* in v. 10b, but their causes differ radically. In the latter, the city rejoices *when the wicked perish* (see 10:28; 11:7). The city revels because its own well-being depends on people receiving their just deserts. The proverb assumes that by common grace, the community comprehends morality. This proverb must be held in tension with 24:17: one must not gloat over a fallen foe. The next couplet (vv. 12–13) cautions against despising anyone.

The *blessing of the upright* (see p. 37) means God's bestowal of blessing on them or the blessing they bestow on the city through their beneficent presence and prayers (cf. 10:6). Either way, the upright mediate the divine blessing that elevates the whole environment (cf. Gen. 18:26; 39:5).[15] *City* (see 8:3). *Is exalted* means "is built up" literally and figuratively, but since the means of building is speech (i.e., a "spoken blessing"), it must have a metaphorical sense here. *By the mouth of the wicked* is a fitting parallel to "blessing" since the latter is a verbal benediction (see 10:6). The metaphor *is destroyed* signifies the slander that demoralizes and demolishes the city "built up" by the upright.

12–13 This couplet further describes the character and speech of the wicked and the righteous (cf. vv. 9, 10b, 11b) and protects vv. 10–11 from misinterpretation.

Those who have no sense (see p. 50). *Despise their neighbors* (see 1:7; 6:30) refers to holding others, even God, in contempt and is rooted in pride (see Pss. 31:18; 123:4). *But the understanding* (see "Intellectual Terms for the Wise and Righteous," p. 36) *hold their tongues* so as not to destroy the community. Such a person has the discretion not to vent his thoughts and feelings (cf. 12:23; 13:3;

---

14. Meinhold, *Sprüche*, 189–90.

15. M. L. Malbim, *The Book of Proverbs*, ed. C. Wengrovand and A. G. Zornberg (Jerusalem: Feldheim, 1973), 112.

17:14, 27)—very hard when one is anxious (Jer. 4:19) or insulted (Gen. 34:5; 1 Sam. 10:27; 2 Sam. 13:20; 2 Kgs. 18:36; Job 13:5). The antithetical parallelism suggests that the wise have been "belittled" (NRSV) by the senseless. Still, they wait for the right time and place to speak (cf. 12:23; 15:2, 28; Isa. 41:1), even as *I AM* does (cf. Isa. 42:14; Hab. 1:13 with 2:2–3), and they do not respond in kind (cf. 26:4; Gal. 6:1).

Verse 13 teaches the protection of private communication, because otherwise rebels are advantaged and friendships disrupted. Its imprecise antithetic parallels suggest that the slanderer is disloyal and the loyal do not slander. *Whoever goes about as a slanderer.* Jeremiah and Ezekiel portray slanderers as hardened liars and deceivers bent on destroying their victims (see Jer. 6:28; 9:3; Ezek. 22:9). The connection with v. 12 is now clear: contempt leads to slander, but the prudent keep silent. *One who reveals* wantonly uncovers. *A secret* refers to the conversation among friends, and especially their secret plans (cf. 11:13; 20:19; Ps. 83:3). Even in court, a secret must not be divulged (25:9). *The faithful in spirit* is a person who is loyal and reliable in character. Such a person is *one who conceals a word* (or "matter"; see 1:6) that, if leaked, will sever friends.

14–15 In the final couplet, v. 14 balances the teachings on the prudent use of silence (vv. 12–13) with the prudent use of speech. Both vv. 14 and 15 juxtapose imprudent action that brings disaster with prudent action that gives security, but v. 14 pertains to civic matters and v. 15 to personal business.[16]

A community needs wise counsel and wise counselors to achieve success. Our equivalent proverb is "Two heads are better than one." *Where there is no guidance* implies that "guidance" (see "Intellectual Terms for the the Wise and Righteous," p. 36) is more important than physical strength, albeit it should not be pitted against heroic strength (cf. 8:14; 21:31). Without it *a people* (the whole community) *falls.* Verse 14b suggests that without wisdom, external hostile forces prevail. The Hebrew verb glossed *but safety [lies]* implies helping those in trouble rather than rescuing them from it.[17] *A multitude of counselors* is the many competent people whose arguments and counterarguments produce a plan that is guaranteed to succeed in spite of danger.

Verse 15 presents the disaster of losing one's safety and security by entering into the imprudent situation of *becoming surety for a stranger* (see on 6:1). *One suffers harm grievously* (see 13:20). *But one who hates* (see 1:22) *clapping [hands]* (see on 6:1), a gesture that functions as a "speech" act that seals the deal, *is one who is secure*, unburdened by worry or risk of financial ruin (see 6:2–15).

---

16. Garrett, *Proverbs*, 125–26.
17. So J. F. Sawyer, *TDOT*, 6:442, s.v. *yāša*.

Benevolence and Community (11:16–22)

The theme now shifts to benevolence and its rewards for oneself in contrast to selfishness and its harm for oneself (11:16–27). The subunit's frame contrasts a gracious woman who obtains honor (v. 16) with an imprudent beauty devoid of honor (v. 22).

16–17 This proverb pair is connected by a common theme, which is also the theme of the whole subunit: noble character traits bring true rewards, but base traits are bereft of benefits.

Gracious woman (sg.) contrasts with *violent men* (pl.). She is "weaker" in gender and in number. Nevertheless, she *lays hold of* what is better, namely, *honor* (social esteem), which has no temporal limits. By contrast, violent men gain only fleeting *wealth* (see 11:28; 23:5), which, though favorable (Prov. 3:16; 8:18; 13:8; 14:23; 22:4), can also separate from God (30:8) and provide false security (11:28) and which does not necessarily bring social esteem. In the end, their tyrannical achievements undermine them: their names will rot (10:7) and their wealth will disappear (23:5). Social esteem, however, is more desirable than riches (22:1; cf. 31:10–31). Thus her "grace" is better than their brute force.

Those who are kind (*ḥesed*) deny themselves to help a needy neighbor, but paradoxically *they benefit themselves*. By contrast, *the cruel*, or "merciless," willfully inflict pain on others but paradoxically *harm their own flesh*. In the book of Job, hurting one's flesh is worse than losing all of one's possessions (Job 1:12; 2:4–6). The one who upholds the paradoxes is *I AM*, as vv. 20–21 assert. According to Paul, kindness is a fruit of walking by the Spirit (Gal. 5:16–23).

18–19 A concentric pattern binds vv. 18 and 19. The couplet also pairs two metaphors, "sowing righteousness" (v. 18b) and "pursuing evil" (v. 19b), suggesting that the deceptive and true wages of v. 18 are defined as life and death in v. 19 (see 10:16).

A	*A wicked person* is one who works for a deceptive wage,	v. 18a
B	but *one who sows righteousness* [works] for true pay.	v. 18b
B'	Yes, indeed! *The righteous* attain life,	v. 19a
A'	but the *one who pursues evil* attains death.	v. 19b

A wicked person (see pp. 45–46) is depicted as a person who *works for a deceptive wage*. The wicked painstakingly perform their selfish work thinking it will bring them good, but all their selfishness earns them in the end is destruction and death, as the rest of the couplet elaborates (see 1:10–18; 10:2, 25; 11:4; cf. Rom. 6:21). By contrast, the benevolent are implicitly compared to a farmer *who sows* (scatters) *righteousness* like seed. Such a "farmer" *[works for] true pay.* "True" is added because in farming, the harvest can be uncertain; not so in the moral sphere (cf. Pss. 19:11; 37:3–6; Isa. 32:17–18; Matt. 19:29; Rev. 22:12).

True and deceptive pay are defined and escalated respectively as life and death in v. 19. Dramatic *Yes, indeed!* underscores the truth about to be stated— namely, *the righteous attain life* (see "The Wise and Their Rewards: Life," pp. 41–42), while in contrast, *whoever pursues evil attains* eternal *death.*

20–21 "God's attitude toward individuals (disgust/pleasure) in v. 20 corresponds to the outcome of their lives (inescapable trouble/deliverance) in v. 21."[18]

The antithetic parallelism of v. 20 contrasts *people with perverse* (twisted) *hearts* with *those who are blameless in their ways* (see p. 37). The perverse oppose God and community to serve self; the blameless are fully committed to serving others. Also contrasted are God's responses: the former *are an abomination to* I AM and the latter *find his favor.* Only *I AM* hands out life and death. The proverb calls for humans to transform their affections in line with God's affections. No other options are granted.

The antithetic parallelism of v. 21 contrasts the subjects, *evil person* and *such as are righteous,* and their respective predicates, *will not go unpunished* and *will escape.* What the righteous "escape" is death (see v. 19; cf. 10:2; 11:4). The strong initial assertion *be sure of this* affirms that the wicked will not be freed but the righteous will, despite the reality that justice is often perverted so that the wicked escape punishment while the righteous are persecuted.[19] The proverb is based on God's nature, not on observation.[20]

22 This single-line sarcastic proverb forms an inclusio with v. 16, thereby dividing vv. 16–21 from vv. 23–28. It draws an absurd comparison between a decorative gold ring in the snout of the unclean pig, which roots in swill, and the superficial beauty of an unwise woman who immerses her beauty in evil. *A gold ring* enhances a person's attractiveness (Isa. 3:21; Ezek. 16:12; Hos. 2:13). The metaphor *in the snout of a pig* evokes the pig's habit of eating swill and rooting in dung while oblivious to tarnishing the precious ornament in its snout. *Beautiful woman* refers to her outward beauty, usually regarded

---

18. Garrett, *Proverbs,* 126–27.

19. So Meinhold, *Sprüche,* 196. According to Fox (*Proverbs 10–31,* 539), "The intensity of the asseveration here, as in 11:19, suggests that the author is insisting on an outcome that visible reality would often contradict."

20. So Van Leeuwen, "Proverbs," in *NIB* 5, 119.

positively as a God-given gift that attracts the opposite sex (see 2:16; 1 Sam. 25:3; Esth. 2:7; Job 42:15). One *who turns aside* deviates from what is normative through conscience and learned through special revelation. *Discretion* here denotes the God-given gift of discrimination that enables good judgment (1 Sam. 25:33; Job 12:20; Ps. 119:66).

The proverb implies that having left whatever sound judgment she once had, the woman has transformed herself into a boorish animal in her dress, speech and behavior. In fact, she is worse than a pig. The sow by nature is boorish; the woman "turned aside" from her dignity. The beauty which should have enhanced her now appears foolishly wasted. Instead of being honored by her natural gift, she finds ridicule. The corresponding verse in the frame (v. 16) teaches that priority must be given to grace and honor over tyranny and wealth. Verse 22 teaches that priority must be given to the inner grace of discretion over outward beauty. This lesson is particularly applicable to young unmarried men. Knut Heim helpfully makes this point, but he mistakenly thinks this is its primary meaning: "Specifically, the proverb warns men not to make fools of themselves by marrying socially inept women simply because of their good looks."[21]

Desires and Paradoxical Fulfillment (11:23–27)

Verses 23 and 27 form a frame around this subunit. They are yoked together by the catchword "good" in the A versets and by generalizations about people's desires and their fulfillment. Within this frame, vv. 23–25 flesh out the paradox that givers gain while abusers abuse themselves (see vv. 17–21).

23 This verse intensifies 10:28. *The desire of the righteous* (see 10:24b) denotes their aspirations rooted in their nature to benefit others. *Is only good* (see 3:27) means both that they desire only good for others, even at their own expense (see vv. 23–25), and that they obtain only good for others and themselves. Since to requite good with evil is unjust, the moral Sovereign obligates himself to requite good with good. *The hope of the wicked* (cf. 10:28) *is wrath*: the wrath the wicked hoped to inflict on others boomerangs on them.

---

21. K. M. Heim, "A Closer Look at the Pig in Proverbs xi 22," *VT* 58 (2008): 13–27. Heim identifies the pig as the young man. But his novel identification depends entirely on the context of the book of Proverbs as a whole, not on the proverb itself. The proverbs, however, interpret themselves by their parallels. The broader context enriches that interpretation even if it is not decisive for its meaning. Nothing in the proverb itself signals that the pig is an incomplete metaphor for a man (cf. 11:22), and nothing in the immediate context suggests this narrow interpretation.

They hoped to prosper by plundering others, but God rewards them with wrath instead.

24 The principle that "the tight-fisted man ends up poorer and the open-handed man richer"[22] links this verse to vv. 25–26. Both halves of v. 24 bring together contradictory elements, creating paradoxes in order to clarify what is not obvious. *The one who scatters* is one who disperses widely, generously, and freely. What is scattered may be supplied from the parallel in v. 24b: "what is right," or what benefits the community. The needy are the unspecified receivers of the generosity. *And* adds the surprising paradoxical truth that generous people who deplete themselves by scattering are in fact *increased still more* (that is, more than what they gave away). By contrast, *the one who withholds from what is right* paradoxically *comes only to lack* life's necessities and riches. Giving charity "has been compared to the suckling of a child. The more the child suckles, the greater becomes the mother's supply of milk."[23] The paradox pertains to philanthropy, not personal investment. Other immoral causes of physical want are laziness (14:23), hastiness (2:15; 28:22), wickedness (13:25; cf. 10:3), intemperance (21:17), and imprudent generosity (22:16).

25–26 Agricultural metaphors and the catchword "blessing" link this proverb pair. The truth of reciprocity stated in v. 24 is elaborated in v. 25 by two images: "fat" from animal husbandry and "drench" from horticulture. The double image guarantees that reciprocity for generosity is certain (see 10:26). *A life bestowing blessing* refers to doing one's duty to the needy (v. 24), including praying (cf. 10:6). Paradoxically, such a giver *will be fattened*. This metaphor connotes abundance, satisfaction, and health (cf. Deut. 31:20). The metaphor *as for those who drench* implies a parched land needing water—an implicit comparison to the poor. *They in turn will be soaked* underscores the reciprocity between generosity and self-gain through abundant harvests, here symbolized by the metonymy of water, "soaked."

The paradox that the generous gain and the illiberal lose is illustrated in v. 26 by the example of selling grain, presumably at market value, in contrast to hoarding it in a famine to up the price. *One who withholds* may refer to merchants who refrain from selling their grain to inflate its price and thus exploit others to advantage themselves (cf. Amos 8:4–8). *Grain symbolizes life's necessities, not its luxuries. People curse them.* However, only God can effect a curse, and so they look to him for its fulfillment (cf. Exod. 22:22–24; Amos

22. Aitken, *Proverbs*, 126.
23. Greenstone, *Proverbs*, 122.

8:4–8; Jas. 5:4).[24] *Blessing [is] on the head* probably refers to the benedictory words whereby the praying people mediate the divine blessing to the righteous *one who sells it* (see on 10:6; Job 29:13).

27 The unit trumpeting the theme that benevolence benefits concludes with a generalization about the desires (see v. 23) of two contrasting seekers. *Diligently* means despite difficulty. *Seeks good* signifies caring for others, since "evil" in verset B refers to harming others. *Will find favor* is a metonymy for God's blessing. *Whoever searches for evil* refers to a person who carefully and energetically seeks to harm one's neighbor even to the point of death (see 11:19). *It will come to them* expresses the inexorable moral law of reciprocity administered by the moral Sovereign (see 1:26–27; cf. Esth. 7:10; Ps. 57:6; Gal. 6:7; 2 Thess. 2:10–11). The proverb admonishes the reader to be like Jesus, who did good and was rewarded with eternal life (Matt. 25:35–36; Acts 10:38–40; Phil. 2:5–11; Jas. 1:27). The truth "seek and you will find" takes on new meaning: what you seek for others you will find for yourself (cf. Matt. 6:33; 7:7).

Certain Gain or Loss (11:28–31)

Verses 28–30 continue the theme of gain and loss, but now with an emphasis on their certainty. The unit ends with a climactic proverb in v. 31.

28 The antithetical parallels of v. 28 contrast those who rely on wealth to save them versus righteous people, as well as their respective destinies, a fatal fall versus flourishing. The parallelism is imprecise, implying that the righteous do not rely on their wealth and those who do are not righteous (see 10:15). *Those who rely on their wealth* do not share it with the needy but zealously protect it since it is their basis of hope. *They will fall* is an incomplete metaphor for violent death and destruction. Riches may be a blessing (cf. 3:14–15; 8:18; Gen. 24:35; 2 Chr. 1:11–12; Job 42:11–12), but trusting in them is both foolish (Mark 10:21–25) and fatal, since they cannot save from death (cf. 10:2, 15; 11:4; 18:11; 28:11; 30:7–9). By contrast, the righteous ground their faith in the unswervingly reliable God (see 3:5; 16:3, 20; 22:19; 28:25; 29:25), seek his favor (11:27), and share their wealth. As a result, they are blessed and *like foliage . . . sprout.* The simile connotes the sprouting of fresh, vigorous life, the opposite of "to fall."

29–30 These verses elaborate the two images of v. 28. Verse 29 develops

24. The point of this proverb was illustrated during the early days of the 2020 coronavirus pandemic, when some people flocked to their local retailer and purchased its entire supply of masks, gloves, and hand sanitizer in the hope of selling them later at exorbitant prices. Eventually the government brought in legislation threatening severe penalties on the hoarders and many ended up donating their supplies and losing even their purchase price.

the tragic downfall of the fool (v. 28a) with the image of a house reduced to wind, and v. 30 explicates the flourishing of the righteous (v. 28b) with the image of a fruitful tree.

Those who ruin their household denotes people who harm those with whom they have relationships, including, by metonymy, slaves and servants. One who *inherits the wind* ends up with nothing (see Job 15:2; 16:3; Eccl. 1:14; Isa. 26:18; Jer. 5:13; Mic. 2:11). *A fool is a slave to the wise in heart.* Having lost their property, fools lose their freedom and become subjects to the competent, who can direct the energy of fools to positive ends. The fool's miserliness ends in misery and slavery.

Verse 30a portrays the healing words and deeds of the righteous as the fruit of the tree of life, to which v. 30b adds that their fruit is so appealing that it attracts people to eat it, whereupon they are saved from death. *Fruit* refers to the benefits that the righteous produce in the community by their words and deeds. *Tree of life* is a sustained metaphor connoting healing and abundant, eternal life to all who eat of it (cf. 3:18). *"Takes lives"* is an intentional irony. The collocation occurs six other times in the Bible, always in the sense of "to kill." But the mind rejects linking that meaning with being *wise* and forces one to the opposite meaning: saving them.[25] This interpretation conforms with 13:14: the righteous both produce eternal life and, by their attractiveness, save others from death.

31 A climactic proverb[26] asserting crime does not pay concludes this section. Using an *a fortiori* argument, it moves from a confident proposition (verset A) to a second, implied proposition (verset B). Verset A states the confident premise, *if*, which is concluded in verset B's "how much more." *The righteous person* links vv. 30a and 31. *Repaid* is a legal term normally denoting compensation for damages but here denoting punishment. *The earth* denotes the historical realm, the land of the living,[27] where the righteous are disciplined. *How much more* introduces the implicit proposition. The combination of *the wicked* (see "Ethical Terms for the Wicked and Fools," pp. 45–46) and *the sinner* (see 1:10) denotes their guilt before God for their crimes against humankind. "Are repaid" is gapped in verset B. "In the land" is not gapped in verset B since the verset probably intends to distinguish between the present ("in the earth") remedial punishment of the righteous and the future punishment of the wicked beyond the historical present. The proverb suggests that

25. So William H. Irwin, "The Metaphor in Prov. 11,30," *Bib* 65 (1984): 97–100.
26. This is the first time the climactic form "how much more" occurs.
27. Fox, *Proverbs 10–31*, 545.

if the righteous do not escape divine discipline (v. 31a), how much less will sinners escape it (v. 31b). The righteous are disciplined by *I AM* within history, "in the earth," which they will inherit, so as not to be condemned along with the world (3:11–12; 1 Cor. 11:32). By contrast, the wicked may not receive their just deserts on the earth (within their lifetimes; see 3:1–12). Rather, their judgment occurs when they are finally torn from the land (2:21–22; 10:30).

Two Subunits on Speech and Deeds (12:1–28)

¹One who loves instruction is one who loves knowledge,
    but one who hates correction is an ignoramus.
²A good person obtains favor from *I AM*,
    but a crafty person he condemns.
³A human being is not established through wickedness,
    but righteous people are not uprooted.
⁴A noble and virtuous wife is the crown of her husband,
    but like rottenness in his bones is a shameful wife.
⁵The plans of righteous people are totally just;
    the guidance of wicked people is full of deceit.
⁶The words of wicked people are a bloody ambush,
    but the mouth of upright people delivers them.
⁷Overturn the wicked and they are no more,
    but the households of the righteous stand firm.
⁸According to their prudence people are praised,
    but a person with a warped mind will be held in contempt.
⁹Better to be one who is held as worthless and yet has a slave
    than to be one who exalts self and lacks bread.
¹⁰The righteous know the desires of their animals,
    but the mercy of the wicked is cruel.
¹¹People who work their land are filled with food,
    but the person who pursues fantasies has no sense.
¹²The wicked person desires the stronghold of evil people,
    but the root of righteous people endures.
¹³In the transgression of [their] lips is the trap set for evildoers,
    and so the righteous person escapes from distress.
¹⁴From the fruit of their mouth people are filled with good things,
    and the deeds of their hands return to them.
¹⁵The way of fools is right in their eyes,

but a wise person listens to counsel.

¹⁶As for fools, their vexation is revealed on the same day,
  but the shrewd person ignores an insult.

¹⁷A trustworthy witness declares what is right,
  but perjurers [declare] deceit.

¹⁸There is one who speaks recklessly like the stabbing of a sword,
  but the tongue of the wise is a remedy.

¹⁹A truthful lip is established forever,
  but a lying tongue is [only] for a moment.

²⁰Deceit is in the heart of those who plan evil,
  but those who counsel peace have joy.

²¹No sort of malevolence will happen to the righteous person,
  but wicked people are full of harm.

²²Lying lips are an abomination to *I AM*,
  but those who show trustworthiness find his favor.

²³The shrewd person conceals knowledge,
  but the heart of fools cries out folly.

²⁴The hand of the diligent will rule,
  but the slack person will become compulsory labor.

²⁵Anxiety in an individual's heart weighs it down,
  but a good word cheers it up.

²⁶The righteous search out their confidential friends,
  but the way of the wicked leads them astray.

²⁷Those who are slack do not roast any game for themselves,
  but a diligent person [roasts] the precious wealth of the land.

²⁸In the path of righteousness is life,
  and the journey of its byway is immortality.

Chapter 12 consists of two subunits of equal length dealing with speech and deeds (vv. 1–14, 15–28). Each half begins with an educational proverb contrasting the teachableness of the wise with the incorrigibility of the fool (vv. 1, 15) to excite the son to accept the teachings that follow. Each half concludes with a synthetic proverb promising the righteous person life now and forevermore (vv. 14, 28).

Each subunit is divided into partial subunits that commence with a proverb broadly categorizing the righteous and the wicked and conclude with proverbs that affirm the permanence of the former and the impermanence of the latter: vv. 1–3, 4–7, 8–12, 13–14 and vv. 16–19, 20–23, 24–28.

The First Subunit (12:1-14)

Introduction (12:1-3)

The introduction characterizes the wise and foolish as open or closed to shaping.

1 This proverb echoes the vocabulary of the Prologue—*instruction* (1:2), *knowledge* (1:2), and *correction* (1:25, 29-30)—and its aim to set youth on the way of life by inclining them toward the parents' teachings and away from folly. The disciple's characterization as *one who loves* instruction signifies passions that are ablaze to act wisely. *But one who hates correction* stands outside the divine realm of wisdom and *is an ignoramus*. "Ignoramus" is parallel with "animal" in Ps. 73:22. Such a person lacks "the rationality that differentiates humans from animals."[28] By spurning correction, incorrigibles alienate themselves from the Holy One, and so, due to original sin, their thinking and behavior become beastly (cf. Ps. 32:9).

2 The teachable and unteachable are now characterized as good and crafty respectively. *A good person* (see v. 1a) beautifies and benefits the community's welfare. Such a person *obtains favor from* I AM, the source of all good (Mark 10:18; Gal. 5:22; Jas. 1:17) and the only One who can bestow life and prosperity (cf. 8:35; Isa. 58:11). *A crafty person* (*'îš mezimmôt*; see 14:17), the opposite of "a good person," designates the brute (v. 1b) who devises evil stratagems to advantage self by disadvantaging others. *He condemns*, the opposite of finding favor, means that *I AM* finds the crafty guilty of violating the norms of wisdom and so hands them over to death.

3 The good and crafty are now characterized chiastically by their wickedness and their righteousness, and their endurance under *I AM*'s favor or condemnation is contrasted as impermanent and permanent. *A human being* (every person with no exceptions) *is not established* (will not endure) *through wickedness* (see "Ethical Terms for the Wicked and Fools," pp. 45-46). By contrast, *righteous people* ("the wise," v. 1, and "the good," v. 2) *are not uprooted*—they will endure.

Speech and One's Household (12:4-7)

This partial subunit begins with a proverb contrasting two kinds of wives (v. 4) and is drawn to conclusion by contrasting the endurance of their households (v. 7).

---

28. Chou-Wee Pan, *NIDOTTE*, 1:691, s.v. *bʿr*.

4 Wise and foolish wives are contrasted by the metaphors of an outward crown and inward bone decay. The contrast suggests that the shameful wife robs her husband of social standing and the noble wife strengthens him by giving him social honor and empowerment to rule in the community (cf. 31:23). *Noble and virtuous* is a hendiadys for the Hebrew *ḥayil* (see 31:10 and Ruth 3:11, its only other uses with "woman"). With respect to women, it refers to spiritual and physical strength, noble character, and competence (Ruth 3:11; Prov. 14:1; 31:10–29). *Wife* (a real woman; but see 9:13). She *is the crown* connotes that she is her husband's most prominent social adornment and empowers him to rule (see 4:9; 31:10–31; cf. Job 19:9). *Husband* (*baʿal*) means broadly "lord." Peter upheld Sarah as an ideal wife because in her heart she called Abraham her "lord" (*kyrios*, 1 Pet. 3:6; cf. *ʾādôn*, Gen. 18:12). The proverb assumes her husband is wise and righteous and sacrifices himself for her good (cf. 1 Pet. 3:7). *A shameful wife* connotes that the husband risked marriage to gain dignity and stature but instead received the opposite. She undermines him by being unfaithful (2:17), contentious (19:13; 21:9, 19), impious, and incompetent. Metaphorically, she is *like rottenness*, or decay, *in his bones* (cf. 12:4; 14:30; Hab. 3:16).[29] "Bones" connotes his fundamental physical and psychical structure. As the decay progresses, his inner happiness and outer usefulness are sapped "till at last . . . the whole life of the man falls to ruin."[30] Marriage is serious; a wife either makes or breaks a man at home and in the community (see 14:1; 18:22; 19:14; 31:10–31). The Mosaic law permitted divorce from a wife who corrupted the home's holiness (Deut. 24:1–4; cf. Matt. 19:3–12).

5 The plans of the righteous and the wicked are diametrically opposed to each other. *Plans* and *guidance* (see "Intellectual Terms for the Wise and Righteous," p. 36) are means of achieving goals. Those *of righteous people* (see "Ethical Terms for the Wise and Righteous," pp. 36–37) *are totally just* (lit. "are justice"; see "delights" in 8:30); those *of wicked people* (see "Ethical Terms for the Wicked and Fools," pp. 45–46) are *full of deceit* (lit. "are deceit"). To succeed, self-serving goals demand deception (cf. Jer. 17:9; Matt. 15:19). Judas used a deceptive kiss to betray Jesus (Matt. 26:47–49).

6 This proverb shows how these contrasting plans are executed. The son again meets the seductress (see "The Unchaste Wife," pp. 53–57) and sinners (1:10–19; 2:12–15; 4:14–19; 6:12–19), who are characterized by perverted speech. *Wicked people* effect their deceptive plans through their *words*. Both the content of their words (false accusations, bribes, etc.; see 1:11–14; 10:11, 18) and the style of their words (e.g., sinister signals, flaming rhetoric; see 6:12–13; 10:10;

---

29. NLT and GNT paraphrase "rottenness" with "cancer."
30. Delitzsch, *Proverbs*, 252.

16:27) aim to murder innocents. Metaphorically, their speech is *a bloody am-bush*, connoting that it entraps and kills unsuspecting citizens (1:10–14; 11:5–7; cf. 1 Kgs. 21:1–14). Their words, however, are countered by the healing *mouth* (speech; see 15:4) *of upright people* (see p. 37). It *delivers them* (saves them from death) directly as a result of speaking the truth in court and indirectly by their counsel and teaching.

7 As plans (v. 5) give rise to words (v. 6; see 16:27), words give rise to desti-nies (v. 7). *Overturn* refers to the sudden reversal of a hoped-for condition.[31] Here it is a metaphor for God's judgment (cf. 12:2, 22; Gen. 19:21, 25, 29). He will sentence to death *wicked people,* who scheme to deceive their victims (v. 5) and who spin words to ambush them (v. 6). *And they are no more.* Their future elimination is irreversible (see 2:21–22; cf. 1 Kgs. 15:4; Esth. 7:10). *The households of the righteous stand firm* implies that their households are built on firm foundations, suitable for weathering devastating storms (10:25, 30; 12:3, 12; cf. Matt. 7:24–27). The fate of Noah's family in contrast to that of his generation instantiates this proverb.

Deeds and Property (12:8–12)

This partial subunit begins by contrasting generally the characters of those having or lacking good sense (v. 8) and concludes with an aphorism contrast-ing their permanence and impermanence (v. 12; cf. vv. 3, 7).

8 *According to their prudence* (see p. 35) *people are praised* (given public acclamation bestowing social honor; cf. Gen. 12:15; 2 Sam. 14:25; Ezek. 26:17). In 3:4, "prudence" is linked with "good repute" (cf. 13:15a). "Our Lord's *wisdom* was also *commended,* not only by the popular voice (Matt. 7:28, 29), but even by the testimony of his enemies (John 7:46)."[32] *But the person with a warped mind* is unable to see reality and so is dishonest. Such a person, though praised mo-mentarily, eventually *will be held in contempt.* This aphorism, however, should be held in tension with others. The wise are not always thanked (see Eccl. 9:15), and apostates praise the wicked (28:4). On his return, however, Christ will certainly commend the wise (Matt. 5:11–12; Luke 12:42–44; 2 Cor. 10:18).

9 The general saying of v. 8 is now applied specifically. To live comfortably as a nobody is better than pretending to be rich while poor (cf. 15:17; 30:8–9). *Bet-ter* is *one who is held as worthless.* Modest people endure society's slights in or-

---

31. K. Seybold, *TDOT,* 3:423, s.v. *hāpak.*
32. Bridges, *Proverbs,* 135.

der not to live above their means. That such a person *has a slave* (or servant) to
help shows that in the biblical world, even those of modest income had slaves.
Today, those of modest means own dishwashers, vacuum cleaners, computers,
and so on. *One who exalts self* pretends to be wealthy to command honor.
Lacks bread shows that the honor is feigned; in reality the self-exalting person
is starving. Petty people unwisely spend their sparse resources to keep up vain
appearances. Their slavery to human opinion dooms them to shame.

10 If the wise care for their animals, how much more will they show mercy
to their slaves/servants. *The righteous* (see "Ethical Terms for the Wise and Righteous," pp. 36–37) *know* (listen to and empathize with) *the desires* (see *Nepeš*
[Traditionally, 'Soul']," p. 32) *of their animals* (domesticated quadrupeds). The
Creator cares for creatures (cf. Deut. 11:15; 25:4; Pss. 36:6b; 104:14, 17; Jonah 4:11);
they too share in his Sabbaths (Exod. 20:10; 23:11–13; Lev. 25:1–7). The proverb
likely argues from lesser to greater by implication: if animals must be shown
mercy, how much more humans. By contrast, if the wicked are cruel to the
lesser creation, who can entrust them with the greater? *Mercy* denotes the tender yearnings and love of a superior for a helpless inferior based on bonds of
common grace. However, here, attributing mercy to *the wicked*, who neither fear
God nor help others, is sarcastic. Their compassion is in fact *cruel* (see 5:9).

11 The economic proverbs now turn from one's workers to one's own work.
People who work exert effort to produce something. *Their land* is their economic base. The proverb is not exalting agriculture above other legitimate
pursuits; the Bible mentions other trades favorably (cf. Exod. 28:3; 36:1; 1 Sam.
8:13). Rather, agriculture is exemplary of all honest work. *Is filled with food.*
Those who work the creation are in turn provisioned by it. By contrast, *the
person who pursues fantasies* (gambles or get-rich-quick schemes that bypass
hard work; see 21:5–6) *has no sense* to preserve their lives. *I AM* backs the
creation order that demands and rewards honest work, not hasty wealth (see
10:3; 12:2).[33] Sometimes, however, poverty results from uncontrollable factors
such as tyranny or natural disaster (see 10:4; 28:3).

12 The text and philology of this proverb are difficult.[34] Out of depravity,
the wicked person desires (or craves) and so acts to possess *the stronghold of
evil people.* Since the wicked lack the true security that comes from a righteous
character, they seek an outward defense obtained illegally by plundering their
victims (see 1:10–19; 11:16); they vainly imagine their ill-gotten gain is a forti-

33. This proverb is repeated with a different ending in 28:19.
34. For the textual difficulties and their resolutions, see Waltke, *Proverbs 1–15*, 529.

fied city (see 18:11). By contrast, *the root* (an incomplete metaphor connoting stable life) *of righteous people endures* because their security emanates from their inner character.

Conclusion: Words and Deeds (12:13–14)

These verses are united by "lips" and "mouth," organs of speech. The sinner's speech leads to death (v. 13), the righteous person's speech to good things (v. 14)

13 Sinners trap themselves by their lies and slander, while the innocent escape from the deadly trap. *In the transgression* (see 10:12) *of [their] lips* (see 10:13) *is the trap set* depicts lethal speech designed to surprise and destroy innocent victims. *For the evildoers* implies that they made the snare to trap the righteous, but unwittingly their slander traps them instead. Similar ironies occur in 18:7 and 29:6, where again the schemers are caught by their own schemes (see 1:16). *And* favors this meaning because it implies that as a result of the evildoer becoming trapped, *the righteous person escapes from distress*. Sometimes the immoral snare the righteous, but when the tables are turned, the wicked are trapped while the innocent escape (see 3:34; cf. 1 Kgs. 2:22–23; Dan. 6:7–8, 24; Matt. 27:25).

14 The concluding synthetic proverb affirms that good things reward good speakers and good workers. *The fruit of their mouth* likens the wise person's godly teachings to a tree's beneficial fruit: they reveal character, come forth naturally, and nourish the community. *People* (that is, righteous speakers) *are filled with good things*. As their good fruit fed others, good now returns and feeds them. Similarly, the *deeds of their hands* (the beneficial actions of the righteous) *return to them*, thus affirming the wisdom principle that deeds and destiny are inseparable. *I AM* is the one who upholds the deed-destiny nexus and reciprocates the doer's good deeds (see 12:2; 19:17). "The meanest exercise of love will be abundantly and eternally recompensed."[35] Jesus promised eschatological rewards to those who left everything to serve him (Matt. 19:28–29).

The Second Subunit (12:15–28)

Following an introductory educational proverb (v. 15), the main body of the second subunit consists of proverbs on words (vv. 16–23) and works (vv. 24–27)

---

35. Bridges, *Proverbs*, 139.

and is drawn to a conclusion with a sublime proverb trumpeting the claim that the righteous keep their relationship with *I AM* forever (v. 28). The inclusio "way" frames the subunit.

Introductory Educational Proverb (12:15)

15 Verse 15, like the Prologue (1:8–9:18; cf. 10:1; 12:1), defines "wise" and "fool" in terms of their reception or rejection of authoritative counsel. The imprecise antithetical parallels suggest each line should be completed by the other. Thus, the fool does not listen to counsel, and the wise do not establish what is right by their own opinions. *The way* (see 1:15) *of fools* (see "Intellectual Terms for the Wicked and Fools," pp. 47–48) *is right in their own eyes* (in their own opinion; see 3:5, 7), but they are incessantly doing evil in *I AM*'s eyes (cf. Judg. 2:11; 3:7; 17:6; 21:5). By contrast, *a wise person* (see "Intellectual Terms for the Wise and Righteous," pp. 34–35) is one who *listens to counsel* (see 1:25).

Wise and Foolish Speech (12:16–23)

This partial subunit on the use and abuse of the mouth is framed by matching proverbs in the outer frame (vv. 16 and 23). Verse 22 lays the theological foundation for the whole unit: *I AM* upholds the moral order with reference to speech.

16 This verse, admonishing self-control, transitions from the introduction to the ethics and theology of speaking (vv. 17–22). *Vexation* means being upset or incensed. Sages regarded this a dangerous emotion requiring restraint (cf. Job 5:2). A foolish son vexes his father (17:25) as the fool does the wise (27:3) and a foolish wife her husband (21:19), yet the wise respond coolly. By contrast, the fool's vexation *is revealed on the same day*—it is disclosed publicly and immediately. Fools flag themselves with their pugnaciousness (cf. 20:3), revealing their intolerant, uneducable attitudes. Their tempers control them, cause havoc, and shame them. By contrast, *the shrewd person ignores an insult*. Instead of responding emotionally to an indignity (see 3:35; 6:33; 9:7; 11:2), the wise person anticipates the dangerous blowback of such a reaction and chooses to overlook the affront. Verses 17–19 clarify that in this way the shrewd can respond reasonably and effectively.

17 The character of a witness affects a judicial decision. *A trustworthy* (or "honest"; see p. 38) *witness declares what is right*. A judge can count on such a witness to assure a right verdict. By contrast, *perjurers* are the antonym of the "trustworthy witness" (12:17; Ps. 119:29–30; Isa. 59:4; Jer. 5:1–2; 9:3). Witnesses have personal knowledge of the facts and so are obliged to testify. The accused's life or death depends on reliable witness testimony (14:25). Ancients lacking modern forensic methods to independently verify the facts relied on the crucial evidence of eyewitnesses for establishing the truth (12:17; 14:5, 25; 18:21; 19:5, 9, 28; 21:28; 24:28; 25:18; 29:24; Exod. 23:1–3; Lev. 19:15). *Deceit* refers to words that aim to mislead the judge and undermine justice by declaring the righteous guilty and the guilty innocent (cf. 1 Sam. 22:9–10; 1 Kgs. 21:1–14; Matt. 26:60–61; John 2:19–21). The *lex talionis* principle demands perjurers suffer the same fate they intended for their victims (Deut. 19:16–19). Qoheleth, however, notes the universal human experience that where justice should be, "wickedness was there" (Eccl. 3:16), a reality experienced by Naboth and Jesus.

18 The psychic damage of the thoughtless "tongue" is here compared to the physical damage of the lethal sword and contrasted with the wise tongue that heals. *Recklessly* (or "thoughtlessly"; see Lev. 5:4; cf. 13:3) comes from the root *bāṭā'*, which also describes the impetuous speech of Moses at the waters of Meribah (Ps. 106:32–33). Such speech is *like the stabbing of a sword.* This simile signifies intentional and insensitive slaughter. The English idiom "their words went right through me"[36] similarly captures the piercing, lethal action of rash speech. By contrast, *the tongue of wise people is a remedy* because it reconciles harmful conflicts (cf. v. 20). The sequence of thoughts may connote that their speech soothes the hurt of reckless speech and cures its fatal wounds (cf. vv. 6, 25). Wise speech aims to create peace, not to win by dominating others.

19 Truth commends itself by its enduring nature in contrast to the transient nature of lies. *A truthful lip* speaks what conforms to reality and to *I AM*'s moral order and so *is established,* a divine passive (i.e., by *I AM*), *forever.* By contrast, *a lying tongue,* instead of finding *I AM*'s favor, is an abomination to him (12:2, 22) and so *is [only] for a moment.*[37]

20 The imprecise parallelism of this proverb suggests that each line should be completed by the other: the deceitful are joyless, and peace promoters do not plot evil. *Deceit,* an essential ingredient for the wicked to succeed (see 12:5), is rooted *in the heart* (see "Heart," p. 32) *of those who plan evil.* Their cold, calculated, skillfully executed plans are morally reprehensible because they aim to harm the innocent (see 1:16). But the antithetical parallel "joy" suggests that their plans boomerang, and so they hurt themselves instead (see 10:6, 11). By contrast, *those who counsel peace* (reconciling action devoid of desire to damage others) *have joy* (cf. 10:28; Rom. 7:22). In Proverbs, "coun-

---

36. Plaut, *Proverbs,* 147.

37. For the textual difficulties and their resolutions, see Waltke, *Proverbs 1–15,* 529.

selors" always occurs in reference to a group; here it refers to any competent group of counselors. Unlike evil-plotters, peacemakers have no fear of evil boomeranging on them.

21 This freedom from harm of the righteous is contrasted with the harm that comes to the wicked. Although deceivers aim violence at the righteous (v. 20a), *no sort of malevolence will happen to the righteous person* (cf. 22:8a). This promise stands in light of the final outcome (see "Does Proverbs Promise Too Much," pp. 44–45). Within God's kingdom, everything, including trouble, ends in what is best so that the promise and the reality are in complete harmony (see 3:5; cf. Gen. 50:20). Romans 8:28 should be translated, "God works together with those that love him to bring about good" (NIV note). "He supports them in testing, delivers them out of it, and sanctifies them by it."[38] By contrast, *wicked people are full of harm.* Here, "full of" refers to the totality of harm that the wicked will experience.

22 The Agent who effects the contrasting fates of the wicked and the righteous is now revealed to be *I AM*, who from the shadows watches over his own (cf. 12:2, 22; Ps. 91:1, 10). *Lying lips* is a synecdoche referring to fools who distort facts carelessly, thoughtlessly (12:17), or intentionally (vv. 19b, 20a). That they *are an abomination to* I AM signifies that liars so repulse him that he removes them (cf. 3:32). *Those who show* refers broadly to people's actions, without restricting it to their speaking. *Trustworthiness* is a metonymy for the good deeds that spring out of their reliable characters. *Find his favor* means that they are accepted by *I AM* and so enjoy his protection and prosperity (see 12:2).

23 The closing frame contrasts fools, who cannot hide their hubris, with the shrewd, who shroud their knowledge. While *the shrewd person* saves wisdom for the right occasion, *fools* create havoc by incessantly spouting their insolent speech (cf. 12:16; 13:16). The shrewd *conceal knowledge* because neither pride to parade their knowledge nor rage to wreak harm drives them. They wait for the right situation to speak (cf. 3:7; 10:14a; 11:13; cf. Matt. 7:6). Until then, they hide it from fools, who hate it, and from situations where it might do more harm than good.[39] This is something Job's three friends had to learn (cf. Job 32:6, 18, 19; Eccl. 3:7; Amos 5:13; Matt. 7:6; 16:20; 17:9; John 1:12; 2 Cor. 12:1–6). *But the heart* (the words and actions) *of fools* loudly *cries out folly* (words and deeds of moral turpitude; see 5:23).

---

38. Bridges, *Proverbs*, 144.

39. Compare the Egyptian *Instruction of Amenemope*: "Better is one whose speech is in his belly than he who tells it to cause harm" (*AEL*, 2:159).

Diligent Work and Good Speech (12:24–27)

These proverbs link prudent speech with prudent work, disallowing any separation between these two essentials of wisdom (cf. 10:1–15; 12:4–12, 13–14).

24 The verse encourages diligence by contrasting the fates of the diligent and the slackers. *The hand of diligent people* (see 10:4), who are self-disciplined (cf. Gal. 5:22–23), will stay independent, attain power, and so *will rule. But* the *slack person* (see 10:4), who is undisciplined, *will become compulsory labor* (labor imposed as a form of taxation without the laborer becoming an outright slave; see Josh 17:13; Judg. 1:28–30, 33–35; Isa. 31:8; cf. Exod. 1:11). Solomon imposed compulsory labor extensively (1 Kgs. 5:13–16; 9:21), and its victims revolted against Rehoboam (12:18). Ironically, the hand that avoids labor ends up slaving away. "To put it bluntly, the diligent rise to the top and the lazy sink to the bottom."[40]

25 A good word can encourage the depressed (v. 18b). *Anxiety* denotes extreme emotional distress caused by the possibility of losing something vital to life (cf. Jer. 38:19; 49:23). *In an individual's heart* underscores that worry strikes at a person's core, causing the person to totter. *Weighs ... down* signifies an unbearable burden, such as a depressed psyche (cf. Ps. 44:25; Lam. 3:20). *A good word* is speech that effectively offsets the threat behind the anxiety. Whereas anxiety can zombify a person, the personal, pleasant, timely, and wise word restores with encouragement and hope (15:30; 25:25; cf. 1 Sam. 2:24). The distraught writer of Lamentations was uplifted by recalling *I AM*'s unfailing love and by self-talk: "*I AM* is my portion; therefore I will wait for him" (Lam. 3:21–24). A good word *cheers it up* (see 5:18; 10:1), as Jacob's spirit revived when he learned that Joseph was alive in Egypt (Gen. 45:27; cf. 1 Kgs. 8:56; Ps. 119:92; Prov. 15:23; 16:21, 24; 25:12; Isa. 35:3–4; Acts 16:28–34; 2 Cor. 1:4; Phil. 4:4).

26 A good word comes from a good person. Without such a friend, a person can stray to death. This proverb urges extreme caution in choosing one's bosom friend; it could be a matter of life or death. *The righteous search out* (undertake a careful examination in order to find what is hidden) *their confidential* (or bosom) *friend*. The righteous are always on the lookout for indications of incorrigibility (cf. 12:1, 15), deceit (12:20), garrulity (12:23), and unreliable conduct (20:17, 19, 22) in their companions. By contrast, *the way of wicked people leads them astray* since their "way" precludes having close friends who

---

40. Ross, *Proverbs*, 973.

encourage them in the ways of righteousness. Here, straying refers "to the trouble which befalls the wicked; they lose their way and meet disaster."[41]

27 As in v. 24, this proverb weighs *a diligent person* against *those who are slack*. Couch potatoes *do not roast any game for themselves* because they will not exert the effort to catch it or cook it. The animals are there, but they are too lazy. "Whether as non-finisher or non-starter, the indolent man throws away his chances."[42] By contrast, the diligent takes advantage of God's benevolent bounty and "roasts" (gapped in v. 27b) the game Providence provides. *The precious wealth of the land* is a metonymy for the wild animals in the field—the riches of the hunt. As the fool starves spiritually in the midst of abundant teaching (10:21), the slacker starves physically in the midst of abundant food.

Conclusion (12:28)

28 This concluding synthetic proverb declares that the righteous keep their relationship with God forever. *The path of righteousness* denotes the road of life traveled in the ethical sphere of piety toward God and self-sacrifice toward neighbors. A person may choose this road, but only *I AM*, who maintains the moral order, determines that righteousness *is* the sphere of abundant *life* (see "The Wise and Their Rewards: Life," pp. 41–42). He ushers those on that path into eternal fellowship with him (see 2:19; 3:18, 22; 10:11). *And the journey (derek;* see 1:15) *of its byways* narrows the broad course of one's lifestyle to the specific aspect of righteousness, the consequence of which is declared to be *immortality* (*'al-māwet*), the reading of the majority of codices within the Masoretic tradition. However, some scholars consider the MT corrupt and prefer the reading "unto death" (*'el-māwet*), the reading found in all the ancient versions and some medieval codices. They read the versets as antithetic instead of synthetic parallels.[43] The Masoretic reading is preferred here for the following reasons.

1. Text critically, *'al-māwet* is the more difficult reading to explain away because it is a unique collocation in Biblical Hebrew. The form of the word used for "no" (*'al*) is used with verbs, not nouns, rendering its use here with the noun "death" inexplicable. Moreover, the difference be-

---

41. J. A. Emerton, "Note on Proverbs 12:26," *ZAW* 101 (1989): 190–98.
42. Kidner, *Proverbs*, 99.
43. So Fox, *Proverbs 10–31*, 560; and REB, GNT, HCSB.

tween the MT and the ancient versions pertains to a vowel, and vowels were not represented in the consonantal text until about A.D. 600. That is to say, the difference is oral, not written. MT preserves a firm oral tradition; the ancient versions do not.[44] In sum, both the internal and external textual evidence favors MT, not the versions.

2. Philologically, in Ugaritic (ca. 1400 B.C.) and in post-biblical Hebrew, 'al-māwet is the term for "immortality," showing this meaning was continuous "from second millennium B.C. Syria to post-biblical Jewish literature."[45]

3. Contextually, units within this section of Collection II regularly end in synonymous or synthetic parallelism, and new units begin with an educational proverb. Given the reading 'al-māwet, the relationship of 12:28 to 13:1 matches that of 11:31 to 12:1 and 12:14 to 12:15.

4. Theologically, the book has consistently implied the immortality of the righteous (see 2:19; 10:2, 16; 11:4, 19; 12:3, 7, 12, 19; see "Does Proverbs Promise Too Much," pp. 44–45). Thus, its explicit expression here is unsurprising.[46] "Nothing is more natural than that the Chokma in its constant contrast between life and death makes a beginning of expressing the idea of *athanasia* [i.e., 'without death']."[47] The RSV read "to death," but the NRSV returned to "no death," presumably because it found the textual evidence too compelling. Commentators often reject this interpretation on the basis of the dogmatic position that there is no afterlife in the Old Testament, not for exegetical reasons.

Good Teaching, Ethics, and Living (13:1–25)

> [1]A wise son [listens to][a] a father's instruction,
>> but a mocker does not listen to rebuke.
> [2]From the fruit of a person's mouth one eats good things,
>> but the appetite of the treacherous craves violence.
> [3]Those who guard their mouths protect their lives,

---

44. *IBHS* §§1.6.3h–m.

45. J. F. A. Sawyer, "The Role of Jewish Studies in Biblical Semantics," in *Scripta Signa Vocis: Studies about Scripts, Scriptures, Scribes and Languages in the Near East Presented to J. H. Hospers by His Pupils, Colleagues, and Friends*, ed. H. Vanstiphout and Johannes Hendrik Hospers (Groningen: E. Forsten, 1986), 204–5.

46. Contra Lucas (*Proverbs*, 105), who states, "The textual uncertainty is too great to make this the one verse in Proverbs which reflects a belief in the after-life."

47. Delitzsch, *Proverbs*, 194.

but those who open their lips wide have terror.
⁴The appetite of sluggards craves, and they have not,
 but the life of the diligent is fattened.
⁵A righteous person hates a false word,
 but a wicked person becomes a stench and comes to feel
  ashamed.
⁶Righteousness guards the blameless way,
 but wickedness overturns the sinful [way].
⁷There is one who pretends to be rich yet has nothing,
 and [there is] one who pretends to be poor yet has great wealth.
⁸The ransom of people's lives is their riches,
 but the poor person does not listen to a rebuke.
⁹The light of righteous people shines brightly,
 but the lamp of wicked people is snuffed out.
¹⁰There is strife only with pride,
 but with those who take counsel [there is] wisdom.
¹¹Wealth [gotten] by unsound means dwindles,
 but those who gather by hand increase [their wealth].
¹²Expectation deferred sickens the heart,
 but a tree of life is desire fulfilled.
¹³Whoever despises an [inspired] word will be ruined by it,
 but whoever fears a commandment will be rewarded.
¹⁴The teaching of the wise is a wellspring of life,
 turning [one] aside from deadly snares.
¹⁵Good judgment wins favor,
 but the way of the treacherous leads to their destruction.
¹⁶Every shrewd person takes cover through knowledge,
 but a fool spreads out folly.
¹⁷A wicked messenger perishes through evil,
 but a faithful envoy brings healing.
¹⁸The person who ignores instruction meets with poverty and
  disgrace,
 but the one who heeds correction will be honored.
¹⁹A desire that comes to pass is pleasant to the soul,
 but an abomination to fools is to depart from evil.
²⁰Walk with the wise and become wise,
 for whoever associates with fools suffers harm.
²¹Trouble pursues sinners,
 but good things reward the righteous.

²²A good person gives [wealth] as an inheritance to grandchildren,
　　but the wealth of a sinner is stored up for the righteous.
²³The unplowed field of poor people yields plenty of food,
　　but there is a being swept away through injustice.
²⁴Those who hold back their rod hate their children,
　　but whoever loves them seeks them diligently with discipline.
²⁵The righteous eat until their appetite is satisfied,
　　but the belly of the wicked lacks [bread].

a. "Listen to" in 13:1b is gapped in 13:1a (cf. v. 22).

XEvery word in v. 1 except "rebuke" (*gəʿârâ*) resonates with the vocabulary of the Prologue (chs. 1–9), which admonishes the son to listen to the parents' instructions. Verse 2 trumpets the chapter's theme: through morally good teaching and behavior one eats what is materially good. The catchwords "eat" and "appetite" (vv. 2, 25) frame the unit whose sayings escalate from implicitly admonishing the son to listen to his parents (v. 1) to implicitly admonishing parents to discipline their sons (v. 24).

The chapter divides into four subunits based on subject matter: speech (vv. 2–6), wealth (vv. 7–11), longings satisfied (vv. 12–19), and eternal destiny (vv. 20–25).

Introductory Educational Proverb (13:1)

1 The introductory rearing proverb sharply contrasts *a wise son* (see 10:1) with *a mocker* (see pp. 48–49). The former listens to *a father's* chastening *instruction* (see 1:2). The latter disses moral *rebuke* (*gəʿârâ*; cf. 1:22; 9:8). *Gəʿârâ* denotes a morally indignant protest against wrong. One rebuke to a wise person is more effective than a hundred blows on a fool (17:10). The sharp contrast warns the son not to be like the mocker. The Suffering Servant, who prefigures Jesus Christ, models a wise son. He submitted to painful discipline to "learn obedience" (Isa. 50:5; Heb. 5:8).

Speech and Industry (13:2–6)

The first subunit consists of two quatrains about speech (vv. 2–3, 5–6) centered on a proverb pertaining to industry (v. 4). The subunit concludes in a typical way by promising endurance for the righteous and destruction for the wicked.

2 Verset A duplicates 12:14a (cf. 18:20) but with a different nuance. The imprecise parallelism between *the fruit of a person's mouth* and *the appetite* (see *Nepeš* [Traditionally, 'Soul']," p. 32) *of the treacherous* (see "Ethical Terms for Wicked and Fools," p. 46) implies that the speaker producing edible fruit is loyal to the covenant community while the disloyal do not produce edible fruit. *One eats good things*—that is to say, wise speech spiritually and materially benefits both the speaker and the listener (cf. 12:14a). Verset B also contains a double-entendre: the appetite of the treacherous *craves violence* (see 3:31)—the harm they do to others redounds upon themselves. The contrast between versets also implies that the disloyal abhor valuable instruction and the loyal abhor violence.

3 The catchword "mouth" links vv. 2 and 3. The mouth that imparted good words (v. 2) now restrains bad ones and so protects life (v. 3a). Good and bad speech are matters of life and death (see "The Wise and Words," pp. 39–40). On its own, the proverb warns against imprudent ego-speech, but read with v. 2, it refers more specifically to violent speech that terrorizes the speaker (cf. 10:14; 21:23). The contrast of *those who guard their mouths* and *those who open wide their lips* implies that the former are cautious, not garrulous; the latter are garrulous, not cautious. The contrast of *protect their lives* and *have terror* implies that the tight-lipped are terror-free and "big mouths" risk their lives. Proverbs 21:23 expands v. 3a to a full proverb. Sirach 28:25 teaches, "Make balances and scales for your words, and make a door and a bolt for your mouth."

4 A play on both senses of *nepeš* ("appetite," v. 2; "life," v. 3) shifts the thought from speech to industry. Success requires good speech plus industry. The "appetite of the treacherous" ravages the community by their treacherous speech (v. 2b); here *the appetite of sluggards* would, if allowed, drain the community of its resources. What sluggards *crave and have not* are the "good things" of v. 2a. In v. 3a, the taciturn person's life is protected; here the *life of the diligent* (plural) *is fattened*, implying that their appetite is abundantly satisfied, including their hunger for God (see Pss. 42:1; 63:1). The contrast assumes that God richly provides for all the needs of the diligent but denies resources to the sluggard (Ps. 128:2). Bridges comments, "The sluggard desires the gain of diligence without the diligence that gains. He would be wise without study, and rich without labor."[48]

5 Those whose lips produce and eat good fruit (v. 2a), who protect their lives through wise speech (v. 3a), and who through industry have every appetite satisfied (v. 4b) are now defined as *a righteous person* (see 1:3; 10:2–3). The righteous person passionately *hates* any *false word* because of love for *I AM*

---

48. Bridges, *Proverbs*, 151.

who hates lies and loves truth. By contrast *a wicked person*, whose selfishness destroys both society and personal relationships, *becomes a stench*—that is, such a person is exposed and so becomes repulsive to society. Furthermore, a wicked person *comes to feel ashamed* (cf. 19:26; Isa. 33:9; 54:4). Public disgrace and personal embarrassment often occur in contexts of calamity (Jer. 15:9; Mic. 3:7).

6 Righteousness is personified as a protector and wickedness as a supplanter, escalating the fates associated with each to an eternal dimension. *Righteousness* (see pp. 36–37) *guards the blameless* (see p. 37) *way* (see 1:15). *But wickedness* (see "Ethical Terms for Wicked and Fools," pp. 45–46) *overturns the sinful [way]* (see 1:10). The metaphor "way" connotes that righteousness and wickedness have their appropriate destinies built into them. The truthful ways of the righteous protect them, but lies subvert sinners. Proverbs 22:12, using the same verb, names *I AM* as the ultimate Agent who protects and frustrates in the realm of ethics. Solomon does not pit immediate and ultimate causes against each other; rather, he views *I AM*'s works through the ethical order *I AM* has established and upholds (see 2:8, 11).

Wealth and Ethics (13:7–11)

This subunit focuses on "wealth," a catchword that frames the unit (vv. 7, 11).

7 This proverb is wonderfully ambiguous and can be read in several ways.[49] Read as it is in the text, it condemns pretenders. The impoverished fool pretends to be rich both to give the appearance of wisdom's success and to command social respect (see 12:9), while the rich fool pretends to be poor to avoid helping the needy. Both are frauds. First, they defraud society: the poor fool by receiving from it undeserved honor and the rich fool by depriving it of charity (1 Tim. 6:18). Second, they defraud *I AM*. One pretends to have received *I AM*'s blessing; the other denies his gracious gifts. When exposed, these liars become a social stench and feel ashamed.

8 This proverb notes the advantages of wealth and the disadvantages of poverty. The imprecise parallelism suggests that a guilty person with riches can be motivated to heed a deadly moral rebuke since he can save himself by paying a ransom. But the penniless poor person cannot be motivated in the same way.[50] *The ransom of people's lives is their riches* assumes that normal

---

49. For the other ways of reading the proverb, see Waltke, *Proverbs 1–15*, 557.

50. Fox (*Proverbs 10–31*, 564) considers this interpretation convoluted. He thinks the rich man would not heed rebuke if he could redeem his life with a ransom. However, the

people will give all they have to preserve their lives (Job 2:4) and that the offended party will accept it.[51] By contrast, a guilty *poor person does not listen to a rebuke* (see v. 1b). With no means, and therefore no hope of redemption, the poor person disregards the threatening rebuke. With *I AM*, however, there is forgiveness for those who repent (Prov. 28:13; 2 Chr. 7:14). Without that hope, sinners would not heed *I AM*'s rebuke (cf. Ps. 130:3–4).

9 This proverb contrasts the enduring wealth of the righteous with the extinction of the wicked by comparing the former's shining lamp with the latter's snuffed-out lamp. *The light that shines brightly* symbolizes legitimate wealth and well-being, including long life (24:20; 2 Sam. 21:17; Job 18:5–6; 21:17; 22:28; Lam. 3:2; Amos 5:18, 20). The contrast in the versets points to the enduring life and prosperity of *righteous people* versus the transitory light, and by implication the fading wealth, of *wicked people*. *Snuffed out* (deliberately extinguished) symbolizes the final misfortune and hopelessness of the wicked (see 24:20; cf. 20:20; Job 18:5–6). The divine passive implies *I AM* is the Agent who gives and takes life.

10 The topic of listening to rebuke (v. 8) is here expanded to its effects on others. *There is* signifies "to set in motion." *Strife* refers to the way egotistical people respond to moral rebuke, namely, *only with pride*, the psychological state of having a puffed-up opinion of one's importance and refusing to accept one's God-given place within society. It is the hallmark of fools and evokes strife since it constantly bucks God's moral norms ordering society. In essence, "Where there is strife there is pride." *But with those who take counsel* (that is, the modest who acknowledge their limited knowledge and humbly accept correction from competent counselors) *[there is] wisdom* (see "What Is 'Wisdom'?" pp. 27–28) the knowledge of the right order of things. Living in conformity to that order leads to peace.

11 This proverb teaches the accumulation of *wealth* (see v. 7b) through virtue, not through get-rich-quick schemes or vice. The Hebrew for *[gotten] by unsound means* basically means "puff of air/vapor." The metaphor of getting money from a vapor—that is, out of nothing—suggests what we call "easy

---

imprecise parallelism suggests that a person who can ransom his life listens to rebuke. Instructively, the proverb does not use the negative term "rich man" (*ʿāšîr*; see "The Wise and Wealth," pp. 40–41) but the generic *ʾîš* ("person") qualified by the positive term "wealth." Fox curiously argues further that in no circumstances would accepting a "rebuke" help avert a death penalty. Yet the book of Proverbs insists that those who reject moral rebuke (see v. 1) are on the way of death, not life (see on 1:30; cf. 2 Sam. 12:13).

51. The cuckold, however, will not accept a ransom from the adulterer (see 6:35).

money," which is money obtained illegally.[52] Such money *dwindles*. Instead of these "airy" methods, the book prescribes the time-tested methods of patience, diligence, prudence, generosity, and faith. Therefore, *those who gather by hand*, an idiom meaning a gradual accumulation of wealth (gapped in 11b) *increase* it. Though unstated, *I AM* created and upholds the nexus between quick wealth and its dwindling and between patient wealth and its increase. The proverb is paralleled in 12:11; 20:21; 28:22.

Fulfillment through Wisdom and Frustration through Folly (13:12–19)

The inclusio created by "desire fulfilled" and "desire that comes to pass" (vv. 12b, 19a) frames this subunit and proclaims its subject matter. The inner framing inclusio, "the one who despises an [inspired] word" and "the person who ignores instruction" (vv. 13a, 18a), states its complement.

12 This verse contrasts the effects of the unfulfilled expectations of the godless with the fulfilled desires of the godly. When *expectation* (the longing for good fortune to replace misfortune) is *deferred* (interminably delayed) it *sickens the heart* (see p. 32). In such hopelessness, the person stumbles in psychological despair to death. By contrast, the fulfilled desires of the righteous are like feasting on the fruit of the tree of life. *Desire fulfilled* denotes the fruiting of deep aspirations. Metaphoric *tree of life* (see 3:18) functions as the antithesis of sickness in verset A. The one who eats of its fruit is revitalized with eternal life and encouraged to live, plan, and hope for the future. The framing of the proverb with v. 19 implies that the wise/righteous are in view. They may find their hopes deferred temporarily, but they never lose hope, for they know *I AM*, who keeps his word (see vv. 13–14).

13 The psychological states described in v. 12 are now invested with the theological reasoning that they depend on rejecting or accepting *I AM*'s inspired commands. The proverb contrasts the ruin of one who *despises* (see 1:7) *an [inspired] word* (*dābār*) with the reward of one who *fears* (see 1:7) *a commandment* (see 1:8; 3:1). The parallel "commandment" colors "word" with the meaning "inspired word." In Deut. 30:11 and 14, "commandment" and "word" refer to the same divine word. The idea of fearing the command also suggests *I AM*'s word is in view; more specifically, it refers to the teachings of Proverbs. *Will be ruined by it* represents the wicked person as guilty and destined to pay

---

52. According to Plöger (*Sprüche*, 160), wealth gained out of nothing evokes the suspicion of having been obtained illegally, a view also reflected in LXX, Targ., and Syr.

the debt on judgment day. The divine passive points to *I AM* as the Agent. In contrast, the one who fears *I AM*'s commandment *will be rewarded*.

14 A variant of this proverb appears in 14:27, where "fear of *I AM* " replaces "teaching of the wise."[53] *The teaching of the wise, contained in Proverbs*, is pictured as *a wellspring of life* beside a booby-trapped road. The imagery of a spring represents abundant life in fellowship with *I AM* gained by heeding the wisdom of Proverbs. In the book's Prologue, the *[one]* who is *turning . . . aside* is the son (see 3:7) or the repentant uncommitted. Those who turn aside avoid *deadly snares*, a metaphor representing the many dangers—bad speech, bad deeds, wicked men, and wicked women—that capture and kill fools (cf. 1:20–33; 13:19). The sages' good teaching attracts people to drink from its life-giving truth. Consequently, they discern the concealed traps and are fortified to resist them.

15 Heeding the sages' teaching also produces prudence, by which one wins favor with God and humanity. By contrast, the perverse perish. *Good judgment* (lit. "good prudence"[54]; see p. 35) refers to a particular and outstanding moral clarity to perceive the best practices that promote life. Such moral clarity *wins* (produces) *favor*—it is pleasing and attractive to God and society (3:4). But the *way of the treacherous* (pl.; see p. 46) *leads to their destruction*. The contrast implies that prudence and treachery are incompatible characteristics and that winning esteem with God and community is the opposite of being destroyed (cf. Rom. 14:18). Joseph (Gen. 39–41), Samuel (1 Sam. 2:26), David (1 Sam. 18:14–16), and Daniel (Dan. 1:9, 19–20; 6:1–3, 28) all won favor, as did the Lord Jesus Christ (Luke 2:52) and Paul (Acts 27:43; 28:2).

16 This proverb contrasts *every shrewd person* (see p. 35) with a *fool* (see p. 48). The shrewd *take cover* (protect themselves) *through knowledge* (see "What Is 'Wisdom'?" pp. 27–28) which enables them to foresee and evade danger (22:3) and to speak wisely (see 12:23). Jesus had knowledge of what was in humans and so did not commit himself to them (John 2:23–24); and Satan cannot sucker saints because they are on to his schemes (2 Cor. 2:11). By such knowledge, the shrewd survive and thrive. By contrast, the dolt, who despises the deed-destiny nexus, *spreads out* (parades[55]) *folly*, a metonymy for morally

---

53. Heim (*Poetic Imagination*, 355ff.) argues the editor replaced "fear of *I AM*" with "the teaching of the wise" due to his desire to keep this section free of references to *I AM*. Ch. 13 forms the center of one of the longest sections in Proverbs that does not mention *I AM*, the last reference being 12:22 and the next being 14:2.

54. *Śekel-ṭôb* was translated "good repute" in 3:4 (see Waltke, *Proverbs 1–15*, 242).

55. Understood as the metaphorical sense of *yiprōś* ("spreads out").

insolent words and deeds. The antithesis "takes cover" (= "protects himself") suggests that "spreads out folly" entails that fools ruin themselves.

17 This proverb contrasts the character of the wicked messenger and his misfortunes with that of the conscientious envoy and his healing effect on the community. The imprecise parallelism implies that the wicked messenger afflicts his sender and himself (6:6; 26:6) while the faithful envoy benefits his sender and himself. The king's envoy was his plenipotentiary (that is, he was invested with the king's authority) and had to represent him accurately yet flexibly during negotiations. Messengers' success depended on high moral character, and their importance entitled them to privileged treatment. *A wicked messenger perishes through evil*—probably a pun on both the evil he does and the evil that befalls him (see 1:16). By contrast, the *faithful envoy* is represented as a therapeutic agent *who brings healing* to the community. Placing the faithful envoy's work (verset B) after that of the wicked envoy (verset A) may suggest that the former remedies the damage caused by the latter.

18 This proverb, the second from the subunit's end, matches v. 13, the second from its beginning. Both connect reward to being correctible and punishment to being incorrigible (see 3:16; 8:18). *The person who ignores corrective instruction meets with poverty and disgrace*, a hendiadys denoting shameful poverty. By contrast, *the one who heeds correction will be honored*. The imprecise parallelism suggests that honor entails the wealth that gives one social gravitas (cf. 3:9; 4:8; 8:18). The causes of poverty are many: laziness (cf. 10:4–5; 12:24), bloviating instead of working (14:23), pursuing pleasure (21:17; 28:19). But here, a more fundamental problem is in view—namely, disobeying the instruction that will correct these faults. Paradoxically, those who flout formative discipline are disciplined by depletion and disgrace, but those who submit to discipline are honored.

19 This framing inclusio with v. 12 asserts that only the righteous, not fools, will experience the joy of fulfilled desires. Verse 25a validates this interpretation, and other proverbs assert that *I AM* gratifies the desires of only the righteous (10:3, 24; 11:23; cf. 14:16a; 16:17a). According to Kidner, *desire fulfilled* must relate "only to a worth-while object: compare Isaiah 53:11 with Psalm 106:15; Ecclesiastes 2:10, 11."[56] A desire *that comes to pass* is "fulfilled" (v. 12b). Desire realized *is pleasant* (see 3:24) *to the soul* (see "*Nepeš*," p. 32). All life has an appetite for life, but fools will not have it fulfilled because they crave vomit (26:11). *To depart from evil* is *an abomination to fools* (see "Intellectual Terms for the Wicked and Fools," pp. 47–48) since it would spoil their fun. They prefer death to life (v. 14), destruction to favor (v. 15), exposure to

---

56. Kidner, *Proverbs*, 104.

protection (v. 16), perdition to healing (v. 17), and shameful poverty to social dignity (v. 18). In sum, life depends on having its drives and appetites fulfilled. The frustrated fool goes from failure to failure, but the gratified righteous from strength to strength.

The Blessed Future of a Wise Son and the Baneful End of Fools (13:20–25)

After an introductory proverb admonishing the son to join the company of the wise to avoid the danger of fools (v. 20), the last subunit elaborates the topic of good and evil.

20 An admonition commanding to walk with the wise, not with fools, introduces the subunit. *Walk* (see 1:15) *with the wise* (see "Intellectual Terms for the Wise and Righteous," pp. 34–35) admonishes one to live in accompaniment with and "under the instruction, encouragement and example"[57] of the wise (cf. 15:31). Consequently, such a person will *become wise*. Further motivation by way of contrast is provided in verset B. *Whoever associates with fools* entails that fools also shape their companions by exciting their interests, forming their resolutions, and fixing their habits (1:10–19; 16:29; 22:24–25); but fools do so for bad, not for good.[58] Consequently, the fool's comrade *suffers harm* (see 11:15).

21 This proverb personifies misfortune and good fortune to show that the evil sinners inflict on others redounds to destroy them, and the good the righteous bestow on others returns to reward them. *Trouble* is personified as a hunter that *pursues sinners*. The evil they pursued now turns around and pursues them to death. By contrast, *good things*, personified as a benefactor, *reward the righteous* (pl.; cf. Ps. 23:6). The life-giving benefits the righteous bestow on others rewards them in return. "Good" refers to that which is beneficial and beautiful. "Not the smallest good—even 'a cup of cold water to a disciple' (Matt. 10:42), or honor shewn to his servants (Matt. 10:41; 1 Kings 17:16–23)—shall lose its reward (Heb. 6:10)."[59]

22 The good that rewarded the righteous (v. 21b) stays with them, but the ill-gotten wealth of sinners (cf. v. 21a) is transferred to the righteous (cf. 10:2–3; Gen. 31:9, 16; Exod. 12:36; 20:6; Josh. 11:14; Esth. 8:1–2; Job 27:17; Ps. 105:44; Matt. 25:28). Here "good" refers to *a morally good person*. Such a person *gives*

---

57. Bridges, *Proverbs*, 164.

58. Non-biblical sayings express the same truth: "Tell me with whom you socialize, and I will tell you who you are"; and "You will become like the one with whom you socialize" (cited by Meinhold, *Sprüche*, 227). Bridges (*Proverbs*, 164) notes, "It is not left to us to determine whether there shall be any influence [on us]; only what that influence shall be."

59. Bridges, *Proverbs*, 166.

[wealth] as an inheritance to grandchildren; it endures through the generations. *Wealth*,[60] gapped in the A verset, places one in the favorable position of being able to help others, but that of *a sinner is stored up for the righteous* (pl.). The wicked hoard their wealth to satisfy their greed, but eventually Providence will transfer it to the righteous, with whom it will endure forever (2:20–22).

23 This saying qualifies v. 21 by teaching that *I AM*—though he is not named here—ensures the earth has abundant food for the hardworking poor, but sometimes tyrants sweep it or them away through injustice. *The unplowed field of poor people* is the marginal fields of the poor or the land left dormant during the sabbatical year for use by the poor (Exod. 23:10–11; Lev. 25:1–7). The point is that even the unplowed fields provide plenty. The proverb here assumes the poor work hard and collect *plenty of food*. The problem is not God's creation or poor working habits but injustice: *there is a being swept away* (violently destroyed; cf. Gen. 19:15, 17; Num. 16:26; 1 Sam. 12:25; 27:1; 1 Chr. 21:12) *through injustice*. During the early 1930s, the so-called Red Trains of Stalin forcefully expropriated the harvests of Ukrainian farmers, thus creating the Holodomor, a devastating man-made famine. An estimated three to seven million hardworking peasants were starved to death as a result of Stalin's policy of collectivization. This proverb corrects simplistic understandings of the principle of retribution asserted in other proverbs. Injustice exists, and retribution may be delayed to a future beyond death (see "Does Proverbs Promise Too Much," pp. 44–45).

24 This proverb qualifies v. 22 by teaching that loving parental discipline ensures the successful transmission of wealth through the generations. *Those who hold back their rod* of remedial punishment *hate their children*. By contrast, the parent who *loves them seeks them diligently with discipline* (see 3:11–12; 22:6). The proverb assumes, first, that the home is the primary place for transmitting values (see "Setting of Dissemination," p. 20; cf. Exod. 20:12); second, that parents have absolute values, not valuations; third, that folly is bound up in the heart of the child (22:15; cf. Gen. 8:21); fourth, that words alone will not dislodge folly (10:13). The time-tested English proverb, "Spare the rod and spoil the child," is biblical. The New Testament does not abrogate it, and the church should not abandon it (cf. Eph. 6:4; Heb. 12:5–11). "A hard way to wisdom is better than a soft way to death."[61] The apostate West's failure to discipline its children has left it in moral chaos with the result that, in the end, the parent "will hate his son, for he will see him . . . going forth to evil deeds."[62]

---

60. Heb. *ḥayil* means "strength," "power." Here it is a metonymy of effect for valuable property ("wealth").

61. Kidner, *Proverbs*, 51.

62. Rashi, *Proverbs*, 76. Recently, Jordan B. Peterson, a clinical psychologist, has addressed this problem in his popular book *12 Rules for Life: An Antidote to Chaos* (Toronto:

25 This is a proverb on retribution, not moderation. *The righteous* who feed others are reciprocally fed so that they too *eat until their appetite is satisfied* (see *Nepeš* [Traditionally, 'Soul']," p. 32). Here, "eat" is used literally, but it can also be used metaphorically for satisfying the spiritual appetite. Behind their eating is the good hand of the heavenly King, who freely feeds his dominion (Gen. 1:29) in due season so that they are filled (Ps. 104:27–28). By contrast, *the belly of the wicked lacks [bread]*. When the stomach lacks bread, the implication is that the owner has become indigent and will die unless the situation is remedied. Abundance of food indicates a right relationship to *I AM* and the community while its lack signifies a failed relationship (cf. 10:3; Deut. 28:48, 57; Jer. 44:18; Ezek. 4:17). However, this judgment must be viewed from the perspective of the end; before then, people live in an upside-down world (see "Does Proverbs Promise Too Much," pp. 44–45).

Living in Wisdom (14:1-32)

¹As for the wise among women, [each] builds her house,
   but a foolish woman with her own hands tears it down.
²Those who fear *I AM* walk in their being upright,
   but those who despise him are perverse in their ways.
³In the mouth of a fool is a rod of pride,
   but the lips of the wise protect them.
⁴Without cattle the manger is clean,
   but there are abundant harvests through the strength of an ox.
⁵An honest witness does not lie,
   but a false witness is a perjurer.
⁶The mocker seeks wisdom and has not,
   but knowledge is an easy matter to the discerning.
⁷Go from the presence of a foolish person,
   for you will not have known lips of knowledge.
⁸The wisdom of the shrewd is to have insight into their ways,
   but the folly of fools is deceit.
⁹As for fools, each one mocks at guilt,
   but among upright people [there is] favor.

Penguin Random House, 2018) under the provocatively titled chapter "Do Not Let Your Children Do Anything That Makes You Dislike Them." His argument is that if parents, who love their children, allow them to do things that make the parents dislike them, how much more will strangers dislike them. Those other people will punish them, severely, by omission or commission. Don't allow that to happen. Better to let your little monster know what is desirable and what is not, so they become sophisticated denizens of the world outside the family" (144).

¹⁰The heart knows its own bitterness,
and in its joys a stranger does not take part.
¹¹The house of wicked people will be annihilated,
but the tent of upright people will bud.
¹²There is a way that is right in a person's judgment,
but the end of it is the ways to death.
¹³Even in laughter the heart may ache,
and the end of rejoicing is grief.
¹⁴Backsliders will be fully punished because of their ways,
but the good [will be fully rewarded] for their deeds.
¹⁵The uncommitted give credence to anything,
but the shrewd give heed to their steps.
¹⁶ The wise fear and turn from evil,
but a fool gets angry and yet feels secure.
¹⁷A quick-tempered person commits folly,
and a schemer is hated.
¹⁸The uncommitted inherit folly,
but the shrewd are crowned with knowledge.
¹⁹Evildoers will bow down before the good,
and the wicked at the gates of a righteous person.
²⁰Even by neighbors a poor person is hated,
but the friends of a rich person are many.
²¹Those who despise their neighbor are sinners,
but those who show favor to the poor, blessed are they.
²²Do not the planners of evil go astray,
and do not the planners of good meet with reliable kindness?
²³In all strenuous labor there is profit,
but empty talk [leads^a] only to scarcity.
²⁴The crown of wise people is their wealth,
but the folly of fools is folly.
²⁵A truthful witness delivers lives,
but the perjurer is deceitful.
²⁶In the fear of *I AM* is a strong security,
and their children have a refuge.
²⁷In the fear of *I AM* is a wellspring of life
turning [the wise] from the traps of death.
²⁸In a multitude of subjects is the splendor of a king,
but being without a populace fills the potentate with terror.
²⁹Patience is great competence,

but a quick temper is that which exalts folly.
³⁰Life in the entire body is a calm heart,
    but hot passion is rot in the bones.
³¹Whoever oppresses the poor scoffs at their Maker,
    but whoever is gracious to the needy honors him.
³²By their own evil the wicked are thrown down,
    but the righteous take refuge in *I AM*ᵇ in their dying.

a. The elided verb can be inferred from the preposition "to" (*IBHS* §11.4d).

b. "In *I AM*" is not in the text. However, *ḥōseh* ("refuge") is the Qal participle absolute of *ḥāsâ*, which occurs 37 times in the Old Testament, always with the meaning "to seek refuge." Thirty-four times, outside of Prov. 14:32b, *ḥāsâ* is used with reference to taking refuge in God or under his wings. In Isa. 14:32, the afflicted take refuge in Zion, a surrogate for God, and in Isa. 30:2 the prophet uses "to seek refuge in the shadow of Egypt" sarcastically—i.e., the Jerusalemites should have sought refuge in *I AM*. The Qal participle absolute is used one other time outside of Prov. 14:32b, with regard to the "savior of those who take refuge" (Ps. 17:7), which the NIV rightly renders "savior of those who take refuge in you." J. Gamberoni (*TDOT*, 5:71, s.v. *ḥsh*) agrees that the Qal participle has the same "religio-ethical" sense in Prov. 14:32b as in Ps. 17:7. Plöger (*Sprüche*, 176), Meinhold (*Sprüche*, 245), and Waltke independently reached the conclusion that YHWH is the unstated object of *ḥōseh* in Prov. 14:32b.

Thematically, this unit can be divided into three subunits: walking in wisdom (vv. 1–7), not walking by sight (vv. 8–15), and the contrasting characterizations and consequences of social deportment (vv. 15–32).

Walking in Wisdom (14:1–7)

1 This proverb again impresses the son with the importance of having a good wife, for she either makes or breaks the family (see 12:4; 18:22; 19:14). *As for the wise among women* indicates real women are in view. *[Each] builds her house* refers to each woman cultivating the material and spiritual well-being of her household. *But a foolish woman* sharply contrasts with "wise among women," both in number and in sense. The singular may suggest that the foolish woman lives alone and that eventually her house is gone (cf. 9:13–18); destroyed *with her own hands*—due to her own incompetence, her arrogance and incorrigibility, poor speech, hot tempter, and lack of self-control. *It* may refer to whatever house she received through God's common grace or one she had before she apostatized (see 2:17).

2 The antithetical parallel of this proverb contrasts the lifestyles of the pious and the impious by the metaphor of two ways: the straight and the crooked.

Those who fear I AM describes people who intrinsically *walk* (see 1:15; 10:9; cf. 13:20) *in their being upright* (see p. 37). But *those who despise him* are described as *perverse*, which is to say, they deviate from *I AM's* fixed and prescribed moral order (see 2:15) and are therefore abominable to him (3:32). The plural *in their ways* suggests the perverse have no fixed path but zigzag according to their lusts. Their ethics betray their religious affections. Fox comments, "One's conduct is inseparable from his attitude to God, and the former reveals the latter."[63] Joseph's refusal to sin against Potiphar revealed his godly heart (Gen. 39:8–9).

3 This proverb's antithetical parallels contrast the punitive effects of the arrogant fool's talk with the protection afforded by the speech of the wise. *In the mouth* identifies the *rod (ḥōṭer) of pride* as the tongue *of a fool*. Elsewhere, *ḥōṭer* only occurs in Isa. 11:1, where it denotes a new shoot or branch coming out of a stump. Here it is an incomplete metaphor connoting sprouting and flourishing or punishment. Its antithetical parallel "protect" suggests a punitive branch is meant, and in Aramaic *ḥōṭer* can be "rod (for punishment)."[64] *But the lips* (speech) *of the wise protect them* from making haughty, insulting speech that provokes others to react in kind and from the fool's speech that aims to injure them (see 10:11, 14; 11:9).

4 The abstractions connected with building or tearing down a house are now applied to prudent work. Intelligent investment in sources of income, as illustrated by strong oxen, reaps benefits far exceeding the cost. *Without cattle* refers to a situation devoid of laboring animals. *The manger is clean* (empty). By contrast, *there are abundant harvests* (see 3:9) *through the strength of an ox*, the brawny king of domesticated beasts. The singular suggests that if abundant harvests can be had with one ox, how much more could be had with a team of them (cf. 12:10; 27:23–27).

5 This proverb returns to the topic of speaking (see v. 3) but is now focused on the character of a witness (cf. Exod. 20:16; Deut. 19:18). *An honest* (or "reliable"; see 13:17) *witness does not lie*. When tested, a reliable witness is moved neither by entreaties nor by threats to swerve from the truth. *But a false witness is a perjurer* (see 6:19). Verset B repeats 6:19a, suggesting that the topic is the "perjurer." Fox rightly says, "This sentence is not a tautology. It observes that both honesty and deceit are indivisible qualities."[65] A judge can discriminate

---

63. Fox, *Proverbs 10–31*, 572.

64. R. J. Clifford, *Proverbs*, OTL (Louisville: Westminster John Knox, 1999), 143; cf. *HALOT*, 1:307, s.v. *ḥōṭer*.

65. Fox, *Proverbs 10–31*, 574.

between true and false testimonies by discerning the character of the witnesses (see 12:17). A good tree brings forth good fruit and the bad tree bad (Matt. 7:17–18; 12:33–35).

6 Wisdom is not something the proud can seize; only the humble find it. *The mocker* (see pp. 48–49) *seeks* after *wisdom and has not*—he cannot find it. Mockers' arrogance prevents them from humbling themselves under the inspired sages' teachings. Instead of finding the wisdom that corrects them, their pride and their desire for social power bring them back to themselves. Luther's description of the nature of human sin as *homo incurvatus in se* ("humanity curved in on itself") describes the mocker well.[66] By contrast, *knowledge* (see "What Is 'Wisdom'?" p. 27–28) *is an easy matter to the discerning* (see "Intellectual Terms for the Wise and Righteous," pp. 35–36), for they have an intuitive aptitude to attain what they seek.

7 The synthetic parallels of this verse warn the youth to keep far from the teaching of fools since all one will get for them is a belly full of folly. *Go* is an urgent imperative. *For you will not have known lips* (speech) *of knowledge.* The proverb uses litotes. Far from experiencing wisdom, what one will get is an abundance of folly (cf. 17:10; 22:24–25; 23:20; 28:7; 1 Cor. 15:33; 2 Cor. 6:17; 1 Tim. 6:4–5).

Not Walking by Sight (14:8–15)

This subunit warns the youth not to be taken in, as fools are, by appearances.

8 This verse contrasts the wisdom of the shrewd to assess the consequences of their ways with the folly of fools that deceives them and others. *The wisdom of the shrewd* (see p. 35) *is to have insight into* (see 1:2; 8:5) *their way* (see 1:15). By knowing the deed-destiny nexus, the insightful penetrate beyond initial appearances to understand the consequences of their way. *But the folly* (see p. 48) *of fools* (see pp. 47–48) *is deceit* (see 11:1; 12:5, 20). Here "deceit," which normally means to deceive others, may also include self-deception. The shrewd choose their steps according to their moral knowledge to assure themselves of life. By contrast, fools, lacking that moral knowledge, scheme to victimize others, unaware that they are also victimizing themselves.

9 This proverb admonishes one to be upright, not a fool who wrongs and refuses to make restitution. *As for fools, each one mocks* (see 1:22; 3:34; 19:28) *at guilt.* "Guilt" brings punishment (Jer. 5:15) and without restitution, death

---

66. Matt Jensen, *The Gravity of Sin: Augustine, Luther and Barth on "homo incurvatus in se"* (New York: T&T Clark, 2006), 5.

(Ps. 68:21). Under the Mosaic law, the "guilt" sacrifice restored one to *I AM*, and appropriate reparations were necessary to make to one's victims (Lev. 6:1–7). Today, wrongs against God are discharged by the sacrifice of Christ, who offered himself as a guilt offering (Isa. 53:10). *But among upright people* (see p. 37) *[there is] favor* (see 10:32; 11:1). The contrast with "guilt" suggests that "favor" with God and people is meant. Upright people seek to steer clear of guilt-incurring situations. If they commit wrong, they count on Christ's sacrifice and make appropriate restitution to their victims.

10 Apart from God, one knows only one's own bitterness and joy—a merism representing the full gamut of emotions. *The heart* (see p. 32) *knows its own bitterness*, such as barrenness (1 Sam. 1:10), fraud (Gen. 27:34), suffering (Job 7:11), and so on. *And in its joys a stranger does not take part.* One's emotional-intellectual-religious-moral motions are too complex, deep-seated, and individualistic to share with others (cf. 1 Cor. 2:11). The proverb implies the dignity of each individual, teaches to accept being misunderstood (cf. 1 Sam. 18:20; 2 Sam. 6:16; 2 Kgs. 4:27), and cautions against evaluating others by outward appearances (see v. 13). Its truth drives us to pray to the compassionate High Priest, who knows us better than we do ourselves (15:11; 16:2; 21:2; 24:12; 1 Kgs. 8:38; John 14:16–17; Heb. 4:15–16).

11 This proverb implicitly teaches the disciple to walk by faith, not by sight. Paradoxically, the wicked person's house is less secure than the upright person's tent. *The house* connotes a more secure and grand dwelling than a tent (see David's desire to replace *I AM*'s *tent* with a *house* in 2 Sam. 7:4–6). That *of wicked people will be annihilated.* By contrast, *the tent of upright people will bud* (or "sprout"). "Tent" refers to a nomadic tent used as a dwelling. The metaphor "bud" signifies that their households burgeon with life and prosperity. The seemingly unstable nomadic tent of the upright has stood from the time of the forefathers, and its inhabitants not only remain but forever flourish with new life (cf. Pss. 1:3; 92:12–14; John 15:1–17).

12 The center proverb of the subunit warning against walking by sight pointedly gives the reason not to do so. Its repetition in a different context in 16:25 shows its importance. *There is a way that is right* (*yāšār*; see 1:3) *in a person's judgment.* "Person" (*'îš*) sharply distinguishes between the human and God (Num. 23:19; Job 9:32; Hos. 11:9).[67] *The end of it* is its outcome, in light of which the whole must be evaluated. Plural *ways* itemizes the way which the person thought right into its many choices—which in fact were evil, as shown by the outcome *death*. Since death is the ultimate failure, this denouement

---

67. N. P. Bratsiotis, *TDOT*, 1:229, s.v. *'îš*.

shows that the person's choices were wrong. Where a road leads is not always as it appears, because human perception of truth is partial, opaque, and often contrary to reality. Only the omniscient God knows the way of life. He reveals it through his inspired sage, and the disciple must accept that revelation by faith. Jesus Christ, the divine Sage, said that he himself is the Way, the Truth, and the Life (John 14:6).

13 This proverb continues the theme that present appearances are deceptive and true reality is revealed in its outcome (i.e., "the end of it," v. 12b). *Even in laughter the heart may ache.* Outward merriment often masks suffering, *but the end of rejoicing is grief.* Despite momentary merriment, sorrow is the default condition. Life begins with a baby's wail; it ends with a dying gasp. "Since humans die, joy inevitably ends in grief (see 27:1). The party always ends; acts of love cease."[68] This exceptionally pessimistic proverb must be balanced by the book's dominant optimism that the righteous expect joy (10:28), life (10:16–17; 11:19; 13:12), and a future hope (23:17), in contrast to the wicked who have none (24:19–20). By describing the human condition as skewed, the proverb points to a salvation and a hope that lies in a relationship with God that outlasts death. Present moments of joy offer a foretaste of future salvation. The positive affirmation of the next proverb balances the pessimism of this one.

14 The antithetical parallels of this proverb pit *backsliders* (or rebellious and perverse people) against *the good* to admonish the disciple to persevere in faith since *I AM* rewards the faithful while punishing apostates. The inseparable deed-destiny nexus is here applied to abandoning wisdom. After choosing the good way, the disciple must continue in it because the Sovereign ensures that the good deeds of the faithful redound to reward them but the ways of the unfaithful, despite whatever communal good they earlier performed, redound to punish them (cf. Jer. 18:7–10). Apostates will be rewarded, but not as they expected; they *will be fully punished because of their ways.* Plural "ways" denotes all the evil manifestations that carry within themselves the apostate's destruction. But the benevolent *[will be fully rewarded] for their* good *deeds.*

15 This verse cautions the disciple against the naiveté that leads astray. The wise test their way by considering whether each step conforms to true piety and ethics. *The uncommitted* (see p. 47) *give credence to* (rely on) *anything. But the shrewd* (see p. 35) *give heed to their steps.* "Steps," a figurative synonym of "way," signifies lifestyle (see 1:15). By labelling the careless as "uncommitted" and the careful as "shrewd," the proverb motivates the youth to be critical and discerning when listening to others. The imprecise parallels suggest that the

---

68. Van Leeuwen, "Proverbs," in *NIB* 5, 141.

uncommitted do not care about their lifestyles and the shrewd do not rely on human opinion. If God puts no trust in even his holy ones, how much less are human beings and their words reliable (Job 4:18; 15:15; cf. John 2:24). The shrewd, by contrast, implicitly rely on God and thereby order their steps to prevent straying.

Contrasting Social Characterizations and Consequences (14:16–32)

This subunit can be further divided into three partial units. The first (vv. 16–18) uses characterizations to encourage the youth to join the wise and concludes with the promise that the shrewd are crowned with "knowledge." The second (vv. 19–24) encourages them, using mostly ethical terms, to wise ethical behavior by showing the consequences of good and bad social conduct. The last (vv. 25–32) combines four characterizations with the consequences of life or death, concluding climactically that the wicked will be finally ruined but that even in their deaths the righteous take refuge in *I AM*.

Contrasting Wisdom Characterizations and Ethical Behavior (14:16–18)

16 The proverb cajoles the youth to submit their lives to *I AM* and his sages by characterizing *the wise* (see "Intellectual Terms for the Wise and Righteous," pp. 34–35) as having the good sense to turn from evil, a metonymy for death, whereas the incorrigible *fool* (see pp. 47–48) lacks this discernment. *Fear* has *I AM* as its implied object, as suggested by the addition of *turn from evil*, the consequence of fearing *I AM* (see 3:7; cf. 1:16). By contrast, the fool *gets angry* at *I AM* and those who fear him. *And yet* the fool *feels secure* and so unconcerned. The imprecise antithetical parallelism of "who turns from evil" and "who feels secure" suggests that God-fearers are not self-confident and that the cocky fool does not turn from evil and death (cf. 13:19). Paul warned the idolatrous, cocky Corinthians, "If you think you are standing firm, be careful that you don't fall" (1 Cor. 10:12).

17 The proverb continues the theme of folly. In a rare antithetical parallelism where both versets state a negative, it cautions against being either *a quick-tempered person*, who acts impetuously, or *a cold, calculating, deliberate schemer* (*ʾîš mezimmôt*; see 12:2; 24:8). The predicates state why each is bad. The hot-tempered one *commits folly* (see p. 48), a singular collective denoting many specific deeds and consequences that are done to harm others and prompted by moral insolence (see 5:23; 14:1, 8). Hotheads are undisciplined, out of control, unpredictable, and overreact. Sages viewed anger negatively: as cruel (27:4), factious (30:33), and needing to be calmed (15:1; 29:8, 11). Johnson says, "The ideal of wisdom is the quiet man who does not err in anger, or as 17:27 puts it, is 'a calm and understanding man.'"[69] Schemers, by contrast, methodically plot and carry out their ruthless plans. They are *hated*, a metonymy for their rejection and elimination by God and/or the community.

18 This janus proverb draws the first subunit to a conclusion and functions as the opening frame to the next subunit. Synonyms for "crown" (*ktr*, v. 18b; *ʿăṭeret*, v. 24a) promised to the "shrewd" (v. 18b) and "the wise" (v. 24a) form an inclusio around the second subunit (vv. 19-24). Vivid metaphors contrast the uncommitted and the shrewd. Verse 18 warns against being among *the uncommitted* (see p. 47) because they metaphorically *inherit* the ignominy of *folly* (see v. 17). The metaphor is used ironically; normally an inheritance sustains life, but this inheritance destroys its possessor (see 11:29). By contrast, the proverb encourages joining *the shrewd* because they are metaphorically *crowned with knowledge* (see "What Is 'Wisdom'?" pp. 27-28). Their internalization of wisdom enables them to evade danger (see v. 16) and to win dominion and dignity.

Contrasting Consequences of Social Behavior (14:19-24)

19 The notion of the shrewd being crowned with knowledge is now escalated to evildoers bowing before good people. In synonymous parallelism, *evildoers* are equated with *the wicked* and *the good* with *a righteous person* (see 2:20; 4:14). The proverb motivates youth to serve others by means of the paradoxical truth that they will so become the ruling class while the self-serving *will bow down* before them. *At the gates* suggests that the righteous will sit in the place of judgment dispensing justice (see 1:3). This gnomic proverb is not always true to experience; Proverbs recognizes that sometimes the world is morally topsy-turvy (see "Does Proverbs Promise Too Much," pp. 42-45; cf. Heb. 2:8b). Eschatologically, however, it is axiomatic (cf. Gen. 42:6; Exod. 11:8; 12:31-32; 1 Sam. 24:16-21; 26:21; 2 Sam. 19:18-19; Esth. 7:7; Acts. 16:39). Ross says that the proverb is "the ultimate fulfillment of the thought of Philippians 2:10."[70]

20 This proverb contrasts the rich and the poor in terms of their social positions (cf. 19:4, 7) and exposes a hard truth about human nature. *Even by neighbors* (see 3:28) *a poor person is hated* (see 1:22; 14:17). *But the friends of a rich person* (*ʿāšîr*; see "The Wise and Wealth," pp. 40-41) *are many* (see 19:4). The saying asserts that in addition to being funds-poor, the poor person is friends-poor,

69. E. Johnson, *TDOT*, 1:356, s.v. *ʾānaph*.
70. Ross, *Proverbs*, 988.

while the *'āšîr* abounds in funds and friends. Sadly, on the one hand, people desire to get rid of the poor, regardless of their virtue, while on the other, they flock to the rich regardless of their vices because the rich offer benefits without moral demands. In light of this dark reality of human nature, the proverb cautions the youth against being either poor or rich. The former is hated by all; the latter loved by the wrong people. The next proverb implies that redemption from this dark reality of nature is possible (cf. 18:24, which also implies exceptions).

21 This verse prevents misinterpreting v. 20 as a rationalization for shunning the poor. The imprecise antithetical parallelism of "neighbor" and "poor" suggests the sense of "poor neighbor" in both versets. Indeed, *those who despise* (see 1:7) *their neighbor* (see 3:28) *are sinners* (see 1:10; 8:36). By vilifying one's neighbor, one is in violation of God's standards. By contrast, *those who show favor to the poor* denotes those who esteem their neighbors and so accept them and act kindly toward them. Such freely given favor implies piety, mercy, and generosity, not preferential treatment. The laudatory exclamation *blessed are they* (see 3:13; 8:32, 34) holds up the benevolent as exemplars of a right relationship with *I AM* now and joy in the future. "Love your neighbor as yourself" is enjoined in both Testaments (Lev. 19:18; Rom. 13:9–10) but uniquely joined by Jesus with "love the Lord your God" as one of the two greatest commandments (Matt. 22:37–40).

22 The neighbor-hater (v. 21a) is here escalated to one who plots evil against others, and the one who shows them favor (v. 21b) to one who plans good. The rhetorical question *do not* (gapped in verset B) *the planners of evil go astray?* gets the attention of the wise by expecting the emphatic negative answer, "Most *certainly* they do!" "Planners of evil" (3:29; 6:14; 12:20; cf. 6:18), along with *planners of good* (see 2:9; 14:14, 19), metaphorically depicts these planners as craftsmen skillfully fashioning deeds that harm or help others. The former "go astray," a metaphor depicting these evil craftsmen as lost wanderers or staggering drunkards. The metaphor entails that they have left the ethical path for one that harms others and themselves (see 7:25). By contrast, the latter, by staying on the right path, *meet with reliable kindness* (see 3:3).

23 This antithetical proverb fleshes out the "planners of good" as those who through hard, honest work are rewarded with material and circumstantial gains (cf. 10:4–5; Isa. 49:4; Heb. 6:10; cf. John 6:27). *In* qualifies the area of profitability as *all* kinds of *strenuous work*. *There is profit* (*môtār*, lit. "what is left over") signifies the axioms that within God's common grace and created order one gains more from an endeavor than what one expends in it and that the profit is realized in the future, upon completion of the work. So, people live by faith in that hope. By contrast, mere *empty talk* (lit. "but words of lips"; cf. 2 Kgs. 18:20

for the meaning of this idiom) *[leads] only to* deprivation and death. Metaphoric "leads . . . to" suggests a journey leading to a goal. "Only" highlights the unexpected destination of *scarcity* (*maḥsôr*; see 6:32; 11:24), the state of lacking basic necessities. Some proverbs censure verbosity (cf. 10:19; 12:18a; 18:6); others extol the power of words (see "The Wise and Words," pp. 39–40).

24 The reference to "crown" concludes vv. 18–24. Continuing the theme of wealth and poverty begun in v. 20, this proverb specifically escalates the "profit" of v. 23 to an adorning crown. *The crown*, a visible sign of God's favor (see 4:9; 12:4), *of wise people is their wealth* (see 3:16), giving them social gravitas and dominion. Though risky (cf. 1:10–19; 10:15–16; 11:16, 28; 18:11; 30:8–9), wealth can be *I AM*'s reward for virtue (see 3:16; 8:18; cf. 1 Kgs. 3:13; Ps. 112:3). *The folly* (see vv. 17–18) *of fools* (see p. 48) *is folly* is a pun, for the harm they intended for others boomerangs upon themselves (see 14:8, 18; 16:22b). Judas's folly in betraying Christ boomeranged as a noose around his own neck (Matt. 27:5).

Contrasting Characterizations and Consequences of Life and Death (14:25–32)

Excepting v. 28, the final subunit correlates four characterizations with their corresponding consequences of life or death. Verse 28 stands apart, being the first of many royal sayings in the collections. Significantly, it is one of several that have been placed in close proximity to proverbs about *I AM*: 16:1–15; 20:26–28; 21:1–14; 22:11–12; 25:2–7; 29:12–14. According to Whybray, "The main purpose of such juxtaposition seems to be to stress that obedience to Yahweh is particularly important for kings, in whose hands are the lives of all his people."[71]

25 The first characterization is the honest witness versus the false. Verse 25b repeats verbatim v. 12:17b. These verses, along with 19:5, 9, 28; 21:28; 24:28; 29:24, are concerned with justice, which depends on trustworthy witnesses. A *truthful witness* in court with firsthand information is a precise antonym of a *perjurer* (see 14:5), but their predicates, *is one who delivers lives* and *is deceitful* (deliberately deceiving to damage others) are not precisely antithetical to each other, suggesting that a truthful witness eschews deception and thus saves the innocent while a perjurer deliberately deceives in order to harm, not deliver, others (cf. 11:1; 14:8). In ancient Israel, serious accusations carried the death penalty, but the accused could only be convicted on the testimony of two or three witnesses (Deut. 19:15). Although the proverb pertains to the judicial court, it is applicable to "fake news": deliberate disinformation in the

---

71. Whybray, *Proverbs*, 221.

news or on social media meant to harm a rival. The damage is often irreversible. In such circumstances, the wise, who speak the truth, are revolutionaries. As someone has said, "In a time of universal deceit, telling the truth is a revolutionary act."[72]

26–27 "Fear of *I AM*," the second characterization, links vv. 26 and 27. Verse 26 links it to *security* and v. 27 to *life*. Both aspects are necessary. Since evil not only attacks but also attracts, parents must know (and show their family, v. 26b) something both stronger and better.

Verse 26 connects "fear of *I AM*" with the consequence of total security, clarified in v. 27 as security from death. *In the fear of* I AM (see "Fear of *I AM*," pp. 38–39) characterizes the wise and their families holding *I AM* in awe and diligently obeying his teaching. *Strong* (firmly fixed and inviolable; see 8:28b; 10:15) *security* denotes a basis for feeling so confident that one is untroubled by threat. *And their* (i.e., "those who fear the LORD") *children* denotes the obedient offspring down the generations, and not merely immediate descendants (see 4:3; 20:7). God saves families (cf. Gen. 7:1; 18:19; Exod. 20:5–6; Ps. 103:17; Acts 16:31). A life committed to God reaches beyond its own existence. *Refuge* stands in precise parallel with "strong security." The connection of v. 26 to v. 27 by the catchword "fear of *I AM*" suggests that here "refuge" signifies protection from the snares of death.

Verse 27 repeats 13:14 except that *fear of* I AM replaces its synonym "the teaching of the wise." Using the metaphors *wellspring of life* and *traps of death*, the proverb continues to call the disciple to enter with awe into the realm of *I AM*'s inspired word. In that realm is found the abundant life that saves from death.

28 The king above all others must live in the fear of *I AM*. As the chief civil magistrate, his leadership sustains the people.[73] *In a multitude of subjects*, the consequence of wisdom and righteousness (cf. 28:2, 12, 16, 28; 29:2, 4, 14), *is the splendor of a king* (8:15–16). The B verset is the precise antithetical parallel to the A verset: *being without a populace*, the consequence of folly and wickedness, *fills a potentate* (= "king"; see 8:15) *with terror*, a metonymy for ruin (see 10:14–15). The proverb implicitly encourages the disciple to be a competent person who attracts people, not a fool whom people desert. Bridges says of Christ, "How great then is the honour of our heavenly King in the countless multitude of his people" (see 2 Thess. 1:10; Rev. 7:9–10).[74]

72. Unsubstantially attributed to George Orwell.
73. R. D. Culver, *TWOT*, 1:508, s.v. *mālak*.
74. Bridges, *Proverbs*, 168.

29–30 These verses designate the third characterization, the patient versus the impatient. Verse 30 escalates the consequences of understanding and folly to matters of life and death.

Patience means literally "to relax the face," a physiological idiom (Prov. 19:11; Isa. 48:9). Patient people are relaxed when wronged; with checked emotions, they act according to piety and ethics. Instead of seeking vengeance, they trust God and, like him, show great patience with sinners (Exod. 34:6–7; Jonah 4:2). Patience makes space for the sinner to repent. Since patience is godlike and unnatural to humans, it is characterized as great competence (see "Intellectual Terms for the Wise and Righteous," p. 36). By contrast, *a quick temper* means to become angry at injustice so quickly that it occasions sin. *Exalts folly* here means "shows the greatest folly" (cf. 5:23; 12:23; 13:16; 14:24). The hot-tempered impiously and rashly lash out in revenge, and in so doing harm themselves, as Simeon and Levi discovered (cf. Gen. 34 and 49:5–7).

The second proverb of the pair escalates the endorsement of patience by highlighting its psychosomatic benefits. Serenity saves; pique kills. *A calm heart* (see "Heart," p. 32) is *life*—physical life, in contrast to physical death, as shown by the qualifier *in the entire body* (see 4:22; 5:11). *But hot passion is rot in the bones*, a condition that deteriorates to death. "Body" and "bones" refer to both the physical and psycho-spiritual aspects of human nature (cf. 12:4). Inward turmoil from a resentful mind that is self-centered and narcissistic is like bone cancer that rots the framework of the body and shortens a person's life (cf. Sir. 30:24).[75]

31–32 The final characterizing proverbial pair pertains to the oppressor of the poor and the one who is kind to the poor (v. 31) and dramatically contrasts their respective eternal destinies of death and security in God (v. 32).

The hot-tempered person now turns to oppress the defenseless poor and in so doing impugns God's splendor. *Scoffs at* means denigrates the worth or significance of someone or something. Maltreating the poor entails denigrating *their* (the poor people's) *Maker*. Humanity's creation in God's image forms the philosophical basis for social ethics. The antithetical *whoever is gracious* means those who esteem the needy as worthy, accept them, and do acts of kindness for them. *The needy* refers to those who are destitute, vulnerable, and dependent on others for survival.[76] The one who *honors him* (i.e., "their Maker") gives God social weight, thereby earning God's reward (3:9–10).

The consequences of being self-serving and of serving others differ radically

---

75. So Meinhold, *Sprüche*, 244.
76. Cf. W. R. Domeris, *NIDOTTE*, 1:228, s.v. *'ebyôn.*

and paradoxically. *The wicked* (see "Intellectual Terms for the Wicked and Fools," pp. 47–48) *are thrown down*—that is, ruined by the loss of their stability and security (cf. Pss. 35:5; 36:12; 62:3). *By their own evil* probably has the double meaning of the harm they do to others and the calamity that comes to them (see 1:16). *But the righteous* (see "Ethical Terms for the Wise and Righteous," pp. 36–37) *take refuge in* I AM (see the translation notes). *In their dying* designates the circumstance in which the righteous show themselves true worshippers of *I AM*. The imprecise antithetical parallels "refuge in *I AM* in their dying" and "thrown down by . . . evil" suggest that the wicked, whose evil kills them, do not trust in *I AM* even when dying, and the righteous, who trust in *I AM* when dying, are not thrown down by any evil, including death (cf. Gen. 5:24; Pss. 49:14–15; 73:24). Along with the rest of the book, this proverb sees a refuge for the righteous after clinical death (see "Does Proverbs Promise Too Much," pp. 44–45).

Upholding Righteousness with a Gentle Tongue (14:33–15:4)

14:33In the heart of the discerning, Wisdom comes to rest;
    and in the midst of fools, she reveals herself.
34Righteousness exalts a nation,
    but sin is a condemnation[a] to peoples.
35The king's favor [comes][b] to a prudent servant,
    but his fury ruins[c] a shameful [servant].
15:1A gentle answer turns back wrath,
    but a painful word stirs up anger.
2The tongue of the wise adorns knowledge,
    but the mouth of fools gushes forth folly.
3The eyes of *I AM* are in every place,
    watching [vigilantly] evil people and good people.
4A soothing[d] tongue is a tree of life,
    but perversity in it fractures the spirit.

a. Following Van Leeuwen ("Context and Meaning," 58 n. 3), who argues that negative *ḥesed* more probably means "guilt" or "condemnation."
b. The elided verb can be inferred from the preposition "to" (*IBHS* §11.4d).
c. For the textual emendation, see Waltke, *Proverbs 1–15*, 609 n. 5.
d. Or "healing."

After an implicit educational proverb introducing the unit (v. 33), a proverbial pair connects wisdom with a nation's ethics and the king's responsibility to show both favor to the prudent and fury to the shameful (vv. 34–35).

A sequel of four proverbs then cautions against the use of painful words that incite anger and commends the beneficial effects of gentle speech to mend the damage (15:1–4).

14:33 Personified *Wisdom* (see "Illumination and Woman Wisdom," pp. 29–30) *comes to rest* and to rule[77] *in the heart* (see "Heart," p. 32) *of the discerning* (see 1:5), who see through a situation because by faith they have embraced the sages' inspired wisdom. *And* connects the versets in synthetic parallelism and points to Wisdom's positive revelation of herself to both the wise and fools.[78] As for *fools*, she is *in the midst of* (cf. Prov. 15:31) them, not in their hearts,[79] since they hate knowledge (see 1:22; 17:16). Therefore, even though she *reveals herself* to them, they reject her (see 1:29–30). To come to rest and rule in someone's heart is quite different than simply making oneself manifest to a group (see 1:20–33; 8:1–36). This educational proverb admonishes the youth to ensconce the sages' inspired wisdom in their hearts.

34 Wisdom (v. 33) is now connected with ethics and its concerns escalated to the nation. The contrasting subjects of *righteousness* (see pp. 36–37) and *sin* (see 1:10; 5:22; 10:16) implicitly admonishes a nation to conform to God's moral standards in dealing with the citizenry. The predicates give the reason. The former *exalts* (see 4:8; 14:29) *a nation*; the latter *is a condemnation* (see the translation notes), implying subjugation, enmity, and scarcity *to peoples*. This lesson is applied to Israel in particular (cf. Deut. 28:1–14, 15–68; Amos 1–2; etc.). Ultimately, a nation's exaltation depends on its piety and ethics, not on its political, military, or economic might.

35 This moral posture of a nation depends largely on its officials. *The righteous king's favor* (see 11:1; 14:28) *comes to a prudent* (see p. 35) *servant* ('*ebed*; see 11:29). Here '*ebed* denotes a "royal officer" who was obligated and indebted to the king (see 30:9).[80] *But his fury* (or "wrath"; see 11:4; cf. Amos 1:11) *ruins a shameful [servant].* The proverb admonishes the king to promote competence, loyalty, and efficiency in governing and not to tolerate mismanagement and corruption (cf. 16:13, 15; 19:12). It also admonishes officials to be competent and conscientious in their actions and to prepare for promotion by eschew-

---

77. Copps (*TWOT*, 2:562, s.v. *nûaḥ*) suggests the verb has soteriological overtones (i.e., to conquer and rule in Num. 11:25; 2 Kgs. 2:15; Ps. 125:3; Eccl. 7:9; Zech. 6:8).

78. If the disjunctive meaning "but" is adopted (see NASB, ESV), the parallels would be antithetical, pointing out the strikingly different responses of the discerning and the fools to Wisdom.

79. The latter would be true with a singular object but not, as here, with the plural object "fools."

80. *HALOT*, 2:775, s.v. '*ebed*.

ing scandal and criticism. Christ taught this lesson in his parables of the ten virgins, the talents, and the sheep and goats in Matt. 25 (cf. John 12:26).

15:1 This verse is a helpful sequel to 14:35. Anger begets anger. The antithetical parallels imply that the disciple, servant, or king has the emotional restraint to give a *gentle* (or "tender"; see 4:3) *answer* that in both substance and style mollifies the listener (Job 32:3; Prov. 25:5). This measured reaction to an opponent, without compromising truth, *turns back wrath* and restores the adversary. *But a painful word* that inflicts psychic pain *stirs up anger.* "Wrath" in verset A refers to anger's inner emotional incitement, "anger" in verset B to its outward expression. LXX underscores this danger of anger by adding to the proverb's beginning: "Anger slays even the wise" (cf. Eccl. 10:4). Soft speech is like oil on bruised skin that softens and heals it (Judg. 8:1–3); harsh speech is like oil tossed on fire (cf. 1 Kgs. 12:1–16). Nabal's surly speech stoked David's anger; Abigail's sagacious speech softened him and saved her household (1 Sam. 25:10–13, 23–31). David credits her wise speech to *I AM* (25:32–34).

2 This proverb continues the topic of a good "answer" in contrast to a bad "word," naming their instruments, the *tongue* (see 6:17) and the *mouth* (see 2:6), and their sources, the inalienable characters of *the wise* (see "Intellectual Terms for the Wise and Righteous," pp. 34–35) and *fools* (see pp. 47–48). The tongue *adorns* internalized *knowledge* (see 1:2). Here "adorns" means to beautify one's speech, presumably in the manner commended in v. 1. The wise, whose tongues are controlled by love and saturated with knowledge, speak their wisdom in a way that attracts listeners. Instead of brutalizing and so repelling people with their knowledge, the wise state it kindly and tactfully, always aiming to save their audience, not to condemn and destroy it. By contrast, the mouth of uncontrolled fools *gushes forth* naked *folly* (see p. 48), an abstraction of their morally insolent speech that destroys individuals and the community.

3 This saying gives the theological basis for the moral order affirmed in the surrounding proverbs. The anthropomorphism *the eyes of* I AM (see 5:21) signifies his presence in, and evaluation of, a situation. *Are in every place* describes *I AM*'s incommunicable (that is, non-human) attribute of being unlimited or infinite with respect to time and space (1 Kgs. 8:27; Ps. 139:7–10; Isa. 66:1–2; Jer. 23:23–24; Acts 17:28). *Watching [vigilantly],* a communicable attribute, carries the nuance "evaluating" and implies that he will act appropriately (Gen. 31:49; Job 15:22; Ps. 66:7), in accordance with whether *evil people,* who destroy society, or *good people,* who nurture it, are under review. In this way, the unseen but not unseeing God regulates history and guarantees the moral order (see 5:23; cf. 15:11; 16:2; 17:3; 21:2; 24:12; cf. 20:17).

4 The value of gentle speech for healing hurtful speech draws the section to a conclusion. The imprecise antithetical parallels, *the soothing* (or "healing"; *marpe*') *tongue* and *perversity in it* (i.e., the tongue), suggest that the soothing, healing tongue of good people who have integrity (see 13:6) does not distort and subvert the truth, including the moral order and thereby a community or individuals (cf. Ps. 5:9; 12:1–4; 73:8–9). The metaphor *a tree of life* (see 3:18; 11:30) suggests that Paradise may be restored in a broken world through healing speech that gives eternal life to those who "eat" of it. By contrast, the perverse tongue of evil people *fractures the spirit* (see "Spirit," p. 33), a metaphor connoting that perverse speech destroys the vitality of the addressee. The proverb implies that the tongue of good people can heal the hurt spirit caused by the twisted tongue of the perverse (cf. Isa. 50:4; cf. Eph. 4:25).

The Importance of Instruction (15:5–19)

> ⁵Fools spurn their father's instruction,
>> but whoever heeds correction is shrewd.
> ⁶The house of the righteous is a great store of wealth,
>> but in the wages of the wicked is ruin.
> ⁷The lips of wise people scatter knowledge;
>> the heart of fools is not right.
> ⁸The sacrifice of wicked people is an abomination to *I AM*,
>> but the prayer of upright people finds his favor.
> ⁹An abomination to *I AM* is the way of the wicked,
>> but one who pursues righteousness he loves.
> ¹⁰Painful discipline awaits the one who abandons the path [of life];
>> the one who hates correction will die.
> ¹¹Sheol and Abaddon are in full view of *I AM*;
>> how much more the hearts of human beings.
> ¹²Mockers do not like to be corrected;
>> to wise people they do not go.
> ¹³A joyful heart makes the face attractive,
>> but in heartache is a broken spirit.
> ¹⁴A discerning heart seeks knowledge,
>> but the mouth of fools feeds on folly.
> ¹⁵All the days of the afflicted are wretched,
>> but a cheerful heart is a feast continually.
> ¹⁶Better a little with the fear of *I AM*
>> than great treasure and turmoil with it.
> ¹⁷Better a small serving of vegetables with love

than a fattened ox with hatred.
¹⁸The wrathful stir up strife,
but the patient pacify a dispute.
¹⁹The way of the sluggard is like a briar hedge,
but the path of upright people is a built-up highway.

After an introductory educational proverb mentioning the father as the teacher (v. 5), the unit consist of two subunits of seven verses. The first pertains to the consequences of accepting or rejecting instruction (vv. 6–12), and the second to the triumph of a person's spiritual condition over circumstances (vv. 13–19).

The Consequences of Accepting or Rejecting Instruction (15:5–12)

The inclusio "correction" (vv. 5b, 12a) frames the subunit and helps trace the development of the contrast between the correctible wise person and the fool (v. 5), who is escalated in v. 12 to the wisdom-hating mocker.

5 This proverb motivates the youth to internalize the parents' instruction (see 1:8) by labelling whoever rejects it a fool and whoever heeds it prudent. The subject of verset A, *fools* (see pp. 47–48) is antithetically parallel to the predicate of Verset B, *is shrewd* (see p. 35); and the predicate of verset A, *spurn* (see 1:30) *their father's instruction* (or "discipline," *mûsār*; cf. 1:2, 8) is antithetically parallel to the subject of verset B, *whoever heeds* (see 2:8) *correction* (or "rebuke," *tôkaḥat*; see 1:23).

6 This proverb ramps-up the motive to be righteous, not wicked, by contrasting the profit of righteousness with the loss of wickedness. It motivates the disciple by picturing *the house*, the locus *of the righteous* person (see pp. 36–37), as *a great store of wealth*, a metaphor for a house brimming with good things (cf. Jer. 20:5). Such abundance is necessary so that the righteous can help others. The *wages* (see 3:9; 10:16) *of the wicked* (see "Ethical Terms for Wicked and Fools," pp. 45–46) refers to the consequences of their sinful activity, to wit, the *ruin* (see 11:17, 29) of the wicked themselves and possibly of their victims as well (see 10:2, 16; also 8:18, 21; 10:3, 6, 30; 11:3, 5–7, 18; 12:3, 21, 28; 13:6, 9, 21, 25; 14:11, 14, 24, 32; 21:7; 22:8).

7 In addition to storing up abundant goods to help others (v. 6), the righteous, now labelled the "wise," store up knowledge in their hearts to bestow it generously through their speech. Knowledge is foundational to storing up wealth since providing for people's physical needs is temporary; making them self-sufficient is the goal. In both respects, righteous and wise people stand in sharp contrast to the wicked and fools. Although *wise people* (see "Intellectual

Terms for the Wise and Righteous," pp. 34–35) and *fools* (see pp. 47–48) are precise antithetical parallels, *lips* and *heart* (see "Heart," p. 32) complement each other and should be understood to refer to both versets (see 15:14). If the heart is hard, the lips lisp (4:23–24; 6:16–19; 13:14; 16:23). The wise *scatter*—like Johnny Appleseed, freely, widely, and generously—their *knowledge* (see "Intellectual Terms for the Wise and Righteous," pp. 34–35). By contrast, the thought and speech of nescient fools are *not* morally *right* and so profit no one.

8 This verse continues the topic of the "righteous" (cf. vv. 8b, 9b) and the "wicked" (vv. 8a, 9a). Both the subjects, *wicked people* in contrast to *upright people* (see p. 37), and their predicates, *are an abomination to* I AM (see on 3:32) in contrast to *finds his favor* (see 11:1), are precise antithetical parallels. However, *sacrifice* and *prayer* is a broken stereotyped phrase representing worship's two essentials: slaying a costly animal and offering an accompanying petition or intercession (cf. Deut. 26:1–15; 1 Kgs. 8:22–63; 2 Chr. 29:27–28; Ps. 4:6; Prov. 15:29; 21:3, 13, 27, passim). The point is not that *I AM* prefers prayer over sacrifice but that the wicked hope to manipulate God by ritual magic instead of obtaining his mercy by confessing and repenting (28:13). They offer everything except what *I AM* asked for: their heart. By contrast, the upright rightly employ prayer and sacrifice in their pursuit of righteousness.

9 This proverb explains why the sacrifice of the wicked is an abomination to *I AM* (v. 8). The criterion for God's favor is not simply to scrupulously perform the rituals but to accompany them with the passionate pursuit of serving others. *I AM* abhors the sacrifice of the wicked (v. 8a) because *the way* (or lifestyle; see 1:15). *of the wicked* is *an abomination* to him. By contrast *the one who pursues* (as in a chase) *righteousness* (see pp. 36–37) *he loves*, a metonymy of his favorable answer to their sacrifices and prayers. God loves him "who is moved to an active, persistent, and even dangerous search for justice."[81]

10 "Verse 10 draws the conclusion from verses 8–9: 'obey (this) instruction before it is too late!'"[82] The synthetic saying ramps up the consequences of spurning instruction to eternal death, the severest discipline. The adjective *painful* in connection with *discipline* (see 1:2) takes on the particular nuance of hurtful and severe. *Awaits the one who abandons the path* (apostatizes; see 2:13, 17). The path is not qualified, but the parallel "will die" shows that the path *[of life]* is meant (10:17; cf. 12:28). *The one who hates correction* (see 1:23; 15:5) *will die* (see 5:23; 10:21) an eternal death without God. This is the tragic, inevitable end of apostates.

---

81. Plaut, *Proverbs*, 170.

82. Knut Heim, "Structure and Context in Proverbs 10:1–22:16" (PhD diss., University of Liverpool, 1996), 175.

11 *I AM*'s omniscience assures the certainty and justice of the apostate's death (v. 10). The final word of v. 10, "will die," forms the transition to the realm of the dead: "Sheol and Abaddon," the first words of v. 11. *I AM*'s watch over the realm of the dead implies that he is the Agent who sentences apostates to it. His sentence is just because he knows everything in the heart. The proverb uses *a fortiori* argumentation (from greater to lesser; cf. 11:31). If God sees into the realm of the dead in the darkest depths of the earth, how much more transparent to him are surface-dwelling human hearts (1 Sam. 16:7; 1 Chr. 28:9; Jer. 17:10; 1 Cor. 4:4–5; 1 John 3:20; Rev. 2:23). *Sheol* (see "The Grave," p. 50). *Abaddon* (see 15:11; 27:20; Job 26:6) intensifies the grave as the place of destruction. *In full view of* (lit. "in front of") *I AM. How much more the hearts* (see p. 32) *of human beings?*[83] The proverb assumes that *I AM* can and will regulate life and death justly.

12 The concluding proverb (cf. v. 5) aims to motivate the youth to heed the sages' instruction by contrasting mockers (see pp. 48–49) with wise people. The synthetically parallel versets are chiastically arranged around the (Heb. sg.) subject, *the mocker*:

A		does not like
	B	one who corrects
	X	him
	B'	to wise people
A'		he does not go

The outer frame (A/A') presents the predicates moving from negative affections (*do not like*), the heart of the mocker's problem, to negative actions (*do not go*). The inner frame (B/B') presents their qualifiers, *to be corrected* and *to wise people*. The arrogant mocker has no excuse for not devouring life-giving knowledge since the wise have been generously scattering it (15:7). The proverb provides insight into the human heart. Hating correction and shunning the company of the wise means one's heart is set on self-love, not on God, and is headed to death (see John 3:20; Gal. 4:16).

---

83. Fox (*Proverbs 10–31*, 593), referring to a study by M. Carasik, blunts the proverb by stating that in the Bible God is not usually presumed to know what humans are thinking but deduces thoughts from behavior, albeit he recognizes this proverb is exceptional. Other texts assert God knows every human heart—and that is the sharp point of this proverb (cf. Gen. 6; Job 26:6; Pss. 44:21; 139:2–23; 1 Kgs. 8:39; Ezek. 11:5). The New Testament cites several occasions when Jesus Christ, God incarnate, is said to know what people are thinking: Mark 2:8; Matt. 9:4; 1 Thess. 2:4).

The Overcomer's Superiority to Circumstances (15:13–19)

This subunit consists of two partial units. The first presents the superiority of the heart, which triumphs over circumstances (vv. 13–17). The second, vv. 18–19, a proverb pair, draws the subunit to its conclusion by outlining the peaceful person in contrast to the angry and the upright in contrast to the sluggard. They are concrete examples of spiritual dispositions that respectively triumph over or are defeated by circumstances.

The Heart's Superiority to Circumstances (15:13–17)

Read holistically, this partial unit teaches that the cheerful heart (v. 13), which daily overcomes affliction or deprivation (vv. 16–17), is derived from pursuing the sages' knowledge (v. 14). This involves the fear of *I AM* (v. 16) and love of others (v. 17). So far, the proverbs have asserted the connection between wisdom and prosperity and between wickedness and deprivation without qualification, but this partial unit significantly qualifies that deed-destiny nexus.

13 The parallels of v. 13 assume the heart's condition affects both a person's outward appearance and inward spirit. *A joyful heart* denotes an enthusiastically merry psyche. *Makes the face attractive* (see 15:2) assumes that all its features come alive, as the Creator intended. *Heartache* denotes the troubled psyche resulting from folly. It is equated with *a broken spirit* (see p. 33; 15:4; 17:22; 18:14), resulting in depression. The next proverb explains the source of these opposite conditions (cf. 13:12, 17; 14:10, 13; 15:15, 30; 25:13, 20, 25; Sir. 13:25–26). The proverb assumes that a person's inner spiritual state can be discovered by means of the appearance of the person's face.

14 The heart's joy or trouble (v. 13) is traceable to whether it is discerning and seeks knowledge. The wise heart is distinguished from the foolish one by its appetites and speech. *A discerning* (or "insightful"; see pp. 35–36) *heart is* revealed when it *seeks* to satisfy itself with *knowledge*, not by blurting out folly. *But the mouth of fools feeds on (rā'â) folly*. The meaning of *rā'â* is debated. To be sure, the mouth is the organ for eating physical food (cf. 30:20), but how does it eat folly, a spiritual-ethical reality? Probably, "mouth," as elsewhere in Proverbs, is a metonymy for speech. In other words, the fool's mouth gratifies its appetite by spouting out folly, unlike the discerning heart's passion for the sages' knowledge.

15 Continuing the topic of the heart, this proverb trumpets the view that its spiritual condition outweighs material well-being (vv. 16–17). *All the days of the* innocent *afflicted* breaks down their entire life into its daily grind of being physically and economically *wretched*. Nevertheless, the *cheerful (tôb) heart*, a synonym of "joyful heart" (cf. 17:22; 1 Kgs. 8:66 [= 2 Chr. 7:10]; Esth. 5:9), *is a feast*—a lavish banquet. *Continually* matches the metaphorical euphoric gratification of human desire with the afflicted's constant condition of economic deprivation. The proverb does not pit the innocent afflicted against the cheerful heart. Rather, the afflicted in health or wealth may yet have the cheerful heart that enables them to endure and to overcome their wretched circumstances (cf. 2 Cor. 4:8; 6:9–10; Heb. 10:34). The cheerful heart of Prov. 15:15b overcomes all the adversities of 15:15a.

16 The catchword *tôb* ("joyful" or "better") links vv. 15 and 16. Moreover, vv. 16 and 17, a "better than" proverb pair, suggest that even in misery the cheerful heart is grounded in the fear of *I AM* (v. 16) and love (v. 17). Verse 16 teaches the disciple to prioritize religion, not mammon. *Better a little with the fear of* I AM (see "Fear of *I AM*," pp. 38–39) *than great treasure and turmoil with it.* Standing opposite "fear of *I AM*," "turmoil" refers to the inward panic that manifests itself in the tumultuous behavior of the mammon-slave. Such behavior probably involves oppressing others (see Amos 3:9). The connection with v. 15 suggests that economic poverty with spiritual gain is *better than* spiritual poverty with economic gain (cf. 10:2). This "better than" condition shows that the deed-destiny nexus may be reversed for a season (see "Does Proverbs Promise Too Much," pp. 44–45). Eventually, however, *I AM* promises to right the world by rewarding the righteous with material gain and visiting the wicked with material loss in a future outlasting death.

17 This proverb contrasts two meals to teach that love toward one another, which cheers the spirit and forges bonds of friendship during dire circumstances, is *better than* the best circumstances when accompanied with hatred and rivalry that breaks the bonds of friendship. *A small serving* together with *vegetables* describes the most modest meal in quantity and quality. *With love* denotes that the meal is accompanied with the passion of cherishing others and their company. *A fattened ox* represents the king of domesticated animals at its best and functions as a synecdoche for the finest foods (cf. Luke 15:23). *With hatred* denotes the inward emotion of loathing the others at the sumptuous banquet and of desiring to rid oneself of them.

Two Overcomers (15:18–19)

This proverb pair is linked by the theme of two kinds of people: the patient (v. 18) and the upright (v. 19), who respectively overcome the circumstances created by the wrathful and the sluggard.

18 The first overcomer is the patient person who, under control emotionally, pacifies the strife created by *the wrathful* (see 6:34; 15:1). Because the wrathful are not in control of their raging resentments, they react rashly and so *stir up strife* (see 6:14). But *the patient*, who rule their emotions, *pacify* (bring a state of peace and tranquility to) *a dispute*—a synonym and parallel of "strife" (associated with anger in 30:33; Isa. 57:16) and the occasion for all kinds of wrongdoing. The patient, who are numbered with the wise (see 14:29), speedily contain controversy and strife to create "quietness" so that good sense will prevail and wrongdoing will cease. They are greater than the wrathful, for they can rule over the chaos caused by hotheads who cannot control their passions (cf. 25:28).

19 The second overcomer is the upright, whose reward is a free stride, in contrast to the sluggard. *The way of the sluggard* (see pp. 49–50) *is like a briar* (i.e., thorn) *hedge.* The simile denotes an impassible obstruction, and more specifically, an obstruction that pricks and pains. Sluggards want to achieve their goals, but their spiritual condition precludes them; to them, everything is too hard, painful, or dangerous to even try (22:13; 26:13). *But the path of upright people*, who have internalized the sages' teaching, *is a built-up highway* cleared of obstacles and good for travel. The metaphor signifies that those who embrace inspired wisdom find the path to achieving their goals free of obstacles. The imprecise antithesis between the sluggard and the upright shows that the sluggard is not upright (see 6:6–11). Jesus called the slothful servant "wicked" (Matt. 25:26).

Consequences of Righteousness and Wickedness (15:20–29)

> [20]A wise son makes a glad father,
>> but a foolish human being despises his mother.
> [21]Folly [brings][a] joy to one who has no sense,
>> but those who have understanding make [their] going straight.
> [22]Plans are thwarted without counsel,
>> but with a multitude of counselors each plan succeeds.
> [23]One has joy in the apt answer of one's mouth,
>> and how good is a word at the right time.
> [24]The path of life leads upward for the prudent
>> and so turns aside from the grave below.
> [25]*I AM* tears away the house of the proud,
>> but he sets in place the boundary of the widow.
> [26]The plans of an evil person are an abomination to *I AM*,

but pleasant words are pure.

²⁷The greedy for gain ruin their households,

but the one who hates bribes will live.

²⁸The heart of a righteous person ponders [its] answer,

but the mouth of wicked people blurts out evil things.

²⁹*I AM* is far from the wicked,

but he hears the prayer of the righteous.

a. The elided verb can be inferred from the preposition "to" (see *IBHS* §11.4d).

This unit contrasting the righteous and the wicked consists of two subunits. The first pertains to joy in the educational process (vv. 20–23). The second features *I AM*'s involvement in preserving the righteous and eliminating the wicked (vv. 25–29). Verse 24 is a janus.

Joy in Education (15:20–24)

The introductory educational proverb in v. 20 resembles those of 10:1, 12:1, and 13:1. The key word *śmḥ*, which as a verb is glossed by "makes glad" (v. 20a) and as noun by "joy" (v. 23a), frames this subunit on joy in successful child-rearing. The frame suggests a trajectory from the parents' present joy in a teachable son (v. 20) to the son's future joy in being able to answer wisely (v. 23).

20 *A wise son makes a father glad* repeats 10:1a. But *a foolish human being* (*ādām*; see p. 31) replaces 10:1b's "son," and *despises his mother* (15:20b) replaces "brings grief to his mother" (10:1b). Apparently, with the change from "son" to "human being," the apostate son is disowned as a "son" (cf. 4:3) and so dismembered from his family's inheritance. Nevertheless, unlike Prov. 12:1, where the correction-hater is likened to a brute animal (12:1), he is still a human being.[84] The proverb suggests the essential role of parents in teaching the son their wisdom (see 1:7–8; cf. 23:22; 30:17). "Be glad" and "despise" are not a precise match; a son who delights his parents does not despise but respects them, and one who hates them does not make them glad but grieves them.

21 This proverb encourages disciples to seek insight so that their affection (verset A) and action (verset B) will be right (see 2:3). The moral insolence of *folly [brings] joy* (see 10:28) *to the one who has no* moral *sense* to survive (see

84. Meinhold, *Sprüche*, 256.

6:23; 10:23). *But those who have understanding make [their] going straight* on the straight way that leads to life (v. 24). The imprecise antithesis, "folly brings joy" and "make [their] going straight," implies that senseless people recklessly turn aside from the path of duty and life while understanding people stay the course for the joy set before them (cf. Heb. 12:2).

22 In adulthood, counselors replace parents. *Plans are thwarted*[85] *without the open confidential counsel* of intimate friends as they lovingly correct each other until they reach wise resolutions through collaboration. The plans of the wicked, based on their hubris, risk failure, for without correction they tend to be self-serving and unrealistic. *But with a multitude of* skilled and authoritative *counselors each plan succeeds.* A plurality of counselors offsets the individual's limitations. The similar proverb in 11:14 pertains to a nation, but this generalization can refer to any situation where counsel is helpful.

23 The dialogical character of counsel leads to this climactic proverb on the joy the wise experience in giving an apt response. Having accepted the parents' good teaching as a child (v. 20), in adulthood *one has joy in the apt answer* (*bəmaʿănē*) *of one's mouth.* Unlike the English "answer," which may denote an ineffective reply, *maʿănēh* refers exclusively to an effective one. Exclamatory *how* underscores the joy of hitting the nail on the head. *Good* here signifies that the moral *word* is so well composed that it is beneficial to all concerned and so wanted by all. *The right time* refers to an appropriate and opportune time. The effective answer is not given in haste (29:20) but, informed by knowledge, is spoken on the right occasion (10:14).

24 This janus, a synthetic proverb, ramps up the reward of righteousness from present joy to everlasting life with *I AM*—in contrast to the destiny of the wicked, the theme of vv. 25–29. *The path of life* refers to the situation of having an everlasting relationship with the living God. *Leads upward,* as an antithesis to downward in connection with the grave, implies eternal life above and beyond the grave. *For* designates *the prudent* (or "insightful") as the path's beneficiaries. *And so* signifies the logical consequence of v. 24b: being on the upward path, one *turns aside from the grave* (lit. "from Sheol"; see "The Grave," p. 50) *below.* Salvation from the grave is not merely avoiding an untimely death, for then the path of life would be swallowed up in death, negating this proverb and the book of Proverbs.

---

85. The Heb. verb *pārar* essentially means "to bring to nothing."

Destinies of the Righteous and the Wicked (15:25–29)

The inclusio formed by "*I AM*" (vv. 25a, 29a) frames this subunit and gives the whole a theological depth. *I AM* secures those on the path of life and draws near to them to hear their prayers in crises.

25 This proverb qualifies v. 24, for it implies that tyrants tyrannize the weak before the time when *I AM tears away* (see 2:22) *the house* (the indispensable means of support) *of the proud* (the violent tyrants who despise God and stomp on his image-bearers; cf. Pss. 94:2; 140:5). *But he sets in place the boundary of the widow* means that *I AM* puts the widow in a particular life-sustaining land. "Boundary" is a synecdoche for the property essential for life. "Widow" also functions as a synecdoche for all who are vulnerable to oppressors (cf. 14:31; 15:15; 19:17; 22:9, 22; 23:10). When they were too weak to speak, God spoke for the vulnerable through Moses (cf. Deut. 19:14; 27:17), the prophets (Hos. 5:10), and the sages (Job 24:2; Prov. 15:25; 22:28). Jesus raised the widow of Nain's son, presumably so the son could resume protecting his mother (Luke 7:11–17).

26 The catchword "*I AM*" binds this proverb to v. 25 and gives it its theological rationale. Implicitly, "the proud" of v. 25a are now designated "evil" and so an abomination to *I AM*, and "the widow," who represents all the weak and oppressed (v. 25b), is designated as "pure" and so favored by him. *The plans of an evil person are an abomination to* I AM, causing him to withdraw from them and abandon them to certain, eternal death (cf. 1:20–33; 6:16–19; Ps. 16). *Pleasant* (that is, beneficial; see 2:10) qualifies *words* that are so agreeable to *I AM* that he takes delight in them (cf. 2:10). *Pure* means free of any contaminations not consistent with something's essential nature, a notion that passes easily into its figurative use for that which is ethically pure (cf. Eccl. 9:2). Here, "pure" functions as a metonymy for favorable to *I AM* (cf. Mal. 3:16), the opposite of "abomination." Such words and plans shine before *I AM* like the gold in his sanctuary because they are free of all the ethical impurities that damage others, such as lies, distortions, and harshness.

27 The catchword "house" binds this verse to v. 25 and gives the concrete example of bribery as a way the proud (v. 25) and the evil (v. 26) ruin their houses. *The greedy for gain* are, for example, the murderous thugs in 1:10–19, and here, by its parallel, the corrupt shyster—possibly an official. *Ruin their households* is clarified in v. 25 as due to God's act. *But the one who hates bribes* (*mattānōt*) *will live.* Outside of the wisdom literature, *mattānâ*, or the collective singular *mattān*, refers to "gift": something given voluntarily with no expectation of reciprocity (Gen. 25:6; 2 Chr. 21:3; cf. Esth. 9:22; Ezek. 46:16–17). In the wisdom literature, however, a "gift" is always used to influence another (see 18:16; 19:6; 21:14). In Eccl. 7:7, it is given to corrupt the recipient's judgment. Here, the parallel with "greedy for gain" excludes a favorable sense and confirms the bribe is to advantage self by disadvantaging a rival. "Greedy for gain" leaves open whether the bribe is given or received; both are bad (17:8; Exod. 23:8; Deut. 16:19; Ps. 15:5; Eccl. 7:7; Isa. 1:23; 5:23). *Will live* is an imprecise antithesis to "ruin their households," implying that "live" entails the continuation of the good person's house and "ruin their households" entails a Judas-like death (cf. Matt. 26:15; 27:5).

28 This verse is paired with the next by the catchwords "righteous" (v. 28a, 29b) and "wicked" (v. 28b, 29a). Verse 28 contrasts their hearts and speech. *The heart* (see "Heart," p. 32) *of a righteous person* (see pp. 36–37) *ponders* (*yehgeh*; see 24:2) *[its] answer* (*la'ănôt*; lit. "to answer"). Here *yehgeh* means "to reflect, meditate" (cf. Ps. 1:2; 63:5–6; 77:11–12), because considered speech is the opposite of rash talk. The wise have answers (see 15:23) but still think long and hard about what, how, and when to say them (see 15:2). *But the mouth of wicked people blurts out evil things.* The imprecise parallels, the inner "heart" and outward "mouth," as in 15:7, 14, complement one another (see 4:23; cf. 10:20, 31). "Blurts out evil things" in v. 28b assumes that "ponders to answer" in v. 28a has "good things" as its object. The proverb assumes that the righteous have the self-control not to react emotionally but to think before they answer, unlike the wicked, who only want to vent their malice (cf. 10:31–32; 15:1–2). What they "ponder" is how to plunder (24:2).

29 This proverb shifts from speaking about people to speaking about God and gives the theological rationale for being righteous. *I AM is far* signifies that his beneficent presence is remote *from the wicked* (see v. 28). *But he hears* and responds to *the prayer of the righteous.* Assertions about *I AM*'s presence or distance are not theological statements that restrict his omnipresence but religious statements about the availability of his favor (see p. 25).

Section B: Mostly Synthetic Proverbs (15:30–22:16)

For the structure of Collection II, see "Structure," pp. 3–4.

Prologue (15:30–33)

> [30]The light of the eyes makes the heart glad,
>   and good news revives the whole person.
> [31]The ear that listens to life-giving correction
>   dwells among the wise.

³²Those who flout instruction despise their lives,
   but the one who hears correction acquires sense.
³³The instruction that gives wisdom is the fear of *I AM*,
   and humility [comes]ᵃ before honor.

a. The elided verb can be inferred from the preposition "from" (*IBHS* §11.4d).

The prologue (15:30–33) to the second part of Collection II consists of two educational proverb pairs. The first (vv. 30–31) is linked by the Hebrew root *šm'* ("to hear"): "good news" (*šəmûʿâ*, "what is heard") delivered by an illuminated messenger (v. 30) and received by a "hearing" (*šōmaʿat*) disciple (v. 31). The second is linked by the catchwords "instruction"—flouted or accepted (v. 32) and elaborated on as "the fear of *I AM*" to be humbly received (v. 33)—and "correction" (vv. 31a, 32b).

30 The metaphor *the light of the eyes* connotes that the eyes reveal the inner vitality and joy of the bringer of "good news," its parallel in v. 30b. Scripture associates light with righteousness (Prov. 13:9; Matt. 6:22–23) and with life and good fortune (Job 3:16; 33:28; Prov. 4:18; 6:23; 13:9; 16:15). The New Testament connects light with Christ and his disciples (cf. Matt. 4:16; 5:14–16; John 1:4–5; 12:35–36; Eph. 5:8). Proverbs associates light and life exclusively with the wise, implying that illuminated eyes belong to the wise (15:13a). *The heart* (see "Heart," p. 32) refers to the disciple's heart. The sages' life and joy are contagious. *Good news* is a metonymy for the teaching that follows in 16:1–15. It bears repeating, however, that proverbs are contextually meaningful and applicable to many situations. *Revives the whole person* is literally "fattens the bone" (see 12:4), referring to a listener's entire self, both physical and psychical.

31 The receptive organ that inclines the heart and revives the whole person is *the ear* (see 2:2) *that listens to life-giving correction* (or rebuke; see 1:23). A disciple with such an ear *dwells among the wise*—that is, lives with them, continuously ready to hear correction. The hearing ear and seeing eye are God's handiwork (20:12).

32 This proverb ramps up the motivation to accept correction by alluding to suicide in contrast to survival (see 8:36; 15:6, 10): *those who flout instruction* (see 13:18) *despise* (see 3:11) *their lives* while *the one who hears correction* (vv. 5, 31a) *acquires* (see 4:5; 8:22) *sense* (lit. "a heart"; see "Heart," p. 32). To "acquire a heart" signifies to gain the mental and moral capacity to live, as its parallel, "life," in v. 31a makes clear. In 19:8 "acquiring a heart" is equated with "loving oneself," the opposite of "despise their lives."

33 *The instruction that gives wisdom* is grounded in *the fear of* I AM (see

1:7). Wisdom is a matter of the heart. The disposition of *humility* (*'ănāwâ*; see 3:34), equated with the fear of *I AM* in 22:4, ushers the disciple into the company of the sage (v. 31) and, as further motivation, into the company of *I AM*. "Humility" signifies a disposition that renounces self-sufficiency to pursue commitment to *I AM*, who alone is trustworthy to provide life-giving instruction (3:5–7). Commitment to *I AM* always *[comes] before honor* (see 3:16; 18:12; 22:4). Paradoxically, those who strip off their glory before the glorious *I AM* are in the end crowned with the glory and the wealth that give them social esteem (see 3:16; 8:18; 11:16).

The Dance between I AM, Humanity, and the King (16:1–15)

> [1]To humans belong the plans of the heart;
>> from *I AM* [comes] the right answer of the tongue.
> [2]People's ways [are] all pure in their own eyes,
>> but *I AM* is the one who evaluates motives.
> [3]Commit to *I AM* your works
>> and your thoughts will be established.
> [4]*I AM* works everything to its appropriate end,
>> even the wicked person for an evil day.
> [5]An abomination to *I AM* is everyone who is haughty;
>> be sure of this: that person will not go unpunished.
> [6]Through love and faithfulness sin is atoned for,
>> and through the fear of *I AM* is a departing from evil.
> [7]When *I AM* takes pleasure in people's ways,
>> he compels even their enemies to surrender to them.
> [8]Better a little with righteousness
>> than a large income with injustice.
> [9]The hearts of human beings plan their ways,
>> but *I AM* establishes their steps.
> [10]An inspired verdict is on the king's lips;
>> in giving a judgment, his mouth is not unfaithful.
> [11]A just balance and a hand scale are *I AM*'s;
>> all the weights in a pouch are his work.
> [12]An abomination to kings is doing wickedness,
>> for a throne is established through righteousness.
> [13]Kings take pleasure in righteous lips,
>> and whoever speaks upright things he loves.
> [14]The wrath of the king is the messenger of death,

but a wise person pacifies it.
¹⁵In the light of the king's face is life,
and his favor is like a cloud of spring rain.

After the prologue to the second part of Collection II, the first section trumpets *I AM*'s moral sovereignty exercised through his king. It consists of two subunits: *I AM*'s sovereignty as it encompasses human responsibility (16:1–9) and his mediated rule through his righteous king (16:10–15). The two subunits are clearly demarcated by the repetition of key words: "*I AM*" (*yhwh*) in vv. 1–9, except v. 8; and "king" in vv. 10–15, except v. 11. Synonyms for "light" in vv. 1a and 15a form an inclusio around the unit. The two subunits are linked, as Meinhold notes, in four ways: (1) the catchwords "abomination" (vv. 5, 12), "favor" (vv. 7, 13, 15), "wicked"/"wickedness" (vv. 4, 12), and "to atone"/"pacifies" (root *kpr*; vv. 6, 14); (2) both the second verse from the end of the first subunit (v. 8) and the second verse from the beginning of the second subunit (v. 11) lack the key words of their subunits; (3) *yhwh*, however, is found in v. 11, and vv. 8 and 11 pertain to justice; and (4) God expects "righteousness" and "justice" of everyone (v. 8), and the king upholds them (v. 12).⁸⁶

I AM's Rule and Human Responsibility (16:1–9)

A chiastic inclusio, "humans," "heart" // "heart," "humans" (vv. 1a // 9a), frames the first subunit. Also, synonyms for "plan" with reference to humans (vv. 1a, 9a) and the catchword "establish" with reference to *I AM* (vv. 3b, 9b) frame it. Verses 1–3 teach *I AM*'s sovereignty over human initiatives and vv. 5–7 his justice in response to human morality. Verse 4 is a janus. Looking back to vv. 1–3, it asserts that *I AM*'s sovereignty brings everything to its appropriate destiny; looking ahead to vv. 5–7, it asserts that his justice matches the wicked with calamity. In sum, the subunit teaches that humans make plans (vv. 1a, 9a) but the sovereign Lord decides what will be established and will endure as part of his eternal, moral purposes (vv. 1b, 9b).

1 Human planning is necessary but limited by Providence. *To humans belong* gives the earthling the first word, but "from *I AM*" gives God the last word. *Plans* implies careful arrangement. The Hebrew root *'rk* refers to things carefully set in order, such as military troops in Gen. 14:8 or the wood on a sacrificial fire in Gen. 22:9. The agent is *the heart* (see "Heart," p. 32). *From I AM*

86. Meinhold, *Sprüche*, 264.

casts Providence as the ultimate Agent, not human wit (cf. 1 Cor. 3:6–7).[87] Hebrew *ma'ănēh* ("answer") is glossed *the right answer*, since *I AM* does not author an evil or ineffective answer. *Of the tongue* underscores the outward expression, both in substance and style, of the inward plans of verset A.

2 This verse adds a moral dimension to the theme of *I AM's* rule over human initiatives. *People's ways [are] all pure* (ethically) *in their own eyes*, which is to say in their deluded opinion (see 3:7; cf. Job 11:4; 16:7; 33:9; cf. Jer. 17:9). *But I AM is the one who evaluates* (*tōkēn*, meaning "to measure," "to determine the weight," "to gauge"[88]). *Motives* glosses the Hebrew *rûḥôt* (lit. "spirits," "winds"; see "Spirit," p. 33), a synecdoche for a person's heart—specifically, a person's disposition (Eccl. 7:8–9; Ezek. 11:19; 18:31; 36:26) or inner life (Job 7:11; Ps. 78:8), including opinions or desires (cf. Ezek. 13:3), mind (Ps. 77:6), will (cf. Prov. 16:32), and motives (cf. 2 Chr. 36:22). The plural, matching "ways" in verset A, is used because complex patterns of behavior depend on complex motives. Since the final verdict on the purity of one's motives belongs to *I AM*, the best one can do is commit one's motives to *I AM* and depend on him to make them pleasing (16:3, 7; cf. Pss. 19:12; 139:23–24; 1 Cor. 4:5–6; Heb. 4:12–13).

3 Since *I AM* is sovereign over human initiatives (v. 1) and he alone can evaluate the purity of human motives (v. 2), disciples should commit their plans to *I AM* (v. 3a) to establish them permanently, outlasting the wicked person's temporary triumphs (v. 3b). *Commit to* (*gōl'el*; lit. "roll upon"; cf. Gen. 29:3, 8, 10; Pss. 22:8; 37:5) connotes a sense of finality in rolling it away from oneself and onto *I AM* and leaving it there. *Gōl'el* is onomatopoeic; one almost hears the sound of a stone rolling. *Works* refers either to planned (Mic. 2:1) or performed deeds (Gen. 44:15). The faithful must not fret about their effectiveness or purity, for that assessment belongs to God (Pss. 22:8; 37:5; 55:22; 1 Pet. 5:7). Self-confident secular people paradoxically live in fear, while the pious, who know God's sovereignty and their limitations, live in prayer and peace. *And your thoughts* (see 12:5), a metonymy of cause for deeds, conceived out of total commitment to *I AM*, *will be established* (see 4:26). And so inner thoughts become overt historical events in salvation history; as such, they endure, like the elements of *I AM's* cosmos (see 8:27–29).

4 *I AM* directs everything to its appropriate end at the time of judgment. *Works* (see 10:29) *everything* allows no exception, no loose ends. *Its appropri-*

---

87. *Instruction of Amenemope* 20:5–6 reads, "If a man's tongue is the boat's rudder, the Lord of All is yet its pilot" (*AEL*, 2:158).

88. B. K. Waltke, *TWOT*, 2:970, s.v. *tkn*.

ate end is literally "its answer" (see 16:1). Providence works to bring *even the wicked person* (see "Ethical Terms for Wicked and Fools," pp. 45–46) *for an evil day.* In contrast to the righteous, whose plans and deeds are established, the wicked are punished (v. 5b) and defeated (v. 7b).

5 Verse 5b virtually repeats 11:21, and v. 5a is similar to 11:20a but replaces "perverse of heart" with "high of heart." *I AM*'s judgment of the wicked is due to his hatred of human hubris. The wicked of v. 4b are defined more precisely as *everyone who is haughty* (lit. "high of heart"—who consider themselves a cut above God and others[89] and so do not submit to his rule), and the "evil day" of v. 4b is clarified as the time of punishment in v. 5b. The haughty are an *abomination to* I AM (see on 3:32) and so *will not go unpunished.* That repugnant disposition precedes its possessor's downfall (11:2; 16:18). Instead of gratitude for their lives, the arrogant vaunt themselves above the Giver, considering their successes their own achievement (cf. Deut. 8:14).

6 So what do the wise do with regard to sin? Verse 6a gives a remedy for past sin (see v. 5) and v. 6b a preventive measure against future sin. *Love and faithfulness* (see 3:3) in Proverbs refers to human kindness to the needy, not to divine grace to sinners (cf. Gen. 32:10). The epigrammatic nature of the proverb (see "Terseness," pp. 10–11) and the purpose of the book of Proverbs focus on the human virtues that complement the atonement through the sacrificial system (cf. Lev. 1:4; 4:4; 16:21; passim). Unless unfailing love to God and neighbor characterizes the offerer, the sacrificial system is of no avail (1 Sam. 15:22; cf. Matt. 5:23–24; 6:12, 14–15; Luke 7:47; Jas. 1:26–27; 2:8, 12–18). *Is atoned for* (*yəkuppar*, from the root *kpr*) may mean "is covered over," "is expiated/wiped away," "ransom is made for," or "placates"/"mollifies." Since *iniquity* refers to misdeeds against God, "atoned for" is a synonym of "forgiven by God" (cf. Exod. 34:6). *And through the fear of* I AM (see "Fear of *I AM*," pp. 38–39). *A departing from evil* is a double entendre indicating salvation from both the moral aspect of doing evil and its disastrous consequences (see 1:16).

7 As part of their punishment, the wicked in the end surrender to the righteous. *When* I AM *takes pleasure* (see 3:12; Isa. 42:1) *in people's ways* entails that *I AM* accepts (cf. 15:8; 2 Sam. 24:23; Ezek. 20:41) and blesses them (Ps. 44:3), then *he compels even their enemies to surrender* (or "offer peace") *to them.* "Enemies" entails wicked people who, out of deep animus, oppose those whom God favors. The righteous, however, do not avenge themselves but trust God to vindicate them (see 3:34; 14:19; cf. Gen. 26:12–32).[90]

---

89. *HALOT*, 1:171, s.v. *gābah.*
90. See E. A. Martens, "The Way of Wisdom," in *WWis*, 75–90.

8 This "better than" proverb qualifies the assertions of divine punishment on the arrogant and blessings on the virtuous (vv. 5–7). *Better a little* (see 15:16) *with righteousness* (see pp. 36–37) implies that *I AM* does not always bless the righteous with immediate abundance. By contrast, *than a large income with injustice* implies *I AM* may allow the wicked to enjoy their ill-gotten gain for a time before bringing them to justice (see p. 37; 10:2–3). The similarity between 15:16 and 16:8, but with "righteousness" in 16:8a replacing "fear of *I AM* " in 15:16a, suggests that the omission of "*I AM* " is intentional—to wit, he seems absent before he turns the morally upside-down world right side up (cf. 1 Sam. 2:3–10; Ps. 37:16–17; Luke 1:51–53; 1 Tim. 4:8).

9 *The hearts of human beings* (see v. 1) *plan* (see 6:3), a poetic word for the human thinking and strategizing that issue in actions. *Their ways* (see 1:15) extends the frame from one's words (v. 1) to one's entire worldview and praxis. *Establishes* (see v. 3; see on 6:8) *their steps* (lit. "step") is a metaphor for the course of one's life. Not a step is taken apart from *I AM*'s superintendence. As Shakespeare put it, "There is a divinity that shapes our ends, rough-hew them how we will."[91]

The Mediatorial King (16:10–15)

The second subunit consists of three proverb pairs: the king's authority to give just verdicts (vv. 10–11), his moral sensibilities (vv. 12–13), and his judicial action to effect life or death (vv. 14–15). Verses 10–11 are linked by the catchword "justice," vv. 12–13 by plural "kings" and the antonyms "abomination"//"takes pleasure" (vv. 12a//13a) and "wickedness"//"righteousness" (vv. 12a//13a). The merism of death (v. 14) and life (v. 15) binds the final proverb pair.

10 *I AM* enacts divine justice through inspiring his wise *king*—the political mediator between God and people—to give infallible verdicts that uphold justice. Hebrew *qesem* (*an inspired verdict*) elsewhere refers to forbidden pagan divination (Deut. 18:10; 1 Sam. 15:23; Ezek. 21:18–23; cf. Num. 22:7; 23:23) or false prophecy (Jer. 14:14; Ezek. 13:6). Yet here, as its literary context shows, it denotes a legitimate method of reaching a verdict in legal disputes. Divination is the art of discerning the mind of the deity, and so *qesem* is a metaphor to denote the Spirit's empowering the king to reach a swift, accurate verdict (see 8:14–16; cf. 2 Sam. 14:17, 20; 1 Kgs. 3:16–28; Isa. 11:1–5; 1 Cor. 2:11–12). The litotes *is not unfaithful* denotes being loyal to a legally definable relationship of trust, to wit, upholding justice. This epigram presents the ideal of kingship

---

91. *Hamlet*, act 5, scene 2.

and anticipates the Messiah (cf. John 5:19–30). Most of Israel's kings were not ideal, and *I AM* removed or punished them (cf. 2 Sam. 7:14; 1 Kgs. 14:5–11; cf. 1 Kgs. 21).

11 *I AM* assists the king to establish justice by ordaining just weights and measures. *I AM* not only stands behind just weights (Lev. 19:35–36; Deut. 25:13; Job 31:6; Ezek. 45:10), he owns them. They *are I AM's*, for they *are his work* (he made them through human hands). *Balance* refers to a stationary balance with beams and bolts, and *hand scale* to the handheld balance.[92] They are a synecdoche for *all the weights* (see 11:1) and measures. *A pouch* refers to a trader's pouch for storing weights (see Deut. 25:13; Isa. 46:6; Mic. 6:11). This epigram speaks only of *just* (see 1:3) weights; for what *I AM* thinks of unjust weights, see 11:1; 20:23.

12 *An abomination* in relation to ethics usually occurs with "to *I AM*" (see 16:5; cf. 11:20; 12:22), but here uniquely occurs with *to kings*. *Doing wickedness* (see "Ethical Terms for Wicked and Fools," pp. 45–46) is unrestricted in its scope but refers particularly to the king's officials (cf. 25:5) and himself (cf. 29:14). His moral tastes agree with those of Woman Wisdom (8:7) and of *I AM* (6:16; 15:9). *For* is explanatory. *A throne*, a symbol of the king's dominion, *is established* (see 16:3) *through righteousness* (see pp. 36–37; cf. 20:28; 25:5; 29:14; Deut. 17:18–20; Pss. 89:14; 97:2; Isa. 16:5).

13 The king's moral sensibilities embrace both actions (v. 12) and words (Ps 101:7), represented here by *righteous lips* and *whoever speaks upright things* (see p. 37; cf. 8:8). "Doing wickedness" is expressed negatively as an abomination, and speaking what is right is expressed positively as something *kings take pleasure in* (see v. 7) and *he loves*.

14 *The legitimate wrath*—not the uncontrolled outbursts—*of the king* informs his verdict of capital punishment. The metaphor *is the messenger of death* signifies the king's wrath presages death (cf. 19:12; 20:2), allowing time to pacify it. Unlike with the jealous husband (see 6:34), *a wise person pacifies it* through virtues such as humility (15:33), repentance and confession (28:13), renewed community loyalty (16:6), and patience with a gentle answer (15:1; 25:15). For historical illustrations, see Gen. 18:16–33; Exod. 32:9–14; Num. 25:6–13; 2 Sam. 12:7–14; Dan. 2:5–24; Matt. 22:1–14; Luke 13:6–8.

15 *In* the sphere of *the light* (see 15:30) *of the king's face* is a metaphor signifying the ruler's beneficent favor (cf. Num. 6:25; Job 17:12; Ps. 119:13; Jer. 15:9). The figure probably has a solar background.[93] His favor is inseparable from

---

92. *ANEP*, 40 (no. 133), 219 (no. 639).

93. One Ugaritic text reads: "And the face of the sun [i.e., Pharaoh] shone bright on me" (cited in Dahood, *Proverbs and Northwest Semitic Philology*, 36)

enjoying *life* (Job 3:16; 29:4; 33:28, 30; Ps. 56:13). *And his favor is like a cloud* that heralds the revitalizing *spring rain* (cf. Ps. 72:15–17).

Wise and Foolish Speech (16:16–30)

¹⁶To acquire wisdom, how much better than gold!
    And to acquire insight is preferable to silver.
¹⁷The highway of the upright is turning away from evil;
    those who guard their way protect their life.
¹⁸Before a shattering comes pride,
    and before humiliation a haughty spirit.
¹⁹Better to be lowly in spirit with the oppressed
    than to divide plunder with the proud.
²⁰The one who pays attention to a saying finds good,
    and as for those who trust in *I AM*, blessed are they!
²¹The wise of heart is named "Insightful,"
    and sweetness of lips increases persuasiveness.
²²A wellspring of life is prudence to those who have it,
    but the discipline of fools is folly.
²³The hearts of the wise cause their mouths to be prudent,
    and on their lips they add persuasiveness.
²⁴Pleasant words are overflowing honey,
    sweet to the soul and a remedy to the bones.
²⁵There is a way that is right in a person's judgment,
    but the end of it is the way to death.
²⁶The appetites of the toilers toil for them;
    surely their mouths urge them on.
²⁷Troublemakers prepare mischief,
    and on their lips [it] is like a scorching fire.
²⁸A perverse person unleashes conflict,
    and the slanderer alienates a close friend.
²⁹Violent people entice their companions
    and lead them in a way that is not good;
³⁰blinking their eyes, they devise perversity;
    pursing their lips, they bring evil to pass.

This unit of synthetic parallels consists of an introduction (vv. 16–19) and two subunits: the winsome speech of the wise (vv. 20–24) and the destructive speech of the diabolical (vv. 26–30). A center verse (v. 25), uniquely antithetical, warns against the way of self-determination, which leads to death.

Introduction: Security in Wisdom (16:16–19)

The introduction resonates with the vocabulary of the Prologue (cf. 3:13–14; 4:5, 7; 8:10–11, 19). It is framed by the catchword "better" (*ṭôb*, "good," vv. 16, 19). In fact, *ṭôb* frames the whole unit (vv. 16, 29). Verses 16 and 17 focus on the wise defined by ethical behavior and vv. 18 and 19 on their inner disposition. Verses 16 and 17 are linked by the logic of cause (being "upright") and effect (acquiring "wisdom"), and the synonyms "pride" and "proud" link vv. 18 and 19. Verse 19 qualifies verse 18 by implying that the proud for a time exploit the oppressed and are not shattered, and verse 18 explains why it is better to be oppressed for a time—to wit, the proud will be destroyed.

16 *To acquire wisdom* and *to acquire insight* (see 4:5, 7) are *better than gold* and *preferable to silver* (cf. 8:10; see on 3:14). In this context, this is so because wisdom protects life whereas wealth by oppression shatters it. The rhetorical exclamation *how much better . . . !* gives the comparative degree a superlative force.

17 The imagery of roads ("highway" and "way") is used to motivate youth to choose ethical integrity. Dorsey explains the imagery: In Iron Age Israel (1100–600 B.C.), *the highway* was the main prepared thoroughfare and normally passed by cities, not through them. Those wishing to enter the city did so by "turning aside" onto an access road (cf. Judg. 19:11, 12, 15).[94] Here, the metaphor depicts the course of life *of the upright* (see p. 37; 2:7). Those who do not deviate from piety and ethics by definition *turn aside from evil* (see 3:7; 14:16; 16:6), which implicitly likens evil to a condemned city (13:14–15; 15:24). By turning aside from the condemned cities, the upright stay on the unimpeded road to life. Verse 17b escalates the impersonal metaphor of a highway to the dynamic personal metaphor of a person on a journey. Like 2:8, 11, the verset puns on the synonyms "guard" and "protect." *Those who guard their way* (see on 1:15) through great care *protect their life* (see pp. 41–42).

18 The imagery of v. 18 depends on the contrast between "high" in the sense of pride and "low" in the sense of abased. Instead of guarding their way, the proud defy the first principle of wisdom (see 2:5–7; 15:33). Raising their eyes above God and humanity (cf. 30:13), they stumble to their perdition (cf. 18:12). Both versets follow *before* with references to providential and ruinous consequences: *shattering* and *humiliation*. These are followed by the cause—

---

94. D. A. Dorsey, *The Roads and Highways of Ancient Israel* (Baltimore: Johns Hopkins University, 1991), 228–29.

synonyms that sound similar in Hebrew: *pride* (*gāʾōn*; see 8:13) and *haughty* (*gōbah*, whose concrete meaning is "high"; see 16:5).

19 This *better . . . than* proverb (see 12:9; 15:16; 16:8) implies that before the *proud* are destroyed (v. 18), Providence may allow them to oppress the oppressed (15:16; 16:8, 19). The proverb teaches youth *to be lowly in spirit,* which has the noble sense of describing people who through affliction have had their pride knocked out of them and who become humble before God (see 3:34). *To divide the plunder* (see 1:13) is taken from military life (Gen. 49:27; Exod. 15:9; Judg. 5:30; 1 Sam. 30:22–24; Ps. 68:12; Isa. 53:12) or from the judicial and civil injustices of the rich (cf. 1:13; 31:11). Its imprecise antithesis implies the proud became rich by exploiting the lowly, *the oppressed.* "Poverty and humility are natural allies, and impious pride goes with ill-gotten gain."[95]

The Wise Speaker (16:20–25)

A pun on Hebrew *maśkîl al-dābār* (see v. 20a below), along with the catchword "good," functions as a transition from the introduction to the body. The rest of the subunit fleshes out "the good" the prudent speaker finds: community esteem (v. 21), being a well of life (v. 22), increasing persuasiveness in teaching (vv. 21, 23), and being as sweet and healing as honey (v. 24).

20 *Maśkîl al-dābār*, glossed *the one who pays attention to a saying*, can also be glossed "the one who is prudent [or 'competent'] in speech." The former sense best suits the parallel *and whoever trusts in* I AM (see 3:5; 28:25; 29:25). According to this interpretation, the proverb shows a thematic connection with vv. 16–19. The lowly in spirit pay attention to the sages' teachings and trust in *I AM* who inspired them (3:5) and so are wise in heart and speech (vv. 21, 23). The latter sense means that prudent speech reaps the benefits in vv. 21–24. The pun functions as a transition from accepting wise speech to giving it. Before people are competent to win respect for their words (v. 21), they must themselves carefully attend to the words of their teachers. *Blessed are they* (see 3:13).

21 The imprecise parallelism of v. 21 suggests that *the wise of heart* (see 11:29) reveal themselves by using language that influences people for good. Such a person *is* officially *named*, presumably by the community, *"Insightful"* (see pp. 35–36), a sobriquet signifying an elevated status in the community. *And sweetness of lips,* to judge from the contrast with the foreign woman's sweet but false speech (5:3; 7:21), refers to truthful speech. As a metaphor, it signifies

95. McKane, *Proverbs*, 499.

delightful and so appealing speech (16:24); and as a synecdoche it represents total gracious deportment. Such speech *increases* the *persuasiveness* of the teaching. The wise teach truth winsomely and so persuade the community for good and win their respect. The proverb is fleshed out in the life of Christ (Luke 4:22; 19:48; John 7:46).

22 *A wellspring of life* (see 10:11; 13:14; 14:27) *is prudence* (see 3:4; p. 35) *to those who have it* signifies that those who possess prudence become a life-giving spring that is so attractive that others turn aside from folly in order to drink from their teachings (see 10:11; 13:14; 14:27). For Christians, Jesus Christ is a spring of water welling up to eternal life (John 4:14; 7:37). *But* contrasts the pedagogy of fools (v. 22b) with that of the prudent (v. 22a). *The discipline* (corporal punishment, not verbal correction; see 1:2) *of fools is folly* signifies the punishing consequences of fools' moral insolence and rejection of the life-giving water.

23 Winsome teaching (v. 21b) originates in *the hearts* (see "Heart," p. 32) *of the wise* (v. 21a; cf. Matt. 7:17), for their hearts *cause their mouths to be prudent*—that is to say, they have the ability to comprehend a situation and so make a beneficial decision on what to say and how to say it (see "The Wise and Words," pp. 39–40; 1:3). *Lips* is a stock-in-trade parallel to mouth. *They add persuasiveness* (see v. 21b). In short, prudent speech is both beneficial and persuasive in all challenging social situations.

24 The notions of beneficence and persuasiveness are compared to overflowing honey. *Pleasant words* stand in contrast to "evil thoughts" in 15:26, suggesting that the expression denotes a moral as well as an aesthetic quality. *Overflowing honey* means a "honeycomb."[96] Verset B explains the metaphor: honey uniquely is both sweet and remedial (see 4:22). *Sweet to the soul* connotes that the style of the speech is pleasing and attractive to others. *A remedy* connotes that its substance heals those hurt by the fool's damaging words. The synecdoche *to the bones* refers to the restoration of the entire person or community. Normally, medicine is bitter, and what is sweet is not medicinal. Both properties are necessary; were healing words bitter, the tonic would not be consumed and so be of no benefit.

25 The unit's center line repeats 14:12, focusing on the lethal danger of deceptive pride and doing your own thing (cf. 16:18–19). It is a fitting introduction to the second subunit, featuring speech that is destructive to others and to self.

---

96. *HALOT*, 3:1013, s.v. *ṣûp.*

Foolish Speakers (16:26–30)

The second subunit begins with the mixed blessing of toilsome labor that the hungry mouth induces, by God's design, to preserve life (v. 26) in contrast to the four negative malevolent speakers who disrupt the social order against God's design: troublemakers (v. 27), the perverse (v. 28a), the slanderer (v. 28b), and the violent (vv. 29–30). The catalog moves from mischief-makers to its climax with the violent, as is indicated by their seduction of others to join them (v. 29) and by extended depictions of them moving from their evil communications to the crime itself. Their "way that is not good" (v. 29b) is unpackaged in v. 30 as "devising perversity" and "bringing evil to pass."

26 The need for food goads workers to productive work. *The appetite* (*nepeš*; see *"Nepeš,"* p. 32) refers to the basic desires and drives of all animate beings. *Toil* is "the process of work . . . and the trouble that it causes."[97] *For them*—the toilers' cravings serve them well. *Surely* indicates that verset B explains and emphasizes verset A. *Their mouths* is a metonymy for the hungers that *urge them on*. Though work is exhausting and frustrating in the fallen world, still the drive to gratify the appetite drives people to productive efforts, and the Creator does not frustrate these primal, productive drives by denying them gratification (10:31; 2 Thess. 3:10). The history of civilization is unimaginable without them.[98]

27 The first malevolent speaker is the nefarious troublemaker (see 6:12–15). This paragon of evil concocts inflammatory speech (verset A) and then propagates it (verset B). *Troublemakers prepare mischief* (*rāʿâ*, "harm" or "evil") for others. *And on their lips* indicates that the cooked-up evil involves their speech. *[It] is like a scorching fire* (see 6:27) likens the troublemaker to a flamethrower, inflicting permanent, painful, and life-threatening damage on others.

28 To the catalog of malicious speakers this proverb adds two more: a perverse person (see "Ethical Terms for Wicked and Fools," p. 46) and the perfidious slanderer. The *perverse person* overthrows God's social order. Such people's perversity starts in their hearts (6:14; 23:33) and comes out in their speech (cf. 2:12; 8:13; 10:31–32) and eyes (16:30). A perverse person *unleashes conflicts* (see 6:14, 19), setting the community at loggerheads. *The slanderer*[99]

---

97. Schwertner, *TLOT*, 2:925, s.v. ʿamal.

98. "Hunger! That unwearying good of men, so beneficial to the race, so pitilessly cruel to the individual" (W. A. L. Elmslie, cited by Cohen, *Proverbs*, 109).

99. Fox (*Proverbs 10–31*, 622), without offering an argument, suggests the "slanderer" (*nirgān*) is an instance of the "perverse person" (*tahpukôt*) and not a separate villain. The other uses of these words, however, suggests that they signify different types of person.

denotes a malicious gossip who distorts reality and so aims to besmirch and defame others behind their backs, as Israel murmured in their tents against their gracious Sovereign. *Alienates* (separates) *a close friend*—the most intimate relationships (Gen. 13:9, 11, 14). Both types of malicious speaker put others in the worst light (cf. 6:19) and divide people. Talebearers, however, do the most damage because by their murmurings they sever the closest relationships—their own and those of others (cf. 1 Pet. 4:15).

29 *Violent people* (see 3:31) denotes cold-blooded murderers who are driven by greed and hate. They employ the deadly weapons of false accusation and unjust judgment. They *entice their companions* to abet them in their crimes (see 1:11–14). The conjunction *and* points to the logical conclusion: they *lead them* (their companions) *in a way* (see 1:15) *that is not good*, a litotes signifying a way that is "altogether evil and destructive."[100] Proverbs 4:10–19 emphatically warns the disciple against this way because of its tragic consequences.

30 This verse depicts the violent as executing their premeditated evil by gesturing to an accomplice behind the victim's back with their eyes and pursed lips. *Blinking their eyes* recalls the troublemaker's malicious winking in 6:13 (cf. 10:10). To *devise* means "to plan creatively, scheme." *Perversity* connects the violent person with the perverse in v. 28. *Pursing their lips* means they communicate by gesturing, not by speaking. *Brings . . . to pass* means causes to happen. *Evil* (*rāʿâ*) has the same nuance as in v. 27a, with which it forms an inclusio.

The Splendid Crown of Old Age through Righteousness (16:31–17:6)

> ^{16:31}Grey hair is a splendid crown;
> > it is found in the way of righteousness.
> ³²Better to be a patient person than a mighty hero,
> > even one who rules over one's spirit than one who captures a
> > > city.
> ³³Into the bosom the lot is hurled,
> > and from *I AM* [come] all its decisions.
> ^{17:1}Better a dry piece of bread with peace and quiet
> > than a house full of sacrifices with strife.
> ²A prudent slave rules over a shameful son
> > and receives the inheritance in the midst of the brothers.
> ³The crucible is for silver and the furnace for gold,

100. Delitzsch, *Proverbs*, 252.

but the one who tests hearts is *I AM*.
⁴One who pays attention to a malevolent lip is an evildoer;
   one who listens to a destructive tongue is a liar.
⁵The one who mocks the poor reproaches their Maker;
   the one who rejoices over calamity will not escape without
      punishment.
⁶The [splendid] crown of the aged is children's children,
   and the glorious [crown] of children is their fathers.

The inclusio formed by "splendid crown" (16:31; 17:6) frames this unit. Instead of viewing old age as the time of physical weakness and decline, when authority is to be resigned and power handed over to the new generation, the frame views it as a time of authority, status, and dignity symbolized by a crown. The opening frame ascribes this resplendent aura to a person's righteousness (16:31), and the closing frame passes on that splendor to future generations (17:6). The proverbs within the frame largely define righteousness. In 16:31 and 17:1, God's rule has priority over human rule; in 17:1–2, spiritual virtue has priority over carnal advantage; in 17:3–5, God's moral rule has the last word, as seen in his punishment of liars and mockers.

16:31 *Grey hair* is a metonymy for "old age" (20:29) and is to be respected (Lev. 19:32). Its comparison to *a splendid crown* signifies its beauty and authority (see 4:9; Isa. 3:5; 9:14–15). *It is found in the way* (see 1:15) *of righteousness* (see pp. 36–37) and so attainable. The following "better than" proverb qualifies this truth by admonishing patience before winning the crown (cf. 16:18–19). Clinically, before being crowned, the righteous may die prematurely (see "Does Proverbs Promise Too Much," pp. 44–45) and old age brings infirmity (Eccl. 12:1–8).

32 This better-than proverb asserts that spiritual strength to rule self is better than brute strength to rule others (cf. 25:28). *Even* signifies both that *a patient person* (see 14:29) is *one who rules over one's spirit* and that *a mighty hero* is a warrior *who captures a city*. Self-control entails not being ruled by anger (Jas. 1:19–20) and may entail overlooking an offense (see 19:11; cf. 1 Cor. 6:7). The proverb implies that, before being crowned (v. 31), the righteous may have to exercise patience and that old age usually demands self-control with increasing infirmity (Eccl. 12:1–8).

33 *I AM* is the determiner of destiny, as illustrated by *the lot*—a small stone used (where God's will was not revealed and impartial selection was desired) to reveal God's selection of someone or something out of several possibilities. *The bosom* denotes the secret holding area in the fold of the garment above the belt where the lot remained covered and uninfluenced. *Is hurled* signifies that the lot's selection is final because it is ultimately "hurled down" by God (cf. 18:18). *All its decisions*—no exceptions. *[Come] from* I AM traces the human action of "hurling down" back to Israel's covenant-keeping God.

17:1 Spiritual tranquility within a household has priority over its physical feasting (cf. 12:9; 15:16–17). A *dry piece of bread* is small in quantity and unsavory in quality without a savory sauce. *Peace and quiet* refers to the harmony and security of the diners. *Sacrifices* refers to sumptuous feasts held at the home after ritual sacrifices (see 7:14). *With strife* (cf. 1 Sam. 1:3–7; 1 Cor. 11:17–34) may be ironic, for the sacrifices referred to are fellowship offerings and meant to be celebrated with joy (cf. Deut. 12:6–7; Judg. 16:23; 1 Sam. 11:15).

2 *A prudent* (see p. 35) *slave rules over a shameful son* (see 10:5) teaches that leadership depends more on character than primogeniture. The Mosaic law allows a landless immigrant to rule over an Israelite who inherits land (Lev. 25:47). *And* explains the slave's promotion. *Receives* (ḥālaq) is used with "the portion coming to one by law and custom."[101] *An inheritance in the midst of the brothers* validates the slave's status as legal heir of the patrimony.

3 *The crucible* denotes here the instrument that tests *silver* for its purity (cf. Prov. 27:21). The same is true of *the furnace for gold*. Human beings can design instruments to test precious metals, *but the one who tests hearts is* I AM (cf. Pss. 17:3; 26:2; 66:10). He strips bare all pretensions and tests all human hearts to determine their genuineness and purity (cf. 16:2). Presumably, he will justly reward or punish each person according to his or her ethical purity (Job 23:10; 1 Cor. 4:3–5; 1 Pet. 1:7).

4 This proverb's parallels equate *one who pays attention* (see 1:24; 2:2) *to a malevolent* (see 6:12) *lip* (see 16:27) with *one who listens to a destructive tongue* (see 12:19, 21–22) and *an evildoer* (3:7) with *a liar* (6:17). "Destructive tongue" refers to evil speech that brings ruin on others and is often associated with lies and treachery (cf. Job 6:30; Pss. 5:9; 52:2, 7). The proverb thus startles us with the truth that those who listen to lies are themselves liars. "Evil words die without a welcome; and the welcome gives us away."[102]

5 *The one who mocks* (see 1:26) *the poor* (see 10:4). The parallel, *one who rejoices over calamity* (see 1:26–27), provides the reason for the mocker's schadenfreude—to wit, the poor's unfortunate socioeconomic situation. The derision, however, *reproaches* the poor person's *Maker* (see 14:31; cf. Gen 9:6). In effect, mockers mock their Maker "by implying that his handiwork is slipshod."[103] They *will not escape without punishment* from God.

---

101. M. Tsevat, *TDOT*, 4:448, s.v. ḥālaq.
102. Kidner, *Proverbs*, 123.
103. Fox, *Proverbs 10–31*, 626.

6 As *the [splendid] crown of the aged is children's children,* who are pictured as gathered around the aged parents like a crowning diadem, so *the glorious [crown] of children* (see 4:1) *is their fathers.* This does not exclude the mothers of each generation (see 1:8). This complementary aura of splendor proves that the family heritage is ancient, enduring, and true. The proverb assumes the righteousness of its parallel in 16:31, for godless families collapse (17:1) and godless children bring their parents shame (cf. 10:5; 17:2; 19:26).

A Collection of Proverbs on Fools (17:7–28)

[7] An eloquent lip is not fitting for a godless fool;
    how much more [unfitting][a] is a lying lip for a nobleman?
[8] A bribe is a magic stone in the eyes of its owners;
    to whomever they turn, [they think][b] they will succeed.
[9] Whoever would foster love covers over a transgression,
    but whoever repeats a matter separates close friends.
[10] A rebuke penetrates more deeply into a discerning person
    than flogging a fool a hundred times.
[11] Evil people foster only rebellion,
    and a cruel messenger is sent against them.
[12] Meet a bear robbed of her young by a human being,
    but [do] not [meet] fools in their folly.
[13] Whoever repays evil for good,
    evil does not depart from that house.
[14] The beginning of strife is breaking open a dam;
    so before a quarrel breaks out, drop [the controversy].[c]
[15] Whoever pronounces a wicked person innocent
    and whoever pronounces a righteous person guilty,
    both, yes, both of them are an abomination to *I AM.*
[16] Why in the world is there payment in the hands of fools
    to buy wisdom when they have no capacity to learn?
[17] At all times a friend loves,
    and a relative is born for adversity.
[18] One who claps a palm is a human being who has no sense:
    the one who pledges a security in the presence of a neighbor.
[19] Those who love strife love transgression,
    and those who makes their doorway high seek destruction.
[20] A person with a perverse heart does not find good,
    and one with a corrupt tongue falls into evil.
[21] He who begets a fool brings himself grief,

and the father of a godless fool does not rejoice.

²²A joyful heart promotes healing,

but a drained spirit dries up the bone.

²³A wicked person accepts a bribe from the bosom

to divert the paths of justice.

²⁴Wisdom stands ready to serve the discerning,

but the eyes of a fool are [looking] at the ends of the earth.

²⁵A foolish son is a vexation to his father,

and brings bitterness to the one who bore him.

²⁶If even to fine an innocent person is not good,

how much more is flogging nobles against what is upright.

²⁷Those who know knowledge restrain their words,

and an understanding person is cool of spirit.

²⁸Even fools who hold their tongues are thought to be wise,

those who stop up their lips, to be discerning.

a. Inferred from v. 7a.

b. Inferred from the parallel "in the eyes of" in v. 8a.

c. Inferred from the parallel "strife" in v. 14a.

This unit on fools consists of an introduction (vv. 7–9) followed by three subunits (vv. 10–15, 16–20, 21–28), each of which begins with an introductory educational proverb. References to "lips," a metonymy for speech, frame the unit.

Introduction: Catalog of Fools Expanded (17:7–9)

The introduction elaborates and expands the malevolent communicators of vv. 4–5 to include the liar (v. 7), the briber (v. 8), and the gossip (v. 9).

7 *How much more* (see 11:31; 19:10) is a minore ad maius argument: an inference from lesser (verset A) to greater (verset B), from an eloquent fool to a lying nobleman. The polysemous *yeter* means "excellence" (Gen 49:3) but with *lip* is glossed *eloquence*. The litotes *is not fitting* means grotesque (cf. 19:10; 26:1; Ps. 33:1). According to Roth, *a godless fool* (*nābāl*) denotes a sacrilegious outcast, the opposite of a "nobleman," and is "one of the strongest possible terms to denote godlessness"[104] (cf. Job 2:9-10, Pss. 14:1; 39:8; 74:22). Eloquence in a fool is as grotesque as a gold ring in a swine's snout (11:22). *A lying lip* that

104. W. M. W. Roth, "NBL," *VT* 10 (1960): 407.

deceives to hurt is *[unfitting] . . . for a nobleman*, who, unlike the fool, is a powerful and respected member of the king's court (cf. 17:26; 19:6; 25:7) and so, if he is a liar, is even more grotesque than the eloquent fool.

8 Continuing the theme of injustice, *a bribe* (see 15:27) usually pertains to a gift that adversely affects the administration of justice (see 6:35; 17:23; Mic. 3:11) and so comes under God's judgment (Job 15:34; Ps. 26:9–10). *A magic stone* (or "charm") produces favor. *In the eyes of* (that is, "in the opinion of") denotes the fool's self-delusion. *Its owners* denotes the bribers. *They turn* refers to the bribers, who think *they will succeed* in perverting justice. But not with God (Deut. 10:17). Unlike in the nations around Israel, *I AM* censured bribery in his kingdom.

9 The disciple restores broken community by veiling others' sins to win their friendship and by not recounting their failures. *Whoever would foster love covers over a transgression* (see 10:12). By contrast, *whoever repeats* signifies doing something once more, not continually. Heb. *dābār* means either *matter* or "word." The parallel "transgression" favors the former. *Separates close friends* repeats 16:28. "Whereas in 10:12 love . . . disposes a person to forgive an offender, here the motive for forgiveness is a desire for *future* friendship."[105] Ahiqar (VII) commends "a good vessel that covers a word in its heart, and [not] a broken one that lets it out."[106]

Fools and Their Punishments (17:10–15)

10 This proverb protects the preceding proverb from the immoral interpretation that the disciple should sweep sin under the rug. The wise person eschews gossip but rebukes a discerning wrongdoer and flogs a fool (Lev. 19:17). This comparative proverb contrasts the discerning from fools by the way they respond to correction. *A rebuke* (a verbal correction; see 13:1, 8) *penetrates more deeply* (i.e., more effectively reorients the way of) *a discerning person* (see "Understanding," p. 36) than *flogging* (19:25; 23:13–14) *a fool* (see pp. 47–48). *A hundred times* is hyperbole (see Deut. 25:1–3). Bridges notes, "A word was enough for David (2 Sam. 1–7; 24:13, 14). A look entered more in Peter's heart (Luke 22:61) than a hundred stripes on Pharaoh (Exod. 9:34, 35), Ahaz (2 Chr. 28:22), and Israel (Isa. 1:5; 9:13; Jer. 5:3)."[107]

11 Fools may steel themselves against human beatings, but rebels against

105. Whybray, *Proverbs*, 256.
106. *ANET*, 429.
107. Bridges, *Proverbs*, 261–62.

God cannot withstand his death sentence. Fox observes, "An intelligent man gets off with a rebuke, a fool gets beaten; but the rebel is put to death."[108] *Evil people* (see 1:16) *foster* (see 17:9) *only rebellion* (mərî). In its nearly 100 occurrences, mərî primarily refers to people's willful, defiant rebellion against God.[109] Rebels grieve his spirit (Isa. 63:10) and disobey his word (Josh. 1:18). *And* connects their rebellion with God's retribution: *a cruel messenger is sent against him* from the divine throne. The "messenger" is either a metonymy for the Angel of Death (cf. Pss. 35:5–6; 78:49) or a personification of death itself.

12 The incorrigibility of fools is escalated from their steeling themselves against flogging (v. 10) to their becoming more dangerous than an angry bear. The proverb is a unique form of a better-than proverb. *Meet* is a sarcastic command that is not to be taken literally but as a comparative hyperbole to what not to meet. *A bear* is a biblical symbol for anger and ferocity, here exacerbated due to being *robbed of her young* (cf. 2 Sam. 17:8; Hos. 13:8).[110] *By a human being* shows that she lost her young by deliberate human action, not by accident, and so is bent on revenge against the robber. *But* marks the antithetical command in the implicit *a fortiori* argument: *[Do] not [meet] fools in their folly*, which, parallel to "bear robbed . . . by a human being," refers to a sudden outburst of anger against an adversary.[111] In sum: on your own, don't confront a raging fool bent on revenge, for the fool will kill you.

13 But the fool will not get away with repaying evil for good. The versets of this proverb are linked together by the logic of the deed-destiny nexus. Fools' folly in repaying evil for good (verset A) results in an evil guest coming to punish them endlessly (verset B). *Whoever repays evil* (moral insolence that harms; see 1:15) *for good* (see 3:27; cf. Gen. 44:4; Ps. 38:20). Sometimes returning evil for good is glaring (cf. 1 Sam. 25; 2 Sam. 10–13). Often, however, it is so common that it is taken for granted. For example, children spurn their parents, who painstakingly raised them, and humanity spits in God's face after eating the fruit of his orchard (Gen. 3:5–6; Rom. 1:18–32). According to verset B, *evil*, personified as a villainous visitor, *does not depart from* the ingrate's *house*. *I AM* is the Ultimate Agent who avenges the wrong. Proverbs 20:22 admonishes disciples not to avenge themselves but to wait for *I AM* (cf.

---

108. Fox, *Proverbs 10–31*, 630.

109. Deut. 28:18 may refer to rebellion against parents; in Job 17:2, mərî is uncertain.

110. According to G. S. Cansdale (*Animals of Biblical Lands* [Exeter: Paternoster, 1970], 117), in biblical times, the Syrian bear roamed the hilly woods of Palestine, but the last one to live there was killed just before World War II. They weigh up to about 500 lbs (225 kg).

111. Delitzsch, *Proverbs*, 260.

24:19–20; 25:21–22; Deut. 32:35; Ps. 27:14; Matt. 5:38–48; Rom. 12:17–21; Heb. 10:30; 1 Pet. 3:9).

14 This proverb reinforces and intensifies the preceding one: do not even begin to provoke the pent-up anger of a fool. Verset A gives the reason for the admonition in verset B. *The beginning of strife* is implicitly likened to *breaking open a dam*, releasing its dammed-up water. The metaphor implies that the pent-up waters quickly burst out into a raging, uncontrolled cataclysm that does irreparable damage. So, *before an* acrimonious *quarrel* (see 15:18) *breaks out, drop* (or "let alone," "desist from") *[the controversy]*.

15 Nevertheless, one must not be indifferent to justice. This proverb's versets are linked by the emphatic *yes, both of them.* The pronoun's antecedents are a corrupt judge who *pronounces a wicked person innocent* and so acquits that person of punishment (cf. Deut. 25:1; 1 Kgs. 8:32) *and* a judge who *pronounces a righteous person guilty* and so penalizes the righteous person (cf. 17:26; 18:5; 24:23b–25). The proverb corrects the popular misconception that it is better to acquit ten guilty people than to condemn one innocent person. Both *are an abomination to* I AM (see 3:32).

The Friend and Fools (17:16–20)

An introductory educational proverb mocking a fool for trying to buy wisdom (v. 16) is followed by four setting a friend (v. 17) in contrast to two inferior types, escalating from the surety (v. 18) to the violent (v. 19). The surety is not punished by *I AM*, but the violent and all misanthropes are punished by God (v. 20).

16 In dramatic irony, the proverb pictures a fool coming to the sage with money to buy wisdom. The rhetorical question, *why in the world*, does not expect an answer but vents the sage's exasperation at the absurd situation. *Payment in the hands of fools to buy wisdom* is absurd for, as the parallel explains, the fool has no fear of *I AM*, the *sine qua non* of wisdom (1:7). Does the fool interpret literally the sage's figurative admonition to buy wisdom (cf. 4:4, 5, 7)? Fools thinks everything can be had for money, including wisdom, the free gift of God to the faithful (2:6; 8:17; Jas. 1:5), and, perhaps worse, fools think the sage is as materialistic as they are. This fool is as grotesque as one coming with payment to a prostitute to acquire love. Neither love nor wisdom can be bought.

17 *At all times*, as the first word in the Hebrew text, is emphatic. *A friend* (see 3:18) *loves* (see 8:17), for a true friend recognizes the inherent dignity and worth of the other and desires to be with the other in a mutual relationship.

And a relative is born (i.e., was brought forth as child) *for* helping to sustain the family in *adversity*, a state of extreme misfortune (cf. 2 Cor. 12:14; 1 Tim. 5:8). In misfortune, a friend rejoices and weeps with you (Rom. 12:15), and a relative functions as a safety net. Yet even in trouble, the friend's spiritual ties are better and stronger than blood ties (see 18:24; 27:10).

18 But being a loving friend and a helping relative does not entail becoming surety. *One who claps a palm* (see on 6:1) is a metonymy for *one who pledges a security* (or "becomes surety"). A surety *is a human being who has no sense* (see p. 50). The *neighbor* whom the surety is *in the presence of* is a witness to the transaction, not the one to whom the creditor is liable or the one being secured. "One need not, and should not, help others in *every* way."[112]

19 *Those who love strife* (see 13:10) in verbal or physical battle *love transgression* (see 10:12). *Those who make their doorway* (a synecdoche for the house) *high* above their neighbors' exhibit pride. Such arrogant misanthropes *seek destruction*—their own and possibly that of others. The agent of destruction is not stated, but since the "transgression" is against God, we should assume *I AM* is the Destroyer, as happened in the cases of pretentious Shebna (Isa. 22:15–19), Jehoiakim (Jer. 13–19), and Haman (Esth. 7:9–10).

20 The underlying image of this proverb is that of a straight path that a person twists and overturns. *A person with a perverse* ("twisted") *heart* (see 11:20) is also *one with a corrupt* ("overturning") *tongue. And* combines the perverted heart, the governor of all body members (see 4:23), with the commands that issue from the tongue (see 2:12, 14; 8:13; 10:31–32; 16:28, 30). The damnation of a misanthrope is certain, as indicated by the two predicates that match the negative with its reinforcing positive equivalent: such a one *does not find good* (tangible prosperity; see 16:10), but *falls* (a metaphor signifying "to perish"; see 11:14) *into evil* (calamity and a metonymy for the pit; see 1:16). Like the "crooked man" in the nursery rhyme, the evil person can walk only a crooked mile. Only the righteous walk a straight path (see 11:5).

The Fool, Injustice, and the Reserved Speech of the Wise (17:21–28)

The last subunit on fools consists of two parts (vv. 21–24; 25–28), each introduced by educational proverbs (vv. 21, 25) that are closely connected by the catchwords "who begets" (*yōlēd*; masc.; first word of v. 21a) and "who bore" (*yôledet*; fem.; last word of v. 25b), "father" (vv. 21a, 25b), and "fool"; by escalating "grief" (v. 21) to "vexation" (v. 25; see 12:16) and "does not rejoice" (v. 21;

---

112. Fox, *Proverbs 10–31*, 633.

see 5:18) to "bitterness" (v. 25); and by adding mother (v. 25b; see 1:8) to father (v. 21b). The emotional pain inflicted by fools on parents motivates youth to be wise (see 10:1, 23).

21 Fools not only ruin themselves (see v. 20) but also bring misery to their parents. *He who begets* emphasizes that fools owe their very being to their fathers. The misanthropic *fool* (see pp. 47–48), however, does not recognize this fundamental solidarity with the family, and so the father *brings himself grief* (see 10:1). *And* underscores the assessment with a negative equivalent: *the father*, a synecdoche for both parents (see 1:8), is presumably wise, for over *a godless fool* (see 17:7) he *does not rejoice.*

22 This proverb, paired with v. 21, elaborates on the negative psychosomatic effects of v. 21. Interpreted on its own, the proverb admonishes youth to live in such a way that they experience vivifying joy instead of mortifying depression. *A joyful heart promotes healing*[113] essentially repeats 15:13 in the Hebrew text. *A drained spirit* repeats 15:13bβ. The incomplete metaphor *dries up* depicts a negative state of perishing that must be overcome. *The bone* is a synecdoche for the whole person (cf. 2 Kgs. 9:13). The opposite of a dry bone is a fatty one, full of marrow (see 3:8; 15:30; 16:24; Isa. 58:11). As 15:15 makes clear, the difference between exhilaration and depression depends more on one's spiritual resources than on circumstances (cf. Acts 16:25) Depression can be avoided through the fear of *I AM* (3:7–8; 15:16), wisdom (15:24), hope (13:12), and good news (12:25; 15:30).

23 This proverb replaces the wisdom term "fool" with the correlative ethical term *wicked person* (see "Correlative Terms," p. 34), who, probably a judge, *accepts* (see 15:27; Ps. 15:5) *a bribe* (see 17:8). The bribe is taken out *from the bosom* (cf. 16:33), where the briber hides it so it will not be seen in open court. By hiding the bribe, the wicked acknowledge their guilt. Both the giver and receiver of the bribe act *to divert the paths* (the causes and consequences) *of justice* to which the oppressed poor hope to gain access and find life (see 18:5). Although hidden from the public's scrutiny and opprobrium, the evil is not hidden from God (15:11; 16:2; 17:3).

24 Fools also fail because they aim at distant, godless, and unattainable goals instead of attainable *wisdom* (see "What Is 'Wisdom'?" pp. 27–28). Wisdom is personified as one who *stands ready to serve*, an expression often used of a subordinate who stands or serves in the presence of an authority figure (cf. 1:20–23; 8:1–21; 14:6; Deut. 30:11–13; 1 Sam. 2:11; 1 Kgs. 12:6; Esth. 1:10; Jas. 1:5). The one served is *the*

---

113. Heb. *gēhâ* occurs only here in the OT, but its meaning is known from the verb in Hos. 5:13.

discerning (see "Understanding," p. 36). *But* instead of being served by wisdom, *the eyes of a fool*, which is a synecdoche for the fool's direction and orientation (see 4:25; Ps. 119:37), *are [looking] at the ends of the earth*, a metaphor for wrong and unattainable goals. To the Israelites, the phrase connoted places with ungodly ways far removed from the covenant people (cf. Deut. 13:7; 28:49, 64; Ps. 61:2).

25 This educational proverb, paired with v. 21 (see above), introduces the final subunit on fools and punishment. The proverb escalates v. 21 by adding the mother and sharpening "grief" (21a) to *vexation* and *bitterness. And* combines the father's grief to the mother's "bitterness."

26 *If even* suggest that an *a fortiori* argument links the versets. *To fine* is more precise than "to punish" (KJV, NJPS, NLT).[114] Hebrew *ṣaddîq* normally means "righteous person," but in a context that pertains to legal fines, it is better glossed *innocent person* (see v. 15). The litotes *is not good* signifies it is very bad, for it establishes tyranny as the law of the land. If fining an innocent is bad, then *how much* worse is *flogging nobles* (honest officials; see 8:16; 17:7) who uphold justice for all. Flagellation is more shameful and painful than a fine (Deut. 25:1–3). *Is . . . against what is upright* (see p. 37) is a litotes signifying that it is perverse.

27 The final proverbial pair pertains to speech ("words," v. 27; "tongue" and "lips," v. 28) and teaches extreme caution, escalating from restrained speech (v. 27) to total silence (v. 28; cf. Isa. 53:7). *Those who know* (see 1:2; 3:5) *knowledge* (see 1:2) *restrain their words* (see 1:2) because restrained speech best serves piety and ethics (cf. 14:29; 16:32). *And* binds the cause, *a cool spirit* (v. 27b), with the effect of restraint. *An understanding person* (see p. 36) is the parallel to "a person who knows" (see 1:2). The Egyptians used the words "hot" and "cool" in a metaphorical sense to describe two distinct personality types. The latter represents the ideal person—calm and dispassionate—and the ideal mouth, which speaks prudently. The opposite of the cool spirit in Hebrew, Grollenberg argues, is a person filled with the heated excitement of resentment (see 15:18).[115] The measure of a people's wisdom is the extent to which they attain this ideal. Jesus epitomizes this proverb (Isa. 53:7; Matt. 27:14; 1 Pet. 2:23), and James measures wisdom by how much control one has over one's speech (Jas 3:2).

28 This proverb aims to admonish disciples to hold their tongue when provoked, not to conceal their stupidity as in Lincoln's witticism: "It is better to keep your mouth shut and let them think you a fool than to open your mouth

114. In the Qal, the verb means "to impose a fine" (so NRSV).
115. R. P. L. Grollenberg, "A propos de Prov. VIII,6 et XVII,27," *RB* 59 (1962): 40–43.

and remove all doubt." *Even fools* (see pp. 46–47) *who hold their tongue are thought* (by others) *to be wise* (see pp. 34–35). The rare addition of a precisely synonymous parallel, *those who stops up their lips* (see 10:19) *to be discerning* (see "Understanding," p. 36) is highly emphatic.

The Speech of Fools and the Speech of the Wise (18:1–21)

¹Those who separate themselves seek self-gratification;
    against all sound judgment they start a quarrel.
²Fools do not delight in understanding
    but in their hearts' exposing themselves.
³When a wicked person comes, contempt also comes;
    and with shame is reproach.
⁴The words of a person's mouth are deep waters;
    the wellspring of wisdom is a rushing stream.
⁵To show favoritism to the guilty is not good,
    and so deprives the innocent of justice.
⁶The lips of fools come into controversy,
    and their mouths cry out for beatings.
⁷The mouths of fools bring them terror,
    and their lips are a trap for their very lives.
⁸The words of a slanderer are like tidbits;
    they descend into one's innermost being.
⁹Even one slack in his work
    is a brother of one who destroys.
¹⁰The name of *I AM* is a fortified tower;
    a righteous person runs into it and is protected on high.
¹¹The wealth of the rich is their fortified city
    and like a high city wall in their imagination.
¹²Before destruction, a person's heart is high and haughty,^a
    but before honor is humility.
¹³As for those who reply before listening,
    it is to them folly and shame.
¹⁴A person's spirit can endure even sickness,
    but as for a broken spirit, who can bear it?
¹⁵The heart of the discerning acquires knowledge,
    for the ears of wise people seek knowledge.
¹⁶People's gifts make room for them
    and lead them before great people.

¹⁷The first to present cases in disputes seem right,
    until opponents come and cross-examine them.
¹⁸The lot puts an end to conflicts
    and separates powerful [opponents].
¹⁹An offended brother is like^b a strong city,
    and conflicts are like the bolt of a citadel.
²⁰From the fruit of people's mouths their bellies are sated,
    [from] the harvest of their lips they are sated.
²¹Death and life are in the power of the tongue,
    and those who love it—each will eat its fruit.

a. "High" and "haughty" gloss one Hebrew word: *gābâ*.
    b. The MT *mqryt* ("from a fortified city") is better corrected by the LXX, Targ., Syr., and Vulg. to *kqryt* ("like a fortified city"). The sense is better, and scribes sometimes confused *kaph* and *mem*.

By mostly synthetic parallels, this unit contrasts in its almost equal-in-length subunits the antisocial speech of fools (vv. 1–12) and the reconciling speech of the wise (vv. 12–21). Verse 12 is a janus.

The Fool's Antisocial Speech and the Defense of the Righteous (18:1–12)

Introduction: The Fool's Alienation from Society (18:1–3)
Verses 1–3 introduce the misanthropy and incorrigibility of fools (vv. 1–2) and their social disgrace (v. 3). Their moral bankruptcy, garrulously expressed, stands in contrast to the sage's advice to restrain speech (17:27–28).

1 Verse 1 states the unit's theme and problem: *those* (that is, fools) *who separate themselves* (are unsociable[116]) *seek* (or "pursue") *self-gratification*, and, bent on self-indulgence, the misanthropes separate from the community. *Against all sound judgment they start a quarrel*. Hostility and isolation go together, as illustrated by Lot's strife with and separation from Abraham (Gen. 13:5–7).

2 The misanthropes are now identified as *fools* (see pp. 46–47) who *do not delight in*—a litotes for "detest"—*understanding* (2:2; 5:1). *But* sharply contrasts their refusal to listen with their opinionated logorrhea. *They delight in*

116. Hamilton, *TWOT*, 2:733, s.v. *pārad*.

their morally bankrupt *hearts' exposing themselves* (cf. 10:8, 10; 14:3; 15:14). Ironically, fools intend to impress others with their opinions, but in fact they expose their folly. The proverb warns against having a closed mind and an open mouth.[117]

3 The antisocial fool (vv. 1–2) is now identified ethically as *a wicked person* (see pp. 45–46). *When . . . comes* denotes the timing between the cause (the wicked person) and the consequence: namely, *contempt*, which refers either to the wicked person's inner disdain for others or to the evaluation of the wicked person by others (see 12:8; 13:18; 26:1). Both may be intended, but verset B favors the latter interpretation. *With* signifies that *shame* (social dishonor and the loss of public respect) and *reproach* (or "scorn"; see 6:33), which the community heaps on them, are as inseparable as the wicked and contempt.

The Fool's Perverse Speech (18:4–8)

The abstract descriptions of the wicked (vv. 1–3) are now narrowed to instances of their misanthropic speech, framed by the inclusio "the words of" (vv. 4a, 8a). Verse 4 condemns the concealing speech of an ordinary person, v. 5 perverse speech, and v. 8 slander. Verses 6–7 follow the condemnation of perverse speech with a warning against the deadly social consequences of misused speech.

4 The concealing speech of an ordinary person to protect self stands in striking contrast to the open, clear speech of the wise (cf. 8:6–9). *A person* denotes an average person, not the wise (see pp. 34–35). *Mouth* supports the water imagery by picturing the source from which others drink. *Deep waters* in poetry always has the negative connotations of inaccessibility and foreboding danger. *The wellspring* (see 5:18) is a metonymy for life (see 10:11; 13:14; 14:27; 16:22). Verset B mixes the metaphors of "wellspring" and *rushing stream* to convey the notion that the living water *of wisdom* is constantly accessible and abundant.

5 *To show favoritism* is literally "to lift the face of," a metonymy for declaring a person innocent (see 6:35). *Is not good* (see 17:26) is a litotes for meaning abhorrent. Verset B explains: favoritism for the guilty *deprives the innocent of justice* (cf. 17:15; 24:23). This injustice is linked with a bribe in 17:23 (cf. 1 Tim. 5:21; Jas. 2:1–4).

---

117. Kidner, *Proverbs*, 127.

6–7 This proverb pair is linked by the concentric structure of the catchwords:

A		"lips of fools" (v. 6a)
	B	"their mouths" (v. 6b)
	B'	"mouths of fools" (v. 7a)
A'		"their lips" (v. 7b)

and by the common theme of the damage of bad speech. The fool's afflictions due to abusive speech escalate from controversy (v. 6a) to beatings (v. 6b) to terror (v. 7a) to death (v. 7b). The theme of reciprocity is expanded and intensified in the unit's concluding proverb pair (vv. 20–21).

The lips of fools come into controversy implies that fools start quarrels to damage others. However, their actions boomerang to flog them (see 10:6): *and their mouths cry out for* (or "summon") *beatings.*

The parallel of the lethal trap (v. 7b) explains the reason for the fool's terror (v. 7a; see 10:14). *The mouths of fools [bring] them terror* (and ruin; see 10:14), *and their lips are a trap* set by God's law of *lex talionis for their very lives.*

8 This proverb is repeated in 26:22 after a proverb on strife. *The words* (cf. v. 4) *of a slanderer* (see 16:28) *are like tidbits* (swallowed greedily). *They descend into one's innermost being,* the deepest and most complete stratum of a person's psyche. Because slander penetrates so deeply into a person, it remains indelibly and permanently etched and effective. Since gossip is so contagious and irresistible, the wise quarantine it by not repeating it (see 16:28; 17:9; 26:20) and by avoiding talebearers (20:19).

Conclusion: The Fool's Plundering of the Community and the Defense of the Righteous (18:9–12)

The Fool Plunders (18:9)

Emphatic and comparative *even* signals an *a fortiori* argument. If even the passive slacker destroys others, how much more the active *gossip.* What the two inferior types have in common is that both plunder their victims in a way that is easily overlooked. Verset A presents the topic, *the person who is slack in their work* (an idle procrastinator); and verset B presents the consequences by the metaphor *is a brother* (a relative; cf. "partner/companion of" in 28:24) *of one who destroys.* When people do not perform their responsibilities, their charges, such as fields and animals, come to ruin just as much as when plunderers strip their victims of their possessions (24:34). So also gossips, however easily overlooked, plunder their victims.

The Defense of the Righteous in I AM *(18:10–12)*

True security of the righteous in *I AM* (v. 10) is underscored by a contrast with the false security of the rich in their wealth (v. 11). Verse 12 reinforces that truth, threatening the high and haughty with destruction (v. 12a) and promising the humble honor (v. 12b).

10 *The name*, a character description, not merely a label of identification, *of* I AM refers to Israel's covenant-keeping God, who reveals himself in Proverbs and who upholds its teachings (see 3:5). *A fortified tower* denotes a storehouse that by its strength and height is firmly fixed and inviolable (see 14:26). People fled to such towers when attacked (Judg. 9:46–53; Ps. 61:34). When attacked by fools, such as the gossip, *the righteous* (see pp. 36–37) *run* quickly, decisively, and with all diligence *into it*, namely, *I AM* and his teachings, by praying to *I AM* (15:8) and not avenging themselves (17:18) nor bribing officials (18:16) nor losing hope (18:14). And so they are *protected on high*, inaccessible to harm.

11 By contrast, *the wealth* (cf. 10:15; 28:11) *of the rich* (who do not trust in *I AM*; see 10:15; 28:11) in their deluded *imagination* is *a fortified city* with, according to the parallel, a *high* wall. In case of enemy attack, the threatened people retreat to the elevated city behind its walls. From this height (that is, their wealth) the rich think that they can ward off their attackers. To be sure, their wealth can afford them temporary protection (cf. 10:15), but not final protection, as, for example, from a terminal illness. The security of the rich in their visible wealth is a chimera; the security of the righteous in their invisible God is substantial.

12 As 15:33 brought the introduction (15:30–33) to the unit of 15:30–16:15 to closure, so this janus verse, which repeats verbatim 15:33b, brings 18:1–11 to closure, while also functioning as part of the introduction (18:12–15) to the next subunit (18:12–21). As part of the closure, note the conceptual sequence from destroyer (v. 9) to true and false protection (vv. 10–11) to the destinies of destruction and honor (v. 12). As part of an introduction, note the inclusio of the haughty *heart* (v. 12) and the discerning heart (v. 15). Verse 12a matches 16:18a but, after repeating *before destruction*, it substitutes *a person's heart is high and haughty*, implying that the "high and haughty" set themselves against

God and humanity (see 16:5). *But before honor is humility* (see 15:33) implies *I AM* is the Agent of these contrasting destinies.

The Reconciling Speech of the Wise (18:13–21)

The second subunit pertains to the handling of conflict and speech. A wise person upholds justice, resolves conflicts, and speaks powerfully.

Introduction: The Incorrigible Fool and the Humble and Teachable Wise (18:13–15)

13 As is typical, an educational proverb introduces the second subunit. *Those who reply before listening* implies that fools interrupt that to which they should be listening—otherwise the sage would not commend fools to listen—in order to spout their own opinions (see 18:2; cf. Sir 11:8). *Is to them* signifies the disadvantages that come from impertinent and imprudent speech, namely *folly* (see p. 48) *and shame* (that is, such a person "becomes subject to scorn, insult, and mockery, and is cut off from communication"[118]).

14 Verse 12 contrasts the future honor of the humble with the future destruction of the haughty. Verse 14 (cf. 15:13; 17:22) contrasts *a person's* heroic *spirit* (see "Spirit," p. 33) that *can endure* to the finish line in spite of awful *sickness* (that is, all sorts of adversities) with *a broken spirit* (depression; cf. 15:13; 17:22) that none *can bear*. The latter is expressed as a question ("who can bear?") expecting an emphatic negative response: "No one!" Such a person cannot cross the finish line. These two radically antithetical parallels, pitting honor against destruction and fortitude against failure, suggest that before crossing the finish line and so to honor, the humble may face extreme adversity[119] (cf. cf. 1 Sam. 30:6; Job 1:21; Rom. 8:36–37; 2 Cor. 12:10). If so, v. 14 qualifies v. 12 in this introduction.[120]

15 *The heart* and *the ear*, the interdependent inner and outer receptacles (see 2:2), are the inalienable possession of *the discerning* and *wise people* that causes them to *seek* (cf. 2:1–5; 19:20) and enables them to *acquire knowledge* (cf. 14:6). Like the conundrum in Aristotle's ethics that one must be virtuous to become virtuous,[121] so also the sages taught that one must be wise to become

---

118. S. Wagner, *TDOT*, 7:186, s.v. *klm*.

119. Cf. Meinhold, *Sprüche*, 304.

120. Cf. Meinhold, *Sprüche*, 304.

121. See J. R. Wilson, "Biblical Wisdom, Spiritual Formation, and the Virtues," in *WWis*, 298.

wise and one must pre-possess knowledge in order to increase it (cf. 1:5; Matt. 25:29; Phil. 3:10–16). By implication, the author of virtue must be God, not self (see on 30:2–3).

Teachings about Justice and Conflicts (18:16–19)

The setting of vv. 16–19 is best imagined as the courtroom, and its concern is settling disputes.

16 *Gifts* (*mattān*; see 15:27; 21:14) in Proverbs, aside from 19:6, is used for benefactions given for selfish interests to gain an advantage over others and so thwart the aim of Proverbs: righteousness, justice, and equity (1:3). *People's* distinguishes earthlings from the heavenly Sovereign. *Make room* connotes giving relief (Gen. 26:22; Ps. 4:1). Presumably, the bribers are in trouble, and their gifts clear the way and open doors that normally bar access to elites. *For them* signifies the unfair advantage. The personified bribes *lead them* as a shepherd to the goal of presenting their case *before great people* (see 25:6)—that is, influential people closely associated with the king (cf. 2 Sam. 7:9; Neh. 11:14; Jer. 5:5; Jonah 3:7; Mic. 7:3; Nah. 3:10). If these "great people" accept bribes to give the rich advantage over the poor, they cannot be trusted to give just verdicts.

17 Moreover, for justice to prevail, both accuser and accused must be given equal consideration (cf. Job 29:16). *The first to present cases* refers to prosecutors. *Disputes* in connection with *seem right* (or "righteous") points to its legal sense. *Until their opponents* (a metonymy for a defense attorney) *come* vividly represents the defendant or the defender stepping up to present their defense. To *cross-examine them* means "to probe" the accusers with cognitive and analytical examination and testing[122] (cf. Deut. 19:16–18) and connotes that the search is diligent, penetrating, and difficult because something is hidden and elusive (cf. 25:2, 27; 28:11). Those who advocate believing the accuser unconditionally and refuse to cross-examine the complainant vigorously to establish the facts condemn themselves as corrupt (cf. Acts 24:10).[123]

18 Some conflicts cannot be resolved, as is evidenced by the fact of hung juries. Verses 18 and 19 form a proverb pair on resolving what seems irreconcilable conflicts (v. 19) by *the lot* (see 1:14; 16:33). That the lot, hurled down from

---

122. M. Tsevat, *TDOT*, 5:149, s.v. *ḥāqar*.

123. The recent "Me too" movement that arose in North America resulted in drawing attention to a previously hidden phenomenon of powerful men taking advantage of vulnerable women. However, one of its negative aspects was that some people began touting the view: "Believe all women," which amounted to accepting their accusations without question. This proverb denies that assertion with its call to vigorously investigate all accusations.

the Sovereign, *puts an end* may mean it decides how to end a legal action.[124] In that case, *conflicts* here uniquely means lawsuits. *Separates* connotes parting amicably, not in hostility. *Powerful* probably refers to physical might. When the courts cannot resolve a matter, it is better to let the "omnicompetent" *I AM* settle a dispute through one throw of a die than to allow the litigants to fight, for in battle, the victor may not be in the right and the defeated party may not be reconciled to the victor. For those who submit to the lot's impartial verdict, it adds the spiritual virtues of self-denial, humility, patience, and faith (Josh. 7:14–18; 1 Sam. 14:40, 42; Jonah 1:7).

19 *Offended* here means "to suffer a breach (of a brotherhood) due to a perceived crime." *Brother* probably means "brother" by choice (a dearly loved companion; see 2 Sam. 1:26; Neh. 5:10) rather than "blood brother." In view is someone in close relationship with another who feels wronged and has cut himself off from the other with a deep sense of personal injury. The difficulty of getting past this psychological barrier that litigants erect to protect themselves from reconciliation is *like* breaching *a strong city* and *like* opening *the bolt of a citadel.* The most vulnerable part in a wall was the gate, which needed a very strong inner bolt to resist attack (see Judg. 16:3; 1 Kgs. 4:13; Neh. 3:3; Isa. 45:2; Ezek. 38:11). Nevertheless, the lot ends the conflict and enables "that confidence will be re-established, injuries forgiven and friendship renewed."[125]

Teachings about the Power of Speech (18:20–21)

The concluding proverb pair is bound together by the speaking body parts ("mouth," "lips," and "tongue"); the notions of eating, of being sated, and of the power of speech, including over life and death; and the catchword "fruit," the first word of v. 20 and the last word of v. 21.

20 *From the fruit of people's mouths* pictures words as things people consume (that influence them; cf. 1:31; 12:14; 13:2; 15:14, 15). *Their bellies*—a synecdoche for a speaker's whole person—*are sated,* a metaphor for the consequences of one's speech to its full and consummate measure (cf. 1:31). The change of the agricultural metaphor from the orchard to the grain field and probably the escalation from "fruit" to *the harvest* emphasizes the notion of being fully sated. The fruit/harvest that the speaker eats may be good or bad (contrast "good things" in 12:14; 13:2; cf. "life" or "death" in 18:21b; cf. 10:16). The metaphor entails that the speaker's effect on the listener is either good or

124. So Albright, "Canaanite-Phoenician Sources," 10.
125. McKane, *Proverbs,* 520.

bad. The rare repetition of *sated* emphasizes maximally the notion of reaping what you sow in words (Gal. 6:7).

21 *Death and life* (see 2:18, 19; 5:5, 6; 8:35, 36; 13:14; 14:27; 16:14, 15) is a merism comprehending all manner of weal and woe for both the listener and the speaker. The merism speaks not only of clinical death and life but of relationships within community or the lack of them. The deadly tongue destroys a community and its owner. The life-giving tongue creates community and blesses its owner with abundant life. *In the power of* is literally "in the hand of," a metaphor signifying "in the power, care, or authority of" (Gen. 16:6; Num. 31:49; Job 1:12).[126] *The tongue* represents speech. *Those who love it* designates people who "are in love with language; they use it fastidiously, they search for chaste expression and precise meaning, . . . they know what language is for and how it can best be used to achieve its purpose."[127] Their purpose may be good (producing life) or bad (producing death); in either case, *each will eat its fruit* (see v. 20).

Wealth and Wisdom in the Court and in the Home (18:22–19:22)

> [18:22]One who finds a wife finds good
>> and so obtains favor from *I AM*.
> [23]The poor person speaks pleadingly,
>> but the rich person answers rudely.
> [24]A person who has unreliable companions is about to be broken,
>> but there is a friend who sticks closer than a brother.
> [19:1]Better is a poor person who walks in integrity
>> than those who twist their lips, for they are fools.
> [2]If even desire without knowledge is not good,
>> how much more will those who hasten with their feet miss the
>>> way.
> [3]The folly of humans overturns their way,
>> but their hearts rage against *I AM*.
> [4]Wealth attracts many companions,
>> but as for the poor, their [close] companions separate
>>> themselves.
> [5]A perjurer will not escape punishment,
>> and a witness who lies will not escape.

126. *BDB*, 391, s.v. *yād*.
127. McKane, *Proverbs*, 514–15.

⁶Many seek the favor of a nobleman,
  and the generous person has everyone for a companion.
⁷Every brother of the poor hates them,
    how much more their close companions become distant from
      them.
    Though the poor pursue them with pleadings, they are not to
      be found.
⁸Those who get sense love their life;
    whoever heeds understanding will soon find what is good.
⁹A perjurer will not escape punishment,
    and a witness who lies will perish.
¹⁰Luxury is not fitting for a fool;
    how much more [unfitting] for a slave to rule over princes.
¹¹A human being's prudence yields patience,
    and one's splendor is to pass over transgression.
¹²The fury of the king is like the roaring of a lion,
    but his favor is like dew on vegetation.
¹³A foolish son is destruction for his father,
    and a wife's quarrelings are a leaky roof that drips constantly.
¹⁴A household and wealth are an inheritance from fathers;
    but from *I AM* is a prudent wife.
¹⁵Laziness casts [one] into a deep sleep,
    and a slack person hungers.
¹⁶Those who keep a commandment keep their life,
    but those who despise their ways will die.
¹⁷Whoever shows grace to the poor lends to *I AM;*
    and for their deeds, he will repay them.
¹⁸Discipline your son, for surely there is hope,
    and to killing him do not set your desire.
¹⁹A hothead is one who incurs a penalty;
    surely if you deliver [one], you will do so again.
²⁰Listen to counsel and receive discipline
    so that you may be counted among the wise in your final
      destiny.
²¹The plans in the heart of a person are many,
    but as for the counsel of *I AM*, it will take place.
²²What people desire in a human being is unfailing kindness;
    better is a poor person than a liar.

284

This unit on wealth and poverty in the court and in the home can be divided into three subunits marked by introductory educational proverbs (18:22–19:7; 19:8–15; 19:16–23).

Poverty, Wealth, and Companions (18:22–19:7)

After an introductory proverb about the most intimate human relationship—that of a man and his wife (18:22; cf. 11:16, 22; 12:4)—the first subunit is about the moral ambiguities of wealth in community. The rich attract companions and the poor lose them. The subunit begins with the poor person's supplications (18:23) and ends by saying they are of no avail (19:7).

18:22 Verse 22a echoes and v. 22b repeats the words of Woman Wisdom in 8:35: "The one who finds me finds life and so obtains favor from *I AM*." Aitken comments that it is "as if to say that finding a good wife is on par with finding wisdom."[128] The *one who finds* entails a diligent seeker for a *wife. Finds good* signifies a delightful and beneficial situation (cf. 12:4; 19:13; 31:10–31; Deut. 24:1). LXX qualifies her as "a good wife" (cf. 4:3). *And so obtains favor from I AM* (see 8:35; cf. Jas 1:17). God's favor rests on those who fear him (cf. 16:5). The apostle Paul, however, commends, not commands, the better way of singleness to be fully engaged in *I AM*'s business (1 Cor. 7:25–35).

23 This ideal conjugal situation gives way to a bad social situation due to human depravity. *The poor person* (see 13:8) *speaks pleadingly* (cries for favor). However, *the* materially *rich person* (see "The Wise and Wealth," pp. 40–41), a correlative term for the foolish/wicked (see 10:15; 18:11; 28:11), *answers rudely*, that is, with a shamelessly unyielding response (see 14:20–21). The poor have no choice but to plead, but the rich can choose how to answer and so are accountable. A Jewish proverb says, "In order to chase away beggars one needs a rich person"[129] (cf. Ps. 28:2, 6; Matt. 5:7).

24 This bad social situation now gives way to a bad and good one. *Unreliable companions* (*rēʿîm*; see 3:28) refers to partners who fail in adversity. *Broken* in Isa. 24:19 is used of the earth being rent asunder. By contrast *there is a friend* (see 14:28) *who sticks closer than a brother* through weal and woe (cf. 17:17). The predicates are imprecise, suggesting that the man with run-of-the-mill friends is about to be ruined for want of one true friend; and the man with one true friend is not ruined. The Lord Jesus instantiates the true friend (cf.

---

128. Aitken, *Proverbs*, 153.
129. Cited by Meinhold, *Sprüche*, 309.

John 15:12–15; Heb. 2:11, 14–18). The significance of friends lies in their quality, not their quantity.

19:1 This proverb turns from the failed social relationships of the poor to their successful ethics in contrast to the rich. The imprecise antithetical parallel of *a poor person* (see 18:23; cf. 13:8) and *fools* implies that the poor person is wise and the fools are rich. The imprecise parallels *who walks in integrity* (in total dedication to wisdom; see "What Is 'Wisdom'?" pp. 27–28) and *who twist their lips* imply that the poor speaks the truth and the liar despises wisdom. The poor person's way is better than that of the liar, for it is blessed (20:7) and secure (cf. Job 4:6) and *I AM* is its protective shield (2:7). In contrast, the liar is headed for calamity (17:20; cf. 22:5). The poor may be miserable for a moment, but the unethical rich are doomed for an eternity. Better to live by faith than by sight.

2 By an *a fortiori* argument (see 17:28; 18:9) that reasons from the lesser (verset A) to the greater (verset B), this proverb escalates the rich fool's folly from being a liar (19:1) to overt sinful actions to get rich. *If even desire* (greed) *without knowledge* of the sages' teachings *is not good* (a litotes for being evil) *how much more will those who hasten* (forcing themselves to act quickly to gratify their greed without regard to moral consequences;[130] see 21:5; 28:20; 29:20; Exod. 5:13; Josh. 10:13). *With their feet* couples greed (v. 2a) with feet that carry it out (v. 2b). *Miss the way* (see Prov. 1:10, 15) refers to a lifestyle that fails God's standard of conduct and is therefore a sin that incurs punishment (see 19:3; cf. 11:31; 13:6; 14:22).

3 By a pun on "way," the consequence of missing *I AM*'s "way" (v. 2) is unpacked by *I AM*'s overturning the rich fool's *way. The folly* (see p. 48) *of humans* (see p. 31) is synthetically paired with *their hearts* (see "Heart," p. 32), and the imprecise parallels *overturns their way* and *rages against* I AM imply that when stubborn, arrogant fools suffer the consequences of their sin, they *rage* in extreme anger (cf. Isa 30:3) and hostility (cf. 2 Chr. 26:19) *against* I AM. Instead of repenting of their sin, the earthlings remain convinced that their sinful way is right, and so they storm against *I AM*, whom they aim to dethrone.

4 The socioeconomic limitations of money can be seen in friendships outside the covenant community. The proverb's antithetic parallels juxtapose (1) *wealth* with *the poor* (see 10:15); (2) *many companions* with *even their [close] companions* (rēʿîm)—a term used elsewhere only of friends outside the covenant community (cf. Gen. 26:20; Judg. 14:20; 15:2, 6; 2 Sam 3:8; Prov. 18:23; 19:7); and (3) *attracts* with *separate themselves*. In view are typical neighbors, not spongers (cf. 14:20; 19:7). Run-of-the-mill friends crowd around wealth,

---

130. "A characteristic of money-making people" (*HALOT*, 1:23, s.v. ʾwz).

hoping to enrich themselves through it. Even a bosom friend without wisdom dissolves the relationship when the demands become too burdensome (cf. 17:17; 19:24b).

5 As v. 3 threatens punishment of those who hasten to get rich in v. 2, v. 5 threatens the punishment of the liar of v. 1, probably with reference to a courtroom setting. A rare precise synonymous parallelism, *a perjurer* (see 12:17) *will not escape punishment* (see 6:29), *and a witness who lies will not escape* punishment, emphasizes the certainty of a perjurer's punishment. The ultimate Agent who unmasks the perjurer and inflicts punishment is *I AM* (see 19:3; cf. 16:1–9).

6 Continuing the courtroom setting, this proverb expands the danger of wealth from its attracting sycophants (v. 4a) to its perverting justice by buying corrupt friends. *Many* (the masses) *seek the favor of a nobleman* (see 8:16; 17:7). Seeking favor to meet a need is not wrong (cf. 1 Sam. 25:1–9; Job 11:19; Esth. 7:1–2). *And* introduces another situation that is wrong. *The generous person* (one who has the character of "gift giving" and is seeking a favor; cf. 18:16; 21:14) *has everyone*, including the nobleman and witnesses, *for a companion* (someone who can do a favor; see v. 4), implying their friendship has been bought and so disadvantages the poor and thwarts righteousness, justice and equity (see 1:3). The wise, who care for the poor (see 14:21), depend upon *I AM* for his benefactions and so are free from this moral jeopardy. Sometimes the disciple has to stand apart from the masses.

7 As v. 6 expands the thought of v. 4a, v. 7 escalates the thought of v. 4b. *Every brother* (the blood relatives who should provide for needs in adversity; cf. 17:17) *of the poor hates them.* We should assume that these brothers are like Jeremiah's unfaithful brothers (Jer. 12:5–6). This lesser situation in the *a fortiori* argument becomes the premise of the greater wrong: *How much more their close companions* (outside of the true covenant community; see v. 4) *become distant* (spatially and emotionally) *from them.* Verset 7aα intensifies verset 7aβ to emphasize that friendship outside of the covenant community is based solely on material benefits. This is not true of covenant keepers, who show unfailing kindness (see 19:17, 22). *Though he pursues them* (i.e., both unfaithful brothers and false companions) *with pleadings, they are not to be found* to help him.

Wisdom in the Court and in the Home (19:8–15)

The second subunit is linked to the first (18:22–19:7) by the catchword "good" in their introductions, by the repetition of v. 5 in v. 9, and by the juxtaposition of "hate" (v. 7a) and "love" (v. 8a).

In the Court (19:8–12)

8 *Those who get sense* (see 15:32) and *heed understanding* (the implicit cause; see 2:8; 9:16) are predicated as those *who love their lives* (an implicit consequence and a unique expression in Proverbs; cf. 29:24). Since "to love" means to desire something so strongly that one strives to be with it, the expression means to preserve one's life. The parallel *will soon find good* (see 18:22) intensifies "life" to "abundant life."

9 Verses 9 and 10 are linked by "not." Verse 9 repeats v. 5 with the exception that it replaces the litotes "will not escape punishment" (v. 5a) with the positive assertion *will perish*. In contrast to the wise—the subjects of v. 8—perjurers will perish. See on v. 5.

10 In contrast to "the good" that is fitting for the wise (v. 8), v. 10 states two things that are unfitting in an *a fortiori* argument (see 19:2). *Luxury* ("good . . . living, a life of pleasure"[131]) *is not fitting for a fool* (see pp. 47–48). This lesser evil is the premise for the greater evil: *How much more [unfitting] for a slave to rule over princes*—that is, to become king (cf. 30:22). The fool's high-living validates the fool's incorrigibility, and worse yet the rebellious slave—certainly not a wise slave (see 14:35; 17:2)—afflicts the entire community with insubordination to wise rulers. To judge from 30:22–23, when rebels become rulers, they become drunk from the feeling of power and their rulership devolves into despotism. Agur also links these—a prosperous fool and a ruling slave—as intolerable social situations (see 30:22).

11–12 This proverb pair links prudent forbearance when one is wronged (v. 11) with the legitimate fury of the king, presumably against evildoers (v. 12; cf. 16:14).

A human being's (see p. 31) *prudence* (see p. 35) *yields patience* (see 14:29). Such a person is self-controlled (16:32) and calms a controversy (15:18). *One's splendor* (see 4:9) implicitly compares the prudent person's forgiveness of sin to wearing beautiful adornments. *To pass over* (a figure meaning "to forgive"[132]) *transgression* wins a person honor (cf. 20:3) and is due to love (10:12; 17:9) The prudent person who forgives sin reflects the glory of Israel's forgiving God and fulfills the Lord's prayer (Luke 11:4).

I AM's earthly king does not forgive the unrepentant sinner but metes out just punishment (16:10–15; Rom. 13:4). The antithetical parallels of verse 12

---

131. *HALOT*, 4:1769, s.v. *ta'ănûg.*
132. BDB, 717, s.v. *'ābar.*

pit *the fury of the king*, which presages his just punishment, against *his favor* (11:1; 14:35). One is made to feel these malevolent and benevolent effects by the imagery of *like the roaring of a lion* and of *like* life-giving *dew on vegetation*, the same images of Jacob's rule among the nations in Mic. 5:7–8. As king of the beasts, the lion tramples its victims into subjection and fatally mauls them with none to deliver. Lions are agents of *I AM's* judgment, sent by him (1 Kgs. 13:24–28; 20:36; 2 Kgs. 17:25–26; Isa. 15:9). "Dew on vegetation" is life-giving, salubrious, refreshing, and heavenly (cf. 2 Sam 23:3–4; Hos. 14:5).

In the Home (19:13–15)

Verses 13–14 pertain strictly to the home: son and wife (v. 13), chattel and wife (v. 14). Verse 13 presents a dysfunctional home: a foolish son and a quarrelsome wife. Verse 14 presents a functional home: household and property and a prudent wife. Verse 15 links the foolish son with laziness, the same coupling as in 10:1, 5.

13 *And* links the synthetic parallels of the foolish son who from below the father undermines his household (verset A) and the nagging wife who from alongside him drives him out of it (verset B). *A foolish son is destruction*, which is to say total destruction, *for his father* because the father is bereft of a "staff" to sustain him in his old age or one competent to preserve the family wealth after him. In bitter irony, *a wife's quarrelings* (see "conflicts" in 6:14; 18:18) are likened to *a leaky roof. That drips continually* has in view the poles of roofs, overlaid with such material as clay, which were prone to leak in heavy rains. The first place a man expects good and the last place he expects an attack is from his wife (see 25:24). Yet under his own roof he is being constantly assaulted by a nagging woman who never lets up. His only escape from the torment is to abandon his house altogether.

14 By contrast, the functional family successfully passes on its *household* (see 11:29) *and wealth* (see 3:9) through the generations, and the *prudent wife from* I AM competently manages it. *Are an inheritance* (see 17:2) *from fathers* (see 4:1–3). The prudent wife preserves the inherited wealth through her moral competence to understand the problems of running a household and to successfully manage them (see 31:10–31). Normally a wife was selected by parents (Gen. 24:3–4; 38:6), though Samson is a tragic exception that proves the rule (Judg. 14:2). However, in spite of all human activity in this connection, the wise know that success in this attempt and fortune in life do not depend on human beings but on Providence. One finds favor with *I AM* through wisdom nd, implicitly, in this way obtains from him a competent wife

sh son (v. 13) who squandered the father's inheritance (v. 14) is
now considered as having a slack hand (cf. 10:1, 4–5; 6:6–11; 24:30–34). Personified *laziness* (see "The Sluggard and the Senseless," pp. 49–50) *casts [one] into a deep sleep (tardēmâ)*, rendering one oblivious to danger and unable to rouse oneself. *Tardēmâ* describes a deep, heavy sleep phenomenon that is rarer than ordinary sleep.[133] *And* connects the physical consequence to the spiritual cause. *A slack* (see 10:4) *person hungers* (see 10:3). This fate is similar to that of drunkards and gluttons (23:21).

Educating the Son to Show Kindness to the Needy (19:16–22)

The third subunit is framed by educational proverbs promising life (vv. 16, 23), albeit v. 23 is also a janus. The subunit's core (vv. 18–21) consists of two pairs of rearing proverbs: the first addressed to the father (vv. 18–19) and the second to the son (vv. 20–21). Each pair is linked in Hebrew by catchwords: *nś' npš* ("set your desire," v. 18), *nś' 'nš* ("incurs a penalty," v. 19), and *'ēṣâ* ("counsel," vv. 19, 20). The two pairs are linked by the catchword root *ysr* ("discipline," vv. 18, 20). Sandwiched between the frame and the core are two proverbs teaching kindness to the poor (vv. 17, 22). The unit is punctuated with sayings of *I AM* (vv. 17, 21, 23), who upholds the moral order, which rewards the kind with abundant life (vv. 17, 23) and punishes the unkind with death (see "Retribution for the Wicked," p. 50). Teaching one's children to be kind to the poor is a matter of life and death.

16 *Those who keep a commandment* (see 1:8) *keep their life*, an obvious pun on "keep," meaning both "to heed scrupulously" and "to protect scrupulously" (see 2:8, 11). *Those who despise* (cf. 1:17) *their ways* (see 1:15) treat their conduct and its consequences with contempt, and so, sinful from birth and cut off from the living God, they *will die.*

17 This proverb turns to the subunit's goal in youths' education: to show kindness to the poor with the motivation that *I AM* will reward them (cf. 14:21, 31; 22:9; 28:27). *Whoever shows grace* (cf. 14:31) *to the poor* (see 10:15) *lends to I AM* teaches that in giving generously to the destitute they are figuratively giving a loan to *I AM*. The parallel explains the figure: *for their deeds, he will repay them. I AM,* who made the poor, assumes their indebtedness, and so he will repay the lender in full with interest (cf. 11:17, 25; Pss. 41:1–3; 112:5; Matt. 25:31–40; Luke 6:38; Jas. 1:27). Thus, the wise stand with the poor, unlike the world (see 19:7).

---

133. J. G. Thomson, "Sleep: An Aspect of Jewish Anthropology," *VT* (1955): 423.

18 The father is commanded *discipline your son*, verbally to prevent acts of folly and corporally to prevent their repetition (see 1:2; cf. 3:12). The motivation is *for surely there is hope* (see 10:28). The parallel *to killing him do not set your desire* implies both that "hope" is a metonymy for life and that a failure to discipline the son is tantamount to killing him. The proverb assumes that folly is bound up in the heart of the child and that the rod of discipline will drive it out (22:15; cf. 13:24; 22:6; 23:13–14; 29:15). In Proverbs, discipline is based on love, never on an intention to harm (cf. 3:12; 4:4; 13:24).

19 This proverb narrows the one in need of discipline to *a hothead* (cf. 6:34; 15:1, 18; 16:14) who responds to an ill-perceived wrong with uncontrolled, irrational negative passion (cf. 19:11), and, as the parallel implies, damages others. *Incurs a penalty* (cf. 17:26) implies that the agitated hothead damages the perceived, yet innocent, offender and so must make restitution. Continuing to address the father, the sage warns that *surely if you deliver [one]* (a hothead from a just penalty), *you will do so again.*

20 From directly addressing fathers, the first proverb of this pair (vv. 20–21) moves to directly addressing youth. *Listen to counsel* (see 1:25), for it shapes character and quells waywardness. *And receive discipline* (see 1:2) escalates the first command from hearing outwardly to inwardly and spiritually receiving it. Typically, a motivation accompanies such admonishments: *so that you may be counted among the wise* (see "Intellectual Terms for the Wise and Righteous," pp. 34–35), who inherit abundant life (v. 16; see "The Wise and Their Rewards: Life," pp. 41–42), *in your final destiny* (from 'aḥărît). 'Aḥărît occurs thirteen times in Proverbs and refers to the final outcome of a way of life (16:25; 23:18; 24:20; cf. Deut. 32:29). Here, it refers to the future hope that nothing, including clinical death, can cut off. Verse 27 will make clear, however, that one must persevere in the teaching to guarantee this outcome.

21 The second proverb of this pair guarantees this outcome by a pun on "counsel," meaning "plan," with an emphasis on God's plan of behavior to be obeyed (v. 20) or his fixed plan of the deed-destiny nexus (see 1:25). *The plans in the heart* (see p. 32) *of a person* refers to the creative calculations within human thought, weighing matters one way and then another. *The counsel of I AM* refers to God's immutable will (see 1:25). The imprecise juxtaposition *are many* with *it will take place* implies that the many human plans may or may not occur, but God's single plan of the deed-destiny nexus will occur (Ps. 33:11; Isa. 7:7; 14:24; 46:10; cf. Prov. 21:30–31). In sum, the wise can trust God to bring about their promised destiny regardless of human machinations.

22 The penultimate proverb of the subunit, like its counterpart (v. 17), instructs youth to be unfailingly kind to the needy and not to be selfish. Verset A states both truths by the ambiguity of "desire," which may refer to good (cf.

20:24) or bad desires (cf. 18:1; 19:2), and by a pun on Hebrew *ḥesed*, which may mean either "unfailing kindness" or "shame." According to the first interpretation, *what people* rightly *desire in a human being is unfailing kindness* (see 3:3; 16:6), for it benefits them. According to the second interpretation, "the wrong desires [i.e., self-gratification] of human beings are their shame" (see 14:34). *And* adds a complimentary truth: *better* (that is, better off[134]) *is a poor person than a liar* (cf. 6:19). In the imprecise antithetical parallels "unfailing kindness" and "liar" suggest that the needy counted on the liar for help. In that sense, it is better to be a poor person from whom no one expects help (see 19:7) than a liar from whom help was expected (25:19). According to the second interpretation, the imprecise parallels suggest that a selfish person tells lies in order to gratify greed. Since that is shameful, it is better to be poor than corrupt (see 19:1).

The Pedagogy and Punishment of Fools (19:23–20:11)

19:23The fear of *I AM* is surely life;
    fully satisfied, one dwells not met with harm.
24Sluggards bury their hand in the pan;
    they do not return it to their mouth.
25Flog a mocker, and the uncommitted will become prudent;
    and if one corrects the insightful, they discern knowledge.
26The one who ruins [his] father, driving out [his] mother,
    is a shameful and disgraceful son.
27Cease, my son, listening to instruction
    in order to stray from words of knowledge!
28A rebel witness mocks at justice,
    and the mouths of the wicked swallow iniquity.
29Punishments are established for mockers,
    and beatings for the back of fools.
20:1Wine is a mocker, and beer is a brawler;
    and everyone who staggers by them is not wise.
2The roaring as of a lion is the terror struck by the king;
    those who anger him forfeit their life.
3Abstaining from strife brings glory to the individual,
    but every fool starts a quarrel.

---

134. Fox (*Proverbs 10–31*, 659) notes that when "better" is predicated of a person in the "better than" proverbs, it means "better off" for the person and not "more beneficial" to others.

⁴Sluggards do not plow from winter on;
    then they ask for [a crop] in the harvest, but there is none.
⁵The counsel in a person's heart is deep waters,
    but an understanding person draws it out.
⁶As for many human beings, they all proclaim their unfailing
        kindness;
    but a conscientious person who can find?
⁷As for those who walk in blamelessness as righteous people,
    blessed are their children after them.
⁸A king is one who sits on a throne of judgment,
    winnowing all evil with his eyes.
⁹Who can say, "I have cleansed my heart;
    I am pure from my sin"?
¹⁰As for differing weights [and] differing ephahs—
    indeed, both of them are an abomination to *I AM*.
¹¹Even youth in their evil deeds dissemble.
    So, is their conduct pure? Or is it upright?

The new unit on the pedagogy and punishment of fools is introduced by an educational proverb that implicitly admonishes readers and hearers to fear *I AM* (19:23). The unit consists of two subunits: one on fools in need of punishment (19:24–20:1)[135] and one on the king cleansing the kingdom of fools (20:2–11).

A Catalog of Four Fools and Their Punishment (19:23–20:1)

After the educational proverb (19:23), the catalog of those who flunked their education escalates from the sluggard, who harms himself (19:24), to the shameful son, who destroys the family (19:26), to corrupt witnesses, who undermine justice (19:28), to the brawling drunkard, who endangers everyone (20:1; cf. 26:9). At the center point stands a sober warning in a rare address to the son: do not neglect your parents' teaching (19:27).

19:23 Verse 23a, a variant of 14:27, summarizes the sublime benefit of *the fear of* I AM (see "Fear of *I AM*," pp. 38–39), namely, that it *is surely life*. Verse 23b explicates this life as *fully satisfied* (abundant; see 18:20) and protected. *Dwells* (*yālîn*; see 15:31) entails the primary idea of "to remain at night," the time of danger. *Not met with* physical *harm* clearly expresses the notion of protection.

135. For this analysis, we are indebted in part to Meinhold, *Sprüche*, 2:325.

24 *Sluggards* (see pp. 49–50) *bury their hand* (from finger tips to forearm) *in the pan* (a flat dish) full of food. But, unable to exert the slightest effort, *do not return it to their mouth.* Thus, the sluggard starves to death in spite of God's abundant provision.

25 The sage commands *flog* (see 17:10, 26) *a mocker* (see pp. 48–49) not as a pedagogic correction—mockers are beyond correction (see 9:7)—but for the benefit of *the uncommitted,* who *will become prudent* (see p. 35; cf. the variant 21:11). For the mocker, flogging is penal, but for the uncommitted, it is remedial, for they will understand the connection between sin and pain and so eschew sin (cf. Deut. 13:11; 17:13; 1 Tim. 5:20). By contrast to the necessity of correction through pain on mockers for the sake of the uncommitted, *if one* verbally (see 3:12) *corrects the insightful* (see pp. 35–36), *they discern* the *knowledge* to fear *I AM,* which is the beginning of wisdom (1:7; see 1:5; 4:18). In other words, mere words are insufficient to correct those who have committed themselves to being uncommitted (see 1:22–32).

26 The next flunkey is the shameful son. *The one who ruins* (see 11:3) *[his] father* is talking about the father's property. Fools may ruin their fathers by passive sloth (10:5), by squandering the family fortune in riotous living (29:3; cf. Deut. 21:18–21; Luke 15:11–14), or by cursing them (20:20; 30:11). Here they seize their inheritance prematurely, as indicated by *driving out [his] mother* (evicting her; cf. Mic. 2:9; cf. Matt 15:3–6). The ingrate, who dishonors his parents, *is a shameful and disgraceful son* (see 10:5), for he brings public opprobrium on his parents for their failure in raising him (see 27:11) and also on himself.

27 Plöger comments, "It seems to me that v. 27 wants to give a reason, in an unusual form, for the shameful behavior of the son as pictured in v. 26."[136] The son's apostasy progresses from rejecting parental instruction (v. 27a) to straying from wisdom (v.27b), to crime against his parents (v. 26). *Cease* (or "refrain from"; see 10:19) *... listening to instruction* so obviously contradicts the teaching of this book (see 1:8, 10, 15; 2:1; 3:1, 11, 21; *passim*) that the sage felt he could safely use sarcasm. The NIV captures the intention by a conditional clause: "cease listening ... and you will stray." *In order to stray,* unconsciously like sheep, *from words of knowledge.* Without constant attention to wisdom, depraved human beings unconsciously stray from it. Even Solomon, the paragon of wisdom, strayed when he ceased listening to his own proverbs.

28–29 Verses 28–29 form a proverb pair by the catchwords "mock"/"mocker"

---

136. Plöger, *Sprüche,* 227.

and "justice"/"penalties." Verse 28 identifies the revolutionary as the cause of injustice, and v. 29 asserts flogging as the appropriate penal response.

The next flunkey is the scofflaw. *A rebel (bǝliyyaʿal;* see 6:12; 16:27) *witness* (see 12:17) *mocks at justice* (see pp. 48–49). The perjurers in Naboth's trial are called *bǝliyyaʿal* (1 Kgs. 21:10, 13); that story testifies to the lethal danger of lying witnesses (cf. Prov. 18:21). *The mouths of the wicked*—a metonymy for corrupt witnesses—*swallow iniquity* (the abuse of power to harm or destroy; see 6:12). The triple pun may signify that: (1) the wicked witnesses greedily devour the trouble their lies are making as tasty morsels;[137] (2) they literally consume the exquisite food obtained from their lies (cf. 1:12; 4:17; 21:20; Job 16:5; 20:12–15); or (3) they have to swallow the harmful consequences of their lies that Providence will justly dish out to them (see 1:31; 10:6; 16:4; cf. 18:20). The paired proverb (v. 29) confirms the third interpretation.

Punishments refer to God's acts of judgment that are penal, not remedial in purpose. The agents are not specified, but they may be the sword, famine, wild beasts, or plagues (cf. Ezek. 14:21). *Are established* denotes that the punishments are part of God's moral and immutable deed-destiny nexus *for mockers* (see pp. 48–49). *And* also, in addition to the divine punishments, human hands inflict *beatings for the back of fools* (see pp. 47–48). These punishments are penal, not remedial in purpose, since fools (27:22) and mockers are incorrigible (9:7–8).

20:1 The drunkard—and today one may legitimately add addicts to other kinds of drugs—caps off the list of dunces. The catchword "mocker" and the association of "beatings" and "brawlers" suggest intoxicants are a potential cause of the punishments in 19:29. In verset A, *wine* (see 3:10; 9:2) *is a mocker and beer* (any alcoholic beverage, not just the mildly intoxicating barley beer) *is a brawler* personifies "wine" and "beer" as villains to warn the youth in verset B that they destroy wisdom, which promotes life: *and* so *everyone who staggers by them is not wise.* The drunkard lacks consciousness and self-control and so, lacking the essential life-sustaining wisdom, dies. This proverb, along with 21:17; 23:19–21; and 31:4–5, concentrates on the negative side of the intoxicants. Proverbs 3:10 and 9:5, however, view wine and beer as symbols of prosperity and blessing. The same ambivalence is found elsewhere in the Old Testament (cf. Lev. 10:9; Num. 6:3; Isa. 28:1–5; Amos 6:6 with Gen. 27:28; Exod. 29:40; Deut. 14:26).[138]

---

137. Delitzsch, *Proverbs,* 291.
138. See Fitzsimmonds, in *NBD,* "Wine and Strong Drink," 1255.

The King Cleanses His Realm of Fools (20:2–11)

The second subunit begins with the king's powerful roar, threatening judgment on the wicked (v. 2) and concludes with the reality of universal human depravity (vv. 9–11). Sandwiched within the unit is a second catalog of four fools: the contentious (v. 3), the sluggard (v. 4), the conniver (v. 5), and the hypocrite (vv. 6–7).

2 The fools of both catalogs (19:24–20:1; 20:3–7) are handed over to the righteous king, God's surrogate, to receive their death sentences (see 16:1–9, 10–15). *The roaring as of a lion is the terror struck by the king* repeats 19:12a, except that the king's "fury" gives way to his victim's "terror." Verset B explains the metaphor: it is incited by anger and presages the victim's death: *those who anger him* (the king) *forfeit their life* (cf. 16:10–15; 19:12; 20:8, 28). Fools ought to appease the surrogate's roar immediately, but they are senseless (cf. 16:14).

3 *Abstaining from strife* (see 15:18) *brings glory* (see 3:35) *to the individual. But every fool* (see pp. 47–48) *starts a quarrel* (see 17:14; 18:1). The antithetical parallels "abstaining from strife" and "starting a quarrel" are fairly precise antonyms, but "every fool" and "glory to the individual" are not, suggesting that the fool has no social honor and the one who has social honor is no fool.

4 *Sluggards*, who are too lazy to eat the food on their plate (19:24; see pp. 49–50), *do not plow*, for it entails doing the arduous work of preparing the ground (cf. Isa. 28:24).[139] *From winter on* is added because plowing began about December, and winter designates the Palestinian rainy season from mid-October to April. In other words, it is the only time for plowing. *Then* having idled their time watching others plow, sluggards turn up at harvest demanding a crop (cf. 12:11; 28:19). *They ask* (šāʾal, lit. "he asks," which can also mean "demand"; see 2 Sam. 3:13) *for a [crop] in the harvest* (see 6:8) from April to May. *But there is none*, for in God's moral law of reciprocity, neglect leads to loss, sin to death, and selfishness to self-victimization. Malbim applies the proverb to all youths: "Similarly, youth is the time to prepare the seed-bed of one's character for moral wisdom to take root."[140]

5 The conniver cannot outsmart the wise (v. 5). Heretofore in Proverbs, *counsel* has referred to the counsel from the wise (1:25, 30; 8:14; 12:15; 19:20) or to the immutable will of *I AM* (see 19:21). But hereafter it has the weakened sense of "advice" from a peer or an inferior (20:18; 21:30) or *in a person's heart* (see "Heart," p. 32). *Deep waters* is a pejorative metaphor (see on 18:4), signi-

---

139. H. Ringgren, *TDOT*, 5:221, s.v. ḥāraš.
140. Malbim, *Proverbs*, 204.

fying that the counsel is hidden and potentially dangerous (cf. Jer. 17:9). By contrast, *an understanding person* (see 10:23), through fear of *I AM* and ethical purity, *draws it up*, a metaphor representing the ability to expose the conniver's unfathomable counsel hidden beneath its verbal surface (cf. Ps. 41:6; Matt. 12:25; Mark 12:15; Luke 5:22; 6:8; 11:17; John 2:24–25; 13:11).

6 Probably, the conniver within (v. 5a) is the hypocrite without (v. 6a) and the insightful person (v. 5b) is conscientious (v. 6b). *As for* points to the *many human beings* (see p. 31); *they all proclaim their unfailing kindness* (*ḥesed*; see p. 38). *But* introduces the antithesis between the many and the exceptional and between profession and reality. *A conscientious* (or trustworthy) *person who can find?* expects the answer: "Hardly anyone" (see v. 7; cf. 31:10). The rarity of such a person is viewed within an evaluation of the human condition in general. Thus, the proverb gives youth insight into human hypocrisy and instructs them to seek the rare friend with the granite quality of being conscientious in unfailing kindness, and to be such people themselves.

7 The repetition of *as for* couples v. 7 with v. 6 and nuances the pessimism of v. 6 by focusing on the rare conscientious person, now characterized as one of *those who walk in blamelessness* (see p. 37) *as righteous people* (see pp. 36–37). As their reward, their immediate lineal descendants realize life to the full extent intended by the Creator: *blessed* (see 3:13) *are their children after them.* Righteous people die in peace, knowing that their family's spiritual and economic patrimony has been securely passed on to their immediate successors. However, a child may hate *I AM* (cf. Ezek. 18:20) and be unwise despite having had righteous parents (cf. 5:12–13; Deut. 21:18).

8 Verse 2 presented the king's awesome power to judge; verse 8 presents his heavenly authority and universal justice. *One who sits* denotes the king's authority (Ex. 18:13; Matt. 5:1; 23:2). *A throne* (see 9:14) is also the symbol of royal authority and is associated with justice (2 Sam. 15:2–4; 1 Kgs. 7:7; Ps. 122:5; Isa. 16:5). In Israel, *I AM* is the initiator and guarantor of enthronement (cf. Ps. 2:6; 2 Sam. 7:13, 16; 1 Kgs. 1:13, 17; 2:24). And God's spirit of justice rests on his anointed king (Isa. 11:1–5; 28:6). *Of judgment* refers to the formal judicial process as a whole. *Winnowing* means separating and driving off in different directions (cf. 20:26). *With his eyes* signifies the king's keen discernment of *all evil*, a metonymy for all morally depraved people who destroy the kingdom (cf. Ps. 5:5; Heb. 4:13). Righteousness at the top of the administration was essential to undergird Israel's judicial system.

Verse 8 also functions as a janus, forming an inclusio with v. 2 and beginning an alternating pattern with vv. 8–11:

A   The king's justice (v. 8)
   B   Universal human depravity (v. 9)
A'   I AM's justice (v. 10)
   B'   Human depravity even in youth (v. 11)

The alternating structure shows that God stands behind his surrogate king's judgment. The omniscient God sees all evil, and his king's eyes search it out (vv. 5, 8). In spite of human cleverness, no one escapes. Their universal justice, however, is tempered by the reality of universal human depravity (vv. 9, 11). The king's actions in ridding his kingdom of evil (v. 8) must be tempered by the reality that no one is sinless (v. 9). Similarly, I AM's revulsion with deceit (v. 10) is tempered by the reality that humans practice deceit from their youth (v. 11). By alternating the proverbs in this way, the collection implicitly matches justice with grace.

9 This proverb qualifies vv. 7 and 8. *Who can say, "I have cleansed* (purified) *my heart* so that *I am* morally *pure from sin?"* anticipates the answer, "No one." Although the righteous king roots out all evil (v. 8), the compassionate also recognize that no human being can cleanse his or her heart from sin (v. 9; cf. Job 4:17; 14:4; 25:4). When profiled against God, all human beings are found lacking in moral purity (cf. 8:21; 1 Kgs. 8:46; Job 15:14–16; Pss. 14; 19:12; 32; 51:5–6; 143:2; Eccl. 7:20–29; Jer. 17:9; Ezek. 18:31; Rom. 3:9–19). The proverb engenders humility and implicitly instructs people to throw themselves through the purple veil on the mercy of both God and their king (see 15:3, 11; 16:10–15). The final court of appeal is God's throne (see v. 10), which is a throne of grace (Heb. 4:16).

10 This proverb throws the full weight of God's righteous justice behind the king's throne (v. 8) and keeps the compassion of the preceding proverb from being abused. Standard weights and measures require legal sanction to enforce their authority. The king (2 Sam. 14:26) and the priests (Exod. 30:13) set the standard, and I AM stands behind them (11:1; 16:11; 20:23[141]; Lev. 19:35; Deut. 25:13–16; Ezek. 45:10). *Differing weights* (a light stone for selling and a heavy one for buying) pertain to measuring by a scale. *Differing ephahs* is literally "an ephah and an ephah." "Ephah" refers to the largest dry measure of a container in antiquity—approximately 22 liters (almost 10 pounds). *Indeed, both of them are an abomination to I AM* (see 17:15b).

11 I AM's revulsion with deceit (v. 10) is tempered by the reality that human beings are deceitful from youth (cf. Gen. 8:21). *Even* introduces the *a fortiori*

---

141. All these proverbs explicitly link I AM's name in the abomination formula with them.

argument. If even *youth* (see 1:4; 22:6, 15; 23:13) *in their evil deeds dissemble*, then how much more will adults "fake it."[142] The questions *So is their* (the youths') *conduct pure* (see 16:2; 20:9)? *Or is it upright?* demand the answer no. Thus the proverb again instructs disciples both to abhor sin and show mercy to the sinner and, when they commit evil and act hypocritically, to throw themselves through the purple veil upon the heart of God.

Speech and Commerce (20:12–19)

> ¹²As for the hearing ear and seeing eye,
>   indeed, both of them *I AM* has made.
> ¹³Do not love sleep, otherwise you will become poor.
>   Open your eyes and be filled with food.
> ¹⁴"Bad, bad," say the buyers—
>   and when they have it in hand, then they boast.
> ¹⁵There is gold and an abundance of corals,
>   but a precious vessel is lips that speak knowledge.
> ¹⁶Take away the garment when one becomes surety for a stranger,
>   and for a foreigner impound it.
> ¹⁷Food gotten by deceit is sweet to people,
>   but afterward their mouth is filled with gravel.
> ¹⁸Plans are established with counsel,
>   so, with guidance make war.
> ¹⁹Whoever goes about as a slanderer divulges secrets,
>   so do not get involved with a silly chatterer.

This unit consists of an introductory educational proverb pair (vv. 12–13) teaching to accept wisdom and to be alert and a concluding proverb pair (vv. 18–19) teaching to seek counsel from the wise, not from a gossip. The body deals with imprudent speech in business practices, escalating from lying in the bargaining process (v. 14) to the risk of promising to be security for a stranger (v. 16) to outright deception (v. 17).

12 To enable his people to live wisely, *I AM* created two organs: ears and eyes. In Proverbs, *a hearing ear* is almost always associated with hearing and obeying the instruction of the wise. The conjunction of it with *a seeing eye* could signify that the latter means to read and obey their instruction (cf. "have I not written for you," 22:20). More probably, however, by the catchword "eye" it should be connected with "open your eye" in v. 13 and so signifies being

---

alert. *Indeed, both of them* I AM *has made* since learning the proverbs by ear and keeping the eye alert to apply them are necessary to live abundantly.

13 The imperative *do not love* aims to effect moral improvement by the power of spiritual words. *Sleep* can be good (see 3:24), but the warning *otherwise you will become poor* associates the sleep with a sluggard, who is worse than a fool (6:9–10; cf. 26:12 with 26:17). To *open your eyes* means to stop being unaware of dangers and opportunities and to become awake and vigilant to such things. The imperative *be filled* expresses an assured promise. *Food*, a necessity for life that drives people to work (see 16:26), is a synecdoche for life and property (see 6:9–11; 24:30–34).[143]

14 The introduction segues into the body by moving from not losing property through apathy (v. 13) to not gaining it through folly and wickedness (that is, by disadvantaging others). The catchword "food" (vv. 13, 17) links the unit's introduction with its body. The repetition, *"bad, bad"* (see 1:16) *say the buyers* represents the buyers' persistent haggling to compel the seller to lower the price. *And when they have it in hand, then they boast*—they praise themselves. The buyers' bragging shows both that they are wicked for knowingly taking advantage of the seller and that they are impious, for one should boast only in *I AM* (cf. Pss. 49:7; 52:superscript; Jer. 9:23–24; 27:1; 49:4; 2 Cor. 10:17).

15 A proverb commending wise speech, using the metaphor of precious jewelry, functions as a corrective to the foolish and wicked speech of the marketplace (esp. v. 14). *There is gold* (see 11:22) is escalated to *and an abundance of corals* (see 3:15)—an oxymoron of an abundance of scarcity. Both gold and coral are enduring, beautiful, and valuable and so coveted in the marketplace. *But*, antithetically, *a* single *precious vessel*, which implicitly is more scarce, enduring, beautiful, and therefore desirable than gold and coral jewelry, is *lips that speak knowledge* (that is, speech informed by Proverbs).

16 Putting up security for a stranger/foreigner is another expression of imprudent speech in the marketplace (see 6:1–5). Verse 16 is repeated verbatim in 27:13. *Take away* has the nuance of being against the owner's will. *One's garment* denotes the guarantor's basic possession for protection from cold and nakedness, and, when pledged, symbolizes the whole body (see 6:1–5; Exod. 22:25–27; Amos 2:8). *When one becomes surety for a stranger*—to wit, the debtor (see 6:1; 11:15). "Stranger" (*zār*) in parallel with "outsider/foreigner" (*nokrî*) means a debtor outside of the covenant community (cf. 5:10; Job 19:27; Ps. 69:8; Obad.

---

143. One of Ivan's students provided a sharp paraphrase of this proverb: "No one becomes a someone while sleeping."

11). *Foreigner* (or "outsider") is another metonymy for the debtor. *Impound* (that is, seize; see Job 22:6; 24:3, 9) *it* (the guarantor's garment). Failure to compensate the creditor could result in the guarantor's slavery (cf. 2 Kings 4:1). The TEV captures the thought: "Anyone stupid enough to promise to be responsible for a stranger's debts ought to have his own property held to guarantee payment."

17 Foolish speech (vv. 14, 16) is now escalated to false speech. *Food* (see v. 13) is a synecdoche for satisfying any drive, including sex (cf. 9:17).[144] *Gotten by deceit* here probably means obtained through deceptive speech, as suggested by the context and the parallel, "mouth." *Is sweet to people* (the liars). *But after* points to the effect of lies. *Their mouth* initiates a metaphor for their having "to eat" the results of their lies. *Is filled* expands the metaphor to signify the deceiver is so crammed that nothing else can fit and denotes the liar's final, unrelieved, awful pain. *With gravel* completes the metaphor, and to judge from its only other use (cf. Lam. 3:16), is a metonymy of cause: gravel breaks the teeth so that the liar can no longer speak or eat and so dies awfully.

18 The conclusion (vv. 18–19) is based on the introduction. Sensible people seek the sages' opinions before taking action and accept their rebuke after mistaken action (cf. 11:14; 15:22; 24:6).[145] *Plans are established with counsel,* presumably informed by the sages' teaching and backed up by *I AM,* for otherwise they fail the test of time (see 19:21). *So* logically connects the versets. *With guidance make war* (*milḥāmâ*). All 319 occurrences of *milḥāmâ* in the Bible refer to armed conflict between nations or parties. The proverb envisions the disciple as a king, since warfare belongs to kings (cf. 24:5–6; Eccl. 9:13–18). However, "war" is probably a metaphor for any hostility confronting a leader (cf. 21:22; Luke 14:31–33). The proverb admonishes youth to make certain, before employing force against an enemy, that the goals and methods are consistent with wisdom.[146]

19 Seek counsel with the wise, not with a fool. *Whoever goes about as a slanderer divulges secrets* to the detriment of the confider. While seeking counsel, one often shares a confidence. So *do not get involved* (do not share a confidence; cf. 14:10) *with a silly chatterer,* one who handles words carelessly. Verse 19a reprises 11:13a, which adds the antithetic parallel "a trustworthy per-

144. So M. Lyons, "Rashi's Commentary on the Book Proverbs" (paper submitted in partial fulfillment of the requirements for the degree of rabbi, 1936), 106; Farmer, *Proverbs and Ecclesiastes,* 58.

145. So Farmer, *Proverbs and Ecclesiastes,* 89.

146. See Bruce K. Waltke, *Finding the Will of God: A Pagan Notion?* 2nd ed. (Grand Rapids: Eerdmans, 2016): 150–68.

son keeps a secret" (cf. 1 Tim. 5:13). Sirach 8:17 likewise cautions, "Take no counsel with a fool, for he can keep nothing to himself."

Trusting I AM to Avenge Wrongs through His Wise King (20:20-28)

20As for those who curse their father and their mother,
  their lamp will be snuffed out in pitch darkness.
21As for an inheritance gained in haste at the beginning,
  in its latter end it will not be blessed.
22Do not say, "I will repay evil!"
  Look expectantly to *I AM*, and he will avenge you.
23An abomination to *I AM* are differing weights,
  and deceptive balances are not good.
24From *I AM* are the steps of a person;
  and as for human beings, how can anyone understand their
    way?
25It is a trap for a human being to say rashly, "Consecrated,"
  and after [making] the vows to examine [them].
26The wise king winnows the wicked,
  and brings back the cart wheel over them.
27The words of human beings are the lamp of *I AM*,
  shedding light on all their innermost parts.
28Kindness and reliability guard the king;
  he upholds his throne with kindness.

This unit consists of an introduction to children implicitly commanding them not to curse parents and seize their inheritance (vv. 20–21), a body commanding not to seek revenge but to trust *I AM* (vv. 22–25), and a conclusion implicitly commanding the king to punish the wicked and protect the needy (vv. 26–28).

Introduction: Honoring Parents (20:20-21)

20 The introductory proverb condemns children who curse parents and forges a link with the theme of bad speech in vv. 14–19. *As for someone who curses* (*məqallēl*, "to declare worthless"[147]) *their father and their mother* refers to publicly defaming and dishonoring parents, hoping to get their inheritance

---

147. For this use of Piel, see *IBHS* §§24.2–3.

early (v. 21). Instead, *their lamp will be snuffed out* (see 13:9), a metaphor for premature death. *In pitch darkness* paints the child's untimely death as tragic and irreversible. As children curse their parents, so *I AM* curses them (Deut. 27:16). The Law commands children to honor their parents (Deut. 5:16; cf. Matt. 15:3–6; Eph. 6:1–3) and makes cursing parents an offense punishable by death (Exod. 21:17; Lev. 20:9).

21 The above interpretation of the reason a child curses parents is validated by its apparent pairing with v. 21. The antonym of "to curse" is "to bless," making "cursing" (v. 20a) and "not blessed" (v. 21b) semantic twins. By some skullduggery (see 19:26), the children seize their *inheritance* (see 17:2; 19:14), the family fortune handed down from parent to child. Verset A depicts *the beginning*, when the greedy child seizes the inheritance. Verset B depicts *its latter end: it will not be blessed* (see 10:6) by God, from whom all blessings flow (cf. Ps. 128:4). In sum, God will punish the child and impoverish the inheritance.

Body: Trust God, Not Self, to Avenge Wrong (20:22–25)

The body consists of two couplets: vv. 22–23, which are linked by the catchword "*I AM*," and vv. 24–25, which are linked by the catchword "human being." The couplets themselves are united by the catchword *I AM* (vv. 23–24). The mortal earthling should trust *I AM*, not self, because God is just (vv. 22–23) and sovereign (vv. 24–25).

22 Verse 22a proscribes vengeful speech in response to evil (see vv. 14–20; 1:16), and v. 22b prescribes to *look expectantly to I AM* for justice no matter how long he delays (Pss. 25:3; 62:5; Luke 18:7–8; 1 Pet. 2:23; 4:19). Thus, it pits avenging self against trusting the divine Avenger (see 24:29; cf. 17:13). *Do not say* to yourself or to another "*I will repay* (seek satisfaction for) *evil*" (see 1:16). *He* (I AM) *will avenge you*, for a wrong against the wise is a wrong against God himself (Deut. 32:43). Vengeance belongs to God, not to the limited and biased human victim (cf. 16:7; Deut. 32:35; 2 Sam. 3:39; Rom. 12:17–21; 1 Thess. 5:15).

23 This proverb, which restructures 20:10 and resembles 11:1, receives its distinctive nuance from the context of trusting the true Avenger. The situation of being sold or selling merchandise by false weights is an example of one in which *I AM* must avenge wrong. *An abomination to* I AM *are differing weights* is a metonymy of cause for the justice that he will execute (see 20:10). *Deceptive balances* (see 11:1) *are not good* (see 16:29). According to 16:11, *I AM* created the scales; therefore, every deceitful practice touches him. Moreover, it also touches him since Israel is his adopted family (Exod. 4:22–23).

24 *From* I AM (see 16:9) identifies Israel's covenant-keeping God as the ultimate author of the *steps* (each decision and activity; see 16:9) *of a person* (*geber*, "a man in his strength"; see "Words for 'Humankind' in Proverbs," p. 31). The question *how can anyone* (*'ādām*, "human being"; see p. 31) *understand their way* expects a negative answer: "It is impossible." "Their way" escalates the individual steps to the entire direction and destiny within which everyone acts (see 1:15). People do not understand their ways because God makes the actual direction and destiny of their free actions serve his hidden plan. Mortals choose their way and their steps, but *I AM* actualizes the divine goal (see 16:1, 4).

25 Since *I AM*, not human beings, controls the future (v. 24), it is imprudent for the human being to make reckless vows (cf. 27:2). This proverb warns youth against talking (verset A) before thinking (verset B). *It is a trap* (see 12:13) *for a human being* (see. v. 24) *to say* (that is, to vow, as the parallel shows; see 7:14) *rashly,* "*consecrated.*" Consecration, in this case by a speech act, sets someone (cf. Judg. 11:30; 1 Sam. 1:11) or something (cf. Lev. 27:10, 33; Num. 18:17; 30:1–16) apart as God's property. *To examine* entails cogitating afterward whether the vow was wise or foolish. Jephthah's rash vow cost his daughter her life and derailed the rulership he sought (cf. Judges 11). Whether wise or foolish, all vows must be paid exactly (Deut. 23:21–23; Eccl. 5:1–6).

Conclusion: The King Judges the Wicked and Protects the Needy (20:26–28)

26 *I AM* avenges wrongs (v. 22) through *the wise king*, whom he ordains to uphold the moral order (see 16:1–9, 10–15; 20:2; Rom. 12:17–13:7). As in 20:8, the agricultural imagery of *winnows* (scatters) pictures the king ridding his kingdom of *the wicked*. Although *and* suggests the threshing occurs after the winnowing, logically the threshing precedes the scattering. The dischronology emphasizes that the king so thoroughly separates the wicked from the righteous that his subsequent scattering of them is total. *The cartwheel* is the wheel of the threshing cart (cf. Isa. 28:27). *He brings* it *back* to go over the "grain" repeatedly to ensure thoroughness. The wheels of the threshing cart were fitted with sharp iron or stone that cut the sheaves as they repeatedly drove over them, separating grain from chaff. *Over them* implicitly likens the wicked to chaff that the wind blows away (cf. v. 8; Ps. 1:4). The metaphor implies thoroughness, not torture. Annihilation without separation is unjust; separation without annihilation is worthless. The proverb finds its fulfillment in the eschatological messianic kingdom. Only the King of kings can make this separation complete (cf. Mal. 3:2; Matt. 3:12).

27 Sandwiched between proverbs pertaining to the king scattering the wicked (v. 26) and defending the righteous (v. 28), v. 27 assures youth that they can trust *I AM* to avenge them (v. 22), for God is moral (v. 23), sovereign (v. 24), and omniscient (v. 27). Verset A represents his omniscience by the metaphor of a lamp, and verset B gives the interpretation. *The words* (lit. "breath" that comes out as words[148]) *of a human being* (see v. 24) *are the lamp* (cf. 20:12; 6:23) *I AM* uses to *shed light on all*, without exception, *of a* person's *innermost parts*. This latter phrase is literally "chambers of the belly" (see 18:8; 20:30), an Egyptianism denoting the human heart, where the truth about a person resides. In sum, a person's speech serves as *I AM*'s flashlight to expose the human thought, expression, and will in the darkest recesses of that person's life.

28 This proverb matches the king's judgment on the wicked (v. 26) with his *kindness and reliability* (see p. 38) to his otherwise helpless subject who appeals to him for justice (see v. 22). *Guard* personifies these two virtues as protecting *the king*. The king *upholds his throne*, the symbol of his authority and dominion, *with kindness* ("and reliability" is gapped). *I AM* supports and safeguards his king (cf. 2 Sam. 7:15; Pss. 2:6ff.; 18:35; 20:2; 41:3; Isa. 9:6) through these virtues (cf. 2:7, 11). This proverb and the entire unit find their final fulfillment in Jesus Christ (see Ps. 72:1, 2, 4; Isa. 16:4b–5; 1 Thess. 1:10).

Doing Righteousness and Justice (20:29–21:31)

> 20:29The splendor of choice young men is their strength,
>   and the majesty of the aged is their grey hair.
> 30Bruising wounds scour away evil,
>   and blows [polish] the innermost being.
> 21:1The king's heart in *I AM*'s hand is a channel of water;
>   on all who please him, he turns it.
> 2People's every way may seem upright in their own eyes,
>   but *I AM* is the one who evaluates hearts.
> 3To do righteousness and justice
>   is more desirable to *I AM* than sacrifice.
> 4Haughty eyes and an audacious heart—
>   the unplowed field of the wicked—produce sin.
> 5The calculations of a diligent person lead only to profit,
>   but everyone who hastens [to get rich] comes only to lack.

---

148. Van Leeuwen, "Proverbs," in *NIB* 5, 188.

⁶The acquisition of treasures by a lying tongue
    is the windblown breath of those seeking death.
⁷The violence of wicked people drags them away
    because they refuse to do justice.
⁸The ways of guilty people are crooked;
    but as for pure people, their deeds are straight.
⁹Better to dwell on a corner of the roof
    than in a house shared with a contentious wife.
¹⁰The appetite of wicked people craves evil;
    their neighbors do not find favor in their eyes.
¹¹Through fining a mocker, the uncommitted become wise,
    and through paying attention to a wise person they gain
        knowledge.
¹²The Righteous One pays attention to the household of a wicked
      person—
    the One who casts down wicked people to calamity.
¹³As for those who stop their ear to the cry of the poor,
    indeed, they themselves will also cry out and not be answered.
¹⁴A gift given in secret subdues anger;
    a* bribe in the bosom pacifies strong wrath.
¹⁵The doing of justice brings joy to the righteous person
    but terror to people who do iniquity.
¹⁶A human being who strays from the way of prudence
    will come to rest in the congregation of the dead.
¹⁷The one who loves pleasure is a destitute person;
    the one who loves wine and olive oil will not become rich.
¹⁸A wicked person is a ransom for the righteous,
    and a treacherous person comes in the place of the upright.
¹⁹Better to dwell in a desert land
    than to dwell with a contentious and vexing wife.
²⁰A desirable supply of food and oil are in the dwelling place of the
      wise,
    but fools gulp theirs down.
²¹The one who pursues righteousness and kindness
    will find life, prosperity, and honor.
²²A wise person scales the city wall of warriors,
    and pulls down its strong security.
²³Those who guard their mouths and their tongues

guard their lives from distresses.

²⁴Insolent, presumptuous people—Mocker is their name—
  behave with insolent fury.

²⁵The craving of sluggards kill them
  because their hands refuse to work.

²⁶All day long they crave greedily,
  but the righteous give without sparing.

²⁷The sacrifice of wicked people is an abomination;
  how much more [when] they bring it with evil intent.

²⁸A false witness will perish,
  but a person who listens well[b] will testify successfully.

²⁹The wicked person becomes brazen,
  but as for the upright, they discern their ways.

³⁰There is no wisdom and there is no understanding
  and there is no counsel that can stand before *I AM*.

³¹A horse is prepared for the day of war,
  but success belongs to *I AM*.

a. The ascensive "and" is left untranslated.
b. "Well" is added as a *constructio ad sensum*.

The theme of trusting *I AM* to avenge wrongs against oneself characterized the previous unit (20:20–28), which concluded with the motif that the king will protect the needy. It is now qualified by a unit on doing righteousness and justice. The unit consists of an introduction (20:29–21:2), a main body (21:3–29), and a conclusion (21:30–31).

Introduction: Educating the Young Sanctioned by *I AM* and His King (20:29–21:2)

The introduction consists of two semantic couplets discussing (1) the implied pedagogical responsibility of the older generation (the wise) to the younger ("choice young men," 20:29), who may require flogging (20:30); and (2) *I AM* as the one who sanctions this instruction through his "king" (21:1–2).

20:29 *Choice young men* and *their strength* (their vital power; see 5:10) are juxtaposed with *the aged* (see 17:6) and *their grey hair*, a metonymy for wisdom (see 16:31). The strength of youth is their *splendor* (see 4:9; 19:11), and the aged wear their grey hair in *majesty* (see 14:28), validating the way of wisdom.

These adornments signify their mutual dependence. Though physically weak, the aged and wise lay down the tracks along which the immature but powerful youth advance the faithful community to abundant life.

30 Remedial punishment is part of moral instruction. *Bruising wounds* from *blows* (cf. Isa. 1:6) *scour away* tarnishing *evil* (see 1:16) from *the innermost being* (see 18:8; 20:27), leaving the core of the personality brilliantly polished to do good.

21:1 *I AM*'s blessings on the wise through his anointed king are also part of moral instruction. As the hearts of individuals direct their every action (see "Heart," p. 32; 4:23), *the king's heart* determines the nation's direction toward good or bad. That it *is in* I AM's *hand* means that it is under God's sovereign control (see 16:14–15; 19:12; 20:2). The king, who steers the people, is himself steered by the just God. *Is a channel of water* is a metaphor communicating that he blesses the people. *On all* refers to every needy person in his realm (see 20:28). *Who please him* (*I AM*) restricts *I AM*'s blessings to the wise. *He* (*I AM*) *turns it* (the king's heart). *I AM* is the Farmer, the king's heart is the flexible channel; and *I AM*'s well-watered garden is the godly and needy. In sum, the proverb instructs youth to be pleasing to *I AM* in order to receive his favors through his king (cf. Gen. 20:6; 41:37–45; Ezra 1:1; 6:22; 7:27; 9:9; Ps. 106:46; Dan. 2:48; 3:30).

2 Verse 2 is a variant of 16:2, replacing "ways" (pl.) with *way*, "pure" with *upright* (see p. 37), and "motives" with *hearts*. The last change links this proverb to v. 1 by the catchword "heart." Conflicts of moral assessment between the holy God and a depraved human being will arise, but only the omnicompetent God rightly assesses the human *heart* and so rightly determines who deserves his blessing (cf. 15:11; 17:3; 24:12).[149] God will not direct life-giving water on fools. Self-distrust must be matched by bold confidence in *I AM,* who keeps his promises to bless the upright (see 3:5; 16:3).

Main Body: On Doing Righteousness and Justice (21:3–29)

The main body, introduced by a janus stating the unit's theme (v. 3), is followed by three subunits (vv. 4–8; 10–18; 20–29) separated by the refrain about "the contentious wife" (vv. 9, 19; cf. 19:13–14). The first subunit focuses on the defeat of the wicked; the middle subunit on the triumph of the righteous over

---

149. Therese of Lisieux said, "Our Lord does not look at the greatness of our actions, not even at their difficulty, but at the love with which we do them."

them; and the last subunit on the lasting gratification and establishment of the righteous and the demise of the wicked. The catchword "wicked" forms an inclusio (vv. 4b, 29a).

 Janus: *I AM*'s Desire for Righteousness and Justice (21:3)

3 The catchword "*I AM*" links verses 2 and 3. "To do righteousness and justice" (see 1:3) looks back and qualifies the abstraction of "who please him" (v. 1) and clarifies the standard by which God evaluates the heart. The phrase looks ahead to the body's three subunits (see vv. 7b, 15a, 21; cf. v. 25). By positive comparisons, the proverb sets forth what counts with God: *to do righteousness and justice*, the aim of Proverbs (see 1:3). The comparison *is more desirable to I AM than sacrifice* does not disparage sacrifices but teaches, along with many other Scriptures, that ethics count for more with God than rituals (cf. 15:8; 20:25; 1 Sam. 15:22; Ps. 51:7ff.; Isa. 1:11–14; Matt. 23:23; Mark 12:33–34). The New Testament disposed of some of the ceremonial laws (cf. Matt. 12:7; Mark 7:19; Acts 10:9–16, 34–35; 15:19–20) but deepened the moral laws (Matt. 5–6; 22:37–39).

An Analysis of the Wicked and Their Downfall (21:4–8)

The body's first subunit escalates wicked people's sin and their judgment. Their sin is escalated from their arrogance (v. 4) to their avarice (v. 5)—expanded to becoming rich through lying (v. 6a)—to "violence" (v. 7a) to their impenitence (v. 7b). They condemn themselves by their twisted path to escape detection (v. 8a). Their downfall is escalated from the evaluation that they are sinners, implying God's judgment (v. 4b), to their "lack" (v. 5b) to their losing everything on the way to death (v. 6b)—expanded by their being dragged away (v. 7)—to the divine verdict of "guilty" (v. 8a).

4 First up are the megalomaniacs who reject righteousness and justice. *Haughty* (lit. "rising") *eyes*, which look down on others, symbolize an impious and unethical pride. God and Woman Wisdom detest them (6:16–17; 8:13). *And* probes beneath the arrogant eyes. They peer out of an *audacious* (lit., "wide of"; see 18:16) *heart*. The Hebrew idiom denotes unrestrained thoughts and ambitious plans. Verset B explains the cause and consequence of this haughty heart by the metaphor of *an unplowed field*. Similarly, the hearts of *the wicked* (see pp. 45–46) *produce sin* because they lack good instruction. Guilty before God for their impiety and villainy, they deserve death (cf. 16:5, 18; 18:12; 29:23; 30:13–14).

5 The next culprits: those hasty to get rich. *The calculations* (see 6:18) *of a diligent person* (see 10:4) consist in wise planning in contrast to ill-conceived and misdirected actions (cf. 11:24–28). The diligent creatively plan within the boundaries of the teachings of Proverbs. *Lead only* (that is, unexpectedly) *to profit*. Contrary to the expectations of the wicked, the diligent gain more than they invested (cf. Rom. 2:7; Heb. 6:12). By contrast *everyone*, without exception, *who hastens to get rich* (without reckoning with the divine moral order) *comes only to lack* (loses what is essential to life).

6 The hasty to get rich of v. 5b are associated with *the acquisition of treasures by a lying tongue*, and "their lack" is escalated to the vanishing breath of those seeking death. For the moment, liars have treasures acquired from the innocent, but in the end they are *windblown breath*, a metaphor signifying that their ill-gotten treasures are fleeting and will disappear. Ironically, the treasures procured through deception are themselves deceptive: they are as insubstantial as breath. *Of those seeking death* can rightly be interpreted in two ways. First, "death" is a metonymy for their tainted treasure—that is to say, the sought-after ill-gotten treasures carry a divine death sentence with them. Second, instead of finding the fortune they hoped for, deceivers find that they unwittingly seek death and so lose everything (cf. 13:11; 20:17).

7 The same fate awaits the violent. Verset A asserts the sin of *wicked people* and its consequence, and verset B asserts the cause. Their fraudulent acquisition of treasures may also involve *violence* (see 1:10–15). Metaphoric *drags them away* likens them to fish in a net (cf. 1:17, 19; 11:3, 5, 6, 8, 18; 12:13, 26; 13:21; 14:14; 15:6). This is so *because they refuse to do justice* (see p. 37). Clearly, the wicked had opportunity to repent (see 1:20–33). The catchword "justice" with 21:3b implies that *I AM* is the fisherman.

8 The climactic verdict against the arrogant (v. 4), the hasty (v. 5), the deceiver (v. 6), and the violent (v. 7) is "guilty," entailing their judgment. *The ways* (which is *their deeds* in the parallel; see 1:15) *of guilty people* (a unique term in Heb.) *are crooked* (also a unique term in Heb.). "Crooked" is the antonym of *straight* (elsewhere rendered "upright"; see 1:3; 3:6; 11:3; 14:12). Since straight is a metaphor for living in accordance with the teaching of Proverbs, crooked means to deviate in various ways from its teaching. Indeed, the wicked detest the straight/upright (see 29:27). The imprecise parallels "guilty" and *pure* (free of impurities; see 16:2) show that the motives of the former are not free of moral dirt and that the latter are free of self-love and wholly given to loving God and neighbor. Sincere and honest, the pure can be counted on (8:7–9; Rom. 6:10–11; Phil. 2:19–22; Titus 1:15).

Refrain: The Contentious Wife (21:9)

The dramatic shift from wicked people to the quarrelsome wife forms a sharp division between the body's subunits. This better-than (see "Parallelism," p. 12; 12:9; 15:16, 17; 16:8) proverb, repeated in 25:24, evaluates the loneliness and discomfort of *dwelling on a corner of the roof* as better than being *in a house shared with a contentious wife* (see 19:13; 26:21). The solid, flat roofs of Palestinian houses supported people (Deut. 22:8; cf. Josh 2:6; Judg. 16:27; 2 Sam. 11:2; 16:22; 18:24), and on hot summer nights they slept on them (1 Sam. 9:25–26). This proverb, however, does not envision sleeping on the roof on a balmy evening. According to the synoptic parallel in 21:19, which replaces the roof with a desert, the proverb envisions dangerous exposure to weather. Ironically, while her lord (cf. Gen. 18:12; 1 Pet. 3:6) lives alone, exposed and unprotected on the roof, his intended helpmeet lords over him securely within (cf. Gen. 2:18). The proverb instructs the son to be one who finds *I AM*'s favor and thus a wife who, in mutual love, submits to him and builds up the household (see 12:4; 14:1; 31:12; cf. Deut. 24:1; Matt. 5:31–32; 19:1–12; 1 Cor. 7:10–16; Eph. 5:21–33). No Scripture instructs husbands to control their wives. The proverb also instructs the wife to eschew pride, for only with pride is there strife (13:10).

Justice and the Righteous versus the Wicked (21:10–18)

The body's second subunit continues the theme of justice but pertains more specifically to the contrast of the righteous and the wicked. "Wicked" may serve as a catchword with the preceding subunit (vv. 4, 7). It forms an inclusio around this subunit (vv. 10a, 18a).

10 What pollutes the behavior of the wicked is their taste for evil. *The appetite* (trad. "soul"; see "*Nepeš*," p. 32) *of wicked people craves* (see 10:3) *evil* (*rāʿ*; see 1:16). In fact, they cannot sleep *until* they have done evil (4:16a). And if "their sleep is torn away unless they make [somebody] stumble" (4:16b), how much more *their neighbors do not find favor*—a metonymy for acts of kindness (cf. 14:21)—*in their eyes* (cf. 14:21). Delitzsch thinks "does not find favor in their eyes" refers to the steely look that shows no compassion to the needy. Instead of helping their neighbors, they brutalize them (see 1:11–14; 4:16–17). Wisdom changes this hard appearance (Eccl. 8:1). The next proverb suggests how to escape this condemnation (see 21:12; cf. Matt. 12:33–35).

11 The uncommitted are saved from greed through a successive twofold educational process. First, *through fining* (see 17:26) *a mocker* (see pp. 48–49), *the uncommitted* (see p. 47) *become wise* (see pp. 34–35). Second, *through pay-ing attention* (1:3) *to a wise person they gain knowledge* (see p. 28) and enter the ranks of the wise (see 15:31). Reproving, even beating, mockers is worthless to the mockers (9:7–8; 15:12), but penalizing them monetarily has the value of educating the receptive uncommitted (see 19:25).

12 The fining of the mocker by a human authority is escalated to the pun-ishment meted out by *I AM*, who topples all the wicked. Moreover, whereas the uncommitted pay attention to the wise and gain abundant life, *I AM* pays attention to the wicked and hands them over to *calamity* (*ra'*, physical "evil"; see 1:16). *The Righteous One*[150] *pays attention to the household of a wicked person* and *casts* that person *down* (see 13:6) with all *wicked people* (Heb. pl.; see 21:4, 7) as a group. "To calamity" is added for emphasis (cf. 13:6; 19:3).

13 That the unrepentant wicked will not be rescued (v. 12) is now taught with a focus on *those who stop their ear to the cry of the poor* (see 21:10). Some-one who is victimized will cry out with utmost urgency, and that cry functions as an accusation or appeal against the oppressor (Jer. 20:8). Thus, v. 13a im-plies both the cruelty and insensitivity to justice of the hard-hearted (cf. Job 31:13–40; Neh. 5:1–11). "When the heart is hard, the ear is deaf" (18:23; 24:11–12). Verse 13b answers this hardness with the *lex talionis* consequence: *indeed* links the consequence to the cause. *They themselves* (the calloused wicked) *will also cry out* for help *and not be answered* by I AM (21:7, 12) at the time of the judg-ment (see 1:28–29). The merciful obtain mercy; the callous will not be pitied (cf. Ps. 109:6–20; Matt. 18:23–35; 25:31–46; Jas. 2:13).

14 The wicked's callousness to the poor is escalated to their accepting a self-serving *gift* (or "bribe"; see 15:27; 17:8, 23; 18:16; 19:6; cf. Exod. 23:8). Whereas they can resist the indigent's cry for justice, they cannot resist bribes. The bribe's perversion of justice is symbolized by its being *given in secret*, taken from concealment *in the bosom* (see 17:23). Here the bribe is given or taken because it *subdues anger*, the outward expression of *strong* inward *wrath* for a perceived wrong (cf. 6:35). Assuaging wrath through virtue is positive (cf. 15:1; 29:8), but pacifying it through a bribe, which perverts justice, is a vice.

15 After a proverb about *I AM* upholding justice (v. 12) and two negative proverbs about injustice (vv. 13–14), verse 15 notes the contrasting responses to justice of the righteous and the wicked. *The doing of justice brings joy* (see 10:28) *to the righteous person* (see pp. 36–37) *but terror* and ruin (see 10:32) *to*

---

150. Although *ṣaddîq* always refers to a human being elsewhere in Proverbs, here it refers to God because it is in apposition to "the One who casts down the wicked," who can only be *I AM*. The same substantive adjective is used for *I AM* in Isa. 24:16.

people who do iniquity (see 10:29b) states a truth about the contrasting psyches of the righteous and the wicked without giving a reason (see v. 18).

16 Using the metaphor of a "way," verset A presents the foolish journey of *a human being who strays* (see 7:25; 10:17; 14:22) *from the way* (see 1:15) *of prudence* (see p. 35; 1:3; 21:12). Every journey has a goal. Ironically, renegades rebel, hoping to settle down in peace and prosperity, but they *will come to* their *rest in the* hapless *congregation of the dead* (*rəpā'îm* ; see 2:18), their ultimate, not necessarily their premature, end (cf. 11:19; 14:12). Isaiah sharply contrasts the death of the *rəpā'îm*, who while living were tyrants, with the death of *I AM*'s saints. Of the former, he predicts: "Those *rəpā'îm* do not rise. You punished them and brought them to ruin; you wiped out all memory of them" (Isa. 26:14). Of the latter, however, he sings: "Their bodies will rise . . . the earth will give birth to her *rəpā'îm*" (Isa. 26:19).

17 One way of straying from prudence is to love pleasure. *The one who loves pleasure* and so pursues it (see 18:21) is concretized in the parallel as *the one who loves wine* for drinking *and olive oil* for anointing the body (cf. 27:9; Amos 6:6), both symbolic of festive pleasure (cf. Luke 6:24; 12:20; 16:25). The synonymous versets also match the consequences. *Is a destitute person* is a prolepsis, representing the future as present (e.g., "As soon as he walked into the room, he was a dead man"). *Will not become rich* is a litotes for becoming poor. Pleasure from virtue is a token of God's blessing and a cause of celebration (cf. 10:28; 12:20; 15:23). But when people pursue pleasure as an end in itself, they dethrone God (cf. 2 Tim. 3:4) and bring upon themselves unrelieved grief (cf. Luke 16:25).

18 The reason justice brings joy to the righteous and terror to the wicked is now given (cf. v. 15). *A wicked person is a ransom* (see 6:35) *for the righteous* (see 21:12, 15). This commercial imagery likens the ruin of the sensualist (v. 17) to their becoming a "ransom" (compensation money to buy someone out of trouble; cf. Exod. 21:29-30; Prov. 13:8; Isa. 43:3). The metaphor represents the righteous as in the place of trouble because the wicked plotted it. But since the wicked, not the righteous, are the expendable members of society, the Righteous One turns the tables against them, releases the righteous, and pops the wicked into their place. *Even* represents verset B as underscoring and clarifying verset A. *A treacherous person comes in the place of the upright.* Consider Haman replacing Mordecai on the gallows (Esth. 7:10).

Refrain: The Contentious Wife (21:19)

Verse 19 matches v. 9 in three ways: (1) its notion of a contentious wife destroying the closest social relationship, (2) its structure as a better-than proverb, and (3) its function of dividing units. It escalates v. 9 in two ways: (1) by replacing as the lesser of two evils "a corner on a roof" with *a desert land*—an uncivilized place far from home and where the husband can barely eke out his existence (cf. Job 24:5); and (2) by adding the descriptor *vexing* (see 12:16) to the contentious wife.

The Endurance of the Righteous and the Death of the Wicked (21:20–29)

The third subunit contrasts the eternal endurance of the righteous with the death of the wicked. It consists of two partial subunits: vv. 20–23 on the advantages of the wise and vv. 24–29, which catalogs types of the wicked—namely, the insolent, the sluggard, the hypocrite, the liar, and the brazenly wicked.

20 "Oil" functions as a catchword with v. 17. *A desirable supply [of food] and oil are in the dwelling place* (lit. "in the pasture") *of the wise.* The animal husbandry metaphor of "pasture" connotes provision, security, and peace. "Food" or grain, which was harvested in the spring, and olive "oil," pressed in the fall, function as a metonymy for continual, yearlong provisions. *But fools*, like dogs, *gulp theirs* (their supply of food) *down* probably connotes greedily eating before others do and a lack of restraint—instant gratification (cf. 1 Cor. 11:20–22).

21 This verse explains the reason for the truth of v. 20 by defining the "wise" as *the one who pursues*, as in a chase, *righteousness* (see pp. 36–37) *and kindness* (see p. 38). *Will find* adds to their reward of food (v. 20a) *life* (see pp. 41–42), *prosperity, and honor* (cf. Matt. 5:6; 6:32–33; Luke 6:38; Heb. 6:10).

22 *A wise person* (see vv. 20–21) is implicitly likened to a warrior to signify victory over evil. The wise person single-handedly launches the attack and *scales* (lit. "goes up") *the city wall of warriors.* The attack of the wise, who do justice and kindness, entails that the opposing warriors are fools, who are hard-hearted evildoers. The metaphor signifies that the wicked outnumber the wise, fight fiercely, and have strong defenses. Nevertheless, the solitary pursuer of righteousness prevails. The wise person *pulls down* (note the antithesis to "scales") *its strong security*, a double metonymy for the city wall and the defeat of its defenders. In spite of insurmountable odds, including famine, nakedness, the sword (Rom. 8:35), and spiritual forces of evil in heavenly places (Eph. 6:12), Christ builds his church through saints who wear God's armor (Isa. 59:17; Eph. 6:10–18).

23 Verses 22 and 23 are linked by military motifs, moving from the offense of the wise on evil to their defense against it. *Those who guard* (šōmēr) *their mouths and their tongues*, metonymies for speech that normally occur in parallel versets (cf. 10:31; 15:2; 31:26), *guard* (*šōmēr*) *their lives from distresses* (the numerous miseries that stem from rash speech; see 1:27). The pun on *šōmēr*, which in verset A means "to take care to do something" and in verset B means "to take care to protect" links the versets in a cause-consequence construction (see 11:12; 12:23; 13:3; 15:28; 29:20; Jas. 3:5–8).

24 The topic shifts dramatically from the overcoming wise (vv. 20–23) to their antagonists, beginning with the mocker. Mockers, who elsewhere are said to attack the pious unmercifully (Pss. 86:14; 119:51), are *insolent* and *presumptuous people*. The "presumptuous person" (Heb. sg.) is *yāhîr*, a rare word used elsewhere only of a tyrant (see Hab. 2:5). The sobriquet *Mocker* (see pp. 48–49; 1:22; 21:11) *is their name* signifies their character and connotes the mocker is a pariah (see 24:8). They *behave with insolent fury*—literally "fury of pride," a bloated opinion of their importance (see 11:2; 13:6) and the spiritual source of their antagonism against the wise.

25–26 Verses 25–26 are a pair. They are linked both by "they" (v. 26; Heb. sg.), whose antecedent is "sluggards" (v. 25; Heb. sg.), and by the catchword "to crave."

Verse 25a states the cause: *the cravings*, a metonymy for life-sustaining nourishment, *of sluggards* (see pp. 49–50) *kills them*. Verse 25b explains the oxymoron that sluggards' craving food kills *because their hands refuse to work*. A person's God-given appetite is meant to provoke the hands to produce the God-given food that gratifies the appetite and sustains life. But since sluggards' hands refuse to work, their frustrated appetite drives them to the grave.

Verse 26 intensifies the sluggards' cravings (vv. 25a, 26a) by modifying *they crave* with the adverbs *greedily* and *all day long* (i.e., constantly). By contrast, the *righteous* (see 10:3; 21:3, 12, 15, 18) *give without sparing*. The imprecise antithetical parallels suggest both that the righteous do not give to sluggards and that self-indulgent sluggards have nothing to share with the truly needy. But the righteous provide the deserving needy with abundant life.

27 At the center of the catalog of evil types stands the hypocritical worshipper, labelled "wicked," a term applicable to all the rest. Verse 27a essentially repeats v. 15:8a. Verse 27b uses the *a fortiori* argument *how much more* (see 11:31; 19:7) to escalate the certainty of *I AM*'s rejection of the sacrifice *when* (implied) *they* (i.e., *wicked people*) *bring it* (the common idiom for offering a sacrifice; see Gen. 4:3; Num. 15:25; Mal. 1:13) *with evil intent* (or "scheme," *bazimmâ*). Here *bazimmâ* denotes a devious plan to hurt the community by manipulating the cult. One can imagine the hypocrite feigning piety to lead others astray and make them easy prey (see 7:14; cf. 2 Sam. 15:7–13; 1 Kgs. 21:9–12; Prov. 7:14–15; Matt. 23:14). In the process, the wicked would make God a minister of sin.

28 A witness is one who has observed the event or who can testify based on knowledge (Lev. 5:1). *A false witness* deliberately deceives to pursue a hidden, selfish agenda. Though for a moment the hypocrites have their say, in the end they *will perish*, implying their hidden agenda was uncovered and their testimony rendered worthless (see 10:28; esp. 19:9). By contrast, *a person who listens well* (attentively and objectively) gives credible testimony and so in the end *will testify successfully*, acquitting the innocent and sentencing the guilty. This is how God listens (15:29). The Ultimate Agent, who vindicates the true witness and silences the false when the courts do not (Deut. 19:19), is the God of truth.

29 The effrontery of the wicked person brings the catalog of wicked types to a climactic conclusion. *The wicked person* (see pp. 45–46) *becomes brazen* (see 7:13), meaning cheeky and shameless. Perkei Abot 5:20 says that an impudent face is headed for Gehenna. *As for the upright* (see p. 37), *they discern* (choose with moral discrimination; cf. 14:8) *their way* (all the decisions and the entire direction and destiny of their life[151]).

Conclusion: *I AM*'s Sovereignty over People and Kingdoms (21:30–31)

Certainly, the wicked impudently defy God and his wisdom (v. 29), but no human power can stand before *I AM* (vv. 30–31). The catchword "*I AM*" links this proverb pair, which, together with the introduction (vv. 1–2), forms a frame around the core of the unit (vv. 3–29), affirming *I AM*'s sovereignty over humanity in general (vv. 2, 30) and over kings and their armies in particular (vv. 1, 31). Behind the victory of the wise/righteous over the wicked/fools stands invincible *I AM*.

30 Humans—even the upright—cannot consummate their journeys independently from *I AM* because it is he who has the final say in realizing their goals. The threefold anaphora that introduces the first three clauses and the assonance in the Heb. text of the final â (*ḥokmâ* = *wisdom*, see 1:2; *təbûnâ* = *understanding*, see 2:2; *ʿēṣâ* = *counsel*, see 1:25) are hammer blows that drive home the truth: not even the best of human wisdom *can stand before I AM*. Everything in the proverb stops at the divine name, giving *I AM* the full majesty and weight due his name. Obviously, the sages' wisdom is not in view, for *I AM* gave it birth (8:22–31), and it does not oppose *I AM*. The proverb pair of vv. 30–31 does not negate human wisdom and counsel (see 24:6) but puts it into perspective (cf. 16:1, 9; 19:21; Ps. 33:10–11; Isa. 8:10; 14:27; Acts 2:23; 4:27–28; 5:34–39; 1 Cor. 1:18–25; 3:19).

---

151. McKane, *Proverbs*, 562.

31 In verset A, the war horse concretizes the human wisdom and counsel alluded to in v. 30. Verset B, which positively asserts *I AM*'s success, complements the conclusion of v. 30 that this human wisdom and counsel will not succeed against *I AM*. In this proverb pair, *I AM* has the final word. The proverb assumes that a war *horse*, a synecdoche for all war machinery, *is prepared* through human wisdom, specifically *for the day of war.* Verset B, however, warns the king and his counselors against trusting horses and chariots (Ps. 20:7). *Success* (see 2:7) *belongs to I AM* (21:1, 30). Solomon multiplied horses (1 Kgs. 10:26–28), but such secular capability threatened Israel's faith in *I AM* and drew heavy criticism from Moses and the prophets and sages (cf. Deut. 17:16; Ps. 33:16–17; Isa. 31:1; Hos. 1:7; Zech. 9:10). Mic. 5:10–15 equates trust in military hardware with idolatry and witchcraft. This proverb was part and parcel of the king's godly guidance before battle (see 20:18; 24:6; cf. 2 Chr. 32:2–8).

Wealth and Moral Instruction (22:1–16)

> [1] A good name is more desirable than great riches,
>   and to be esteemed is better than silver and gold.
> [2] Rich and poor meet together;
>   *I AM* is the maker of them all.
> [3] The shrewd person sees evil and hides,
>   but the uncommitted pass on and pay the penalty.
> [4] The wage for humility—the fear-of-*I-AM* sort—
>   is riches, honor, and life.
> [5] Snares—the bird-trap sort—are in the way of the perverse;
>   those who would preserve their life keep far from them.
> [6] Dedicate youth according to what their way dictates;
>   even when they become old, they will not depart from it.
> [7] The rich person rules over poor people,
>   and the borrower is the slave to the lender.
> [8] Those who sow injustice will reap empty deception,
>   and the rod they wield in fury will fail.
> [9] As for the generous, they will be blessed
>   because they give from their food to the poor.
> [10] Drive out the mocker so that contention might depart
>   and strife and disgrace might cease.
> [11] As for those who love a pure heart,
>   whose lips are gracious, they will have the king as a friend.

^{12}The eyes of *I AM* protect knowledge,
  and so he subverts the words of the treacherous.
^{13}The sluggard says, "A lion is outside.
  In the midst of the plaza I will be murdered."
^{14}A deep pit is the mouth of unfaithful women;
  the one cursed by *I AM* falls into it.
^{15}Folly is bound up in the heart of a youth,
  but the rod of discipline will remove it far away.
^{16}Those who oppress the poor to increase [riches] for themselves
  [and] who give gifts to the rich come only to lack.

The final unit of Collection II consists of two subunits: on wealth and moral instruction (vv. 1–9) and on treacherous speech and moral instruction (vv. 10–16). Framing the unit is an introduction (vv. 1–2) and conclusion (vv. 15–16) linked by the catchword "rich." The other catchword, "*I AM*" (vv. 2, 4, 12, 14), punctuates the whole.

Wealth and Moral Instruction (22:1–9)

1 The introduction raises the topic of wealth by relativizing its value compared with a good name. Social favor with God and people is better than material wealth. "A good name" and "to be esteemed" function as metonymies of wisdom's effect. *A good name* is the expression of the outward beauty and benefits that come from inner wisdom. *Is more desirable* (see 21:3) *than great riches* (see 3:16). *To be esteemed* (lit. in "good favor") *is better than* (see "Parallelism," p. 12) *silver and gold*, the specific equivalents of "great riches." Material wealth is good, but a good reputation is better (cf. Eccl. 7:1). Wealth can be obtained apart from virtue (cf. 11:16), but a good name cannot be. Wisdom gives both (see 3:14).

2 The second proverb, a janus, looks back to the topic of wealth and ahead to the topic of *I AM*'s sovereignty. Rich and poor both owe their lives to a common Maker and are accountable to him. Verset A pictures this commonality: *rich*, who in Proverbs are cruel and impious (see 10:15; 28:11), *and poor*, who in in Proverbs are destitute through no fault of their own (see 10:4; 13:23), *meet together*. Verset B explains the common factor of their face-to-face encounter: *I AM is the maker of them all*, meaning *I AM* excludes no one due to economic status (cf. 14:31; 17:5; 29:13; Job 34:19). The rich should remember that their treatment of the poor is equated with their treatment of their Maker (14:31; 17:5), and the poor should remember not to despise, envy, or revolt against the rich (3:31) nor to sycophantically ingratiate themselves to them nor to compromise their conscience to win their favor.

3–4 This proverb pair protects v. 2 from misinterpretation. While rich and poor have a common Maker (v. 2), human folly leads *ultimately* to impoverishment, be it one's own (v. 3) or others' (v. 4).

The antithetical parallels of v. 3 symmetrically juxtapose (1) the topics of *the shrewd person* (see p. 35) versus *the uncommitted* (Heb. pl., suggesting they are more numerous; see p. 47); (2) the predicates *sees* (with moral discernment the connection between) *evil* (and its misery) versus *pass on* (or "keep on going"); (3) and the consequences that the one *hides* from *I AM* 's just scourges versus the others who *pay the penalty*. If the uncommitted do not develop the moral astuteness to spot danger and avoid it, they too will be fined when the scoffers are penalized (21:11). The shrewd discern the connections both between generosity and enrichment and between tyranny and impoverishment and so protect themselves by avoiding evil. The uncommitted fail to see these connections and take no precaution to find salvation while they can (1:32; cf. Isa. 26:11).

Verse 4a offers the cure whereby the uncommitted can in part become shrewd: to wit, *humility* (see 15:33), which is the renunciation of human sufficiency. Particularly, it is the sort of humility associated with *the fear of* I AM (see "Fear of *I AM*," pp. 38–39). The proverb motivates youth to accept this sort of humility by the metaphor of its *wage*, to wit, *riches* with *honor* (see 3:16; 18:12) and, supremely, *life* (see pp. 41–42). Without these other benefits, riches are socially worthless and vaporous.

5 This proverb escalates the preceding pair from the uncommitted, who do not watch where they walk, to the perverse, who walk in a way filled with *snares*, specifically *the bird-trap sort* of nets used by fowlers (see 7:23). The metaphor refers to temptations such as easy sex (2:16–20) and easy money (1:10–19). The snares are laid *in the way* (see 1:15) *of the perverse* (see 2:15). Verset B presents the way of escape: *Those who would preserve* (or "protect"; see 2:8) *their life* (see pp. 41–42) *keep far* (see 19:7) *from them* (the bird traps).

6 This proverb admonishes the wise pedagogue, especially the parent, to orient youths away from their innate folly by starting them on the right way. *Dedicate* here means to start the youth off with a strong commitment to religious and moral direction. *Youth* (or "a child"; Heb. sg. *naʿar*; see 1:4; 20:11). *Their way* (see 1:15) refers to someone or something dictating the orientation of their dedication. The innate way of youth according to Prov. 9 is folly (see 22:15; see p. 48). This well-known proverb teaches that the religious and moral initiation of the youth must be oriented from the start to counteract their uncommitted foolishness. As a consequence, *even when they grow old, they will not depart from it* (that is, the "way" of verset A). This gnomic proverb must not be pushed to mean that the parent or authority is ultimately responsible for the youth's entire moral orientation. Other proverbs recognize a youth's freedom to choose sin and apostatize by joining with villains (1:11–15) and whores (5:11–14).

7 The harsh reality is that the rich enslave the poor (the destitute). *The rich person* (see 22:2; 10:15) *rules over* (or "lords it over"; see 12:24) *poor people* (see 22:2; 10:4) by enslaving them with loans: *a borrower is a slave to the lender.* The metaphor of slavery implies the rich person charges interest from the destitute borrowers, who otherwise could not maintain their life. In the biblical world, the interest rate could range from as low as 20 percent for money to as high as 50 percent for grain. These high interest rates kept borrowers in perpetual debt and stripped them of their freedom. Charging interest from the destitute is forbidden in the Law (Exod. 22:25; Lev. 25:36–37; Deut. 23:19), excoriated by the prophets (Ezek. 18:8, 13, 17; 22:12), and censored by the sage (Prov. 28:8). Nevertheless, Israel's ability to grant loans to nations is regarded as a sign of God-given prosperity (Deut. 28:12) and Israel's need to borrow from them as the withdrawal of God's blessing (28:44).

8 In the future, *I AM* will end the tyranny of the rich (v. 7), and in the present, their tyranny is remedied by the generous, whom *I AM* rewards. *Those who sow . . . will reap* metaphorically depicts the deed-destiny nexus that informs Proverbs (cf. Job 4:8; Hos. 8:7; 10:12–13; Gal. 6:7). *Injustice* consistently involves "crimes of a social, property, or commercial nature."[152] Ironically, the unjust sowed a crop of injustice, but the riches they reap are an *empty deception,* for they will come to nothing. In verset A, the unjust lose their property; in verset B, they lose their power. *The rod* symbolizes the power and authority of the tyrant to subjugate and oppress others. It *will fail* because righteous *I AM* upholds the principle of *lex talionis* (cf. 10:28; 11:18; 12:3; 13:9, 25; 21:12; 24:19–20; 28:22).

9 *As for the generous* (lit. "good of eye") sharply contrasts them with the tyrannical rich and their reward (v. 8). The generous *will be blessed* with abundant provision and protection (cf. 10:6–7; 11:24–26). The Agent is *I AM,* for from him all blessings flow. Verset B explains why they are blessed: *because they give from* some of *their* limited *food to the poor* without expecting repayment. Whybray comments that this "clearly reflects the economic situation

---

152. R. Knierim, *TLOT,* 2:849–50, s.v. *ʿāwel.*

of the giver, who is able to spare something for the truly destitute, but from a limited budget rather than from great wealth."[153]

Treacherous Speech, Wealth, and Moral Instruction (22:10–16)

The second subunit consists of three proverb pairs (vv. 10–11, 13–14, 15–16) and a janus proverb (v. 12).

10–11 The introductory pair implicitly admonishes youth to accept the parents' teaching by noting the reality that mockers have no friends whereas the wise have the king as a friend.

Drive out the mocker (the worst of fools; see pp. 48–49) is a command to forcefully drive the mocker from the community. The command is not addressed to a particular individual but to the wise in general, who must assume the responsibility of authority. *So that contention,* personified as the mocker's twin, *might depart* (see 12:13) with the evicted mocker. Verse 10b clarifies v. 10a: *And strife and disgrace* (see 3:35) *might cease.* Van Leeuwen comments, "The matter of boundary definition, of inclusion and exclusion . . . is crucial, for without it no group, even the family of God, can have identity with integrity."[154] And Kidner says, "What an institution sometimes needs is not reform, but the expulsion of a member."[155]

As for focuses attention on the wise, the opposite of mockers. *Those who love* and so pursue (see 1:22) *a pure* (see 15:26) *heart* (see "Heart," p. 32) is a metonymy for the wise. Verse 11a features their inward heart's purity, v. 11b their outward and amiable speech that flows from a pure heart (see 4:23–24): *whose lips* (parallel with "heart" also in 10:8; 16:21; 24:2; cf. Job 33:3; Ps. 21:2) *are gracious.* The pure heart is mentioned first to protect elegant speech from being a mere facade (cf. 26:25). *They will have the king as a friend.* An upright attitude and high moral competence in speech are the prerequisites for a career in the palace (cf. 25:5), but the proverb pertains to any moral leadership.

12 This janus verse puts a saying about *I AM* back to back with a royal one (v. 11b; cf. 14:27–28) and continues to push youth to obey the faithful teaching and not to place confidence in false doctrine. The anthropomorphism *the eyes of* I AM (see 5:21; 15:3) is also a synecdoche for *I AM* himself. They *protect* and thus preserve the *knowledge* based on Proverbs (see p. 28). *And so* marks the logical connection between the cause, the moral awareness of *I AM* (v. 12), and

---

153. Whybray, *Proverbs,* 320.
154. Van Leeuwen, "Proverbs," in *NIB* 5, 198.
155. Kidner, *Proverbs,* 148.

the consequence, to wit, *he subverts the words of the treacherous* and brings them to a dead end so that his truth alone endures.

13–14 This proverb pair exemplifies two kinds of speech by the treacherous: the sluggard's (v. 13) and the harlots' (v. 14). The sluggard looks for easy money and harlots offer easy sex.

The sluggard (see pp. 49–50) *says, "A lion is outside. In the midst of the plaza I will be murdered."* "Murder" (*rāṣaḥ*) elsewhere denotes taking innocent human life either intentionally ("murder") or unintentionally ("manslaughter"; see Exod. 20:13; Num. 35:6, 11, 16, 30). Here, the deluded sluggard uses it uniquely of an animal to portray himself as an innocent victim. In other words, anyone forcing sluggards to go to work at the plaza is guilty of murdering them. The claim is absurd. In ancient Israel, lions were plentiful (see Ps. 104:20–21) but not in the cities and certainly not in broad daylight in the fortified plazas bustling with soldiers, merchants, and crowds. For sluggards, no idea is too eccentric or fantastic to keep them from laboring. Ironically, what really "murders" them is their laziness, not lions.

The femme fatale who loomed so large in Collection I (2:16–19; ch. 5; 6:20–35; ch. 7; 9:13–18) is again met at the close of Collection II. Now, however, the singular unfaithful woman gives way to the plural "unfaithful women." If one harlot's victims are many (see 7:26), those of several must be legion. *A deep pit* (cf. 23:27) is a metaphor that connotes danger and death. The metaphor here represents *the mouth*, a metonymy for speech (cf. 5:3; 9:17; 23:27; 30:20), as a hidden trap of danger and ruin. Seductive speech is part and parcel of illicit sex (5:3). *Unfaithful women* (see 2:16) designates unfaithful wives who stalk the streets to seduce young men. *The one cursed by* I AM experiences damnation by the fact that he *falls into it* (the harlot's "mouth-trap"). The image depicts the man who falls into her clutches as pillaged of everything he has, even of his life (cf. 23:28; see 5:10–11; 6:32–35; 7:23).

15–16 Verse 15, matching v. 6, escalates the admonition to start youth off on the right way to using the rod to keep them on it. The strong discipline is essential to protect the youth against *I AM*'s curse of casting him into the pit of the unfaithful women (v. 14). *Folly*, not purity, *is bound up* tightly *in the heart* (that is, the very constitution) *of a youth*. Whybray describes this as "the doctrine of 'original folly.'"[156] *The rod of discipline* (see 13:24) *will remove it far away*. Since folly incurs *I AM*'s curse (v. 14b; cf. Eph. 2:3), this proverb seeks to protect the youth from eternal death through the parents' relatively light sting. External bodily harm heals the internal moral rot.

---

156. Whybray, *Proverbs*, 125.

As in vv. 6 and 7, vv. 15 and 16 link moral correction of youth with taking care of the poor. The last proverb of Collection II aptly pertains to social justice with reference to wealth. The parallels, *those who oppress the poor* and those *who give gifts* describe two kinds of self-aggrandizers. "Gifts were given to the rich not out of love, but to secure their favor," says Toy.[157] In this enjambment, *to increase [riches] for themselves* is gapped in v. 16b. *Come only to lack* chastises trampling down the poor and currying favor with the rich. The juxtaposition of the one who takes money from the poor, who need it, with the one who gives to the rich, who does not need it, exposes the folly. This unit makes clear that the paradoxical outcome for such evildoers is due to the eyes of *I AM*, who protects his moral imperium (see "Retribution for the Wicked," p. 50; 14:31; 15:25; 17:5; 22:12, 23).

---

157. Toy, *Proverbs*, 420.

The Thirty Sayings of the Wise

(22:17–24:22)

For the demarcation of the Thirty Sayings of the Wise as Collection III of Proverbs and for its structural analysis, see "Structure," p. 4.

Many scholars believe that the Thirty Sayings of the Wise is related to the Egyptian *Instruction of Amenemope* (ca. 1186–1069 B.C.). The structural marker for the third collection, "Have I not written for you thirty sayings?" (22:20a), resembles the last chapter of the Egyptian *Instruction of Amenemope*: "Look to these thirty chapters." In Egyptian literature, the number thirty symbolizes a complete and perfect teaching, and we should assume the same for Proverbs.

SAYING 1: PROLOGUE (22:17–21)

[17]Incline your ear and hear the sayings of the wise,
    and pay attention to my knowledge,
[18]because [it is] lovely when you keep them in your belly,
    [when] they are fixed together on your lips.
[19]In order that your trust may be in *I AM*,
    I cause you to know today, even you!
[20]Have I not written for you thirty[a] sayings
    as advice and knowledge
[21]to teach you to be honest in speaking reliable words,
    to bring back reliable reports to those who commission you?

a. The meanings of both the written MT *šilšôm* ("formerly [?]") and the oral MT *šālîšîm* ("officer" > "noble") are questionable. In that light, many text critics emend the vocalization, without changing the consonants, to *šəlōšîm* ("thirty") because there are thirty sayings and the first eleven of the sayings resemble the initial sayings of Amenemope's thirty.

The prologue consists of two couplets (vv. 17–18, 20–21) around a center line (v. 19). Verses 17–18, pertains to the son and admonish him (v. 17) with motivation (v. 18) to accept the "sayings of the wise." Verses 20–21, which pertain to the father, define his sayings (v. 20) and his purpose in writing (v. 21). The center line is a janus, looking both back to the son in v. 19a and ahead to the father in v. 19b. More importantly, it grounds accepting the thirty sayings in trust in *I AM* to uphold their truth (cf. 3:5–6).

17–18 The admonition to accept *the sayings of the wise* (see 1:6) escalates from *incline your ear* (see 4:20) *and hear* (see 1:8) to *pay attention*. The learning process progresses from the outward ear that acquires the wisdom (v. 17a) to the interior heart set on its acquisition (v. 17b) to preserving it in the belly (v. 18a) to the outward lips that represent it to others (v. 18b; cf. 4:20–27). The parallels "the sayings of the wise" and *my knowledge* imply that Solomon, who is the only plausible antecedent of "my," is adopting and adapting the sayings of his peers (see "The Relationship of Proverbs to the Wisdom Literature of the Surrounding Cultures," pp. 23–24).

Because [it is] lovely (exceedingly beautiful and attractive) *when you keep* (carefully protect and memorize) *them. In your belly* may be a shortened form of the Egyptianism "in the casket of your heart" (see 18:8; 20:30). *Fixed* signifies both that they endure and are ready to be applied. *Together on your lips* both collectivizes the thirty sayings and individualizes them to be spoken at the right time.

19 The sayings of the wise are adapted by Solomon as from Israel's covenant-keeping God. *In order that your trust may be in* I AM implies that, albeit they originated in common grace, Israel's holy God inspired them as part of special revelation. The reasoning entails he will validate them in salvation history (see 3:5–6). The antecedents of the pronouns "I" and "you" are respectively Solomon and the fictive son of the Prologue to the book of Proverbs (1:8–9:18). The son's faith is not in the sayings per se but in the God of the sayings. *I,* Solomon, *cause you,* my son, *to know* represents the son as actively involved in internalizing the inspired king's wisdom. *Today* refers to each day of the son's life, for which he is to have the sayings always on the ready (cf. Heb. 3:13; 4:7 with Ps. 95:7). *Even you!* emphatically concentrates the application of the sayings on the son. Within the canonical context, every member of the church is reckoned as the son (cf. Heb. 12:5).

20–21 In Hebrew, a question such as *have I not written* calls for strong affirmation. It entails that the sayings, which were earlier represented as transmitted orally, are also transmitted in writing and accurately preserved. *For you* emphasizes the father's tender concern for his son. *Thirty* (see the translation notes). *As advice and knowledge* qualifies the sayings as authoritative.

The aim of this knowledge is to make the son a trustworthy speaker. Through these sayings, a leader ensures that the entire chain of command will be honest. *To teach you* founds this ethical behavior on trust in *I AM*. Honest (*qōšṭ*), a unique term, signifies "the quality of a man whose speech and actions conform to what reality is and requires."[1] If *qōšṭ* refers to human character, *speaking reliable words* is that character's expression. *Those who commission you* (see 10:26; cf. 13:17; 15:23; 26:6), according to Cody, refers to "one of those important persons . . . who tells his councillors, diplomats, emissaries, to look into various situations on which he expects reliable reports."[2]

SAYINGS 2–11: A DECALOGUE OF SAYINGS ABOUT WEALTH (22:22–23:11)

22:22Do not rob poor people because they are poor,
   and do not crush the afflicted in the gate;
23because *I AM* will plead their case,
   and so he will despoil those who despoiled them of life.
24Do not associate with hotheads,
   and with wrathful people do not get involved;
25lest you learn their ways,
   and so you fetch a snare for your life.
26Do not be among those who strike a palm,
   among those who pledge securities for loans.
27If you do not have the means to repay,
   why should your very bed be taken from under you?
28Do not move an ancient boundary
   that your ancestors have set.
29Do you see people who are skillful in their commission?
   They will present themselves before kings;
   they will not present themselves before obscure people.
23:1When you sit down to eat with a ruler,
   mark well what is before you,
2and place a knife in your gullet
   if you are a glutton.
3Do not crave his delicious morsels,
   for that is deceptive food.
4Do not become weary to make yourself rich;

---

1. A. Cody, "Notes on Proverbs 22,21 and 22,23b," *Bib* 61 (1980): 424.
2. Cody, "Notes," 423.

stop [trusting] in your own insight.
⁵Will you let your eyes glance at riches?
[If you do], they are not.
Surely, without question, they will make a set of wings for
themselves;
like an eagle, they will fly toward the heavens.
⁶Do not eat the food of a stingy host;
do not even desire their delicious morsels;
⁷because as they calculate within themselves, so are they.
"Eat and drink," they say to you, but their heart is not with you.
⁸As for the morsel of food that you have eaten, you will vomit it,
and you will have wasted your pleasant words.
⁹In the ears of fools do not speak,
because they will show contempt for your prudent words.
¹⁰Do not move the ancient boundaries;
and do not enter the fields of the fatherless,
¹¹for their Defender is strong;
he will plead their case against you.

This decalogue of sayings is structured as a chiasm:

A			Do not exploit the poor, for *I AM* defends them		22:22–23
	B		Do not get involved with hotheads		22:24–25
		C	Do not become surety, *for you may lose everything*		22:26–27
			D	Do not move boundary stones	22:28
				X The skillful stand before the king	22:29
			D'	Do not be greedy for deceptive food or money	23:1–3, 4–5
		C'	Do not eat with a stingy host, *for you will vomit and gain nothing*		23:6–8
	B'		Do not speak with fools		23:9
A'			Do not exploit the fatherless, for *I AM* defends them		23:10–11

Sayings 2 and 11 (22:22–23 = A; 23:10–11 = A'), which both prohibit exploitation of the vulnerable, form an inclusio around the decalogue. Their threats that *I AM* protects the vulnerable, unique within this decalogue, color the whole with "the fear of *I AM*." It is precisely at 23:11 that the sayings similar to the *Instruction of Amenemope* disappear. As for the pivot (22:29 = X), by centering this uniquely positive, didactic saying on how to succeed in the middle of nine prohibitions, Solomon deliberately makes it the most important saying of this decalogue.

Saying 2 (22:22–23)

22 *Do not rob poor people* means do not take violently and permanently whatever property the destitute may have. *Because they are poor* explains why the poor are a tempting target for the rich and powerful to exploit: namely, they lack the monetary strength to resist the attack of the powerful. The metaphor *crush* (or "pulverize") signifies the eradication of the poor person's free citizenship: they are brought to a state of bankruptcy and pressed into a state of dependence.[3] *The afflicted*, often in parallel with "the poor," denotes those who have been victimized (Job 34:28; Ps. 82:3; Isa. 10:2; 11:4; Amos 2:7). *The gate* is a metonymy for the rulers, elders, and merchants who carry on the economic, social, and political life of the community. The proverb envisions rich merchants, who manipulate the economy, in cahoots with corrupt magistrates (cf. Exod. 23:1–9; Lev. 19:13; Deut. 27:25; Ezek. 18:7ff.; Mic. 2:1–11; 3:1–12; 6:9–16; 7:1–6).

23 The son must not deceive himself by thinking corrupt people can victimize the vulnerable with impunity. This is so *because* I AM himself is their Protector. The afflicted can bring their claim to his heavenly court where he *will plead their case*—contend against injustice on their behalf. *And so* marks the progression from their committing their case to their Prosecutor to his becoming the Judge handing down a death sentence, exacting life for life. He *will despoil* (or "plunder") *those* (i.e., the rich and powerful) *who despoil them* (the poor) *of life*. In other words, he will render a death sentence. When human justice fails the poor, their offended Maker (14:21; 17:5) takes their brief and will avenge them (Exod. 22:22–24; Deut. 10:17–18; Ps. 72; Isa. 1:23; etc.).

Saying 3 (22:24–25)

24 Associating with a hothead is as self-destructive as robbery, but whereas *I AM* sentences the plunderer of the afflicted to death, he has built into the ways of hotheads their own self-destruction (cf. 1:16; 29:6). *Do not associate with* (emphatically, *do not get involved with*) *hotheads*. Hotheads are fools. Their judgment is clouded by irrational thought. They act impetuously—often in a terrifying way. They are incapable of restraint. This is so because the visibly distraught hotheads are inwardly *wrathful people*—that is, full of anger.

---

3. Meinhold, *Sprüche*, 381.

25 The danger is that *you* will *learn their ways*. "Ways" is a metaphor signifying the hothead's patterns of behavior, such as calling everyone who angers them "stupid." By merely associating with a hothead, one becomes fatally involved without even realizing it. The hothead's habits are both infectious and lethal: *and so fetch a snare* (a lethal hidden danger) *for your life*. The metaphor is ironic. One avoids fatal traps; one does not fetch them to kill oneself purposefully.

Saying 4 (22:26–27)

26 *Do not be among those who strike a palm*, the gesture that seals a guarantee, is explained by *among those who pledge securities for loans*, which are guarantees to pay off the borrower's loan should the borrower default (see 6:1–5; 11:15; 17:18; 20:16; 27:13).

27 To motivate the son, the father threatens him with the loss of all his possessions. *If you do not have the means to repay* (see 6:31). The one securing the loan must have the financial resources when they become the surety, but future financial reversals, out of the surety's control, may expose the surety to financial disaster. The hypothetical question, *Why should your very bed be taken from under you?*, is an implied criticism and censure of becoming a surety, dramatically representing the consequences of defaulting on payments. "Bed" presumes the son is a person of means, since ordinary people slept on the floor (Judg. 4:18). "Very" represents the bed as his last valuable possession.

Saying 5 (22:28)

Do not move an ancient boundary refers to the time when Joshua distributed the land by casting the lot (Josh. 14–19; cf. Deut. 19:14; 27:17). *That your ancestors have set* refers to the activity of the first families in marking out the boundaries when they settled the land. The crime of moving boundary markers was easy to do and hard to prove. A rogue would probably only move the boundary marker by an imperceptible amount each time, but over the years it adds up to a sizable land grab.

Saying 6 (22:29)

This pivotal saying aims to motivate the son to become competent in his occupation in order to rise to his highest social and economic potential in the service of kings. *Do you see* presents the condition of keeping a sharp lookout for *people skillful in their commission* or occupation in order to emulate them, in contrast to avoiding hotheads and fools. Such people *will present themselves* (firmly take their stand) *before kings* (cf. 16:10, 12–15; 19:12; 20:2; 21:1). The plural "kings" suggests the savants enjoy international reputations. To put it negatively in order to highlight the upward mobility, the capable *will not present themselves before obscure people*. Since poor people do not hire or give commissions, "obscure people" refers to low officials in the chain of command under the king. The Lord Jesus taught in parables that the one who is trustworthy in the small matters of this world will be entrusted with much in his coming kingdom (Matt. 25:14–30; Luke 19:11–27; cf. John 12:26).

Saying 7 (23:1–3)

This saying consists of two conditional situations with admonitions (vv. 1, 2), a prohibition (v. 3a), and a reason for it (v. 3b).

1 The first conditional situation is *when you sit down to eat with a ruler*, or one above you in the chain of command. *Mark well* (be sure to discern) *what is before you*, which is "the deceptive food" of v. 3.

2 *And* adds the second conditional situation: *if you are a glutton*, to wit, unable to restrain your greedy appetite. The situation of dining with a ruler is the moment to showcase your discipline and self-control. The stakes are high—so much so that, if you know you cannot restrain your appetite, full abstinence is best. The hyperbole *place a knife in your gullet* is like the English "bite your tongue" and Jesus's command to "pluck out your eye" (see Matt. 5:29). The hyperbole stresses the need for total abstinence if you are unable to curb the appetite. The saying teaches one to acknowledge if one is a glutton and to abstain totally from the temptation.

3 *Do not desire* (see 10:24; 13:4) *their delicious morsels* (*maṭ'ammôtāyw*). *Maṭ'ammîm* is a key word in Genesis 27 to indicate Isaac's character flaw of loving tasty food. The reason for the prohibition is that the situation is false: *it is deceptive food* (lit. "food of lies"). It appears the official is treating you to a sumptuous dinner, in which case desiring the joyous cuisine would be appropriate. But in truth, the official is testing your character: whether you are able to restrain your appetite when tempted.

Saying 8 (23:4–5)

This saying consists of two admonitions (v. 4) with a reason (v. 5).

4 The first admonition, *do not become* physically *weary* by toiling *to make yourself rich* (see 10:4), is clarified by the second (verset B). *Stop* (*ḥădāl*) means "refrain from" in the sense of not even beginning to do something (cf. Num. 9:13; Deut. 23:22; Amos 7:5). The terse poetry elides *[trusting]*. *In your own insight* (or "cleverness") represents the human, apart from God, as the authority of moral behavior (see 3:5). While verset B should be understood as a universal prohibition against trusting in one's own understanding, verset A shows that it particularly applies to the inherent human trait of seeking security through money. When wealth is acquired wisely and righteously, it is a blessing (see 3:16; 8:18; 10:22; 12:27; 14:23–24; 22:4; 28:20); when acquired impiously, a curse (10:2; 11:4, 18; 20:17; 22:4: 28:20).

5 The rhetorical question *will you let your eyes* (see 3:7) *glance at* (*tāʿûp*; lit. "let fly") *riches* represents the activity of chasing wealth as acceptable to the son but not to the father. *[If you do]* is added to smooth the broken syntax of the Hebrew text. *They are not* (*ʾênennû*) is a terse one-word clause in the Hebrew text, matching their sudden nonexistence. Verset B strongly underscores that truth in three ways: (1) by employing two emphatic adverbs, *surely* and *without question*; (2) by the metaphor *they will make a set of wings for themselves*; and (3) by intensifying the metaphor to that of the swift and powerful *eagle* disappearing into the sky. *They will fly toward the heavens* adds to the metaphor of the swift eagle the notion that it evades capture. So it is with riches.

Saying 9 (23:6–8)

6 *Do not eat the food of a stingy host* escalates in the essentially synonymous parallelism to *do not even desire their delicious morsels* (see v. 3a). "A stingy host" (lit. "evil eye") is the opposite of a generous person (lit. "good eye"; see 22:9; cf. Deut. 15:9; Sir. 14:10). According to 28:22, the stingy are eager to get rich.

7 The reason for the prohibition is that the situation is false. *Because as they calculate within themselves, so are they.* The host's inner thoughts represent their true identity, which is hostility, though his outward words are friendly: "*Eat and drink.*" But why would the stingy host feign friendship? A similar saying in the Egyptian *Instruction of Any* (8:10–13) provides an answer: "Attend to your position . . . ; it is not good to press forward. . . . Do not intrude on a man in his house, enter when you have been called; he may say, 'Welcome,' . . . yet deprive you of his thoughts. One gives food to one who is hated, supplies to one who enters uninvited."[4] Evidently, the host is bound by oriental custom to be polite to the uninvited guest. Accordingly, the onus for the false situation

---

4. *AEL*, 2:142.

is as much on the imposing guest as on the stingy host. A freer translation is "do not insist on eating the food of a begrudging host."

8 Verse 8 asserts the negative consequences of this false situation. *As for the morsel of food that you have eaten* assumes a situation after the meal. *You will vomit it* dramatically represents hypocritical food as repulsive and indigestible (cf. Lev. 18:25–28; 20:22; Jonah 2:10). In other words, the false situation you created in your greed backfires and sickens you. *And,* in addition, your carefully crafted words to win favor and wealth from your host will have no effect; you will gain nothing, and so *you will have wasted your pleasant words.* In sum, you will find the false meal both foul and futile. The saying implies the need to evaluate whether a person is generous or stingy.

Saying 10 (23:9)

It is also futile and foolish to speak to a fool. *Ears* is a metonymy for the heart, since the ear is the gateway to the heart, where decisions are made (2:2; 15:31). The phrase connotes that the good words spoken to the *fool* (see pp. 48–49) are clear, direct, and urgent. To *speak* refers to the process of making a complete address. The prohibition (*do not*) is reasonable *because they will show contempt* (cf. 9:8; 17:10; 27:22) *for your prudent* (see p. 35) *words,* which shows that the words contain moral insight. Woman Wisdom appeals to fools to listen but does not speak her wisdom to them (cf. 1:22, 32; 9:7–8). However, the proverb must be held in tension with 26:5: a reasoned response to folly is necessary. The proverb teaches that one must spiritually discern people's receptiveness before responding to them in order to predict the effect of one's words on them.[5]

Saying 11 (23:10–11)

10 *Do not move the ancient boundaries* repeats 22:28a. Here, it is escalated by the additional admonition, *do not enter the fields of the fatherless.* "Fatherless" refers to children bereft of paternal protection (cf. Job 29:12; Ps. 10:14). They, like the poor in the opening frame, are vulnerable and so tempt the rich and powerful to exploit them. The culprits will not succeed. *I AM,* who owned all the fields in Israel, granted them as a perpetual usufruct (property to be used freely but responsibly) to each Israelite family to guarantee their right to life in the holy land as long as they kept covenant (see 22:28). This usufruct

---

5. *The Instruction of Ankhsheshonq* 7:4 admonishes, "Do not instruct a fool, lest he hate you" (*AEL*, 3:165).

was represented by boundary stones and was to be jealously guarded as the family's permanent inheritance (cf. Lev. 25:23–28; 1 Kgs. 21:3). Unfortunately, by securing the sanction of corrupt courts, land-grabbers could take away the fields of the powerless (cf. 1 Kgs. 21:1–16).

11 If the human courts that *I AM* established to protect the poor fail, *I AM* himself will protect them by punishing their oppressors (cf. Deut. 16:18–17:13). *Because their Defender* (gō'ălām), a metonymy for *I AM, is strong*—that is, able and willing to act as their redeemer. The *go'el* is the nearest relative of a needy person and responsible to protect needy relatives (Lev. 25:47–54) and their property (Lev. 25:25–35), even avenging them if they are murdered (Num. 35:12, 19–27; Deut. 19:6, 12; Josh. 20:2–3, 5, 9). *He will plead their case against you* refers to the time of judgment, when *I AM* condemns the oppressor and vindicates the innocent (Prov. 14:31; 15:25, etc.).

SAYINGS 12–20: AN OBEDIENT SON (23:12–24:2)

[23:12] Apply your heart to instruction,
   your ear to words of knowledge.
[13] Do not withhold discipline from youth;
   for if you strike them with a rod, they will not die.
[14] You must strike them with a rod
   and deliver them from the grave.
[15] My son, if your heart is wise,
   my heart will be glad—yes, mine.
[16] And my inward parts will leap for joy
   when your lips speak what is upright.
[17] Do not let your heart be envious of sinners,
   but be zealous for the fear of *I AM* all the time.
[18] Surely there is a latter end;
   your hope will not be cut off.
[19] Listen, yes you, my son, and become wise,
   and direct your heart in the way.
[20] Do not be among wine bibbers,
   among those who gorge themselves with meat.
[21] Because those who imbibe and are profligate become destitute,
   and drowsiness clothes them in rags.
[22] Listen to your father who begot you,
   and do not show contempt for your mother when she
      grows old.

²³Buy truth and do not sell
    wisdom and instruction and insight.
²⁴The father of a righteous son surely shouts in exultation,
    and the one who begets a wise son rejoices in him.
²⁵Let your father and your mother rejoice,
    and let the one who bore you shout in exultation.
²⁶Give to me, my son, your heart,
    and let your eyes take pleasure in my ways.
²⁷Because an unchaste wife is a deep pit,
    and the unfaithful woman is a narrow well.
²⁸Indeed, she lays an ambush like a robber
    and increases the traitors among men.
²⁹Who has "Woe!" Who has "Alas!"
    Who has bitter conflicts? Who has complaint?
    Who has bruises needlessly?
    Who has flashing eyes?
³⁰Those who linger over wine;
    those who come to search out jugs of mixed wine.
³¹Do not look at wine when it is an alluring red,
    when it sparkles in the goblet,
    [when] it goes down smoothly.
³²In the end, it will bite like a snake
    and poison like a viper.
³³Your eyes will see incredible sights,
    and your mouth will speak what is perverse.
³⁴And you will become like one sleeping on the high seas,
    like one sleeping on top of the mast.
³⁵"They hit me, but I am not hurt;
    they beat me, but I do not know it.
    When will I wake up
    so that I may continue to seek it yet again?"
²⁴ᐟ¹Do not envy evil people,
    and do not crave to be with them,
²because their hearts ponder violence,
    and their lips speak malice.

The first seven sayings of this subunit (sayings 12–18: 23:12, 13–14, 15–16, 17–18, 19–21, 22–25, 26–28) share the same educational theme and sound very much like both the Prologue to Proverbs as a whole (1:8–9:18) and the prologue to the Thirty Sayings of the Wise in particular (22:17–21). To these are appended two sayings (sayings 19 and 20: 23:29–35; 24:1–2) that elaborate on the warning against the drunkard in saying 16 (23:19–21) and the prohibition not to envy sinners in saying 15 (23:17–18).

Saying 12 (23:12)

This verse marks the beginning of a new unit. It pictures the son bringing his heart and ear to Solomon's authoritative teachings mediated through his parents. *Apply* is literally "bring." *Your heart* (see "Heart," p. 32) *to instruction* (*mûsār*; see 1:2) and *your ear* (see 2:2) *to words of knowledge* (see 19:27) complement each other. The heart and ear work in tandem. The inner heart must open the outer ear to allow the ear to reshape the heart (cf. 2:2; 15:31; 18:15; 19:27). In 2:2, priority was given to the ear; here, it is given to the heart. Solomon brings the two together in his prayer for a "hearing heart" (1 Kgs. 3:9; cf. Prov. 20:12).

Saying 13 (23:13–14)

13 The thirteenth saying advances the twelfth by admonishing the son, who submitted himself to instruction (*mûsār*, v. 12a) to become himself a disciplinarian of youth. *Do not withhold discipline* (*mûsār*, here not rendered "instruction" as in v. 12a because of the parallel, "rod") *from youth* (Heb. sg. *na'ar*; see 1:4; 22:6) is explained in verset B as flogging youths on the back, because that sort of discipline is lifesaving. *For* segues into the reason. *Strike them with a rod* refers to a severe, but not fatal, flogging to cleanse the youth and to prevent repeated folly (19:25; 20:30). *They will not die* from the corrective flogging. The parallel in v. 14b suggests that death refers to eternal, not clinical, death (cf. 5:23; 10:21; 15:10; 19:16, 18). The disciplined youths can expect clinical death, but the grave will not hold them. Severe discipline is not cruel; withholding it from callous youths is. However, the chastening rod must be applied with love and respect (see 4:3). Parents who brutalize their children cannot hide behind the rod doctrine of Proverbs.

14 *You must strike them with the rod* repeats v. 13b but escalates the admonition from the conditional "if" to the obligation "you must." *And* (= "and so") *you will deliver their lives from the grave*. Bridges asks, "Is it not better that the flesh should smart, than that *the soul should die?*"[6]

---

6. Bridges, *Proverbs*, 429.

Saying 14 (23:15–16)

Saying 14, a couplet (vv. 15–16), continues the theme of admonishing the son to heed parental teaching. Verse 15 persuades him to accept the parents' wisdom by conditioning their joy on the son's wisdom. Verse 16 escalates the persuasion by shifting from gladness to leaping for joy (10:1; 15:20; 17:21, 25; 23:24–25; 27:11).

15 Verse 15a presents the condition, an implied admonition, and 15b the consequence. *My son* (see 1:8) *if* (see 2:1) *your heart* (see "Heart," p. 32) *is wise* (see "Intellectual Terms for the Wise and Righteous," pp. 34–35), *my* (the father, who represents both parents; see 1:8) *heart will be glad* (see 5:18). *Yes, mine* (lit. "I"); the pleonastic pronoun, featuring the father, focuses psychologically on his own heart's rapture, thus making a connection between the son's wise heart and the father's glad heart (that is, his psychological health).

16 As saying 13 (vv. 13–14) advanced from the son accepting the father's teaching (saying 12; v. 12), so also in saying 14 the father advances from motivating the son to have a wise heart (v. 15) to motivating the son to have upright lips—that is to say, to become an educator himself. The conditional clauses regarding the advance from the heart to the lips frame the couplet (vv. 15a, 16b). The consequences regarding the father's exhilaration are given concentrically in the couplet's inner core (vv. 15b, 16a). The first consequence shifts from "my heart" to *my inward parts* (*kilyôtāy*; lit. "my kidneys"), a synecdoche for the father's emotions. Both the heart and the kidneys designate the whole of the inner person. The second consequence escalates from "will be glad" to *will leap for joy*, an expression of extreme euphoria through such actions as singing, dancing, shouting. *When your lips speak what is upright* means when the son's speech conforms to *I AM's* fixed moral order.

Saying 15 (23:17–18)

17 Saying 15 complements the son's "wise heart" of saying 14 in two ways. First, by the prohibition *do not let your* wise *heart* (see v. 15) *be envious* (have wrong zeal) for the stolen property *of sinners* (see 1:10–19). And second, by contrast (*but*), make your heart *zealous* (have right zeal) *for the fear of* I AM (see "Fear of *I AM*," pp. 38–39), emphatically *all the time*.

18 The outcome of pursuing the fear of *I AM* as one's only goal (v. 17) is an unending beatific future (see vv. 13–14) that is repeated in 24:14 and that is apprehended by faith (see v. 14b). The blessed future escalates in this subunit from "will not die" (v. 13b) to "deliver from the grave" (v. 14b) to "your hope will not be cut off" (v. 18). Those who build their lives on that vision please

God. *A latter end* refers to the certain end that results from constantly fearing *I AM*. *And* adds a second situation. *Your hope* (the future, when God reverses the present ill-gotten fortune of sinners by punishing them with privation but rewarding the righteous with prosperity; see 10:2–3) *will not be cut off.* The hoped-for abundant life will not be annihilated (Matt. 6:33).

Saying 16 (23:19–21)

19 *Listen, yes you, my son* commands the son's attention and focuses it on the instruction to steer clear of profligates (v. 20). *And direct your heart in the way* puts a fine point on the command to listen. Verses 20–21 will define "in the way." Although "and then take strides in the way of your heart" is a tenable translation,[7] it does not fit well the rest of the saying. If the son's heart is going in the right direction, a promise that he will not be among profligates seems more appropriate than a prohibition commanding him not to be among them.

20 Kidner labels the prohibition of v. 20, with its rationale in v. 21, "from revelry to rags."[8] To *be among* connotes being in the company of or being identified with a group. *Wine bibbers* (drunkards or addicts) and *those who gorge themselves with meat* (or "those who make light of precious meat and squander it for themselves"; that is, gluttons) epitomize self-indulgence and profligacy. The latter phrase implies that these gluttons gorge themselves on animal flesh without regard to the animal or the needs of others (cf. Luke 21:34; Rom. 13:11–14; 1 Cor. 5:11–13; 1 Tim. 3:3; Titus 1:7).

21 *Because* signals the prohibition's rationale. Those self-indulgent ones *who imbibe and become profligate* will become indigent (verset A) due to the drowsiness that accompanies drunkenness and gluttony (verset B). Like the sluggard, they *become destitute* (see 20:13)—social pariahs (cf. 6:9–11; 19:15; 20:13). The destitute are unable to sustain their lives. *And* compounds the reason. *Drowsiness* connotes inability to be vigilant or valiant to protect property. Personified drowsiness *will clothe them in rags*—torn pieces of cloth that offer neither protection nor social acceptance.

Saying 17 (23:22–25)

This saying remarkably escalates saying 14 (vv. 15–16) and, in similar logic to it, presents the admonition to accept the parents' teaching in the first half (vv.

---

7. So Fox, *Proverbs 10–31*, 736.
8. Kidner, *Proverbs*, 152.

22–23) and the motivation to give the parents exuberant joy in the second half (vv. 24–25). The two couplets are framed by "your father who begot you" (v. 22a) and "the one/mother who bore you" (v. 25b). That notion also unifies the second couplet (vv. 24b, 25b). The saying uniquely stresses the role of the mother in birthing and raising the son (cf. 1:8), evincing the home, not a school, as the locus for transmitting the Thirty Sayings of the Wise.

22 For the splitting up of the stereotypical phrase for parents, *your father* and *your mother*, see 1:8; 10:1. Thus, the admonitions *listen* and *do not show contempt*—a litotes for continuously adhering to the teaching—pertain to both parents. Similarly, the merism the one *who begot you* and *when she grows old* spans the whole life of both parents in relationship to their son, from his birth to their old age (cf. 30:11, 17). Disrespect for parents is one of the signs of the distressing times to come (2 Tim. 3:1–4).

23 *Buy truth and do not sell* means that the son so greatly values the parents' wisdom that no price is too high to stop him from obtaining it and no offer is high enough to tempt him to part with it (cf. 2:4; 3:14–15; 4:7). The metaphor of "selling wisdom" describes someone with a spiritual attitude that counts the world-and-life views of sinners as better than the inherited *wisdom and instruction and insight*, the same three values for right living that open the book's preamble (1:2).

24 This didactic verse, though lacking a logical connector to the admonitions in vv. 22–23, implicitly supplies their motivation for the admonitions of the first couplet. The rare synonymous parallelism makes the verse emphatic. Verset B paraphrases verset A: *the father* by *the one who begets* (see v. 22); *a righteous son* by its correlative term, *a wise son*, and *surely shouts in exultation* by *rejoices in him*.

25 The second couplet is linked to the first by the catchword "rejoice" (vv. 24b, 25a). The transformation of the didactic saying of v. 24 into the petition *let your father and your mother rejoice* confirms that v. 24 functions as motivation to heed the admonition of vv. 22–23. As the synonymous parallel of v. 24b intensifies v. 24a, so once again the synonymous parallel of verse 25b reinforces and intensifies v. 25a, replacing "your mother" with *the one who bore you* and "rejoice" with *shout in exultation*. Obviously, the son brings them joy by heeding the admonitions of the first couplet. That the parallel features the mother and not the father to frame the unified saying is truly remarkable in Proverbs.

Saying 18 (23:26–28)

The femme fatale, prevalent in the Prologue (see 2:15–19; 5:1–23; 6:20–35; 7:1–27; 9:13–18) and mentioned once in Collection II (22:14), is encountered again in the Thirty Sayings as the climax to the subunit on the obedient son. She is both deadly (v. 27) and deadly effective (v. 28). The son's only protection is committing his heart and eyes beforehand to the father, who represents God to the son (2:6; 3:5–6).

26 *Give to me . . . your heart, and let your eyes . . . in my ways* (see 23:19) enjoins the son to give these crucial body parts to the father's ways (see 1:15), not to the ways of the adulteress. *Take pleasure* depicts the father's teachings as a path that the son should delight in to keep the son from wandering into the temptress's trap. What gives one pleasure depends on one's prior spiritual disposition. Accordingly, the heart's commitment (verset A) informs the eye's pleasure (verset B). To ask for the son's heart, which rightfully belongs only to God, implies that the father, with Solomon's inspired wisdom on his lips, speaks as God's substitute (see 2:7).

27 *Because* segues into the reason to give these crucial body parts to the father; namely, to protect the son from *the unchaste wife*, who is *the unfaithful woman* (see pp. 55–56). The hunting metaphor of *a deep pit* signifies either her house or, more aptly, her sexual orifices of mouth and vagina (cf. 22:14). She engages in sex for lust or money, not for creating a lasting relationship. She is now compared to *a narrow well*, having the same extra-linguistic referent as "deep pit." In poetry, the well, a source of refreshing water, is a common metaphor for sex. "Narrow" signifies the frustration this paramour creates. The adulterer comes expecting to have his sexual passions satisfied. Instead, he is frustrated because his illicit partner, who is incapable of intimacy, cannot satisfy his passion. Moreover, after his encounter, he finds himself trapped (cf. Jer. 38:6).

28 The passive metaphors of a pit and well now give way to a more active metaphor: *Indeed, she lays an ambush like a robber,* a simile explained in 1:10–14. But instead of ravaging him by brute force, she traps him by her seductive speech. *Increases the traitors among men* suggests that she has seduced multiple men to abandon their loyalty to God and the covenant community. To her hardened heart, however, such behavior is as common as eating a delicious meal (see 9:17).

Appendix: Sayings 19 and 20 (23:29–24:2)

The riveting warning against wine in saying 19 expands on the warning against drunkards in saying 16 (23:19–21) by shifting from the danger of associating with drunkards to the danger of wine itself. Saying 20 (24:1–2) elaborates on the command against envying sinners in saying 15 (23:17–18).

Saying 19 (23:29–35)

The previous saying unmasked the seductive siren as a triumphant trapper; this saying uncovers wine as a venomous viper. Both are hidden, deadly traps. King Lemuel's mother (31:3–4) and Sirach also link the dangers of women and wine: "Wine and women lead intelligent men astray" (Sir. 19:2; cf. Hos 4:10–11). M. E. Andrew analyzes this satirical song in Proverbs as follows: a riddle (v. 29) with an answer (v. 30), a commandment (v. 31) with a consequence (v. 31), further consequences in direct address ("making the hearer feel as though he were already drunk," vv. 33–34), and a conclusion in the drunkard's own words (v. 35).[9]

29 The sixfold anaphora *who has* binds the riddle in an escalation of the drunkard's social problems. First, one hears cries of *"Woe!"* and *"Alas!"* which, if addressed to the drunkard, express threat and denunciation (cf. Num. 21:29; Jer. 13:27). Next, the boozer's problems escalate to *bitter conflicts* and *complaint*, denoting a person's grievance, and then from these grievances to *bruises*. The bruises probably result from floggings or fights (see 20:30). *Needlessly* shows that the drunkard's troubles were all due only to profitless drunkenness. *Flashing eyes* concretizes his pugnacity, but the meaning of the phrase is uncertain.

30 The riddle's answer is *those who linger over wine*, escalated to *those who come* (that is, engage in a destiny-affecting activity) *to search out jugs of mixed wine*. The wine bibbers mix spices or herbs and honey into the wine to make the wine sweeter, more enjoyable, and longer lasting (see 9:2; cf. Isa. 5:11).

31 The satirical riddle now gives way to a command, calling the youth to avoid addiction by nipping it in the bud. As noted at 20:1, the Bible and Proverbs speak both favorably and unfavorably of intoxicants. This command prohibits giving wine an opportunity to work its charm and seduce the son into addiction. When one is charmed by its color, its sparkle, its goblet, and its delectable taste, one should shove it aside. The command details wine's allurement to the eyes and palate. *Do not look at wine when it is an alluring red* is expanded to *when it sparkles* (or "gleams") *in the goblet*. To wine's alluring appearance is added its delectable taste: *[when]* (gapped) *it goes down smoothly*. The command is a hyperbole. To stop looking at wine implies one has been looking at it, and the statement "when it goes down smoothly" means one has even begun imbibing it. The exaggeration means, "Stop drinking it."

---

9. M. E. Andrews, "Variety of Expression in Proverbs XXIII 29–35," *VT* 28 (1978): 102–3.

32 The deadly *end* of gazing at and drinking wine exposes its true identity and so the rationale for the prohibition. *It will bite like a snake* (inflict pain) *and poison like a viper* (kill). Like a poisonous viper, wine's lethal danger strikes unexpectedly.

33 The father now turns to directly address the son about wine's delusions and perversions. In this way, he forces the son to experience firsthand the nightmarish effects of wine. *Your eyes will see* is a figure for hallucinating. The Hebrew word glossed *incredible sights* could denote "disgusting things." Wine's hallucinatory effects are escalated from not seeing straight to not speaking straight: *Your mouth will speak what is perverse.* Instead of seeing things as they are, the inebriated fool sees an upside-down world, and the drunkard's perverse speaking represents a topsy-turvy moral order.

34 From perverse speech to precarious sleep, this verse underscores wine's disastrous effects by vivid and dramatic similes. *And you will become like one sleeping,* oblivious to the real world. *On the high seas* refers to the sea beyond the horizon, where great waves undulate ceaselessly. The simile portrays the drunkard as physically nauseated and staggering, mentally unaware of peril at a time when one's wits are most needed to survive. The peril is escalated to *like one sleeping* in the crow's nest *on top of the mast,* where the ship's rocking is greatest.

35 The mocking song is drawn to conclusion by having the desperate drunkard confess in first person: *They hit me, but I am not hurt.* The foolish boast reveals the drunkard's insanity; sober people protect themselves. *They beat me, but I did not know it* escalates the drunkard's anesthesia to total unawareness of the precarious plight. Hebrew "beat" is used of Jael, who with tent peg in hand, struck Sisera the fatal blow (Judg. 5:26; cf. Ps. 141:5). *I do not know it* shows that the dipsomaniac is the exact opposite of the wise, whose senses are open to know. Verset B escalates the plight: boozers learn nothing from beatings. Instead, they are so addicted that, even before waking up, they crave more of the stupefying poison, whatever the cost. *When will I wake up so that I may continue to seek it* expresses the wino's determination to obtain the venomous wine. *Yet again* underscores that the souse's seeking is not an isolated occurrence. Aitken comments, "The passage describes more than a night's drinking and a morning's hangover. It describes the increasingly degenerative effect, physical and mental, of the habitual drinker and the alcoholic"[10] (cf. John 8:34–36; 1 Cor. 6:10–11).

10. Aitken, *Proverbs,* 124.

Saying 20 (24:1–2)

Both the prohibition (v. 1) and the rationale (v. 2) of this saying are double-sided.

1 The double prohibition of this verse escalates from not envying depraved sinners (verset A) to not consorting with them (verset B). The prohibition *do not envy evil people* assumes evil people have enviable traits or property. *And do not crave to be with them* assumes they are successful. No one is tempted to join evil people unless they are successful in their quest for easy money.

2 *Because* signals the double rationale for the double prohibition. The double rationale moves from describing the evildoers' wanton violence (verset A) to their mendacious speech (verset B) in order to repulse the son from embracing their wicked worldview and perverse praxis. *Their hearts* (see "Heart," p. 32) *ponder violence*. Their inward hearts express themselves on *their lips* that *speak malice*. Their contemplative, violent acts of destruction and their veiling of their horrendous behavior with deceptive and treacherous speech is so repulsive that one intuitively recoils from mimicking or joining them (cf. 1:11–14). In the interim, while sinners plunder and deceivers prosper, the righteous live by faith (Prov. 3:5; 2 Cor. 5:7; Heb. 11:1).

SAYINGS 21–25: STRENGTH IN DISTRESS (24:3–12)

³By wisdom a household is built,
and by understanding it is established,
⁴and by knowledge its rooms are filled
with all kinds of precious and pleasant wealth.
⁵A wise person prevails by might;
a person of knowledge musters strength.
⁶Surely by guidance you must wage war;
victory is won through many counselors.
⁷Wisdom is too high for fools;
in the gate they must[11] not open their mouths.
⁸As for those who plan to do evil,
they will be named "Schemer."
⁹The schemes that come from folly are sin,
and an abomination to humanity is a mocker.
¹⁰If you show yourself lax in the time of crisis,

---

11. The *yiqtôl* form is interpreted as obligatory (see *IBHS* §31.4g).

your strength is meager.
¹¹Deliver those being taken to death,
    even hold back those swaying and being led to slaughter.
¹²If you say, "We knew nothing about this,"
    does not even he who weighs motives discern [the truth]?
    As for him who protects your life, does he not know,
    and will he not repay people according to their conduct?

The five sayings of this subunit of the Thirty Sayings motivates the son to grasp the wisdom that will give him strength and strategy in conflict.

Saying 21 (24:3–4)

This introductory educational saying admonishes the son to build his household and accumulate wealth by wisdom, not by plunder (see vv. 1–2). Its two verses are linked by employing "wisdom," "understanding," and "knowledge," the same agents in the same sequence that *I AM* used when he "established" the world (3:19). These are the virtues Proverbs aims to inculcate in youth (1:2). Moreover, they are foundational to "the fear of *I AM*" (1:7).

3 The synthetic parallels of v. 3 escalate the making of *a household* (see 11:29) from *is built* (see 14:1; cf. 2 Sam. 7:13) to *is established* (see 3:19; 8:21). *By wisdom* and *by understanding* occur at the beginning of the clauses to focus on the means of building. Unless a household is built on the wisdom revealed by *I AM*, it is no more firm than a house of cards.

4 This verse narrows "household" down to *its rooms* and escalates "is built" and "is established" to *are filled with all kinds of precious and pleasant wealth* (see 3:15).

Saying 22 (24:5–6)

This saying implicitly calls for wisdom to equip one with strength (v. 5) and strategy (v. 6), both of which are necessary for any undertaking, but especially for war. Wisdom provides all that is necessary for victory over every enemy that attacks the wise person's household (cf. 11:14; 15:22; 20:18; 21:5, 22).

5 *A wise person* (geber-ḥākām) *prevails by might* asserts that the wise person possesses a fixed and inviolable protective security. *A person of knowledge musters strength* asserts that the person has an empowering inner vital energy. The word order of the Hebrew text keeps the focus on wisdom and knowledge, not on their effects: might and strength. Mustering vital energy is essential to producing anything successful (see 31:17), but "prevailing by might" is used primarily with war (v. 6) and speech (v. 7).

6 Counsel and strategy are also essential for success. *By guidance* (see 1:5), the means of victory, *you must wage war* (see 20:18). Verset B, which repeats 11:14, qualifies this war as successful: *victory is won through* (by means of) *many counselors* (see 11:14). The deliberations of many counselors, who with a spirit of humility learn from each other, guarantee that the finally agreed-upon strategy will succeed.

Saying 23 (24:7)

This saying acts as a caution to the preceding saying (vv. 5–6) by pointing out the incompetence of fools to speak on public policy issues. Thus, it implicitly commends becoming competently wise. Verset A states the cause. *Wisdom is too high for fools* means that they lack wings of piety and humility that will enable them to soar high enough to attain the heavenly wisdom needed for public affairs (see 8:15–16). Verset B states the consequences. *In the gate*, where public policy is formed (see 1:21), *they must not open their mouths*. Fools must not be allowed to shape public policy or settle disputes. Having rejected revealed wisdom, they are not competent to speak authoritatively and constructively. If they had prudence—which they don't—they would keep their mouths shut (17:28).

Saying 24 (24:8–9)

Verses 8–9 are connected by the catchword "scheme." This saying also functions as a caveat to saying 22 and escalates the sage's evaluation in saying 23 that the fool must keep silent (v. 7) to the public's condemnation of a schemer whose roots are in folly. The divine evaluation that such scheming is sin (v. 9) justifies the public's censure.

8 *As for those who plan to do evil* describes plotters who coldly plot to further themselves at the expense of others. Their cold calculations to defraud society show that they are neither intellectually dull nor emotionally impulsive. Verset B states the consequence: *they will be named "Schemer,"* a moniker given them by the community that despises them (see 21:24). To be saddled with a bad name means becoming a pariah.

9 Whereas the derivatives of wisdom are strength and strategy, the derivatives of *the schemes that come from folly* (see p. 48) *are sin*. Those schemes are rooted in being a *mocker* (see pp. 48–49). This verse escalates the public's disapproval of fools from branding them "schemers" (v. 8) to regarding them as *an abomination* (see 3:32). A healthy society regards them as such because "sin" signifies transgressions against *I AM*, who establishes a well-ordered society.

Saying 25 (24:10–12)

The catchword "strength" links this saying with saying 22 (vv. 5–6). The strength derived from inspired wisdom is needed especially in crises. If fortified strength signals a person's wisdom (v. 5), then meager strength in crisis signifies the lack or loss of wisdom (vv. 10–12). The saying is connected with sayings 23 (v. 7) and 24 (vv. 8–9), which pertain to antisocial behavior, warning youth against complicity with them by passivity. The saying is unified by specifying "the time of crisis" (v. 10) as when people are "being taken to death" (v. 11). It also specifies "if you show yourself lax" (v. 10) as self-talk that excuses oneself from helping in the crisis (v. 12).

10 The sage uses shame to motivate the son to obtain and show wisdom's strength. To *show yourself lax* is a symptom that *your strength*—and so your wisdom (see v. 5)—*is meager,* qualitatively and quantitatively. The lack of resolute strength is due to cowardice, fear, indolence, or carelessness. *The time of crisis* (see 11:8) refers to the distress of others (see vv. 11–12). Conduct in crisis reveals a person's strength or lack of it. "It is . . . in adverse circumstances that [a person's] powers of endurance are stretched and an estimate of his toughness and stamina can be made."[12] In sum, v. 10 spurs the son to be courageous and deliver the perishing in their time of need (vv. 11–12).

11 In vv. 11–12, the sage motivates the son to show courage against those who victimize the innocent by threatening them with death. *Deliver those being taken to death* commands him to meet his moral obligation to those threatened with death. *Even* signals that 11b is epexegetical. *Hold back* (save or spare) *those swaying* (tottering and about to fall off). *Slaughter,* the killing of a perceived enemy, is ethically neutral. But v. 12 shows that, here, the slaughter is a crime that God will punish and so, implicitly, it is murder. The admonition does not specify how the innocent are slaughtered and asks the son to determine the appropriate means of deliverance (e.g., law, force, or ransom). The saying exemplifies any situation in which the wise have an obligation to deliver innocent people from criminals.

12. McKane, *Proverbs,* 400.

12 To the injustice of not helping the helpless (v. 11), this verse adds the injustice of lying to escape liability. *If you say* introduces the hypothetical lie of ignorance as the excuse for ignoring the admonition. *We knew nothing* uses the plural to signal that the defendant is part of a group. Also, it obviates the potential question, if the son felt incapable to help, why he did not call on others for assistance. The antecedent of *about this* is the fact that the innocent victims were "being taken to death." Verset B demolishes the lie. The rhetorical question *does not* expects an emphatic positive answer (see 14:22). *He who weighs motives (I AM;* see 16:2) *discern* (see 1:2; 2:5). *[The truth]* is added to represent the unstated object of "discern," namely whether it was cowardice or ignorance. The description of *I AM* as *him who protects your life* prepares the way for his just retribution. *And* having discerned motives *will he not repay people according to their conduct?* In sum, the omnicompetent Sovereign will act justly, unlike the passive coward. If the son turns away from helping victims, *I AM*, who protects their lives, will turn away from helping him. Fox comments, "God, who protects *you*, cares that you defend others."[13]

SAYINGS 26–30: PROHIBITIONS AGAINST INVOLVEMENT WITH THE WICKED (24:13–22)

> [13]Eat honey, my son, because it is good,
>> and honey from the comb is sweet on your palate;
> [14]so know wisdom is like honey for your life.
>> If you find wisdom, then there is a blessed future,
>> and your hope will not be cut off.
> [15]Do not lay an ambush as a wicked person against the dwelling
>>> place of the righteous;
>> do not plunder their resting place.
> [16]For if the righteous fall seven times, then they rise;
>> but the wicked stumble in calamity.
> [17]When your enemies fall, do not rejoice;
>> when they stumble, do not let your heart shout in exultation;
> [18]otherwise I AM will see,
>> and it will be evil in his eyes;
>> and he will turn away his wrath from them.
> [19]Do not fret because of those who forge evil;
>> do not envy the wicked;

---

13. Fox, *Proverbs 10–31*, 747.

²⁰for the evil person has no blessed future;
>the lamp of the wicked will be snuffed out.
²¹Fear *I AM,* my son, and the king;
>with [intriguing] officials do not get involved.
²²Because disaster from them suddenly appears,
>and who knows what ruin the two of them can inflict?

The final subunit of the Thirty Sayings also consists of five sayings, the first of which, implicitly and as is typical, encourages the son to obtain wisdom. All five sayings are proverb pairs consisting of double admonitions or prohibitions in the odd verses (vv. 13, 15, 17, 19, 21) with reasons in the even verses (vv. 14, 16, 18, 20, 22). The endearing term "my son" frames the subunit (vv. 13a, 21a). After the implicit admonition to obtain wisdom, the subunit forbids involvement with the wicked. The stakes are high. Eternal life awaits the wise (vv. 14a, 16a) and eternal death the wicked (vv. 16b, 20, 22). The three middle sayings are linked by the word *ra'* ("evil," "calamity").

Saying 26 (24:13–14)

The introductory saying consists of two positive admonitions with reasons: eat honey because it is beneficial and good (v. 13), and know wisdom because it promises eternal life (v. 14). "So" shows that the first command functions as an analogue of the second. The metaphor of honey for wisdom has three facets: (1) physically eating is analogous to spiritually "knowing" (internalizing); (2) wisdom, like honey, is medicinal but, remarkably, tastes sweet (see 16:24); and (3) the palate, the seat of taste (v. 13b), matches "life" (v. 14b), the seat of vitality. In sum, internalizing honey and wisdom alike is pleasurable and quickening.[14] But the analogy breaks down in v. 14b because, unlike honey, wisdom's pleasure is eternal.[15]

13 *Eat* entails a command to have a right relationship with God (cf. Gen. 2:16). Food is God's good gift, and eating and joy go together (Deut. 28:17–18, 31, 33, passim; Prov. 13:25). Though the command functions as a metaphor, the father also intends his son to eat *honey* literally *because it is good.* It is medicinal and pleasurable. Verset B escalates and underscores honey's delight: *honey from the comb* (cf. 16:24) *is sweet on your palate,* which is the seat of taste.

14 *Know* (experience and internalize) revealed *wisdom* (see 1:2). *Is like honey*

---

14. God's word is also likened to honey in Pss. 19:10; 119:103; Ezek. 3:3; Rev. 10:9–10.
15. Cf. Malbim, *Proverbs,* 248.

glosses the implied ellipsis. *For your life* (*nepeš*; see "*Nepeš*," p. 32). The reason (v. 14b) essentially repeats 23:18 but transforms it into a conditional clause: *if you find wisdom, then . . .* The outcome of internalizing wisdom is unending delight.

Saying 27 (24:15–16)

The subunit's first double prohibition (v. 15) prohibits partnering with the wicked to plunder the righteous (see 1:10–19). The rationale (v. 16) entails that the wicked may not get their just punishment until the end, when the righteous rise from their being plundered. In other words, before they attain eternal life, the wise/righteous may first be utterly ruined (see "Does Proverbs Promise Too Much," pp. 44–45). This is the pattern for many saints (see Heb. 11), and it is best exemplified in the death and resurrection of Jesus Christ. Both threat and promise demand faith that God upholds his moral order (cf. 3:5–6; 22:23; 23:11; 24:18, 21).

15 *Do not lay an ambush* (see 1:11, 18; 7:12; 12:6) is escalated to *do not plunder* (see 11:3), thus including the property of the righteous. *As a wicked person* hypothetically pictures the son as an apostate. *The dwelling place of the righteous* is their place of provisioning. *Their resting place* is their place of repose and restoration.

16 *For if* segues into the rationale and introduces the condition. The antithetical parallelism juxtaposes "the righteous person" (= *the righteous*; Heb. sg.; see "Ethical Terms for the Wise and Righteous," pp. 36–37) with a plurality of *the wicked* and the righteous person falling and rising with the falling and not rising again of the wicked. *Fall* here probably refers to violent destruction effected by the ambush of the pillaging wicked. *Seven*, a symbolic number, signifies special sacredness (Exod. 23:15; 25:37; 29:30) or completeness—the totality of a cycle (6:31; 9:1; 26:16, 25). The intensification shows that the righteous are subject to unmerited suffering. But although their lives appear to end in final ruin, it is reversed: *then they rise*. Since the righteous rise after a violent and final fall, their recovery means their resurrection from death. By contrast, the wicked *stumble* and fall *in calamity* (see 1:33) from which they will never rise.

Saying 28 (24:17–18)

The previous saying promised that the wicked will fall (v. 16b); this saying prohibits the son from gloating over their punishment. Gloating is contrary to praise of the One from whom all blessings flow and exalts self by denigrating the defeated. God would rather suspend his retributive justice than tolerate abhorrent gloating. Rejoicing is appropriate when the wise celebrate God's establishment of justice by eliminating the wicked (see 1:20–33).

17 *When your enemies fall, do not rejoice* is essentially repeated; albeit more emphatically, in the synonymous parallel: *when they stumble, do not let your heart shout in exultation.* Joy for the triumph of the righteous over the wicked is good (see 1:20–33), but cold and calloused rejoicing at another's misfortune is evil.

18 *Otherwise* signals that v. 18 provides the validation for the double prohibition of v. 17. The reason the son should reject cruel and arrogant schadenfreude is to avoid the situation that, if disobeyed, will result in the wicked getting off the hook—at least temporarily. Each clause of this verse presumes a divine attribute, moving from God's omniscience (v. 18aα) to his moral sensibility (v. 18aβ) to his righteous and just response (v. 18b). First, *I AM will see and,* consequently, *it will be evil in his eyes.* God's moral character eschews all cruelty, arrogance, and cynicism toward people (cf. Obad. 10–12; Zech. 1:15). *And* subsequently *he will turn away his wrath from them* (the enemies). Some think that the purpose of the proverb is to explain how to ensure that one's enemy receives retribution, a notion they consider cold and unpleasant.[16] In truth, the proverb prohibits gloating because it pollutes justice and thwarts it by the introduction of another sin. Positively, the son should weep, not rejoice, at the tragic desecration and destruction of God's image (cf. Job 10:8–9). Other texts even enjoin positive assistance to a needy enemy (Exod. 23:4–5; Prov. 25:21; Matt. 5:38–48; Rom. 12:20–21). In his mercy for the wronged, God establishes justice; but he has no pleasure in the death of the wicked.

Saying 29 (24:19–20)

This saying protects the preceding one from misunderstanding. Even if the judgment of the wicked is temporarily delayed due to the son's gloating, in the end they will be annihilated. *I AM's* stay of execution is only long enough to deprive the gloaters of their malicious schadenfreude. That leads to the prohibition not to envy their temporary prosperity. The saying escalates the fall of the wicked (vv. 16b–17) to the eternal darkness that befalls them.

19 *Do not fret* means not to get burned up emotionally (become angry). The same form of the verb occurs also in Ps. 37:1, 7, 8, and, as here, in parallel with *do not envy* (see 23:17) *the wicked* (cf. Ps. 37:1). The parallels suggest that envy ignites one's internal fury. *Because of those who forge evil* (see 17:4) implies that evildoers prosper. Paupers are not envied. But envying the ill-gotten gain of the wicked is foolish, since God will destroy them, as the next verse makes clear.

16. E.g., McKane, *Proverbs,* 404.

20 *For* segues into the reason: *the evil person has no blessed future* (see 23:18a). *The lamp of the wicked will be snuffed out* is a divine passive; *I AM*, the righteous avenger, is the unexpressed Agent (see v. 21). This metaphor for premature death repeats 13:9 (see 20:20). When *I AM* extinguishes the lamp of the wicked, their ill-gotten gain will be righteously redistributed. No sensible person envies self-destructive property. In sum, keeping the extinction of their lamp in view will extinguish burning envy.

Saying 30 (24:21–22)

The final saying builds on the preceding one, pointing to *I AM* and his king as the agents who deliver retribution. Both will render to rebellious royals such certain, sudden, and sweeping disaster that no one knows its limits. The double admonitions of v. 21 are matched by the double reasons in v. 22.

21 The father's love for his son prompts the admonition *fear* I AM (see "Fear of *I AM*," pp. 38–39), *my son* (see 1:8). *And* also fear *the king*, God's vice-regent on earth to effect his rule, dispensing life and death (see 16:10–16). The admonition to fear the king as one fears God is unusual (see 1 Pet. 2:17) and shows that the sage regarded the king's earthly throne as the legitimate representation of God's heavenly throne (cf. Matt. 17:24–27; Rom. 13:1–5; Titus 3:1). The proverb is fulfilled in Jesus Christ, the King of kings. Fearing *I AM* and his king means one must *not get involved with [intriguing] officials*—to wit, with rebels who seek to grab power and position through intrigue (cf. 30:32–33). The admonitions imply that the way to advancement is to revere legitimate authority and avoid involvement in plots to undermine it and seize power for oneself.

22 *Disaster* (see 1:26) *from them suddenly appears.* The punishment that *I AM* and the king inflict will descend unexpectedly. Verse 22b represents their punishment as being of unknown limits. *Who knows* here means that no one knows. *What ruin the two of them* (*I AM* and the king) *can inflict.*

Further Sayings of the Wise
(24:23–34)

For the structure of this collection, see "Structure," pp. 4–5.

SUPERSCRIPTION (24:23A)

²³ᵃThese also are sayings of the wise.

The Hebrew of the prose superscription contains only three words, which in the Masoretic tradition is too short to justify a separate verse. *Also* adds this second collection of sayings authored by the wise (cf. 22:17) to the proverbs of Solomon (10:1), probably with his imprimatur.

JUDGING AT COURT (24:23B–25)

²³ᵇTo show partiality in giving a verdict is not good.
²⁴Those who say to the guilty, "You are innocent," peoples will
    curse them;
  communities will strike them with a curse.
²⁵Those who establish what is right, it will be pleasant;
  on them will come a blessing that brings good.

    The first saying pertains to rendering just judgments and the community's contrasting responses to the unfair and fair judge. The former is cursed, the latter blessed. The contrasting responses are the reason why it is not good to show partiality in court.

    23b This rare one-line proverb uses a litotes to assert forcefully that partiality in justice is neither admirable nor beneficial. The Hebrew glossed *to show partiality* (cf. Deut. 1:17; 16:19; Prov. 28:21) literally means "to take note of a face." The blindfold on the well-known image of Lady Justice symbolizes the danger of showing partiality in the administration of justice by taking note of a person rather than a person's deeds. *In giving a verdict* points to a court situation and suggests the original addressees were budding officials and courtiers (see "Setting of Composition," pp. 18–20). The litotes *is not good* is an emphatic understatement; that is to say, giving such a verdict is bad (see 16:29; 17:26; 18:5; 20:23).

24 Quoting an unjust judge's verdict of acquittal dramatizes the partiality of the unjust judge. *Guilty* and *innocent* gloss terms that, outside of a judicial context, are normally translated by "wicked" and "righteous" respectively (for "wicked," see pp. 45–46; for "righteous," see pp. 36–37). *Peoples will curse them* assumes God's common grace that enables people to distinguish right from wrong (see 11:26). *Communities*, a stock-in-trade parallel to "peoples," *will strike them with a curse* connotes that they look to God to punish the unjust judge, whom no godless human authority punishes.

25 Conversely, in common grace, the community blesses *those who establish what is right*. The antecedent of *it will be pleasant* (see 3:17) is defined in verset B as God's *blessing* (see 10:6; 11:26) *that brings good* (see 2:20). By praying God's blessing on those who administer them according to divine law, the people promote the integrity and orderliness of the community.

CORRECT SPEAKING (24:26)

> [26]One kisses lips—
> the one who gives an honest reply.

Honest judging now gives way to honest speaking (26b), which is compared to a kiss, the symbolic expression of love (26a). *The one who gives an honest reply* refers to a person of candor and truth. *Kisses the lips* expresses a strong bond of affection and solidarity between the two participants. The phrase is unique in the Bible (cf. Song 4:11; 5:13), but Meinhold verifies the use of "kisses the lips" in Sumer and Ugarit and during the New Kingdom period in Egypt.[1] Fox thinks it is synonymous with "kisses the mouth" (Gen. 41:40). There, Pharaoh says to Joseph, "All my people will kiss your mouth."[2] This saying teaches the disciple to express his devotion to his partner by giving a straight answer.

1. Meinhold, *Sprüche*, 411, citing O. Keel, *Das Hohelied*, Zürcher Bibelkommentare (Zürich: 1986), 48–50.
2. Fox, *Proverbs 10–31*, 773.

POSITIVE BEHAVIOR IN WORK (24:27)

²⁷Establish your out-of-doors work,
  and prepare it in the fields for yourself.
  After [doing that], then build your household.

No reason is given for the admonition to establish one's source of income before building a household because common sense validates it. *Establish* (make ready and fix; see 16:9) *your out-of-doors work*, narrowed to *prepare it* (cf. Job 15:24) *in the fields* refers to plowing and planting the fields and orchards so that they produce fruit. It is *for yourself* because it is in one's own best interest. Only *after [doing that]*, but just as surely, *build your household* (see 3:33; 11:29). Building a household requires wealth, and that requires timely work (see 10:4–5). Farming is an exemplar of work, standing in for any occupation.

WRONG SPEAKING (24:28–29)

²⁸Do not be a witness against your neighbor without reason;
  you would not convince with your lips, would you?
²⁹Do not say, "As they have done to me, I will do to them;
  I will pay those people back according to their conduct."

Though vv. 28 and 29 constitute one saying, each verse is a distinct admonition. Verse 28 prohibits needlessly becoming a hostile witness against a neighbor, and verse 29 prohibits getting even with a neighbor.

28 Verset B of this synonymously parallel pair concretizes verset A. *Do not be* (see 22:26; 23:31) *a witness* (see 12:17) *against your neighbor* (see 3:28) *without reason* (without legal obligation to testify). Eyewitnesses do have a legal obligation to testify, but this warrantless witness abuses the legal process to incriminate another as a means to get revenge (see v. 29). The rhetorical question, *You would not convince* (presumably the triers of fact) *with your lips* (that is, your mere words), *would you?*, implies a negative answer. According to 26:17, meddling in someone else's dispute is folly.

29 This verse defines the warrantless witness of the previous verse as falsely testifying to get revenge. *Do not say, "As they have done to me, I will do to them"* envisions seeking present revenge for a past offense. Verset B specifies the act of revenge: *I will pay those people back according to their conduct.* The law allowed the principle of *lex talionis* (an "eye for eye") for community justice (Exod. 23–25; Lev. 24:19–20; Deut. 19:19) but not for personal revenge. An offended party must still love a neighbor (Lev. 19:18) and commit the offense to God and his magistrate to adjudicate (see 16:4–7, 10–15).

BAD BEHAVIOR IN WORK (24:30–34)

³⁰I passed by the field of the sluggard,
> even the vineyard of one who lacked sense.
³¹And behold, the whole of it had grown up as all sorts of nettles;
> its surface was covered with all kinds of weeds,
> and all its stone wall was thrown down.
³²And I saw; I paid attention;
> I observed; I accepted a lesson.
³³A little sleep, a little slumber,
> a little folding of the arms to lie down,
³⁴and poverty will come on you like a vagrant,
> and scarcity like an armed man.

An anonymous striding sage (see 24:23) passes the vineyard of the snoring sluggard and observes a hostile creation marching to attack the sluggard. A once-verdant vineyard is now a web of weeds, and its vigilant wall is now a useless stack of stones (vv. 30–31). If impersonal creation attacks sluggards, how much more their spiritual adversaries. In v. 32, the center line of the poem, the sage engages his mind to understand what he observed in vv. 30–31. From his observation, he infers a lesson that he articulates in vv. 33–34: untimely naps enable personified poverty, which never sleeps, to plunder all you inherited. The wasted vineyard is exemplary of any inheritance that is lost through negligence. The lesson is similar to that of 6:10–11.

30 Through synonymous parallelism representing the sage's personal encounter (*I passed*), *the field of the sluggard* is specified and clarified in as *even the vineyard of one who lacked sense* (see 6:32). The vineyard in particular was chosen to illustrate the need for industry due to the painstaking labor it took to create, maintain, and vigilantly protect such a valuable field (cf. Isa. 5:1–6).

31 *And behold* presents the audience with a dramatically new and present perspective on the field. *The whole of it* without exception *had grown up as all sorts of nettles*. Hebrew "nettles" (*qimməśōnîm*) appears in two other contexts of devastating judgment (cf. Isa. 34:13; Hos. 9:6). The synonymously parallel *its surface was covered with all kinds of weeds* underscores the hostile takeover of the vines by weeds. Hebrew "weeds" (*ḥărullîm*) appears in relation to *I AM*'s devastation in Job 30:7 and Zeph. 2:9. If the field is not weeded in the spring, then weeds take over the cursed ground (cf. Gen. 3:17–19). All the heirs need to do is to maintain what their fathers have bequeathed them. But sluggards have no brains to see that and preserve their lives. *All its stone wall was thrown down* by the law of entropy, personified as a troop of marauders.[3]

32 The center line forms the transition from observation (vv. 30–31) to lesson (vv. 33–34). Verset A, *I saw; I paid attention*, is synonymously paired with verset B: *I observed; I accepted a lesson.*

33–34 These verses essentially repeat 6:10–11. See the exposition there.

3. Ralph Waldo Emerson ("Man the Reformer," in *Harvard Classics*, vol. 5 [New York: Grolier, 1937], 48–49) notes that "every species of property is preyed on by its own enemies, as iron by rust; timber by rot; cloth by moths; provisions by mold, putridity, or vermin. . . . And whoever takes any of these things into his possession, takes the charge of defending them from this troop of enemies."

Proverbs of Solomon from Hezekiah's Men
(25:1–29:27)

For the structure of this collection, see "Structure," p. 5.[1]

SUPERSCRIPTION (25:1)

[1]These also are proverbs of Solomon, which the men of Hezekiah
the king of Judah copied and collected.

These also are proverbs of Solomon (see 1:1; 10:1) suggests that the final editor
(see "The Final Editor," p. 9) reckoned this collection (chs. 25–27) an appendix to Solomon's own collections (10:1–22:16; 22:17–24:22). *Which the men of
Hezekiah the king of Judah* (715 to 686 B.C.) *copied and collected*—that is, transmitted and arranged as a unified appendix. The proverbs in 25:2–25 were likely
originally addressed to budding court officials, a setting the superscription
confirms (see "Setting of Composition," pp. 18–20). The Lord Jesus may have
instantiated 25:6–7 to guests at a wedding feast (Luke 14:7–11), and Jude (v. 12)
applied the image in 25:14 to unproductive people.

THE COURT HIERARCHY AND THE CONFLICT OF THE RIGHTEOUS
AND THE WICKED (25:2–27)

[2]The glory of God is to hide a matter,
    but the glory of kings is to search out a matter.
[3]As for the heavens with reference to height
    and the earth with reference to depth
    and the heart of kings, there is no searching out [of them].

---

1. It cannot be stated strongly enough that our exegesis of Prov. 25–27 draws heavily on
Van Leeuwen, "Context and Meaning."

⁴Remove the dross from silver,
  and a vessel comes forth for the silversmith.
⁵Remove a wicked official before a king
  that his throne may be established by righteousness.
⁶Do not honor yourself before a king,
  and in the place of great people do not stand.
⁷Better one says to you, "Come up here,"
  than one humiliate you before a noble.
What your eyes have seen,
  ⁸do not bring hastily to trial;
otherwise, what will you do in its end,
  when your peer puts you to shame?
⁹Plead your case with your peer,
  but do not divulge another's confidence,
¹⁰otherwise an arbiter will pronounce you guilty,
  and the accusation against you never depart.
¹¹Apples of gold in a silver sculpture
  is a decision made appropriate to its circumstance.
¹²A gold earring, even an ornament of fine gold,
  is a wise arbiter's rebuke upon a listening ear.
¹³Like the coolness of snow at the time of harvest
  is a trustworthy messenger to the one who sends him;
  he refreshes his master.
¹⁴Clouds and wind and no rain
  is a person who boasts of a gift never given.
¹⁵Through patience a ruler is persuaded,
  and a soft tongue shatters a bone.
¹⁶[If] you have found honey, eat [only] what you require;
  otherwise, you will have more than enough of it and vomit it.
¹⁷Make your foot scarce, [and turn away] from your neighbor's
    house;
  otherwise, they will have more than enough of you and hate
    you.
¹⁸A war club or a sword or a sharpened arrow
  is one who testifies against a neighbor as a false witness.
¹⁹A decaying tooth or a turned foot
  is reliance on a treacherous person in the time of adversity.
²⁰One who puts off a garment on a cold day,
  [one who pours] vinegar on a wound,

357

[is] one who sings songs to a heavy heart.
²¹If those who hate you are hungry, give them food to eat;
and if they are thirsty, give them water to drink;
²²for burning coals you are taking [and heaping] on their head,
and *I AM* will repay you.
²³Like a north wind that brings forth rain,
a sly tongue [brings] a face struck by a curse.
²⁴Better to dwell on a corner of the roof
than to share a house with a contentious wife.
²⁵Cold water to a weary person
and a good report from a distant land.
²⁶A muddled spring, a ruined fountain
[is] a righteous person who sways before the wicked.
²⁷To eat honey excessively is not good,
nor is it honorable to search out weighty matters.

After the superscription, ch. 25 can be divided by poetics into two units (vv. 2–15, 16–27). The inclusio formed by "king" and "ruler" (vv. 2, 15) frames the first subunit and one formed by "honey" and "eat" (vv. 16, 27) frames the second. Thematically, the first subunit concerns matters of the royal court; the second explores human conflict in general. *Kābôd* ("glory" or "honor") forms an inclusio around the entire section (vv. 2, 27).

Introduction (25:2–5)

Two proverb pairs trumpeting the unit's twin themes introduce this section: vv. 2–3 establish the God-king-subject hierarchy, and vv. 4–5 present the fundamental, unremitting, and all-encompassing conflict between the righteous and the wicked.

God-King-Subject Hierarchy (25:2–3)

The first pair brings the glory of God and kings into close proximity while subordinating kings to God. Both obtain glory by their inscrutability: God by concealing his wisdom in his acts of creation and of history (v. 2a), kings by thoroughly searching out affairs of state (v. 2b). God's inscrutability even to the king, however, sets him high above the king, while the king's incomprehensible knowledge and impenetrable motives set him high above his subjects (v. 3). In sum, vv. 2 and 3 set up a hierarchy of wisdom and power: God, king, subjects.

2 *Glory of God* means the social weight that comes to or is bestowed on him. *To hide a matter* means to conceal it from sight. The use of the name "God" (*'ĕlōhîm*) instead of YHWH, and possibly also the reference to the heavens and earth in v. 3, may suggest "matter" refers to his acts of creation. Since the king searches out military, administrative, and judicial matters, God's acts in history may also be in view. *The glory of kings* (see 16:10-15) *is to search out a matter* means that kings achieve social weight by investigating and penetrating human motives and deeds in a judicial setting. To act as a wise judge is an essential part of the king's glory (see 8:15), which entails the skill to search out the core of a conflict.

3 The king who thoroughly investigates others is himself so lofty that he is inscrutable to his subjects. *The heavens* refers to the dome-like sky. *With reference to height* emphasizes loftiness (cf. 30:4). *The earth* together with "the heavens" is a merism for the vast, complex cosmos. *With reference to depth* does not refer to the underworld but emphasizes the apparently limitless extent of the earth below human feet. *And* links *the heart of kings* with the unfathomable cosmos. *There is no searching* (see v. 2b). The parallelism between the vast cosmos and the king's heart takes the breath away. As in 16:10-15, the ideal king is in view. So also, the person with the Holy Spirit investigates all things (1 Cor. 2:15-16).

The Conflict of the Righteous and the Wicked in Court (25:4-5)

This proverb pair advances the wise king's activity from his investigating matters of the state (v. 2) to his elimination of corrupt officials. The comment about purifying silver (v. 4) illustrates the real topic of purifying the king's officials in v. 5. As the silversmith can only produce a vessel with silver purified of dross, so the king's throne (his dynasty) can endure only when wicked officials are eliminated (cf. 20:8, 26). A solid building cannot be built of marred material.

4 *Remove* (or "if you remove") *the dross from silver, and* (or "then") *a vessel comes forth for* (to the benefit of) *the silversmith.* The proverb directly connects the cause (purifying the silver) with the consequence (the beneficial vessel) to emphasize the fundamental necessity of purification.

5 *Remove* (see v. 4a) *a wicked official before a king that his throne* (the chair that symbolizes his reign; cf. 2 Sam. 3:10; 7:13, 16; 14:9) *may be established* (see 16:3, 12) *by righteousness.* This proverb likewise directly connects the cause and consequence to emphasize the necessity of removing all corrupt officials to establish an enduring dynasty (cf. 2 Sam. 7:14; 1 Kgs 2:24, 33, 46; 8:25; 9:5-7).

A Decalogue of Proverbs for Courtiers (25:6–15)

The next ten proverbs pertain to the education of courtiers and fall into two equal halves: admonitions (vv. 6–10) and sayings (vv. 11–15). Except for v. 15, they consist of proverb pairs.

Admonitions for Courtiers (25:6–10)

6–7a This proverb pair warns the courtier not to take it upon himself to barge into the higher-ranking social spheres of the king and his nobles. It is better that superiors elevate him based on his aptitude than that he overreach his limits and risk a reprimand and shame that will curtail his career prospects (cf. Luke 14:8–11). *Do not honor yourself before a king* prohibits self-exalting oneself to a rank or dignity one does not have. *The place of great people* is where people of rank and influence congregate. *Do not stand* cautions the courtier not to join in the activities of men of rank and influence on his own initiative. *For* (v. 7a) substantiates the prohibition. *Better one* (a superior official) *says to you, "Come up here* (to the higher position of ranking people)," *than one humiliate you before a noble* by demoting the courtier to a lower status (see 16:19). Promotion by superiors creates confidence that one has merited the higher position. Self-promotion leads to insecurity from the fear that one may be discovered to lack merit, resulting in demotion. The proverb encourages courtiers to advance themselves rightly (cf. 1 Sam. 15:17; 18:18; 1 Kgs. 1:5, 30; Matt. 18:1–4; John 13:1–15; 3 John 9–10).

7b–8 To humility, this pair adds assiduous preparation. It admonishes against rushing to court with impetuous lawsuits based on partial evidence. *What your* (the courtier's) *eyes have seen, do not bring hastily to trial* because, despite being an eyewitness to a crime, the courtier may have only a keyhole view of the situation and may misinterpret it. It is unclear whether the courtier is the victim or the litigant in the case. *Otherwise* points to the potential harm to the courtier's career if he loses the case. The rhetorical debasing question *what will you do in its end* assumes the courtier loses the case, leading him to gasp, "Nothing!" The courtier's career will be derailed when his opponent shows that the courtier jumped to conclusions without fully investigating what he saw. He will lose his case *when your peer* (the opposing litigant) *puts you to shame.* "Shame" denotes public dishonor or ignominy due to a failed risk. Our Lord advocated correcting an offending brother in private first, then with a witness, and only then to the church (Matt. 18:15–17).

9–10 To punctilious preparation, this pair adds confidentiality. Keeping confidence is more important than winning a case. *Plead your case with your peer* denotes arguing a case in order to win it. *But* presents a situation that may exclude arguing one's case, namely, when one must *not divulge another's confidence* (see 11:13). One should not smear another's name to clear one's own or someone else's. "There is no success which is achieved at the price of our own integrity or someone else's hurt."[2] *An arbiter* refers to the judge hearing the case, who upon recognizing the breached confidence *will pronounce you guilty* of disloyalty. *And the accusation* (an injurious report) of disloyalty *against you* will *never depart*. Betraying a confidence will ruin one's career.

Sayings for Courtiers (25:11–15)

11–12 To confidentiality (vv. 9–10), add appropriate speech and reproof. Kidner captures the thematic connection of this pair: "Finely said [v. 11], finely taken [v. 12]."[3] The harmony between a decision and its circumstance bestows beauty and value on the finely crafted pronouncement (v. 11), and the harmony between the rebuke and its acceptance enhances its beauty and value (v. 12). A proper decision (v. 11b) is likened to gold apples and the appropriate circumstance to a silver sculpture. *Apples of gold in a silver sculpture* means that the artist either engraved a sculpted figure or laid the apples in it. *A decision made appropriate to its circumstance* is a decision given at the right time and in the right way (cf. 15:23). The comparison to the apple refers to the loveliness of a proper decision and the gold to its great value.

The matching proverb (v. 12) implicitly compares the sage who reproves a wrongdoer to an ornate gold earring and the one who listens to the ear that wears it. *A ring of gold* probably designates a man's earring, not a woman's nose ring. *Even an ornament of fine gold* qualifies the earring as the work of an artist. *Is a wise arbiter's decision* (that is, his rebuke) *upon a listening ear* (a person whose heart engages what it hears).

13–14 To appropriate speech and reproof this pair adds reliability, represented positively by the reliable envoy (v. 13) and negatively by the unreliable windbag (v. 14). The trustworthy envoy is likened to *the coolness of snow*. During the hot summers, laborers brought snow and ice from the high mountains and stored them in snow houses or snow caves to cool their drinks. The Bible reports a fatal heat stroke *at the time of harvest* (cf. 2 Kgs. 4:18–20). *A trustworthy envoy* is dispatched to investigate and report on facts. *He re-*

---

2. Plaut, *Proverbs*, 258.
3. Kidner, *Proverbs*, 158.

freshes his master. Just as cold water invigorates the harvesters for work, so knowing that an envoy will faithfully discharge his mission invigorates *the one who sends him* for his duties.

The complementary proverb (v. 14) contrasts the faithful envoy to one who reneges on giving a gift. The parallelism matches a man *who boasts of a gift* with *clouds and wind,* which are a harbinger of rain, and matches *he did not give* with *no rain.* The comparison suggests that the one who reneges has vociferously promised his gift, creating great expectations, and then sunk them in disappointment. Since rain is essential for life, the comparison may also connote that the gift is essential for the well-being of the deceived. Presumably, the boaster deceives victims to defraud them and thus, instead of giving life, takes it away (cf. 2 Pet. 2:19; Jude 12).

15 This single proverb, after seven proverb pairs, closes the decalogue with reference to a "ruler," forming a semantic link with vv. 2–3 on the topic of the king. To appropriate speech and reproof, this verse adds patience and gentleness. *Through patience a ruler is persuaded* avers that the courtier can bring the ruler to his way of thinking by his longsuffering, open, and warm disposition. *And* adds *a soft* (or "gentle"; see 15:1) *tongue,* which refers to speech that does not grate or hurt. *Shatters a bone* is a metaphor for "is persuaded" (cf. 14:17; 15:1; 16:14; 1 Cor. 9:20–22; Gal. 5:22–24; 2 Tim. 2:24–26). Garret comments, "Fracturing the bones here refers to breaking down [a person's] deepest, most hardened resistance to an idea."[4]

General Human Conflicts (25:16–27)

Though the second subunit pertains to general human conflict, v. 18 returns to the court in a strict sense.[5]

Resolving Conflicts (25:16–22)

Apart from the positive admonition in vv. 21–22 to resolve human conflict, vv. 16–22 present human conflict negatively and without resolution.

16–17 This proverb pair promotes the virtue of moderation and restraint. Excess can make even good things like honey (v. 16) and neighborliness (v. 17) become loathsome. Verse 16a admonishes one not to overindulge, and v. 16b gives the reason. *If you have found honey* refers to wild, uncultivated honey,

---

4. Garrett, *Proverbs,* 207.
5. See p. 356, n. 1.

accidently discovered and so all the more delightful (see Judg. 14:8–9, 14, 18; 1 Sam. 14:26–27). As *I AM* commanded humanity to eat the good food in the Garden (Gen. 2:16), so the sage commands the son to *eat* the good honey (see 24:13), but he qualifies the amount by *what you require*. The reason: *Otherwise, you will have more than enough of it*, eating beyond the point of satisfaction, *and vomit it*. "Too much of anything is good for nothing" (cf. Sir. 37:29).

Verse 17 applies the principle of moderation and self-control learned by experience in the realm of gastronomy to a warning about being a good neighbor in the social realm. The admonition entails keeping one's visits rare and leaving a neighbor longing for, not loathing, one's companionship. It assumes that neighborliness, like honey, is good and beneficial to both parties and does not aim to chill friendship. *Make your foot* (a synecdoche for the whole person) *scarce* (low in availability and high in value) *[and turn away] from your neighbor's house*. The reason: *Otherwise, they will have more than enough of you and hate you*. Similar English-language proverbs are "Familiarity breeds contempt" and "Guests, like fish, stink after three days." → *lol* !

18–20 In addition to sound plays, the next three proverbs are linked by the same syntax (a figurative comment involving more than one feature in verset A and the topic in verset B) and by the theme of conflict between neighbors. The theme is developed by katabasis, descending from the perjurer (v. 18) to the undependable (v. 19) to the tactless (v. 20), all of whom should be avoided.

Verse 18 denounces the treachery of a false witness (see 6:19; 14:5; 19:5, 9, 28; 24:18; cf. Exod. 20:16; Deut. 5:20) by comparing a false witness to three deadly assault weapons (v. 18a) to make the disciple shrink in horror at the thought of perjury. *One who testifies against a neighbor as a false witness* is depicted as one who beats out a neighbor's brains with *a war club*, as piercing a neighbor's bowels with *a sword*, and as killing a neighbor with *a sharpened arrow*.

Verse 19 shifts from the actively treacherous to a fair-weather neighbor who passively fails to live up to expectations in a crisis. *Reliance on a treacherous person* (one who reneges on promises) *in the time of adversity*, when faithfulness is most needed, is compared to a *decaying tooth*, on which one cannot bite, and a *turned* (lame) *foot*, on which one cannot walk. Such "friends" are worse than worthless; they are frustrating and painful.

Verse 20 showcases the insensitive and inept speaker by implicitly comparing the incompatibility of one singing joyful songs to a sullen heart to the incongruity of taking off a warm garment on a cold day and to pouring stinging vinegar on a wound. All three foolishly inflict pain with no therapeutic value. The two figurative situations, *one who puts off a garment on a cold day* and *one who pours vinegar on a wound* pertain to senselessly hurting the body. *One who sings songs to a heavy heart* pertains to senselessly hurting the heart. A timely song can be therapeutic (cf. 1 Sam. 16:15-23; 19:9; Job 30:31), but untimely songs are damaging to the spirit (cf. Ps. 137:1-4; Sir. 22:6a). The sensitive know how and when to mourn and how and when to rejoice (Eccl. 3:4; Rom. 12:15; 1 Cor. 12:26; Heb. 13:3).

21-22 This proverb pair instructs one on how to resolve conflicts with neighbors "who hate you," perhaps due to one's own folly. Van Leeuwen observes, "Whereas 'eating' too much causes conflicts in vv. 16-17, giving to eat resolves conflict in vv. 21-22."[6] The proverb admonishes the wise to show sympathy and compassion to a neighbor's plight by meeting the neighbor's urgent need with sympathy and compassion in a tangible way, and immediately. The proverb illustrates the neighbor's plight as the urgent need of food and drink and instantiates the commandment to love neighbors in the very practical way of feeding them (cf. Exod. 23:4-5; Lev. 19:17-18; Job 31:29-32; Prov. 24:17-18). *If those who hate you* (see 25:17) *are hungry, give them food to eat; and if they are thirsty, give them water to drink.* "Water," instead of wine, suggests that the disciple should meet the enemy's basic needs (cf. 9:5; 25:25).

For signals why one should meet an enemy's needs. First, it will bring the person to godly repentance of hating you (v. 22a), and second, *I AM will repay you* (v. 22b). The food and water of v. 21 are now implicitly compared to *burning coals.* The significance of the phrase *taking [and heaping] on their head* is debated. Some scholars think that heaping fiery coals on a person's head is a form of punishment and of appeasing one's need for vengeance. But the parallel, "*I AM* will reward you," negates that interpretation. The book of Proverbs categorically rejects taking personal revenge (17:13; 20:22; 24:17-18). According to most interpreters, "coals of fire" is a morally good deed that pleases *I AM*. The LXX understands it this way and so adds the word "good" to the end of v. 22b: "*I AM* will reward you for your good." The apostle Paul, using the LXX text, forbids the taking of revenge and abstracts from it the principle of overcoming evil with good (Rom. 12:17-21).

Most scholars agree with Augustine and Jerome that the phrase refers to the "burning pangs of shame" felt when good is returned for one's evil—a shame leading to repentance. Morenz points to an Egyptian penitential ritual that validates this view. According to the narrative of Cha-em-wese, the thief Cha-em-wese returned a stolen book by carrying a basin of fiery coals on his head. Carrying the fire signified his remorse, shame, and correction. Israel probably did not practice this ritual, but the metaphor as it existed in

6. Van Leeuwen, "Context and Meaning," 85.

Israel is elucidated by it.[7] The reward from *I AM* is presumably for achieving reconciliation between the two persons involved.[8] Our Lord exemplified and established the precept when he gave his life for his enemies and so reconciled them to God (Rom. 5:8; 2 Cor. 5:17–21).

Unexpected Conflicts (25:23–27)

The first four proverbs of this partial subunit present universal truths with metaphors in their A versets and their topics in their B versets. They consist of a proverb pair using weather imagery and second pair using water imagery. The first pair pertains to unexpected conflicts due to bad speech, and the second contrasts restoration with ruin, again advocating doing good to resolve conflict. Verse 27, a single proverb, concludes the unit.

23 The first proverb compares the unexpected damage of the slanderous tongue (verset B) to the icy blast of a north wind that unexpectedly brings rain (verset A). In Israel, people expected rain from the west wind. The north wind was welcome because it cleared the sky and aided ships traveling south. The point of the comparison *like a north wind that brings forth rain* is that rain from a north wind is hidden and so unexpected and damaging. Hidden slander similarly brings unexpected damage. *A sly tongue [brings]* (gapped) *a face* (the outward manifestation of the inner spirit; see 7:13; 15:13) *struck by a curse* (see 22:14:24:24). Secret speech is by nature malevolent; otherwise, why hide it? When the unsuspecting victim gets wind of the slander, the damaging effects will be writ large on the victim's face.

24 The proverb about the nagging wife repeats 21:9 verbatim. See the exposition there.

25 This proverb compares hearing good news from afar to refreshing a spent person with a drink of cold water. Giving *cold water to a weary person* energizes the person to keep on going (Gen. 16:7; Exod. 17:1–6; Num. 20:11; Judg. 15:18–19). "Weary" (*ʿāyēpâ*) signifies the person is almost completely devoid of energy due to hunger or thirst and so unable to continue living. Such a person desperately needs reviving, and "cold water," which represents the best remedy, will do the trick. This physical remedy functions as a metaphor for the spiritual remedy, to wit, *a good report from a distant land*. To people weary from uncertainty or anxiety about a situation in a far-off place that they cannot control, hearing good news will disperse anxiety and energize them to carry on.

---

7. S. Morenz, "Feurige Kohlen auf dem Kaput," *TLZ* 78 (1953): 187–92.
8. Whybray, *Proverbs*, 368.

26 The perseverance of a weary person is now contrasted with the wavering righteous person's lack of perseverance. The vacillations of the compromised righteous are compared to feet that muddy a spring, and their imminent downfall as they yield to the wicked is likened to a ruined fountain. *A muddled spring* depicts an important fresh water source that has been befouled, and *a ruined fountain* refers to the destruction of another important water source. Together, they depict the deadly effects, on others and on self, of a *righteous person who sways* (morally falters) *before the wicked*; both will perish. In Proverbs, the righteous triumph over the wicked; never do the wicked force the righteous to yield (11:8; 12:21; 14:19; 16:7; 21:12; 24:15–16). Here, the righteous fall by their own fault.[9] There is no guarantee that the righteous person's current blessed state will continue in the future, as Solomon himself tragically illustrates (cf. 19:27; 1 Kgs. 11:1–8; 2 Kgs. 23:13). Battle weariness, fear, or a desire to please others can lead to compromise. This will disappoint and imperil those who have relied on the righteous for their spiritual life. All must endure to the end to save themselves and their communities (11:19; cf. 11:31; Matt. 24:13, 42–51).

27 The concluding proverb compares cogitating on a weighty matter (verset B) to overeating honey (verset A). *To eat* beneficial *honey excessively is not good; nor is it honorable to search out* by a cognitive and analytical process *weighty* (that is, unfathomable) *matters*, a reference to the ineffable things of God and the king (see vv. 2–3). The introductory proverb (25:2) refers to searching out a matter that is appropriate to divine and human inquiry, but the concluding proverb proscribes humanity's search of matters that lie beyond its reach (cf. Deut. 29:29). Investigating profundities that belong to transcendence, such as the complexities of God's governance of the universe and of the inspired king's heart, is not honorable. There, the appropriate response is to fear *I AM* and to depart from evil (Job 28:28) and to accept *I AM*'s revealed wisdom (cf. Job 28:12–28; Ps. 131; Prov. 30:1–6).

SEVEN PERVERTED TYPES OF HUMANITY (25:28–26:28)

> 25:28 A breached city, which has no wall,
>   a person whose spirit has no restraint.
> 26:1 As snow in summer and rain in harvest,
>   so honor is not fitting for a fool.
> 2 As a fluttering bird, as a flying sparrow,
>   so an undeserved curse does not come to pass.

9. Meinhold, *Sprüche*, 170.

³A whip for a warhorse, a bit for a donkey,
and a rod for backs of fools.
⁴Do not answer fools according to their folly;
otherwise, you will become like them—even you!
⁵Answer fools according to their folly;
otherwise, they will become wise in their own eyes.
⁶People who chop off their feet, who drink violence,
are those who send messages by the hand of a fool.
⁷Legs dangle from one who is lame,
and a proverb dangles in the mouth of fools.
⁸Like one who binds a stone in a sling
is a person who gives honor to a fool.
⁹A thornbush in^a the hand of a drunkard,
and a proverb in the mouth of fools.
¹⁰An archer who pierces every passerby,
and one who hires a fool, and one who hires those who pass by.
¹¹As a dog returns to its vomit,
so fools repeat their folly.
¹²Do you see people who are wise in their own eyes?
There is more hope for a fool than for them.
¹³A sluggard says, "A [fierce] lion is in the way;
a lion is in the plaza!"
¹⁴A door turns on its pivot,
and a sluggard on a couch.
¹⁵Sluggards bury their hand in the pan;
they are too weary to return it to their mouth.
¹⁶A sluggard is wiser in his own eyes
than seven men who give a judicious answer.
¹⁷People who grab the ears of a dog passing by
are those who become engaged in a dispute not their own.
¹⁸Like one gone mad, who shoots
flaming missiles and deadly arrows,
¹⁹so is a person who deceives a neighbor
and says, "Am I not only joking?"
²⁰Without wood, a fire goes out;
and when there is no slanderer, a conflict calms down.
²¹Glowing charcoal to embers and wood to fire
and a contentious person to kindling strife.
²²The words of a slanderer are like tidbits;

they descend into one's innermost being.
[23]Silver dross glazed over a potsherd
  are smooth[b] lips and an evil heart.
[24]With their lips enemies dissemble,
  and in their inner being they harbor deception.
[25]If they make their voice charming, do not trust them,
  for seven abominations are in their hearts.
[26]Their hatred is concealed by deception;
  their evil is revealed in a congregation.
[27]Whoever digs a pit will fall into it;
  those who roll a stone, it will return to them.
[28]The lying tongue hates those oppressed by it,
  but the smooth mouth works ruin.

a. "thorn that goes up into."
b. "Smooth" represents *ḥlqym*, retroverted from *leia* of LXX, rather than *dōlaqîm* ("burning") of MT.

This section warns against seven types of depraved people: the undisciplined (25:28), the fool (26:1–12), the sluggard (26:13–16), the busybody (26:17), the mischief-maker (26:18–19), the slanderer (26:20–22), and the personal enemy of the wise (26:23–28).

The Undisciplined (25:28)

As with the proverbs in 25:23–27, so also v. 28a presents a metaphor that illustrates the topic in v. 28b. *A breached city, which has no wall* is defenseless since its primary protection has been razed by an outside enemy. It is now vulnerable to all manner of trouble. So is *a person whose spirit* (see "Spirit," p. 33) *has no restraint.* Such people's self-control, which would have protected them as the wall protected the city, is non-existent (cf. 2:11). Thus, paradoxically, their own unchecked animal drives plunder them like an outside enemy. This is so because (1) the unrestrained are vulnerable to the wicked and to temptation from without (see 7:21–22), (2) sin will overpower them from within (cf. Gen. 4:6–7), and (3) society will punish them for whatever damage their unchecked passions cause others (cf. 10:6; 14:17, 29; 15:18; 19:11, 19; 29:22). Paradoxically, those with unrestrained passion have the spiritual strength to resist *I AM*, whose wisdom would otherwise fortify their inner self and so safeguard them from death (see ch. 2; 14:29; 17:27). A fruit of the Holy Spirit is self-control (Gal. 5:22–23).

The Fool (26:1–12)

The key word "fool" (*kəsîl*; pl. *kəsîlîm*) occurs in every verse of this unit except for v. 2. The catchword *kābôd* ("glory" or "honor") links this section to the preceding one, where it formed an inclusio (25:2, 27). One must neither seek the glory that belongs to God and kings (25:2–27) nor give glory to fools (26:1–12). The theme of the unit is what is unfitting and fitting for a fool.

Introduction (26:1–3)

The unit's introduction is unified by structure and theme. Pairs of comparisons in the order of creation (vv. 1a, 2a, 3a) illustrate the truths in the social order (vv. 1b, 2b, 3b). Their common theme pertains to what is unfitting and fitting: "Honor is not fitting for a fool" (v. 1) and "a rod [is fitting] for . . . fools" (v. 3). Verse 2 functions as a comparison and contrast with v. 1. As for comparison, uttering a curse on an innocent person is as unfitting as giving honor to a fool. As for contrast, whereas giving honor to a fool will cause great damage—like snow in summer—uttering a curse against an innocent person will do no damage because it will not come to rest. Van Leeuwen notes that, in v. 1, something good (honor) is wrongly given to someone bad (a fool) and, in v. 2, something bad (a curse) is wrongly given to someone good (an innocent person). In v. 3, something bad (a rod) is rightly given to someone bad (a fool).[10]

1 The social damage resulting from honoring a fool is compared to the anomaly and calamity of *snow in summer and rain at harvest*. Snow and rain in summer mean that times are catastrophically out of sync (cf. 1 Sam. 12:17). In summer, they damage the grain harvest and cause it to rot. *So* (similarly) *honor is not fitting for a fool*. The notion of unfitting implies a standard—namely, the standard revealed in the Proverbs. Its teachings produce an abundant life. Fools despise this wisdom, and giving them honor emboldens them in their deadly folly. Honoring them is a characteristic of an upside-down, damned society (cf. 2 Sam. 15:1–12; 1 Kgs. 12:1–20).

2 Humans may unfittingly honor a fool; but when they curse the wise, the Moral Governor vetoes their curse. An unfulfilled, underserved curse in the social order is likened to a fluttering bird in the created order that flies about with (implicitly) no place to land. *So an undeserved curse will not come to pass* because the curse has no place (that is, no guilty person on which) to roost. This reason is validated by other texts teaching that a deserved curse will come

10. Van Leeuwen, "Proverbs," in *NIB* 5, 224.

to pass (cf. Deut. 28:15; Josh. 6:26; 1 Kgs. 16:34; 2 Kgs. 2:24; Prov. 30:10; 1 Cor. 16:22; Gal. 1:8–9). Since *I AM* is the source of blessing and cursing, the unfitting and undeserved curse is ineffective because *I AM* vetoes it. "They may curse, but you will bless" (Ps. 109:28; cf. Num. 22:6 and 23:11).

3 *A whip* was used as a goad *for a warhorse* (see 21:31); *a bit* was used to restrain and control both a horse and *a donkey*. Both animals required tremendous energy to train, and even after taming, they demand great energy to motivate them for useful activity. *And* introduces the topic: *a rod for the back of fools.* The predicate, "is fitting," is gapped in both versets. In sum, brute force, not words, is fitting to goad and govern animals and fools. It is a language they both understand (cf. 10:13; 19:29; 1 Cor. 5:5; 11:29–30).

Body (26:4–10)

The body of the unit consists of two subunits: two admonitions prescribing correction as fitting for the fool (vv. 4–5) and five sayings proscribing honor for a fool because it is unfitting (vv. 6–10).

Correct a Fool (26:4–5)

In addition to caning fools to control them, the wise give fools fitting verbal answers (vv. 4–5). The apparent contradiction between the admonitions "do not answer fools" and "answer fools" is resolved by their differing reasons. It is unfitting to answer fools in the same manner they speak in (cf. 2 Pet. 3:9): impetuously, vindictively, harshly, or falsely. The instructor would thus fall into the condemnation of fools. The wise overcome evil with good (25:21–22). Nevertheless, by their knowledge and understanding, the wise expose and rebut the content of what fools say. They do so for the good of fools—otherwise, they would become confirmed in their way of death. Both proverbs are absolutes and applicable at the same time. One must rebut the content of what the fool says but never in the style of a fool.

4 *Do not answer fools* (see v. 1) *according to* (in a similar style to) *their folly* (see p. 48); *otherwise, you will become like them—even you!* Implicitly, even the wise would be condemned with the fool if they adopted the proud and unloving style of fools. God does not show favoritism (cf. 18:5; Rom. 2:1–11).

5 The reason for answering fools according to their folly (verset A) is to ensure fools do not replace *I AM*'s wisdom with their own (verset B). *Answer fools according to* (with an answer that addresses) *their folly* (see v. 4a). *They will become wise in their own eyes,* or confirmed in replacing *I AM*'s wisdom with their own and so replacing life with death.

Do Not Honor a Fool (26:6–10)

The following five proverbs return to the introduction's form, using negative images from the created order to condemn fools by what is unfitting for them in the social order. Duane Garrett astutely shows that the men of Hezekiah compiled these sayings in a chiastic structure:[11]

A		Committing important business to a fool	v. 6
	B	A proverb in the mouths of fools	v. 7
	X	Honoring a fool	v. 8
	B'	A proverb in the mouths of fools	v. 9
A'		Committing important business to a fool	v. 10

The pivot trumpets the composition's big idea: that it is unfitting to honor a fool (cf. v. 1). Verses 6b, 7b, 9b, and 10b, surrounding the pivot, illuminate how one unfittingly honors fools: by educating them with proverbs (vv. 7b, 9b) or by hiring them (vv. 6b, 10b). Verses 6a, 7a, 9a, and 10a illuminate why it is unfitting to honor fools in these ways. Hiring them or educating them with proverbs is not only absurd and worthless (vv. 6a, 7a) but, even worse, dangerous both to those who honor them and to society at large (vv. 9a, 10a).

6 *Those who send messages by the hand of a fool* are as bizarre and absurd as *people who chop off their feet* and as dangerous as people *who drink* (an incomplete metaphor for poison) *violence*, a metonymy for severe damage and even death. The senders hope the messenger will be an extra pair of feet to carry the message to the recipient, but by hiring a fool whose independent spirit and arrogance will invariably mess up the delivery and offend the recipient, the senders cripple themselves and, worse yet, prompt the recipient to physically retaliate against them. By exaggerated sarcasm, the proverb warns the wise against hiring a fool as a press secretary.

7 *Legs dangle from one who is lame* designates a person whose legs cannot carry the person's weight or be used for walking. *A proverb dangles in the mouth of fools* because it carries no weight (authority) and gets the fool nowhere. It is folly to educate fools by putting proverbs in their mouths (see 17:16). Even if they learn them, in their rejection of wisdom, they misappropriate them to serve their pride (14:3). The proverb makes them look like the hypocrites they are and so carries no authority (cf. Matt. 7:3–5; Luke 4:23; Rom. 2:21).

8 The pivot lampoons *a person who gives honor* (social weight) *to a fool*. The one honoring a fool is like *one who binds a stone in a sling*. A stone was

11. Garrett, *Proverbs*, 212–13.

never bound in the sling, since its purpose was to fly to the target when the sling was released. A bound stone would keep whirling dangerously around the slinger's head. The proverb escalates verse 1: giving honor to a fool is not only unseemly but also absurd, ineffectual, and dangerous. Warriors hurl the stone out of the sling to protect themselves, and so should people fling the fool out of society to protect themselves and their community.

9 This proverb returns to the folly of a proverb in the mouth of a fool, escalating its lack of value to the fool (v. 7) to the damage it inflicts on others. Verse 9 juxtaposes a hazardous thornbush in the drunkard's hand with a proverb in the fool's mouth. The parallelism linking the versets equates *a thornbush* with *a proverb* and *the hand of a drunkard* with *the mouth of a fool*. A thornbush in the hand of a staggering drunkard senselessly wounds and lacerates the bodies of others. Similarly, a proverb spoken by a fool senselessly and seriously wounds the heart (or mind) and spirit of others, as illustrated by Job and his three insensitive, arrogant "friends" (Job 16:1–4; 19:2; cf. Prov. 10:32; 11:9, 11; 12:18; 14:3).

10 This proverb returns to the folly of hiring fools, escalating their worthlessness and danger to self (v. 6) to their extreme danger to a community. Here, however, the prime folly is that of the fool's employer, albeit the fool's as well. To the *one who hires a fool* the proverb adds the *one who hires those who chance to pass by* the hirer. Both employers are as reckless and as dangerous as *an archer who pierces every passerby.* In other words, these employers are, in effect, like mass shooters!

Conclusion (26:11–12)

The conclusion implicitly elaborates the theme that wounds, not words, fit a fool. Verse 11 pillories fools as incapable of self-improvement, but v. 12 opens a door of hope for their salvation.

11 This proverb underscores the stubbornness of the fool by an intentionally repulsive simile. *Fools* are juxtaposed with the contemptible *dog* and *repeat their folly* with the dog's return *to its vomit*, a metonymy for eating it. In other words, the incorrigible nature of fools causes them to repeat their bizarre, repulsive, and dangerous behavior (see vv. 6–10) The Bible's thirty-two occurrences of "dog" reckon it unclean (cf. Exod. 22:31) and detestable (cf. 1 Sam. 17:43). Dogs ate garbage and carcasses and licked the blood of the dead (e.g., 1 Kgs. 14:11; 21:23–24). The vomit occurred because the stomach violently rejected something introduced through the mouth. To return and eat the vomit again, therefore, is absurd, detestable, and dangerous. In both the image and the topic, the body rejects the emetic (vomit and folly), but a debased fool craves it again (cf. 4:16–17)! The proverb is applied in the New Testament in relation to those who "have escaped the corruption of the world" but have become "again entangled in it and overcome" by it (2 Pet. 2:20–22).

12 This verse does not evaluate fools but uses them as the standard for comparison with *people who are wise in their own eyes* (see 3:7; 26:5). That *there is more hope for a fool than for them* opens a door of hope for the salvation of fools, presumably by caning (v. 3) or rebutting them before they become "wise in their own eyes" (v. 5). Worse than a fool is a confirmed fool. Although fools do not learn from their mistakes (v. 11), timely physical and verbal correction can save them from fortifying themselves in their own conceit (cf. Isa. 50:11; Matt. 21:31; John 9:40–41; 1 Cor. 3:18; 8:2).

The Sluggard (26:13–16)   folly + conciet = sl-sjard

This unit escalates the inferior types of people to a more pernicious stage by adding conceit to folly (cf. vv. 5, 16). It is one of three collections that feature the sluggard and sloth (see 6:6–11; 24:30–34). The key word "sluggard," occurring in every verse, unites it. The sluggard descends morally from inability to leave the house (v. 13) to inability to get off a couch (v. 14) and finally to inability to even bring a hand from dish to mouth (v. 15). Sluggards may appear comical, but the climactic verse represents them as wiser than the wise in their own eyes, making them much worse than fools (v. 16; cf. v. 12). The poem's frame represents the sluggards' problem as psycho-spiritual. Their irrational fear condemns them to house arrest (v. 13), and their irrational pride prevents their correction (v. 16). The poem offers them no solutions. The ludicrous images may be intended to shame sluggards into action (cf. 6:6–11), and they certainly warn all people that laziness thwarts talent, position, wealth, and power.[12]

13 This proverb is a variant of 22:13 (see the exposition there),[13] where the sluggard justifies sloth more explicitly: "I will be murdered."[14]

14 Again, the proverb uses an image (*a door turns on its pivot*), this time to satirize the *sluggard on a couch*. Both the door and the sluggard move within a narrow range and get nowhere. The satire may connote that both are anchored: the door to its pivot and sluggards to their comfort zone. The pivoting door,

---

12. Van Leeuwen, "Context and Meaning," 108.

13. The two verses use different, but synonymous, words for lion: *ărî* (22:13) and *šaḥal* (26:13).

14. See Fox, *Proverbs 10–31*, 798.

however, is profitable because its job is to pivot, whereas the sluggard hinged to a bed accomplishes nothing.

15 Verse 15a repeats verbatim 19:24a. The variant, *they are too weary to return it to their mouth*, clarifies "they do not return it to their mouth" (19:24b). "Weary" signifies a state of mental and spiritual fatigue. Sluggards are so allergic to work that the very thought of it exhausts them.

16 The concluding saying uses *seven men who give a judicious answer* as the standard of comparison for the delusion of the *sluggard* that he *is wiser in his own eyes* than they. "Seven" symbolizes the perfection of their answer. That is probably why Artaxerxes and Xerxes had seven advisors (Ezra 7:14; Esth. 1:14). A fool may be saved from being a confirmed fool according to v. 12, but no resolution is given to save the sluggard from his delusion.

Four Kinds of Troublemakers (26:17–28)

The section featuring seven types of depraved humans is brought to completion by a unit on the final four malevolent, antisocial types who cause dissent, mostly by their speech (see 6:12–15, 16–19; 16:27–30). The unit escalates from the busybody (v. 17) to the mischief-maker (vv. 18–19) to the slanderer (vv. 20–22) to the hateful enemy (vv. 23–28).

The Busybody (26:17)

17 The striking image of *people who grab the ears of a dog passing by* illustrates the folly of *those who become engaged in a dispute not their own*. The dispute, which itself entails getting hurt (see 17:14), is likened to a semi-wild dog (see v. 11). Its dynamic equivalent would be a jackal. Grabbing it by its sensitive ears inevitably means getting hurt. That the dangerous dog is "passing by" connotes the needlessness of interfering in the dispute. The wise do not insert themselves into a dispute between other people that does not involve their interests—a valuable lesson in foreign affairs.

The Mischief Maker (26:18–19)

The comparative *like* (v. 18) . . . *so* (v. 19) construction is usually found within one verse (see 26:1, 2, 8), but here it spans two that together present the mischief maker as one who disguises lethal havoc by deception. The negative image, *one gone mad, who shoots flaming missiles and deadly arrows* illustrates the danger of *a person* (the mischief maker) *who deceives a neighbor* with the rhetorical question *"Am I not only joking?"*, expecting an affirmative answer. The verb "deceive," however, shows that the mischief-maker intended to harm the neighbor by words or deeds. Mischief-makers who cloak their wrongdoing or harmful speech as joke are mass killers, not pranksters. Their question betrays them as liars and hypocrites, mean and cynical (cf. 6:10; 24:12). A mad person's evil may not be intentional, but the mischief-maker is cunning and intentional; regardless, they both inflict horrible tragedy. The problem of mischief-makers is spiritual; they lack kind affections.

The Slanderer (26:20–22)

Hezekiah's editors (see 25:1a) now profile the slanderer, who destroys the community by inflaming strife (see 6:12–15, 16–19). Slanderers sustain strife (v. 20), inflame it (v. 21), and transform the society into their own image (v. 22). The chiastic frame of "slanderer" (vv. 20b, 22a) intimates that "a contentious person" (v. 21b) is a coreferential term for the "slanderer." Verses 20–21 present two sides of the same coin—namely, that the inflammatory speech of slanderers incinerates the community (v. 21) and their absence restores shalom to the community (v. 20). The words of slanderers are so destructive because people devour their inflammatory libel like tasty tidbits (v. 22a), making a deep impact on them (v. 22b). The community that tolerates the slanderer is also culpable for tolerating conflicts that tear it apart.

20 The image of fire dying without fuel (verset A) represents bitter conflicts ceasing without a slanderer (verset B). The precise parallelism matches *without wood* with *when there is no slanderer* and *a fire goes out* with *a conflict calms down*. Van Leeuwen defines "slanderer" as the type of fool who attempts "by verbal calumny to wrongfully attack another's rights, reputation, or authority to secure his own will"[15] (see 16:28; Deut. 1:27). Slanderers trade in innuendoes, half-truths, and exaggerated facts (cf. 10:18). Their lies whip up strife so strong that it divides even the closest of friends (16:28). Without such people patently seeking their own will by defaming others, even bitter and old conflicts die down (cf. 22:10).

21 This proverb reverses the previous image and escalates the danger of the slanderer from keeping a controversy alive to starting one. Adding *glowing charcoal to embers and wood to fire* heats the fuel until it combusts. *And* combines the image with its topic—that is, *a contentious person* who is *kindling* (inflaming) *strife*. By implication, a community must rid itself of the slanderer to have peace.

---

15. Van Leeuwen, "Context and Meaning," 111 n. 2.

22 If the community does not rid itself of a slanderer, the slanderer's yeast will leaven the whole batch of dough (1 Cor. 5:6; Gal. 5:9). This proverb repeats 18:8 verbatim but functions as a janus between the second and third triplets on inferior types. Looking back, it draws to conclusion images of the slanderer but reverses the image/topic form used to this point, with *the words of a slanderer* preceding *like tidbits*. Looking ahead, the verse anticipates the next triplet with its focus on the hidden inner dimension of conflict.

The Hateful Enemy (26:23–28)

Lastly, the compilers feature the hateful enemies of the wise. The command "do not trust them" (v. 25) shows that the wise are the haters' target and states the aim of the partial unit. Compositionally, it is made up of two triplets of sayings. The first triplet depicts the enemies' deception (vv. 23–25), the second their destruction (vv. 26–28).

The Enemies' Deception (26:23–25)

23 This proverb warns the wise that behind the enemy's attractive veneer lurks an evil heart. Verset A presents a striking metaphor from the physical realm to illuminate a truth in the social realm in verset B. *Silver dross* is the scum that remains after the silver has been extracted by the smelting process. Because of its silvery gloss, it was used to glaze ceramics. Here, it is compared to *smooth lips* (see 5:3; 7:21) to signify that flattery is as deceptive and as cheap as what looks like silver but in fact is nothing but cheap dross. An *evil heart* is compared to *a potsherd* that is *glazed over* to signify that the reprobate is as worthless as a broken piece of pottery. The combined image implies that the enemy's outwardly smooth (flattering) speech cloaks a hidden and evil agenda.

24 This verse forms a pair with v. 25. Together, they represent enemies as concealing by their mode of communication the deceit in their hearts. The synthetic parallels combine the outward, deceptive speech of enemies (v. 24a) with their inner and true malevolent intention (v. 24b). *With their lips* (their speech) *enemies* (see 25:21) *dissemble* (disguise the facts or their intentions under a false appearance). *In their inner beings* (a metonymy for "heart"), they *harbor deception*. Here, speech is the disguise of the enemies. What they say is not their true intention, which is to mislead or harm their victims (e.g., Gen. 3:1–5; 4:8; 34:15–25).

25 This climactic verse reveals the moral of the triplet: an admonition to see through the enemy's facade of hypocrisy and to not trust them (verset A) because they are totally dedicated to deadly deceit that the godly abhor (verset B). Once again, the admonition is given after underscoring the enemy's deception. *If they* (the enemies in v. 24) *make their voice charming* (a metonymy for their beguiling speech; see 5:3; 8:4), *do not trust them* (rely on them for future support). *For* signals the explanation. *Seven abominations are in their hearts.* Symbolic "seven" signifies the full panoply of their wicked thoughts and deeds that the righteous deplore. The admonition entails that the godly must make a judgment about the trustworthiness of people's character and the truthfulness of their words.

The Destruction of Enemies (26:26–28)

The final triplet concludes the catalog of seven perverted types by predicting that the enemies' own lying tongues will overthrow them. Verse 26a presents the enemies' hate and deception, v. 27a that their deception will bring them affliction, and v. 28a that their hatred afflicts others. The triplet's B versets underscore through repetition that liars will be punished.

26 The antithetical parallels instruct the wise that although their enemies disguise their deception, they will be exposed. *Their hatred is concealed by deception* repeats the theme of the preceding triplet and underscores that the spiritual enemy of the wise will diabolically aim to win their trust by deception in order to destroy them. However, *their evil* (their deception to ruin the wise) *is revealed* (exposed publicly, a metonymy for "punished") *in the congregation*, the judicial assembly that will judge and punish the enemy's evil deeds (cf. 5:14).

27 The synthetic parallels of an ill-fated trapper and a doomed stone roller reinforces v. 26 by the divine principle of *lex talionis*. *Whoever digs a pit*, as one would to catch and kill an animal, depicts the enemy's cunning deception and deadly intention, reinforcing v. 26a. *Falls into it* reinforces v. 26b. *Whoever rolls a stone* depicts someone rolling a stone uphill—a stone too heavy to carry. This is an extreme effort to dispatch the godly. *It will return to them* and, by implication, crush them, also reinforcing v. 26b. The enemies' deception and their extreme efforts to vanquish the righteous now turn around and destroy them (cf. Num. 23:10; Esth. 7:10; Dan. 6:24; 2 Tim. 4:14). This "poetic justice" is in the hands of the Sovereign (cf. 10:3, 29; 16:4; 1 Cor. 3:19; 2 Tim. 4:14).

28 The climactic parallels of this verse contrast the painful blows that the lying tongue inflicts on others with the knockout blow it inflicts on itself. *The lying tongue* is matched with *the smooth mouth*, both metonymies for the enemies' dissembling (v. 23a) and charming speech (v. 24a). *Hates*, the liars' inner motive, is matched with *works*, its outer effects. Finally and climactically, the versets contrast *those oppressed by it* (the hurt, but not fatally crushed, righteous) with *ruin* (or "calamity"). The latter forces a double take, since at first it seems to refer to the hated's but on reflection refers to the haters' ruin. That interpretation best fits the context of the parallel B versets of this triplet, best explains the difference between the hurt (but not fatally crushed) and the fatally ruined, and best fits the optimistic theology of the book. In sum, villains victimize themselves.

Friends and Neighbors (27:1–22)

¹Do not boast about tomorrow,
  for you do not know what a day may bring forth.
²Let a stranger and not your own mouth praise you,
  an outsider, and let not your own lips praise you.
³The weight of a stone and the burden of sand—
  but the vexation of a fool is heavier than both.
⁴The cruelty of wrath and the torrents of anger—
  but who can stand before jealousy?
⁵Open rebuke is better than concealed love.
⁶The wounds of a friend are faithful,
  but the kisses of an enemy are too excessive.
⁷A sated person tramples down a honeycomb,
  but for a hungry person, every bitter thing is sweet.
⁸Like a bird that flees from its nest,
  so are people who flee from their home.
⁹Olive oil and incense make the heart glad,
  and the sweetness of one's friend comes from passionate
    counsel.
¹⁰Your friend and your father's friend do not forsake,
  and the house of your relative do not enter in the time of
    distress.
  A close next-door neighbor is better than a relative who is far
    off.
¹¹Be wise, my son, and make my heart glad,
  so that I might answer them who reproach me.
¹²Shrewd people, who see evil, hide themselves;
  the uncommitted, who pass on, are fined.
¹³Take away the garment of one who becomes surety for a stranger;
  and for a foreign woman impound it.
¹⁴As for those who bless their neighbor with a loud voice early in
    the morning,

it will be reckoned to them as a curse.
¹⁵A leaky roof in a cloudburst
and a contentious wife are alike.
¹⁶Those who shelter her shelter wind,
and oil meets their right hand.
¹⁷Iron is sharpened with iron,
and a person sharpens the face of a friend.
¹⁸The one who protects a fig tree will eat its fruit,
and those who guard their master will be honored.
¹⁹As, looking in water, a face looks to a face,
so a human being's heart looks to a human being.
²⁰Sheol and Abaddon are never satisfied,
and the eyes of humankind are never satisfied.
²¹The crucible is for silver and the furnace for gold,
and people are tested according to their praise.
²²If you grind fools in a mortar,
in the midst of groats with a pestle,
their folly will not depart from them.

This is the fifth of seven sections in Collection V (see p. 5). The verb *hallēl* ("to boast" or "to praise"), the first word in v. 1 and the last word in v. 21, frames the section. Verse 22 may be a janus. Synonyms for "friend" (*ʾōhēb*, v. 6; "neighbor," *rēaʿ*, vv. 9, 10a, 14, 17; "next-door-neighbor," *qārôb*, vv. 10b, 14) sound the theme of this manual on friends and neighbors.

A rearing proverb (v. 10) divides the section into two units (vv. 1–10, 11–22). Tricola draw the units to conclusion (vv. 10, 22; cf. v. 27). An alternating thematic structure also unites them:

A		To whom to listen for praise: Strangers	vv. 1–2
	B	Relationships to avoid: The foolish, angry, jealous	vv. 3–4
		C Teachings about friendship	vv. 5–10[16]
A'		To whom to listen for rearing: Parents	vv. 11–12
	B'	Relationships to avoid: The wicked, hypocrite, shrew	vv. 13–16
		C' Teachings about friendship	vv. 17–22[17]

16. The framing proverbs (vv. 5 and 10) are better-than proverbs.

17. In vv. 17–21, an analogy from the order of creation in verset A teaches the truth about the order of redemption in the verset B. Verse 22 also teaches moral truth from the order of creation but breaks the pattern.

First Unit on Friends and Neighbors (27:1–10)

The first unit consists of five couplets, respectively on the topics of receiving praise from strangers, not self (vv. 1–2); the vexation of fools, hotheads, and the jealous (vv. 3–4); the beneficial wounds of a loving friend (vv. 5–6); the causes and loss of the most intimate relationships in the home (vv. 7–8); and the benefits a true friend (vv. 9–10).

To Whom to Listen for Praise: Strangers (27:1–2)

The catchword *hallēl* ("boast," "praise") links this couplet that censures boasting about tomorrow (v. 1) and self (v. 2) and commends praise from an outsider. The couplet implicitly calls for humility before God and modesty before a stranger.

1 *Do not boast* (praise yourself; see v. 2) *about tomorrow.* "Tomorrow" refers to the immediate future and functions as a metonymy for expectations of success. The reason: *you do not know what a day may bring forth.* If the most immediate and visible future is beyond human control and uncertain, how much more the distant future. Only God controls the mortal's destiny. Nevertheless, Proverbs commends planning for the future (11:14; 15:22; 20:18; 21:5; 24:6, 27).

2 To *praise* (*hillēl*) means to favorably judge another's virtue and express admiration by extolling it to others. The precise synonymous parallels *a stranger, not your own mouth* and *an outsider, not your own lips* could not be more emphatic. A stranger has no self-interest, and so the evaluation is credible (cf. v. 21). Self-praise destroys a person's relationship with God and with people: *I AM* detests the proud, and people dislike a boaster. Self-praise may elevate people beyond their competence, leading them to fear demotion or in fact to be demoted and shamed.

Relationships to Avoid: The Foolish, Angry, and Jealous (27:3–4)

People with irrational and destructive emotional excitements are insufferable (v. 3) and incapable of friendship (v. 4). They should be avoided to create the spiritual milieu in which friendship flourishes.

3 Physical burdens that exhaust a person's strength and cause extreme discomfort and misery are lighter and easier to bear than the emotional burden of a fool's vexation. *The weight of a stone* refers to one so heavy that it is unliftable, and *the burden of sand* refers to beach sand and connotes its immeasurable weight (Job 6:3). *But the vexation* (see 21:19) *of a fool* (see pp. 47–48) is *heavier* (even more unbearable) *than both* burdens.

4 Also to be avoided are *wrath* (see 6:34) and *anger* (see 15:1). Their two "sidekicks" are unmerciful *cruelty* and *torrents* of overwhelming destruction (i.e., cataclysmic floods). But anger—unlike jealousy—can be withstood. Rhetorical *who* asserts emphatically that none *can stand before jealousy*. David stood his ground before his brother Eliab's angry outburst (1 Sam. 17:28), but he fled from Saul's jealousy (1 Sam. 18:9).

Teachings about Friendship (27:5–10)

5–6 How one responds to the wrongdoing of a fool differs from how one responds to the wrongdoing of a friend. Friendship with a fool is impossible, but a true friend does not shrink from correcting error. Comparative paradoxes link this couplet on friendship: "open rebuke" is better than "concealed love," and "faithful wounds" are better than hypocritical "kisses."

Open rebuke (see 1:25) *is better* (benefits life more) *than concealed love* suggests that corrective criticism proceeds openly and directly, even severely (cf. v. 6a), but remains caring and concerned with the best interests of the erring person. Indeed, hidden love is selfish, for the "lover," out of cowardice or laziness, refuses to risk self in the best interests of the beloved. Open, loving rebuke is potent; hidden love, like winking at a girl in the dark, is useless. The famous command to "love your neighbor as yourself" (Lev. 19:18; see Matt. 22:39) is preceded by the neglected command to "rebuke your neighbor frankly" (Lev. 19:17).

In an antithetical proverb, v. 6 presents two oxymorons: "friendly wounds" and "wounding kisses." *Wounds* are a metaphor for painful but necessary words (see v. 9). "Wounds" are normally inflicted by an enemy; but when inflicted by *a friend* (*ʾōhēb*; see 14:26), they *are faithful*—they demonstrate devotion and loyalty to the erring person. *Kisses* are normally associated with a friend; but when given by an enemy, they are hypocritical and symbolize their disdain for and infidelity to the one kissed (see 5:3–4; 7:13; Matt. 26:49). The imprecise antithetical parallels "faithful" and *excessive* suggest that profuse kisses are insincere, deceitful, or sycophantic.

7–8 This couplet metaphorically warns the son to gratify his appetites with a good wife (v. 7)—to marry a good, not nagging, woman. Satisfaction in the wrong woman leads to contempt of a good wife (v. 7a), and lack of satisfaction in a good wife leads to enjoyment of a bad woman (v. 7b). Van Leeuwen links vv. 7b and 8: "The satisfied husband is content and does not wander like an errant bird from the nest. . . . People controlled by lust and hunger do not discriminate."[18]

A sated person tramples down something as sweet and healthy as *a honeycomb* (see 16:24). The proverb implies that the person, such as a husband, has sated himself with something obnoxious and unhealthy, such as an adulteress. As for *a hungry person*, whose drives and appetites are unsatisfied, *every bitter thing*, which a healthy appetite rejects, *is sweet*. People so sated by wrong things that they despise good things and people so hungry that they perceive every harmful thing as sweet are both sick. Similarly, the person who does not find spiritual satisfaction in true religion chases after any idolatry and, sated by it, will despise true religion.

A bird that flees from its nest refers to a bird permanently[19] fleeing its place of refuge due to a distressful situation (cf. Isa. 16:2; Jer. 4:25; 9:10b). *People who flee from their home* implies a crisis, such as a nagging wife. Cut off from the security of their home, they are exposed and vulnerable (cf. 19:13; 21:9, 19; 27:15). The proverb is not faulting the man as a feckless gadabout but warning the son to marry a good wife who will gratify his appetites (see 5:15-19). Malbim interprets it spiritually as the soul fleeing from its proximity to God.[20]

9-10 Friends (the catchword of this couplet) are of great value for giving counsel (v. 9) and support in time of need (v. 10).

The beauty of *olive oil* on a person's body (cf. 21:17) and the fragrance of *incense* on their clothes make the person's *heart glad* because they induce a sense of well-being. Similarly, *the sweetness*, a metonymy for what is pleasant and agreeable and a metaphor for what is delightful to the psyche, *of one's friend* (*rēaʿ*; see v. 10) *comes from* the friend's *passionate*, not disinterested, *counsel*, which also induces a sense of well-being.

When disaster strikes, turn to a tried, tested, nearby family friend, not a far-off relative (cf. 18:24). *Your friend* denotes a socially close neighbor who helps in need. *Your father's friend* further defines the friend as a family friend whose faithfulness has lasted over two generations. *Do not forsake* (that is, ignore) "in the time of distress" (gapped). *And* introduces the other side of the same coin: *the house of your blood relative do not enter in the time of distress.* Verset B provides the rationale: *A close next-door neighbor* denotes one who resides close by, in physical proximity and in spiritual sympathy (cf. Lev. 21:3;

---

18. Van Leeuwen, "Proverbs," in *NIB* 5, 230.
19. Cf. Fox, *Proverbs 10–31*, 806.
20. Malbim on Proverbs 27:8.

Ruth 2:20; Ps. 148:14). Such a neighbor *is better than a relative who is far off* in space and in sympathy. The proverb should be held in tension with 17:17.

Further Teachings on Friends and Friendships (27:11–22)

The rearing proverb in v. 11 is paired with v. 12 by their initial synonyms: "wise" and "shrewd." They form an inclusio with their antonym, the "fool" (v. 22). Within this frame, vv. 13–16 are negative, warnings against being surety (v. 13), the hypocritical friend (v. 14), and the shrewish wife (vv. 15–16). Verses 17–21 are positive, teaching the values of true friendship by analogies from the order of creation.

To Whom to Listen for Rearing (27:11–12)

11 The twofold command *be wise* (see 6:6), *my son* (see 1:8) and so *make my heart glad* (see 27:9) with the motivation *so that I might answer* (lit. "return a word"; cf. 16:1) *them who reproach me* appeals to the son's desire to honor his father, whose significance, worth, competence, and dignity have been denigrated (see 14:31). Since the father cannot boast of his accomplishments (27:1–2), he appeals to the son to vindicate him by displaying the wisdom that he has taught him (cf. Ps. 127:4–5; 2 Cor. 3:1–3; 1 Thess. 2:19–20; 3:8). Those who denigrate God the Father need only to look at his Wisdom, the Lord Jesus Christ.

12 This proverb repeats 22:3 with only miniscule stylistic variations (see the exposition there). It segues the introductory couplet into proverbs on evils to be avoided.

Relationships to Avoid: The Wicked, Hypocrites, and Shrews (27:13–16)

13 This verse essentially repeats 20:16, but changes "outsider" (*nokriyyām*) to "foreign woman" (*nokriyyâ*; see "unchaste wife," p. 54). Here, a foolish guarantor has agreed to pay the debt of a foolish stranger, who had indebted himself to the unchaste woman. Both the guarantor and the debtor are in her hands. The proverb instructs the disciple to have nothing to do with these fools.

14 Hypocritical friends are revealed by their ostentatious and untimely greeting. *Those who*, like a priest before a congregation, *bless* (see 3:33) *their neighbor* (or "friend," *rēʿēhû*; see 27:9–10) *with a loud voice* do so to be heard by everyone. *Early in the morning* signifies "at rising time" and connotes eagerness and zeal to bless the neighbor. Their unnatural voice and timing, however, betray them as hypocrites who use God, the Agent of blessing, in their pretense of being trustworthy neighbors. But God will have none of it. Therefore, the hypocrite's illocution *will be reckoned* by God *as a curse to* (that is, upon) *them.* "God will not be mocked. A person reaps what they sow" (Gal. 6:7).

15–16 The antecedent of "her" (v. 16) is the "contentious wife" (v. 15), linking the two verses as a couplet. She is like a leaky roof, a storm wind, and slippery oil.

A contentious wife (see 21:9) and *a leaky roof in a cloudburst*—both of which are unexpected, deceptive, irritating, and unbearable—*are alike.* In a torrential downpour of misfortune, the man runs to his home for cover, but his leaky roof provides him no shelter. Likewise, he married expecting to find good, but his wife, instead of protecting him from the slings and arrows of misfortune, makes his home insufferable and his life miserable by her nagging (see vv. 7–8).

The weather imagery of a cloudburst is now escalated to a storm wind. *All* those *who* attempt to *shelter her* (that is, restrain her) *shelter wind*—in this context, an unrestrainable storm wind, such as a tornado, that sets everything in motion. The third image—she is like *oil that meets his* (probably the husband's) *right hand*—reinforces that she cannot be restrained because it is impossible to grasp and hold oil. Oil refers to delightful olive oil (see v. 9), and the right hand is the position of majesty and privilege. Her husband's powerful right hand should have protected her, and she should have delighted her husband as fragrant olive oil. Her belligerence makes neither possible.

Teachings about Friendship from the Order of Creation (27:17–22)

17 *Iron*, the exceedingly hard, raw metal, *is sharpened with iron*, a metonymy for the hammer that the smith used to fashion the durable and powerful iron into a sharp tool (e.g., a knife) or weapon (e.g., a sword). Were the raw iron sentient, the beneficial sharpening would be painful. *The face of a friend* (or "neighbor") is a pun, since the working edge of a sword or knife is called its "face" (see Eccl. 10:10). Here, "face" may be literal; as a mirror of the soul, a face shows feelings of pain or anger. It could also be a synecdoche—as the most important part of a person—for the whole person.[21] The proverb does not say *how* one person sharpens another. Elsewhere, however, "sharpened" is used metaphorically of mouth and tongue (Ps. 57:4; Isa. 49:2), suggesting *a person sharpens* is a metaphor for dialogue. Ronald L. Giese Jr. argues that "sharpening the face" is a negative image for victims becoming angry because

---

21. A. S. van der Woude, *TLOT*, 2:1000–1001, s.v. *pānîm*.

they have been violently assaulted by their neighbor.[22] Giese's essay helpfully contributes the notion that sharpening entails pain and violence, but it fails to take adequate account of the positive intent of the analogy of iron sharpening iron. A sharpened tool is better than a dull one. Though hard and violent, the pounding hammer produces an effective tool in the end.[23] By the sufferings *I AM* inflicted on his Servant, the Sovereign Lord gave him a well-instructed tongue (Isa. 50:4).

18 *The one who protects* (see 2:8) *a* precious *fig tree will eat its* sweet, life-sustaining *fruit* is an analogy for *those who guard* (see 2:8) *their master* (see 25:13), who *will be honored* with wealth and social dignity (see 3:9). The analogy of the inexorable nexus between investment and reward from the order of creation illustrates, not proves, that in the order of redemption, the person who observes sovereignly established relationships between master and servant will be duly and appropriately rewarded (cf. Matt. 25:21, 23; John 12:26).

19 *As, looking into water, a face looks to a face* refers to seeing the reflection of one's face in the water. *So a human being's heart* (see "Heart," p. 32) *looks to* (is reflected in) *a human being.* One can evaluate one's disposition, motives, and behavior by looking to others and seeing in their honest compliments (see 27:2), constructive criticism (vv. 6, 17), and earnest counsel (v. 9) an image of one's true character.

20 The personification *Sheol and Abaddon are never satisfied* represents death as never experiencing a sense of fulfillment no matter how many victims it devours. Similarly, *the eyes of humankind* have appetites that *are never satisfied* (Eccl. 6:7–9). The unsatisfied eye is used as a metonymy for that part of the psyche that stimulates greed and covetousness (cf. Eccl. 2:10; 4:8; 1 John 2:16). The comparison of human greed with the ruthless, insatiable grave suggests that human craving is also ruthless and insatiable. The lust of the eye led Eve and Adam to transgress social boundaries. The proverb teaches the son to live within boundaries and not according to his insatiable appetites. In Christ, Christians find rest (cf. 4:13–17; Matt. 11:28; John 6:35; 7:37; Phil. 4:11–13), and in his Spirit, self-control (Gal. 5:22–23).

21 What people praise and who praises them (that is, their reputation) are now compared with the two images of a *crucible* that tests the purity of *silver*

---

22. R. L. Giese Jr., "'Iron Sharpens Iron' as a Negative Image: Challenging the Common Interpretation of Proverbs 27:17," *JBL* 135 (2016): 61–76.

23. Giese ("Iron Sharpens Iron," 76) looks outside the proverb to argue that "sharpening the face" is a negative image of a person honing a neighbor by going on the attack. The parallel within the proverb itself, however, connotes improving the raw iron into an effective instrument, and we should assume the same for the parallel, "the face of a friend/neighbor."

and a melting *furnace* that tries the genuineness of *gold*. The same two images for testing are used in 17:3, but there *I AM* tests whereas here the *people are tested* (true character is revealed) *according to their praise*—that is to say, who or what they praise (see 28:4) or from whom they receive praise (cf. 29:27). Musicians praise their composers, readers praise their authors, and the godly praise *I AM*. Likewise, the immoral adulate adulterers, and the covetous revere the rich (Ps. 49:18). The curses of sinners are the honor of saints (cf. Luke 6:26).

22 The section's concluding proverb illustrates the incorrigibility of a fool in the order of redemption by the analogy of grinding grain drawn from the order of creation. But instead of the two orders being similar, they are dissimilar. *If you grind fools* (see pp. 47–48) *in a mortar . . . with a pestle* signifies severe discipline, such as by a rod. *In the midst of groats* implies that the severity of the discipline is comparable to the severity of grinding dried grain that successfully removes the unwanted husks to yield the edible groats. By contrast, however, the fool's *folly,* unlike the husks, *will not depart from them* in spite of severe discipline. Words will not change a fool's behavior (25:3). A rod may coerce a person to do what is right (10:13), but it will not convert the heart (27:22). Divine grace that regenerates the heart is the fool's only hope for salvation (cf. 26:11).

Caring for "Flocks and Herds" (27:23–27)

²³Be sure you know the condition of your flocks;
  pay attention to [your] herds.
²⁴Wealth does not endure forever,
  and certainly not a crown from generation to generation.
²⁵If the grass is removed, then the new growth appears;
  and if vegetation of the mountains is harvested,
²⁶the young rams will provide your clothing,
  and your he-goats the price of a field.
²⁷And you will have enough goats' milk
  for your food, for the food of your household,
  and for the life of your servant girls.

This longer poem, a janus between the two clusters of Collection V (see "Structure," p. 5), consists of an admonition to look after one's flocks and herds (v. 23) with negative (v. 24) and positive (vv. 25–27) substantiation. Unlike money and status, which are depreciating and not self-renewing resources (v. 24; cf. 23:4–5), animals are a self-renewing and an increasing source of wealth. In plentiful pasture (v. 25), they provide clothing and money to buy land (v. 26) and enough milk to feed the entire household, including the milk-maids (v. 27).

The reference to a crown (v. 24) shows that caring for flocks and herds in the order of creation is an analogy for the wise king's diligent and vigilant care for his subjects in the order of redemption (2 Sam. 12:2, 4; 22:22; 23:1–6; Ezek. 34). By caring for them, he establishes his crown. On the democratized literary level, however, the crown symbolizes any high status or wealth. By its nature, a proverb has applications beyond its specific reference.

23 The admonition commands the son as an owner of flocks (that is, a ruler over subjects) to become intimately and personally concerned with the well-being of his wards. *Be sure you know* and its emphatic parallel, *pay attention*, instruct him to have an intense and intimate, not merely a superficial, relationship with them. *The condition* (or "well-being") is literally "faces" (*pānîm*; see v. 17). *Your flocks and your herds* refers to the gamut of domesticated quadrupeds. For the son to involve himself fully and personally with his flocks will take industry, kindness, and other virtues of wisdom.

24 *Because* introduces the admonition's negative (v. 24) and positive (vv. 25–27) substantiations. Negatively, *wealth does not endure forever*; it does not continue unceasingly. *And certainly not a crown*, the symbol of kingship, *from generation to generation*. Both wealth and a crown are transitory, perishable, and depreciating commodities.

25 They can be retained, however, by diligence and constant vigilance, as illustrated by providing rich pastures for the flock. Verse 25a presents the condition of removing the wild grass as fodder for the animals and the promise that if it is removed, it will replenish itself. In the conditional clause, *grass* refers to the wild grass that grows in Israel's rainy season and that was valuable as fodder for the animals. *Is removed* (taken for fodder) entails the diligent and timely work of harvesting it. *Then the new grass appears* refers to new grass available for grazing. This promise of replenishment entails that the Creator also sustains his creation by renewing it with rain. *Vegetation of the mountains* refers to the wild plants that grow on the highlands of Palestine and on which the flocks could also feed. *Is harvested* unites the Sustainer's good created order, including mountains, vegetation, and seasonal rains, with the human wisdom to diligently reap it at the right time.

26 This verse points to the riches provided by the males of the flocks, and v. 27 to the wealth from its females. *The young rams*, one type of domesticated animal, *will provide* the wool for *your clothing*. Another type, *he-goats*, "will provide" (gapped) *the price*—the money received from their sale, which can be used to purchase *a field*. The livestock provide both usable commodities and money to purchase property. This kind of incremental wealth greatly increases the family's wealth over the generations, enabling them to care for the destitute.

27 *And* adds the plentiful supply of milk as another consequence of careful shepherding. *You will have enough . . . milk*, a comprehensive term for an indispensable source of nutrition. The milk is qualified as *goats'* because goat milk was by far the choice animal nutrient in the ancient Near East, being richer in protein and more digestible than cow's milk. *For your food* (that is, your personal food) is expanded to *for the food of your household*. The *servant girls* are milkmaids, signifying that the abundant milk is totally self-perpetuating. It provides life for those who milk the goats, which in turn feeds the household that looks after the goats. If one wisely looks after one's animals, they will provide rich rewards. And if, in the social order, the king takes care of his subjects, his crown will endure.

On Rearing, Ruling, and Relationship with God (28:1–29:27)

²⁸:¹The wicked flee though no one is pursuing,
  but the righteous are confident like a lion.
²Because of the transgression of a land, its princes are many;
  but because of a discerning person, a person who knows
    [wisdom],
  what is right endures.
³A destitute person[a] and one who oppresses the poor—
  a rain that washes away and there is no food.
⁴Those who abandon instruction[b] praise the wicked,
  but those who keep instruction strive against them.
⁵Evil people do not discern what is right,
  but those who seek *I AM* discern everything.
⁶Better destitute people who walk in integrity,
  than [people who walk in] the crookedness of double-dealing
    ways, though they are rich.
⁷A discerning son guards instruction,
  but one who associates with profligates puts his father to
    shame.
⁸Those who increase their wealth by taking interest of any sort
    [from the poor]

gather it for those who are gracious to the poor.
⁹Those who turn a deaf ear to hearing instruction—
  even their prayers are detestable.
¹⁰Those who mislead the upright into an evil way—
  they will fall into their own pit;
  but the blameless will inherit good things.
¹¹Rich people are wise in their own eyes,
  but a discerning poor person searches them out.
¹²When the righteous triumph, the splendor is great,
  but when the wicked rise up, mortals must be searched out.
¹³Those who conceal their transgressions will not succeed,
  but the one who confesses and abandons them will obtain
    mercy.
¹⁴Blessed is the human being who trembles [before *I AM*]
    continually,
  but those who harden their heart will fall in calamity.
¹⁵A roaring lion and a ravenous, charging bear
  is a wicked ruler over destitute people.
¹⁶A leader who is lacking in understanding multiplies extortion;
  the one who hatesᶜ ill-gotten gain prolongs days.
¹⁷Human beings oppressed by shedding the blood of life
  will flee to the pit. Let no one restrain them.
¹⁸The one who walks as a blameless person will be helped,
  but the double-dealing crook will fall into a pit.
¹⁹The one who works the land is filled with food,
  but the one who pursues worthless ventures is filled with
    poverty.
²⁰A conscientious person abounds in blessings,
  but one who hastens to get rich will not escape punishment.
²¹To show partiality is not good;
  even for a portion of food, a personᵈ may commit a crime.
²²Misers are hasty for wealth,
  but they do not know that poverty will come to them.
²³The one who reprimands human beings about their conduct
    finds favor,
  not the deceptive flatterer.
²⁴Those who rob their father and their mother while saying, "There
    is no crime,"
  are companions to those who destroy.

²⁵The unrestrained appetite stirs up strife,
    but the one who trust in *I AM* will be fattened.
²⁶Those who trust in their own heart are fools;
    but one who walks in wisdom will be delivered.
²⁷As for the one who gives to the poor, there is no lack,
    but those who shut their eyes abound in curses.
²⁸When the wicked rise up, human beings hide themselves,
    but when they perish, the righteous thrive.
²⁹:¹Those who are often reproved [and] harden their necks
    in an instant will be broken, and without remedy.
²When the righteous thrive, the people rejoice,
    but when a wicked person rules, people groan.
³Those who love wisdom make their father glad,
    but those who associate with prostitutes squander [his] wealth.
⁴A king through justice establishes a land;
    but whoever exacts contributions or gives them tears it down.
⁵People^e who flatter their neighbors
    spread a net for their feet.
⁶In the transgression of an evil person is a snare,
    but the righteous person shouts for joy and is glad.
⁷The righteous involve themselves in court decisions for the poor,
    but the wicked do not understand involving themselves.
⁸Mockers cause a city to pour forth anger,
    but the wise turn back anger.
⁹If a wise person confronts the fool in court,
    [the fool] rages and scoffs, and there is no calm.
¹⁰Bloodthirsty people hate the person of integrity,
    and as for the upright, they seek to kill each of them.
¹¹Fools give full vent to their rage,
    but a wise person finally stills it.
¹²As for a ruler who pays attention to deceptive words,
    all his attendants become wicked.
¹³Poor and oppressor meet together;
    I AM is the one who gives light to the eyes of both.
¹⁴As for a king who judges the poor through truth,
    his throne is established forever.
¹⁵A rod and reproof give wisdom,
    but an undisciplined child brings its mother shame.
¹⁶When the wicked thrive, transgression abounds;

but the righteous will gaze on their downfall
[17]Discipline your son so that he will give you rest,
and he will give delight to you.
[18]Without revelation the people fall into anarchy,
but blessed is the one who carefully obeys instruction.
[19]Slaves are not disciplined by words;
though they understand, they do not respond.
[20]Do you see people who are hasty with their words?
[there is] more hope for fools than for them.
[21]A slave pampered from youth
afterward will be insolent.
[22]A hothead stirs up strife;
a wrathful person is one who abounds in transgressions.
[23]People's pride will bring them low,
but the lowly in spirit will lay hold of honor.
[24]Those who are an accomplice with a thief hate their life;
they hear the divine curse but will not testify.
[25]Panic induced by a human being lays a snare,
but the one who trusts in *I AM* will be protected.
[26]Many are they who seek the face of a ruler,
but justice for an individual comes from *I AM*.
[27]An unjust person is an abomination to the righteous,
but the upright in their ways are an abomination to the wicked.

a. Heb. *geber* ("strong man"; see "Words for 'Humankind' in Proverbs," p. 31).
b. "Instruction" (28:4, 7, 9; 29:18) is a translation of Heb. *tôrâ* (see 1:8).
c. *Qere* sg.; *Ketiv* pl.
d. Heb. *geber* ("strong man").
e. Heb. sing. *geber* ("strong man").

Bruce Malchow argues that Hezekiah's men organized this second section of Collection V into four parts by strategically placing proverbs contrasting "the righteous" and "the wicked."[24] The section begins and ends with proverbs using these catchwords (28:1; 29:27). Within this outer frame are four other proverbs using this contrast (28:12, 28; 29:2, 16). Thus, these framing proverbs divide the section into its four subsections (28:1–12; 28:13–28; 29:2–15;

24. Malchow, "A Manual for Future Monarchs," 238–45.

29:16–27).[25] The single line proverb teaching the ultimate destruction of the hard-hearted wicked (29:1) is sharpened by being centered between the framing proverbs 28:28 and 29:2.

Meinhold, independently observing the four subsections, comments, "[They] shed light, each from a particular primary emphasis, on the structure of connections between a relationship with God, rearing, and rulership."[26] We propose these headings to the subsections around the center line:

I   Relationship to Instruction as a Measure for Ruling and Gaining Wealth (28:1–12)

II   The Importance of One's Relationship with God for Ruling and Gaining Wealth (28:13–27)

III   Center Line: Sudden Death for the Hard-Hearted (29:1)

IV   Rearing and Ruling Proved Worthwhile in Dealing with the Poor (29:2–15)

V   Rearing and One's Relationship with God (29:16–27)

The section's dozen explicit or implicit references to the ruler or the court (28:2, 3, 15, 16, 28; 29:2, 4, 7, 9, 12, 14, 26), especially in its framing proverbs, give this section a royal color, leading Malchow to plausibly entitle it "A Manual for Future Monarchs."[27] Budding officials were the original addressees of Egyptian instruction (see "Setting of Composition," pp. 18–19), albeit their directives for a successful life are often couched, like this manual, in universal terms. (E.g., "Wrongdoing has never brought its undertaking to port."[28]) In any case, this "manual," unlike Egyptian instruction, has been democratized in Proverbs for all of Israel's youth (see "Setting of Dissemination," p. 20). The section's rhetorical structure, however, is not dependent on an original royal setting. The career of the Lord Jesus Christ validates the truth of Proverbs.

---

25. Wilson (*Proverbs*, 291) notes that "righteous" versus "wicked" occurs at the end of the sections in ch. 28 and at the beginning of the sections in ch. 29. S. Liew ("Social and Literary Context of Proverbs 28–29" [PhD diss., Westminster Theological Seminary, 1991], 105ff.) notes their stitching pattern: "wicked" (W)/"righteous" (R) (28:1); R/W (28:12); W/R (28:28); R/W (29:2); W/R (29:16); R/W (29:27).

26. Meinhold, *Sprüche*, 464.

27. Malchow, "A Manual for Future Monarchs."

28. *The Instruction of the Vizier Ptah-Hotep* (ANET, 412).

Relationship to Instruction as a Measure for Ruling and Gaining Wealth (28:1–12)

This subunit features the theme of submitting to "instruction" (*tôrâ*), particularly with regard to wealth. The just handling of wealth enriches all; injustice impoverishes the victim immediately and the oppressor ultimately.

Introductory Framing Proverb (28:1)

The psychological insecurity of the wicked (see "Ethical Terms for Wicked and Fools," pp. 45–46) is contrasted with the psychological confidence of the righteous (see pp. 36–37; cf. 29:27). *The wicked flee though no one is pursuing* implicitly compares the paranoia of the wicked to that of warriors or prey fleeing when no enemy is pursuing (cf. Lev. 26:17, 36). By contrast *the righteous* (see pp. 36–37) *are confident like a lion*, the proverbial fearless king of beasts (cf. 30:30). Paradoxically, the wicked, who do not fear God, live in fear of people, but the righteous, who fear God (1:7), do not fear people. Both psychologies are grounded in reality: *I AM* safeguards the righteous and damns the wicked (see Eph. 2:1–3).

Instruction and Righteous Government (28:2–6)

2 *Because of the transgressions* (that is, the crimes) *of a land* (a metonymy for the land's inhabitants), *its princes* (officials with delegated power) *are many*. When a nation abandons *I AM*'s moral order, a massive bureaucracy is necessary to keep an eye on its people. By contrast, *because of a discerning person, one who knows [wisdom], what is right* (the moral standard) *endures*. The imprecise antithesis implies that the many bureaucrats do not know wisdom and so maintain neither justice nor their own positions. But discerning rulers maintain both justice and their own position. In short, corrupt rulers are many both in quantity and in succession.

3 The social catastrophe of a tyrant, who pounces on the produce of the poor, is compared with the natural catastrophe of a shearing downpour that strips the fields. The parallels match hardworking people with poverty and a tyrant, probably a ruler, with a destructive rain. *A destitute man* (*geber*; see the translation notes) refers to a "strong man" forced into poverty. *One who oppresses the poor* refers to a tyrant who strips hard workers of their produce. This social chaos is compared in the emblematic parallel to cosmic chaos: *a rain that washes away* (destroys the crops) *and there is no food*. The imprecise parallelism of "a destitute strong man" and "there is no food" suggests that the strong man has no food because the oppressor has plundered the food that the strong man's strength produced.

4 The antithetical parallelism of this proverb contrasts *those who abandon* (reject) the sages' inspired *instruction* (see the translation notes) with *those who keep instruction*. It also contrasts their attitudes and actions. The former *praise the wicked* (cf. 27:21). People praise what they admire; rebels against God make celebrities of the wicked. By contrast, those who fear God, by their spiritual nature, *strive against* the wicked. One's spiritual mettle can be tested by whom one praises or strives against.

5 A person's intellectual clarity and moral acumen hinge on a proper relationship to *I AM*. *Evil people*, whose moral compass is wrecked by their rebellion against God, *do not discern what is right* and correct[29] and are unaware that divine justice awaits them. By contrast, *those who seek* the wisdom and will of *I AM discern everything* that, according to the parallel, is right and correct (e.g., caring for the poor and restoring community harmony by punishing evildoers and vindicating the innocent) and are aware that *I AM* will reward them in due course. The imprecise parallelism implies that the disciple discerns what is right by seeking the moral will of God.

6 This better-than proverb emphasizes that acting with integrity, even while destitute, benefits oneself and others more than acting deceitfully though rich. *Better destitute people who walk in integrity* repeats 19:1. *Than [people who walk in] the crookedness* (lit. "twisted[ness]") *of double-dealing ways* (something that is false in multiple ways), *though they are rich*. The rich (see 28:11) commit two wrongs: defrauding the poor and making themselves appear righteous. Farmer insightfully comments that better-than proverbs are "concerned with the hidden costs involved in making choices. Some desirable things come with undesirable conditions attached."[30] The proverb challenges the disciple to count the cost and live by faith.

Further Instruction and Righteous Government (28:7–11)

7 The antithetical parallels of this proverb pit *a discerning* (cf. v. 2) *son* against the *one who associates with profligates*. The former is defined as one who *guards* the *instruction* inspired by the covenant-keeping sages and handed down by the faithful parents. The latter implicitly abandons that wisdom. By choosing

---

29. For this rarer meaning of *mišpāṭ*, see Exod. 28:30; Judg. 13:12; Job 32:9.
30. Farmer, *Proverbs and Ecclesiastes*, 72.

to identify with reckless squanderers the foolish son *puts his father to* public *shame* (see 10:1; cf. 27:11). The Mosaic law prescribes that a profligate, stubborn son be stoned to death by the community (Deut. 21:18–21).

8 Providence will transfer the profits of the creditor to those who are gracious to the poor. *Those who increase their wealth by taking interest of any sort [from the poor]* refers to the rich getting richer by charging interest— about 30 percent in that economy—on loans given to the poor (see 22:7). Charging interest kept the poor in perpetual poverty. The Mosaic law, also assuming the borrower is destitute, prohibits an Israelite charging interest from a fellow Israelite (see Exod. 22:25; Deut. 23:20). *Gather it for those who are gracious to the poor* breaks this cycle of abuse. The proverb presumes that *I AM*, the Protector of the poor, is the Agent effecting the transfer (see v. 9). The mediator in this divine economy is the righteous person to whom God entrusts wealth.

9 Like v. 8, this proverb asserts the doctrine of reciprocity. "If a man . . . is deaf to instruction, then God . . . is deaf to prayer."[31] *Those who turn a deaf ear to hearing* (lit. "turn aside their ear from") the inspired *instruction* (tôrâ; see 1:8) will find as a consequence of their rebellion that *even their prayers are detestable* to God (see 15:8, 29). Not hearing instruction implies disobedience to it. If rebels' supplicatory prayers are detestable to God (see 3:32), how much more detestable is their criminal behavior.

10 The antithetical parallelism pits *those who mislead the upright into an evil way* (cf. Matt. 18:6) with the blameless (see p. 37). In poetic justice, the seducer *will fall into their own pit* (the evil trap that they dug for their upright victims) and *the blameless*, who resist the temptation, *will inherit good things* (what is delightful and desirable). The upright are corruptible (see 9:15), but they can defend themselves by hiding God's truth in their hearts (1:8–9; 2:1–22; Ps. 119:10).

11 The antithetical parallelism of this proverb contrasts *rich people* (10:15; 18:11), who are now clearly defined as those who *are wise in their own eyes* (self-reliant; see 3:7; 26:12), against the *discerning poor person* who *searches them out*. Though destitute of earthly wealth, the discerning poor person is rich with divine wisdom and through the purity of their moral acumen can probe and uncover the rich person's deceptive motives and self-serving activities. According to the apostle Paul, the Holy Spirit, who indwells Christians, empowers them to search out all things (1 Cor. 2:15).

---

31. Toy, *Proverbs*, 499.

Concluding Framing Proverb (28:12)

This framing proverb (see above) asserts that a people's fortunes depend on whether the righteous or the wicked come to power (cf. 11:10–11; 14:34; 28:28; 29:2, 16). Its antithetical parallels pit the cause of their fortunes, *when the righteous triumph,* against the cause of their scarcity, *when the wicked* (see pp. 45–46) *rise up* (*ûbəqûm,* "to take over" or "to rise to power," perhaps by military action, as supported by the military terminology of "triumph" in verset A). The parallels also juxtapose the different results, *the* public *splendor* (probably a metonymy for the reemergence of the people) *is great* in contrast to *mortals must be searched out* (for they have hidden themselves; cf. 1 Sam. 13:6–7; 1 Kgs. 17:2–3; 18:4; 19:1–4). But with the victory of the righteous, they emerge to celebrate (cf. 1 Sam. 14:22; Esth. 8:17).

The Importance of One's Relationship with God for Ruling and Gaining Wealth (28:13–27)

I AM and the Ruler (28:13–18)

Malchow observes that every verse of this subunit specifies a type of wicked person: the concealer of transgressions, the hard-hearted, the wicked ruler, the hurry-to-be-rich oppressor, the partial, the greedy, the flatterer, the robber of parents, the self-confident, and those who raise their eyes to avoid seeing the poor's need.[32]

Apart from the frame (v. 28; see v. 12), the unit begins and ends with sayings pertaining to one's relationship with *I AM* (vv. 13–14, 25–27), forming an inner theological frame. Within its theological frame, apart from vv. 17–18, the unit pertains to proper and improper methods of acquiring wealth: hard work and benevolence on the one hand and get-rich-quick schemes and stinginess on the other. The theological frame prevents the teaching from becoming mere moral instruction; it's based on faith in God, who upholds and reveals the moral order.

13 In this proverb pair (vv. 13–14), the unrepentant sinner of v. 13 is escalated to the hardened sinner in verse 14. Verse 13 asserts God's mercy and defines true repentance. *Those who conceal their own transgressions* (see 10:12) describes people who rebel against God and cover up their offenses against others. *They will not succeed* because God (the presumed Agent) will not allow

---

32. Malchow, "A Manual for Future Monarchs," 241.

them to reach their goal. By contrast, *those who confess and abandon them* (transgressions) *will obtain mercy.* "To confess" entails praising God for his greatness (one cannot hide sin from him), his justice (he has the right to punish the sinner), and his grace (he forgives and delivers; cf. Josh. 1:9). Proper repentance involves a double action: acknowledging sins and abandoning them. Such a person *will obtain mercy* (*yəruḥām,* always used for mercy extended from a superior to an inferior). Mercy is voluntary, yet its availability motivates sinners to repent (Ps. 51:13). People may avoid humbling themselves, but they cannot avoid that God knows and will punish sin. How much better it is to give him glory by acknowledging this and experience his mercy (see Ps. 32:3–5; Isa. 1:16–18; Hos. 14:1–3; 1 John 1:8–9; cf. Job 31:33–34)!

14 This proverb warns youth to not harden their hearts, for the hard-hearted will be defeated and ruined. The oxymoron *blessed is the human being* (see 3:13) *who trembles . . . continually* is probably an equivalent of "fear of *I AM.*" Trembling here refers to reverent fear, not to fear of bondage; it is caution, not distrust. Such God-fearers maximize life as God intended it. Their opposites are *those who harden their hearts.* Hardening the heart results in a fixed heart that cannot move in a new direction. The hard-hearted is frozen in unbelief and defiance to God (Exod. 7:3; Ps. 95:8) and is destined to *fall,* a metaphor for defeat/destruction (11:5, 14, 28; 13:17; et passim). *In calamity* signifies the ruin that belongs to vile behavior (see 10:27; 14:2, 27; 15:33; 1 Cor. 10:12; Phil. 2:12; 1 Pet. 4:8).

15 This emblematic proverb compares *a wicked ruler over destitute people* to a hungry lion and ravenous bear. *A roaring, hungry lion* symbolizes the strength and ferocity of the tyrant's swollen appetite. The compounding image intensifies and certifies the tyrant's danger and damage: *a ravenous, charging bear* depicts one that attacks savagely and suddenly to satisfy its hunger (see 17:12). The ruler unleashes his ferocity, brutality and violence over the needy and defenseless poor. Ironically, the defender of justice and protector of the poor turns on them and viciously brutalizes them. Fox comments, "If the king's growl is menacing even when he is not wicked (19:12; 20:2), how much more frightful are wicked . . . rulers"[33] (cf. Dan. 7:1–8; Luke 22:25).

16 The antithetical parallels pit the morally senseless leader piling up extortions against those who hate all unjust gain (cf. Jer. 22:13–19). *A leader who is lacking in understanding* (incompetent by lack of the sages' wisdom) *multiplies extortions* (resorts to corrupt schemes). By contrast *the one who hates ill-gotten gain* ("rip-offs"; see 1:19) *prolongs days* both of others and themselves. The

---

33. Fox, *Proverbs 10–31,* 827.

imprecise parallelism suggests that the rip-off haters are political leaders and that those who practice extortion shorten their own and other's lives. This is so because *I AM* upholds the moral order.

17 As vv. 15 and 16 were linked by the topic of oppressive rulers, this proverb forms a pair with v. 18 by the topic of the consequences of "oppression" (*ʿšq*, v. 17a) and being a "crook" (*ʿqš*, v. 18b): going to the pit. *A human being who is oppressed*, likely by a guilty conscience due to *shedding the blood of life* of an innocent victim, now becomes a fugitive from life. Consequently such a person *will flee* (see 28:1) *to the pit* (the entrance of the grave) in the hope of escaping inward torment. The command *let no one restrain them* warns others not to help them evade their divinely appointed fate. In *lex talionis*, the oppressors are now the oppressed and will forfeit their own life for the innocent blood they shed. The Lord Jesus did not restrain blood-shedding Judas from his fatal destiny (Matt. 27:3–5).[34]

18 The antithetical parallels pit *the one who walks as a blameless person* against *the double-dealing crook*. These contrasting subjects are matched by contrasting consequences. Those who serve *I AM* and the community *will be helped* by *I AM*. If God obliges those who hear the cry of the innocent to help (Deut. 22:27), how much more will the merciful and just God effectively help the oppressed (see 18:10; cf. Luke 11:11–13). But double-dealing crooks *will fall* to their final ruin, *into a pit*.

Wealth by Hard Work versus Haste (28:19–24)

19 This verse and v. 20 form a pair contrasting the gaining of wealth by just and unjust means. Verse 19 essentially repeats 12:11, but instead of "lacks sense" (12:11b), v. 19b reads *is filled with poverty*. The proverb pits people who earn their livelihood steadily through honest toil within God's moral order against *one who* (without honest toil, implicitly) *pursues worthless ventures* outside of it. Since *I AM* is the Agent who obliges himself to reward virtue, we should assume "worthless" ventures violate God's law. Dishonest ventures include bribery (v. 21), stinginess (v. 22), deception (v. 23), robbing parents (v. 24), and greed (v. 25). *I AM* will ensure that the contributor to the communal wealth is filled with food while the unjust taker is ironically filled with the want of life's necessities. Recall that Proverbs looks at the final end of the

---

34. In his novel *Crime and Punishment*, Fyodor Dostoevsky masterfully explored the inner workings of a murderer's conscience leading him to the pit of despair, alienation, and guilt.

moral order, not the exceptions before then (see "Does Proverbs Promise Too Much," pp. 44–45).

20 This proverb's matching antithetical parallelism pits *a conscientious person*, who out of inner stability is honest and dependable, against *one who hastens to get rich* (see 10:4; 13:11). The former, says McKane, "has sufficient integrity and humanity to enable him to possess wealth without being corrupted by it."[35] The imprecise parallels of the subjects suggest that the one in a hurry to get rich lacks the honesty that comes from inner stability. The versets also contrast the different results. The divine Agent causes the conscientious person to *abound in blessings* (fertility, peace, and prosperity). By contrast, the dishonest person who takes shortcuts and cheats others for a quick buck *will not escape punishment* (sterility, poverty, and defeat).

21 Taking a bribe is a slippery slope. Eventually one will be persuaded to commit a crime for the smallest of bribes. The litotes, *to show partiality is not good*, emphatically censures showing favoritism to anyone for a bribe. The clause repeats 24:23 without adding "in giving a verdict." Ironically, *even for a portion of food* (a regular meal; see Gen. 18:5; Judg. 19:5; 1 Sam. 2:36; 28:22; 1 Kgs. 17:11) *a person* (who is able to work and earn a living; see the translation notes) will *commit a crime*. The word "bribe" is not used, but the parallelism implies that the showing of partiality was in exchange for a gift. The debasing greed and degeneration that results from accepting bribes is underscored by the willingness to be corrupted for as little as a meal.

22 Miserliness is another false step to getting rich. The briber tries by disregarding justice (v. 21), the miser by disregarding compassion (see 28:27). Verset A presents the cause, stinginess, and verset B the consequence, want. *Misers* (lit. "a person of an evil eye"; see 23:6; cf. 22:9) *are hasty for wealth* (see 3:9). *They do not know* expresses the fundamental moral problem of fools and the wicked: they have not internalized the fixed moral order of the deed-destiny nexus. *That poverty* (a personification of the lack of food) *will come to them. I AM* will ensure that only righteous people, who serve others, not self, finally hold wealth in his kingdom.

23 Deception by flattery is added to the catalog of foolish ways to get rich. The antithetical parallels pit *the one who reprimands human beings about their conduct* (see 27:6; cf. 15:12) against *the deceptive flatterer* (lit. "one who causes his tongue to be smooth"; see 2:16; 5:3). Flattery aims to deceive and trap victims in order to cheat them. The parallels also contrast the respective conse-

35. McKane, *Proverbs*, 626.

quences. The rebuker *finds favor*—probably from *I AM* and the community, including the corrected (cf. 3:4; Gal. 6:1–2). The flatterer does *not*.

24 The catalog of get-rich-quick schemes climactically ends with the most reprehensible of all evils: the robbing of parents. The subject is *those who rob their father and their mother* (cf. 19:26) *while saying, "There is no crime."* Such people rationalize their villainy with excuses such as, "Eventually it will be all mine anyway" (see 19:14) or "They can no longer manage their finances." Verset B, a variant of 18:9b, adds the consequence: far from being family members, such people *are companions to those who destroy* people. Clifford comments, "Children have no more right to their parents' property while they are living than a brigand from outside the family."[36]

Wealth by Trust in *I AM* and Generosity versus Stinginess (28:25–27)

25 This proverb returns to the theme of a right relationship with *I AM* (cf. vv. 13–14), the theological underpinning of Proverbs. Verse 25 forms a pair with v. 26 that contrasts those who find their security in *I AM* (v. 25b) with those who feel secure in their own understanding (v. 26a). Its antithetical parallels contrast the subjects: *the unrestrained appetite* with *the one who trusts in* I AM (see 3:5; 16:20; 18:10; 28:5; 29:25). They also contrast the predicates: *stirs up strife* (see 15:18) with *will be fattened* (see 11:25). The insatiable appetite of the greedy leads them into conflict because they transgress social boundaries. Those whom the greedy violate then fight back. Thus, wars are started (see Jas. 4:1–2). The righteous, however, do not transgress boundaries, for they rely on *I AM*, the ultimate cause of their "fattening."

26 *Those who trust* (or "feel secure") *in their own heart* (or opinions) are now contrasted with *the one who walks in wisdom* (who conforms to the sages' revealed wisdom). The self-confident live in a fool's paradise, and no one can tell them otherwise. The contrast implies the depravity of the human heart and its need to be redirected by the sages' heavenly wisdom. The contrasting results, *are fools* and *will be delivered* are imprecise, implying that the hardened fools will not escape their justly deserved punishment (11:29; 14:14) and that the wise will escape when *I AM* punishes the fools (1:32–33; 2:20–22).

27 This concluding proverb on proper and improper ways of gaining wealth asserts the paradoxical principle of divine reciprocity: benevolence leads to abundance and stinginess to scarcity. Implicitly, the benevolent trust *I AM* to reward them (19:17; 22:9), but the stingy, trusting their own wisdom (see v. 26a), selfishly hoard their wealth (cf. Matt. 25:40 with 25:41–46). Its im-

---

36. Clifford, *Proverbs*, 247.

precise antithetical topics, *the one who gives to the poor* and *those who shut their eyes*, suggest that the latter ignore the pleas of the poor and fail to help them. The imprecise predicates, *there is no lack* and *abound in curses*, imply that the generous do not lack either the necessities or luxuries of life. "Abounding in curses" (note the plural) refers to curses that bring blight on every area of life (cf. Deut. 27:15–26; 28:15–45). In God's economy, which is against natural reason, the generous do not lack and scrooges will not escape punishment.

Concluding Framing Proverb (28:28)

This framing proverb, like 28:12 and 29:2, asserts the importance of having the right kind of government for a community. *When the wicked rise up* and become dominant (see 28:12b), *mortals hide themselves* (see 22:3; 27:12) to avoid harm from the tyrants. By contrast, *when they perish, the righteous thrive* (increase and become powerful). The imprecise parallelism suggests that when the righteous increase, the people come out of hiding (see 28:12a; 29:2a), something that oc-curred during the reign of Hezekiah, whose men collected these proverbs (25:1; see 2 Chr. 29–30, esp. 30:13–27; cf. Esth. 8:17; Acts 12:23–24). The proverb implies that the devastating destruction of the wicked that enables the righteous to rise is from *I AM*. This is the hope of humanity suffering under tyranny.

Center Line: Sudden Death for the Hard-Hearted (29:1)

This center line (see above) emphasizes the danger of not listening to moral cor-rection. *Those who are often reproved [and] harden their necks* describes people who, as an animal hardens its neck to resist the yoke, repeatedly and willfully defy correction to conform their lives to wisdom (cf. 1:24–31). Hardening the neck is a recurring complaint against Israel (see Exod. 32:9; 2 Chr. 36:13–16; Neh. 9:29; Isa. 48:8; Jer. 17:23; Zech. 7:11–12; Acts 7:51). Verset B presents the fatal consequence, repeating 6:15: *in an instant* (when least expected) *they will be broken and without remedy*. Implicitly, the sinner's sudden, final shattering is from *I AM*. When the opportunity to repent finally ends, the incorrigible fool will have no hope of salvation (see 1:22–32; 28:14, 18; Heb. 10:26–27).

Rearing and Ruling Proved Worthwhile in Dealing with the Poor (29:2–15)

The framing proverb of v. 2 introduces the third unit, whose main body (vv. 3–15) is demarcated by the inclusio formed by "father" (v. 3a) and "mother" (v. 15b). Mentioning only the mother is unique in Proverbs, corroborating that the breaking apart of the compound "father" and "mother" (cf. 1:8; 10:1) is deliberate.

In the second position, vv. 4 and 14, reference is made to the king. Verse 7 functions as a janus between two subunits (vv. 3–6, 8–15). The catchword "righteous" links the janus with v. 6 and "poor" with v. 14.

Framing Proverb (29:2)

This single framing proverb again asserts the importance of righteous rather than wicked leadership for public morale. The imprecise contrast of the causes, *when the righteous thrive* and *when a wicked person rules*, probably implies in this "Manual for Rulers" that the righteous flourish due to magistrates who serve their subjects and not themselves. As for the consequences, in the former case, the *people rejoice* with spontaneous shouts of joy for their prosperity, but in the latter case, *people groan*. Statesmen use their offices to serve the people; mere politicians see their offices as prizes they won and the means to enrich themselves.

Joy and Stability through Righteousness (29:3–6)

The catchwords "person" (*'îš*) and "glad" (*śmḥ*) frame this subunit (vv. 3a, 6b). Positively, the unit pertains to stability: of wealth (v. 3), of a land (v. 4), and of one's self (vv. 5–6). Negatively, it presents three ways in which wealth can be squandered: the prostitute (v. 3), a corrupt king (v. 4), and the flattering or scamming neighbor (vv. 5–6). However, the victims of these fraudsters are also culpable: by associating with prostitutes, by participating in bribes, and by being gullible to flattery.

3 *Those who love wisdom make their father glad* essentially repeats 10:1 and 15:20 (cf. 27:11). The imprecise antithetical parallel, *those who associate with prostitutes squander [his] wealth*, implies that the wisdom-lover keeps far from women who exploit sex for money (cf. 7:6–10) and in so doing not only stay on the path of wisdom but also save the family wealth (cf. 5:7–10). In contrast, the son who wastes the family fortune on prostitutes brings his parents shame (cf. 31:3; Luke 15:30).

4 The antithetical parallels contrast *a king* administering his realm *through justice* with a "person of contributions," an ambiguous term that probably embraces two meanings: *whoever exacts . . . or gives them. Contributions*, a liturgical term that denotes donations to the temple, is probably a satirical metaphor for bribes, blackmail, and other types of ill-gotten gain demanded by the usurper who sits on God's throne (cf. 2 Thess. 2:4). To maintain justice, the king keeps a sharp eye that detects and disallows these corrupt practices. The consequences are precisely antithetical: the former *establishes* (lit. "causes to stand/endure") *a land* (a metonymy for its citizens; see 25:25), while the latter *tears it down* (see 11:11), a strong term for a successful attack that destroys its object. A king who governs justly will make his kingdom steady on the inside and impregnable from the outside, but a king who governs through "contributions" divides his people and renders the kingdom vulnerable to enemy attack.

5–6 These verses are a proverb pair, for both refer to deceitful people by hunting metaphors ("net" and "snare") to signify that they plunder their victims. The flatterer seduces his victims into a sense of false security to plunder them. *People* (see the translation notes) who instead of working hard and contributing to the community economy, deceitfully *flatter their neighbors* do so to take them off guard and so steal their wealth. "Flattery is different from encouragement," says Longman, "because the latter is based on truth."[37] The consequence, *spread a net for their feet,* applies to the neighbors' feet (see v. 5) and their own (see "evil" in 1:16). The next verse clarifies that while the net is intended for the neighbor, it actually snares the evil person (cf. Job 18:7–10).

The metaphor *in the transgression of an evil person is a snare* implies that the rebellious act against God and that their harm against a neighbor involve deception, such as the flattery of v. 5 (cf. 12:13). *But the righteous person,* the intended prey, *shouts for joy and is glad,* implying that the righteous escapes the snare and that in fact the snare destroys the deceiver, giving the righteous the last word in this subunit and in life.

Janus (29:7)

The antithetical parallels of this janus proverb precisely contrast the topics of *the righteous* and *the wicked* and imprecisely predicate one of their essential differences. *The former involve themselves in* (lit. "know"; see 27:23) *court decisions for the poor* and oppressed, which impact their rights. By contrast, the wicked, who care only for their own interests, *do not understand involving themselves* in this way (cf. 28:5; Luke 18:1–5; Acts 24:26–27). The wicked person's ignorance of the plight of the oppressed is due to apathy, not intellectual deficiency. A litmus test for being righteous or wicked is one's involvement with the innocent poor (see 4:18–19; 10:32; 21:10; 24:11; 29:10; Gen. 4:8; Job 29:12–17).

---

37. Tremper Longman III, *Proverbs* (Grand Rapids: Baker Academic, 2006), 502.

Peace through Righteousness (29:8–15)

The second subunit is demarcated by the inclusio formed by the catchword *ḥkm* ("wise people," v. 8b; "wisdom," v. 15a) and its theme pertaining to restoring peace and security through righteous courts.

Three Morally Inferior People (29:8–11)

Verses 8–10 present three morally inferior types of people: mockers (v. 8), the raging fool (v. 9), and murderers (v. 10). Verse 11, which returns to the fool, offers a necessary corrective to the raging fool: the wise person silences the fool and has the final word.

8 This proverb pits intractable *mockers* against the calm *wise*. The former *cause a city* (that is, its citizens) *to pour forth anger*, for they inflame a community's latent resentments against one another to a boiling point by scoffing at the moral order, distorting truth, and inciting people's passions through heated rhetoric. "They are those who take a bad situation and intensify it into a riot"[38] (13:10; 22:10). By contrast, the wise *turn back anger* by addressing the real issues with real solutions. They call the community to repent of wrongdoing (28:13), to trust God (16:1–3), to care for others, not self (v. 7), and to speak calmly, truthfully, and graciously with each other (12:18; cf. Isa. 28:17). They may also restore calm by taking the fool to court (v. 9).

9 *If a wise person confronts the fool in court,*[39] the latter *rages and scoffs* (flies off the handle and rants and raves in an attempt to have the case tossed out of court) *and there is no calm* (that is, the fool will not stop). Wise people, however, calmly submit their case to arbitration, confident that the evidence-based claim will win in the long run. The proverb advises the disciple to ignore the irrational response of fools should they become involved in litigation with them.

10 The internal revulsion experienced by *bloodthirsty people* (see 1:11) who *hate the person of integrity* is escalated in verset B to attempted murder: *as for the upright, they* (the bloodthirsty) *seek to kill each of them*. By placing this proverb between others that pertain to bringing fools to court (v. 9) and finally

---

38. Longman, *Proverbs*, 503.

39. The court setting is suggested by *nišpaṭ*, the Niphal of *špṭ*, which means "an action that restores the order of a disturbed (legal) community" (G. Liedke, *TLOT*, 3:1393, s.v. *špṭ*). However, Fox (*Proverbs 10–31*, 837), Wilson (*Proverbs*, 299), and others assume a non-legal setting where the wise and the fool enter into a personal dispute. The proverb would then be warning the wise about the futility of engaging the fool in debate.

silencing them (v. 11), the context suggests that the murderer will be sentenced by the wise through due process of law.

11 This proverb returns to the wise and the fool but advances it beyond v. 9 to the final scene of their conflict. When the fool rages, the wise person's competence stills it. *Fools give full vent to their rage* (*rûḥô*; lit. "his wind"), probably expressed in a barrage of words. But *a wise* person has the last word and *finally stills it* (*yəšabbəḥennâ*, from the root *šbḥ*). Elsewhere *šbḥ* only occurs in connection with *I AM*'s power to still the stormy sea (Pss. 65:7; 89:9). That sense fits here, for the wise still the fools' "wind." By sound arguments delivered in a cool spirit with a gentle tongue—and if all else fails, by corporal punishment (26:2–5; 29:15)—the wise finally end the fool's raging and its damage to the community.

Rulers and the Court (29:12–15)

This partial subunit returns to the subject of rulers and gives more specific direction about wise procedures in court.

12 Verset A presents the topic, which is also the cause: *A ruler who pays attention to deceptive words* refers to any ruler who through indifference to truth or cynicism about God and humanity is persuaded by lies to injure the weak. Verset B presents the comment, which is also the consequence: *All his attendants* (his sub-officials) *become wicked* (see pp. 45–46): *Qualis rex, talis grex*—like king, like people. Lindsay Wilson comments, "There is great power in modelling. . . . The negative example of a king's behavior . . . results in all the lower officials becoming wicked. They put into practise what they see in the actions of those in authority."[40]

13 This theological proverb sandwiched between royal sayings is a variant of 22:2, but instead of "rich and poor" it has "poor and oppressor." Verset A states the social inequalities of the oppressed and their oppressors, but verset B asserts their ontological equality. *Poor and oppressor* represent both ends of the social spectrum. *Meet together* (see on 22:2). Verset B asserts what they have in common: *I AM is the one who gives light to the eyes of both*; that is to say, both are his creatures and so should respect one another as such.

14 *A king who judges the poor through truth* reestablishes the disturbed harmony of his realm by punishing oppressors and delivering the victims through careful application of justice. Unlike the ruler who listens to deceptive testimony (v. 12), he carefully investigates offenses and probes witnesses to get

---

40. Wilson, *Proverbs*, 300.

to the truth of the matter. Because he conforms his rule to the nature of the Eternal, *his throne*, the symbol of his rule, *is established forever* (cf. 20:28; 25:5; 29:4). Just so, Christ's kingdom will never be toppled.

15 A rearing proverb finishes the inclusio formed by the broken stereotypical phrase, "father" (v. 3a) and "mother" (v. 15b), drawing the unit on rearing and ruling to a conclusion. *A rod and reproof* could be a hendiadys meaning "rod of correction," but judging from 26:3–5 they are better interpreted as signifying physical punishment and verbal reprimand. According to the parallel, *an undisciplined child* has not been disciplined by caning and scolding (cf. 13:24; 19:18; 20:30; 22:6, 15; 23:14). Such instruments of discipline *give wisdom* "to the youth" (gapped); the undisciplined child *brings its mother shame*. Implicitly, undisciplined youth lack wisdom and so bring shame on their lax parents (cf. 3:11–13).

Rearing and One's Relationship with God (29:16–27)

Within the framing proverbs (vv. 16, 27), the fourth unit consists of a decalogue of sayings in two equal halves (vv. 17–21, 22–26). Sayings in the first half alternate between the settings of the home and society. They aim to teach youth on the necessity of discipline both in the home and in the nation. The second half warns them against reprobates: the angry (v. 22), the proud (v. 23), and the thief's accomplice (v. 24). Verses 25–26 form a pair instructing them to trust in *I AM*. The whole unit is concluded by sayings about *I AM*, calling for fear of and trust in him (vv. 25–26; cf. 28:25; 29:13).

Introductory Framing Proverbs (29:16)

When the wicked thrive (*rəbôt*; root *rbh*), *transgression abounds* (*yirbeh*; root *rbh*) implies that the impious and their transgressions sometimes abound for a while (cf. 10:2), but not forever: *The righteous will gaze on their downfall.* The righteous will outlive the wicked and see the Eternal's just order established (see 10:2–3, 24, 28; cf. Gen. 7:23; 19:28; Exod. 14:30; Ps. 54:7; Rev. 11:15). The resurrection of Jesus Christ proves this truth.

The Necessity of Discipline (29:17–21)

17 As with 28:7 and 29:3, a rearing proverb again introduces the subunit. Verset A states the admonition and the motive. Every admonition in Proverbs contains motivation, even when not explicitly stated.[41] *Discipline your son* (see 19:18) addresses the disciple as a parent and implies the home as the location for teaching the wisdom. The motive is *that he will give you rest*, the delightful state of being undisturbed and being free from physical distress and emotional anxiety. Verset B escalates the motivation with *he will give delight to you*, a metonymy for such emotional luxuries as peace (v. 17), joy (vv. 2, 6), and honor (v. 15) as well as the physical rest that the wise son provides for the parents in their old age. The proverb, by its epigrammatic form, presents the truth but cannot present the full story (see "Terseness," pp. 10–11; 22:6). The motivation in three rearing proverbs of this unit (28:7; 29:3; 29:17) is for the parents' benefit; only v. 15a relates to the child's benefit.

18 This second rearing proverb turns from the home to the community. According to J. G. Janzen, this proverb "first characterizes the (desperate) situation of a people for whom there is no means to true wisdom . . . [and] then identifies the critical issue for the members of a people who possess such a means."[42] *Without revelation* (ḥāzôn, the nominal form of ḥāzâ) probably refers to the absence of the sages' inspired wisdom, since the parallel "instruction" refers to the sages' teaching (see 2:5). In 24:22, the sage used ḥāzâ to signify his insight. The parallel, *as for the one who carefully obeys instruction* (tôrâ; see 1:8; 28:4), implies that where the inspired wisdom is present, the critical issue is whether people opt to obey it. Where a society lacks the sages' wisdom to guide it, presumably due to a failure in rearing youth and in exemplary leadership, *the people fall into anarchy*. But where people communicate and obey the sages' revelation, they become worthy of the pronouncement *blessed* (see 3:13). Delitzsch comments: "People are only truly happy when they earnestly and willingly subordinate themselves to the word of God."[43]

19 This proverb returns to the home and the theme of effective rearing and expands it to include the foolish slave. The inspired sage assumes human depravity in spite of moral understanding and that discipline is needed to correct it (cf. 22:6; 26:3). Mere words are insufficient. *Slaves are not disciplined by words* assumes folly is in the heart of indentured workers and asserts that words are insufficient to drive it out of them. *Though they understand* what is right, they do not by nature respond appropriately by repenting and renouncing their wrongdoing (see 28:13;

---

41. P. J. Nel, *The Structure and Ethos of the Wisdom Admonitions in Proverbs* (Berlin: de Gruyter, 1982), 64.

42. Janzen, "The Root *pr'*," 397.

43. Delitzsch, *Proverbs*, 432.

cf. Isa. 66:3b–4). Whybray cites Papyrus Insenger 14:11: "If the rod is far from his master, the servant will not obey him."[44] Biblical law did not allow caning "at any cost" (see Exod. 21:20–21, 26–27; Deut. 25:3). By responding to measured discipline, a slave could become wise and even replace a disgraceful son (17:2).

20 This verse protects v. 19 against an interpretation minimizing the power of words. *People who are hasty with their words* describes those who use their words without regard to the moral order. *There is more hope for a fool than for them* repeats 26:12 verbatim. The fool's speech is rash and reckless (cf. 12:23; 14:16; 15:2), but the amoral damn themselves (Jas. 1:19). They may not blurt out their folly, but they coolly and calmly calculate what to say to manipulate people to serve their, not others', interest.

21 This proverb returns to the theme of disciplining slaves (v. 19), tracing their lives from their youth to their destiny. *Slaves pampered from youth* (lit. "if one pampers his slave from youth") presents the condition or cause: allowing a slave to lead an easy and undisciplined life during their trainable years. *Afterward* transitions to the logical end of the pampering. *They will be insolent* (*mānôn*). Mānôn is found only here, and its meaning is deduced from the context, which is negative. Indulging a slave is not kindness. Instead of stimulating gratitude to their owner, diligence in work, and respect for others, coddling makes them ungovernable and brings their masters shame and loss.

Spiritually Inferior Types versus Those Who Trust *I AM* (29:22–26)

22 First on the list of degenerates to be dodged is *a hothead* (lit. "angry person"), who is *a wrathful person* who *stirs up strife* (see 15:28; 22:24). "Anger" describes the physical visage and "wrath" the inner emotional condition. Hotheads *abound in transgressions* against God's moral ordering of society. Their resentment of others causes them to pick fights with others for the smallest reason. They are ruled by their passions, and their belligerence shows that they love transgression.

23 The arrogant are accented next: *people's pride* is pitted against *the lowly in spirit*. "Pride" derives from a root meaning "to be high." "In pride a person rejects the need for dependence on God or his laws and despises moral or social limitations that regulate behavior according to the highest good for others."[45] In contrast, the lowly (Job 5:11; Prov. 16:19) depend on God and submit to his moral ordering of society. The humble seek the highest good of

---

44. Whybray, *Proverbs*, 403.
45. Gary V. Smith and Victor P. Hamilton, *NIDOTTE*, 1:788, s.v. *g'h*.

others instead of demanding their own rights. The imprecisely paralleled contrasting consequences, *will bring them low* and *will lay hold of honor*, suggest that the lowly will be exalted and the proud will lose social esteem, property, and whatever else was gained by violating the rights of others (cf. Matt. 19:30; 23:12). *I AM*, not an impersonal law, guarantees this outcome.

24 *Those who are an accomplice with a thief* refers to those who agree to help a thief and share in the loot (cf. 1:10–19; Ps. 50:18; Isa. 1:23–24). Such people *hate their life*—they unnaturally devalue their own lives and so put them at risk. Verset B explains: *They hear the divine curse but will not testify.* According to Lev. 5:1, if a case could not be solved by other means, a public curse[46] was proclaimed. Whoever knew about the matter was then required to come forward and testify or else have the curse land on them. Oxymoronically, the accomplice lies by his silence. People join a thief to better their life; instead, they lose it. Blessed is the person who does not join sinners (Ps. 1:1).

25 The accomplices of a thief may refuse to testify because they fear people more than they fear God. This proverb teaches that such people will not survive judgment and offers the solution: trust in *I AM* and experience his protection (cf. Ps 56:11). *Panic* (or "terror") *induced by a human being lays a snare* that fatally traps him. The panic-stricken do not act rationally. In mortal fear of what others may do, they allow themselves to be manipulated by their depraved dictates and in the process incur God's wrath (cf. 1 Sam. 13:8–14; 15:10–29). By contrast, *the one who trusts in* I AM (see 3:5) *will be protected* (see 18:10–11).

26 The proverb's antithetical parallels imprecisely contrast those who seek an audience with a ruler by performing various courtesies, presumably to subvert justice, with those who seek justice from *I AM*. Implicitly, the *many*, especially the rich (see 19:6), excludes those who trust in *I AM* for justice. The expression *who seek the face of a ruler*—used elsewhere only in 1 Kgs. 10:24—signifies seeking a favorable audience with him by "a display of courtesy"[47] (cf. 28:5), probably including a bribe. In contrast to the "many," *an individual* implies a minority status. The outlier seeks a favorable audience with *I AM*, knowing *justice comes from* I AM. Such an individual fears *I AM* and so submits to God's laws. The proverb does not preclude seeking justice from the ruler, but it does prohibit seeking a ruler's judicial interference apart from the fear of *I AM* (see 1:7).

---

46. According to C. A. Keller (*TLOT*, 1:113, *s.v. 'ālâ*), Heb. *'ālâ* ("a public charge," NIV) indicates the curse is a legal aid for securing an oath. Jacob Milgrom (*Leviticus 1–16*, AB [New York: Doubleday, 1991], 293–96) agrees, glossing *'ālâ* with "public imprecation."

47. G. Gerleman, *TLOT*, 2:252, *s.v. bqš.*

Concluding Framing Proverb (29:27)

The concluding framing proverb contrasts the antipathy that the righteous and the wicked feel toward each other's ways. *An unjust person,* who acts against the social, economic, and property rights of others, stands in contrast with *the upright in their way,* whose deportment does not transgress God's established boundaries. The former's behavior *is an abomination* (see 3:32) *to the righteous,* who serve the community, not themselves; the latter's lifestyle *is an abomination to the wicked,* who serve themselves, not others. Fox, citing Saadia, notes: "Not everyone will love you if you are righteous; some people will hate you. But this must not cause discouragement."[48] Van Leeuwen notes: "Tolerance is not an adequate response to evil."[49]

48. Fox, *Proverbs 10–31*, 848.
49. Van Leeuwen, "Proverbs," in *NIB* 5, 247.

The Sayings of Agur Son of Jakeh
(30:1–33)

In the MT,[1] Collection VI, "The Sayings of Agur," is a rhetorical and thematic unity in three parts:

I	Introduction: Agur's Confessions and Prayers	vv. 1–9
II	Main Body: Seven Numerical Sayings	vv. 10–31
III	Conclusion: A Warning Not to Exalt Oneself	vv. 32–33

The introduction and conclusion teach *I AM*'s people to submit to both the authority of God's word (vv. 1–9) and to the king (vv. 32–33) and the sayings in the main body teach to renounce greed and hubris and to live within divinely established moral and social boundaries.

INTRODUCTION (30:1–9)

[1]The sayings of Agur son of Jakeh. An oracle.[a]
   The inspired utterance of the man[b] to Ithiel.
   I am weary, O God, but I can prevail.[c]
[2]Surely I am too stupid to be a man;
   indeed, I do not have the understanding of a human being.
[3]Indeed, I have not learned wisdom,
   nor have I attained to the knowledge of the Holy One.
[4]Who has ever ascended to heaven and come down?
   Who has ever gathered up the wind in his fists?

---

1. To establish Solomonic authorship of the whole book of Proverbs, LXX removes the names of Agur and Lemuel from the superscripts of chapters 30 and 31 and inserts 30:1–14 between 24:22 and 23 and 30:15–31:9 between chs. 24 and 25, leaving 31:10–31 at the end of ch. 29.

Who has ever wrapped up the waters in his robe?
Who has established all the ends of the earth?
What is his name? And what is his son's name?
Surely you know!
⁵Every word of God is purified;
he is a shield to those who take refuge in him.
⁶Do not add to his word,
otherwise he will convict you and you be proved a liar.
⁷Two things I ask of you;
do not withhold [them] from me before I die.
⁸A deceitful lie keep far from me.
Poverty or riches do not give me;
provide me my quota of food;
⁹otherwise I may be sated and dissemble and say, "Who is *I AM*?"
or I may become poor and I steal, and so do violence to the
name of my God.

a. Heb. *maśśâ* normally means a "prophetic burden" (cf. Jer. 23:33–39, NRSV).

b. Traditionally, Heb. *nə'um haggeber* has been translated "the man said," but the use of the collocation in Num. 24:3; 2 Sam. 23:1 shows it refers to prophetic speech.

c. Traditionally, this line has been translated, "To Ithiel and Ukal." But the repetition of the addressee's name would be unique, Ukal is not a Semitic name, and "to" is unexpectedly not repeated. More probably, MT *lə'îtî'ēl* should be revocalized to to *lā'îtî 'ēl* ("I am weary, God") and *'ûkal* be interpreted as a verb ("I am able").

The introduction consists of a superscription identifying the literary genre, author, and addressee (v. 1a) followed by a summary statement of Agur's episte-mology (v. 1b–6)—to wit, wisdom cannot be found apart from revelation. Agur thereupon prays to be truthful in speech and modest in possessions (7–9).

Superscription (30:1a)

If Ithiel is an apprentice official (cf. v. 32), the otherwise unknown *Agur son of Jakeh* is a sage and probably a high court official, which is common in Egyptian instruction literature (see "Setting of Composition," pp. 18–19) and would match the royal authorship of the other six collections. His *sayings* are an inspired *oracle*, a word underscored by the phrase *the inspired utterance of the man*. The immediate addressee, *Ithiel*, stands in for God's people, the implied audience.

Summary Statement of Orthodox Epistemology (30:1b)

I am weary, O God alludes to Agur's inability to know wisdom through human reason (see vv. 2–4); *but I can prevail* alludes to his hope to find truth through Israel's Scriptures (see vv. 5–6). He develops his epistemology with four confessions.

Orthodox Epistemology: Five Confessions (30:2–6)

Confession 1: Inability to Find Wisdom by Human Reason (30:2–3)

Paradoxically, by confessing that he cannot attain wisdom innately or from uninspired sages, Agur displays divine wisdom and takes his first step toward becoming truly wise and fully human. So, this first step of wisdom—to acknowledge one's lack of wisdom—must be a gift of God.

2 Agur's self-abasement—*surely I am too stupid* (or "brutish") *to be a man*, intensified by the parallel *I do not have the understanding of a human being*—may be hyperbole (see Ps. 22:6; cf. Job 25:4–6; Ps. 73:21–22), but it factually acknowledges a person is subhuman without inspired wisdom. His confession expresses deep reverence.[2]

3 He continues to abase himself: *I have not learned wisdom* from uninspired sages (cf. Isa. 5:21; 19:11–12; 29:14; Jer. 8:8–9). The parallel, *nor have I attained* (lit. "know") *to the knowledge of the Holy One*, equates wisdom with a personal relationship with the One who transcends mortals ontologically and stands apart from them morally (see 2:5; 9:10). Fallen and finite humans are unable to grasp the enigma of the human situation (cf. Job 28:12–22) and so cannot live in accordance with divinely established moral order apart from sympathizing with the mind and will of God.

Confession 2: Wisdom Is Dependent upon Comprehensive Knowledge (30:4a)

To be wise, one must transcend the relativity and depravity of a purely human epistemology. Only the Holy One in heaven sees the whole and so sees it clearly. H. Blocher argues, "If . . . reality is all of one piece . . . nothing is independent of God, and nothing can be truly interpreted independently of

---

2. Clifford, *Proverbs*, 26.

God."[3] Humanity can know certainly only if it knows comprehensively. Damming up water was once thought to be always good and forest fires always bad. With more comprehensive knowledge, we now know that damming up water may hurt the environment and forest fires may sustain it. This dilemma of relativity has been noticed by postmodernists. But unlike Agur, who finds its solution in a relationship with God (vv. 4–6), they conceive the contradiction that therefore humans can have no absolutes—except for this one!

Agur's second confession is founded in four "who" questions that showcase unaided humanity's inability to know how to behave. The first question (*Who has ever ascended to heaven and come down?*) establishes the unbridgeable gap between the earthling and heaven and so excludes the mortal from the comprehensive knowledge upon which wisdom depends (see "Wisdom's Delight in the Created Order," pp. 162–64). *Who has ever gathered up the wind in his fist?* and *Who has ever wrapped up the waters in his robe?* point to the Sustainer of the cosmos. The last question (*Who has established all the ends of the earth?*) points to the Creator and implies his omniscience (see Prov. 8:22–33). The Sovereign's mastery over the earth in time and space implies and demonstrates his comprehensive knowledge and so his capacity and wisdom (cf. 8:22–31; Job 28:12–28).

Confession 3: *I AM* Alone Possesses Omniscience (30:4b)

The third confession asks the disciple to answer the first of two "what" questions in v. 4b: *what is* this Sovereign's *name* and elicits the implied second confession as an answer. Based on the rest of the Old Testament, the answer must be "*I AM*" (cf. Job 38; Exod. 3:13). As the creator and sustainer of the whole earth, Israel's covenant-keeping God alone possesses comprehensive knowledge.

Confession 4: Israel Is the Son of *I AM* (30:4b)

The epistemological dilemma that the Holy One is separated from humanity by an unbridgeable gulf (see Agur's second confession) is further resolved by his second "what" question inviting the disciple to confess himself as God's "son." As a good Father, *I AM* teaches his son his wisdom. The question *What is the name of his son?* entails both understanding the significance of being a "son" and knowing the son's name. In Proverbs, "son" always denotes the son whom the wise father teaches (cf. 4:3). From other Old Testament texts, it can be deduced that the son's

---

3. H. Blocher, "The Fear of the LORD as the 'Principle' of Wisdom," *TynBul* 28 (1977): 21.

name is "Israel" (see Exod. 4:22; Deut. 14:1; 32:5–6; Isa. 43:6; Jer. 3:4; Hos. 11:1).[4] In the New Testament, Jesus Christ is the quintessential Son of God, and all those baptized into him are God's children, whom the triune God instructs.

Agur's exclamation *Surely you know!* implies the question, "Don't you?" The question echoes God's challenge to Job in a similar context (38:3). This rhetorical exclamatory question elicits the unspoken second and third confessions. In an erudite Regent College master's thesis, Bruce's student J. Pauls comments that, by asking the questions "Who?" and "What is his name?" rather than the more traditional epistemological question "How does one know?" Agur "radically reshapes the crisis of knowing . . . as a crisis of relationship. . . . The resolution to the epistemological crisis is defined in relational rather than intellectual categories. True wisdom is found in a responsive and receptive relationship with Yahweh, who is wisdom's sole possessor."[5]

Confession 5: *I AM* Revealed Wisdom in the Holy Scripture (30:5–6)

Agur finally confesses that the Holy One and his wisdom, which are otherwise unknown and inaccessible (vv. 2–4), are known through the inspired Scriptures. B. S. Childs remarks, "As an answer to the inquirer's despair at finding wisdom and the knowledge of God, the answer offered is that God has already made himself known truthfully in his written word."[6]

5 Agur cites David's confession of the reliability of God's word (cf. 2 Sam. 22:31 [= Ps. 18:30]). *Every word of God is purified* utilizes imagery of the refiner's cleansing precious metal to assert the truthfulness of Scripture. The imagery of God as *a shield to those who take refuge in him* represents God as a warrior. The imprecise parallelism of the purity of God's word and God's protection assumes that the faithful disciple knows God through Scripture and trusts him according to his inspired revelation (see 3:5–6). This is true even in death (see 14:32).

6 In verset A, Agur cites Deut. 4:2 and 12:32 to restrict God's word to a canon of Scripture (see v. 1; Rev. 22:18–19) which, with regard to the Old Testament, was reckoned as such by ca. 165 B.C. *Do not add to his words*, the so-called canonical formula, warns Israel not to add to or subtract from any part of God's word and implies the authority and inviolability of Agur's sayings (see v. 1). Verse 6b states the reason: *otherwise he may convict you and you be proved a liar*

---

4. The striking parallel in Baruch 3:36 confirms this interpretation.

5. J. Pauls, "Proverbs 30:1–6: 'The Words of Agur' as Epistemological Statement" (ThM thesis, Regent College, 1998), 124.

6. Childs, *Introduction*, 556.

and so be excluded from the way of eternal life. Agur makes no attempt to validate by human reason Scripture's absolute claim for its reliability and authority. Such an attempt would make finite human reason the final arbiter of truth. The finite mind can neither derive nor certify infinite truth; only the Holy Spirit can certify the truth of Scripture to obedient children (cf. Matt. 11:25–27; 16:13–17; John 5:45–47; 8:47; 10:2–6; 1 Cor. 2:11–16; 2 Cor. 3:14–4:6; 1 Thess. 1:5). In sum and in short, orthodox epistemology is based on "the fear of *I AM*" (see 1:7).

Petitions for Truthfulness and Modest Property (30:7–9)

Agur's prayer in vv. 7–9 functions as a janus to his numerical sayings. "Two things" looks ahead to the numerical sayings in vv. 10–31, and his petition to be kept from "deceitful lies" looks back to his warning against adding to God's word and being proved a liar (v. 6). This prayer implies that his sayings are true and that he will not be proved a liar (cf. v. 1).

7 Agur now shifts from addressing Ithiel to addressing God: *I ask of you.* Only the living God, the Holy One of Israel, can satisfy the spiritual and physical needs expressed in his *two things.* The addition *do not withhold [them] from me before I die* adds urgency to his petitions and may imply that he prays "with all the intense earnestness of a dying sinner."[7]

8 His first petition, *a deceitful lie keep far from me*, is a request to be radically truthful. His second petition, *poverty or riches do not give me*, anticipates his numerical sayings that proscribe greed and prescribe moderation. Verset B presents this second petition again positively: *provide me my quota of food.* "Food" functions as a synecdoche for all of one's needs, and "my quota" depends on one's station in life (e.g., whether one is single or married, a governor or governed; cf. Exod. 16:18; Neh. 5:17–18; Matt. 6:11; 1 Tim. 6:8).[8] Agur's ideal is the golden mean in possessions, not in moral behavior per Aristotle.

9 His reasons for this golden mean are that he neither disown *I AM* nor dishonor his name. On the one hand, if he has too much (*otherwise I may be sated*), even Agur may *dissemble* (act against his better knowledge) and haughtily ask, "*Who is* I AM?"—that is, say, "I have no need to depend on *I AM* or reason to obey him" (cf. Deut. 8:12–14). On the other hand, if Agur became indigent (*I may become poor*) he would need to *steal* to survive *and so do violence to the name of* (a metaphor for defaming) . . . *God.* His stealing would

---

7. Bridges, *Proverbs*, 596.

8. R. W. Byargeon ("Echoes of Wisdom in *I AM*'s Prayer," *JETS* 41 [1998]: 353–65) shows that the Lord's prayer (Matt. 6:9–13) echoes the structure and theology of Agur's prayer.

imply he does not trust God to provide for his needs and that he is a hypocrite. In sum, the glory of God, not his own need, motivates Agur's two requests.

MAIN BODY: SEVEN NUMERICAL SAYINGS (30:10–31)

¹⁰Do not slander a slave[a] to his master,
 otherwise he may curse you, and you become liable.
¹¹A generation—they curse their fathers
 and do not bless their mothers.
¹²A generation—[they are] pure in their own eyes
 but are not cleansed from their excrement.
¹³A generation—how they raise their eyes!
 And [how] they lift up their pupils!
¹⁴A generation—their teeth are swords
 and their jawbones are butcher knives
 to devour the poor [and eliminate] them from the earth,
 and the needy from humanity.
¹⁵The horse leech has two daughters: "Give!" "Give!"
 They are three things that are never satisfied,
 four that never say, "Enough!"
¹⁶Sheol and the barren womb,
 the land that is never satisfied with water, and fire, which never
  says, "Enough!"
¹⁷As for the eye that mocks a father and shows contempt for the
  grey hair of a mother,
 the ravens of the wadi will peck it out,
 and the vultures will devour it.
¹⁸They are three things that are too wonderful for me;
 and as for four, I do not know them:
¹⁹the way of an eagle in the sky, the way of a serpent on a rock,
 the way of a ship in the heart of the sea, and the way of a man
  with a virgin.
²⁰This is the way of an adulteress:
 she eats and wipes her mouth and says, "I have not done
  iniquity."
²¹Under three things the earth trembles,
 under four it cannot endure:
²²under an official when he becomes king
 and an outcast who becomes full of food;

417

²³under a hated woman when she gets married
  and a maidservant when she dispossesses her mistress.
²⁴As for four things, they are small creatures of the earth,
  but they are extremely wise:
²⁵ants are a people without strength,
  and so they store up their food in the harvest.
²⁶Rock badgers are a people without numerical strength,
  and so they place their houses in the rocks.
²⁷Locusts have no king,
  and so all of them go forth dividing into companies.
²⁸A wall lizard you can catch with two hands,
  but it lives in the king's palace.
²⁹They are three creatures that excel in their stride,
  and four that excel in their movement:
³⁰the lion is a hero among animals
  and does not turn back from the face of anything;
³¹the strutting rooster and the he goat
  and a king no one dares to resist.

a. Or "official."

The seven numerical sayings are rhetorically and thematically unified.

Rhetorically, the seven[9] numerical sayings are arranged into two groupings, distinguished by the second group having an *initial* titled line involving a numeral.[10] The macrostructure of the two groups of three (vv. 11, 15a, 15b) and four (vv. 18, 21, 24, 29) sayings mirrors the microstructure of the numerical echelon ("three . . . four") in the title lines (vv. 18, 21, 29). Each group is introduced by a one-verse saying in contrast to sayings of more than one verse. Here is a sketch of the structure:

First Group: Renouncing Greed	vv. 10–16
Introductory one-verse saying	v. 10
Saying 1	vv. 11–14
Saying 2	v. 15a
Saying 3	vv. 15b–16

9. The number seven signifies divine perfection in the Bible.
10. Note the numerical title line of the third saying is not initial but tucked away in a parallel: v. 15b.

Second Group: Living within Boundaries	vv. 17–31
Introductory one-verse saying	v. 17
Saying 4	vv. 18–20
Saying 5	vv. 21–23
Saying 6	vv. 24–28
Saying 7	vv. 29–31

After the introductory sayings, the first saying of each group begins with a fourfold anaphora: *dôr* ("generation," vv. 11–14) and *derek* ("way," v. 19).[11]

Thematically, numerical sayings, says Aitken, "never press their lesson, but leave it to the reader to ponder and tease it out."[12] We infer that these numerical sayings collectively aim to preserve the divinely established moral and social order. The introductory sayings of both groupings proscribe hubris against government (v. 10) and parents (v. 17), and both introductions threaten the violators with death, and so provide the motivation for renouncing greed (vv. 11–16) and living within established boundaries (vv. 18–31); these actions sustain the divinely established social order founded on accepting authority (v. 17) and not abusing it (v. 10).

First Group: Renouncing Greed (30:10–16)

Introductory Saying: Abusing Authority in Government (30:10)

The first introduction proscribes abuse of authority in government: *Do not slander an 'ebed* (a *slave* or "official"; cf. 16:28; 18:8; 25:23; 26:20, 28) *to his master*. The saying assumes that the unjustly slandered *'ebed* has been found guilty by his superior and, having no other recourse for justice, appeals to God to punish the slanderer: *otherwise he may curse you*. Agur's threat (*and you become liable*) refers to divine punishment and entails that the curse is deserved, for it lands on the guilty (see 26:2).

Saying 1: The Greedy Generation (30:11–14)

Unlike the other numerical sayings that have different referents, this saying lists four characteristics of one generation (a discrete age group, like baby

---

11. These two introductory anaphoras are complemented in the conclusion by the three-fold anaphora of polyvalent *mîṣ* ("churning," "stirring," "wringing," v. 33).

12. Aitken, *Proverbs*, 232.

boomers and millennials in our time). The evils of the depicted generation escalate from demeaning parents (v. 11) to devouring the poor (v. 14). The catchword "their eyes" links vv. 12 and 13.

11 This *generation* not only dishonors their fading *fathers* and *mothers* (cf. Exod. 20:12; Deut. 5:16; Lev. 19:3), they *curse* them (cf. v. 10), a capital crime (Exod. 21:17; Deut. 27:16), and *do not bless* those to whom they owe their own lives (see 10:6). These children demean their parents, hoping to obtain their inheritance faster (cf. 20:21) and avoid caring for them (Matt. 15:3–6), but instead will obtain a premature, demeaning death (20:20; 30:17).

12 Furthermore, this *generation* is *pure* (free of ethical contamination) *in their own eyes*—which is to say, not actually; they are deluded (Prov. 16:2). In truth *they are not cleansed from their excrement*, a gross metaphor for their moral defilement and stench.

13 Though covered with excrement, they think themselves much better than others, as signified by the rhetorical *how*.[13] *They raise their eyes* (see 6:17) symbolizes their supreme superciliousness, intensified by the synonymous parallel *they lift up their pupils*. Their raised eyes reveal their arrogant hearts (Ps. 131:1; Prov. 21:4).

14 Their *teeth* and *jawbones* are grotesquely represented as *swords* and *knives*—unique metonymies for speech, signifying that it is cruel, insensitive, and lethal. As explained in verset B, their speech slices and dices *the poor* and *the needy* in order to *devour* (that is, cannibalize) *them* and so *[eliminate] them from the earth* and *from humanity* itself (cf. Micah 2:2–3). "They withhold good from those to whom it is due" (3:27) and lie to crush the defenseless poor in the court (Prov. 22:2; cf. Ps. 10:8–9; Eccl. 4:1; Isa. 3:15; Amos. 2:6–7; 4:1; Mic. 2:1–3; 3:1, 9).

Saying 2: The Insatiable Leech (30:15a)

The greed of the evil generation morphs into a second saying about greed. The parasitic *horse leech* has *two* organs: one to suck blood, the other to attach itself to its host. It is personified as a mother with *two daughters* who demand, "*Give!*" "*Give!*" The saying warns against the danger of tolerating a parasite. The double-sucking leech symbolizes either an individual of inordinate lusts or a wicked person (e.g., a thief or a welfare scammer), both of whom suck out the life and wealth of a society. The insatiable appetite of the parasite must be quickly eliminated; otherwise it multiplies and does ever more damage.

---

13. *HALOT*, 2:551, s.v. *māh*.

Saying 3: Four Insatiables (30:15b–16)

This is the first explicit numerical saying, though it is not line-initial (see p. 418). In sayings having a numerical echelon, such as *they are three things . . . four*, the higher number is the real number and states what the items have in common. Here, they have the common characteristic of *never satisfied*, personified by *never say, "Enough!"* They are divided into two pairs: *Sheol*, which ever yearns to end life, and *the barren womb*, which ever yearns to produce life (cf. Gen. 30:1; 1 Sam. 1; Luke 1:5–25); the arable *land*, which *is never satisfied with* enough *water* to sustain crops, and *fire*, which ever destroys the harvest. As the created order is ever engaged in an unending battle between life and death, similarly in the moral order, the wise ever strive against evil without ever attaining utopia.

Second Group: The Wisdom of Living within Boundaries (30:17–31)

The second group of numerical sayings moves from order within the home to order within society to order within the state.

Introductory Saying (30:17)

Verset A presents the cause, which is rebellion against parental authority: *the eye* (see vv. 12, 13; the eye reveals the child's haughty inner disposition) *that mocks a father* and mother *and shows contempt* (clarifying "mocks") *for the grey hair* (which represents wisdom) *of a mother* and father. Verset B presents the fatal consequence with two metaphors using unclean (cf. Lev. 11:15) carrion birds (cf. Isa. 34:11; Jer. 16:3–4). *I AM* feeds these birds (Job 38:41), so they represent his judgment. *The ravens of the wadi will peck it out.* Their plural number and their feeding in a barren environment indicate the total elimination of the defiant child. *The vultures will devour it* implies that the carcass is unburied, symbolizing its tragic and shameful end. The doubling of the metaphor indicates the certainty of punishment.

Saying 4: Four Awesome Ways and One Awful Way (30:18–20)

Four creations amaze Agur, climaxing with human erotic love (vv. 18–19). His awe of human eros between a man and his virgin stands in stark contrast to his disdain for the adulteress, who reduces sex with many men to nothing more than eating a meal (v. 20).

18 The four *ways* that are listed in v. 19 are *too wonderful for* Agur because they exceed normal expectations and so evoke his praise and admiration. *I do not know them* expresses his inability to fully appreciate such wonders (cf. Job 42:2–3).

19 The four wonders all move within their appropriate and difficult environments in an easy, intriguing, gracious manner without leaving a trace and without being taught, and yet they reach their goals. The first two pertain to animals and the latter two to human creation and behavior. What amazes Agur about *the way of an eagle* is its artless, yet so artful, gravity-defying and seemingly endless circling high *in the sky*. *The serpent on a rock* amazes because it appears to glide over the rock despite lacking legs and anything to grasp. Agur probably chose *a ship*, not a fish, both to turn away from animal skills to human skills and for its gliding motion in common with the other three things. *In the heart of the sea* (the remote, open seas) evokes the ship's defiance of the unfathomable depths. *Of a man with* (or "in") *a virgin* refers to the first experience of sexual intercourse, the goal of romantic love, limited in this case to one man and woman. All four ways demonstrate the paradox of freedom within boundaries.

20 *This is the way of an adulteress*, a married woman who has sexual liaisons with other men (see 2:16). *She eats* (a metaphor signifying her sexual activity) *and wipes her mouth* (she leaves no trace of her immoral act). Her self-condemning quote, "*I have not done iniquity*," vividly dramatizes her lack of conscience about smashing the boundaries of ordered society. The way of the man and his virgin enhances life; the way of the adulteress undermines it.

Saying 5: Four Upside-Down Social Situations (30:21–23)

The adulteress who upsets the divine moral order morphs into a saying that is a sober commentary on a world turned upside-down by human hubris. Verse 22 pertains to men attempting to usurp power in society and v. 23 to women attempting to usurp authority in the home. The saying motivates the wise, who bring life to a culture, to prevent upstarts from seizing power and reddening it with blood.

21 The title line introduces the *four* upstarts *under* (the saying's catchword) whose weight *the earth* (its social order; see 29:4) *trembles* (breaks up) and *cannot endure*.

22 Society collapses from *under* the leadership of *an official* (*'ebed*; see v. 10) *when he becomes king*. An official's primary responsibility is loyalty to the king. The saying implies an unfaithful official who usurps the divinely ordained throne (cf. 1 Kgs. 16:9–20; 2 Kgs. 8:7–14). The hubristic usurper will prove to be a tyrant. Society also collapses *under* an asocial *outcast* (a sacrilegious fool) *who becomes full of food* (cf. 9:5; 30:9, 15, 16). The fool has been on a starvation diet; feeding him rewards vice and makes him more arrogant and dangerous.

23 A home is threatened when it comes *under* the control of a *hated woman*. That she is hated shows she is the opposite of the prudent wife (12:4; 18:22; 31:10). *Gets married* connotes that the quarrelsome woman who cannot rule her own tongue now rules the home against the divinely established social order. The home can also be ruined by an uppity *maidservant*, the female counterpart to the *'ebed* in v. 22. That *she dispossesses her mistress* means she takes possession of the home, as Hagar attempted to do (Gen. 16:4). To succeed, the rebellious maidservant must first steal the affections of her mistress's husband. To maintain domestic stability, a man must marry wisely and then remain true to his wife, as Abraham did.

Saying 6: Four Wee but Wise Beasties (30:24–28)

In contrast to the four upstarts who upend the social order (vv. 22–23), this saying lists four exemplary wee beasties who, in this parable about brains over brawn, have divine wisdom that enables them not only to survive but also to thrive. The saying is a parable since Agur is a sage, not a zoologist.

24 *They are small* (that is, vulnerable and without offensive or defensive power) *creatures of the earth*. Yet *they are extremely wise* (see pp. 34–35).

25 *Ants are a people* personifies the ant. They represent people *without strength* to overcome their enemy or defend themselves. Their compensating wisdom is that *they store up their food in the harvest*. Likewise, the wise exercise prudent foresight, discipline, and industry in a timely manner (see 6:6–8). For example, the disciple should store up the sages' wisdom now so that when tested by the wily adulteress or wicked villains, he will not succumb (cf. 1:10–14; 6:22). Christians know that now is the time of salvation (2 Cor. 6:2); after death, it is too late (see 1:28; cf. Heb. 9:27).

26 *Rock badgers* are limited by their being a *people without numerical strength*. Their compensating wisdom is that *they place their houses in the rocks*, making them inaccessible to predators (Ps. 104:18). The moral: the wise find their security outside themselves in God as he is known in the inspired sages' teachings (see 3:5; 22:19). Christians find their safety in the Rock, Christ Jesus.

27 The vulnerability of *locusts* is that *they have no king* to lead and protect them. Their compensating wisdom: *all of them go forth dividing into companies*. Locusts are well known for their amazing ability to form gigantic swarms that wreak devastation on apocalyptic scales. How much more should God's people under God's kingship advance God's kingdom by fighting in unison against the enemy, not one another.

28 The vulnerability of the *wall lizard*[14] is that it *can be caught with two hands*. Instead of presenting a compensating wisdom, the saying asserts the reward of wisdom: *it lives in the king's* luxurious and protected *palace*. The wise, though vulnerable, will dwell in the highest residence of the realm. Christians will reside forever in the dwellings that the Son of God is preparing for them (John 14:1–3).

Saying 7: Four Stately Marchers (30:29–31)

The palace-dwelling wall lizard morphs into four stately creatures who stride majestically over their spheres of influence. The wise, knowing how to compensate for their vulnerability, march with their heads held high, fearing no one but God. The first three animals, supreme leaders in the natural realm, lead up to the fourth, the stately king in the human realm. The connection to the king and the personification of the lion as a "hero" implies that the three animals function as a parable for human rulers. The wise son should walk in stately fashion, cowering before nobody, knowing that through wisdom he has power and ability to rule (see 8:14–15) and that *I AM* establishes his step and protects the wise.

The title line identifies the unifying feature of the saying's *four* figures: they *excel in their stride*—that is, *in their movement*. *The lion* is personified as a *hero* and thus strong, presenting a stark contrast to the preceding weak animals. *Among animals* is added to emphasize its surpassing its fellow creatures in strength and capability. *And does not turn back from the face of anything* signifies its heroism.

The rest of the stately marchers are *the strutting rooster, the he-goat,* and *the king no one dares to resist*.

CONCLUSION: A WARNING AGAINST SELF-EXALTATION (30:32–33)

> [32]If you play the fool in exalting yourself,
>   and if you scheme to do so, clap your hand over your mouth,
> [33]for [as] the churning of cream produces butter
>   and as the wringing of the nose produces blood,
>   so the "pressing out" of wrath produces strife.

The concluding saying warns Ithiel, upon whom God has not bestowed royalty (see v. 1), not to make a play for a higher position such as that of the heroic

---

14. Or "spider"; the Heb. is disputed.

king; otherwise, he will get a bloody nose and set strife loose in the community. The saying protects legitimate authority and the community from conflict.

32 *If you play the fool* (see pp. 47–48) is specified as *exalting yourself* (cf. 25:6; Num. 16:3; 23:24). This folly disrupts the divinely established social order. *And if you scheme to do so* further specifies the usurpation as a planned coup (cf. 24:9). *Clap your hand over your mouth* suggests that the self-exaltation involves boasting. It has the sense of "shut up immediately" (cf. Job 40:3–5).

33 *For* introduces the reason to stop exalting self. The three comparatives speak of self-exaltation as a sustained pressure that inevitability changes something's very nature. The simile *as the churning of cream produces butter* signifies that self-exaltation has an inevitable effect. The second simile about self-exaltation and its inevitable effect (*as the wringing of the nose produces blood*) safeguards the first comparison from being misinterpreted as beneficial. The third metaphor (*the pressing out of wrath produces strife*) clarifies the inevitable damage to society. The usurper's disdainful pressing down of a community by self-ambition squeezes the people's anger beyond its limits and so breaks out in strife (cf. 30:22). The Protestant Reformers broke out against popes who exalted themselves above the word of God.

The Sayings of Lemuel
(31:1–31)

Following its superscription, the Sayings of King Lemuel contains two distinct poems: the first a poem on the noble king (vv. 2–9) and the second an acrostic on the noble wife (vv. 10–31).

SUPERSCRIPTION (31:1)

¹The sayings of Lemuel, a king—
an oracle that his mother taught him.

Many commentators suggest the superscription only covers the poem about the noble king (vv. 1–9), but based on Egyptian analogies, Kitchen extends it to the poem about the valiant wife (vv. 10–31): "If verses 10–31 be excluded then the resulting first 'work' of only 9 verses becomes ludicrously brief and the supposed second 'work' of vv. 10–31 becomes an isolated poem with no title [or preamble] . . . [and becomes] an anomalously foreign body in Proverbs."[1]

Verse 1a identifies the genre of both works as *sayings* (see 1:6) and its author as King *Lemuel* ("Dedicated to God"). This king is unattested in Israel's history and so is probably a proselyte. *A king* further identifies the sayings as "royal instruction," a genre that aims to equip rulers to discharge their duties wisely and justly. Verse 1b further identifies the "sayings" as a prophetic *oracle* (see 30:1) and explains its authorship: *his mother taught him* (see 1:8), either as the author or more probably as the conveyer of a tradition whose origin is unknown (see 4:1–4). Queen mothers influenced kings, but there is no parallel in ANE literature of a mother's wise sayings (see 1:8; 4:3; 6:20). The faithful,

---

1. K. Kitchen, "Proverbs and Wisdom Books of the Ancient Near East: The Factual History of a Literary Form," *TynBul* 28 (1977): 100–101.

through the Holy Spirit, heard the voice of God in the tradition, an inspired editor added it to Proverbs, and so it became part of the Holy Bible.

THE NOBLE KING (31:2–9)

²Listen,ª my son! Listen, son of my womb!
    Listen, son of my vows!
³Do not give your strength to women,
    and your sovereign power to those who destroy kings.
⁴It is not for kings, Lemuel, not for kings to drink wine,
    nor for rulers to crave intoxicants;
⁵otherwise he may drink [them] and forget what is decreed,
    and lest he change a verdict for every oppressed person.
⁶Give² intoxicants to the one who is perishing,
    wine to those who are bitter!
⁷Let them drink and forget their poverty,
    and remember no more their misery.
⁸Open your mouth for the mute;
    to give judgment for everyone fading away.
⁹Open your mouth, judge righteously,
    and issue edicts for the poor and needy.

a. For the meaning of Hebrew *māh*, see Waltke, *Proverbs 15–31*, 503–4 n. 14.

The saying of the noble king exhibits the following structure:

I	Introductory admonition to hear		v. 2
II	Admonitions to show restraint		vv. 3–7
	A	With regard to women	v. 3
	B	With regard to intoxicants	vv. 4–7
		1 Not to become drunk and forget edicts that protect the poor	vv. 4–5
		2 To give intoxicants to the poor to forget their misery	vv. 6–7
III	Admonition to give new edicts for the poor		vv. 8–9

As in the Thirty Sayings of the Wise, a warning against immoral women

2. Indef. pl.

(v. 3; cf. 23:26–28) is linked with a warning against intoxicants (vv. 4–7; cf. 23:29–35). Six of the eight verses on the noble king pertain to caring for the poor (vv. 4–9), and four of these pertain to liquor (vv. 4–7). The latter four consist of a negative didactic couplet (vv. 4–5) and two positive admonitions (vv. 6–7).

2 Through a threefold repetition of *listen* (*māh*), Lemuel's mother strongly admonishes him to "take heed" of her sayings. She couches the typical *listen my son* in tender terms (*son of my womb, son of my vows*), wherein she traces their close relationship backward from the present to his development in her womb and to her vows before pregnancy. Her vows probably were that if God gave her a son, she would dedicate him to live according to God's wisdom (cf. 1 Sam. 1:11).

3 In the first command, the queen warns against unrestrained sexual gratification: *your strength* and *sovereign power* are metonymies for all that contributes to making a strong dynasty. *Those who destroy kings* is a metonymy for *women*, as those who do not build up the home (2:16–19; 5:1–23; 6:20–35; 7:1–27; 14:1) but instead destroy dynasties, corrupt the king's power, distract his attention from serving the people, undermine his good judgment, and squander the nation's wealth (see 13:22). David's obsession for Bathsheba led to flagrant violations of justice.

4–5 In the first couplet, the queen warns kings not to drink wine because intoxicants, like obsession with women, undermine the just decrees established to protect the poor (v. 5; cf. 20:1; 21:17; 22:22; 23:20–21, 29–35). *Otherwise he may drink [them] and forget what has been decreed* concerning justice *and lest he change a verdict* already given in favor *of every oppressed person.*

6–7 The second couplet may be a citation of an older saying that was originally addressed to people in general and is now applied specifically to Lemuel (in contrast to v. 4). *Give intoxicants to the one who is perishing and wine to those who are bitter* is pure sarcasm, not a proposed welfare program to offer this "opiate" to the masses. Taken literally, her command would be contrary to wisdom (cf. 19:27). Drinking to drown distress solves nothing. The sarcastic command aims to debunk intoxicants as useless. The misery of the poor needs to be alleviated by the king protecting them, as indicated in the next couplet.

8–9 She again addresses Lemuel. The king must speak up for the marginalized (cf. v. 20). *Open your mouth*, repeated at the beginning of both v. 8 and v. 9, means "speak up," clarified in vv. 8b and 9: *to give judgment* (judicial verdicts) and to *judge righteously* (deliver the oppressed). The metonymy *for the mute* implies the poor lack a voice to defend themselves in the court (cf. Ps. 72:1–4, 12–14; Jer. 22:15–19). They may be too illiterate to counteract the judicial sophistry of the powerful wicked, too inarticulate to state their case convincingly, too poor to obtain relevant evidence, too lowly to command respect, and too vulnerable to abuse by bribery. The king, therefore, is their only human defense against the ungodly. *Everyone fading away* is another metonymy for *the poor and needy*.

THE VALIANT WIFE (31:10–31)

¹⁰*aleph*   A valiant wife who can find?
    Her price is far beyond corals.
¹¹*bet*   The heart of her husband trusts in her;
    he does not lack spoil.
¹²*gimel*   She does him good and not evil
    all the days of her life.
¹³*dalet*   She diligently selects wool and flax,
    and works with her glad palms.
¹⁴*he*   She becomes like trading vessels;
    she brings her food from afar;
¹⁵*waw*   and she arises [like a lioness] while it is still night
    and provides prey for her household
    and the quota [of food] for her servant girls.
¹⁶*zayin*   She considers a field and purchases it;
    from the fruit of her palms she plants a vineyard.
¹⁷*khet*   She girds her loins with strength;
    she strengthens her arms for the task.
¹⁸*tet*   She perceives that her trading is good;
    her lamp [of prosperity] does not go out at night.
¹⁹*yod*   Her hands she holds out to the doubling spindle;
    her palms grasp the spindle.
²⁰*kaph*   Her palms she spreads out to the poor,
    and she holds out her hands to the needy.
²¹*lamed*   She is not afraid for her household on account of snow,
    for all her household is clothed in scarlet.
²²*mem*   Coverlets she makes for herself;
    her clothing is fine linen and [wool dyed with] purple.
²³*nun*   Her husband is respected at the city gate
    when he sits with the elders of the land.
²⁴*samek*   Garments she makes and sells;
    sashes she supplies to the merchants.

²⁵*ayin*   Strength and majesty are her clothing,
and so she laughs at the coming days.
²⁶*pe*   Her mouth she opens with wisdom,
and loving teaching is on her tongue;
²⁷*tsade*   [she is] one who watches over the affairs;
the food of idleness she does not eat.
²⁸*qoph*   Her sons arise and pronounce her blessed;
her husband [rises] and praises her:
²⁹*resh*   "Many daughters do valiantly,
but you surpass all of them."
³⁰*shin*   Charm is deceitful and beauty is fleeting;
as for a woman who fears *I AM,* she should be praised.
³¹*tav*   Extol her for the fruit of her hands,
and let her works praise her in the gates.

The paean of praise to the valiant wife draws Proverbs to its close. It is structured as an acrostic, in which the initial letter of each verse follows the sequence of the Hebrew alphabet. This achieves a sense of totality and completeness ("everything about the subject from A to Z"). The acrostic is also structured logically:

I	Introduction: Her value		vv. 10–12
	A	Her general worth inferred from her scarcity	v. 10
	B	Her specific worth to her husband	vv. 11–12
II	Body: Her activities		vv. 13–27
	A	Her cottage industry	vv. 13–18
	B	Janus	v. 19
	C	Her social achievements	vv. 20–27
III	Conclusion: Her praise		vv. 28–31
	A	From her family	vv. 28–29
	B	From all	vv. 30–31

The encomium's three stanzas progress from her husband's trust in her (v. 11) to his political empowerment by her (v. 23) to his praise of her (v. 28). The body also proceeds logically from her income generated by her weaving skills and expanded through her trading (vv. 13–19) to her accomplishments on that economic base (vv. 20–27).

As for genre, Al Wolters classifies the poem as heroic (recounting a hero's mighty deeds—usually military exploits).[3] Erika Moore agrees: "Heroism in the battlefield is transposed . . . to a woman's *vita activa* in home and community." Moore adds that the valorous wife is "a spiritual heir of Israel's ancient heroes" and "a champion for those around her by her diligent application of wisdom." So, the valorous wife is "a heroic figure used by God to do good for His people, just as the ancient judges and kings did good for God's people by their martial exploits."[4]

But does the encomium praise a real woman or a personification of Wisdom, as in the Prologue (1:20–33; 8:1–36; 9:1–6)? If she is a personification of wisdom, then the poem instructs the son to embrace Wisdom as a wife to help him provide for the family (cf. 4:4–9). If, however, she is a real woman like Ruth, who is also praised at the gates as a "valiant woman" (*ēšet-ḥayil*, Ruth 3:11), then she emerges as an important contributor to the economy of the family and the community. The exegesis that follows validates that she is a real woman. In fact, every occurrence of "woman" (*'iššâ*) in Proverbs refers to a real woman (see 12:4; 14:1; 18:22; 31:3).

But how real is she? Murphy's rhetorical question, "Who could possibly achieve in many lifetimes what she achieves in these verses?" implies that no one could.[5] However, as Fox notes, "there are a great many women whose activities equal the ones described in Prov. 30:10–31 [*sic*]." He adds that most nineteenth-century "American farm wives . . . would need a broad array of skills in handicraft, agriculture, poultry farming, and commerce, as well as home economics and child-rearing, and [they] would work from before dawn to after dark . . . while remaining generous and God-fearing."[6]

Of course, the valiant wife is not the family's sole breadwinner. Up to now, Proverbs focused exclusively on the son's character and work. This paean of praise to the valiant wife assumes that the husband has founded the home on a sound economic foundation (24:27). On that firm foundation, his wife can settle down and function at her maximum capacity.[7]

---

3. Al Wolters, "Proverbs XXI 10–31 as Heroic Hymn," *VT* 38 (1988): 446–57.

4. Erika Moore, "The Domestic Warrior" (unpubl. paper submitted to Bruce Waltke for OT 813: Proverbs, Westminster Theological Seminary, 1994), 18.

5. Murphy, *Proverbs*, 245.

6. Fox, *Proverbs 10–31*, 910.

7. On a humorous note, Ivan knew a gifted single woman who engaged a reputable online matching service to help her find a life partner. All the male responders would ask her one question: "Are you a Proverbs 31 woman?" After several such inquiries, she began to respond, "I am. And are you a Proverbs 1:1 to 31:9 man?"

The valiant wife has been canonized as a role model for all Israel for all time. Wise daughters aspire to be like her, wise sons seek to marry her (v. 10), and all wise people aim to incarnate her virtues.

Introduction: Her Value (31:10-12)

10 The initial words, *a valiant wife* (*ʾēšet-ḥayil*), immediately focus attention on the sage's subject. *Ḥayil* denotes "competent strength" (Prov. 12:4; cf. Ruth 3:11; Ps. 84:7) and membership in a select group (cf. Gen. 47:6; Exod. 18:21), including a warrior class (2 Kgs. 24:14, 16). The itemization of her deeds in the body of the poem defines specifically what *ḥayil* means. Were the question *who can find?* real, the expected answer would be *"almost* no one," not "no one," since she is married and so was "found" by her husband. The question, however, is rhetorical, to awaken within the implied audience the desire to find such a wife and be like her and to imply that she is precious, rare, and attractive, as indicated by the assertion *her price is far beyond corals* (see 3:14). The assertion is based on the ANE practice of obtaining a wife by means of a bride-price (see 4:5-7).[8] A valiant wife is a gift from God (19:14) and must in part be sought by prayer (15:29; 16:3; Jas. 1:6).

11 That *the heart of her husband trusts in her* is remarkable, for apart from this text and Judg. 20:36, Scripture condemns trust in anyone or anything apart from *I AM* (cf. 2 Kgs. 18:21; Ps. 118:8-9; Isa. 36:5; Jer. 5:17; 18:10; 48:7; Ezek. 33:13; Mic. 7:5). This remarkable exception elevates the valiant wife to the highest level of spiritual and physical competence. The claim implies that this couple enjoys a robust relationship. His trust is well-founded: *he does not lack spoil* (*šālāl*), a military metaphor implying that the woman wins life's essentials through strategy, timely strength, and risk in a depraved world. C. Yoder notes that *šālāl* occurs elsewhere only in 1:13, where the gang tempts the son to obtain spoil by joining them. Thus the word may form an inclusio for the book as a whole: whereas the son is warned to avoid the sinners and their illicit spoil (1:10-19), here the "spoil" he receives from his valiant wife is licit and most desirable.[9]

12 This verse defines the extent and duration of her value. *She does him,*

---

8. C. R. Yoder ("A Socioeconomic Reading of Proverbs 31:10-31," *JBL* 122 [2003]: 432) confirms that this is a reference to the wife's "purchase price," which in this case is considerable (cf. Gen. 24:10; 29:18).

9. Yoder, "Proverbs 31:10-31," 434 n. 25.

intentionally and deliberately, *good* (see "Ethical Terms for the Wise and Righteous," pp. 37–38) a metonymy escalated to the emphatic litotes *not evil*. The body of the poem will define "good" primarily in terms of her economic benefit. *All the days of her life* means she never fails her husband.

Body: Her Activities (31:13–27)

The body of the acrostic consists of two halves (vv. 13–18, 20–27), with v. 19 functioning as a seam stitching them together.

Her Cottage Industry (31:13–18)

The first half of the poem's body lists the valiant wife's contributions to the family economy. She starts by establishing a "cottage industry," producing clothing from raw materials. She uses the money earned from the trade of the textiles to purchase a field that she converts into a valuable, productive vineyard (see 24:30).

13 *She diligently selects wool and flax* suggests that a positive attitude drives her work in making thread from the raw materials of animals and vegetables respectively. *And she works with her glad palms* signifies her competence at manual labor. Her goal is to produce clothing from scratch.

14 The success of her weaving industry provides enough income that she can trade for exotic foods from far-off places. The simile *she becomes like trading vessels* signifies her savvy and diligent trading. That *she brings her food from afar* signifies that she is not confined to locally farmed fare but can furnish her family with delicacies from faraway fields.

15 To the figure of a trading fleet, the poet adds the figure of (probably) a lioness. *And she arises [like a lioness] while it is still night* belongs to hunting imagery and should not be taken literally; a lioness hunts food by night, but not an aristocratic woman! The figure implies that she puts the well-being of her household above her own comfort. *And provides prey (ṭerep) for her household* metaphorically depicts this God-fearing wife as a predator providing food for her young. The shocking image signifies provisions acquired through great effort, prowess, and ingenuity and commends the valiant wife's ability in provisioning her home.[10] The parallel *and the quota [of food] for her servant girls* underscores her success. She not only feeds the members of her

---

10. T. T. McCreesh, "Wisdom as Wife: Proverbs 31:10–31." *RB* 92 (1985): 41.

direct family but also those of her extended household, who further enrich the household.

16 Furthermore, *she considers* (she puts together a workable plan to obtain) *a field*, and after examining it from all angles, she executes her plan *and purchases it*. *The fruit of her palms* refers to the textiles she made with her "glad palms" (v. 13). *She plants a vineyard* represents her as the agent and assumes that the field was dug up and cleared of stones before planting the choice vines; afterward, a watchtower would be built and a winepress hewed out of a huge rock (see Isa. 5:2).

17 She undoubtedly accomplished these achievements with hired workers or indentured slaves (v. 15). Nevertheless, *she girds her loins* (puts on a waist-cloth that extends to the middle of the thighs) refers to putting on the standard clothing of a worker or soldier[11] to prepare for some "kind of heroic or difficult action"[12] (cf. Exod. 12:11; 1 Kgs. 18:46; 2 Kgs. 4:29)—a fitting metaphor for the physical and spiritual *strength* demanded for her accomplishments in textiles, culinary art, and farming. Thus girded, *she strengthens her arms*, signifying both her capability and her tenacity to complete *the task*.

18 The rewards that she gains from all her hard work motivate her to keep going: *she perceives that her gain* (profit) *is good. Her lamp does not go out at night* probably does not mean that she works late into the night. It is not wise to be a workaholic, working day and night; a person needs adequate sleep (cf. Ps. 127:2). More probably, the symbol means that she has enough money and so does not have to save oil by snuffing out the lamps. A Middle Eastern proverb says, "He sleeps in the dark," meaning, "He has not another penny in the house."[13] Toy comments, "In a well-ordered house the lamp burned all night . . . as a sign of life; its extinction marked calamity (Jer. 25:10; Job 18:6)."[14] In sum, the symbol signifies her enduring prosperity (cf. Prov. 13:9; 20:20; 24:20).

Janus (31:19)

Verse 19 functions as a seam uniting the two sections of the body. On the one hand, its theme forms an *inclusio* with v. 13, concluding the unit on the wife's textile manufacturing (vv. 13–18) by developing her collection of raw wool and flax for her textiles (v. 13) to the actual making of thread, as signified by reference to the spindle (v. 19). On the other hand, it is linked with the second half of the body by its concentric structure with v. 20:

---

11. Waltke and Houston, *Psalms as Christian Praise*, 137.
12. Van Leeuwen, "Proverbs," in *NIB* 5, 261.
13. Gemser, *Sprüche*, 110.
14. Toy, *Proverbs*, 545.

A	Her hands she holds out to the doubling spindle,		v. 19
	B	her palms grasp the spindle.	
	B'	Her palms she spreads out to the poor,	v. 20
A'	and she holds out her hands to the needy.		

According to Wolters, the *doubling spindle* was grasped "either . . . for making two-ply or three-ply yarn out of previously spun threads."[15] *Her palms grasp the spindle* reinforces the picture of her skill and industry. Van Leeuwen comments, "The hands that grasp to produce open wide to provide [v. 20]."[16]

Her Social Achievements (31:20–27)

The second half of the poem's body lists the valiant wife's contributions to the household and the community. It does so with a chiastic structure.

A		Spreads palms to the poor		v. 20
	B	No fear of snow		v. 21a
		C	Household clothed in scarlet	v. 21b
			D Makes coverlets and clothing for herself	v. 22
			X Husband respected at the gate	v. 23
			D' Makes garments and sashes for merchants	v. 24
		C'	Wife clothed with strength and dignity	v. 25a
	B'	Laughs at the future		v. 25b
A'		Opens mouth with wisdom, looking after household		vv. 26–27

A/A', which feature body parts, suggest that the wise words of her mouth (A') inform the deeds of her hands (A) and, *mutatis mutandis*, the wise deeds of her hands give credibility to the wise teaching of her mouth. B/B' refer to her confidence in facing the future by means of negative and positive synonyms: "no fear" and "laughs."[17] C/C' explains her confidence: she has protected her household from the snow without (v. 21a) and fortified herself with strength within (v. 25a). D/D' specify her textile products: two for herself and two for the merchants. X emphasizes by means of the pivot the poem's central message: the valiant wife's accomplishments empower her husband to lead the nation

---

15. Wolters, "The Meaning of *Kîšôr*," *HUCA* 65 (1994): 103.
16. Van Leeuwen, "Proverbs," in *NIB* 5, 262; cf. Eph. 4:28.
17. For "laugh" and "no fear," see Waltke, *Proverbs 1–15*, 528–29 n. 169.

in righteousness and justice. This message is further enhanced by a hierarchical escalation, with her contributions ascending from the poor (v. 20) to the household (v. 21) to herself (v. 22) to her husband (v. 23).

20 Pride of place is given to her kindness to the poor. Whereas the king opens his mouth to defend their interests in court (31:8–9), the valiant wife opens her hands to meet their physical needs. *Her palms she spreads out to the poor* means either that she invites them home by gesturing to them or that she hands them material aid (22:9). *And she holds out her hands to the needy,* who live hand to mouth, parallels the first line in meaning.

21 The list of her activities returns to her textile industry, not as a source of income but as a means to protect the family from the cold. *She is not afraid* (not agitated by anticipated danger) *of snow* that threatens life. *Her* immediate *household* is escalated to *all her household,* presumably including her slaves and servants. *Scarlet,* the color of the thread, is a metonymy for costly wool (see v. 22; cf. 2 Sam. 1:24; Jer. 4:30), for linen cannot readily be dyed.

22 *Coverlets she makes for herself.* Fox notes that this is the only mention of the competent wife looking after herself and is important because it shows that she does not neglect herself even while helping others.[18] "Coverlets" (see 7:16) refers to bed coverings that made the bed soft, comfortable, and elegant. *Her clothing* is made of the finest textiles from plant and animal material. *Fine linen* from Egypt and *[wool dyed with] purple* from a Phoenician seashell were costly imports and so connote wealth and luxury (cf. Judg. 8:26; Song 3:10; Ezek. 27:7, 16; Acts 16:14).

23 *Her husband is respected* for several reasons: he is free of domestic worries, and his prosperous household builds his reputation;[19] the apparel with which his wife adorns him (see v. 21b) also enhances his prestige, as do his wife's character and genius, which are praised at the gate (see 31:31); they are a crown on his head (see 12:4). *The gate* (see 1:21; cf. Job 29) symbolizes the city's collective authority and power. *When he sits* is a figure for proclaiming authoritative counsel and teaching (cf. Gen. 19:1; 2 Sam. 18:24; 19:8; 1 Kgs. 22:10). *With the elders* means her husband is among the highest authorities of the city. Before the monarchy, elders maintained order in the community (Ruth 4:1–12). During the monarchy, the elders became members of the nation's aristocracy. Their main duty was to provide wise counsel (cf. Ezek. 7:26 with Jer. 18:18; also Job 12:20; Ezek. 27:9). *Of the land* suggests their authority extends beyond the borders of the local city. Far from lounging around, this empowered husband works mightily for the good of the nation.

18. Fox, *Proverbs 10–31*, 896.
19. McKane, *Proverbs*, 669.

24 *Garments she makes and sells* continues the list of her economic contributions to the household. *Supplies* is a synonym for "sells." In Isa. 3:24, *sashes* refers to pieces of fashionable women's dress. Perhaps "[under]garments" and outer "sashes" are a merism for all kinds of fine clothing.

25 The valiant wife is not only "not afraid" (v. 21a) but even laughs at any prospect of future danger (v. 25b). *Strength* denotes powerful energy, while *majesty* signifies the magnificence that elevates her above her peers. In the Old Testament to put on *clothing* is symbolic of showing one's true character.[20] The praise attributes to her the best qualities of both youth and old age ("power and splendor"; cf. 20:29). Like a warrior, *she laughs* at her metaphorical enemy, *the coming day*—the indefinite future with all its potential alarming prospects. Christians put on the full armor of God so that they can stand when evil days come (Eph. 6:10–11).

26 Climactically, *her mouth she opens with wisdom*, which she was taught (see "Intellectual Terms for the Wise and Righteous," pp. 34–35) and which now informs what and how she speaks. Specifically, *loving teaching* (or the teaching of kindness) *is on her tongue*, matching her loving activities in serving others. She practices what she preaches. Her teaching is informed by the content of Proverbs, as Christian teachings are additionally informed by Jesus Christ, the One who is greater than Solomon (Matt. 28:18–20).

27 To successfully manage her household, she adds vigilance to her instruction. That *[she is] one who watches* means she keeps a sharp eye *over the affairs* of her household to quickly deal with problems and maintain order. The metaphor *she does not eat the food of idleness* stands in sharp contrast to the pathetic sluggard.

Conclusion: Her Praise (31:28–31)

King Lemuel's mother concludes her encomium to the valiant wife by citing the family's praise of their valorous mother and wife (vv. 28–29) and then by calling on the community to praise her (vv. 30–31). The woman so concerned for others now becomes the central concern and praise of others. The woman who otherwise does "not fear" (v. 21a) yet "fears *I AM*" (v. 30b). Wise Christians will be rewarded with their Lord's praise: "Well done, good and faithful servant!" (Matt. 25:22).

---

20. Whybray, *Proverbs*, 429.

Praised by Her Family (31:28–29)

28 She arose early to provide for her household (v. 15), now *her sons arise,* presumably in her presence, to show their respect for her (see Job 29:8; Isa. 49:7). They *pronounce her blessed,* signifying that they esteem her and declare that she is living life optimally, as the Creator intended. *Her husband [rises] and praises her;* the content of his praise is given in v. 29.

29 The poet quotes the husband's superlative praise of his wife verbatim: *Many daughters* (a synonym for "women" in poetry; cf. Gen. 30:13; Song 6:9) *do valiantly (ḥayil).* This is the very quality that the poet said was most rare among women (v. 10); so exceptional, however, is the wife's valor that by comparison valiant women are plentiful. Even granting that, *you surpass all of them.* The husband's hyperbole does not intend to negate that she is a model of excellence to which all the daughters of Israel strive.

Praised by All (31:30–31)

30 The shift from "you" back to "she" signals that the poet takes over from the husband. The verse pits the *charm* and *beauty* of some women against "a woman who fears *I AM.*" A woman who possesses charm and beauty but does not fear *I AM* is not praiseworthy because her beauty is *deceitful*—to wit, it is *fleeting.* "Charm" deceives because it promises a lifetime of happiness that it cannot deliver. The sages' ideal woman possesses both beauty and piety (see 5:19). The antithetical parallelism, *as for a woman who fears* I AM (see 1:7), *she should be praised* implies that inner spiritual beauty does not deceive because it never fades.

31 The encomium is brought to a climax with an intensifying synonymous parallel commanding that those "in the gates" (see v. 23) praise her splendid accomplishments, first directly (*extol her for the fruit of her hands*—a figure for her numerous and splendid works) and then indirectly (*let her works praise her in the gates*). Her works praise her to the extent that they are publicly acknowledged and acclaimed. C. S. Lewis writes, "If we do not admire [what is praiseworthy], we shall be stupid, insensible, and great losers."[21]

---

21. C. S. Lewis, *Reflections on the Psalms* (New York: Harcourt, Brace & World, 1958), 92.

Index of Authors

Index of Subjects

442

Index of Scriptures